THEY CHANGE THEIR SKY

THEY CHANGE THEIR SKY:
THE IRISH IN MAINE

Edited by Michael C. Connolly

Preface by Senator George J. Mitchell

The University of Maine Press
Orono, Maine 2004

The paper used in this publication meets the minimum requirements of the American National Standard for Information Sciences—Permanence of Paper for Printed Library Materials, ansi z39.48–1984. Book design by Michael Alpert. Index by Mary E. Lawrence. Printed and bound in the United States of America.

Cover illustration: *Alewife Cove, Late Day* (detail), oil on canvas, 2003, by Holly E. Gilfillan Ready

.08   07   06   05   04   1   2   3   4   5

ISBN: 0-89101-110-2 (paperback)
ISBN: 0-89101-111-0 (hardcover)

Caelum non animum mutant qui trans mare current
–Horace

They change their sky but not their soul who cross the ocean

TABLE OF CONTENTS

A GALLERY OF PHOTOGRAPHS AND OTHER
ILLUSTRATIONS FOLLOWS PAGE 186

PREFACE

MAINE'S PEOPLE ARE DIVERSE. Some trace their origins back thousands of years to this region's aboriginal settlers. Others stake their claim to be among its original European settlers, the English and mainly Protestant ancestors of our dominant ethnic group and the source of the stereotypical "Downeast Yankee." The place names of our state reveal the significance of these two early influences. Imagine the widespread gaps in any map of our state if we were to eliminate Native American and English place names.

The story of Maine's people, of course, does not end there. The southward migration of thousands of French Canadians in the nineteenth and early twentieth centuries forever changed the face of Maine, and that of all of New England. And the story continues with the late twentieth century and current arrivals of refugees from Asia and Africa, especially in Maine's largest cities. A Portland High School graduation ceremony these days includes students with surnames from Somalia, Cambodia, or Vietnam joining those from earlier places of origin such as Italy or Ireland. Today over fifty different languages are spoken in the Portland School District, the most prominent, other than English, being Somali, Spanish, Arabic, Khmer, and Vietnamese.

In Lewiston a significant Somali population has developed along the Androscoggin River, where a French enclave held near exclusive sway for over one hundred years. Such change is not without its difficulties, nor was it easy in the nineteenth and early twentieth centuries. It still calls for tolerance, understanding, and empathy. The persistent stereotype, which suggested that Maine is lacking in racial and cultural diversity, has been thoroughly debunked. A state that produces an Edmund Muskie and a Bill Cohen, and that features gubernatorial contests between McKernan and Brennan, or Baldacci and Cianchette, cannot be viewed as exclusively the domain of any one ethnic group. Maine today is ethnically diverse, and it is strengthened by this diversity.

They Change Their Sky, edited by Michael Connolly, describes part of the history of Maine's diversity. This is a story, in ten essays, about one of Maine's leading ethnic communities, the Irish—the first non-Anglo-Saxon and largely non-Protestant wave of immigrants that would change the face of Maine. The Irish would pave the way for other immigrant groups to follow.

This book contributes to the understanding of Maine as a more complex state and region than many had previously believed. Even within the Irish migration itself there was widespread variation, depending upon time and place of arrival. Many factors contributed to these immigrants' difficult decisions to pull up stakes on the northwestern fringe of Europe and recreate their lives here on the northeastern fringe of the United States.

The story of the Irish in Maine is different from that of the Irish in Boston, New York, or Chicago, or, for that matter, any other place, primarily because Maine is more rural than these other possible destinations. Maine presented a unique set of circumstances for new Irish arrivals, which shaped their futures here. The story is different, too, in that it is largely unknown. Certainly in comparison to the Irish of Boston, Maine's Irish for the most part have been largely ignored by history and historians. One could argue that they represent a more typical story of the Irish in America. They settled in a region they would never dominate culturally or politically and were thus forced, by reason of this minority status, to adapt where necessary and to persist and endure where possible. Is this not the history of our country?

They Change Their Sky draws a complex picture of Maine's Irish, beginning with the earliest Irish settlers, mainly Scots-Irish, Presbyterians from the northern province of Ulster who arrived in the early eighteenth century. My work for peace and reconciliation in Northern Ireland has taught me that historical amnesia never succeeds in the long term and, therefore, it is imperative to chronicle the experience of this group—as in the first essay by R. Stuart Wallace—especially as they represent the very first wave of Irish settlers in Maine. The next three essays that address the Irish settlement of late eighteenth- and early nineteenth-century Lincoln, Washington, and southern Aroostook counties are critical foundation studies of the Irish Catholic experience in our state. The Irish settlers in these three areas, as distinct and distant as they are from each other, displayed common patterns of endurance, creativity, and sacrifice. The example of Benedicta, in particular, is the story of an experiment in American immigration history: could the Irish be transplanted from one rural and agrarian community to another?

The essay on the Irish of Lewiston presents a story not well known even in that city or in the state. The widespread assumption has been that the French arrived in a nineteenth-century city that had yet to experience immigration. The infrastructure of Lewiston, however, was at least in part built by Irish labor. Likewise the story of the Fenian invasion of Canada in the years immediately following the Civil War is largely unknown, especially its Washington County component; this essay adds to the understanding of the survival of Irish political aspirations in Maine, far from the Anglo-Irish rivalries then raging within Ireland itself.

The four essays that deal with the Irish in Maine's largest city, Portland, provide other examples of the diversity of this group. The degree and depth of political and social organization already displayed in the nineteenth century reveals the survival and transference of skills and tactics learned in Ireland. The essay on "mutually single" Irish women opens windows of understanding concerning not just women alone, but the larger issue of mutual support within the whole Irish-American community. Evidence of Irish nationalism among early twentieth-century Portland longshoremen, while not at all unexpected on its own, supports and extends the thesis of the earlier essay on nineteenth-century social and political organizations in this city.

Finally, the concluding essay, by Kenneth E. Nilsen, on the usage and prevalence of the Irish language among the Portland Irish community is both surprising and deeply revealing. It demonstrates the extent to which a separate and unique language, the foremost evidence of a distinct culture, survived and indeed flourished in a sea of English. The compelling stories, translated directly from the native Gaelic (Irish), are full of the humanity and character of these Irish Mainers, providing a fitting end to the book.

Editor Michael C. Connolly, publisher Michael Alpert of the University of Maine Press, and all ten contributors to *They Change Their Sky* have produced a readable and compelling collection of essays which inspire as many questions as are answered in this single work. It will, undoubtedly, be a catalyst for future research and publication in the fields of state, local, and ethnic history in Maine. I am pleased to rec-ommend this book to all readers within and beyond the boundaries of our state.

I am especially grateful that the authors have collectively decided to transfer all royalties generated by the sale of this book to the creation and maintenance of the Irish Heritage Center located at the former Saint Dominic's Church, Portland's first Catholic church building. I have been an enthusiastic supporter of the Irish Heritage Center since its inception, and this generous contribution is both welcome and appropriate since both this book and the Center honor and preserve what is past. *They Change Their Sky: The Irish in Maine* and the Irish Heritage Center both represent a living community whose future remains as bright and varied as its past. The Irish changed their sky but not their souls when they crossed the ocean to America and to Maine; and like every group that has become part of our society, they have changed Maine for the better.

–Senator George J. Mitchell

ACKNOWLEDGEMENTS

THE TITLE OF THIS BOOK was inspired by a quote by the Roman philosopher, poet, and critic Horace (65–8 BCE) found in Thomas Cahill's bestseller *How the Irish Saved Civilization* (1995). Horace's words were recalled by a ninth-century Irish monk who was a follower of Saint Gall, "the greatest of all [of Columbanus'] spiritual sons." This anonymous monk was laboring in the Celtic monastic site that would bear its founder's name, Saint Gallen, near Lake Constance in north-eastern Switzerland. We only know him to be from the eastern province of Ireland. He was then living thousands of miles away from his home and working in relative silence – but his words and thoughts spoke to me over 1000 years later.

> In the ninth century, one of [Gall's] spiritual sons, a Leinsterman, sitting in the now enormous scriptorium of the towering monastery on Lake Constance, would put together a commonplace book containing bits of all his favorite readings . . . and in Irish his own perfect poem about his cat, Pangur Ban. Thinking no doubt of his Irish home, the scribe also writes down this sentence from Horace: "Caelum non animum mutant qui trans mare current" ("They change their sky but not their soul who cross the ocean")—a good maxim for all exiles and, in this context, a reminder of the constancy of Irish personality. (Thomas Cahill, *How the Irish Saved Civilization*, 193)

An early stimulus for the writing of this book came from former Governor Joseph E. Brennan who, in the course of a speech given many years ago, spoke of the need for someone to document the history of the Irish in Maine. Brennan himself epitomizes the social mobility experienced by many of this group. The son of Irish immigrants, he was able to take advantage of first-rate educational opportunities at Cheverus High School in Portland, Boston College, and the University of Maine School of Law, to rise to political prominence as a state legislator, Attorney General, U.S. Representative, and two-term Governor of

Maine. I subsequently discovered that the home of Governor Brennan's maternal ancestors and that of my paternal ancestors was the same – the tiny townland of Callowfeenish in the heart of the Irish-speaking Gaeltacht area of Connemara, County Galway, Ireland. His father, John, and my grandfather, Coleman, labored together along the waterfront as members of the Portland Longshoremen's Benevolent Society.

One of the first scholars to to document the history of Maine's Irish was James H. Mundy in *Hard Times, Hard Men: Maine and the Irish 1830–1860* (1990). The book was based on his Master's thesis (1970), which ultimately resulted in his Ph.D. dissertation (1995) at the University of Maine, Orono. Jim Mundy must be commended for this pioneering work and for its catalytic effect on historical research in this area. Largely in recognition of Mundy's research and publications, especially on Bangor and the Irish in the "Queen City," an editorial decision was made not to include a separate essay on Bangor in this collection. As important as Bangor is to the state and to the fate of the Irish in Maine, it seems that Mundy's research provides a substantial foundation for those interested in further pursuing that subject specifically.

My academic interest had been in the field of labor and ethnic study for some time, leading to "The Irish Labour Movement 1916-1918" (Master's thesis, University College Dublin, 1977). After many happy years of hearing stories about colorful Irish longshore characters from my father, Michael Francis Connolly, and his best friend, Larry Welch, I decided to do my doctoral dissertation on this topic. What emerged was "The Irish Longshoremen of Portland, Maine, 1880–1923" (Boston College, 1988). For me, it was a labor of love, and a way to recognize the many thousands of Irish dockworkers, who, like the monk in St. Gallen, labored away in relative obscurity. My work aspired to give them voice.

On June 5, 1999, The Maine Historical Society presented an Irish-American Roundtable discussion. This was largely organized by William David Barry of the MHS and supported by Cindy Murphy, Stephanie Philbrick, Christine Albert, Nicholas Noyes, and the society's executive director, Richard D'Abate. This roundtable presentation brought together scholars from many areas of ethnic and local history, and reunited me with a colleague I had first met at an academic conference in October 1988 at Salve Regina College in Newport, Rhode Island. Ed McCarron was then researching the Kavanaghs and Cottrills of mid-coast Maine while a graduate student at the University of New Hampshire. Our paths had crossed twice—perhaps this was serendipity. I would like especially to thank Ed for his collaboration on this project, including his assistance with the Bibliography and discussion about the larger issues in Maine and Irish-American history. About one year after the MHS Roundtable, I proposed a book on the Irish in Maine using some of the presenters from the earlier academic session and contacting others who were working in this area. Nearly everyone contacted responded with enthusiasm, and the project was underway. The inspiration for the Overview came during a Labor Day weekend, 2002, visit to a lovely B&B on Vinalhaven Island. I had to get out of bed several times during the night to scratch down small details for the Overview, lest they be forgotten.

Michael Alpert of the University of Maine Press was supportive from the start, but, of course, wanted to see the revised drafts of the essays. These were completed and sent to the Press in the spring of 2003 and the rest, as they say, is history. I would like to take this opportunity to personally thank Michael for his enthusiasm and very helpful criticism along the way. He saw the value of this work, and wanted it to be a foundational study that could be used as a major resource for many years to come. Along those lines he counseled me to create an extensive bibliography for the use of future scholars. Michael's imprint is firmly on this book. Many thanks also go to Betsy Rose of the University of Maine Press for her masterful editorial work.

Where would a book like this be without its talented and creative contributors? The ten scholars who composed these essays have each put their own distinctive stamp on this book and its composition. They were, from the beginning, extremely enthusiastic and responsive, and they made my work most enjoyable. To these writers go my sincere thanks and admiration. They bring different styles and emphases to this book, and this diversity is part of the book's strength.

At this stage, as I attempt to acknowledge and thank all those who have contributed to the publication of this book, I want to thank my life partner and *anam cara* (soul friend), Becky Hitchcock, for all her support and comfort. She has given me the loving environment in which a task such as this could be undertaken and completed. For all that you have done, and continue to do, I say from the bottom of my heart, thank you. Thanks also go to Becky's children, Dan and Abby, for their interest in this work, and for their understanding.

Saint Joseph's College of Standish, Maine has given me the platform from which I could reach this goal. St. Joe's has provided me a living for the past nineteen years, since I started as a replacement, part-time faculty member in 1984. Much more than that, however, the college actively encourages the academic goals of its faculty. Since achieving tenure and promotion in 2001, I have felt even more connected to this institution. Here, I wish to offer a special thanks to the Vice President for Academic Affairs and Dean of the College, Daniel Sheridan, for his personal interest in my success. He has placed scholarship on the pinnacle where it belongs in a liberal arts college, and SJC has benefited greatly from his leadership. The Dean's secretary, Julie Moore, has been supportive of my efforts at SJC from an early date, and to her I offer my thanks and congratulations upon her upcoming graduation. She is a role model for perseverance and dedication. Two of my colleagues, out of the many that offer regular support, stuck by me when the slogging was tough; and for that reason, I would like to offer my special thanks to Jonathan Malmude, Chair of the History Department, and Ed Rielly, Chair of the English Department.

Technical support is crucial in such an undertaking. In this regard I wish to thank the faculty secretaries at SJC, Elaine Moesel and Eileen Morton, for their gracious assistance at critical times. Suzanne Murphy of the Graduate and Professional Studies Summer Program has often transported this book in its many forms from Standish to Portland. I also would like to offer my thanks to the Information Systems staff—to Eric Tremblay, Skip Williamson, and, especially to Jackie Mulholland for her expertise. Also thanks go to Linda Galluccio of Graduate and Professional Studies, who assisted at a critical juncture. Reg Hannaford, with his Classical language expertise, was able to help me more fully understand the Latin roots of the book's title. His free-style translation of Horace included the following: "Where one lives does not change one's essential spirit," and "Even if you cross the sea, the old sod is still in your soul."

Two of my work-study students assisted greatly in the preparation of the Bibliography and should be publicly thanked: they are Kris Kimball and Matt Crellin, both members of the SJC Honors Program. Nathan Warecki of Stonehill College in North Easton, Massachusetts, assisted Ed McCarron in collecting sources for the Bibliography. Matt Barker and Bill Barry did an enormous amount of digging into the resources of the Maine Historical Society, and their work added greatly to the scope of this book. Works of other academics have been consulted in the preparation of the Bibliography, but especially I wish to thank Tim Meagher for his inspiring work about Worcester, Massachusetts, *Inventing Irish America*, the Bibliography of which was widely consulted and used for this work.

The Irish-American Club, especially its current president, Bob Kearney, and the Irish Heritage Center and its current board president, Joe Moran, are both strong advocates for this work. P. Vincent "Vinny" O'Malley, in this matter as with anything to do with Irish affairs in Portland, has been tireless in his efforts. In particular I wish to thank Linda Hogan for her support and for all of her many skillful efforts as project director in behalf of getting the new Irish Heritage Center (IHC) off the ground in a successful way. John O'Dea, the current IHC Executive Director, has been enthusiastic in supporting this book.

Senator George Mitchell, the Honorary Chair of Fundraising for the IHC, graciously agreed to write the Preface for this book. Each time I have met Senator Mitchell, whether in Belfast, Northern Ireland, or in Portland, he is always giving something of himself. For the gift of this Preface, and for all you have done for the state of Maine and for peace in Ireland, I and we say thank you so very much.

Bill Barry of the Maine Historical Society and Ann Surprenant of the University of Maine, Orono have graciously assisted by serving as peer reviewers of this work and by offering their advice and counsel as to its improvement. The advice of these scholars has greatly enhanced the scope and nature of the book. Dr. Francis C. "Bud" McGrath of the University of Southern Maine English Department, a friend and colleague for over fifteen years, provided a critical reading of the manuscript at an important juncture. Many others have helped in many large and small ways. Christine Albert of the Maine Historical Society was enormously helpful in the creation of this book's illustration gallery. Bruce Glasier of WCSH television provided information on early Irish sports heroes. Tom Gaffney of the Portland Public Library's Portland Room provided information on John Ford. Aileen Carroll must be commended for her years of volunteering at the Portland Public Library, especially her work on the Healy Collection of books of Irish and Catholic interest. John Coyne of South Portland, formerly of Gray Street in Portland, has over the years generously given me Irish books and copies of *Irish America* and *Ireland of the Welcomes* which I have enjoyed and from which I have profited. We are all very grateful for the generosity of artist Holly Ready in allowing us to use for our book cover an original piece of art showing the expansive Maine sky over the ocean near her home in Cape Elizabeth. The connection between this beautiful painting and the book's title and concept will be readily apparent to all. Thank you, Holly.

Sr. Marie of the Visitation Nicknair, O.P., studied the unique Maine Irish settlement of Benedicta in southern Aroostook County while doing graduate research at Boston College. John Munroe of the Saint Joseph's College Theology Department and Graduate and Professional Studies assisted in procuring a copy of the Nicknair study for this book. Christine Qualey Heskett of Portland kindly shared her memories of growing up in Benedicta along with source material about the Irish community still living there.

Three good friends in the Irish community of Portland were influential. One was Dorothy Healy, formerly of Westbrook College, founder of the Maine Women Writers Collection, and a strong supporter of all things Irish. The second, Tom Wilsbach of the Portland Public Library, is my idea of a "Renaissance man." Just ask Tom, I say, and he usually knows the answer, or at least as a good librarian he knows where to find it. Thanks, Tom, for your many years of good friendship, good music, and good counsel. The third, Claire Foley, remains one of my strongest links to Irish culture in so many ways. Her love of the Irish language and of Irish dance (especially set dancing) have long been inspiring. She has introduced me to her family, both here and in Ireland, and this has added to my enjoyment on both sides of the Atlantic. Claire has given unselfishly to assist many groups associated with Ireland. She has been declared "Irish Person of the Year" by the Irish-American Club, was influential in setting up the Portland Irish set dancing class, was presented with a special recognition for her work in support of the Maine Irish Children's Program, and was recognized as a Community Leader in the Irish community by the Center for Cultural Exchange. Presently she is giving her time again, this time to the new Irish Heritage Center. In addition to all of this, Claire was instrumental in setting up many of the interviews of Portland's Irish speakers conducted by Dr. Kenneth Nilsen beginning in 1984. For all of this, and for innumerable strong cups of tea and good *comhra* (conversation), the best that I can do is to say to her, *go raibh míle maith agat, a Chlár.*

Ken Nilsen has put Portland on the map as an Irish-speaking enclave. He has helped to record many of its last Irish speakers in their native language, on audio and videotapes in interviews that he conducted starting in 1984 and continues to analyze, translate, and publish up to the present. Many families in Portland now have a momento of their deceased relatives, and the Irish community here has a record of its cultural ties with that quintessential element of culture, one's native language. For his gentleness and love of the language, for his many years as a teacher of both Irish and Scots-Gaelic, and for this gift to the future I say thank-you, *a chara*, for your many contributions to the Irish in Maine. A special word of thanks should go to the Busby family of Portland, the family of Portland's greatest *seanachi* (a person who remembers and transmits their own cultural legacy in the form of history, genealogy and stories). Pat Malone was such a person, and when he died in 1985 in the midst of a rare hurricane, I remember thinking that it took a very big wind to carry away his spirit. *Gó ndeanaigh Día trochaire ár a anam.*

In memory of Francis O'Brien, "the dean of Maine's antiquarian book dealers," and the heart of Portland's Irish intellectual community, whom I had the great pleasure of knowing. I am happy to report that work in the areas of his scholarly interests continues. Two of Francis's good friends, Bill Barry, of the Maine Historical Society, and William B. Jordan, Jr., formerly of Westbrook College, continue to labor in the field. They have also been influential on my work, and I wish to thank them both for supporting my small efforts in this area that they know so well.

–M.C.C.

THE IRISH IN MAINE: AN OVERVIEW

THE IRISH IN MAINE: AN OVERVIEW

by Michael C. Connolly

THE IRISH CAME TO MAINE WITH COURAGE AND HOPE. Their story is as exciting and varied as that of the state of Maine itself, but it is woefully under-chronicled and, therefore, largely unknown. *They Change Their Sky: The Irish in Maine* represents an attempt to address this historical omission. The threads are there; what is necessary is for historians to weave these threads together into a logical, understandable, and compelling narrative. In this effort to chronicle the history of Maine's Irish, I have been joined by nine other scholars, each with their own expertise and unique slant on history. My role as editor of this work, over and above the choice of these essays for inclusion, has consisted of working with the publisher and the individual authors, as needed, in fine-tuning their work. An extensive bibliography has also been created with the help of several contributors and interested parties. Finally, I have created this synthesizing chapter on "The Irish in Maine: An Overview." My purpose in this overview is to create a scholarly framework through which the subsequent essays may be viewed. The overview is more descriptive than academically complete in the hope of providing present and future scholars with guidance toward possible areas of related research. All the contributors to this volume of Maine and ethnic history, as well as its publisher, hope that, together with our bibliography, this book may stimulate additional research and publication in these fields for years to come.

There are many areas of special interest through which one could approach the broad topic of the Irish in Maine. Among the multiple prisms through which to view this subject I have chosen to address the following four: labor, politics, religion, and culture (a topic which embraces the immigration process, language, sports, the arts, and social/cultural organizations).

LABOR

Most ethnic groups in America initially gravitated toward certain predictable labor and occupational niches. This pattern had two major causes. First, the host community of established settlers exerted a certain degree of control over the availability and distribution of jobs. This control would remain in effect over time and place, and it would even survive the replacement of these earlier settlers with subsequent dominant groups as time passed. Newly-arriving immigrants in the American mosaic have almost universally been forced to start at the very bottom rung of the socioeconomic ladder. For Irish men in Maine, this translated into planting potatoes in Benedicta, digging canals in Lewiston, working in timberland and sawmills in northern and central Maine, and working alongshore in Portland, or in heavy construction labor throughout the state. Likewise, for Irish women, the ubiquitous positions as domestic servants in the homes of prominent Yankee families, along with other types of service-related labor, would be safe and dependable entry-level jobs.

With the passage of time, and the inevitably slow but steady rise of the Irish up the occupational ladder, new work opportunities arose. New ethnic groups subsequently arrived in Maine to take the place of the Irish on the bottom rung. Eventually the occupational domain of the Irish expanded to include manufacturing positions, politically-appointed jobs, and public service positions such as police officers; Irish women could obtain jobs such as department-store clerks, government welfare workers, or telephone operators. Concentrations of Irish men or women in certain areas would become almost stereotypical in Maine and throughout America. What this clearly represented, of course, was gradual upward social mobility on the one hand, and ethnic cohesiveness on the other.

The labor movement itself was such an occupational niche, and by the late nineteenth century, the Irish were playing an increasingly prominent role in union organization.[1] The crucial role of documenting the history of the laboring classes in Maine has been painstakenly pursued over the past several years by Charles A. Scontras of the Bureau of Labor Education. His efforts on behalf of Maine's workers will aid future historians of labor and social research, and Scontras must be publicly acknowledged for his diligent work in this much-neglected area.[2]

By the late twentieth century, the Irish continued to have an important presence in the AFL-CIO; this group is still being led by Irish labor leaders such as Edward Gorham and Charles O'Leary, its current and immediate past-president, among others. Union records provide a rich source of data on the question of labor and ethnicity.[3]

POLITICS

Politics was always closely related to jobs, especially in the years before the rise of the modern civil service in the early to mid-twentieth century. With this change, merit replaced political patronage and ethnic identity as the chief criteria for being hired. Many Irish political bosses, notably and stereotypically Mayor James Michael Curley of Boston, attempted to preserve the old system and with it, their own political power.[4] As the Irish in Maine rose up the occupational ladder and formed and led unions, they simultaneously joined and eventually became prominent leaders within the Democratic Party. Maine's Republicans in the mid-nineteenth century were, not unlike the majority white Anglo-Saxon Protestant (WASP) community elsewhere in America, often sympathetic with nativist concerns regarding the rapid increase in immigration, especially from Catholic Ireland.[5] Another cultural factor, in addition to the obvious religious differences that drove the Irish in Maine and elsewhere away from the Republican Party, was the prohibitionist bent of prominent Republicans. Leaders of this movement included, among others, Portland Mayor Neal Dow, whose "Maine Law" in the nineteenth century became the legal basis for the American experiment with national prohibition between 1920 and 1933.[6]

One additional factor dividing the Irish from the Republicans and driving them toward the Democratic Party in the mid-nineteenth century was the issue of race and the Civil War.[7] Working-class Irish were not, as a group, proponents of the abolition of slavery in America, although there were notable exceptions to this rule. Irish workers and African Americans often competed for jobs in this country in similar occupational niches. Both of these groups were simultaneously striving for wider acceptance within American society. This competition and their shared status as part of the lower class seemed to exacerbate the tendency toward racism. Many contemporary historians have written on this topic of "whiteness" and acceptance by the larger American community.[8]

As the Irish gained political voice through the writing of Finley Peter Dunne and his character "Mr. Dooley," so did Mainers chuckle at the homegrown wisdom of Maine's folk hero, "Major Jack Dowling," created by Seba Smith. Politics, of course, offers natural competitors an alternative to actual physical violence. Verbal fisticuffs, although often stinging, do not always result in actual bloodshed; and the Irish in Maine as elsewhere soon learned the ropes here as they had on the other side of the Atlantic. Most often within the protective ranks of the Democratic Party, at least initially, the Irish in Maine climbed the political ladder to achieve more power and a greater degree of security than would have been possible without political representation. By the late twentieth century, Irish-American political leaders such as Joe Brennan could be elected to two terms as Governor, while George Mitchell could gain national and international respect and recognition as a man of peace.[9]

RELIGION

Religion and the Roman Catholic Church have always been strongly identified with Ireland and Irish immigrants to America. It is important to remember, however, that there were Irish in this country and in this state long before the Potato Famine of the mid-nineteenth century. These were the Scotch-Irish or Ulster-Scots, primarily Presbyterian in religion, who fled discriminatory treatment by Anglican elites in both Great Britain and Ireland. Many of these earliest Irish immigrants participated in the founding of this country and its earliest institutions, and several of their progeny would go on to serve as presidents of the United States. In Maine, the Scotch-Irish landed as early as 1718.[10]

Roman Catholicism would represent the faith of the vast majority of Irish immigrants into America and Maine who arrived subsequent to the mass starvation and resultant out-migration caused by the potato blight of the late 1840s. In Ireland this catastrophe would initiate a "devotional revolution" in the church.[11] An estimated one million Irish died of famine-related illness and starvation, and well over one million additional Irish emigrated, many to America.[12]

Among the first Irish Catholic settlements in Maine were those of the Newcastle and Damariscotta area in the mid-coast region. Here two Irish merchants by the name of James Kavanagh and Matthew Cottrill would anchor an important self-supporting community and subsequently provide for the founding of St. Patrick's Church (1808), the oldest standing Catholic church in New England.[13] By 1822 the rural parish of North Whitefield would also have its own church, St. Denis, predating both of the larger urban parishes of Bangor and Portland.

In Portland, a Galway-born Dominican, Father Charles Ffrench, was largely responsible for the construction of that city's first Catholic church, Saint Dominic's, in 1833.[14] This building would predate the founding of Bangor's first Catholic church, Saint Michael's (1834), by just one year and Saint John's (1855) by twenty-two years. Although there were significant contrasts among cities such as Bangor, Ellsworth, and Portland in the antebellum years in their treatment of newly-arrived Irish Catholics, strongly nativist tendencies had to be confronted to some degree in all locales.[15]

Connections between Maine and Massachusetts, established before Maine's independence from the Bay State and admission into the Union in 1820, have remained strong in the years since. This is especially true in episcopal matters. Jean Cheverus, an émigré from the French Revolution, visited the Catholics of Portland and beyond in the spring of 1822. He would eventually be known as Bishop John Cheverus of Boston, the first bishop of the Diocese of Boston that then included the state of Maine. His name, of course, is today memorialized in the form of the Jesuit-run college-preparatory high school in Maine's largest city.[16]

Boston's second bishop, Benedict Fenwick, in 1834 would be largely responsible for the establishment of a rural, agrarian, Irish-Catholic settlement in southern Aroostook County that would bear his name, Benedicta.[17] In the early years of the twentieth century the Diocese of Portland, by then including all of the state of Maine, would be served by Boston-born William O'Connell (1901–1906), who would subsequently be named Bishop of Boston and Cardinal. His relationship to his Maine successor, Bishop Louis S. Walsh, was reportedly cold, primarily, it would seem, because of financial irregularities.[18]

Another important connection between religion and Irish ethnicity has been the ubiquitous and highly influential presence in Maine of the Sisters of Mercy. This religious order was founded in Dublin, Ireland in 1832 by Mother Catherine McAuley.[19] The expansion of the Sisters of Mercy into America would be the life's work of Frances Warde (Rev. Mother M. Xavier Warde) in the years 1843-1883. The Mercy institutions founded by Frances Warde stretched from Pleasant Point in Perry, Maine to Eureka, California, literally spanning the North American continent.[20]

In Maine, the earliest Mercy schools, hospitals, and convents associated with Frances Warde were in Bangor (1865), North Whitefield (1871), Portland (1873–1882), Old Town (Indian Island, 1878), Perry (Pleasant Point, 1879) and Princeton (Peter Dana Point, 1879).[21]

Bishop Bacon's desire to have the Sisters of Mercy in Portland encountered many obstacles. In an effort to satisfy the French-Canadian immigrants in Maine, who resented Irish-American domination of the hierarchy and the schools, he had invited French-speaking Canadian Sisters of Notre Dame rather than Sisters of Mercy to teach at the Cathedral School in Portland.[22]

The withdrawal of the Sisters of Notre Dame to Canada in 1873 provided the opening for the Sisters of Mercy to serve Bishop Bacon in Portland as they were already doing in Bangor and North Whitefield. "If Bangor was picturesque, if North Whitefield was loved, Portland was beautiful."[23] In Portland, the Sisters of Mercy founded Queen's Hospital, which became known as Mercy Hospital. The Sisters also organized St. Elizabeth's Academy for Girls, which, in 1915, changed its name to St. Joseph's College. The college later moved to its present site in Standish, on the former Verrier estate, on the shore of Sebago Lake. In addition to these early sites in Maine, the Mercy Sisters had missions in the north, including Benedicta, Houlton, Presque Isle, and Eagle Lake, all in Aroostook county; in the east, at Calais and the two Passamaquoddy reservations; in the west, at Farmington and Rumford; and in the south, in Biddeford and Sanford, as well as many points in between.

The Irish domination of the leadership of the Maine diocese would continue well beyond Bishop Bacon, as can be seen by the unbroken string of Irish surnames of bishops serving from the mid-nineteenth century through the early twenty-first century:

> David William Bacon (1855–1874)
> James Augustine Healy (1875–1900)
> William Henry O'Connell (1901–1906)
> Louis Sebastian Walsh (1906–1924)
> John Gregory Murray (1925–1931)
> Joseph Edward McCarthy (1932–1955)
> Daniel Joseph Feeney (1955–1969)

Peter Leo Gerety (1967–1974)
Edward Cornelius O'Leary (1974–1988)
Joseph John Gerry (1988–2004)
Richard Joseph Malone (2004–   )[24]

This nearly embarrassing string of success for the Irish represents a corresponding disappointment for Catholics of other ethnic backgrounds, especially Franco-Americans.[25] A major point of contention within the church, which was certainly related to the question of ethnicity, concerned the control of financial resources, the complex question of who actually owned and controlled church property, including its parish schools.[26]

The first African American Catholic Bishop in America was James Augustine Healy of the Diocese of Portland (1875-1900).[27] In this same period the premier American labor organization was the Knights of Labor (KOL), a quasi-secret, oath-bound organization also led by an Irishman, Terence V. Powderly of Scranton, Pennsylvania. In part because of the secret oath, and in part because of the perceived radical agenda of the Knights, Bishop Healy became known as "the foremost Episcopal opponent of the order [KOL] in the United States."[28]

The 1920s brought a new nativist threat to Maine's Roman Catholics, including the Irish, in the form of the Ku Klux Klan (KKK). This organization, which had its origins in the American South during the Reconstruction period after the Civil War, was experiencing a new era of expansion. Now, in the aftermath of World War I, the Klan expanded its perennial animus toward black Americans and now added other target groups such as Jews, Catholics, and most non-Anglo-Saxon immigrants in general. In Maine, the KKK focused its attention on Irish, Italian, and French Catholics.[29] Maine's Bishop Louis S. Walsh spent the last years of his life fighting the Klan's growing influence in the state, and defending the church and its parochial schools from the nativist impulse. In 1923 the Klan supported a successful referendum measure to change Portland's mayoral system to a city manager form, one which it has to this day. Since the city manager would be hired by a smaller nativist-run group instead of being elected by a largely Irish populace, Bishop Walsh concluded, "the Anti-Catholic feeling is now on top."[30]

Other interesting anecdotal stories abound from this period that point to the suspicion with which the dominant, Yankee Protestant community was viewed by the minority, Irish Catholic community.[31] The social stereotyping of the Irish by nationally known figures such as the political cartoonist Thomas Nast, and other later cartoon characters, such as *Maggie and Jiggs*, caused pain in many Irish homes, leading to anger and a reciprocal stereotyping of the Yankees by the Irish themselves.[32]

CULTURE

The issue of Irish culture and its survival under the new sky of this American land is also intriguing. Culture includes the immigration process, language, sports, the arts, and cultural or social organizations. Perhaps the most obvious cultural questions should begin by focusing on why the Irish left the land of their birth (as Irish emigrants) and how they survived culturally in the land of their choice (as Irish immigrants).

As previously noted, the earliest Irish immigrants arrived in Maine well before the famine period of the mid-nineteenth century. Representative of this early Irish presence is the family of Jeremiah O'Brien, who was born in Scarborough in 1740—the son of Morris O'Brien, a native of Cork, Ireland—and died in Machias in 1818. In 1775, Jeremiah led a force of rebels, including several of his brothers, in the seizure of the British armed schooner *Margaretta*. This episode has often been referred to as the first naval engagement of the American Revolution, and it occurred only a short time after the pivotal military encounters at Lexington and Concord. O'Brien was subsequently captured by the British while commanding the privateer *Hannibal*. After serving time on a guard-ship, he later escaped from an English prison and returned to Brunswick and later Machias, Maine. Jeremiah's brother, John O'Brien, commanded an American privateer aptly named *Hibernia* and was successful in capturing several British army officers. This period is contemporary with the British burning ("pacification") of Falmouth (later Portland), Maine, an act that was prominently included in the list of grievances against the "Tyrant" (King George III) outlined in the American Declaration of Independence: "He has burnt our towns . . ."[33]

Many Irish immigration studies have analyzed the phenomena of "chain migration" or the practice of "assisted immigration" whereby earlier-arriving members of a family would actively encourage and financially sponsor other family members to join them in America.[34] Other studies have reviewed the persistence of cultural traits that survived the wrenching process of upheaval and displacement.[35]

Maine's Irish often represented the "push-pull" struggle that demographers have demonstrated. According to this theory, most people will
stay at home unless or until they experience simultaneously the negative "push" factors in their own region and the positive "pull" factors
of a "distant magnet" like the United States. Demographers are more
specific, however, in this regard. They have concluded that rates of emigration soar only when the negative "push" factors such as discrimination, unemployment, crop failure/famine, overcrowding, and lack of
opportunity at home are counterpoised by limitless opportunity abroad.
The "pull" factors in Maine, and elsewhere in America, would have
included positive employment opportunities, less rigid social control,
abundance of food, open space, and the prospect of "freedom" in all its
alluring and ill-defined forms. Pull factors to Maine were enhanced if
the potential immigrant could anticipate a welcome from family,
friends, or the other Irish acquaintances on this side of "the Pond."
Chain migration was thus facilitated.[36]

One particularly unique aspect of this pattern, at least in the case of
Portland, was the very high percentage of Irish immigrants who spoke
Irish (Gaelic) as their primary language. This was, of course, a consequence of their emigration from Irish-speaking (Gaeltacht) regions, such
as Cois Fharraige or Connemara in County Galway.[37] Kenneth E.
Nilsen's final essay in this book deals effectively and sympathetically
with this phenomenon. Nilsen's work, especially in documenting many
of the oldest surviving members of this linguistic tradition in Portland
in the 1980s–1990s, guarantees that here, at least, the "great silence"
will not be absolute. Seán de Fréine, in *The Story of the English
Language*, gave voice to the Elizabethan English acknowledgement that
if a person's "tongue [language] be Irish, their heart must needs be Irish,
too."[38]

Sport in America has always provided an avenue for minority groups
or newly-arriving immigrants to compete on a level playing field with
more established groups. Many sports such as boxing, for example,
require a highly individual effort, pitting one person's strength, stamina
and heart against another. Sport, therefore, became a vehicle and in
many cases a metaphor for realizing social mobility both within one's
own ethnic group and, in few but notable cases, in the larger society as
a whole. Witness, for example, the role played by the great Irish boxing
champion, John L. Sullivan. He was, of course, a hero well beyond the

confines of the Irish neighborhoods of his native Boston. All Americans wished to "shake the hand that shook the hand of the great John L."[39]

Arguably it was in baseball that the Irish made their most profound contribution to sport in America. Baseball historian David Q. Voigt, in his opus *America Through Baseball*, writes that the game was "a primary vehicle of assimilation for immigrants into American society and a stepping stone for groups such as Irish Americans." In fact, the Irish influx helped create an anti-English backlash that reduced the popularity of cricket in the U.S. and helped solidify baseball as the "national game."[40] A popular 1911 baseball song, "They're all good American Names," by Jean Schwartz and William Jerome, sums up this connection between Irish ethnicity and our national pastime in a humorous fashion:

> Jennings and McGann, Doyle and Callahan.
> Hanlon, Scanlon, Kirk and Donlin,
> Devlin, Keeler, Walsh and Conlin.
> Joe McGinnity, Shea and Finnerty,
> Farrell, Carroll, Darrell, and McAmes.
> Connie Mack and John McGraw
> All together shout hurrah!
> They're all good Irish names.[41]

In Portland, Sylvanus Lyng earned enough from stabling horses and racing them on a track in Ligonia, near the Rolling Mills section of South Portland, to enable him to build a substantial Greek Revival home in 1846 on the crown of Munjoy Hill. This home, noted for its architectural style, overlooked the Atlantic Ocean and, if Lyng looked eastward far enough, to Ireland itself.[42] As the builder and owner of one of the first Irish homes on the Hill proper, Lyng represented upward social mobility in its purest and most literal form, moving from the traditional Irish neighborhood at the base of Munjoy Hill to its pinnacle. His wealth came from horse racing, a sport much beloved by the Irish throughout history. In boxing, another sport much loved by the Irish, middleweight Coleman Patrick "Coley" Welch (see gallery, plate 6) in the 1930s and 1940s and light heavyweight James "Irish Jimmy" McDermott, albeit from Massachusetts, in the 1960s thrilled crowds of Irish boxing fans in Maine and elsewhere with their pugilistic successes against all comers.[43] The rosters of many school and social sports teams in Maine would be filled with Irish surnames, especially in the late nineteenth and twentieth centuries. John "Bull" Feeney, later better known as the acclaimed American film director John Ford, first made a name for himself on the football playing fields of Portland High School, which he attended between 1910 and 1914.[44] Coach James J. "Fitzy" Fitzpatrick's name now adorns "the Stadium" as Portland's premier football field was previously known, and the Fitzpatrick Award is annually presented to the outstanding football player in the state of Maine.

Far away from the playing fields, the Irish in Maine were also making contributions in the arts and humanities. James Sullivan produced the first history of Maine in 1795; Irish-born architect Henry Rowe designed buildings in Portland; Frederick N. Crouch, the English composer of Irish music, enlivened the Portland scene and beyond with popular songs such as "Kathleen Mavourneen"; and Tommy Glynn from Portland was for a time acclaimed as "the world's greatest banjoist." Later in the nineteenth century, landscape painters such as George McConnell and Thomas F. O'Neil achieved a measure of success. Interest in art and literature among Maine's Irish-American population probably peaked between 1900 and 1910, or so at least thought Portland-born philanthropist James A. Healy. In the middle of the twentieth century Healy wrote to bookman Francis M. O'Brien, "I'm not surprised to learn from you that interest in Irish history or literature is non-existent in Portland, that is, among the Irish."[45]

Indeed, among many Maine Irish families, a career in art or scholarship was seen as "getting above one's-self" and, therefore, not encouraged. Thus many artistically talented Irish youth were forced to work outside of their community. Francis and John Ford (see gallery, plate 4) found fame in the Hollywood film industry:

> The story of how [John] Ford came to Hollywood has become a legend. He grew up as John Martin Feeney in the Munjoy Hill section of Portland, Maine, the son of Irish-speaking parents in an Irish Catholic immigrant community. His older brother Francis, a handsome scapegrace driven out of Portland by a bit of local scandal, had lost touch with the family for several years, drifting into an acting career in the fledgling film industry in Los Angeles, where he had emerged as an important director as well as a successful leading man. Meanwhile, back in Portland, their mother Abby, who as a native Irish speaker had never learned to read and write English, was an enthusiastic fan of the new silent films being shown at

the Empire Theater. On a weekend in 1914, the inevitable happened. Abby Feeney returned to announce to her family that she had just seen her eldest son, listed in the credits as Francis Ford, in a starring role. They contacted Francis through his studio, and he made a short triumphal visit to his old hometown. Shortly thereafter, some weeks after graduating from [Portland] high school, John Martin Feeney was on his way to join his older brother in Los Angeles.[46]

Among other Irish exiles from Maine, poet Louise Bogan became part of the New York literary scene; Maxine Elliott became an acclaimed stage actress; and Leo Connellan went to Connecticut and became that state's Poet Laureate.

Occasionally, talent remained within the state, as was the case of nationally-known actor Bartley McCallum, who built a summer theater on Peaks Island, or Francis M. O'Brien who owned and managed a famous antiquarian bookshop in Portland, a gathering place for literati who visited the city. One of the great contributors was Portland native James A. Healy, who made his money in New York but returned to present Colby College with a superb collection of Irish literature. Healy also gave some of the first fine examples of modern painting to the Portland Museum of Art. In recent decades renewed connections between Maine and Ireland, the availability of traditional and newer Irish music, and an awakened interest in scholarship concerning Ireland and Irish culture have led to a rapidly improving situation.[47]

Finally on the larger issue of culture, there is a growing concern for the preservation and celebration of Irish culture, as it has survived in this northeastern corner of our country. The Irish American Club (IAC) of Maine at the turn of the twenty-first century has a membership of over 600.[48] It is a non-political and non-sectarian organization welcoming people of diverse views and faiths, with a love of maintaining Irish culture as a common denominator. Traditionally, the IAC has sponsored trips to Cape Cod, Nova Scotia, and Ireland. Additionally they offer Irish language classes taught by Mary Concannon of Norwood, Massachusetts (who has local ties to South Portland), and Irish *ceili* dancing taught by Brendan and Mary McVeigh, originally from Belfast, Northern Ireland and now living in South Casco, Maine. The IAC often joins with its counterpart group in Norwood, Massachusetts for a summer picnic and dance on the grounds of Southern Maine Community College in South Portland, featuring live Irish music.[49]

Although the club's average membership is aging, an influx of younger members such as its current president, Bob Kearney, is taking it in new directions. One of the most exciting examples of new thinking is the Irish Heritage Center (IHC) which has opened in the former Saint Dominic's Church (on the corner of State and Gray Streets in Portland's West End) after having been recently purchased from the City of Portland. The new IHC will be the home for the IAC for the foreseeable future, consisting of a library and a space for language classes, research, club meetings, dances, and public events. It is an exciting time for this organization, the largest Irish social group in Maine.[50]

The Maine Irish Children's Program (MICP), originally created in 1984 by Father John Feeney and Rev. Alex Cairns, among others, has served the cause of peace in Northern Ireland. It sponsors several children of both major faiths to stay for extended periods with local families in the peace and quiet of a Maine summer—far from the rancor, discord, and turmoil of home.[51] Maine's most famous connection to Northern Ireland is, of course, the work of our own Senator George J. Mitchell, who helped to negotiate the Belfast (Good Friday) Agreement of 1998.

In addition to specifically Irish social organizations, there are many cultural groups within Maine that promote Irish events on a regular basis. Prominent among these is the Center for Cultural Exchange (CCE), formerly Portland Performing Arts.[52] In one of its early initiatives, the House Island Project, participants worked with four different ethnic communities in southern Maine, including the Irish, to find creative ways for the communities to meet their self-defined cultural needs. Saint Patrick's Day and weeklong celebrations at the CCE often feature visits by some of Ireland's premier music groups, along with film, dance, and lectures on issues of Irish interest.[53]

REVIEW OF ESSAYS

The ten essays that make up this book are examples of the type of scholarship that will serve to fill the gaps in our knowledge of the history of the Irish in Maine. This collection is by no means exhaustive, nor was it intended to be. It is, however, representative and diverse. Each writer has brought her or his expertise and curiosity to this project. In addition, diverse regions of Maine are represented, from Portland in the south to Benedicta and Aroostook County in the north.

R. Stuart Wallace deals with a topic too often overlooked by ethnic historians, the Scotch-Irish emigration of the early eighteenth century. It has often been jokingly remarked that a sure way to start a fight among any group of Irish in this country is to ask the question, "How many Irish presidents have there been in the United States?" JFK is always cited, and often Ronald Reagan or Bill Clinton, but many of the earlier presidents came from forebears who were among the eighteenth century Scotch-Irish (Ulster Presbyterian) migration here.[54]

Historians agree that the first considerable immigration of the Scotch-Irish took place in 1718, when five vessels from Ireland landed in Boston. Most of the newcomers moved on to the frontier of the districts of New Hampshire and Maine. These unsettled regions had certain attractions for the Scotch-Irish, or perhaps it would be nearer the truth to say that they seemed less unattractive to them than they did to the English settlers. The Scotch-Irish wanted freedom from control and interference at all costs. They had left Ulster in protest against the impositions of the established (Anglican) church and the landlords. To obtain freedom, they were ready to move into territories then inhabited by native peoples, where they might face conflict.[55] Wallace's essay describes the situation of these earliest Ulster settlers in Maine and in North America as a whole, nearly sixty years before the Revolutionary War and the emergence of the new nation they helped to create.

In 1718, Brunswick was among the first Maine settlements to receive Scotch-Irish immigrants. One of the newcomers, the Rev. James McKean, was a grandfather of the first president of Bowdoin College. Orr's Island was named for Joseph Orr, an Ulster weaver and companion of a Dublin-based ancestor of the shipbuilding Skolfield family of mid-coastal Maine. A later group of Scotch-Irish who resettled from New Derry, New Hampshire around 1769 founded the town of Belfast further down the coast, where, according to tradition, the toss of a coin allegedly decided whether it would become Belfast or Londonderry.[56] (This story recalls the reported manner in which the name of Oregon's largest city was chosen by competing settlers from Boston and Portland, Maine.)

Wallace's essay details early events from Purpooduck (after 1763 a part of Cape Elizabeth, and after 1898, South Portland), Merrymeeting Bay (the confluence of the Kennebec and Androscoggin Rivers near modern-day Bowdoinham), and "Georgia" (the land east of the Kennebec River claimed by rival land proprietors). It includes early historical records from coastal towns such as Warren, Bristol, Bremen, Boothbay, and Southport, among others, and is therefore of great interest in this provincial, pre-Revolutionary period.

"Facing the Atlantic," by Edward McCarron, deals with the growth of one of Maine's first significant Irish Catholic communities, that of Damariscotta and Newcastle in Lincoln County. It is, in part, also the story of two remarkable families, the Kavanaghs and the Cottrills, who came from the same region of southeastern Ireland (Inistioge, County Kilkenny) along the River Nore. This essay represents not only a chronological continuation of Wallace's essay but also a geographical extension, as the focus shifts slightly to the coastal region east of the Kennebec. It was in the mid-coastal region that these pre-famine Irish Catholics, joined by the Scotch-Irish, would carve out small entrepreneurial empires along this eastern frontier in the years that Maine was still a district of Massachusetts. McCarron's work challenges several assumptions, among them that early American coastal trading communities were homogenous; he demonstrates that a healthy degree of ethnic and even religious diversity existed among them. This merchant community somehow survived the period following the implementation of the 1807 Embargo Act, when, according to Edward Elwell, "grass literally grew on the wharves."

This essay also chronicles a vigorous trade between mid-coast Maine and several ports in Ireland that were especially covetous of Maine's leading export crop of the time, timber. Upon their return to America, these Maine ships would often complement their cargo with Irish passengers bound for Boston or, in some cases, Maine itself. McCarron cites several specific examples of this human cargo, that although smaller in number than those going to the larger metropolitan regions on the Atlantic coast, would have strongly influenced the more sparsely populated Maine coast. Atypically, some of these Irish emigrants gravitated inland to smaller "upcountry towns" such as Windsor or Whitefield, among the few cases in New England where rural Irish settled in rural settings. "Facing the Atlantic" sets the stage for an analysis of Irish immigration even further "downeast" in Washington County, and also for the rural development of Benedicta in southern Aroostook County.

"Ireland along the Passamaquoddy" is the work of independent scholar Fidelma McCarron (*Ní Chairbre or Carbery*), a native of

Drogheda, County Louth, Ireland who now resides on Munjoy Hill in Portland. This essay moves our focus as far to the east as one may go and still be in the United States. It also has some intriguing ties with the final essay in this volume (by Ken Nilsen) which explores the extent to which Gaelic (Irish) was spoken in Maine. This is a study of marginality, within Ireland and in America. It focuses on Rathlin Islanders who traveled from the northeasternmost point in Ireland to settle along the Passamaquoddy and Cobscook Bays, at the northeasternmost point in America. The resemblance does not end with geographical similarities. It is worth reflection that in both the region of origin and the region of destination, these marginal settlers were looking out, across narrow stretches of ocean, to proximate, albeit foreign, land: Scotland in the case of Rathlin Island, and Canada in the case of Washington County. The depopulation of the former led to the growth and vibrancy of the latter. Demographic patterns were also similar, with Rathlin Islanders living in kin-based farm clusters (or *clachans*). In easternmost Maine the chain migration, which would be repeated in other Maine-based Irish communities, led to similar social/familial systems. Extended family units moved, in some cases en masse, from the Old World to the New. In Rathlin, the family farms were often cooperative, based on an extended family functioning as a single unit of production. This necessity often proved to be a virtue along the rocky coast of downeast Maine.

As Fidelma McCarron notes in the third essay in this book, another rich cultural repository of the Irish is language. Referring to the research of Augustine McCurdy on Rathlin Irish, she concurs with him that apparently in many cases "Rathlin Irish was spoken upon first arrival" in the Passamaquoddy region. She relates an interesting case of intergenerational and interethnic name-calling on Rathlin which appears similar to the playful, yet derogatory, nicknames often given to first- and second-generation Irish in Portland. In Maine the Irish-born were often called "greenhorns" (new arrivals), "amadans" (fools), or "spailpins" (itinerant farm laborers) by their second-generation Irish-American children. The linguistic favor was returned by the first-generation Irish, who sometimes referred to their progeny collectively as "narrow backs" or "country borns." The well-known Welsh geographer E. Estyn Evans shares a concern with Fidelma McCarron and McCurdy regarding the marginality of Rathlin: "Rathlin Irish, now almost gone, but long preserved in the upper end, was much closer to Scottish than

Irish Gaelic, and this gives a clue to the island's history, for it was a stepping-stone between the two countries and its ownership was long disputed."[57]

Fidelma McCarron sensitively captures the essence of place when she cites Chris Crossman's opinion that "islands may be the last places where self-reliance is coupled with a keen sense of community." This unique sense of community, found in both Rathlin and easternmost Maine, is constantly being challenged by the isolation and lack of opportunity that drives the young away. As Maine islands and other isolated communities lose their schools, the light of survival burns less bright. A Rathlin islander spoke of this concern in the period just after World War II when he was asked if the island way of life could be preserved: "No, it'll not stay, for there's nobody to come after us. [The school had been closed] for want of children [who had sought work in Scotland]."[58] Uncannily, these two worlds, Rathlin Island and Passamaquoddy Bay, tied together by a common people, yet separated by three thousand miles of the North Atlantic, seem to share a common present and, perhaps, future.

"A Brave New World" is Edward McCarron's treatment of a unique Irish demographic experiment, the creation of the southern Aroostook town of Benedicta. It was designed as an ethnic and religious Utopia—a place where rural Irish tenant farmers, hard-pressed by economic, political, and religious travails in their own native land, could achieve their dreams of political and religious freedom and, of course, claim a plot of land to call their own.

In 1823, Boston's first bishop, Jean Cheverus, was appointed to the See of Montarban in his native France because of concern about his ailing health. Two years later, Pope Leo XII appointed Benedict Fenwick as successor to Cheverus.[59] Less than a decade later, in 1834, Bishop Fenwick announced plans to create an agrarian community on the northern frontier of his diocese, in a newly-created southern Aroostook township that would bear his name, Benedicta. Although his larger dream to build a Catholic seminary there never materialized (Holy Cross was built in Worcester, Massachusetts instead), Fenwick's goal was instantly embraced by 134 Catholic families, mostly Irish in ethnicity.

Benedicta marks an important experiment in the history of American immigration. Ed McCarron cites works on Catholic-sponsored immigration by authors such as James P. Shannon, Sister Mary Gilbert Kelly,

O.P., and Marvin R. Connell. Ed McCarron also discusses the idea that moving from old-world substistence farming to new-world "market-oriented" farming presented nearly insurmountable difficulties for Benedicta's settlers. Lawrence McCaffrey, in his often-cited work *The Irish Diaspora in America*, has further developed this thesis, as have other historians.

In Maine, Bishop Fenwick's Utopian dream did not change the demographics of the northern half of the state; rather, they were changed by the steady and sizable immigration of French-Canadian Catholics from the Beauce region of Quebec, as well as from Acadian areas of the Maritime Provinces. Remarkably, though, a small but notable Irish Catholic community based on farming did form and was sustained in Benedicta. Family surnames like McAvoy, Rush, and Qualey were and are still widely represented. Place names, too, as witnessed by a simple perusal of the DeLorme Company's *Maine Atlas and Gazeteer*, can speak volumes about a region's history. In the immediate vicinity of Benedicta township one can find the following Irish geographical influences in this small section of the great expanse of northern Maine: Casey Road and Sweeney Road; Lawler Ridge and Cruddin Ridge; Logan Brook, Tracy Brook, and Connerly Brook; Plunkett Pond, Flinn Pond and McAvoy Pond.

In "Irish Organizations and the Irish Community of Nineteenth Century Portland, Maine," Matt Barker uncovers a virtual gold mine of societies, fraternal and sports associations, political parties, religious and temperance groups, Irish-support endeavors and myriad other social organizations of the Irish community of Maine's largest city. The sheer scope of his research demonstrates not only Barker's energy as a researcher, but also the energy, vitality, and creativity in nineteenth-century Portland.

Up to this point in *They Change Their Sky*, the essayists have analyzed the Irish impact on smaller towns and rural development in Maine. Barker's essay introduces the topic of Irish influence in urban areas of the state, more often the norm for the Irish in America. Among the many intriguing elements of the time period covered in this essay, I will highlight only a few. The Irish of the nineteenth century, unlike the eighteenth-century Ulster immigrants described in Stu Wallace's essay were primarily Roman Catholic. Barker mentions early contacts with Portland by the first two bishops of Boston, Jean Cheverus and

Benedict Fenwick. The latter appointed Father Charles Daniel Ffrench from Galway, Ireland to be Portland's permanent pastor and founder of its first church, Saint Dominic's. This ecclesiastical decision was significant in that "The appointment of Ffrench to Portland is the first known example of a connection between County Galway and Portland that continues to this day."

The nativist reaction to the famine-era tide of Irish immigration was ferocious in the mid-nineteenth century. Martin Scorsese's fascinating film *The Gangs of New York* (2002) is based largely on racial and ethnic incidents that occurred in the infamous Five Points neighborhood of New York City.[60] Northeast of Portland, in Ellsworth, Maine, the infamous case of Father John Bapst is well-known locally.[61] Portland's Father John O'Donnell, a contemporary of Father Bapst, protested against the societies that were formed "for the avowed purpose of persecuting Irishmen." Although religious and ethnic tensions reached a high point in the 1850s, not all non-Catholics were hostile toward their Catholic neighbors. On June 18, 1851, local Protestant entrepreneur John Bundy Brown, who employed many Irish laborers in his sugar factory on the Portland waterfront, attended a mid-summer picnic sponsored by the Young Catholic Friends Society. According to Barker, Brown wrote in his diary, "weather very pleasant. Catholic picnic to the islands to-day . . ."

What was the reason for increased inter-ethnic violence, both north and south of Portland? Jim Mundy has suggested that the obvious personality differences between Father John Bapst and Father John O'Donnell were crucial. Another obvious factor would be the actual size of the Irish community in Portland as compared with Ellsworth. Most importantly, however, would have been the relative need for labor in Portland, perhaps offering a rationale for J. B. Brown's patronage of an Irish-Catholic picnic in the midst of this nativistic hysteria. Even today large American business concerns often promote a more open immigration policy, especially during periods of rapid economic growth, and accordingly the mid-nineteenth century corresponds with the building of the rail link between Portland and Montreal. The Grand Trunk Railroad, originally called the St. Lawrence and Atlantic, was completed in 1853, thus assuring a transport-related boom in labor opportunities in Maine's leading entry port (*entrépot*). The themes that Barker discusses regarding nineteenth-century Portland are continued later in this book by my essay, which looks at early twentieth-century nationalistic ties between Portland laborers and Ireland.

"The Irish Experience in Lewiston: 1850-1880" by Margaret Buker Jay extends the analysis of the Maine Irish on the "urban frontier," this time along the Androscoggin River. Today, Lewiston is seen as a predominantly Franco-American city with a newly emerging Somali population. However, between Lewiston's earliest origins and the influx of large numbers of French-speaking Catholic mill operatives in the late nineteenth century, the Irish had their moment. Buker Jay writes that not until the 1870s was Irish dominance of the unskilled labor pool challenged. She cites the relative number of Canadian immigrants within the labor force rising from 13% in 1870 to 44% in 1880.[62] Buker Jay cites an 1871 report by the city physician which inauspiciously linked the two groups together: "I cannot avoid the conclusion that very much of the sickness of the city, especially among the Irish and the French population, is caused by the overcrowding of tenements, with the consequent impure atmosphere within doors, and by poisonous gasses from decaying vegetable and animal matter about the dwellings." Not a favorable assessment for either group.

Buker Jay reports that the first documented Roman Catholic religious service in Lewiston did not occur until 1850, in the home of Patrick McGillicuddy; by the time of the nativist hysteria, around 1855, McGillicuddy's home was being used for Catholic services under the direction of Father McLaughlin. It was subsequently burned by a mob of Know-Nothings. The water hose was cut so that the fire-fighting efforts were ineffectual, and "the building was ruined." However, economic necessity, especially for cheap, unskilled labor, once again trumped zenophobia. By mid-century, the tradition of hiring only American-born employees slowly gave way, and the Irish would be the first beneficiaries of this relaxation of policy.

Between 1850 and 1880, even a few skilled employment opportunities presented themselves. The Irish of Lewiston, who had originally largely come as canal- and ditch-diggers and heavy-construction laborers, were now moving up the socio-economic ladder. Ironically this change occurred at precisely the same time that they were being overwhelmed in numbers by waves of French immigrants from Quebec and the Maritimes. Buker Jay concludes that "unskilled day labor, which has furnished employment for the majority of Irish immigrants, accounted for only about twenty percent of the occupational distribution of the second generation."

Buker Jay's essay provides a fascinating study of ethnic conflict, tension, and eventual relaxation in a major Maine mill town of the nineteenth century. The Irish, as usual, were at the center of action, caught between the Yankees, such as Benjamin Bates, on the one hand, and the new French ethnic majority with their mayor, Dr. Alonzo Garcelon, on the other. Most did not succeed as dramatically as Patrick McGillicuddy, Timothy Murphy, or Patrick Many, as described in Buker Jay's essay; but they survived and made an impact.

Gary W. Libby's "Maine and the Fenian Invasion of Canada" forms the next section of this book. It details a well-documented 1866 incident in which supporters of an Irish Republic, the Fenians, threatened an assault on Maritime Canada from their bases in Eastport and Calais. Fenians were willing to use violence, if necessary, to gain their political goals, which were to distract Britain and to hurt that colonial power in distant Canada, where it was most vulnerable, thus aiding the cause of Irish freedom. A series of skirmishes on and around Campobello Island resulted, preceding the larger, better-planned raids made from near Niagara, New York, and St. Albans, Vermont.[63]

The "comic opera" that played out in the spring of 1866 was in reality a very serious policy decision by a group of American Fenians. Their goal was to hit the British at their weakest link (Canada) rather than focusing on the ultimate goal of the liberation of Ireland, which in the mid-1860s was heavily fortified in anticipation of an expected insurrection. Libby describes the origins of the Fenian movement on both sides of the Atlantic. He then analyzes the predictable split in this organization: nearly every Irish political group throughout history has split into factions, thus worsening their chances of success. This tendency, together with a highly effective network of British spies and paid informers, usually doomed these insurrections to "triumphant failures."[64]

The incident's chronological proximity to the recently-ended American Civil War is no mere coincidence. The presence of so many Irish soldiers in the Civil War can, in part, be explained by the desire of some to acquire weapons and military skills for a possible later battle with Great Britain for the freedom of their country of ancestry, Ireland. "The Hero of Gettysburg," Gen. George G. Meade, was dispatched to Maine by the Secretary of War, Edwin Stanton, to "cool out" the

Fenians with as little publicity as possible." Meade arrived by train in Portland on April 19, 1866, and immediately proceeded by steamship to Eastport. His presence symbolized the seriousness with which both the American and British governments took this Irish republican threat.

Libby alludes to some of the differences between Canadian and American Irish in an attempt to explain the greater tendency of the latter to support the Irish republican, and especially the Fenian, cause. Compared to their fellow countrymen in the U.S., the Canadian Irish were more rural, isolated, diffused, and threatened by the "mob loyalism" of fellow Canadians of British stock, including the members of active Orange Order Lodges throughout much of British North America.

Although most of the action described in Libby's essay occurs in and around Passamaquoddy Bay in Washington County, there are several excerpts which deal with Portland-based Fenians involved in the Eastport and later the St. Albans episodes. He mentions Daniel O'Connell O'Donoghue from County Kerry, who was center (or leader) of the large Fenian group in Portland. Also mentioned is William McAleney of County Derry, who was the Portland center of the competing Fenian factions. Perhaps the central figure in this intrigue was one B. Doran Killian, the Fenian treasurer, who initially proposed the seizure of Campobello Island, just over the Canadian border from Eastport, and its use as a base from which to negotiate for a British withdrawal from Ireland. Historians will long debate whether these episodes represented a "comic opera," an "Eastport fizzle," or, together with subsequent and more famous raids from other parts of the northern United States, a case of high international political intrigue.

"Mututally Single: Irish Women in Portland, Maine 1875–1945" by Eileen Eagan and Patricia Finn, both of the University of Southern Maine, forms the next section of this book. In the late nineteenth century, single Irish women were migrating to North America at higher rates than women of other ethnicities, according to prominent historians such as Janet Nolan and Hasia Diner. Eagan and Finn address the question of what happened to these single women once they arrived in Maine. The answer is compelling in its rationality: these women, many of whom would remain single, formed other supportive relationships to take the place of the stability provided by traditional marriage. "Mutual support" would often occur within the family, through what sociologists and demographers refer to as vertical and horizontal extension of the nuclear family. Sisters, cousins, and aunts, among others, became parts of these extended families; the only thing missing from the traditional formula was a husband.

Eagan and Finn create an academic/theoretical paradigm and then proceed to flesh out this model with real-life Portlanders. Various methods were used, including oral interviews and research in local newspaper, institutional, and governmental documentation. A central institution for these women was, of course, the Catholic Church. Whether by providing welfare (St. Elizabeth's Orphanage) or education (St. Elizabeth's Academy for Girls, renamed Saint Joseph's College after 1915), the Sisters of Mercy in Portland played a central role in supporting young women.

Traditional occupational niches, such as domestic worker, are, of course, discussed; but to this list are added opportunities such as teaching, hotel and department store work, public welfare, and small business. In later years, opportunities arose in all levels of the secure and well-paid (and eventually unionized) telephone industry. Comparing local with national sources, the authors conclude that by 1920 when one-quarter of women nationally worked outside the home, the number was higher in Portland, averaging one-third.

In other New England cities, conditions for women seeking employment between 1880 and 1900 were limited. "Irish-born women also seemed incapable of exploiting opportunities among the city's fastest growing female occupations . . . Irish immigrant women also suffered from competition and prejudice."[65] Certainly both in Worcester and Portland these conditions would change over time. By the early twentieth century, many of the Irish women seeking employment opportunities were well-adjusted Irish Americans, familiar with local customs, and they were at ease with working outside of their homes. In these efforts, as this essay reveals, they were mutually supported by others in similar situations. In some ways this essay spans the lifetime of single Irish women in Portland from "Bridget the domestic" to "Rosie the riveter."

This book's penultimate essay is my effort to tell the story of the survival of a profound sense of "Nationalism Among Early Twentieth Century Irish Longshoremen in Portland, Maine." My essay connects with Matt Barker's. Picking up Barker's thread, the essay begins with Charles Stuart Parnell and Michael Davitt's Land League of the 1880s and even earlier, Civil-War-era groups, such as the Irish American Relief Association (IARA).

The major thrust of this essay, however, is the twentieth century and, in particular, the events on both sides of the Atlantic during the years of the Anglo-Irish War (1919–1921). It must have been a harrowing time to be Irish and Catholic in America. The nativist KKK was again on the rise, especially in northern states such as Maine. In Ireland, the might of the British "Black and Tans" and other irregular military forces were occupying large sections of republican (pro-independence) Ireland, while the Government of Ireland Act (1920) proposed the partition of the six most northeastern counties of the province of Ulster. Thus Ireland would be granted dominion status, as an Irish Free State (and not a republic), and this "concession" would come at the terrible cost of Irish unity.

The longshoremen of the Portland Longshoremen's Benevolent Society (PLSBS) were possibly the most solidly Irish work force in Portland at this time, and they numbered well over 1,000. This essay looks at the question of support for Ireland and Irish nationalism through the lens of this union and its members. During these turbulent years, especially 1919-1921, Portland was visited by several Irish dignitaries, such as Judge Donald F. Cohalan, Robert Lindsay Crawford, and Lord Mayor Donal O'Callaghan. Visits such as these reflect the significance of Portland as a center of Irish nationalist causes, albeit small in population.

Although this essay focuses on local responses to broader national and international political developments, I also look at the wider picture to see what was going on simultaneously in larger metropolitan areas, such as New York, with their significant Irish population bases. Portland was arguably only a backwater, but it was, at least, aware of the global picture and played its occasional piece in the drama, often the tragedy, being acted out in these pivotal years in Ireland.

The final essay in this book is Kenneth Nilsen's tribute to speakers of the Irish language, "The Galway Gaeltacht of Portland, Maine." Because of the geographical source of Irish chain migration into Portland, largely from Gaelic-speaking regions of Cois Fharraige and Connemara in County Galway, Nilsen writes, "It is quite possible that Portland has the highest percentage of Irish speakers among its Irish-born residents of any American city in the twentieth century."[66]

Nilsen's analysis of Irish-speaking Portlanders derives from interviews, many of them videotaped, with sixteen Irish speakers (in Irish) and five persons conversant with the Portland Gaeltacht (in English) from 1984 to 2003. Of these Nilsen credits two in particular, Mary Kilmartin and Pat Malone, both now deceased, with having not only "a remarkably high level of Irish fluency . . . [but also] very impressive stories of Irish folklore and tradition." (See gallery, plates 44–45.)

Conversations with the sixteen Irish-speaking interviewees make up the bulk of this essay, and a chart in the endnotes (Table 1) gives useful information concerning each interviewee's birth and death dates, place of origin, date of arrival in Portland, and the nature of their work. Of particular interest is their place of origin. The one exception is Nan Foley (née Connolly) who was born in Portland but taken to Cois Fharraige in Ireland where she lived from ages three to eighteen, returning to Portland a fluent Irish speaker. All the rest were born in one of three Irish-speaking districts in County Galway: Cois Fharraige, Corr na Móna, or Seana Faracháin. Nilsen's ability to discern the differences among these dialects gave him a tremendous advantage in gaining the confidence of each of the interviewees. Uniformly the interviewees believed Nilsen to be a native Irish speaker rather than a native New Yorker, clearly a great compliment to his mastery of the nuances of the language, or what the Irish refer to as "having the blas."

One final morsel of information may be gleaned from Nilsen's interviews which provides an interesting connection to Eagan and Finn's conclusions in their essay: all five of the female Irish speakers, at some point in their lives, labored as domestic workers. What a curious sight and sound it must have been to see and hear these native Irish speakers working in the proper Yankee homes of Portland's Western Promenade or other fashionable inner-city districts. This was *Upstairs, Downstairs* with a Gaelic twist. The story ends sadly but predictably with Nilsen's finding that "Irish was an oral language spoken only within a certain network of acquaintances . . . [and therefore] Irish speakers only rarely passed Irish on to the second generation in the twentieth century."[67] As was prophesized by the famous Blasket Island writer and native Irish speaker, Tomás Ó Crohan (*Ó Criomhthain*), in his influential work, *An tOileánach* (translated by Robin Flower as *The Islandman*), "their likes will not be seen again."

1. One example of an Irish-American labor leader with a Maine connection was Elizabeth Gurley Flynn, whose father was a Maine granite cutter. She writes about his experiences and their influence on her family in her autobiography, *The Rebel Girl: An Autobiography of my First Life 1906–1926* (New York: International Publishers, 1973), originally published as *I speak my own piece*, 1955. Equally famous as a female Irish labor leader was Maria Harris "Mother" Jones.

2. Charles A. Scontras, *Organized Labor and Labor Politics in Maine, 1880–1980*, University of Maine Studies, 2d ser., no. 83 (Orono: University of Maine Press, 1966); *Organized Labor in Maine: Twentieth Century Origins* (Orono: University of Maine Press/Bureau of Labor Education, 1985); *Organized Labor in Maine: War, Reaction, Depression, and the Rise of the CIO 1914–1943* (Orono: Bureau of Labor Education, University of Maine, 2003); *The Socialist Alternative: Utopian Experiments and the Socialist Party of Maine, 1895–1914* (Orono: University of Maine Press/Bureau of Labor Education, 1985); and *Two Decades of Organized Labor and Labor Politics in Maine, 1880–1900* (Orono: University of Maine Press, 1962).

3. Michael C. Connolly, "The Irish Longshoremen of Portland, Maine 1880–1923" (Ph.D. diss., Boston College, 1988). The entire collection of the records of the longshoremen's union (PLSBS, ILA local 861) is housed in the Maine Historical Society. This is the exception to the rule, however, as most labor records are not now safely housed in a manner that will make them accessible for future research. See also Charles J. O'Leary, "A History of Organized Labor in Maine during the New Deal," Special Collections, Fogler Library, University of Maine, Orono.

4. See Michael C. Connolly, "The First Hurrah: James Michael Curley versus the 'Goo-Goos' in the Boston Mayoralty Election of 1914," *Historical Journal of Massachusetts* 30, no. 1 (winter 2002).

5. See Allan R. Whitmore, " 'A Guard of Faithful Sentinels': The Know-Nothing Appeal in Maine, 1854–1855," *Maine Historical Society Quarterly* 20, no. 3 (winter 1981). For a broader regional analysis of this nativist phenomenon, see Tyler Anbinder, *Nativism and Slavery: The Northern Know Nothings and the Politics of the 1850s* (New York: Oxford University Press, 1992). Also see Anbinder, *Five Points* (New York: The Free Press, 2001). The Five Points neighborhood is the setting for Martin Scorcese's film, *The Gangs of New York*, which focuses on the animosity between the Irish-Catholic immigrants and the nativists in that city.

6. Neal Dow, *The Reminiscences of Neal Dow* (Portland, ME: Evening Express Publishing Co., 1898); Frank L. Byrne, *Prophet of Prohibition: Neal Dow and His Crusade* (Gloucester, MA: Peter Smith, 1969). For an older assessment of Dow, see A. A. Miner, "Neal Dow and His Life Work," *The New England Magazine* 10, no. 4 (June, 1894); and on the early drive for prohibition see Ian R. Tyrrell, *Sobering Up: From Temperance to Prohibition in Antebellum America, 1800–1860* (Westport, CT: Greenwood Press, 1979). See also William David Barry and Nan Cumming, *Rum, Riot, and Reform: Maine and the History of American Drinking* (Portland: Maine Historical Society, 1998). This is the catalog of an exhibit that ran from June 1 to October 31, 1998 at the Maine History Gallery, MHS.

7. Michael C. Connolly, "Black Fades to Green: Irish Labor Replaces African-American Labor Along a Major New England Waterfront, Portland, Maine, in the Mid-Nineteenth Century," *Colby Quarterly* 37, no. 4 (December 2001): 367.

8. See Noel Ignatiev, *How the Irish became White* (New York: Routledge, 1995); David R. Roediger, *The Wages of Whiteness: Race and the Making of the American Working Class* (London: Verso, 1991); and Dale T. Knobel, *Paddy and the Republic* (Middletown, CT: Wesleyan University Press, 1986).

9. See George J. Mitchell, *Making Peace* (Berkeley: University of California Press, 1999). Perhaps one of Governor Joseph Brennan's greatest political accomplishments was his nomination of former federal attorney George Mitchell to fill a vacant seat in the U.S. Senate following the elevation of Senator Edmund S. Muskie to Secretary of State during the Carter administration. From this position, Mitchell was instrumental in returning the U.S. Senate to Democratic Party control, resulting in his elevation to Majority Leader. After his retirement from the Senate, Mitchell worked tirelessly to help negotiate the Good Friday (Belfast) Agreement in Northern Ireland in April of 1998. Mitchell's work on behalf of Maine and Ireland continues, especially in the crucial field of education. He is currently serving as Chancellor of the Queen's University of Belfast and is largely responsible for the Mitchell Scholarships, totaling about 130, roughly one for every public high school in the state of Maine. The Senator George J. Mitchell Scholarship Research Institute may be reached at 22 Monument Square, Portland, ME 04101 and at 207-773-7700. Their website is http://www.mitchellinstitute.org.

10. See the essay in this book by R. Stuart Wallace. See also William David Barry, *Bryce McLellan and his Children, 1720–1776* (Portland: University of Southern Maine, 1973); William Willis, "The Scotch-Irish Immigration to Maine, and Presbyterianism in New England," *Collection of Maine Historical Society* 6 (1859); Maude Glasgow, *The Scotch-Irish in Northern Ireland and the American Colonies* (New York: G. P. Putnam's Sons, 1936); and Marjorie R. Fallows, *Irish-Americans: Identity and Assimilation* (Englewood Cliffs, NJ: Prentice Hall, 1979).

11. Emmett Larkin, "The Devotional Revolution in Ireland, 1850–1875," *American Historical Review* 77, no. 3 (June 1972): 625–52; see also his study of the period following in *The Roman Catholic Church in Ireland and Fall of Parnell, 1888–1891* (Chapel Hill: University of North Carolina Press, 1979).

12. The literature on the famine is voluminous. The best current source is arguably Christine Kinealy, *This Great Calamity: The Irish Famine 1845–52* (Dublin: Gill and Macmillan, 1994). See also her latest work, *The Great Irish Famine: Impact, Ideology and Rebellion* (New York: Palgrave, 2002). Perhaps the best-known work on the famine is Cecil Woodham-Smith, *The Great Hunger* (New York: Harper and Row, 1962). See also Joel Mokyr, *Why Ireland Starved: A Quantitative and Analytical History of the Irish Economy, 1800–1850* (Winchester, MA: Allen and Unwin, Inc., 1983).

13. See Edward McCarron's essay on Lincoln County in this book as well as his other publications cited in that essay and in the Bibliography. Also see two works of William Leo Lucey, *The Catholic Church in Maine* (Francestown, NH: Marshall Jones, 1957); and *Edward Kavanagh, Catholic, Statesman, Diplomat from Maine, 1795–1844* (Francestown, NH: Marshall Jones Company, 1946). For

the latest work on the Catholic Church in Maine, see Vincent A. Lapomarda, *The Catholic Church in the Land of the Holy Cross: A History of the Diocese of Portland, Maine* (Strasbourg, France: Les Editions du Signe, 2003).

14. See Fr. Hugh Fenning, "The Conversion of Charles Ffrench," *The Watchman* 28, no. 53 (summer 1961). I am indebted to Irish teacher and historian extraordinaire Donal Taheny of Wood Quay, Galway for this reference. See also "History of St. Dominic's Parish," *Saint Dominic's, 175 Years of Memories, 1822–1997,* ed. Michael and Marilyn Melody (Portland ME: Smart Marketing, Inc., 1997).

15. See James Mundy, *Hard Times, Hard Men: Maine and the Irish 1830–1860* (Scarborough, ME: Harp Publications, 1990), 37–38. For a comparison between two of these Maine cities and their dramatically contrasting priests (Portland's Fr. John O'Donnell and Ellsworth's Fr. John Bapst), see 156–66. For the history of nativism in Maine, see Whitmore, " 'A Guard of Faithful Sentinels'."

16. For information on Cheverus, See Lucey, *The Catholic Church in Maine,* as well as Matthew Jude Barker's essay in this book. The Maine Historical Society holds a manuscript collection concerning Cheverus. See Cheverus to E. Kavanagh, 20 March 1821 (Maine Historical Society Collection 420, vol. 1); and Kavanagh to William King, 7 January 1832. See also Walter Muir Whitehill, *A Memorial to Bishop Cheverus, With A Catalogue Of The Books Given By Him To The Boston Athenaeum* (Boston: Athenaeum, 1941).

17. See Edward McCarron's essay on Benedicta in this volume. See also Sister Marie of the Visitation Nicknair, O.P., *Bishop Benedict Fenwick and the Origins of the Benedicta, Maine Community* (Augusta, ME: O'Ceallaigh Publications, 1992). My thanks go to John Munroe of the Theology Department and the Graduate and Professional Studies program at Saint Joseph's College (Maine) for procuring a copy of this study. I am also very grateful to Mrs. Christine Hescott (née Qualey) of Portland who was born and raised in Benedicta. Mrs. Hescott graciously shared with me several documents concerning the history of this township as well as enjoyable conversation and anecdotes about her family and life there. She still has family in Benedicta.

18. James M. O'Toole, *Militant and Triumphant: William Henry O'Connell and the Catholic Church in Boston, 1859–1944* (Notre Dame, IN: University of Notre Dame Press, 1992). In part the reason for this chill was the poor financial condition in which O'Connell allegedly left the treasury of Portland and Bishop Walsh, his successor. Walsh alleged that O'Connell had taken funds from Portland when he was promoted to the Boston Diocese.

19. Mary C. Sullivan, *Catherine McAuley and the Tradition of Mercy* (Notre Dame, IN: University of Notre Dame Press, 2000).

20. Kathleen Healy, *Frances Warde: American Founder of the Sisters of Mercy* (New York: The Seabury Press, 1973).

21. Mary Raymond Higgins, RSM, *For Love of Mercy: Missioned in Maine and Andros Island, Bahamas 1883–1983* (Portland: Sisters of Mercy, 1995).

22. Healy, *Frances Warde,* 392–93.

23. Ibid., 393–95.

24. See http://www.catholic-hierarchy.org/diocese/dpome.html.

25. See Michael J. Guignard, *La Foi, La Langue, La Culture: The Franco-Americans of Biddeford, Maine* (By author, 1982) and "Maine's Corporation Sole Controversy," *Maine Historical Society Quarterly* 12, no. 3 (winter 1973). Maine

was not the only state facing this issue, as can be seen in Edward Kantowicz, *Corporation Sole: Cardinal Mundelein and Chicago Catholicism* (Notre Dame, IN: University of Notre Dame Press, 1983).

26. Guignard, "Maine's Corporation Sole Controversy."

27. The most thorough current biography of Healy and his family is James M. O'Toole, *Passing for White: Race, Religion, and the Healy Family 1820–1920* (Amherst: University of Massachusetts Press, 2002). See also Albert S. Foley, S.J., *Bishop Healy, Beloved Outcaste: The Story of a Great Priest whose Life has Become a Legend* (New York: Ferrar, Straus, and Young, 1954); and other works by Foley cited in the Bibliography. See also Josephine Kelly, *Dark Shepherd* (Patterson, NJ: St. Anthony Guild Press, 1967).

28. Henry J. Browne, *The Catholic Church and the Knights of Labor* (Washington DC: Catholic University Press, 1949), 128. See also Terrence V. Powderly, *The Path I Trod* (New York: A.M.S. Press, 1940) for a revealing recounting by Powderly of an emotional meeting between these two rival Irish leaders during an organizing trip by Powderly to Portland. Also of interest is Fergus Macdonald, *The Catholic Church and the Secret Societies in the United States* (New York: U.S. Catholic Historical Society, 1946). The Catholic hierarchy in both Ireland and America tended to perceive organizations such as the Knights of Labor as being radical, especially if their agenda would tend to increase the power of the organization/union/state at the expense of the Church/individual/family. This remained true even if the agenda, as in the case of the KOL, was merely social democratic (mildly socialistic).

29. John Syrett, "Principle and Expediency: The Ku Klux Klan and Owen Brewster in 1924," *Maine History* 39, no. 4 (winter 2000–01): 219. See also Rita Mae Breton, "Red Scare: A study of Maine Nativism, 1919–1925" (master's thesis, University of Maine at Orono, 1972); Edward Bonner Whitney, "The Ku Klux Klan in Maine: A Study with Particular Emphasis on the City of Portland" (master's thesis, Harvard University, 1966); Harold Boyle, "When the Klan Campaigned in Maine," *Maine Sunday Telegram*, 23 April 1978; and John Higham, *Strangers in the Land: Patterns of American Nativism, 1860–1925* (New Brunswick, NJ: Rutgers University Press, 1955).

30. See the Bishop Louis S. Walsh Diaries (Chancery of the Roman Catholic Diocese of Portland). Look in the early 1920s for several references to his struggle against the KKK. There are anecdotal reports from Catholics who, at the urging of their priests and perhaps even Bishop Walsh, changed their political affiliation from Democrat to Republican in order to defeat Ralph Owen Brewster in the Republican primary prior to the gubernatorial election of 1924. The tactic almost succeeded, but Brewster narrowly won the primary with active Klan support and easily won the general election on September 8, 1924. See John Syrett, "Principle and Expediency," for more detail on this period.

31. These anecdotes, mainly from the Portland area, range from the highly believable to the merely speculative, and in that spirit they are offered here. They include a report of a Portland Irish-Catholic businessman serving as a liaison between Gov. Owen Brewster, who was elected with the open support of the KKK, and Bishop Walsh over the question of school funding; a report that the fire brigades responding to a devastating fire at the KKK Portland headquarters on Forest Avenue were "unavoidably delayed"; an allegation that lunch buckets

(connoting lower social class) were strongly discouraged from being displayed on Congress Street (Portland's major commercial/business thoroughfare); Irish citizens' belief that the Thirteen Club centered at Munjoy Hill's Saint Lawrence Congregational Church was, in reality, a secretive group affiliated with Portland's elite for the purpose of social control; a belief that the main Catholic church building in Portland (The Cathedral of the Immaculate Conception) was built facing away from Congress Street rather than on Portland's central artery, also for social reasons, as was Saint Dominic's Church built facing Gray Street rather than the much more prominent State Street.

32. Many studies have been published on this topic of stereotyping. Perhaps the best known is Perry Curtis, *Apes and Angels: The Irishman in Victorian Caricature* (Washington, DC: The Smithsonian Institution Press, 1971). See also Morton Keller, *The Art and Politics of Thomas Nast* (New York: Oxford University Press, 1968). In the case of *Maggie and Jiggs* (aka *Jiggs and Maggie*, or *Jiggs*, or by its authentic title *Bringing Up Father*) many Irish saw this as humorous self-parody, but others judged it to be insulting and reflecting the social stereotyping of the Irish in the early twentieth century when they were climbing socially but had not yet "arrived." The strip's creator, George McManus, launched the series in the Hearst newspapers on January 12, 1913, and it became one of the longest-running comic strips in American history. McManus's themes focussed on Jiggs' "uninhibited naturalness" and his "socially ambitious wife and daughter's feelings of shame about him, and his consequent desire to escape from the pretensions of his new social world." It was an Irish "Beverly Hillbillies" that featured copious amounts of corned beef and cabbage, alcohol, and card games with his cronies at the corner saloon, Dinty Moore's. See Ron Goulart, ed., *The Encyclopedia of American Comics* (New York: Facts on File – A Promised Land Production, 1990): 51–52. Available at the Maine Historical Society.

33. See Donald A. Yerxa, "The Burning of Falmouth, 1775: A Case Study in Imperial Pacification," *Maine Historical Society Quarterly* 14, no. 3 (winter 1975): 119–60. On O'Brien see the following: Andrew M. Sherman, *Life of Captain Jeremiah O'Brien, Machias, Maine* (Morristown, NJ: The Jerseyman Office, 1902); Thomas P. Cahill, *A Short Sketch of the Life and Achievements of Captain Jeremiah O'Brien of Machias, Maine* (Worcester, MA: Harrigan Press, Inc., 1936); and John O'Brien, "Exertions of the O'Brien Family, at Machias in the American Revolution," *Collections of the Maine Historical Society* II (Portland: By the Society, 1847): 242–49. One of only two surviving Liberty Ships, the *S.S. Jeremiah O'Brien* was built in 1943 at the New England Shipbuilding Corporation in South Portland, Maine. It is currently berthed at Pier 45, Fisherman's Wharf, San Francisco. See Herbert G. Jones, *Portland Ships are Good Ships* (Portland: Machigonne Press, 1945). See also one of several web sites such as www.geocities.com/jeremiahobrien/obrien.html, dedicated to this ship that participated in the Allied invasion of Normandy in 1944.

34. Kerby A. Miller, *Emigrants and Exiles: Ireland and the Irish Exodus to North America* (New York: Oxford University Press, 1985). For an analysis of earlier Irish immigration see Kerby A. Miller, Arnold Schrier, Bruce D. Boling, and David N. Doyle, *Irish Immigrants in the Land of Canaan: Letters and Memoirs from Colonial and Revolutionary America, 1675–1815* (Oxford: Oxford University Press, 2003).

35. Robert E. Kennedy, Jr., *The Irish: Emigration, Marriage, and Fertility* (Berkeley: University of California Press, 1973). See also Mícheál D. Roe, "Contemporary Catholic and Protestant Irish America: Social Identities, Forgiveness, and Attitudes Toward *The Troubles*," *Éire-Ireland* 37, nos. 1 and 2 (spring/summer 2002): 153–74.

36. Seamus Grimes and Michael C. Connolly, "The Migration Link between Cois Fharraige and Portland, Maine, 1880s to 1920s," *Irish Geography* 22 (1989). See also Michael C. Connolly, "The Next Parish West of Galway: The Irish Diaspora of Portland, Maine," *House Island Project* (Portland: Portland Performing Arts, 1996); and three articles by Matthew J. Barker, "From Galway to Maine: The Story of an Immigrant Family," *Galway Roots, Clanna na Gaillimhe* 4 (1996–97); "John Ford and The Feeney Family of Galway and Portland, Maine," *Galway Roots/Clanna na Gaillimhe* 5 (1998); and "The Last Time We Shared Stone Soup," *Portland Monthly Magazine* (October 2000). For the most comprehensive coverage of this Galway-Portland link in the local newspapers see John Healy (writer) and John Ewing (photographer), "Irish Roots: From Galway to Casco Bay," *Maine Sunday Telegram* (22 December 1991): 1A, 13–14A; *Portland Press Herald* (23 December 1991): 6A; *Portland Press Herald* (24 December 1991): 1A, 6A; *Portland Press Herald* (25 December 1991): 1A.

37. Kenneth E. Nilsen, "Thinking of Monday: The Irish Speakers of Portland, Maine," *Éire-Ireland* 25, no. 1 (spring 1990): 6–19; Nancy Stenson, "Beagáinín: The Use of Irish Among Immigrants to the United States," *New Hibernia Review* 2 (1998): 116–31; and Seán de Fréine, *The Great Silence* (Cork: Mercier Press, 1978).

38. See Robert McCrum, William Cran, and Robert MacNeil, *The Story of English* (New York: Viking Press, 1986). This is the companion book to the PBS series of the same name. See especially Episode 8, "The Loaded Weapon," regarding the Irish influence on both English and American-English dialects. Perhaps the new Irish Heritage Center in the old Saint Dominic's Church (Portland) will one day house a collection of these and other materials in both English and Irish. Kenneth Nilsen has translated his Irish-language interviews in Portland into English for his essay in this book. He is currently compiling an Irish-language transcription of these same interviews.

39. Michael T. Isenberg, *John L. Sullivan and His America* (Urbana: University of Illinois Press, 1988).

40. Ron Kaplan, "The Sporting Life: The Irish Influence in Baseball," *Irish America* (February/March 2003): 54. See also Edward J. Rielly, *Baseball: An Encyclopedia of Popular Culture* (Santa Barbara, CA: ABC-CLIO, 2000).

41. Kaplan, "The Sporting Life," 54.

42. William David Barry and Arthur J. Gerrier, *Munjoy Hill Historic Guide* (Portland: Greater Portland Landmarks, 1992). This citation is for 8 Sherbrooke Street on the corner of Waterville Street on Munjoy Hill. Lyng's equivalent in Lewiston would have been Patrick Many (see Margaret Buker Jay's essay in this volume). As owner and proprietor of Lewiston's only racetrack, the Androscoggin Trotting Park, among other ventures, Many was able to own property valued at over $25,000 in the mid-1870s.

43. See J. Donald MacWilliams, *Yours in Sport: A History of Baseball, Basketball, Boxing and Bowling in Maine* (Lewiston, ME: Twin City Publishers for the

Monmouth Press, 1967). For boxing specifically see Dick Redmond, *The Maine Boxing Records Book 1922–2000* (Greenville, ME: Moosehead Communications, 2000). Welch in 140 fights (1936–49) compiled a record of 108 wins, 26 losses, and 6 draws (with 51 knockouts). McDermott in 72 fights (1962–71) compiled a record of 52 wins, 17 losses, and 3 draws (with 29 knockouts). I am grateful to Bruce Glasier of WCSH television news (Channel 6 in Portland) for these references. MacWilliams' and Redmond's books contain information about many more Irish sports figures.

44. Bill Levy, *John Ford: A Bio-Bibliography* (Westport, CT: Greenwood Press, 1998); Joseph McBride, *Searching for John Ford: A Life* (New York: St. Martin's Press, 2001); and William C. Dowling, "John Ford's Festive Comedy: Ireland Imagined in *The Quiet Man*," *Éire-Ireland* 36, nos. 3 and 4 (fall/winter 2001): 190–211. Tom Gaffney of the Portland Public Library also made me aware of the following works available at the Library: Peter Bogdanovich, *John Ford* (Berkeley: University of California Press, 1968); Tag Gallagher, *John Ford: The Man and His Films* (Berkeley: University of California Press, 1986); and Scott Eyman, *Print the Legend: The Life and Times of John Ford* (New York: Simon and Schuster, 1999).

45. William David Barry, "James Healy, We Hardly Knew You," *Portland Monthly Magazine* 9, no. 3 (May 1994): 11. I am indebted to Barry for his assistance in the area of the Irish and the arts.

46. See Dowling, "John Ford's Festive Comedy," 194–95.

47. As evidence of this renewed scholarship see Mundy, *Hard Times, Hard Men*. See also the work of University of Southern Maine English professor Dr. Francis C. "Bud" McGrath, *Brian Friel's (Post) Colonial Drama: Language, Illusion, and Politics* (Syracuse: Syracuse University Press, 1999); *The Sensible Spirit: Walter Pater and the Modernist Paradigm* (Tampa: University of South Florida Press, 1986); and *Ireland's Field Day Theatre Company* (forthcoming). Another young Maine academic doing work in this area is Dr. Angela B. Gleason of Union, a graduate of Saint Joseph's College in Standish, Maine and a Fulbright scholar. See her "Adamnan in the Tenth and Eleventh Centuries: A Literary Revival" (M. Phil. thesis, Trinity College Dublin, 1997); and "Entertainment in Early Ireland" (Ph.D. diss., Trinity College Dublin, 2002; a published version of this is forthcoming).

48. Founded in 1973, the Irish-American Club of Maine can be reached via its mailing address, P.O. Box 1683, Portland, ME 04104-1683, or by phone, 207-780-0119. Its website is www.maineirish.com, and its email address club@maineirish.com.

49. The connection between the Irish of Portland and Norwood, Massachusetts is mentioned in Kenneth Nilsen's essay in this volume, but much more research should be done in this area.

50. A mailing address for the IHC is P.O. Box 7588, Portland, ME 04112-7588. Its website is http://www.maineirish.com and its email address, info@maineirish. com. Linda Hogan was the original director of early fundraising efforts, currently being chaired by Sabrina Loring, and Senator George J. Mitchell is the Honorary Capital Campaign Chair. John J. O'Dea is the IHC Executive Director.

51. The MICP's mailing address is P.O. Box 3122, Portland, ME 04104, and their phone number, 207-282-3939. This organization was founded in 1984 by Father John Feeney, Patricia Corey, Philip Curran, Bruce Webb, Joe Denson, and Anne Scanlon, among others. It was later joined by Rev. Alex Cairns, Claire Foley,

Joanne Baribeau, Susan and Bruce Schuyler, and many others. Since 1991 the Schuylers have served as co-directors of MICP. This program has depended on contacts within Northern Ireland for students to travel to Maine. Programs there such as Protestant and Catholic Encounter (PACE) and Community Relations in Schools (CRIS) were early sponsors of this Belfast-Maine Children's Program. Eamonn and Maureen McMillan were enthusiastic early supporters; now deceased, they are both missed by their many friends in Maine. Other Northern Irish volunteers who worked with MICP were Beryl McKee, Regina Millan, and John Herron, among countless others. Currently Pat Morgan of the North East Education and Library Board coordinates efforts between Maine and Northern Ireland. All these people and the many hundreds of volunteers who aided them have strongly served the cause of peace and justice, both in Northern Ireland and here in Maine.

52. This organization, formerly known as Portland Performing Arts, is largely the creation of James "Bau" Graves and Phylis O'Neill. The location and mailing address for CCE is One Longfellow Square, Portland, ME 04101, the telephone number is 207-761-0591. Its website is http://www.centerforculturalexchange. org and the e-mail address is info@centerforculturalexchange.org. The CCE has recently become even more active in the area of multicultural education and out-reach, and has become a tremendous resource for Maine individuals and groups interested in this subject. A forthcoming book by James Bau Graves with the working title of *Cultural Democracy* will be published by the University of Illinois Press.

53. *House Island Project* (Portland: Portland Performing Arts, 1996). This Project facilitated the extended visits to Maine by traditional Irish musician Seamus Egan of the band Solas and Irish set dancer Tony Ryan of Galway for the purpose of teaching local Mainers their specialties.

54. See Patrick Griffin, *The People with No Name: Ireland's Ulster Scots, America's Scots Irish, and the Creation of a British Atlantic World, 1689–1764* (Princeton, NJ: Princeton University Press, 2001). See also Andrew Greeley, "The Success and Assimilation of Irish Protestants and Catholics in the United States," *Social Science Research 72*, no. 4 (1985).

55. E. Estyn Evans, "Old Ireland and New England," *Ireland and the Atlantic Heritage* (Dublin: The Lilliput Press, 1996), 114. I am indebted to Ed McCarron for this reference. See also, in the same source, Evans' article "The Scotch-Irish: Their Cultural Adaptation and Heritage in the American Old West." For the demographic implications of this early Ulster immigration, see Fallows, *Irish-Americans*. Fallows intriguingly asserts that because of this early source of Irish migration to America, and its strong ties with Presbyterianism, a surprisingly high number of Irish in this country are Protestant.

56. Evans, *Ireland and the Atlantic Heritage*, 114–15.

57. Evans, *Ireland and the Atlantic Heritage*, 122. On the question of the survival of the Gaelic languages on Rathlin and the historic context of language displace-ment there, three very important works should be consulted: Nils M. Hulmer, *The Irish Language in Rathlin Island, Co. Antrim* (Dublin: Hodges, Figgis, 1942); T. F. O'Rahilly, *Irish Dialects Past and Present* (Dublin: Browne and Nolan, Ltd., 1932); and Wallace Clark, *Rathlin: Its Island Story* (Coleraine: Northwest Books, 1988). I am very grateful to Kenneth Nilsen for these three references.

58. Evans, *Ireland and the Atlantic Heritage*, 126.

59. Nicknair, *Bishop Benedict Fenwick*, 11–12.

60. See Anbinder, *Five Points* and *Nativism and Slavery* for a wider historical account of these nativist-Irish rivalries.

61. See Mundy, *Hard Times, Hard Men*, especially Chapter 7, for the infamous and violent Ellsworth case and a description of the more civil contrasting situation in Portland in the same mid-nineteenth century period.

62. See the works of Michael J. Guignard, especially *La Foi, La Langue, La Culture* and "Maine's Corporation Sole Controversy." See also the new film by Ben Levine, *Waking Up French, Reveil: The Repression and Renaissance of the French in New England* (Rockland, ME: Watching Place Productions, 2002) for a depiction of the struggle of the French against the nativism of the KKK in the 1920s. Also see Gerard J. Brault, *The French Canadian Heritage in New England* (Montreal: McGill University Press, 1986), and Raymond Breton and Pierre Savard, eds., *The Quebec and Acadian Diaspora in North America* (Toronto: Multicultural History Society of Ontario, 1982).

63. There are numerous books and articles available on the Fenians and/or the Irish Republican Brotherhood. See Leon O'Brion, *Fenian Fever: An Anglo-American Dilemma* (New York: NYU Press, 1971); Brian Jenkins, *Fenians and Anglo-American Relations During Reconstruction* (Ithaca, NY: Cornell University Press, 1969); and Michael Ruddy, "An Irish Army in America," *Civil War Times* 42, no. 1 (April 2003): 32–40. This article refers to the incident described in this essay as the "Eastport Fizzle" (38).

64. Many Irish and Irish-American revisionist historians in recent years have viewed violent or revolutionary episodes, such as the Fenian movement of the 1860s, with less sympathy than did earlier, more traditionalist, nationalist writers. As an example of this Irish historical revisionism, see Ruth Dudley Edwards, *Patrick Pearse: The Triumph of Failure* (New York: Taplinger Publishing Co., 1978). This historiography, which is generally more critical of the armed struggle and of traditional physical-force republicanism, resulted, in part, from the continued carnage in Northern Ireland since the most recent resurgence of "The Troubles" in the late 1960s.

65. Timothy Meagher, *Inventing Irish America: Generation, Class, and Ethnic Identity in a New England City, 1880–1928* (Notre Dame, IN: University of Notre Dame Press, 2001): 46–47. The works most often cited on this subject are Hasia R. Diner, *Erin's Daughters in America: Irish Immigrant Women in the Nineteenth Century* (Baltimore: Johns Hopkins University Press, 1983), and Janet A. Nolan, *Ourselves Alone: Women's Immigration from Ireland, 1885–1921* (Lexington: The University Press of Kentucky, 1989). An example of a more recent study would be Diane M. Hotten-Somers, "Relinquishing and Reclaiming Independence: Irish Domestic Servants, American Middle-Class Mistresses, and Assimilation, 1850–1920," *Éire-Ireland* 36, nos. 1 and 2 (spring/summer 2001): 185–201.

66. See Nilsen's previously published study of Portland, "Thinking of Monday: The Irish Speakers of Portland, Maine." Nilsen's published research on Portland is cited in Nancy Stenson's "Beagáinín: The Use of Irish among Immigrants to the United States," 117–18.

67. For an analysis of the state of the Irish language in contemporary Ireland see Brian ÓCuív, *A View of the Irish Language* (Dublin: Stationery Office, 1969); Tomás de Bhaldraithe, *The Irish of Cois Fhairrage, County Galway: A Phonetic Study* (Dublin: Dublin Institute for Advanced Studies, 1945); and Kenneth E. Nilsen's publications. A useful collection of contemporary scholarship, in the form of eleven essays, may be found in a Special Issue of *Éire-Ireland* 38 (*Language and Identity in Twentieth-Century Irish Culture*), nos. 1 and 2 (spring/summer, 2002).

ESSAYS

THE SCOTCH-IRISH OF PROVINCIAL MAINE: PURPOODUCK, MERRYMEETING BAY, AND GEORGIA

by R. Stuart Wallace

INTRODUCTION

THE MIGRATION OF IRISH PROTESTANTS from Ulster to British North America in the eighteenth century was part of the long-standing English effort to establish "plantations" in foreign lands. This was a policy that called for the replacement of "native" peoples with subjects loyal to the Crown. The policy required justification. By the late sixteenth century, British colonizing interests had determined that native peoples could be removed if they were non-Christian, or "pagans"; if they were nomadic, hence "barbarians"; and if they had no title to the land in the first place. Native peoples were deemed without title if they had not "improved" the land, which in English terms meant they had not cultivated the land.

English colonizing policy took shape during the reign of Queen Elizabeth, and the primary objective was Ireland. As English attitudes toward the Gaelic Irish hardened in the late sixteenth century, it became easier to justify brutality. The native Irish were seen as hea-thens and barbarians, deserving subjugation or worse. Efforts to colo-nize Ireland were soon followed by colonial ventures in North America. Veterans of Irish colonial wars came to America determined to displace another native people. By the seventeenth century, Native Americans were being described in language previously used for the Gaelic Irish.

The first wave of Ulster emigrants to come to New England in 1718 may not have thought of themselves as part of a grand colonizing plan, but they soon participated in the plan, just as their Scottish ancestors had participated in earlier efforts to colonize the northern counties of Ireland, historically known as the province of Ulster. Boston land speculators and government officials were quick to use Irish immigrants as settlers on frontier lands in Maine, where they displaced Native Americans from some of their traditional hunting and fishing grounds. Frontier warfare was the obvious result. Before long, Scotch-Irish attitudes toward Native Americans hardened. The Indian foe was seen as heathen and barbaric, and Irish and Scotch-Irish settlements in Maine were seen as being justified because the land was "idle" and awaiting cultivation.[1]

This essay is written from the perspective of the Scotch-Irish settlers. It presents their point of view and does not deal with relations between white Europeans and Native Americans in Maine. That is an enormously important subject, but one that is beyond the scope of the present work. This essay deals primarily with relations between the early Scotch-Irish settlers on the Maine frontier and their more numerous and powerful English fellow settlers further to the south.

* * * * *

On March 5, 1719, the Reverend William Boyd, a recent immigrant from Ulster, was invited to dine with Judge Samuel Sewall in the latter's Boston home. As the "advance scout" of many of the early Ulster settlers to come to Boston, Boyd felt responsible for their welfare. As they dined, he discussed an alarming rumor with Sewall. According to street talk in Boston, Governor Vaudreuil of Canada had warned New Englanders that he could no longer "hold back" his Native American allies. The frontier regions of northern New England might once again run with blood. To Boyd, the prospects were very disturbing. Many of his fellow immigrants had departed for the coast of Maine, the "eastern parts," and it was certain that more would follow. Their very presence on the eastern frontier was causing uneasiness among Native Americans loyal to Vaudreuil's government.[2]

Potential conflict with the French and their Native American allies was only one of many troubles encountered by Irish and Ulster immigrants in Maine in the early eighteenth century. The soil, the topography, and weather conditions presented challenges as well. Even more troublesome were Boston political leaders and land speculators. Political and economic turmoil in Massachusetts, compounded by the ethnic and religious bigotry of "the people of New England," meant nothing but trouble for the Irish Presbyterians struggling to make a living along the coast of Maine. It was only with the greatest of difficulty that some of the immigrants managed to gain a foothold in the eastern parts for the crown of England.

Although a few Irish migrants had found their way to New England in the seventeenth and very early eighteenth centuries, it was not until 1718 that Irish migration to New England began in earnest. In that year, ships sailing from ports in northern Ireland, or Ulster, arrived in Boston harbor. Most of these immigrants were Presbyterians of Scottish descent. While they generally rejected the ethnic label "Irish," which they felt was tainted with Catholicism, they could not arrive at a generally acceptable substitute label. It was left for their descendants to popularize the term Scotch-Irish, or sometimes, Scots-Irish. Unfortunately, their arrival in Boston coincided with a period of high unemployment, famine, and even an outbreak of smallpox. They were not welcome. On the other hand, their arrival came at a time when the frontier regions of British North America were considered relatively safe for settlement. A number of land speculators in Boston were looking for families to settle their lands in Maine and elsewhere. Hence, the Irish immigrants who were so unwelcome in Boston were more than welcome in Maine.[3]

No sooner had they arrived then groups of Scotch-Irish immigrants began petitioning for grants of land. On October 31, 1718, the Reverend Archibald Boyd and the Reverend James MacGregor petitioned the Massachusetts House of Representatives on behalf of twenty-six others for a "Tract of their vast Land, in such a Place as they shall think fit, where they may without Loss of Time, settle themselves & their Families." In this petition, Boyd and MacGregor asked for no particular piece of land, but they did indicate that forty more families of their acquaintance would join them "as soon as they hear of their obtaining Land for Township."[4] Two weeks later, John Armstrong, an early leader, and thirty-four other Irish immigrants petitioned the House of Representatives for a tract of land at Casco Bay.[5]

Their timing was good. Massachusetts leaders wanted to resettle some of the towns in Casco Bay that had been deserted during Queen Anne's War (1700-1713). On November 19, 1718 a committee of the house reported favorably on the general principles of both of the "Irish" petitions, but the specifics of Armstrong's petition needed revision; the requested tract of land was already inhabited. The committee went on to recommend that a township be set aside for the various petitioners. It would be six miles square, and eighty house lots of approximately one hundred acres each would be surveyed and marked.[6]

Accounts of the first winter at Casco Bay are sketchy and contradictory. Several Scotch-Irish families apparently sailed immediately for Casco Bay upon receiving word that the House of Representatives supported their venture. They probably sailed on the *Robert*, led by James MacGregor's brother-in-law James McKeen and the Reverend William Cornwall.[7] Numbers are harder to determine. Some secondary accounts place the migration to Falmouth at between sixteen and twenty families; a more recent account indicates the number was higher.[8] The most substantial piece of evidence survives in the form of a petition for relief. On December 2, the Massachusetts House received a petition from the town of Falmouth, complaining that "there are now in town about 300 souls, most of whom are arrived from Ireland, of which not one half have provisions enough to live upon over the winter, and so poor that they are not able to buy any, and none of the first inhabitants so well furnished as that they are able to supply them." The House responded by voting "the Poor Irish People" one hundred and fifty bushels of Indian meal.[9]

Because they had arrived so late in the year, there was little the immigrants could do about either shelter or food. A few may have built crude huts at the "Purpooduck" section of Falmouth (later Cape Elizabeth and now, part of modern South Portland) before winter came, but others spent an uncomfortable winter aboard the *Robert*. Miraculously, none died.

Finding the coast of Maine to be at least as inhospitable as the people of Boston, much of the group left the area in the spring. While some returned to Boston, others apparently sailed for Pennsylvania.[10] An unknown number of the Scotch-Irish who had wintered in Casco Bay chose a third alternative. They sailed for the mouth of the Merrimack River, in the hopes of finding good farmland along the Massachusetts or New Hampshire frontier. This group became the nucleus of the successful Scotch-Irish town of Londonderry, New Hampshire, which in turn spawned Scotch-Irish settlement throughout south central New Hampshire. Meanwhile, a small number of the Scotch-Irish elected to

remain at Falmouth, including John Armstrong, one of the early leaders. Yet the number staying behind was small. In 1725, there were only
seventeen families living at Purpooduck and "Spurwink," and not all of
these were known to be Scotch-Irish immigrants.[11]

More substantial and promising Irish settlements took place further
east, in the coastal region between the Kennebec and Penobscot Rivers.
These resulted from the speculative efforts of a number of proprietors
of ancient claims to lands in Maine. In 1713, Massachusetts authorities
re-established its old Committee of Eastern Claims and Settlements to
look into a number of old land claims in Maine and to enhance settlement in the "eastern parts." The settlements in and around Casco Bay
were only one of the committee's concerns; the Pejepscot and
Lincolnshire Company proprietors were another.[12]

On November 5, 1714, Thomas Hutchinson, Adam Winthrop, John
Watts, David Jeffries, Stephen Minot, Oliver Noyes, and John Ruck of
Boston, along with John Wentworth of Portsmouth, New Hampshire,
purchased a seventeenth-century claim for lands around Merrymeeting
Bay for the sum of £140.[13] They called themselves the Company of
Pejepscot Proprietors. The original claim dated back to 1632, but its
shares had passed through a number of hands over the next eighty years
with no effect on settlement along the Androscoggin or Kennebec
rivers. By 1714, the area was ripe for settlement, and the new proprietors began immediately to plan at least two townships within their territory. The proprietors asked the Massachusetts General Court to provide some protection for the settlers on their lands. They also asked
that the settlers be exempted from taxes for seven years and that they
be assisted in efforts to support a minister. In return, the proprietors
would lay out three of four towns, settle fifty families in each, provide
temporary funds toward a minister's salary, and spend at least £400
toward construction of a fort. The General Court approved the plan, and
the towns of Brunswick and Topsham were off to a slow but well-
planned start.[14]

Yet there remained the problem of enticing settlers to come to the
Pejepscot Company lands in the vicinity of Merrymeeting Bay. The proprietors offered prospective settlers one hundred acres of land per family
and free transportation to Merrymeeting Bay from Boston. This must
have helped, for in a memorial dated November 15, 1716, the proprietors petitioned the House of Representatives for a detachment of sol-

diers, stating that they had begun a small settlement and a fort at Small Point, near Georgetown. There was some activity further inland as well, for Brunswick became a township in 1717, and one John Cochran, probably an Irish immigrant, became one of the town's first selectmen. At this point, the proprietors entered upon a new phase of development. They decided to entice Irish immigrants to the Kennebec region. For this task, they enlisted the services of Robert Temple.[15]

Temple (1694-1754) was a native of Munster, the southernmost province of Ireland; members of his family had apparently come from England as part of the Cromwellean settlement of Ireland. In 1717, at the age of twenty-three, Temple arrived in Boston with "servants and effects." His plan was to become a landed proprietor of some sort, and toward that end he toured Connecticut upon arriving in New England. He seems not to have found what he wanted there, for a short while afterwards he toured lands along the Kennebec with Pejepscot proprietors Adam Winthrop, Oliver Noyes, and Stephen Minot. The proprietors agreed to give Temple one thousand acres of land if he would arrange for the passage of a number of Irish Presbyterians to the Pejepscot lands.[16]

Temple's activities over the next two years are not particularly well documented. He returned to Ireland for a short while, where he arranged for the voyages of two shiploads of immigrants in 1718 and three more in 1719. He seems also to have been active in Boston. When the ship *Maccalum* arrived in Boston on September 2, 1718, Robert Temple was there to begin negotiations with the ship's master James Law. The vessel had come from Londonderry with "20 odd familys" led by the Reverend James Woodside of Garvagh in the Bann Valley. The group was apparently destined originally for Connecticut, but Temple persuaded them to sail for the Kennebec. On September 8, 1718, the *Maccallum* left Boston for Maine and Merrymeeting Bay.[17]

Between 1718 and 1720, Temple probably encouraged about one hundred families, or approximately five hundred people to settle on Pejepscot lands. Not all of these were Scotch-Irish, and some settlers to the region came independently of Temple's efforts. Some of the immigrants, 150 or more, settled upon Temple's one-thousand-acre tract, located on the eastern side of the Kennebec, in an area Temple chose to call Cork (present-day Dresden). Others started farms in Brunswick, Topsham, Georgetown, and Swan Island. Temple was not an absentee proprietor. At some time before the outbreak of conflicts with Native people, he moved to Cork, built a house, and began to raise cattle.[18]

The spiritual needs of the various settlers scattered around Merrymeeting Bay, most of whom were Presbyterians, were at least temporarily addressed on November 3, 1718. James Woodside, who had taken up temporary residence in Falmouth, was formally called by the townspeople of Brunswick to be their minister for a salary of £40 per year. Woodside and his sons built a garrison on the minister's lot, and, like other residents in the area, began a small farm. Unfortunately, Woodside's brief stay in America was unhappy from the start. On September 10, 1719, the Brunswick town meeting voted to dismiss him: "whereas the conversation of the Reverend Mr. James Woodside is Displeasing to the most of us, which renders us unable to reverence him as our Minister, therefore shall not heare him any Longer as such."[19] The unhappy minister left his sons behind in Brunswick and returned to Boston, where, in the words of Cotton Mather, "poor Mr. Woodside, after many and grievous calamities in this uneasy country, is this week taking ship for London."[20]

By the time Woodside sailed for London, however, the settlers at Merrymeeting Bay were all about to experience "many and grievous calamities in this uneasy country." The Native Americans of Maine, not to mention their French allies, quickly became alarmed at the various English-sponsored settlements along the Maine coast. They were particularly upset by the Irish settlements at Cork, Swan Island, and "summerset"—a portion of Topsham. In July 1720, groups of Native Americans came into Cork, where the Irish immigrants "were threatened to be knocked on the head if they continued there any longer" and hastily fled to Georgetown. Pejepscot proprietor Thomas Hutchinson heard of the episode in a letter written on July 13 by Georgetown leader John Penhallow. The panic-stricken immigrants fully intended to return in flight to Boston, but Penhallow stopped them, allowing only a few women and children to go on. He asked Hutchinson and Governor Samuel Shute for a troop of soldiers, as most of the men in Georgetown had recently been sent to defend Casco Bay.

The Kennebec settlements, and not Casco Bay, had greater need of troops, as they were "more immediately exposed to the rage & malice of the Norridgwalk Indians, who have an insulting fellow of a Jesuit among 'em and is the instigator of Disorder." In the meantime,

Penhallow sent a letter to the Topsham settlers, urging them to "stand their ground," while a number of Cork residents regained their courage and went back upstream to "Hill & secure their Corn." Shute was sufficiently alarmed by the episode to send a detachment of soldiers to Swan Island. In addition, he issued a proclamation forbidding settlers from abandoning their farms. One of those who returned to his home as a result of the governor's proclamation was Scotch-Irish immigrant Alexander Hamilton. As will soon be evident, he would live to regret his act of obedience.[21]

For the next two years, there was an uneasy peace over the Kennebec. Yet the peace was fragile at best, and in September 1721, the Massachusetts House of Representatives was sufficiently upset by the Native Americans at Norridgewock to forbid further trade with them. Apparently the Scotch-Irish settlers at Merrymeeting Bay took the Native American threat seriously as well. In the spring of 1722, prior to the start of full-scale hostilities, authorities in Boston were being forced to warn out "Irish" refugees from Maine.[22]

On June 13, 1722, threats and rumors turned to all-out war along the northern fringes of New England. On that day, Native Americans came down the Kennebec, attacking settlements along the way. Cattle and oxen were killed and homes were burned. Adam Winthrop's mill was burned as was Robert Temple's home. Alexander Hamilton was one of several to be taken captive. John Penhallow, once again writing from Georgetown, informed Lieutenant Governor William Dummer, in Shute's absence, that settlers along the Kennebec and the shores of Merrymeeting Bay "are all flying for shelter, & that no arguments can persuade them to keep their houses."[23]

Some settlers fled to nearby fortifications. The six or seven families remaining in Topsham, for instance, fled to Fort George in Brunswick, although Brunswick itself was attacked at various times throughout the war. The Brunswick garrison, manned by James Woodside's sons, was a target of one Indian assault, and Woodside lost both cattle and provisions.[24] A number of other refugees fled to the supposedly safer fortifications of Georgetown in the early days of the war. Safety here was illusory as well. In July 1722, when Shadrach Walton arrived in Geogetown to take command of troops along the Kennebec, he found the town under attack by at least five hundred Native Americans.[25]

Several young men among the Scotch-Irish immigrants enlisted in local regiments and fought during the war—variously known as Dummer's or Lovewell's War.[26] One of those who stayed behind to fight was Robert Temple, who commanded a garrison at Cork in 1722. Yet Temple soon tired of warfare in the Maine woods. His dreams of becoming a landed proprietor had been dashed, and in the spring of 1724, he abandoned the Kennebec and took up residence in the Ten Hills section of Charlestown, Massachusetts. In these more civil surroundings, Temple resided until his death in 1754.[27]

The vast majority of Irish immigrants living at Merrymeeting Bay prior to the outbreak of hostilities chose to flee rather than fight. Historian Charles Knowles Bolton found the names of 223 Scotch-Irish refugees from Pejepscot lands. Temple claimed that most went to Pennsylvania or Londonderry, New Hampshire, during Dummer's War. Many others went to Boston, where they were hardly welcome.[28]

Dummer's War came at a time when the Scotch-Irish were turning the area around Merrymeeting Bay into a Scotch-Irish "plantation." By the end of the war, however, the few remaining immigrants were scattered. Williamson, in his *History of the State of Maine*, probably underestimated the number of Scotch-Irish in Maine when he stated that throughout the province in 1750, there were only seventeen families that were "Scottish Hibernean, and all presbyterians. . . ."[29] In the region between Kittery and the Kennebec alone, there were probably more than that. Following the war, some Scotch-Irish settlers lived in the Purpooduck area of Casco Bay. Others had settled at Biddeford and near the Saco Falls by 1727, for local officials complained that "Irish" nets were keeping fish from reaching their spawning grounds, and that in turn was upsetting the Indians further upstream.[30] Other Scotch-Irish settlers, including the Reverend Hugh Henry, lived in Scarborough, where the war had so decimated the population that Henry, like his Scotch-Irish predecessor, the Reverend Hugh Campbell, could not collect a living wage. While Hugh Henry's sad case dragged on in York County courts, other Scotch-Irish settlers trickled into Scarborough in the years after the war.[31]

In addition, some Scotch-Irish settlers remained in or near Brunswick, Topsham, and Georgetown. In the Brunswick area, for instance, James Woodside's son William was running a trading post at Pejepscot Falls at the end of the war. The Presbyterian influence remained strong enough in Brunswick for the town to invite the

Reverend Robert Dunlap, a Presbyterian native of Ireland, to be their town minister in 1747, although he had to travel all the way to Boston to be ordained by a fellow Presbyterian.[32]

Yet the war ended efforts by the Pejepscot Proprietors to encourage immigration to their lands. The proprietors seem to have run out of steam. With peace came renewed efforts to bring Scotch-Irish immigrants to Maine, but this time to settlements east of the Kennebec. Leading the charge was an Irishman named David Dunbar; close on his heels came Samuel Waldo and the Lincolnshire Company Proprietors.

The settlement of the region beyond the Kennebec is best understood within the context of the provincial and family rivalries that ran rampant in Massachusetts and New Hampshire in the years after Dummer's War. Merchants and political leaders in both provinces wanted to control the lucrative timber trade of northern New England, including the mast trade, and in order to do this, it was deemed necessary to have both ownership and political hegemony over the forests of Maine and New Hampshire. Authorities from Massachusetts used a literal and somewhat questionable interpretation of their provincial charter to claim virtually all of western and much of northern New Hampshire. As for Maine, there was uncertainty as to where the jurisdiction of Massachusetts ended and that of Nova Scotia began. Hence, Boston leaders were quick to recognize the landed claims of the so-called Lincolnshire Company.

Like the Pejepscot Proprietors, the Lincolnshire Company originated with a land grant made in the 1630s, and like the Pejepscot grant, it went through a long, dormant period until the end of Queen Anne's War in 1713. The Lincolnshire Company, sometimes referred to as the Waldo Patentees or the Muscongus Proprietors, claimed Maine lands between Muscongus Bay and the Penobscot River. The very few settlers attempting to move into this territory had been chased away during various Indian wars, although a stone fort had been built at Pemaquid in 1692. In 1719 and 1720, the Lincolnshire Company began to find settlers for their lands east of Pemaquid. They built a couple of forts along the St. George's River and erected a sawmill in the area. Portsmouth's Thomas Westbrook, a shareholder in the company, was in charge of Lincolnshire operations in Maine. He had been granted ten thousand acres of land by the proprietors in 1720, with the understanding he would reside there and encourage twenty-five families to live along the

St. George's River. That same year, Robert Edwards of Castleburg, Ireland, was asked to populate two entire townships in Lincolnshire territory by bringing over Scotch-Irish families. Neither plan amounted to much, however, as warfare with Native people virtually eliminated the possibility of settlement.[33]

Following Dummer's War, Lincolnshire proprietors Westbrook, Elisha Cooke, Boston merchant Jonathan Waldo, and his son Samuel Waldo took the lead in bringing people to Lincolnshire lands. It is not known how successful they were initially, but their plans to settle Lincolnshire lands soon ran into problems from an unforeseen source.[34]

In 1728, Irishman David Dunbar, a former soldier, was made Surveyor General of the King's Woods "in America and Nova Scotia." His chief function was to encourage the production of naval stores and to protect white pine trees in the forests of Maine and New Hampshire that had the potential to be made into masts. In short, he was the crown official with oversight of the northern New England timber trade.[35]

At the time of Dunbar's appointment, northern New England's logging operations were conducted for the most part by two rival groups of merchants. One group, which included many of the Lincolnshire proprietors, consisted of Boston area merchants with close ties to the Massachusetts government. The other faction was led by New Hampshire's Lieutenant Governor John Wentworth, who had tried unsuccessfully to have himself appointed Surveyor General. The two rival groups of merchants were determined to control as much of the forested territory in Maine and New Hampshire as possible.

Dunbar's appointment caused little stir at first. Although in theory the Surveyor General had the authority to stop the illegal cutting of white pines—a common practice in Maine and New Hampshire—in reality, the laws had been enforced with indifference. Dunbar's predecessor had not even bothered to come to America.

Unlike his absentee predecessor, however, David Dunbar was energetic, abrasive, and controversial. He started stirring up things in New England before leaving England. He determined that the fight to save most of the remaining white pines in North America would have to be fought in the territory beyond the Kennebec, called Sagadahock. London officials were uncertain as to whether this territory belonged to Massachusetts or Nova Scotia. Massachusetts' authorities, and particularly the Lincolnshire Proprietors, were very certain the land beyond the

Kennebec was part of the Bay Colony. Before leaving England for Boston, however, Dunbar convinced London officials that the land between the Kennebec and St. Croix Rivers should be made into a separate province. By the time Surveyor General Dunbar arrived in Boston in 1729, he was also the nominal head of a new province called "Georgia."[36]

Dunbar quickly discovered that the land beyond the Kennebec not only had a few residents, but that extensive logging operations were being conducted in the area by Massachusetts' interests. He was informed that Boston officials did not recognize "Georgia," and that the land in question belonged to the Lincolnshire Proprietors.

Undeterred by his cold reception in Boston, Dunbar wrote to the Board of Trade in October 1729, outlining his plan to rebuild the fort at Pemaquid, naming it Fort Frederick. In his letter, he noted that "a great many hundred men of those who come lately from Ireland," not to mention some earlier Scotch-Irish settlers, wanted to settle on these lands. The recent immigrants he wrote of were apparently some of the same who had been the subject of mob abuse in Boston. According to Dunbar, "the greatest part of those who lately came from Ireland had removed themselves to Pennsylvania upon ill treatment they received here, where a very Numerous Mobb threatened and insulted them as foreigners."[37]

Dunbar claimed that he was literally pressured into starting his new plantation by Scotch-Irish immigrants looking for a place to settle. He originally intended to offer each family between fifty and one hundred acres of land around Fort Frederick, saying in October 1729 that he already had about 250 men ready to migrate to the area. By August 1730, he was advertising for additional settlers. For every forty families, he would grant a township of twelve miles square. Each family would receive a home lot of forty acres and an additional one hundred acres nearby. In all he may have attracted about 150 families to Georgia.[38] A petition dated January 1730, which asked for land in Georgia, was signed by forty-four people, most of whom had Scottish names. Some of those expressing interest in the area were not recent immigrants, however, but Scotch-Irish immigrants from earlier migrations. In June 1730, for instance, Dunbar received a petition from a number of Scotch-Irish settlers in Londonderry, New Hampshire. Encouraged about the possibility of a "plantation" governed by a fellow countryman, these settlers, "originally from north Britain but Last from Ireland," asked Dunbar for a tract of land in Georgia.[39]

Dunbar's Georgia venture was plagued with problems. For one thing, Dunbar did not actually have authority to grant land. At first, he tried to hide his weakness. He noted in a letter to the Board of Trade that there were a number of "Irish Protestants" who "have been very importunate for lands" in Maine. "If I declared to them my power and how I am limitted it would at once put an end to all proceedings here." He almost succeeded in getting formal approval to grant townships, but the Board of Trade cautioned him that courts in London were in the process of determining the legality of the Lincolnshire grant.[40]

Another problem for Dunbar was that a number of Massachusetts' settlers and loggers were already living in Georgia, and they refused to recognize his authority. Dunbar regarded these individuals as little more than squatters to be imprisoned or evicted. He used the Scotch-Irish to carry out his wishes. In September 1730, for instance, one Josiah Glover, who lived east of the Kennebec by virtue of an old Native American deed, complained to Massachusetts authorities that he was accosted by "Eight Irish Men Armed with Guns and Swords" while he and his crew were sailing out for a day's fishing. When Glover and his crew returned, "there came on board the Schooner five or six Irish men Armed with Guns and Clubbs, and in an hostile Violent manner surprised & Seized upon the Informant & his Crew," taking them all to Dunbar's fort at Pemaquid.[41] To his credit, Dunbar defended the actions of his people at Pemaquid, particularly when it came to ethnic slurs. He complained to the Board of Trade that his people were "over and over stigmatized with the name of Irish."[42]

The eager recipient of complaints about Dunbar was the new Massachusetts governor, Jonathan Belcher. Aside from wishing to pursue Bay Colony claims to Sagadahock, Belcher was further motivated by his utter contempt for Dunbar, whom he called "the bull-frog from the Hibernian Ferns." Belcher and Dunbar bombarded the Board of Trade with complaints about one another. At one point, ostensibly in the name of preserving order and avoiding bloodshed, Belcher sent an armed vessel to Pemaquid and arrested four of the Scotch-Irish settlers. Dunbar predictably fired off another complaint to the Board of Trade, saying "this is the justice of this Country to strangers and foreigners as all his Majesty European Subjects are called here."[43]

The Lincolnshire proprietor who was most persistent in attacking Dunbar and his claims to Georgia was Samuel Waldo. As a timber trader and mast agent, Waldo had encountered immediate problems with the new Surveyor General of the King's Woods. To address both personal and company concerns, Waldo finally took his case to London. Dunbar was equally resentful of Waldo, once complaining to the Board of Trade that Waldo had been cutting illegally in the Maine forests, adding that Waldo was also "agent for a number of the Claimants for Vast Tracts of Land in Georgia."[44] In the end, Waldo, Belcher, the Lincolnshire Company, and Massachusetts prevailed over Dunbar. Georgia simply disappeared. Dunbar retained his title as Surveyor General and was appeased for his loss of Georgia when he was named lieutenant governor of New Hampshire following John Wentworth's death.

The Scotch-Irish living in the former Dunbar colony did not fare as well. In 1732, it was estimated that at least fifty or sixty Scotch-Irish settlers were living in the Pemaquid area. Their land "titles" were considered worthless by Massachusetts authorities. In spite of the uncertainty, many chose to remain. Most of the Scotch-Irish who remained lived in the old Dunbar town of Townshend, or present Boothbay. Their plight was summed up pathetically in the 1772 deposition of Townshend resident Samuel McCobb, made to authorities in Boston. The sixty-four-year-old McCobb recounted his migration with Dunbar and "more than 40 others" to Townshend in 1729. House lots were drawn and upon completion of a house "eighteen feet long" and the clearing of two acres of land, the immigrants were given forty-acre lots, with the promise of an additional one hundred acres to follow. Yet Dunbar's departure brought this to a halt. According to McCobb, most of his neighbors were "generally in low circumstances, and most of them (as being from Britain and Ireland) utterly unacquainted with the mode of managing lands in that state." For a while, some earned a living by cutting wood and supplying Boston and other coastal towns with firewood. Yet life was poor, and in 1745, most Townshend residents fled the area when threatened by Indian attack. For unexplained reasons, many returned to Townshend in 1749, where, in spite of "peace" with the Native Americans, the settlers were attacked. Many were carried into captivity; others lived in a small fortress, surviving on a diet of clams and water. In a state of utter poverty, not to mention fear, they survived both King George's War and the French and Indian War, only to be threatened with "Law Suits, Ejectments, if not imprisonments and Ruin," by "three or four opposite setts of claims."[45]

Some of the other Scotch-Irish settlers living east of the Kennebec survived by throwing in their lot with an old enemy. For his part in defending the Lincolnshire Company claim in England, Samuel Waldo was given half of the company shares. He subsequently purchased an additional 100,000 acres of Lincolnshire Company land. Of greatest interest to Waldo were the deposits of lime found along the St. George's River. By 1734, he had financed the construction of a lime kiln in the area at present Warren. But he needed settlers to work his land.[46]

In spite of his past problems with the Scotch-Irish followers of David Dunbar, Waldo wasted no time enticing the Scotch-Irish in Maine, Boston, New Hampshire, and Ireland to migrate to his proposed settlement along the St. George's River. In April 1735, he reached an agreement with twenty-seven Scotch-Irish settlers, on behalf of their families and nineteen others. They were required to build homes along the St. George's by the end of the year, and within two years, if they would clear four acres of land, Waldo would give them each one hundred acres.[47]

In 1736, Waldo was again attracting the Scotch-Irish. In a petition to Governor Belcher, he boasted that he "expects a great number of Irish Protestants to arrive in these parts in a Month or Two having Engaged three ships for that purpose who Passengers your Petitioner has Contracted with to Settle on the Lands there." By year's end, twenty-five to thirty Scotch-Irish families were living in the new settlement.[48]

There is no way of knowing how many Irish settlers Waldo brought to his lands along the St. George's River. Starting in 1740, he began to bring over German settlers as well, and by 1753, his son, Samuel Waldo, Jr., was actively recruiting Scottish settlers for a new settlement at nearby "Stirling." What is known is that the early Scotch-Irish settlers in Warren suffered a plight common to most other Scotch-Irish immigrants in Maine. In 1745, the settlement was attacked by Native Americans, forcing virtually all of the settlers along the St. George's River to abandon their homes. Some returned after a few years in Boston or some other haven. Other refugees left and never returned.[49] Yet the story was the same along the St. George's as it had been in "Georgia" and Merrymeeting Bay. The warning of Native American attack heard by the Reverend William Boyd back in 1719 continued to plague the Scotch-Irish wherever they went in Maine.

By mid-century, the struggling coastal settlements of Maine were familiar with the potato and the "broad Scotch tongue" of Scotch-Irish immigrants. In some communities, only a scattered few were Scotch-Irish; in others, a small but vocal minority occasionally clamored for a Presbyterian minister. During periods of peace, the Scotch-Irish came to Maine in substantial numbers; there was talk of a Scotch-Irish "plantation." During periods of war, the Scotch-Irish fled to Boston; there was talk of Pennsylvania. The closest the Scotch-Irish would come to a "plantation" in Maine came shortly before the American War for Independence, when several residents of Londonderry, New Hampshire, became proprietors and early settlers of Belfast. By this time, the so-called Scotch-Irish were assimilating with non-Irish neighbors and becoming something of a frontier blend of Maine settler.

1. See, for example, Nicholas P. Canny, "The Ideology of English Colonization: From Ireland to America," *The William and Mary Quarterly* 30, no. 4 (October 1973): 575–98; and Canny, *Kingdom and Colony: Ireland in the Atlantic World, 1560–1800* (Baltimore and London: The John Hopkins University Press, 1988). See also Francis Jennings, *The Invasion of America: Indians, Colonialism, and the Cant of Conquest* (Chapel Hill: University of North Carolina Press, 1975), 3–174; Howard Mumford Jones, *O Strange New World. American Culture: The Formative Years* (New York: Viking Press, 1964), 167–79; and Peter S. Leavenworth, "'The Best Title That Indians Can Claime': Native Agency and Consent in the Transferal of Penacook-Pawtucket Land in the Seventeenth Century," *The New England Quarterly* (June 1999): 275–300. A classic example of the mixed images of Native Americans and Celtic Irish may be found in John Josselyn's second voyage to Maine from 1663–1671, where the author reports that Indian men and women were guilty of "hatred to strangers, a quality appropriated to the Old Brittains, all of them Cannibals, eaters of humane flesh. And so were formerly the Heathen-*Irish*, who used to feed upon the Buttocks of Boyes and Womens Paps; it seems it is natural to Savage people so to do." Paul J. Lindholdt, ed. *John Josselyn, Colonial Traveler: A Critical Edition of* Two Voyages to New-England (Hanover and London: University Press of New England, 1988), 90.
2. M. Halsy Thomas, ed., *The Diary of Samuel Sewall, 1684–1729*, 2 vols. (New York: Farrar, Straus and Giroux, 1973), 918.
3. There are a number of general studies of the so-called Scotch-Irish. See James G. Leyburn, *The Scotch-Irish: A Social History* (Chapel Hill: University of North Carolina Press, 1962); Maldwyn A. Jones, "The Scotch-Irish in British America," in Bernard Bailyn and Philip D. Morgan, eds., *Strangers within the Realm: Cultural Margins of the First British Empire* (Chapel Hill: University of North

Carolina Press, 1991): 284–313; and Patrick Griffin, *The People with No Name: Ireland's Ulster Scots, America's Scots Irish, and the Creation of a British Atlantic World, 1689–1764* (Princeton: Princeton University Press, 2001), which is best for the Pennsylvania story.

4. *Journals of the House of Representatives of Massachusetts* (hereafter *Massachusetts House Journals*), 2:65; Charles Knowles Bolton, *Scotch Irish Pioneers in Ulster and America* (Boston: Bacon and Brown, 1910), 240; Charles E. Clark, *The Eastern Frontier: The Settlement of Northern New England, 1610–1763* (New York: Alfred A. Knopf, 1970), 175.

5. *Massachusetts House Journals*, 2:83.

6. *Massachusetts House Journals*, 2:91–92.

7. Edward L. Parker, *The History of Londonderry, comprising the Towns of Derry and Londonderry, N.H.* (Boston: Perkins and Whipple, 1851), 36; Bolton, *Scotch Irish Pioneers*, 205, 207; Jeremy Belknap, *The History of New-Hampshire*, 3 vols. (Dover, NH: 1812), 1:192. See also William B. Jordan, Jr., *A History of Cape Elizabeth, Maine* (Bowie, MD: Heritage Books, 1987): 286–87.

8. Parker says sixteen families went to Casco Bay (*Londonderry*, 36–37). Gordon Woodbury, "The Scotch-Irish Presbyterian Settlers of New Hampshire," *Proceedings of the New Hampshire Historical Society* 4 (Concord, NH: 1906), 143–62, reports that twenty families went to Casco Bay, but that they took another three hundred Scotch-Irish along with them. Woodbury's account stems from a misreading of William Willis, *The History of Portland*, 2 (Portland, ME: Charles Day and Co., 1833), 17. Leyburn, *Scotch-Irish*, 238, says that one-quarter of the group in Boston went to Casco Bay.

9. Willis, *Portland*, 2:17; *Massachusetts House Journals*, 2:104, 106; Parker, *Londonderry*, 37; and William Willis, "The Scotch-Irish Immigration to Maine, and Presbyterianism in New England," *Collections of the Maine Historical Society* (hereafter *Baxter Manuscripts*), 6 (Portland, ME: by the Society, 1859), 11–12.

10. Many who returned to Boston were warned out of town. For the Casco Bay episode, see Bolton, *Scotch-Irish Pioneers*, 203–14.

11. Willis, "Scotch-Irish," 12; Willis, *Portland*, 2:18 and 97; *Massachusetts House Journals*, 9:134. There was a strong enough "Presbyterian" element left in the area, however, for a Presbyterian minister to settle in Falmouth. See *Baxter Manuscripts*, 11:210–11.

12. William D. Williamson, *The History of the State of Maine* (Hallowell, ME: Glazier, Masters, and Co., 1832), 2:81.

13. George Augustus Wheeler and Henry Warren Wheeler, *History of Brunswick, Topsham, and Harpswell, Maine* (Boston: Alfred Mudge and Son, 1878), 21; Roy Hidemichi Akagi, *The Town Proprietors of the New England Colonies* (Philadelphia: University of Pennsylvania Press, 1924), 145–46.

14. Akagi, *Town Proprietors*, 256–57; Williamson, *Maine*, 2:87; Wheeler and Wheeler, *History of Brunswick*, 21–23, 27–30.

15. Williamson, *Maine*, 2:90; *Massachusetts House Journals*, 1:140–41; Wheeler and Wheeler, *History of Brunswick*, 104; Douglas Edward Leach, *The Northern Colonial Frontier: 1607–1763* (New York: Holt, Rinehart, and Winston, 1966), 131. Leach concludes that the Scotch-Irish were lured to America by land speculators.

16. For Temple and the Temple family, see *New England Historical and Genealogical Register*, 10 (1856): 73–77 (hereafter *NEHGR*); Michael J. O'Brien, "The Lost Town of Cork, Maine," *The Journal of the American Irish Historical Society*, 12 (1913): 176–79, 182, 184; Willis, *Portland*, 2:17 n; Willis, "Scotch-Irish," 14–16; Bolton, *Scotch-Irish Pioneers*, 218.

17. Bolton, *Scotch-Irish Pioneers*, 142–45.

18. For the settlement of lands at Merrymeeting Bay, see Bolton, *Scotch-Irish Pioneers*, 215–38; O'Brien, "Cork," 178; Wheeler and Wheeler, *History of Brunswick*, 37, 42, 104. Given Temple's roots in Munster and his choice of the name Cork, is has been suggested that some of the people brought to Maine by Temple were native Irish. See Edward Thomas McCarron, "The World of Kavanagh and Cottrill: A Portrait of Irish Emigration, Entrepreneurship, and Ethnic Diversity in Mid-Maine, 1760–1820" (Ph.D. dissertation, University of New Hampshire, 1992), 5 n. Also see McCarron's essay "Facing the Atlantic" in this book.

19. Quoted in Wheeler and Wheeler, *History of Brunswick*, 355.

20. Bolton, *Scotch-Irish Pioneers*, 220–27; *Baxter Manuscripts*, 10:163–65.

21 Penhallow's letters appear in *NEHGR*, 32 (1878): 21–22. See also O'Brien, "Cork," 180; and Williamson, *Maine*, 2:104.

22. Douglas Edward Leach, *Arms for Empire: A Military History of the British Colonies in North America, 1607–1763* (New York: Macmillan, 1973), 181; Bolton, *Scotch-Irish Pioneers*, 230; *A Report of the Record Commissioners of the City Boston, Vols. 8, 11, 12, 13, 17* (Boston, 1883, 1884, 1885, 1887; hereafter *Boston Record Commissioners*), 13:101.

23. *Massachusetts House Journals*, 5:186; *NEHGR*, 32 (1878): 23. See also O'Brien, "Cork," 181; and Leach, *Arms for Empire*, 181.

24. *NEHGR*, 32 (1878): 23; *NEHGR*, 24 (1870): 25; *Baxter Manuscripts*, 10:163–65; Williamson, *Maine*, 134–35.

25. *NEHGR*, 32 (1878): 25. For a general account of Dummer's War in Maine, see Williamson, *Maine*, 2:111–51; and Samuel Penhallow, *The History of the Wars of New England with the Eastern Indians . . .* (Boston: R. Fleet and Cornhill, 1726).

26. Muster rolls are scattered for the war in Maine, but better than a dozen Irish immigrants fought in Captain John Gayles' company in 1723 and 1724. William Blake Trask, ed., *Letters of Colonel Thomas Westbrook and Others Relative to Indian Affairs in Maine, 1722–1725* (Boston: George E. Littlefield, 1901), 171.

27. O'Brien, "Cork," 182, 184; *NEHGR*, 10 (January 1856): 73–77.

28. Bolton, *Scotch-Irish Pioneers*, 229–38; Willis, *Portland*, 2:17 n; O'Brien, "Cork," 179; *Boston Record Commissioners*, 13:101, 112.

29. Williamson, *Maine*, 2:159.

30. Samuel Jordon to William Dummer, June 8, 1727, *Baxter Manuscripts*, 10:400.

31 On the Henry case, see Neal W. Allen, Jr., ed., *Province and Court Records of Maine*, 6 (Portland, ME: Maine Historical Society, 1975): 178–83; and William S. Southgate, "The History of Scarborough, from 1633 to 1783," *Baxter Manuscripts*, 3:158–59, 208, 212, 220.

32. *Baxter Manuscripts*, 3:443–45; Wheeler and Wheeler, *History of Brunswick*, 729–30.

33. For Lincolnshire Company activities, see Akagi, *Town Proprietors*, 248–50,

257–58, 262; Cyrus Eaton, *Annals of the Town of Warren* (Hallowell, ME: Masters, Smith and Co., 1851), 18–44; and Joseph Williamson, *History of the City of Belfast in the State of Maine, From its First Settlement in 1770 to 1875* (Portland, ME: Loring, Short, and Harmon, 1877), 36–41.

34. Eaton, *Annals of Warren*, 45.

35. For a general discussion of British timber policy in Maine and New Hampshire, see Joseph J. Malone, *Pine Tree and Politics: The Naval Stores and Forest Policy in Colonial New England, 1691–1775* (Seattle: University of Washington Press, 1964), especially 57–123; and Robert Greenhalgh Albion, *Forests and Sea Power: The Timber Problem of the Royal Navy, 1652–1862* (Cambridge: Harvard University Press, 1926), 231–80.

36. There are several secondary accounts of Dunbar and "Georgia." See, for instance, John Johnston, *A History of the Towns of Bristol and Bremen* (Albany, NY: Joel Munsell, 1873), 265–75; Francis B. Greene, *History of Boothbay, Southport and Boothbay Harbor, Maine, 1623–1905* (Portland, ME: Loring, Short and Harmon, 1906), 109–24; and Eaton, *Annals of Warren*, 45–46.

37. Dunbar to Board of Trade, October 9, 1729, *Baxter Manuscripts*, 10:438–40; and *Calendar of State Papers, Colonial Series, America and West Indies, 1574–1738* (hereafter *CSP, CS*), 44 vols. (London, 1860–1969), 36:589, 628, 929.

38. *Boston Gazette*, 10–17 August 1730; *Baxter Manuscripts*, 10:440; Willis, "Scotch-Irish," 18. Dunbar placed the figure somewhat higher. See *CSP, CS*, 38:217.

39. *Baxter Manuscripts*, 11:129–30, 23–24.

40. *CSP, CS*, 37:533; *CSP, CS*, 38:44, 49.

41 *Baxter Manuscripts*, 11:44–46. For a similar complaint, see *Baxter Manuscripts*, 11:21–23. See also *Massachusetts House Journals*, 10:352, 353–54, 362, 385–87.

42. Dunbar to Board of Trade, September 15, 1730, *Baxter Manuscripts*, 11:51. According to Robert G. Albion, Dunbar also burned the homes of Sheepscot River settlers (*Forests and Sea Power*, 262).

43. Belcher to Richard Waldron, 5 June 1732, *Collections of the Massachusetts Historical Society*, 56 (Boston: by the Society, 1893): 145.

44. Dunbar to Board of Trade, December 29, 1729, *Baxter Manuscripts*, 11:1–5.

45. This and other Townshend depositions may be found in Johnston, *Bristol and Bremen*, 268–71; and Greene, *History of Boothbay*, 116–22. The deposition of Samuel McCobb is cited in the new work by Kerby A. Miller, Arnold Schrier, Bruce Boling, and David N. Doyle, *Irish Immigrants in the Land of Canaan: Letters and Memoirs from Colonial and Revolutionary America, 1675–1815* (Oxford: Oxford University Press, 2003): 128–35 (the research of both Edward T. McCarron and R. Stuart Wallace is cited on page 715 of this work).

46. Johnston, *Bristol and Bremen*, 285; Akagi, *Town Proprietors*, 249–50.

47. Eaton, *Annals of Warren*, 49–50; Willis, "Scotch-Irish," 20–21.

48. *Baxter Manuscripts*, 11:169. The petition is dated July 26, 1736. See also Eaton, *Annals of Warren*, 55.

49. Eaton, *Annals of Warren*, 60–63, 66–72, 76–78, 81–86. See also *Boston Record Commissioners*, 17:18, 57–58.

FACING THE ATLANTIC:
THE IRISH MERCHANT COMMUNITY
OF LINCOLN COUNTY, 1780–1820

by Edward T. McCarron

There is a tide in the affairs of men
Which, taken at the flood leads onto fortune;
Omitted, all the voyage of their life
Is bound in shallows and in miseries.
On such a full sea are we now afloat;
And we must take the current when it serves
Or lose our ventures.

–William Shakespeare, *Julius Caesar*, Act IV, scene 3

IN THE YEARS FOLLOWING THE AMERICAN REVOLUTION,
Maine experienced a remarkable expansion in commerce and ocean-
borne trade, a boom that brought prosperity to seaports along the Maine
coast, and attracted a new, and sometimes diverse, merchant community. As historian Joyce Butler remarks, "with its undeveloped land,
resources and commercial potential, Maine represented 'opportunity' to
veterans eager to reap the rewards for their war service, to bright young
men ready to launch careers in law and politics, and to ambitious
European as well as American businessmen."[1] This influx of newcomers was evident in the larger seaports such as Portland, where the
Reverend Thomas Smith recorded in 1784 that "strangers, traders and
others crowd in among us surprisingly."[2] It was likewise felt in the burgeoning outports of Lincoln County, where native New Englander and
immigrant alike entered into the timber trade, shipbuilding and
milling. In the town of Newcastle, for example, one finds master

mariners and traders from the Scottish ports of Greenock and Port Patrick, a shipbuilder and "Gentleman" from Londonderry, and "West India Merchants" from County Kilkenny, by way of Newfoundland. This diversity among the merchant personnel was one of the important features of the trading boom that linked Maine to the wider Atlantic world during the early American republic.

Irish-born merchants and mariners, in particular, pursued careers in the seaports of Lincoln County. At its peak in the early nineteenth century, this Irish merchant community numbered close to thirty individuals, drawn from a variety of beginnings in Ireland. They included merchants such as Thomas McCrate, a Wiscasset factor who shipped timber to the West Indies, Liverpool, and Ireland. Those of merchant rank also included coastal traders such as Thomas McGuire of Waldoboro, whose schooner *Neptune* plied the waters of northern New England during the Federal period. Underpinning this commercial elite were several shopkeepers, country traders, and ship captains—men who were often affiliated with the larger firms by way of kinship, Old World connections, or ethno-religious ties. Many of these men had emigrated in the years following the American Revolution, leaving behind in Ireland a rigid and often discriminatory social, economic, and religious climate in search of new beginnings.

This essay will focus on one of these firms in Lincoln County: the merchant house of James Kavanagh and Matthew Cottrill, based in Newcastle, Maine. At its peak in 1810, their company controlled a lucrative empire that included over two thousand acres of timberland, seven mills, eight ocean-going vessels, and a prosperous trade with the West Indies, England, and Ireland. By using their career as a springboard, this work will explore the social and economic milieu that gave rise to immigrant entrepreneurs in Lincoln County. We will also investigate mid-Maine's timber trade with Ireland, a brief zenith between the 1790s and 1812 that provided the means for immigrants like Kavanagh and Cottrill to enter the ranks of the merchant class and also generated a budding passenger trade with Ireland.

OLD WORLD ANTECEDENTS

Winding gracefully through Kilkenny's rich farmland and prosperous estates, the river Nore reaches its tidal limits at Inistioge, a small town founded at the site of a medieval priory. There in 1764, Matthew Cottrill was born in an attractive townhouse on the village square. The Cottrills were shopkeepers, one of several Catholic families in the parish who managed to preserve a slice of trade and property amidst the social upheavals of the Penal Laws in eighteenth-century Ireland. Matthew likely carried some of this prosperity with him when he emigrated to America in 1784.[3]

Long after his migration to Maine, Cottrill remembered his beginnings along the Nore. In the old churchyard in Inistioge, close by the village square, one finds a headstone that Cottrill commissioned in 1800 in memory of his family:

> Erected by Matthew Cottril, America
> In memory of his father Patrick Cottril
> Died April 7, 1777 aged 52. Also in
> Memory of his mother, Anastasia Joyce,
> Died December 13, 1777, aged 52 [4]

Significantly, this is one of the earliest examples in Ireland of a gravestone commissioned by an immigrant in the New World. It is also noteworthy for its identification of "Matthew Cottril, America"—suggesting that his sense of identity, his sense of opportunity and assimilation in the Atlantic World, had already taken root.

Cottrill's partner in trade, James Kavanagh, was the son of a strong farmer in the nearby townland of Lower Cluen.[5] Kavanagh's father worked a prosperous farm of seventy-six Irish acres in 1782, leased from the local landlord William Tighe.[6] (It is instructive to remember that while Catholics were prohibited from owning land at this time, some—particularly in the fertile regions of southeast Ireland—occupied large leaseholds.) The Kavanagh house in Cluen—a substantial two-story slated farmhouse—was typical of strong farmers during the late eighteenth century. It reminds us that Irish immigrants journeyed from a variety of beginnings, not simply the humble thatched cottages that predominate in Irish America's collective folk memory. (See gallery, plate 14.)

The Kavanaghs were part of a wide network of dairy farms throughout south Kilkenny, farms that took advantage of the profitable butter trade then flourishing in the ports of New Ross and Waterford. During the eighteenth century, butter was one of the mainstays of the southeastern economy and was shipped as provisions to Newfoundland and the West Indies. As historian Louis Cullen and others emphasize, even in quiet inward-looking farm villages like Cluen, one was never far removed from the larger Atlantic world of commerce and opportunity.[7] The merchant trade, in fact, was an important outlet for the younger sons of prosperous southeast farmers. Surviving evidence in Kavanagh family documents suggest that James Kavanagh was apprenticed to the merchant trade in the port of New Ross, County Wexford, in 1771.[8] Kavanagh journeyed as a clerk to the Newfoundland cod fisheries and in 1784, at age twenty-nine, found his way to Boston, where he linked up with his townsman Matthew Cottrill.[9]

MAINE

Seventeen eighty-four, following closely on the conclusion of the American Revolution, was a pivotal year in Irish emigration. Kavanagh and Cottrill were two of many Irish who crossed the Atlantic, a post-war surge one scholar estimates at 20,000.[10] Many of these emigrants were Catholic, and they left not only from Belfast or Dublin but also from the southern ports of Cork, Waterford, Limerick, and New Ross. Economic concerns motivated many to leave. Ireland during the previous two years had endured bad weather, harvest failure, and economic depression—prompting thousands of farmers and artisans alike to seek a better life in the New World. Other factors also prompted the 1784 exodus to America. Contemporary literature published in the wake of the Revolution celebrated the virtues of life in the vast new country. One work, *Letters from an American Farmer* (reprinted in Ireland in 1782 and 1783), opined that America was a refuge for the peoples of Europe, one that promised religious freedom, economic opportunity, and the pursuit of happiness.[11]

Kavanagh and Cottrill responded well to the allure of the New World. They first arrived in Boston with hopes of earning wealth in "the city upon a hill." Initially they worked as traders along the waterfront, insinuating themselves into a world of merchants, mariners, and immigrants.[12] In time, James Kavanagh looked eastward to the timber frontier of Maine. It was a land that captured the imagination, a "wooden world" where trade and opportunity beckoned in the decades following the American Revolution.[13] Indeed, during this period Maine witnessed a remarkable surge in commerce, land settlement, and population growth. Between 1783 and 1820 the population of Maine boomed to close to 300,000 people, many of them newcomers from southern New England who were attracted by new lands in the interior.[14] This rapid growth and peopling of backcountry and waterside was paralleled by political growing pains as well. For much of its history Maine had been part of Massachusetts, "an outpost in every imaginable sense from political and military to demographic and social."[15] Yet with a expanding population during the early national period, and a growing sense of its own political and economic identity, Maine increasingly moved toward separation from Massachusetts and statehood (which it gained in 1820). This heady mix of population boom, economic energy, and political change in the decades following the Revolution attracted a host of entrepreneurs, including James Kavanagh, seeking to make their fortunes in trade and land speculation.

Arriving along the Damariscotta in 1788, Kavanagh would have encountered a number of Irish folk already part of the social landscape. These included immigrants such as Patrick McGuire, a tailor in Boothbay; John O'Brien, the Dublin-born schoolmaster of Thomaston; and John O'Neil, an itinerant laborer in Bristol who was hanged for murder in 1788.[16] Many of the Irish in Lincoln County settled in coastal ports such as Wiscasset and Newcastle, finding work as laborers, mariners, and traders. Others were farmers, who, like their Yankee neighbors from southern New England, were drawn to newly opened lands in Lincoln County. Patrick Hanley, for example, journeyed to Maine in 1771 from his native Tipperary via the seasonal fisheries of Newfoundland.[17] He settled in Bristol, Maine where he hauled timber, carved out a farmstead from the forest, and married Agnes Askins, the daughter of a Scotch-Irish settler. Traces of these early Irish still echo along the old migration corridors into mid-Maine, in place names such as Finn's Brook (Whitefield), MacMahan's Island (Georgetown), McGuire Point (Bristol), and Meaher Road (Whitefield), the latter in an area once known as New Waterford, a speculative venture established by Richard Meagher, a merchant from Waterford city. In the years to come, Finns, Hanleys, and Meaghers would all be pulled into the social and mercantile orbits of Kavanagh and Cottrill.

James Kavanagh, within a few short years of his arrival in Maine, had established a merchant store and wharf in Nobleboro, a prosperous

river town in Lincoln County.[18] In 1794 he entered into business partnership with his countryman Matthew Cottrill—an enterprise that
quickly emerged as the leading merchant firm along the Damariscotta
River. In 1795 they purchased land and valuable waterfalls at
Damariscotta Mills, a rural settlement in the adjacent town of Newcastle. With over 500 acres it was a valuable tract that combined waterpower, timber reserves, and access to the sea. Here they developed a
lucrative complex of sawmills and gristmills, opened a merchant store,
and expanded into land speculation in the interior, a timely strategy
given the number of settlers streaming into the Maine backcountry.[19]

In time the partners divided their empire into distinct spheres of
influence. Kavanagh settled at Damariscotta Mills, where he built a fine
house and managed the company mills. (See gallery, plate 16.) Cottrill,
remaining true to his town origins, opted to establish his seat at
Nobleboro, where he directed the firm's overseas trade and shipbuilding. In this way the two partners secured a virtual monopoly over timber and trading along the Damariscotta. The stepped ascent of
Kavanagh and Cottrill to the pinnacle of their careers was mirrored by
the success of other Maine merchants and frontier entrepreneurs during
the early American republic.[20]

A good place from which to view the accomplishments and interests
of the firm was Nobleboro town, where Matthew Cottrill settled in
1795. Together with Newcastle, its sister village across the river,
Nobleboro was the center of a thriving timber and shipbuilding industry during the early Republic. Indeed, sailing up the Damariscotta
toward the twin villages in 1810, one would have encountered a river-
scape shaped in large part by the timber trade. On the left bank were
commercial wharves and warehouses reaching into the river channel,
the business interests of prominent merchants such as Samuel Glidden
and Nathaniel Bryant. Most striking of all was the island wharf of
Kavanagh and Cottrill, a floating complex of stores and warehouses that
served as the nerve center of their overseas trade. Moored along its 100-
foot dock could frequently be seen one of several square-rigged vessels
in the company fleet, ships that regularly carried timber to the West
Indies, Ireland, and Liverpool and returned home with manufactured
goods for the company stores.[21]

Trade and shipbuilding led to the expansion of the village center in
Nobleboro with stores, warehouses, and small wooden shops lining the

post road that ran through town. Also in evidence were several Federal-style homes that reflected what one historian has called the "ascendancy of capital" along the timber coast of Maine.[22] Most impressive was the townhouse of Matthew Cottrill, overlooking the river and company wharves. (See gallery, plate 15.) Built by Dublin-born housewright Nicholas Codd in 1801, it boasted a five-bay front and a fashionable interior with drawing rooms and dining areas. Cottrill's probate inventory of 1828 provides an invaluable portrait of how these rooms were furnished as well as the luxury afforded a wealthy merchant in the timber trade.[23] Upon entering the house through a columned portico, guests were immediately attracted to the handsome semi-circular staircase, a hallmark of Codd's craftsmanship.[24] Opening off the center hall were spacious rooms furnished in the latest style with Sheraton tables, mahogany chairs, sideboards and game tables. Each room was adorned with wall hangings, including a fine portrait of Matthew Cottrill, painted circa 1805. (See gallery, plate 17.) He is depicted in black frock coat and cravat, a stylish portrayal that, when combined with his straightforward gaze, spoke of a man of substance.

Many of the fine pieces, including a carved secretary desk and tall clock, were most likely commissioned by Boston craftsmen and transported aboard the firm's shipping to Nobleboro.[25] Certainly, it was a house worthy of lavish entertainment, and several celebrated guests, notably Archbishop John Carroll of Baltimore, were treated to Cottrill's Irish hospitality. One must underline, however, that the Cottrill mansion was informed not by Irish precedent but rather from more cosmopolitan examples found throughout the Atlantic World. A stately merchant seat, stylish furniture, and frequent entertainment signaled assimilation to a cultural ideal that was emanating out of England during the period.

Outside the house, guests could have walked through grounds that followed upon the elegant example set by the mansion. Deeds and probate records speak of gardens, orchards, and outbuildings, and along the waterfront one could find a "gandolo" (known locally in Maine as a gundalow), a type of flat-bottomed boat used for hauling bulk cargo, which Cottrill used for travel upriver. It is clear that Cottrill endeavored to create an estate that would communicate his position in the community and present a fashionable front for his fellow merchants in mid-Maine. Yet with all this concern over style and appearance, Cottrill was never far away from the means of his wealth and power. Directly adjacent to his merchant seat stood the company store and wharves, and walking along the avenue behind the house one would have heard hammering and construction—the sound of a busy shipyard.

Shipbuilding was a natural adjunct to the firm's timber and maritime interests. With miles of untapped woodland at their doorstep, and the need for ships to carry lumber to distant markets, many rising merchants such as Kavanagh and Cottrill entered into the shipbuilding trade. As early as 1797 the firm operated a shipyard behind Cottrill's mansion, a yard that produced several sailing vessels by 1820.[26] For the most part these were square-rigged, heavy draft brigs and ships built to serve in the booming West Indies and European trade. The Damariscotta region was a rich source of new shipping during this period. In addition to Kavanagh and Cottrill there were at least five other shipyards within a five-mile radius of Nobleboro—a busy industry that sustained local shipbuilders Nathaniel Bryant, George Barstow, and John Borland, an Ulsterman who owned a shipyard on Great Salt Bay.[27]

The shipyards along the Damariscotta were a major source of employment, attracting a steady flow of artisans into the region. Many came from seaport communities in southern New England, skilled craftsmen who were hit hard by recession and lack of opportunity after the Revolution.[28] Others were recent arrivals from the British Isles, voyagers who carried their skills to the New World.[29] One of these was John Boulger, an Irish-born shipwright who, along with his son Lestshay, worked at the Cottrill shipyard during the early nineteenth century. Boulger learned his trade in Dublin, where he most likely worked at one of the shipyards along the River Liffey. While his motivations for leaving Ireland are unknown, he may have been recruited with promises of work in the Cottrill shipyards—a possibility suggested by his passage aboard the company brig *Atlantic* in 1804.[30]

Company accounts, deeds, and probate records identify at least eight ships owned by Kavanagh and Cottrill and likely built in their shipyard. The names of these vessels suggest much about the interests and loyalties of the two partners. Several vessels bear the name of family members: the brig *Lydia*, for example, named after Cottrill's wife; and the *John and Edward*, christened after the eldest sons of Cottrill and Kavanagh. Other vessels, notably the *Erin* and the *Hibernia*, look back to the Irish origins of their owners and identify the overseas markets for which they sailed. And finally, one finds in the *Fair America* an indication of the reception the partners experienced in the New World and the opportunities that they experienced in the Maine timber trade.

THE MAINE TIMBER TRADE AND IRELAND

From their cockpit on the Damariscotta River Kavanagh and Cottrill directed a far-flung enterprise. They shipped lumber and country produce to the West Indies, and their ships returned laden with molasses destined to be made into rum in their "still house" in Damariscotta Mills. Like fellow timber traders in Wiscasset and Portland they also followed the transatlantic routes to Europe, an increasingly lucrative enterprise for Maine merchants—especially beginning in 1793, after the outbreak of the Napoleonic wars (Anglo-French hostilities that continued intermittently for twenty years).[31] As neutral carriers, New England vessels shipped goods to both combatants and sailed with impunity to ports of call throughout Europe. Kavanagh and Cottrill, for example, sent lumber, potash and barrel staves to Cork, Dublin, and Liverpool, carried high grade salt between Lisbon and Cork, and returned with freight or manufactured goods bound for Boston.[32] The transatlantic trade, however, was not without its risks. During the early 1800s New England vessels and their cargos were regularly seized and confiscated by both France and England.[33] Maine merchants also suffered setbacks of a diplomatic nature. In December 1807, President Thomas Jefferson, in response to French and British seizures, issued a trade embargo with both nations and forbade the clearance of any American ship bound for foreign ports of call. Jefferson's embargo effectively suffocated transatlantic trade in New England for over a year and contributed to the failure of a number of merchant firms along the Maine coast.[34] The firm of Kavanagh and Cottrill managed to weather the storm, however, and resumed shipping timber to Jamaica, Liverpool, and especially Ireland.

At the turn of the nineteenth century, Ireland represented a lucrative market for Maine timber, mast trees and barrel staves; and the firm increasingly directed its overseas trade toward Dublin and Cork. They were not alone. Between June 1810 and September 1811, shipping news in the *Cork Mercantile Chronicle* recorded that 41 timber ships from Maine entered Cork harbor (see Table 1). Some, like the *Nabby* of Wiscasset, offloaded timber and barrel staves "for orders" by Cork merchants. Many, however, simply reprovisioned at Cork and sailed on to Dublin, Belfast, or English ports, especially Liverpool.

TABLE I

New England Vessels entering Cork Harbor
June 1810 – September 1811

Boston Mass.	21	Bath, Maine	2
Wiscasset, Me.	16	Portsmouth, N.H.	2
Portland, Me.	7	Newburyport, Ma.	2
Newcastle, Me.	4	Penobscot, Me	1
Kennebunk, Me	4	Castine, Me.	1
Warren, Me	2	Cohasset, Mass.	1
Waldoborough, Me	2	Plymouth, Mass.	1
Georgetown, Me	2	New Bedford, Mass.	1

Source: *Cork Mercantile Chronicle*, June 1810–September, 1811;
National Library of Ireland, Dublin.

The timber trade between Maine and Ireland was a short-lived but dynamic commerce that flowered between 1790 and 1812. Timber had been in short supply in Ireland since the seventeenth century, a legacy of the systematic stripping of the landscape to fuel iron furnaces in England and to suit agricultural expansion at home. Except for a few isolated reserves on landlord estates in Kilkenny and Wicklow, Irish consumers of timber and building materials depended largely on sources from abroad.[35] Much of this timber was imported from Scandinavia and the Baltic region during the eighteenth century, a pattern that slowly shifted during the Napoleonic Wars in favor of supplies from British North America and the United States, particularly New England and coastal Maine.[36] At its peak in 1811, northern New England was sending over 12,000 tons of timber into Irish ports, thirty-five percent of total imports for the island nation.[37] New England also sent a significant volume of milled lumber and barrel staves to Ireland, the latter being in great demand for the Irish food packing trade. Cork, in particular, with its extensive salt-beef and butter trade to Newfoundland and the West Indies, absorbed a large proportion of barrel staves during the early nineteenth century.

Whereas Irish-born merchants such as Kavanagh and Cottrill routinely sent timber vessels to Ireland beginning in the 1790s, it took Yankee merchants in Maine a bit longer to see a window of opportunity in the Emerald Isle. Customs records for Bath, Maine (among the few that survive for this period) suggest that a direct trade between Maine and Ireland only began to accelerate in the first decade of the nineteenth century. Shipping manifests between 1802 and 1803 reflect that "foreign" voyages from Bath were still primarily directed to the West Indies.[38] This pattern, however, soon began to change, especially after Jefferson's embargo. By 1810 Irish and English ports of call (especially Liverpool) had captured a sizeable share of Kennebec timber. The increasing commerce with Ireland was also reflected in inward foreign manifests for Bath. Vessels arriving from Irish ports in 1811 and 1812 represented twelve percent of all foreign entries on the Kennebec River during these years.[39] Fragmentary evidence from other ports, such as Wiscasset, revealed a similar increase. This upsurge in Irish trade, in part, is explained by diplomatic shifts such as the Non-Importation Act of 1809, which forbade two-way trade with England. Writing to his agents in Glasgow, Abiel Wood, a merchant from Wiscasset, confided, "it will not do to send ships to England or Scotland where duties are enormous without some prospect of freight home, and this we cannot expect till the non importation acts are off." Until then, according to Wood, "we do better in Ireland."[40]

This trade between Maine and Ireland—which gave rise to firms such as Kavanagh and Cottrill—is largely forgotten today. Historians have tended to focus on the primary trading ports (such as Boston and New York) and their significant commerce with Europe and the Orient. Yet the commerce of smaller outports, such as those in mid-Maine, often took place outside the influence of these great trading centers. Wiscasset, for example, maintained an important and direct trade with England and Ireland through much of the Federal period, and was well known to contemporaries in Dublin, Belfast, and Liverpool.

THE BRIG ATLANTIC

The transatlantic timber trade with Ireland and Liverpool was the fulcrum on which the firm of Kavanagh and Cottrill turned. Their trade is articulated in the account book of Captain James Smithwick, master of the brig *Atlantic*.[41] Smithwick was born in Boston in 1770, the son of an Irish trader from New Ross, County Wexford. During the Revolutionary era the Smithwicks owned ships and commercial property on

Fish Street in the North End, and dabbled intermittently in trade between New England and Ireland.[42] Young Smithwick's career eventually took him to coastal Maine where his skills were commissioned by wealthy timber merchants, especially Kavanagh and Cottrill. Through a combination of successful voyages and an advantageous marriage to Elizabeth Jackson, the sister-in-law of James Kavanagh, Smithwick entered into partnership with the firm, acquiring a share in several oceangoing vessels, including the brig *Atlantic*. Between 1800 and 1811 Smithwick made at least eight voyages in the employ of Kavanagh and Cottrill, touching upon Ireland, England, Portugal, and the West Indies. By following one of these voyages, in 1806, we can glimpse a picture of the cargoes and trade routes that characterized the Irish trade of Kavanagh and Cottrill.

Timber ships such as the brig *Atlantic* were among the most distinctive vessels sailing out of Maine during the Federal period. Larger than the coastal schooners and Caribbean traders, they were designed to carry a cumbersome cargo of timber as well as withstand the rigors of a long transatlantic crossing. During the early summer of 1806, planks, shingles, and timber were loaded aboard the *Atlantic*—a cargo that would be sold in Dublin. While ship accounts do not provide precise dates, the transatlantic crossing typically took six weeks. Under Smithwick's command, the *Atlantic* made landfall at Cork and then sailed into the Irish Sea for the port of Dublin. Timber from the vessel, described in the *Dublin Evening Post* as oak, maple, and pine of "superior quality," was auctioned in the timber yards along Sir John Rogerson's quay.[43] Profits were then remitted on account to Kavanagh and Cottrill's correspondents in London to purchase linen and manufactured goods for the return voyage.

Herein lies one of the important features of the Irish timber trade out of Maine. A major objective for merchants in the decades following the American Revolution was the importation of British manufactured goods—in response to local consumer demand for new styles and products from across the Atlantic. New England, however, produced few commodities that could be marketed directly in England without carrying a high duty attached to them. The Irish trade effectively changed the complexion of this trade imbalance. As historian David Doyle explains, by selling their cargo in Cork or Dublin, where it was in heavy demand, American traders were able to "draw on London or Liverpool merchants through bills of credit—often arranged by the Irish firms whom they supplied."[44] Merchants such as Kavanagh and Cottrill, therefore, were able to generate sufficient credit through their timber sale to "fund the importation of British manufactured goods" for their merchant stores.[45] This process is outlined in the letterbooks of Thomas Nickels, a timber trader in Wiscasset. In October 1810, Nickels penned detailed instructions to Captain Francis Preble, who was carrying timber and flaxseed aboard the *Rachel*, bound for Sligo, on the west coast of Ireland:

> Wherever you may conclude to have your cargo sold, be particular to call on good responsible men to do your business (as there are many failures in Ireland) and when your cargo is sold and your disbursements paid; to remit the net proceeds to Messr. Morrill and Borland of Liverpool without delay.[46]

Such remittances could then be credited toward shipments of coal, salt, and manufactured goods on future voyages to Boston.

THE IRISH MERCHANT COMMUNITY

Along with the movement of merchandise and freight across the Atlantic, another consequence of the expanding trade networks between Ireland and Maine was the migration of an Irish elite to northern New England.[47] During the last quarter of the eighteenth century, several enclaves of Irish traders and mariners emerged in coastal towns north of Boston. Mid-coast Maine, in particular, developed an active network of expatriate Irish merchants and mariners scattered between the ports of Wiscasset, Newcastle, and Thomaston. At its peak in the early nineteenth century, this group numbered close to thirty, a loosely-knit fraternity connected as much by timber profits as by ethnic origins (Table 2). In Wiscasset alone they ranged from wealthy transatlantic firms to modest shopkeepers, mariners, even an innkeeper.[48] The firm of Anderson, Child, and Child, for example, a prominent trading house in Liverpool with both Irish and English partners, sent out several associates to establish a branch operation in Wiscasset (just as the lumbering frontier was advancing to the Sheepscot at the turn of the nineteenth century).[49] Among them was John Anderson, from Castlewellan in County Down.[50] Other Irish traders in the town included John O'Dee and Thomas McCrate, from Waterford; and Walter Madigan who emigrated in 1804 to Wiscasset where he opened a shop overlooking Long Wharf.[51] Three of his sons eventually became mariners; the eldest of whom, John Madigan, worked for Kavanagh and Cottrill in Newcastle.

TABLE 2

IRISH MERCHANTS AND MASTER MARINERS
LINCOLN AND KENNEBEC COUNTY, MAINE, 1780–1830

NAME, TOWN, OCCUPATION, PLACE OF ORIGIN

Francis Anderson, Wiscasset, Merchant, County Down
John Anderson, Wiscasset, Merchant, Castlewellan, County Down
Thomas Anderson, Wiscasset, Merchant, County Down
John Borland, Newcastle, Merchant, Londonderry
Edward Bradshaw, Bath, Merchant, County Antrim
Matthew Cottrill, Nobleboro, Merchant, Inistioge, County Kilkenny
Sydenham Davis, Hallowell, Trader, Thomastown, County Kilkenny
Patrick Doyle, Newcastle, Trader, County Kilkenny
Martin Esmond, Gardiner, Merchant, County Wexford
Roger Hanley, Bristol, Trader, County Tipperary
James Kavanagh, Newcastle, Merchant, Inistioge, County Kilkenny
Patrick Keegan, Thomaston, Trader, Dublin
Thomas McCrate, Wiscasset, Merchant, Waterford City
Samuel McCullogh, Boothbay, Mariner, Belfast
Thomas McGuire, Waldoboro, Trader, County Wexford
Patrick McKown, Boothbay, Mariner, Glenarm, County Antrim
Edmund Madigan, Wiscasset, Mariner, Thomastown, County Kilkenny
John Madigan, Newcastle, Merchant, Thomastown, County Kilkenny
Walter Madigan, Wiscasset, Trader, Knockanore, County Kilkenny
James Meagher, New Waterford, Mariner, County Waterford
Richard Meagher, Bristol, Gentleman, County Waterford
William Meagher, Wiscasset, Mariner, County Waterford
John Molloy, Hallowell, Trader, Ireland
William Mooney, Newcastle, Merchant, County Wicklow
John O'Dee, Wiscasset, Trader, County Waterford
Michael Power, Wiscasset, Mariner, Ireland
Richard Power, Jefferson, Trader, County Kilkenny
Thomas Timmons, Bath, Mariner, Dublin

Sources: Naturalization Petitions, Lincoln and Kennebec County, Maine, Record Group 85, Boxes 477-78, 480, NAW; Lincoln County and Kennebec County, Registry of Deeds and Registry of Probate; Gravestone Inscriptions, St. Patrick's Church, Newcastle, and St. Dennis Church, North Whitefield; and Genealogical data.

Kavanagh and Cottrill were arguably the most prominent Irish merchant house in New England during the Federal period. They surrounded themselves with a galaxy of mariners, clerks, and shopkeepers drawn from the distant corners of the Anglo-Celtic world. Their shipmasters included James Smithwick, Daniel McDonnell from Greenock, Scotland, and Robert Askins, the son of immigrants from Londonderry. The firm also employed a network of kin and countrymen who worked as traders and storekeepers. These included Cottrill's nephew John Madigan; his son-in-law William Mooney; and Patrick Doyle, a native of County Kilkenny, who worked at the Kavanagh store in Damariscotta Mills. The two partners also forged connections with Richard Meagher, a trader and justice of the peace who speculated in the Maine backcountry. Meagher's holding along the Sheepscot frontier was christened "New Waterford" after his birthplace in Ireland.[52] Such networks were crucial to the success of Irish merchant houses such as Kavanagh and Cottrill. As historians of Irish migration have recently argued, "Eighteenth century commerce, both within the colonies and with foreign ports, was based almost entirely on credit and, consequently, on networks of personal contacts and trust that were largely shaped by familial ties and ethno-religious affinities."[53]

The Irish merchant community of Lincoln County was linked by more than family connections and timber profits. Several merchants—James Kavanagh, Francis Anderson, and Thomas McCrate—were members of the Charitable Irish Society of Boston, an elite fraternity open to "all gentlemen, merchants and others of the Irish nation or extraction, in or trading in these parts." On occasion they came together to celebrate St. Patrick's Day, and joined a list of members that included Henry Knox and James Sullivan.[54] During the Federal period Knox and Sullivan were perhaps the best-known representatives of the "Irish nation or extraction" in New England. Both men also had important ties to Maine. Henry Knox was born in Boston, the son of Mary Campbell and William Knox, a Scotch-Irish master mariner. Henry made his name during the American Revolution, serving as commander of Continental Artillery, and afterwards was named Secretary of War in the first cabinet of George Washington. Through his wife's inheritance, Knox acquired the Waldo Patent, a vast tract of Maine land between the Kennebec River and Penobscot Bay. From his mansion in Thomaston, called Montpelier, Knox oversaw this frontier empire: directing agents to rein in squatters on his backcountry lands, experimenting with new industries such as lime extraction, and entertaining a host of visitors in grand style. During the early 1800s Knox and Matthew Cottrill were acquaintances when they both served as Trustees for Lincoln Academy in Newcastle. While no record survives of their association, as opportunistic émigrés from the metropolis they would have shared an interest in wresting profits from the land, and a concern for bringing order and cultural refinement to the frontier of Maine.[55]

Cottrill and Kavanagh also had ties with James Sullivan who, on at least one occasion, served as an attorney for the Irish community in Damariscotta. Sullivan was born along the Salmon Falls River in 1744 and grew up with his brothers John and William in the village of Berwick, Maine. Their father, John Sullivan, born into the old Gaelic gentry in Limerick, and their mother Margaret Browne from Cork, had both crossed the Atlantic as redemptioners (immigrants who had to pay for their passage once they arrived in the New World). The elder Sullivan subsequently worked as a schoolmaster in Berwick—a common occupation for Irish emigrants in early New England—and gained local reknown as a linguist, having acquired several languages while living in France after the Williamite Wars.[56] In time the Sullivans assimilated themselves into colonial society in northern New England, illustrated by their membership in the Congregational Church, and most dramatically, by the accomplishments of their children. James served as Governor of Massachusetts from 1807 to 1808, and John as a Major General under Washington in the American Revolution. Still, evidence suggests that both sons continued an interest in Irish affairs and identity. John Sullivan's personal correspondence includes letters to relations to Ireland in which he inquires into family history;[57] and James Sullivan's proprietary venture in the Maine backcountry was named "Limerick," in honor of his father's birthplace in Ireland.[58]

In addition to ties of status, ethnicity, and family tradition, many of the Irish in the Damariscotta region were also joined by bonds of religion. Close to one-half of the Irish merchant community were members of the "Catholic Society of Newcastle, Maine"—a congregation founded in 1798 and visited periodically by priests and missionaries out of Boston. With land donated by James Kavanagh and Matthew Cottrill they built St. Patrick's, "a very neat and elegant chapel" in Damariscotta Mills. Built by Nicholas Codd, it is today the oldest standing Catholic church in

New England.[59] (See gallery, plate 18.) The church was consecrated on July 30, 1808 by Father Jean Cheverus, who would later become the first Bishop of Boston. Writing to Bishop John Carroll in Baltimore, Cheverus described a "numerous and respectable" assembly that day, one that would have ranged from timber traders to Irish farmers who had settled the backcountry community of New Waterford. Indeed the Irish antecedents of this assembly were much in evidence, from the harps that stood out in carved relief over the sacristy doors, to the name St. Patrick's, which Cheverus noted "seems to gratify our friends here."[60]

The Catholic Irish were not the only tradition represented among Erin's merchants in Lincoln County. Also visible were Irish Protestants who peopled the trading communities of several coastal towns.[61] In St. George, for example, Anglo-Irish and Scotch-Irish comprised a notable bloc in the town.[62] Boothbay, likewise, boasted a number of families with roots in Ulster. Robert McKown, for instance, was a ship captain in the timber trade whose father Patrick, also a mariner, came from Ireland prior to the Revolution. When he died in 1779 Patrick willed his son the family house, garden and "estate" in Glenarm, County Antrim, provided that "he go there for it."[63] Much the same picture applied for Wiscasset, where a number of the town's merchant community were descended from Ulster immigrants who had settled the region a generation earlier. The Nickels, Pattersons, Cunninghams, and Boyds—families who figured prominently in the port's timber trade during the Federal period—were all heirs to a migrant stream that left Ulster during the mid-eighteenth century.[64]

This is not to imply, however, that all of the Irish merchants in Lincoln County maintained their Old World traditions and identity. Some, in fact, quickly absorbed the predominant Yankee culture of coastal Maine—acquiring New England styles of houses and attire, marrying Congregational partners, and worshipping at the local meeting house. The experience of Wiscasset merchant Thomas McCrate is representative of this cultural metamorphosis. While likely born into a Catholic family in County Waterford, McCrate (McCraith or McGrath in Gaelic) jettisoned much of his Irish persona upon settling in Maine. He married into a locally prominent family, served as Captain of the town militia, and experimented freely in the diverse religious environment of Maine. At the time of his death in 1835 he held pews in the Baptist, Methodist, and Congregational churches in Wiscasset.[65]

The question remains: to what do we attribute this early migration of Irish traders to coastal Maine? Certainly the lure of material gain and open competition played an important role in attracting outsiders to Lincoln County. Here in the newly opened lands east of the Kennebec immigrants had a better chance of opportunity and upward mobility than in the settled trading communities of Boston or Salem.[66] Indeed, as one recent history of Irish migration asserts: "In the colonial era, aspiring Irish entrepreneurs generally enjoyed greatest success . . . when they could specialize in branches of trade not already controlled by exclusive, non-Irish merchant oligarchies."[67] The timber trade in mid-Maine offered just such an opportunity. One must also credit the role of trade networks in drawing seafaring personnel to Lincoln County. Many early Irish immigrants in mid-Maine came from regions in the Atlantic world that were ports of call for Maine timber ships. Thomas Timmons, for example, apprenticed himself in Dublin aboard an American vessel and subsequently worked as a mariner out of Bath, Maine.[68] In 1812 he captained the brig *Dispatch* which carried timber and masts to the shipbuilding town of Kinsale in south Cork, and returned to Bath with a cargo of high-grade salt from St. Ubes in Portugal.[69] Robert Kelly followed a similar experience in Liverpool, traveling to Wiscasset as an apprentice to Captain David Otis in 1796. Kelly eventually went on to become a shipmaster in his own right, directing timber voyages to Ireland and Liverpool.[70] This pattern of recruitment, which attracted aspiring emigrants from Maine's trading fields in Ireland and Britain, contributed to the cosmopolitan flavor of seafaring towns such as Newcastle and Wiscasset.[71]

Indeed, as scholars have demonstrated, provincial elites in early America were drawn in surprising numbers from the margins of the Anglo-Celtic world.[72] Narrowing economic opportunities at home for the younger sons of gentry, shopkeepers, and large farmers forced an outward-looking perspective on the Atlantic world and a positive inclination toward colonial careers in trade and the military. These emigrant elite, as in the case of the Irish-Protestant merchant community of Philadelphia, or the Hibernian enclaves of mid-Maine, often concentrated their efforts in particular commodities such as flaxseed or timber from which they forged lucrative trade networks with the Old World. As Eric Richards suggests, "They were link-men, commercial go-betweens, of the economy in the wilds of America to the domestic sources of industry and people in . . . Europe."[73] The backgrounds and careers of James Kavanagh and Matthew Cottrill illustrate this phenomenon in striking detail. Coming from the ranks of the up-and-coming middling class in Catholic Ireland, they were nonetheless closed off to advancement in the larger seaports of the realm. In response, they sought their opportunity on the periphery of New England, where risk-taking and entrepreneurial ambitions could find free reign.

THE IRISH PASSENGER TRADE

Commerce in passengers was another facet of the Maine timber trade during the Federal period. Because of their size, westbound timber ships such as the brig *Atlantic* often ran the risk of having to go out with much unoccupied space (European goods carried on the return journey were generally small manufactured wares or luxury items), or entirely in ballast. Paying passengers, therefore, were a boon to shipowners such as Kavanagh and Cottrill. Temporary berths and accommodations could be easily fitted out aboard ship at the Irish port of call, and passengers provided with a modicum of provisions. The ship *North Star*, for example, sailed with 110 passengers from Londonderry to Bath, Maine in 1812, some of whom carried their own provisions and necessities. John Raverly and his family brought on board "One chest, two barrels, one box, and one Bundle bedding."[74] Income from these emigrants often brought in considerable revenues during peak years and, at the very least, it helped to meet shipboard expenses.[75]

Merchants from several ports along the timber coast of Maine participated in this commerce, carrying passengers from Dublin, Belfast, Londonderry, and Cork. Indeed, merchants and shipowners were an important cog in the machinery of emigration to early America, and the promise of profits from the passenger trade played no small part in its inception. As one scholar on immigration suggests, "Between the 'push' of uncomfortable circumstances at home, and the 'pull' of a new land's attractiveness, merchants were the principal ingredient in the sustained movement of people to the New World."[76] One such merchant was Abiel Wood of Wiscasset, who owned a fleet of twenty oceangoing vessels during the early nineteenth century. In 1811, several of his ships, including the aptly named *Shamrock*, were recorded in Dublin offloading timber and taking on passengers bound for Boston and New York. A

passenger list for the *Shamrock*, published in the *Shamrock or Hibernian Chronicle* in 1811, identified sixty passengers, a group recruited
largely from Dublin and its hinterlands. Most of these voyagers
embarked for New York, which by the early nineteenth century had
become the principal magnet in the Irish emigrant trade.[77]

Many of the passengers traveling to America during this era came
with marketable skills, unlike those Irish migrants leaving later during
the famine era of the 1840s. Shipping lists and official statistics, such as
those kept between 1803 and 1806, describe many as farmers, artisans,
and clerks—passengers who most likely emigrated out of personal
choice and paid their own passage.[78] That most of this movement
involved the "middling sort" during the early nineteenth century was
due in large part to the British Passenger Act of 1803, legislation that
sharply raised transatlantic fares on American owned vessels.
Consequently, only the more prosperous and "solid" Irish folk could
afford to sail to America at this time, and most of the poorer sort either
postponed their departure or took passage to Maritime Canada. The
aforementioned *Shamrock* offers a prime example. Upon clearing
Dublin in June, 1811, one customs official declared that "many of the
passengers per the *Shamrock* . . . are very respectable and none under
the degree of mechanics and farmers. Not one servant of either sex
could be obtained from amongst them."[79]

Having said this, however, there is evidence that Irish servants occasionally traveled aboard Maine timber ships during the early Republic.
Captains, for instance, were periodically asked to enlist artisans willing
to indenture themselves in exchange for passage to New England. In
1797, James Kavanagh instructed Captain Robert Askins, sailing to
Dublin aboard the schooner *Hester*, to find "two young men [black-
smiths] acquainted with horseshoeing to indent themselves for one year
each after they arrive here. Each of them to be sober, honest young
men." Kavanagh added that "You should also seek two young women
as servants . . ."[80] It is tempting to interpret this as an extension of the
Irish servant trade which flourished during the Colonial era. More likely,
however, Kavanagh was personally recruiting artisans and domestic servants for his estate in Damariscotta Mills. This is suggested in his
account books that make reference to several Irish servants and "hired
girls."[81] In terms of the larger emigrant trade aboard his timber vessels,
Kavanagh, like other merchants of this period, sought paying passengers.

Passengers traveling from Ireland aboard Maine timber ships were recruited by one of several means. Passage was most often arranged by agents in the major ports, who represented the interest of timber coast merchants. Many agents, such as the firm of Forbes and Fawcett in Dublin, doubled as brokers in the timber trade. Besides auctioning off a ship's cargo of timber, they also advertised details concerning its departure and arranged accommodation for paying passengers.[82] In addition to quayside agents, ship captains also took a hand in recruiting passengers. From pubs, inns, and marketplaces along the waterfront they touted the advantages of their ship and the opportunities awaiting at its destination. Their efforts become understandable when one is reminded that captains regularly shared in the profits of the voyage—profits that included emigrant fares.[83] As Abiel Wood reminded his captains, they would take in "one half of all real neet profits, made in the Cabbin by passengers including the State Rooms . . . ."[84]

An instructive example of the Maine passenger trade can be found in the affairs of the brig *Atlantic*, owned by Kavanagh and Cottrill, and sailing between Ireland and New England in 1804. Upon selling its cargo of timber in Dublin a notice was placed in the *Dublin Evening Post* seeking passengers for the return voyage to Boston, "for which she has excellent accommodation."[85] On July 19, Captain Robert Askins from Bristol, Maine signed twenty-one passengers aboard the *Atlantic*. In order to comply with requirements of the Passenger Act of 1803, Askins recorded each passenger's name, age, place of origin, as well as their height, coloring, and distinguishing features (Table 3).[86] Ralph Moran, for example, was described as a laborer from Raheen, County Kilkenny. He was twenty years of age, five feet eleven inches in height, and of sallow complexion. Moran later settled in Hallowell, Maine, where he married into a Yankee family and farmed fifty acres along the Kennebec River.[87]

TABLE 3
PASSENGER LIST OF THE BRIG ATLANTIC: 1804

"Passengers engaged to sail on board the American brig Atlantic,
Robert Askins master, burden 196 tons, for Boston. Sworn at
Dublin, 19 June, 1804."

Sydenham Davis of Summerhill, Kilkenny. Age 20, height 5'2", dark, farmer.
Ralph Moran of Raheen, Kilkenny. Age 20, height 5'11", sallow, labourer.
Michael Ryan of Thomastown, Kilkenny. Age 22, height 5'7", fair, labourer.
John O'Hara of Kilmurry, Kilkenny. Age 31, height 5'3", dark, labourer.
Walter Madigan of Thomastown, Kilkenny. Age 35, height 6'0", fair, labourer.
    Also his wife Catherine, age 28.
Hugh Heffernan of Clonfert, Kings County. Age 22, height 5'6", dark, labourer.
Andrew Shortall of Thomastown, Kilkenny. Age 21, height 5'10", dark, labourer.
Daniel Nowlan of Tullow, Carlow. Age 21, height 5'10", dark, clerk.
John Boulger of Dublin. Age 36, height 5'5", dark, labourer.
    Also his wife Catherine, age 36.
Samuel Duke of Thomastown, Kilkenny. Age 21, height 5'5", dark, labourer.
Martin Switzer of Navan, Meath. Age 28, height 5'10", fair, labourer.
James Maxwell of Dublin. Age 20, height 5'8", dark, labourer.
William Coonan of Dublin. Age 32, height 5'10", dark, clerk.
William O'Brien of Dublin. Age 20, height 5'6", dark, clerk.
Michael Mallon of Dungannon, Tyrone. Age 33, height 5'6", dark, brewer.
Anthony Kearns of Dunleer, Louth. Age 23, height 5'6", dark, labourer.
Andrew Melvin of Bray, Wicklow. Age 25, height 5'9", dark, clerk.
Thomas Reynolds of Klena, Longford. Age 22, height 5'6", fair, clerk.

Source: *New England Historical and Genealogical Register*, Vol. LXII (1908): 172.

Perhaps the most interesting feature of this passenger list is the strong regional and local identity of its emigrants. Many of those who sailed aboard the brig *Atlantic* were drawn from the southeast of Ireland, particularly County Kilkenny. Thirteen emigrants came from the parish of Thomastown along the River Nore, just upriver from Inistioge. Among them were Sydenham Davis, a gentleman farmer; Samuel Duke, the son of a local apothecary; and Walter Madigan, an artisan traveling with his wife Catherine and four young children. Upon closer examination, one finds that most of these Thomastown folk had earlier connections to Matthew Cottrill, the ship's owner. Walter Madigan, for example, was Cottrill's brother-in-law, and eventually opened a shop in Wiscasset with his assistance.[88] The family of Sydenham Davis, similarly, had close ties with Cottrill's kinsmen in

Kilkenny who acted as witnesses on business transactions concerning the Davis's in Thomastown.[89] Sydenham went on to settle in Hallowell, Maine where he set up shop as a trader and brewer.[90]

The career of Sydenham Davis is an instructive episode in the history of Atlantic trade and migration. The younger son of a Protestant landowner, Davis was drawn to Maine by Old World networks and New World opportunities. By 1808 he had established himself in trade, shipping goods out of Bath and dealing in consignments of flour, rice, and tobacco.[91] He eventually acquired ownership of a vessel, the brig *Montezuma*, which, in 1812, transported timber to Waterford and returned to Bath carrying passengers and barrels of Irish beef. In 1815, perhaps prompted by financial losses, Davis pulled up stakes in Hallowell and sailed for Ireland, one of the few documented return-migrants in the pre-famine era. He subsequently entered into trade in Thomastown and later inherited his family estate, known as Summerhill.[92] Perhaps most intriguing was his venture as an inland broker in Kilkenny for the emigrant trade to Atlantic Canada. In 1818 he advertised berths for St. John's, Newfoundland, and later sought passengers for Prince Edward Island, along with "seventy youngsters . . . for the Labrador fishery."[93] His enterprise as emigrant broker reflects that, despite his cushion of privilege and property in Ireland, Davis did not turn his back on the Atlantic world. His earlier experience in Maine (both as an immigrant and as a businessman) had sharpened his sense of opportunity, especially concerning profits to be made in the emigrant trade.

Many who sailed aboard the brig *Atlantic* in 1804 eventually settled in Lincoln County, Maine. Andrew Shortall, for example, worked as a housewright in Wiscasset. He was also a member of the "Catholic Society of Newcastle," and chose each of his children's godparents from among the Madigan and Cottrill families—understandable given that they were his Old World neighbors along the Nore.[94] Michael Ryan, also from Thomastown, settled in Hallowell. John Boulger, a carpenter whom we met earlier, found work in the firm's shipyards in Damariscotta. Their experience, along with Walter Madigan's, suggests one of the interesting features of a migration managed by merchants: immigrant entrepreneurs such as Kavanagh and Cottrill occasionally tapped into kinship and neighborhood networks to attract labor and settlers from the homeland. For the most part, however, this was a rare occurrence in the New England timber trade. Passengers who traveled aboard

Maine vessels were predominately recruited through agents and captains in the port of origin.

While the majority of emigrant ships in the Maine trade sailed for the larger ports of New York or Boston, timber vessels carrying Irish passengers also made landfall along coastal Maine. The brig *Patty* of Wiscasset, for example, returned to its home port with emigrants from Dublin, as did the ship *Washington*, which landed fifty-one passengers at Wiscasset in 1812.[95] It appears that this larger number of passengers was unusual for vessels returning to the timber ports of Lincoln County. More common were vessels carrying only a handful of emigrants, for reasons noted by Wiscasset merchant Abiel Wood. In 1811, he instructed his shipmasters to always seek passengers for the New York or Boston market, cities that attracted a large contingent of new emigrants. However, "if no freight offers nor any passengers worth going to another port for, you'll in this case take on board Ballast and return direct to this port [Wiscasset], taking at same time each passenger as may offer for this Port."[96]

Thus a small but steady number of Irish immigrants made their way aboard timber vessels into mid-Maine during the early national period, joining the ranks of Irish coming by way of the Maritimes and Boston. That some of these voyagers remained is suggested in local records and naturalization petitions for Lincoln and Kennebec County—which reveal close to three hundred Irish-born settlers between 1790 and 1840.[97] Many of these were of the "middling sort": artisans and traders who peopled the seaports of Newcastle and Wiscasset. They also included farm families who settled in the upcountry towns of Windsor and Whitefield, Maine. Their rural experience and landownership differed sharply from the urban poor who settled in east coast cities during the 1830s and 1840s. Mid-Maine, in fact, represents one of the few locations in the northeast where rural Irish settled in rural settings—a phenomenon that had important ramifications for cultural continuity and identity into the twentieth century.

EPILOGUE

By 1820, Kavanagh and Cottrill's trade with Ireland had all but disappeared—the victim of war, exorbitant duties imposed on American timber, and changing legislation concerning the passenger trade.[98] Some of these changes, in part, were brought on by the ascendancy of the Canadian timber industry, which eclipsed the earlier commerce between Maine, Britain, and Ireland. In the years after 1815, Britain actively choreographed this Canadian trade, importing large shiploads of timber from the Maritime Provinces and initiating a system of preferential tariffs that all but guaranteed its success. This policy, for the short term, hampered New England timber interests in Europe, and those merchants who continued in the trade faced declining fortunes brought on by heavy duties on the British and Irish end.

Despite its meteoric rise and decline, the Maine-Irish trade suggests important patterns, particularly with regard to the Canadian trade that followed in its wake. Many of the established patterns we associate with Maritime-Atlantic commerce during the nineteenth century—its timber cargoes, trade routes, and Irish passenger trade—were briefly established on a modest scale in Maine several decades earlier. Likewise, the opportunities realized by an Irish elite in mid-Maine—notably Kavanagh and Cottrill—were also echoed in Maritime Canada. The histories of St. John's, Halifax, and Charlottetown are punctuated by the stories of Irish emigrants, Protestant and Catholic, who made their fortune in timber, trade, and land speculation.[99]

The Maine timber trade, and the profits and status that it afforded immigrant entrepreneurs, provided an initial launching pad for the Irish into the political arena. This was evident among several second-generation sons of merchant elites in Maine. The most notable of these was Edward Kavanagh, the oldest son of James. Educated at Catholic schools in Montreal and Baltimore, Edward Kavanagh chose a career in law and politics rather than continue in the trans-Atlantic trade of his father. He went on to become the diplomatic representative to Portugal under President Andrew Jackson, and was appointed Governor of Maine in 1843 (the first Catholic Governor in New England).[100]

Today the legacy of Kavanagh and Cottrill in Maine is perhaps best remembered in the elegant Federal period mansions they built along the Damariscotta, and in St. Patrick's Church, which they helped to establish in 1808. These historic sites are emblematic of the firm's ascendancy on the eastern frontier, and they continue to impress all who travel to this region of mid-Maine. One such traveler was poet Robert Lowell who, along with his wife Jean Stafford, lived for a time in a farmhouse in Damariscotta Mills, just down the road from the estate known as "Kavanagh." An excerpt from his long poem, "The Mills of the Kavanaughs," written in 1951, leaves us with an evocative and lasting image of this community and its founder:

> He will abet my thoughts of Kavanaugh,
> Who gave the Mills its lumberyard and weir
> In Eighteen Hundred, when our farmers saw
> John Adams bring their Romish Church a bell,
> Cast—so the records claim—by Paul Revere.
> The sticks of Kavanaugh are buried here—
> Many of them, too many, love, to tell—
> Faithful to where their virgin forest fell.[101]

1. Joyce Butler, "Rising Like a Phoenix: Commerce in Southern Maine, 1775–1830," in Laura Fecych Sprague, ed., *Agreeable Situations: Society, Commerce, and Art in Southern Maine, 1780–1830* (Kennebunk, ME: The Brick Store Museum, 1987), 19.
2. Ibid.
3. Regarding the two partners, Matthew Cottrill's grandson, Edward Madigan, remembered that "These young men came of families of fair means, and of education and it is certain that Matthew Cottrill had pecuniary assistance from his family after coming here." Edmund Madigan, "An Early History of the Catholic Faith in Damariscotta Mills, Maine," 1. A copy of this unpublished manuscript is in the author's possession.
4. The surname Cottrill had several variant spellings during the eighteenth and nineteenth centuries. In Inistioge, County Kilkenny, it is most often spelled Cottril, or Cotterel. In Maine, however, Matthew signed his name as Cottrill (with a double "L" at the end). This is the spelling that I have used throughout this chapter.
5. "Strong farmer" was a term for a tenant farmer in Ireland who held a large and often prosperous leasehold (thirty acres or more). By nature they were commercial farmers who were often associated with dairy and livestock. See Kerby Miller, *Emigrants and Exiles: Ireland and the Irish Exodus in North America* (New York: Oxford University Press, 1985), 48–49.
6. An "Irish acre," or "plantation acre" was a distinct measure of land in Ireland that was larger that English statute acres (the unit of measure also used in America). One Irish acre was equal to 1.62 statute acres. Thus, seventy-six Irish acres equaled to 123.12 statute acres.
7. Louis Cullen, "The Social and Economic Evolution of South Kilkenny in the Seventeenth and Eighteenth Centuries," *Decies* 13 (January 1980): 45–50. On the butter trade see John Mannion, "The Waterford Merchants and the Irish-Newfoundland Provisions Trade," in L. M. Cullen and P. Butel, eds., *Negoce et Industrie en France et en Irlande aux XVIII et XIX Siecles* (Paris: Centre de Recherches Historiques, 1980), 30–31; and Thomas Truxes, *Irish-American Trade, 1660–1783* (New York: Cambridge University Press, 1987), 157–62.

8. A practice ledger book that has on its flyleaf "James Kavanagh, [New] Ross 1771–1772" was used by Kavanagh, as a young clerk or apprentice, to learn lessons in double entry bookkeeping. It is now in the possession of Mrs. Molly Baldwin, Damariscotta Mills, Maine.

9. Kavanagh's Newfoundland connections are suggested in William L. Lucey, "Two Irish Merchants of New England," *The New England Quarterly* 14, no. 4 (December 1941): 633–45.

10. James Kelly, "The Resumption of Emigration from Ireland after the American War of Independence, 1783–1787," *Studia Hibernica* 24 (1984–1988): 79.

11. Ibid., 67.

12. See, for example, the naturalization record of Matthew Cottrill, which described him in 1793 as a "trader . . . principally in the town of Boston." Petition, Record of Naturalization, 1787–1906, Supreme Judicial Court of Suffolk County, Massachusetts, Record Group 85, Vol. I, p. 18; National Archives, Northeastern Records Center, Waltham, Massachusetts (herafter, NAW).

13. The term "wooden world" comes from the pen of a contemporary, Ann Hallowell, who described her arrival in Maine from Boston in 1798. She went on to extol the virtues of life along the "Kennebeck," writing that "This wooden world . . . is by no means such a dull stupid place as you Bostonians may imagine. I assure you that I have only passed four days since my arrival on the river without being engaged in a party without or at home." Ann Hallowell to Ann Eliot, 23 July 1798; Hallowell-Gardiner Papers, Box 2, Folder 4, Oaklands, Gardiner, Maine.

14. The population of Maine leaped from 56,321 in 1783 to 297,325 in 1820. For figures on population growth, see David C. Smith, "Maine's Changing Landscape to 1820," in Charles E. Clark, James S. Leamon, and Karen Bowden, eds., *Maine in the Early Republic: From Revolution to Statehood* (Hanover, NH: University Press of New England, 1988), 15.

15. Clark, Leamon, and Bowden, *Maine in the Early Republic*, 1. For details on the growing movement toward separation, see James S. Leamon, Richard R. Wescott, and Edward O. Schriver, "Separation and Statehood, 1783–1820," in Richard W. Judd, Edwin Churchill, and Joel Eastman, eds., *Maine: The Pine Tree State from Prehistory to the Present* (Orono: University of Maine Press, 1995), 169–92; also, Ronald Banks, *Maine Becomes a State: The Movement to Separate Maine from Massachusetts, 1785–1820* (Middletown, CT: Wesleyan University Press, 1970).

16. On the O'Neil case see *The Massachusetts Spy*, 3 April 1788 and 16 October 1788. Also John Johnston, *History of Bristol and Bremen* (Albany, NY: Joel Munsell, 1873), 374–78.

17. See notes and genealogy on the Hanley family compiled by Paul Hanley Furfey and deposited at the Skidompha Public Library, Damariscotta, Maine. Also see Lincoln County Registry of Deeds (hereafter LCRD) 9:82 and 10:82, and Lincoln County Probate Records (hereafter LCP), Lincoln County Courthouse, Wiscasset, Maine, 17:277–79.

18. The section of Nobleboro that comprised the original Kavanagh store (as well as Matthew Cottrill's house and shipyard which are mentioned in this essay) later became part of Damariscotta, Maine, when it formed in 1848. See George F. Dow and Robert E. Dunbar, *Nobleboro, Maine: A History* (Nobleboro: Nobleboro Historical Society, 1988), 21.

19. On Kavanagh and Cotrrill's business activities, see LCRD 34:67, 35:43, 44:70, 44:181, 44:182. Also see Dow and Dunbar, *Nobleboro*, 44–47. Alan Taylor describes the growth of similar rural industrial centers and millseats in *Liberty Men and Great Proprietors: The Revolutionary Settlement on the Maine Frontier, 1760–1820* (Chapel Hill: University of North Carolina Press, 1989), 156–58; also see Richard Candee, "Maine Towns, Maine People: Architecture and the Community, 1783–1820," in Clark, Leamon, and Bowden, *Maine in the Early Republic*, 54–63.

20. See, for example, Alan Taylor, "The Rise and Fall of George Ulmer: Political Entrepreneurship in the Age of Jefferson and Jackson," *The Colby Library Quarterly* 21, no. 2 (1985): 53.

21. On Kavanagh and Cottrill's holdings in Nobleboro and Newcastle town, see plans of Damariscotta eddy (Josiah Jones, 1811) and Damariscotta River (Ebenezer Flint, 1813) in the Massachusetts State Archives, Maps and Plans, #1742, #1753, Boston. Also see LCRD 34:159, 63:4, 72:236, and 93:188, and the will of Matthew Cottrill, which makes reference to personal and business holdings. LCP 30:155–61.

22. Candee, "Maine Towns, Maine People," 49–58. "Federal style" here refers to the style of architecture that emerged during the Federal Period—between the years 1790 and 1810—when the Federalist party held sway, and when new styles and designs from England were adopted and patronized by New England elites, many of whom, like Cottrill, made their profits in the maritime trade.

23. LCP 28:437–41.

24. On Nicholas Codd's work in mid-Maine, see Arthur Gerrier, "Nicholas Codd," *Biographical Dictionary of Architects in Maine* (Augusta, ME: Maine Historic Preservation Commission, 1991); and records of the Historic American Buildings Survey, Lincoln County (microfilm, Maine State Library, Augusta), HABS no. Me-93, Me-22, Me-84.

25. Most of the wealthy timber barons in Maine patronized craftsmen and furniture makers in Boston, New York, and Philadelphia—thus imitating the material culture and taste of the urban elite. For more on the movement of high-style culture into mid-Maine, see Carolyn Parsons, "'Bordering on Magnificence':Urban Domestic Planning in the Maine Woods," in Clark, Leamon, and Bowden, *Maine in the Early Republic*, 62–82; and Sprague, *Agreeable Situations*, especially the essays by Sprague and Richard Candee.

26. On the Kavanagh and Cottrill shipyards, see Mark Wyman Biscoe, "Damariscotta-Newcastle Ships and Shipbuilding," (Master's thesis, University of Maine at Orono, 1967); and Dow and Dunbar, *Nobleboro*, 46, 61.

27. Dow and Dunbar, *Nobleboro*, 59–66.

28. On the movement of artisans and shipbuilders into mid-Maine see Butler, "Rising like a Phoenix," 22.

29. A good source from which to view foreign-born artisans coming into Lincoln County is the register of British Aliens (including Irish-born) kept by the United States during the War of 1812. In Wiscasset, for example, one finds several foreign-born artisans—including rope maker Nicholas Arter, rigger William Jerrard, and mariner Daniel Dempsey. See Kenneth Scott, compiler, *British Aliens in the United States during the War of 1812* (Baltimore: Genealogical Publishing Co. Inc., 1979), 1–9.

30. On John Boulger, see the passenger list of the brig *Atlantic* in *Handbook of Irish Genealogy* (Dublin: Heraldric Artists, LTD., 1984), 109; Scott, *British Aliens*, 1; and the Federal Census schedules for Newcastle, Maine: 1810, 1820 (microfilm M252, reel 6; and M33, reel 12), NAW.

31. On transatlantic trade and merchant culture in Maine during the early National period, see Butler, "Rising Like a Phoenix." Also see Lawrence C. Allin, "Shipping and Shipbuilding in the Period of Ascendancy," in Judd, Churchill, and Eastman, eds., *Maine: the Pine Tree State*, 297–305; William Baker, *A Maritime History of Bath, Maine and the Kennebec River Region* (Bath, ME: Marine Research Society of Bath, 1973), Vol. 1, especially chapters 13–16; and William Hutchinson Rowe, *The Maritime History of Maine: Three Centuries of Shipbuilding and Seafaring* (New York: W. W. Norton & Company).

32. In 1797, for example, the Ship *Jane*, sailing for Cork with James Noble as master, carried a cargo of 188 tons of oak timber, 66 tons of pine timber, 20,000 hogshead staves, 4,919 feet of oak boards, and 6,000 feet of pine boards. It was sold for 1,708 pounds Irish currency, a sum equivalent to $7,008.71. See James Kavanagh and Matthew Cottrill vs. James Noble, Lincoln County Court of Common Pleas (hereafter LCCCP), Box 348, September term, 1797; Lincoln County Courthouse, Wiscasset, Maine.

33. Kavanagh and Cottrill, for example, had their Ship *Hibernia* confiscated on the open seas and its cargo of timber seized by the French. The firm labored in the courts for years attempting to recover their losses—to no avail. See William L. Lucey, "A Late Report of the Ship '*Hibernia*' Captured by a French Privateer in the Year 1800," *The New England Quarterly* 17 (March–December, 1944): 101–06.

34. For a fine overview of commerce and diplomacy during the early National period, and a detailed perspective on the fortunes and lifestyle of Maine merchants during this era, see Joyce Butler, "Rising Like a Phoenix." Also see Robert G. Albion, William A. Baker and Benjamin W. Labaree, *New England and the Sea* (Mystic, CT: Mystic Seaport Museum, 1972), 60–96.

35. On the timber economy and the cutting of Irish woodland, see Eileen McCracken, *The Irish Woods since Medieval Times* (Newton Abbot, England: David and Charles, 1971); and "Notes on Kilkenny Woods and Nurserymen," *Old Kilkenny Review* (1970): 17–23. Michael Hutcheson's doctoral research at Boston College, "Deforestation in Ireland, c. 1500–1800" (forthcoming, 2004) is also particularly relevant.

36. Hostilities during the Napoleonic Wars caused a disruption in the sea lanes between the Baltic and Britain and consequently opened increased opportunities for neutral carriers from New England.

37. Irish imports of timber and barrel staves from New England are gleaned from "Abstracts of Irish Exports and Imports," 24 vols., 1764–1823, MSS 353–76, National Library of Ireland (NLI), Dublin.

38. RG-36, Bureau of Customs, Bath, Maine, Outward Foreign Manifests (1802, 1803), Box 1, E-267, NAW.

39. RG-36, Bureau of Customs, Bath, Maine, Inward Foreign manifests (1811, 1812), Boxes 1 and 2, E-266, NAW.

40. Abiel Wood to Pott and MacMillan, Glasgow, 21 January 1812, Abiel Wood Letterbooks, Volume III [photocopy], Special Collections, Folger Library, University of Maine, Orono.

41. James Smithwick's accounts for eight voyages (1806–1810), undertaken in the employ of Kavanagh and Cottrill, were presented as evidence in the lawsuit—Elizabeth Smithwick vs. James Kavanagh et al., Lincoln County Court of Common Pleas, January Term, 1821 (microfilm reel # 124), Maine State Archives, Augusta, Maine. Elizabeth (James Smithwick's wife) was suing James Kavanagh for $6,000 owed Smithwick for his share of the voyages when he died in St. Mary's, Georgia in 1811.

42. James Smithwick, Sr. came from New Ross, County Wexford, where the family held property on North Street paralleling the Barrow River (RD 323-73-211858, Irish Registry of Deeds, Henrietta St., Dublin). Henry Smithwick, possibly James' brother, was a mariner working the trade route between Ireland and Boston. His will, probated in Boston in 1778, identified him as being from "the town of Ross McThrew in the county of Waxford" (Ros Mhic Treoin was the Irish vernacular for New Ross). See Suffolk County Registry of Probate, docket #16797. Information on Smithwick's business dealings can be found in the Suffolk County Courthouse, Boston: Registry of Deeds, 121:231, 290:1; and probate office dockets #17375, #17376, and #21185. Also see a family history of the Smithwicks, New England Historical and Genealogical Society, Boston; and references to shipping in the *Boston Gazette*, 26 October 1767.

43. The cargo consisted of 40 tons of oak timber, 20 tons of maple, beech, and birch, 60 tons of pine, and several tons of oak planking and board. *Dublin Evening Post*, 23 September 1806.

44. David Noel Doyle, *Ireland, Irishmen, and Revolutionary America* (Dublin: Published for the Cultural Relations Committee of Ireland by Mercier Press, 1981), 42.

45. Truxes, *Irish-American Trade*, 59. In an era when currency and hard money were occasionally at a premium, the ability to work on credit was absolutely essential. See Butler, "Rising Like a Phoenix," 19.

46. Thomas Nickels to Francis Preble, 1 October 1810, Thomas Nickels Letterbook, Jane S. Tucker Archives and Genealogical Collection, Wiscasset Public Library, Wiscasset, Maine.

47. This was part of a larger migration of Irish merchant elite to early America, as delineated in Doyle, *Ireland, Irishmen and Revolutionary America*, 47–48.

48. The Pitt Tavern in Wiscasset, where traveler John Barnard lodged during a lecturing tour in 1807, was described as being "kept by an Irishmen." The proprietor was William Pitt. See Fanny Chase, *Wiscasset in Pownalborough* (Portland, ME: The Anthoensen Press, 1967), 161.

49. Chase, *Wiscasset in Pownalborough*, 417.

50. On John Anderson, see his naturalization petition in RG-21, U.S. District Court, Portland Maine (September, 1795), Box 1, NAW. Also LCRD 41:55; 42, 223; 47:48, and 48:164.

51. LCRD 78:9 and 79:237.

52. On New Waterford, see LCRD 45:231, 46:14, and 47:187. See also Edward T. McCarron, "Irish Migration and Settlement on the Eastern Frontier: The Case of Lincoln County Maine, 1760–1820," *Retrospection: The New England Graduate Review in American History* 2 (1989): 21.

53. Kerby A. Miller, Arnold Schrier, Bruce D. Boling, and David N. Doyle, *Irish Immigrants in the Land of Canaan: Letters and Memoirs from Colonial and*

Revolutionary America, 1675–1815 (New York: Oxford University Press, 2003), 329. Having said this, there is also evidence that Kavanagh and Cottrill, like other Irish merchants in early America, forged commercial links with non-Irish partners. As Thomas Truxes explains, "merchants in the colonies were forced to modify their parochial Irish interests in order to compete effectively in the Atlantic economy" (*Irish-American Trade*, 108). In their early careers, for example, Kavanagh and Cottrill entered into temporary partnerships with several New England merchants, the most pivotal being the Noble family—an alliance that brought sponsorship, support, and access to business networks in mid-Maine. Arthur Noble, the putative proprietor of Nobleboro, was a witness on behalf of James Kavanagh during his naturalization proceedings. James Noble, his son, was partner with Kavanagh and Cottrill on the ship *Jane* and captained at least one voyage on their behalf to Ireland. The Noble example underlines the diverse networks of patronage and support that underpinned the success of nascent Irish trading firms in early America. On the connections between the Nobles and Kavanagh and Cottrill, see James Kavanagh's naturalization petition, RG-85, Box 480 (Lincoln County), NAW. Also, the courtcase James Kavanagh and Matthew Cottrill vs. James Noble, LCCCP, Box 348, September term, 1797, Lincoln County Courthouse, Wiscasset, Maine.

54. Records of the Charitable Irish Society, Volume I (minutes of 17 March 1800 and 17 March 1802); Massachusetts Historical Society, Boston; and Michael J. O'Brien, *The Irish at Bunker Hill* (Shannon, Ireland: Irish University Press, 1968), 213–14.

55. On Henry Knox's Irish connections see Taylor, *Liberty Men and Great Proprietors*, 38; and Doyle, *Ireland, Irishmen and Revolutionary America*, 188, 192, 196. Concerning Knox's career in Maine, see Taylor, *Liberty Men and Great Proprietors*, 37–47; and Carolyn S. Parsons, "Bordering on Magnificence: Urban Domestic Planning in the Maine Woods," in Clark, Leamon, and Bowden, *Maine in the Early Republic*, 62–82.

56. Charles E. Clark, "James Sullivan's History of Maine and the Romance of Statehood," in *Maine in the Early Republic*, 186; and Doyle, *Ireland, Irishmen and Revolutionary America*, 188. Schoolmaster John Sullivan and his wife Margaret Browne are buried in the family cemetery behind the General John Sullivan house in Durham, New Hampshire. Their gravestones note that they were born in Limerick and Cork, respectively.

57. On the Sullivans, see Charles P. Whittemore, *A General of the Revolution, John Sullivan of New Hampshire* (New York: Columbia University Press, 1961); and *Letters and Papers of Major General John Sullivan*, ed. Otis G. Hammond (Concord, NH: New Hampshire Historical Society, 1930). Concerning John Sullivan's Irish correspondence, see Nanette O'Sullivan to General Sullivan, 15 September 1788; and Phillip O'Sullivan to General Sulllivan, 16 May 1796, in *Letters and Papers* 3:593–97, 632. John Sullivan the immigrant left a fascinating history of his family in Ireland. They were directly related to the O'Sullivan Beare, from County Cork and Kerry, a prominent old Gaelic family who took an active role in the Battle of Aughrim and Limerick during the Williamite Wars. His own father, Major Phillip O'Sullivan, was one of the "Wild Geese" who after the war was exiled to France (where John was raised). For the Sullivan family history, *see Letters and Papers* 3:632–34.

58. On the naming of Limerick, Maine, see Linda Maule Taylor, ed., *Limerick: Historical Notes* (Limerick, ME: Town of Limerick, 1975); and Irene Quenzler Brown and Richard D. Brown, *The Hanging of Ephraim Wheeler* (Cambridge, MA: Harvard University Press, 2003), 54.

59. Robert H. Lord, John Sexton, and Edward T. Harrington, *History of the Archdiocese of Boston* (New York: Sheed and Ward, 1944), 1:612–16, 695.

60. Reverend Jean Cheverus to Bishop John Carroll, 10 July 1808 (typescript), Lord/Sexton/Harrington files, Archives of the Archdiocese of Boston, Chancery, Brighton, Massachusetts.

61. Scotch-Irish and Anglo-Irish immigrants are often mentioned in early town histories in Lincoln and Kennebec County. See, for example, David Quimby Cushman, *Ancient Sheepscot and Newcastle* (Bath, ME: E. Upton and Son, 1882); Johnston, *History of Bristol and Bremen*; James North, *The History of Augusta* (Augusta, ME: 1870; reprinted Somersworth, NH: New England History Press, 1981); Cyrus Eaton, *Annals of the Town of Warren*, 2d ed. (Hallowell, ME: 1877); and Francis B. Greene, *History of Boothbay, Southport and Boothbay Harbor, Maine, 1623–1905* (Portland, ME: Loring, Short and Harmon, 1906). Scotch-Irish traders and mariners are also outlined in several early journals. See, in particular, George F. O'Dwyer, "Captain James Howard, Col. William Lithgow, Col. Arthur Noble, and other Irish Pioneers in Maine," *The Journal of the American Irish Historical Society* 19 (1920): 71–91. Also see R. Stuart Wallace, "The Scotch Irish of Provincial New Hampshire (Ph.D. diss., University of New Hampshire, 1984); and Wallace's essay in this book.

62. Edward T. McCarron, "In Pursuit of the 'Maine' Chance: The North Family of Offaly and New England, 1700–1776," in William Nolan and Timothy P. O'Neill, eds., *Offaly History and Society: Interdisciplinary Essays on the History of an Irish County* (Dublin: Geography Publications, 1998), 339–70.

63. LCP 2:81–82. One source maintains that Robert McKown "went back to Ireland to sell the Glenarm property left him by his father." There he married Ann Grace and "came back to America and settled in Woolwich, where they raised a family." See Greene, *History of Boothbay*, 578.

64. On the Wiscasset merchant community and their antecedents, see family history files in the Genealogy Room, Wiscasset Public Library. Also consult Chase, *Wiscasset in Pownalborough*, and Cushman, *Ancient Sheepscot and Newcastle*.

65. LCP 41:259.

66. This point is also underlined in Miller, et al., *Irish Immigrants in the Land of Canaan*, 328–30.

67. Ibid., 331.

68. See Thomas Timmons' naturalization petition, LCCCP 20:152.

69. RG-36, Bureau of Customs, Bath Maine, Outward and Inward Foreign Manifests (1812), NAW.

70. Naturalization petition, Robert Kelly, Lincoln County Supreme Judicial Court 2:102.

71. This diversity is evident in lists of "British Aliens" during the war of 1812—a definition which included Irish born. See Scott, *British Aliens*, 1–9.

72. On Irish traders in the Atlantic world, see Doyle, *Ireland, Irishmen and Revolutionary America*, 22–50; Truxes, *Irish-American Trade*, especially chapters 4–6; John Mannion, "Irish Merchants Abroad: the Newfoundland

Experience, 1750–1850," in Cullen and Butel, *Negoce et Industrie*, 27–43; and Mannion, "Migration and Upward Mobility: The Meagher Family in Ireland and Newfoundland, 1780–1830," *Irish Economic and Social History* 15 (1988): 54–71. Also see the work of Louis Cullen, especially "The Irish Diaspora of the Seventeenth and Eighteenth Centuries," in Nicholas Canny, ed., *Europeans on the Move: Studies on European Migration, 1500–1800* (New York: Oxford University Press, 1994); *The Emergence of Modern Ireland, 1600–1900* (Dublin: Gill and Macmillan, 1981), 116–18; and "The Social and Economic Evolution of South Kilkenny."

73. Eric Richards, "Scotland and the Atlantic Empire," in Bernard Bailyn and Philip D. Morgan, eds., *Strangers Within the Realm: Cultural Margins of the First British Empire* (Chapel Hill: The University of North Carolina Press, 1991), 96.

74. The passenger list of the *North Star* is located in RG-36, Bureau of Customs, Bath, Maine, Inward Foreign Manifests (1812), Box # 2, E-266, NAW.

75. William Forbes Adams, *Ireland and the Irish Emigration to the New World from 1815 to the Famine* (New York: Russell and Russell, 1967), 68–89; and Truxes, *Irish-American Trade*, 127–28.

76. Peter Moogk, "Reluctant Exiles: The Problems of Colonization in French North America," *William and Mary Quarterly* 46 (July 1989): 464. An instructive example of merchant sponsored emigration can be seen in John Mannion, "Patrick Morris and Newfoundland Irish Immigration," in Cyril Byrne and Margaret Harry, eds., *Talamh an Eisc: Canadian and Irish Essays* (Halifax, Nova Scotia: Nimbus Publishing, 1986), 180–202.

77. The passenger list of the ship *Shamrock* can be found in Donald N. Schlegel, *Passengers from Ireland: Lists of Passengers arriving in American Ports between 1811 and 1817* (Baltimore: Genealogical Publishing Co. Inc., 1980), 32. By comparing ships and captains identified in Schlegel's work with shipping letters for the port of Wiscasset (which record date, names of vessel, owner, and master), one can identify several Maine ships carrying passengers from Ireland. Between 1811 and 1812, for example, one discovers seven vessels from Wiscasset:

Ship, Port of Departure, Master, Owner, Port of Arrival, Passengers

Africa, Belfast, J.Scott, Joseph Wood, N.Y., 105
Shamrock, Dublin, R. McKown, Abiel Wood, N.Y., 60
Huntress, Dublin, T. Ronson, R. Elwell, N.Y., 47
President, Newry, A. Baker, Abiel Wood, N.Y., 92
Perserverance, Belfast, G. Crawford, Abiel Wood, N.Y., 40
Belisarius, Dublin, J. Tinkham, Abiel Wood, Boston, 52
Washington, Dublin, J. Boyington, Abiel Wood, Wiscasset, 51

Sources: *Passengers from Ireland*; and "Sea Letters from the Port of Wiscasset," Box 23, Patterson Papers, Maine Historical Society, Portland, Maine.

78. For an overview of these lists, see Cormac O'Grada, "Across the Briny Ocean: Some Thoughts on Irish Emigration to America, 1800–1850," in T. M. Devine and David Dickson, eds., *Ireland and Scotland, 1650–1850* (Edinburgh: John Donald Publishers, LTD., 1983), 118–30. A full listing can be found in the *New England Historical and Genealogical Register*, Volumes 60, 61, 62, and 66.

79. Schlegel, *Passengers from Ireland*, 32.

80. Kavanagh and Cottrill to Robert Askins, 18 November 1797, cited as evidence in Askins vs. James Kavanagh, et. al., Lincoln County Supreme Judicial Court, Box 453, #39.58 (Lincoln County Court House, Wiscasset, Maine).

81. Kavanagh's household accounts were presented in a lawsuit between him and partner Matthew Cottrill. See Kavanagh vs. Cottrill, LCCCP, 17 April 1819 (microfilm reel #124), Maine State Archives, Augusta.

82. On the role of agents in the passenger trade see R. J. Dickson, *Ulster Emigration to Colonial America, 1718–1775* (Belfast: Ulster Historical Foundation, 1988), 98–124; and Adams, *Ireland and the Irish Emigration*, 78–79.

83. Truxes, *Irish-American Trade*, 134.

84. Abiel Wood to Captain William Heddean, 5 December 1811, Abiel Wood Jr. Letterbooks, Volume 3 [photocopy], Special Collections, Fogler Library, University of Maine, Orono.

85. *Dublin Evening Post*, 5 June 1804 (microfilm), National Library of Ireland, Dublin.

86. The *Atlantic's* passenger list has been published in the *New England Historical and Genealogical Register*, Vol. 62 (1908), 172.

87. Naturalization petition, Ralph Moran, Kennebec County Court of Common Pleas (hereafter KCCCP) 1:390, Maine State Archives, Augusta.

88. Madigan's career as a trader in Wiscasset is revealed in LCRD 78:9 and 79:237. For his family connections, see the will of Matthew Cottrill, in which Cottrill bequeathed property "to my sister Catherine Madigan." Lincoln County Probate 50: 155–61.

89. Irish Registry of Deeds, 425/452/277761 and 424/520/2767887, Henrietta St., Dublin.

90. On Davis' career in Hallowell see Kennebec County Registry of Deeds 20:508, 21:482, 14:291, and 15:55. Also see his naturalization petition, KCCCP 12:189.

91. On Davis's involvement in the coastal trade, see Sydenham Davis vs. Asa Bean, et al., KCCCP 4:177, Maine State Archives, Augusta.

92. P. H. Gulliver and Marilyn Silverman, *Merchants and Shopkeepers: A Historical Anthropology of an Irish Market Town, 1200–1991* (Toronto: University of Toronto Press, 1995), 380, 123, 127.

93. John Mannion and Fidelma Maddock, "Old World Antecedents, New World Adaptations: Inistioge Immigrants in Newfoundland," in William Nolan and Kevin Whelan, eds., *Kilkenny, History and Society: Interdisciplinary Essays in the History of an Irish County* (Dublin: Geography Publications, 1990), 353. The Labrador reference is quoted in Gulliver and Silverman, *Merchants and Shopkeepers*, 90.

94. On Andrew Shortall, see "Baptisms, Marriages and Burials in the Congregation of St. Mary's Church, Newcastle . . . District of Maine [1798–1823]," Portland Diocesan Archives, Portland, Maine.

95. "A list of passengers landed by Capt. Jos. Boyington, August 15, 1812," Jane S. Tucker Archives and Genealogical Collection, Wiscasset Public Library.

96. Abiel Wood to Captain Samuel Coombes, 17 June 1811, Abiel Wood Jr. Letterbooks, Volume 3 [photocopy], Fogler Library, University of Maine, Orono.

97. Figures are drawn from analysis of gravestones in St. Dennis churchyard, Whitefield, Maine, and especially from declarations of intention and naturalization petitions, Record Group 85, Boxes 477–78, 480, NAW. These naturalization

records reveal that in addition to Lincoln County, many arrived by way of Boston, or via timber ships to the Maritimes.

98. A series of new passenger acts in 1816 and 1819 made fares to British Canada less than half the rates to the United States. This meant that after 1815, an increasing number of pre-famine Irish traveling to the New World did so aboard timber vessels bound for the Maritimes. See Adams, *Ireland and the Irish Emigration*, 68–127.

99. See, for example, Cecil J. Houston and William J. Smyth, *Irish Emigration and Canadian Settlement: Patterns, Links, and Letters* (Toronto: University of Toronto Press, 1990), 54–55, 87–90; and Byrne and Harry, *Talamh an Eisc*, particularly the essays by B. C. Cuthbertson, Terrance Punch, and John Mannion.

100. On the career of Edward Kavanagh, see William L. Lucey, *Edward Kavanagh: Catholic, Statesman, Diplomat from Maine, 1795–1844* (Francestown, N.H.: Marshall Jones Company, 1946).

101. Robert Lowell, *The Mills of the Kavanaughs* (New York: Harcourt Brace and World, Inc., 1951), 19.

IRELAND ALONG THE PASSAMAQUODDY: RATHLIN ISLANDERS IN WASHINGTON COUNTY, MAINE

by Fidelma M. McCarron

IN A RECENT ARTICLE in *Maine History*, historian Alan Taylor argues that eastern Maine and the Passamaquoddy region—far from being an insignificant backwater—was actually an important crossroads during the early nineteenth century, one that was open to a variety of cultures and peoples.[1] This is particularly evident when viewed through the lens of Irish immigration. During the first half of the nineteenth century, Eastport and Lubec were portals through which thousands of Irish traveled by coastal schooner and on foot to the "Boston States." While most ventured to Bangor, Portland, and Boston, some Irish families made a permanent home in the eastern corner of Washington County. This essay focuses on the important patterns of migration to Maine during the mid-nineteenth century, exploring a unique case study of chain migration between Rathlin Island and the Cobscook Bay communities of Pembroke, Perry, Trescott, and West Lubec.

In 1850, Cobscook Bay had an air of enterprise and progress. Farming, fishing, shipbuilding, and cutting timber provided opportunities for newcomers. In addition, the Pembroke Irish Works, a thriving foundry situated along the banks of the Pennamaquan River, employed a steady stream of natives and newcomers, many of them Irish. By 1860 there were well over 120 Irish families in Pembroke and West Lubec, most of them drawn by links of family and community. Indeed, these downeast communities illustrate one of the essential patterns of the Irish experience in America: namely, chain migration. Scores of those who settled along the coves of Cobscook Bay ventured from Rathlin Island, a small outcrop of sea-cliff and hardscrabble farms off the coast of Antrim (near the northeasternmost point of Ireland). Between 1841 and 1861—a period punctuated by the Great Famine—the island population declined from 1,010 to 453, many of them migrating to America. Notably, the vast majority of these migrants sought the same destination, the coastal villages of Washington County, Maine. The 1860 Federal Census of this county reveals over 230 people with distinctive Rathlin surnames. In the Catholic graveyards of St. John's (Pembroke) and St. Mary's (West Lubec), clusters of headstones bear silent testimony to homeplaces in "Rathlin Island." Family letters and encouragement, remittances, ready jobs in the iron foundry, and the early Catholic church in Washington County all acted to pull these island people to eastern Maine.

This essay will explore the experience of Rathlin immigrants with a comparative focus: investigating their Old World antecedents; seeking to understand the factors that prompted their departure; exploring the Atlantic routes they traveled; and unraveling the textures of community that they reproduced along the Passamaquoddy. I also seek to underline the larger context of immigration into eastern Maine—especially the contours of the Maritime timber and passenger trade—a migration corridor that brought thousands of Irish voyagers downeast. This migration is still remembered in the folklore of Rathlin Island—where Maine and the Maritimes faintly echo in the living tradition of those families who remained behind.

RATHLIN

Rathlin Island is located in the boiling tides of the North Channel between Ireland and Scotland. (See gallery, plates 19 and 21.) A rocky outcrop of basalt and chalk with hidden valleys and sparkling lakes, it has been a hotly contested middle ground since the earliest times. Early Christian monks took refuge here; marauding Norsemen found a place to plunder; and Irish, Scots, and English at various times exploited its strategic location. In 1746 the Reverend John Gage purchased a long lease of the island from the McDonnells, the Earls of Antrim; and Gage's descendents were resident landlords into the early years of the twentieth century.

In the centuries leading up to the famine, Rathlin was peopled by a variety of newcomers. Reverend Gage recruited weavers and spinners from the Antrim coast as well as a scattering of English families. There was also a fluid movement between Scotland and Rathlin. Island settlers included migrants from the Hebrides, exiles from the Highland armies of Bonnie Prince Charlie in the aftermath of their defeat at the Battle of Culloden (1745), as well as women from the island of Islay who intermarried with families on Rathlin. Some settlers, fleeing landlord and established (Anglican) church discriminatory practices in Scotland, continued to travel the fourteen miles between Rathlin and the Mull of Kintyre. These Scottish connections continued well into the twentieth century as many Rathlin islanders traveled seasonally to the Scottish mainland to seek work.[2] Contemporary writers suggest that many Rathlin folk saw themselves as a people set apart, and spoke of the channel crossing to Antrim as if visiting "a foreign land."[3]

During the nineteenth century, Rathlin featured several distinct communities. In the rugged western reaches of the island (the "Upper End" or Ceann Ramhar), framed by mountains and sea cliff, one would have found kin groups who were primarily Irish speakers and who subsisted on herding, fowling, and sheep raising. The southern townlands (the "Lower End" or Ceann Caol), more fertile and with several navigable harbors, were the home of farming and fishing families. Here the descendants of Scots settlers spoke a distinct dialect of Rathlin Irish that reflected a greater influx of Scots-Gaidhlig and Lowland Scots traditions.[4] Most Rathlin folk lived in kin-based farm clusters, called *clachans*. Families held the land through joint tenancy—leasing holdings collectively from the landlord. Duncan Bradley, for example, who migrated to Lubec in 1831, grew up in a close-knit cluster of cabins in the townland of Ballynegard. The Bradleys worked several holdings (much of it poor land) and lived amidst a scatter of families that included Craigs, McCurdys, and McGuilkins—likely extended kin.[5]

Like most of the families on Rathlin, the Bradleys and their neighbors lived in a "low whitewashed stone and thatch house." And, like most of their neighbors, they subsisted off a variety of pursuits: cattle and sheep raising, tillage of oats and potatoes, fishing, and weaving. Many of the islanders also raised barley and harvested kelp to barter with Scottish boats carrying coal and fuel. A few, living adjacent to the island cliffs, "are very dexterous in seeking for the nests of sea fowl, for which they swing themselves down the face of the precipices by means of a rope secured to a stake on the summit."[6]

In 1831 Duncan Bradley left the intimate world of Ballynegard, bounded by the familiar landscape of farm-cluster, boreen (a narrow lane), and rocky pasture. He walked the parish road to Church Harbor where he took a boat to Ballycastle, on the Antrim mainland. It was the first leg of a journey that would lead him across the Atlantic—first to Eastport and eventually to the quiet farming community of West Lubec, Maine.[7] Bradley was one of the first immigrants to make this journey from Rathlin, but certainly not the last. During a period of twenty-five years, between 1835 and 1860, over 500 islanders left for America, and more than half of these settled in Washington County, Maine.

EMIGRATION

Rathlin people had long been accustomed to migration and movement. For centuries the island was a busy crossroads—a stepping stone along the fluid cultural boundaries between Scotland and Ireland. Islanders, for example, regularly made short voyages to the mainland or Scotland to carry produce and fish to market. Members of the Ordnance Survey in 1830 also noted an outward looking mentality, stating that "a considerable number go to the Scottish [potato] harvests each year."[8] Some were tempted to stay on, settling in Greenock and Glasgow, or working in the burgeoning factory towns of the Midlands. For these folks, then, a seasonal sojourn was simply the first step of a longer journey; recent literature has stressed that many who journeyed to the New World during the early nineteenth century were already on the move in their native localities. Some had left the farms and villages of their youth to live and work in one of the larger factory towns or seaports. Others wandered as journeymen, tradesmen, or seasonal laborers.[9] Rathlin is a case in point. Writing in 1851, Mrs. Catherine Gage, the wife of the local landlord, remembered that prior to the Famine a growing number of young men journeyed to Greenock in Scotland "where they learned the trade of shipwrights." In time, "these young men made voyages to America as ship carpenters, where some of them settled and others brought home such favourable accounts of the country to their friends, that many of them were induced to emigrate there."[10] As John Mannion and Fidelma Maddock assert concerning Irish migration to the Canadas, "Transatlantic migration was a dramatic extension of local moves."[11]

In the decades preceding the Famine, emigration quickened out of Ireland, especially from the province of Ulster as well as the commercial agricultural regions of Leinster and the southeast. This migration was largely in response to the collapse of agrarian prosperity brought on by the end of the Napoleonic wars. During the war the economy boomed in Ireland with Irish farmers supplying a significant share of foodstuffs to the British. The end of the war in 1815, however, brought recession and hardship. Many small farmers who had previously taken out long leases and improved their farmholdings could no longer support a large family or provide land for younger sons. Increasingly, emigration was seen as the only option for aspiring farmers.[12]

One of those who left during this period was Neal Black, who settled as a farmer in Washington County, Maine. In his naturalization petition he notes that he was born at "Roslin" [Rathlin in local dialect] in 1807. He took ship to Saint John, New Brunswick in 1828 and in June 1829 arrived at Eastport, Maine. Black, like many emigrants who crossed the border into Maine, continued on to Boston where he worked for a year. He eventually returned to the Passamaquoddy where he carved out a farm in Trescott, a budding town overlooking the Atlantic.[13]

Canada's Maritime ports, especially Saint John, were the entry-point for many voyagers coming from the north of Ireland. Many, like Neal Black, chose the Canadian route since fares to the Maritimes were less than half the price of passages to America. They sailed aboard timber ships into Quebec, Halifax, Saint John, and St. Andrews, and then made their way south into New England, some by sea transport and others walking the coastal roads passing near Eastport, Belfast, and Portland. Maritime ports such as Saint John also were closely linked with Ulster commercial centers such as Derry. Sources reveal that "Of the 29,000 people who emigrated through Derry in the decade 1816-1826, almost 19,000 [or 65 percent] went to New Brunswick." Houston and Smyth elaborate, "There was in the geography of the Irish trade a set of constraints that funneled emigrants from particular origins to particular destinations."[14] Rathlin lay within the recruitment ground of several Derry shipping firms, such as J & J Cooke, which predominantly traded with Saint John.

Eastern Maine and Washington County have significance for immigration that goes well beyond a Rathlin and Ulster context. During the first half of the nineteenth century, Eastport and Lubec were gateways through which thousands of Irish immigrants traveled on their way to the "Boston States." The Passamaquoddy region—far from being an insignificant backwater—was actually a vital crossroads during the early nineteenth century, one that welcomed a variety of cultures and peoples. It was a migration corridor that linked Atlantic trade routes into the Maritime Provinces with the burgeoning industrial cities of Irish America, especially Boston.[15] Of course, while many immigrants ventured southward, some Irish families made a permanent home in the salt-water villages of eastern Maine.

Naturalization records offer a valuable lens for viewing these migration patterns into Maine and the Maritimes. During the 1840s, scores of Irish immigrants appeared at Washington County courts to declare their intention to become citizens of the United States. Courthouse records often specify place of birth, date of emigration, and ports of arrival. In the July 1844 session of the Supreme Judicial Court in Machias, one hundred twenty-six immigrants appeared before the clerk to petition.[16] Most of those who specified a port of arrival traveled via Saint John, New Brunswick; St. Andrews, New Brunswick; or Halifax, Nova Scotia. They came from a variety of origins, most notably Ireland and England. Thirty-five immigrants, or 28 percent, were from Ulster, and many others hailed from the southeastern counties of Kilkenny, Wexford, Waterford, and Cork. This latter pattern reflects the steady migration stream between southeast Ireland and Canada, one that sent fishermen and immigrant families to Newfoundland and Nova Scotia (some of whom eventually left for America).

As in Neal Black's case, many who arrived in the Maritimes did not go directly to Washington County. Instead, they often worked for several years locally before acquiring property and settling in Maine. Donegal man Hugh McCool, for example, worked for five years in Saint John before coming to Eastport, Maine. Ports like Saint John were magnets for immigrants in need of work or looking for funds to continue their journey. It was one of the premier shipbuilding centers in the British Empire and attracted artisans from a wide swath of beginnings (including Rathlin). Its wooded hinterland also provided opportunity to work in logging camps, lumberyards, and sawmills that supplied the timber that flowed back across the Atlantic on the immigrant ships.[17] These opportunities at the port of arrival were of pivotal importance in the adjustment of new immigrants in eastern Maine. As Houston and Smyth assert, "Temporary work in the colonies could provide immigrants with the possibility of acquiring cash for investment in land."[18]

Some immigrants to Maine ranged far afield before settling down in Washington County. Alexander McQuaig, a stone mason from Rathlin

Island, journeyed first to Scotland and then to New Jersey before home-steading a farm in Trescott. McQuaigs had long traveled to Greenock in search of apprenticeships and jobs.[19] His neighbor in Trescott, Denis O'Donnell, from the "Glan" in County Antrim, declared that he first arrived in Holmes Hole, an isolated inlet in southern New England. From there he ventured to New Bedford, New York City, Savannah, and back to Trescott.[20] Their experience reminds us that many immigrants Down East were on the move before finding the "Maine chance."

WASHINGTON COUNTY

Trescott, along with West Lubec, Pembroke, and Perry, formed the nucleus of Rathlin settlement in the New World. Why islanders first came to these communities on the eastern periphery of New England is still unknown, but several explanations are plausible. First, places like Trescott and West Lubec were still relatively unsettled in the 1820s when the first Rathlin folk moved through. Cheap land was available, fuel was plentiful, and the numerous inlets of Cobscook Bay offered an easy means for transport (especially for islanders accustomed to sea travel). More central, perhaps, in explaining Washington County's attraction to Rathlin folk is chain migration. Communities such as Trescott were among the first to be settled by islanders in the New World—and quickly became a magnet that attracted others. Mannion and Maddock explain the process: "A pathfinder or pioneering family established a base; friends and kin followed through a system of infor-mation diffusion and remittances for fares."[21] In the mid-nineteenth century over 200 islanders followed, drawn to eastern Maine through family letters and encouragement, pre-paid tickets, ready work, and the early presence of the Catholic church at Pembroke and Trescott. This process was echoed in contemporary accounts of Rathlin migration. Mrs. Catharine Gage remembered in her autobiography that early emi-grants sent home such favorable accounts of the New World "that many were induced to emigrate there. They generally succeeded well and always showed great attachment to the home and friends they had left, sending presents of money and encouraging them to join them in the New World and, in numerous instances, paying their passage out."[22] This pattern of chain migration would shift and accelerate during the mid-nineteenth century as a result of the Irish famine.

FAMINE

The Great Famine was a watershed in both the history of Ireland and the experience of Rathlin Island. Between 1845 and 1855 over one million people died in Ireland and it is estimated that upwards of two million emigrated to distant shores. This diaspora—which peopled the industrial cities of England and America, and sent emigrants to such widely dispersed destinations as Australia and Argentina—has only recently been studied on a micro-level.[23] The local experience of famine emigrants at home, and the patterns of chain migration, assistance, and family links they forged in the Atlantic world, still beckon to be fully explored.

Rathlin Island was one of those communities that made the trans-Atlantic leap during the famine era. Rathlin, whose poorer families subsisted largely on potatoes, experienced a marked degree of distress and destitution during the famine. Remarkably, there were no famine-related deaths recorded on the island. Contemporary accounts suggest that only through the response of landlord Reverend Robert Gage (who cancelled all rents due to him), and remittances from family members in America, was Rathlin able to avert a larger tragedy. As Catharine Gage described, "In the beginning of 1847 the distress of the people was very great, their entire crop of potatoes rotted in the ground and they had no visible means of support." Applications for assistance were made by Reverend Gage to a variety of charitable societies and agencies "who were most liberal in their donations of food and money, especially the Society of Friends, so that during this trying season, not one perished for want."[24]

While efforts by Robert Gage played an important role in averting mortality on Rathlin, remittances from family members in America were also crucial in helping to avert a larger tragedy. What is more, folk memory in both Lubec, Maine and Rathlin Island asserts that Gage was not always the benevolent patriarch that he is painted in the historical record. Frank Craig, a Rathlin farmer interviewed in the 1930s by the Irish Folklore Commission, remembered hearing that Indian meal—purchased during the famine by Rathlin immigrants in "America" and shipped aboard the vessel *Erin's Hope*—was commandeered by Robert Gage before it could reach their relations in Rathlin.

He [my father] minded the *Erin's Hope* coming in to the Island, the Irish sent it from America. She had yellow meal. Gage [the landlord of Rathlin] got that. Now listen to this, Gage was the landlord, the Irish paid for that yellow meal to be given free, but Gage made people pay for it. My father's father, my grandfather, was a blacksmith, and he went for his share of the meal off Gage. What did Gage do? Says he, 'You're well fit to pay for it, you have money. Get the money and you'll get your share of meal'. . . . He made money out of that and it given free.[25]

While the precise details of this account cannot be verified today, it echoes stories passed down in the Rathlin community of Washington County, Maine. The Down East version elaborates that the yellow meal commandeered by the landlord was actually purchased by Rathlin families in Pembroke, Maine, who had saved up their wages made in the Pembroke iron works. When their efforts were stymied by officials in Rathlin, they determined to forego any further relief.[26]

Whether one acknowledges contemporary accounts by the Gages, or family tradition and recollections, there was nonetheless a dramatic outmigration from Rathlin during the famine and its aftermath. Between 1841 and 1861 the population of the island plummeted from 1,010 people to 453 (a 55 percent decline).[27] This dramatic decline left a shadow over the landscape and folklore of the island. Walking the hillsides today one still catches the faint echoes of the famine, especially in the abandoned farm clusters and *clachans* which dot the island. The impact of the famine is perhaps most poignantly remembered in the upland townland of Cleggan, where Clogh-na-screeve, the "writing stone," stands. Here, faintly etched in limestone, are the names of some of the islanders who left during the famine—a unique record of their leavetaking for America.[28]

The historical record leaves us but a few faint sketches of this migration from Rathlin. Mrs. Gage tells us that in 1846 "when the potato failure set in . . . the number of emigrants the following Spring amounted to 107, leaving the population considerably diminished."[29] Some immigrants followed family to Scotland. Most, however, took ship to America, traveling aboard timber vessels to Nova Scotia, New Brunswick, and Maine. Rathlin native Maggie McKinley, born in Craigmacagan in the decades following the famine, recalled this exodus:

My grandmother minded the Famine. She said there was a boat come into the bay here that took away over a hundred people, whole families. She had five or six sisters and two brothers and they went away. A wild lot died on the boat going over. From here they went to East Port, Maine, and a lot went to Boston.[30]

Historian Kerby Miller writes, "American grain ships [bringing Indian corn to Ireland] sometimes carried away small groups of people who begged to be rescued from isolated districts such as Rathlin Island."[31] Since many of the American vessels carrying Indian corn to Ireland were registered in New England, this may have represented an opportune chance for Rathlin folk to travel to their relations in Maine.[32]

One of those who left the island in the years surrounding the famine was John McFaul from the townland of Kilpatrick.[33] In many ways his experience encapsulates the story of famine migration from Rathlin. Kilpatrick is rugged and upland, with expansive views of the Mull of Kintyre, in Scotland. In the years before the famine, settlement was concentrated in two *clachans*. Five families—with surnames of McFaul, Black, and McCurdy—worked a harsh world of rocky pasture and upland, herding sheep and depending for survival upon their "lazy beds" of potatoes (or "rigs" as they were known on Rathlin), planted on the hilly slopes. In normal years Kilpatrick offered at best a marginal existence. Weaving provided some subsistence. Sons and daughters also regularly crossed the seas to Scotland as seasonal labor to work the potato harvest. They returned with enough money to tide the family over for another season. This all changed during the famine. Upland clusters like Kilpatrick were among the most devastated on the island (and throughout Ireland).[34] Indeed, by 1850, when government officials made a survey of householders for Griffith's Valuation, the townland was all but empty, with only one house still inhabited.[35]

While many famine families throughout Ireland simply disappeared into the mists of time, we are fortunate that from Rathlin we have a clear picture of the fate of some who made the Atlantic crossing. John McFaul, for example, along with his neighbor Charles McCurdy (likely from Kilpatrick), journeyed to eastern Maine. McCurdy and his family worked as farmer-weavers in the town of Lubec—perhaps following Rathlin antecedents—while McFaul found work in the iron foundry in Pembroke and eventually purchased a small farm on the outskirts of town.[36] They were but a small part of a much larger migration between Rathlin Island and Washington County, one that continued for over a decade. By 1860 there were over 100 Rathlin families in the towns surrounding Cobscook Bay, a colony that comprised a significant percentage of those who left the island in the years surrounding the famine.[37]

FARMLAND AND FACTORY

In the wake of the famine, Rathlin people in Washington County, Maine settled into two distinct "communities": one of them agricultural, straddling the towns of Trescott and West Lubec; the other industrial, centered around the Pembroke Iron Works, a thriving foundry situated along the banks of the Pennamaquan River. (See gallery, plate 22.) The different paths of experience that Rathlin people chose to follow in downeast Maine raise a number of instructive questions. Why, for example, did some emigrants from Rathlin choose industrial jobs over farming? Did family traditions and experience in the homeland define who would be a farmer and who would labor in the foundry? Was there a perception of opportunity and upward mobility that came from working for cash wages? While the answers to some of these questions are still unknown, I would like to explore some tentative explanations. To begin, let us explore these communities in more detail.

In 1860 Trescott and West Lubec, which comprised the heart of the Irish farming district along the Cobscook, boasted seventy-five Irish families. This included forty-one families from Rathlin, fifty-four percent of the emigrants in the two towns.[38] Rathlin families began arriving as early as 1829, a migrant stream pioneered by Neal Black, Duncan Bradley, and Laughlin Black, who acquired land along Cobscook Bay. They joined other Irish families, many of them from Ulster, who were fishing the coves of Cobscook and farming the hardscrabble land straddling Lubec and Trescott—Bartholomew Gillise from Tyrone; Patrick Boyd from Donegal; and John Driscoll from Waterford, to name but a few. This growing community soon attracted the attention of the Catholic Church, which had established an early presence in eastern Maine. Circuit riders from Eastport and missionary priests on the Indian reserve at Pleasant Point ministered to this Irish flock. In 1852 a wooden Catholic chapel was built on a piney rise in Trescott.[39] Consecrated St. Mary's, it served as the geographical focus of the Irish community and it attracted new settlers to the town, many of whom settled within earshot of its church bell.

The 1860 Federal census provides a valuable snapshot of this community. The majority of the Irish were identified as farmers, although there was a scattering of artisans, especially in Lubec. These included Thomas Quirk, a master mason from Rathlin; Francis McBride, who had a shoemaker's shop in the village; and Patrick McEvoy, one of several coopers in the town employed in the packaging of fish. There were also several Irish immigrants among the merchant community in Lubec, including Patrick Gillese, from Tyrone, and Charles Keive, a Donegal man whose shop looked out on the channel separating the mainland from Campobello Island, New Brunswick. From the census one also catches a glimpse into the demographics of this community.

One of the most striking qualities revealed in the record was the longevity of Rathlin people along the Cobscook. In Lubec and Trescott, twelve householders were in their seventies or eighties and one, John Bradley, gave his age as 101! Besides this impressive longevity, what is implied in these examples is the sense of community that was preserved and nurtured among island folk. When emigrant families abandoned Rathlin en masse in the years surrounding the Great Famine they took everyone with them—extended families that ranged from young children to elderly grandparents. This community was subsequently transplanted to Washington County.

John Horan, age eighty-four, along with his sons Alexander and John were among the Rathlin voyagers who settled in Lubec at mid-century. As a pioneering farmer, Horan's experience was perhaps representative of many of his Irish neighbors. His experience also reflects the often-surprising upward mobility open to island folk in the New World. The Horans most likely came from the Demesne lands in Rathlin, which included a densely populated lane of cabins overlooking Church Bay. Many of the families on the Demesne were employed as weavers, flax spinners, and farm laborers—the descendants of artisans recruited from the Antrim mainland by Reverend John Gage in the eighteenth century.[40] They were also among the first to leave the island in the years prior to the famine. By 1850 the eight cabins along the lanes were listed as "unoccupied."[41] John Horan and his sons arrived in Lubec and eventually purchased a plot of land at the head of Federal Harbor, one of the coves opening off Cobscook Bay. By 1850 they had cleared upwards of 100 acres on which they raised potatoes, barley, and flax, reproducing some of the agricultural patterns they knew in Rathlin. Livestock owned by Horan was typical of the saltwater farms bordering Cobscook

Bay. In 1850 he had a yoke of oxen, four milk cows, and fifteen sheep which produced wool enough to clothe his family and a little more beside, to sell to the Pembroke woolen mills.[42]

The prosperity of the Horan farmstead in 1860 was dependent upon a cooperative strategy through which his extended family formed a single economic unit. Rather than homestead farms of their own, his two adult sons (ages thirty-seven and thirty-one) pooled their resources and their work with their father, a cooperative undertaking that led to subsistence and success. The Horans also diversified their economic interests in Lubec. While many of their neighbors had long since abandoned the growing of flax, a laborious and time-consuming process, the Horans continued to spin and weave their summer linen. Only four families in the Cobscook region towns preserved this tradition—all of them from Rathlin Island![43] Like many of the Rathlin farmers in Lubec they also fished on Cobscook Bay. Indeed, fishing was an important adjunct to farming: it provided Irish families with a ready source of cash or credit at the town store. One of the sons, Alexander, also worked in the rural lead mines near Bassett's Cove in West Lubec.

Horan's farm was located on Denbow's Neck Road—one of several Rathlin holdings overlooking Federal Harbor. In the midst of stump-strewn fields and rough pastures stood his farmhouse, a small wood framed structure that was a visible departure from homeland building traditions. Houses on Rathlin were constructed of stone and thatch, a style well suited to climatic conditions. This form, however, quickly became redundant Down East with its bountiful supply of timber. Building styles among the Irish in the Passamaquoddy region largely conformed to examples set by their Yankee neighbors, namely the wood-framed vernacular farmhouses ("Cape Cods") that still dot the landscape of northern New England.

Research in Washington County suggests that cultural continuity among the Irish families was a selective process at best. Rathlin families continued to hold onto their Catholic identity, but in terms of building styles, material culture, and farming, they quickly adapted to the new physical and economic environment. This is expressed clearly in the 1850 agricultural census for Lubec and Trescott. Rathlin farmers such as John Horan became acquainted with new implements and new methods of farming—for example, the use of oxen as draught animals—unknown in the homeland.[44]

With respect to language, it is most probable that early Rathlin families coming to the Cobscook region spoke Irish, as even in 1910 a large number of people in Rathlin (almost two-thirds of the population) were still native speakers.[45] During the period of peak migration to Maine (1830-1860), Rathlin Island was a patchwork of linguistic traditions that reflected its diverse social history. Rathlin Irish, as historian Augustine McCurdy explains, was intermixed with a good deal of Scots-Gaidhlig, and this was not unusual considering the Scottish origin of many of the islanders. The eighteenth century, in particular, brought successive waves of Scottish Highlanders to the island (as mentioned earlier, some had fled following the defeat of "Bonnie Prince Charlie" at the Battle of Culloden in 1745).[46] Some of these refugees were given tenancies or employment by the Gage family. Indeed the migration of Scots-Gaidhlig speakers (who also carried some English or Lowland Scots in their linguistic baggage) "led to a dilution of Rathlin Irish." This was especially true in the Lower End of the island (Ceann Caol), where a distinct dialect emerged, one that was different in grammar and pronunciation from that in the Upper End of the island.[47]

This difference in dialect between the Lower End and the Upper End of the island developed into a friendly rivalry that survived into the twentieth century. As Augustine McCurdy explains:

> The Upper End people spoke, in the main, Irish. They were not impressed with the dialect and ways of the incomers and so they called them 'Cuddins'. This is the Rathlin Irish for a very small fish which used to come into the harbour area in large shoals. They were caught in nets and salted away for the winter. However, this description implied that the Lower Enders were not of much account. The Lower Enders, in turn, called the inhabitants of the Upper End 'Furns' [Gaelic 'forachan']. This is the Rathlin term for puffins and other auks which gather in vast numbers every spring at the cliffs of Cnoc an Tirrive (*Cnoc an Tairbh*—the hill of the bull). Of course, this term implied that the Upper Enders were as wild and untamed as seabirds.[48]

To what extent this rivalry was carried to Maine is unknown, but it seems certain that Rathlin Irish was spoken by many of these immigrants upon their arrival in the saltwater coves of Lubec, Trescott, and Pembroke during the mid-nineteenth century. Few artifacts of this linguistic heritage have survived in the Passamaquoddy region, with the exception of distinctive Scottish trace elements, such as the use of

Archibald, Laughlin, and Duncan as first names.[49] There is also the occasional tantalizing hint embedded in local memory and stories. In the 1940s, John L. McCurdy of Lubec (then a sheriff in Washington County), in his letters to Augustine McCurdy of Rathlin Island, remembered his mother singing Gaelic songs to him when he was a young child. His mother, born in Lubec, in turn had learned the songs from her own mother, who had emigrated from Rathlin during the famine.[50]

PEMBROKE

On the northern shore of Cobscook Bay one finds the town of Pembroke—today a quiet community. In 1850 Pembroke had an air of enterprise and progress. Farming, fishing, shipbuilding, and cutting timber provided opportunities for newcomers. Most importantly, the Pembroke Iron Works (established 1828), a thriving foundry situated along the banks of the Pennamaquan River, employed a steady stream of natives and newcomers—many of them Rathlin Islanders. At its peak the foundry produced 5,000 tons of iron: nails, horseshoes, chain iron, and boiler rivets.[51] By 1860 there were over sixty-eight Irish families in Pembroke, many employed in the iron works. There was also a vibrant community of English families in Pembroke who lived in an enclave called "the English village." Indeed, one detects a distinct ethnic division of labor in the irons works: skilled English puddlers were recruited by the foundry, while Irish were employed almost exclusively in lower scale positions as heaters helpers, puddler's helpers, and laborers.[52] Irish workers in Pembroke were primarily wage earners and lived in company housing within the shadows of the iron yard.

We return to the question posed earlier: Why did some Rathlin people work in the factories when others found subsistence in the soil and the sea? Was it a perception of opportunity? Of cash wages? Kevin Whelan argues that Irish immigrants in nineteenth-century America were informed and opportunistic: they ventured to urban centers and industrial jobs not solely because they were poor, or had limited choices, but because factory work, with steady cash wages, offered the best options for moving ahead.[53] Family letters flowing between Ireland and the New World frequently mentioned the state of the economy and available jobs in America. As one immigrant wrote in 1853, "This is a good country for a labouring man . . . At this time he can earn at least one dollar a day, equal to 4 shillings British. He is in good demand for this sum."[54]

While the lure of employment may have been a factor in Irish migration to the industrial cities of the Northeast, the experience of Rathlin folk in Washington County is perhaps more complex. First, it appears that the choice to work in the industrial setting of Pembroke was dictated in some degree by the timing of migration. Many of the Rathlin people who took up farms along the Cobscook were early arrivals—"pioneers" who are able to purchase available land in the 1830s and 1840s. This window of opportunity was not always available to newcomers arriving after the Famine years, when emigrants left Rathlin with few resources and often out of desperation. Work in the iron foundry, then, was a safety valve that allowed newcomers to find their feet during the first critical years. In time, cash wages at the foundry enabled some immigrants to purchase land in nearby farming communities.

Foundry work was also a safety valve in another important way. The Pembroke Iron Works was at its peak in the 1850s and 1860s—just at the time when a new generation of Irish boys (immigrant and American-born) in towns like Lubec and Trescott were coming of age. These surplus sons—like many of their contemporaries throughout northern New England—faced several choices. Population was increasing and land in coastal Maine was growing scarce. Many had to choose between staying at home in a constricted economic environment, or to look West toward the new frontier of opportunity. Indeed, many of their generation in the 1840s and 1850s homesteaded land in the Midwest.[55] Yet while some of the Irish and Rathlin folk in Washington County followed this westward migration, many others stayed behind. Increasingly, some of this younger generation of islanders opted to work in the foundry, within sight and sound of home communities.

According to the 1860 Census of Pembroke, which recorded Irish workers at the iron works, many were relatively young and in their formative years. Rathlin-born Daniel McFall, twenty-five years of age and residing on his father's farm in Pembroke, worked as a roller at the iron works, along with two of his brothers. Neale McCurdy, an "Iron works laborer," lived within earshot of the foundry in a household with several other young men from Rathlin, including John and James Black, a roller and puddler's helper.[56] These examples suggest a different way of looking at our question. Industrial jobs, rather than simply being a sign of Rathlin folk leaping into the capitalist world of wages and opportunity, may have also represented something more fundamental. Taking a job in the foundry was a way of maintaining a sense of community and a sense of cohesiveness within families. For surplus sons like Daniel McFall and his brothers, factory work may have been a way to postpone out-migration. For those like Neale McCurdy, who as a young boy on Rathlin Island had experienced the wrenching dislocation brought on by the Great Famine, taking a job in the foundry, and working alongside Old World neighbors, was a way to preserve a sense of place and community. Even after the foundry closed in the 1880s and the lead mines folded, Rathlin Islanders from Washington County held onto their cohesiveness and island identity, moving on in groups to new horizons. As one writer reflects, "islands may be the last places where self-reliance is coupled with a keen sense of community."[57]

LEGACY

The Rathlin enclaves along the Cobscook Bay are important for several reasons. First they reflect the growing diversity and pluralism of Maine communities during the mid- to late nineteenth century. Farming, fishing, logging and factory work attracted to Maine a variety of people who settled in burgeoning mill towns and agricultural communities alike. These included Franco-American mill families in Lewiston, Scandinavian farmers in New Sweden, and Scottish, Italian and Finnish granite workers on Hurricane Island—immigrants who envisioned, but not always realized, a new world of opportunity in Maine.[58] Like the Rathlin Islanders of Lubec and Pembroke, their migration was facilitated by families who had gone earlier—pioneers who wrote home of jobs and opportunities and whose assistance often eased the adjustment of newcomers. And like Rathlin folk, their migration was often undertaken to preserve a sense of family identity and community and to pursue opportunities that were beyond their reach, or no longer accessible, in their home places.

The Rathlin migration to Washington County is also significant in that it illustrates the often fluid boundaries and migration corridors that crossed Maine during the nineteenth century. French-Canadian families, for example, moved back and forth between the farming villages of Quebec and the factory towns of Maine and southern New

England. Irish migrants, likewise, used Maine as a stepping stone in what often were extended migration patterns. Between the years 1815 and 1850, in particular, thousands of Irish crossed from the Maritimes into Maine on their way to Boston and beyond. Some of these voyagers, of course, remained Down East—exemplified by the Rathlin communities of Cobscook Bay, the farming enclaves of Aroostook County, and the urban Irish neighborhoods of Bangor and Portland. Their stories have enriched the cultural and religious heritage of Maine and has also proved to be an important legacy for immigrants and newcomers who would follow in their footsteps.

Migration to Washington County brought dramatic changes in experience for Rathlin Islanders. Local traditions and associations from Rathlin slowly faded as they adjusted to a new landscape, new building traditions, and new allegiances—which included celebrating the Fourth of July and, for some, serving in Union Regiments during the American Civil War.[59] In towns such as Lubec and Pembroke, they also came into close contact with a spectrum of newcomers—from New England Yankees to Irish from a variety of counties and localities. Perhaps most striking to island people were their encounters with Native Americans— Passamaquoddy and Maliseet Indians—who lived in remnant groups nearby. Pembroke, as late as 1860, had several Native American "camps," and bands of native people continued to travel the roads and byways of Washington County and trade at local stores.

Yet, despite encounters and adjustments in the New World, a sense of "Rathlin" was still embroidered on the landscape in eastern Maine. We can visualize this in the 1881 Atlas of Washington County—where in West Lubec we find a "little Rathlin" clustered along the shores of Federal Harbor. (See gallery, plate 20.) Here were McCurdys, Blacks, Morrisons, McQuaigs, and Horans, linked by the physical boundaries of field, fence, and farm but also connected by an invisible "map"—one woven together by a web of personal relationships that stretch back to Rathlin Island. Many of these families and associations are gone today, but their memory still survives in the place names surrounding Federal Harbor. Approaching the cove by boat one is impressed by the headlands rising above the water—Horan Head and Black Head—named for the pioneer families along the inlet. Nearby one finds Bradley Mountain and Morrison's Cove. Perhaps most intriguing of all is the elevation on the north side of the cove, called "Cobble Hill." Was this perhaps in memory of Kebble—an upland district of Rathlin cleared during the famine of some of the same families that settled in Lubec? Johnny Horan is silent on this question.

Today the fate of Rathlin Island resembles, in many ways, that of eastern Maine. It was once a busy crossroads—a stepping stone along the fluid cultural boundaries between Scotland and Ireland. During the last century, however, it has suffered from a decline in population, lack of opportunity, and the draw of brighter lights. Yet, both Rathlin and eastern Maine have much to share in their history. At the interface of sea and land the communities of Rathlin and the Passamaquoddy are bound together by the ever-present and ever-changing ocean. In facing the Atlantic they face each other across time and space.

1. Alan Taylor, "Centers and Peripheries: Locating Maine's History," *Maine History* 39 (Spring 2000): 3–15.
2. The most recent and authoritative work on Rathlin can be found in Augustine McCurdy, *Rathlin's Rugged Story: From an Islander's Perspective* (Coleraine, County Derry: Impact Printing, 2000); and *Gaeilge Reachlann: A History of Rathlin Irish* (Rathlin: An tEach Ceannann Dubh Publications [By author], 2002). Also see the pioneering work of Marie E. Daly, "Rathlin Islanders Downeast," *Nexus* 6, no. 6: 196. Patricia McCurdy Townsend (formerly of Lubec), in her detailed family histories and website, has laid the important groundwork for continuing research on the connection between Rathlin and Washington County, Maine. See http://members.tripod.com/~quoddybelle/index
3. Samuel Lewis, *A Topographical Dictionary of Ireland* (1837, reprint 1984), 2:502; *Ordnance Survey Memoirs of Ireland: North Antrim Coast and Rathlin* (Belfast: The Institute of Irish Studies, 1994), 24:129.
4. McCurdy, *Gaeilge Reachlann*, 7; *Ordnance Survey Memoirs*, 24:134; and Wallace Clark, *Rathlin: Its Island Story* (Coleraine, County Derry: Northwest Books, 1988), 131.
5. Tithe Applotment Books (County Antrim, Barony of Cary, Parish of Rathlin Ireland), Northern Ireland Series, Microfilm Reel #139, O'Neill Library, Boston College, Chestnut Hill, Massachusetts.
6. Lewis, *Topographical Dictionary*, 2:502.
7. See Duncan Bradley's Naturalization Petition in Supreme Judicial Court Records, Washington County, Maine, July Term, 1841 (Volume 5), Maine State Archives, Augusta, Maine (hereafter MSA).
8. *Ordnance Survey Memoirs of Ireland*, 24:133.
9. On this stepwise migration, see Bernard Bailyn, *The Peopling of British North America* (New York: Vintage Books, 1988), 20–43. This phenomenon is also reflected in studies on Irish migration. See, for example, David Fitzpatrick, " 'A peculiar tramping people': the Irish in Britain, 1801–70," in W. E. Vaughn, ed., *A New History of Ireland: Ireland Under the Union* (Oxford: Clarendon Press, 1989), 5:627–32; Edward Chafe, "A New Life on 'Uncle Sam's Farm':

Newfoundlanders in Massachusetts, 1846–1859," (Master's thesis, Memorial University, St. Johns, 1982); and Edward T. McCarron, "Altered States: Tyrone Migration to Providence, Rhode Island during the Nineteenth Century," *Clogher Record* 16, no.1 (1997): 145–61.

10. *A History of the Island of Rathlin, by Mrs. Gage* (Coleraine: J. Margaret Dickson, 1995), 87. These accounts are corroborated in the writings of Dr. J. D. Marshall, who visited Rathlin in 1834. He noted that a number of men journeyed to Glasgow and Greenock to learn the trade of ships carpenter, and others took ships to America. "In one of the years preceding his visit, upwards of forty had left for America and during the summer of 1834 sixteen had emigrated. . . ." See McCurdy, *Rathlin's Rugged Story*, 38.

11. John Mannion and Fidelma Maddock, "Old World Antecedents, New World Adaptations: Inistioge Immigrants in Newfoundland," in William Nolan and Kevin Whelan, eds., *Kilkenny History and Society: Interdisciplinary Essays on the History of an Irish County* (Dublin: Geography Publications, 1991), 371.

12. Kerby Miller, *Emigrants and Exiles: Ireland and the Irish Exodus to North America* (New York: Oxford University Press, 1985), Chapter 6.

13. Declaration of Intention, Neal Black, Washington County District Court, Eastern District, Records Volume 9, September term 1847, MSA.

14. Cecil J. Houston and William J. Smyth, *Irish Emigration and Canadian Settlement: Patterns, Links, and Letters* (Toronto: University of Toronto Press, 1990), 90, 31–35. It is probable that many of the Rathlin emigrants left from Derry. In 1847, for example, a ship, the *Charles Napier*, departed Derry for Saint John, New Brunswick, carrying several Rathlin families—Blacks, McCurdys and McFauls. See McCurdy, *Rathlin's Rugged Story*, 44.

15. This pivotal migration corridor through eastern Maine has, with the following notable exceptions, received scant attention from students of Irish America. See William Forbes Adams, *Ireland and Irish Emigration to the New World from 1815 to the Famine* (New York: Russell and Russell, 1967); Marcus Lee Hanson, *The Atlantic Migration, 1607–1860* (Cambridge, MA: Harvard University Press, 1940); and Marcus Lee Hanson, "The Second Colonization of New England," *The New England Quarterly* 2 (1929): 539–60.

16. Supreme Judicial Court Records, Washington County Maine, Volume 8 (July Term 1844), MSA.

17. Houston and Smyth, *Irish Emigration and Canadian Settlement*, 204.

18. Ibid., 128.

19. See, for example, Sean McCouaig, "McCouaig Family Ships," *The Glynns: Journal of the Glens of Antrim Historical Society* (Cushendall, Co. Antrim: The Glens of Antrim Historical Society, 1998), 70–73. On Alexander McQuaig, see his naturalization petition, Supreme Judicial Court Records, Washington County Maine, Volume 10 (22 September 1847), MSA.

20. The travels of Denis O'Donnell are outlined in his declaration of intention, Supreme Judicial Court Records, Washington County, Maine, Volume 9, July Term 1847, MSA.

21. Mannion and Maddock, "Old World Antecedents, New World Adaptation," 371. On the importance of chain migration in Irish movement and settlement, see David Fitzpatrick, "Emigration, 1801–70" in Vaughn, *A New History of Ireland*, 5:600–603; Houston and Smyth, *Irish Emigration and Canadian Settlement*,

90–95; and Miller, *Emigrants and Exiles*. For a specific case study of chain migration from Tipperary, see Bruce Eliot, *Irish Emigrants in the Canadas: A New Approach* (Montreal: McGill-Queen's University Press, 1988).

22. *A History of the Island of Rathlin by Mrs. Gage*, 87.

23. Robert J. Scally, *The End of Hidden Ireland: Rebellion, Famine, and Emigration* (New York: Oxford University Press, 1995); Tyler Anbinder, "From Famine to Five Points," *American Historical Review* 107, no. 2 (2002); and Edward T. McCarron, "Famine Lifeline: The Transatlantic Letters of James Prendergast," in David Valone and Christine Kinealy, eds., *Ireland's Great Hunger: Silence, Memory and Commemoration* (Lanham, MD: University Press of America, 2002), 41–62.

24. *A History of the Island of Rathlin by Mrs. Gage*, 87. It appears that Robert Gage also took direct responsibility for securing food and relief. In 1847 he purchased thirty-two barrels of Indian corn meal and three tons of Carolina rice—most likely intended for Rathlin. See McCurdy, *Rathlin's Rugged Story*, 43.

25. Cathal Poirteir, ed., *Famine Echoes* (Dublin: Gill and Macmillan, 1995), 198.

26. The story of Pembroke's efforts to sent Indian meal to Rathlin during the famine was told to me by Patricia McCurdy Townsend, whose family emigrated from Rathlin Island to Lubec, Maine in the years surrounding the famine.

27. Clark, *Rathlin: Its Island Story*, 140.

28. Clogh-na-screeve is described in Clark, *Rathlin: Its Island Story*, 140. It still stands in Cleggan and is remembered by natives of the island. Telephone interview with Noel McCurdy of Rathlin Island, 28 May 2002.

29. *A History of the Island of Rathlin by Mrs. Gage*, 87.

30. Poirteir, *Famine Echoes*, 245.

31. Miller, *Emigrants and Exiles*, 295. Augustine McCurdy also notes that in 1847 there is a record of Robert Gage negotiating with the J&J Cooke Shipping Line.

32. American Consulate records, for example, kept a record of American ships provisioning in Cork and carrying Indian corn to a variety of locations in Ireland. Many of these were "belonging" to ports in Maine. See "Dispatches from United States consuls in Cork, 1800–1906," National Archives, Microfilm Publications, microfilm D 359, Roll 1.

33. John McFaul's origins in "Kilpatrick, Rathlin Island" are recorded on his gravestone in St. John's Cemetery, Pembroke, Maine. It records that he died in 1867, at age seventy-seven.

34. On the famine's effect on Ireland, and the devastation of marginal uplands, see F. H. A. Aalen, Kevin Whelan, and Matthew Stout, *Atlas of the Rural Irish Landscape* (Cork: Cork University Press, 1997), 87–92. See also Miller, *Emigrants and Exiles*.

35. Griffiths Valuation of Tenements, Parish of Rathlin Island, townland of Kilpatrick (Microfiche, County Antrim, fiche #4), O'Neill Library, Boston College.

36. 1860 Federal Census, Washington County, Maine, Towns of Lubec and Pembroke, Series 653, Roll # 455.

37. Marie Daly, of the New England Historical and Genealogical Society, estimates that of the 550 people who emigrated from Rathlin between 1841 and 1861, at least 230 with Rathlin names settled in Washington County, Maine. See Daly, "Rathlin Islanders Downeast," 196.

38. Figures are gleaned from the 1860 Federal Census.

39. On Eastport and the missions of Trescott and Lubec, see William L. Lucey, *The Catholic Church in Maine* (Francestown, NH: Marshall Jones Co., 1957), 70–79, 115, 144.

40. My research points to the fact that all of these emigrants—including the Horans—were leaseholders rather than landowners. There were only three property owners on the Island in 1861, the largest by far being the Gage family. The remaining families, seventy-five in all, were tenants of Gage. See McCurdy, *Rathlin's Rugged Story*, 44–45.

41. The Demesne lands in 1834 listed a John Horan as leasing just over two acres, and Edward Horan with eight acres. See Tithe Applotment Books (County Antrim, Barony of Cary, Parish of Rathlin Island), Northern Ireland Series, Microfilm Reel #139, O'Neill Library, Boston College. By 1850, these holdings are listed as "unoccupied" in Griffith's Valuation of Tenements, Parish of Rathlin Island, Demesne townland (Microfiche, County Antrim, fiche #4), O'Neill Library, Boston College.

42. Information on the Horan farm can be found in the Industrial, Agricultural, and Social Census, 1850, Washington County, Maine (Vol. 131), Microfilm Roll #2, MSA.

43. Industrial, Agricultural, and Social Census, 1850, Washington County, Maine (Vol. 131), Microfilm Roll# 2, MSA. It was very unusual to grow flax and make linen homespun in 1860—with the availability of factory cloth. See Clarence Day, *History of Maine Agriculture, 1604–1860 (University of Maine Bulletin 56, no. 11 [April 1954]):* 155. Yet, it was still certainly a tradition on Rathlin Island, where in the years before the Famine (and before widespread mechanization of weaving) "nearly every house [in Rathlin] had a weaving loom." McCurdy, *Rathlin's Rugged Story*, 42.

44. 1850 Agricultural Census.

45. McCurdy, *Gaeilge Reachlann*, 15. In 1835 there were six schools on the island, two of which (in the western townlands of Cleggan and Ballygill) continued to teach Irish. The active promotion of culture by such schools and their committed teachers throughout the nineteenth century was responsible for the preservation of the Irish language on Rathlin into the early years of the twentieth century. The local authority on linguistic traditions of Rathlin Island is Augustine McCurdy. Much of my discussion of Irish and Scots-Gaelic is drawn from his *Gaeilge Reachlann: A History of Rathlin*. For his efforts to reinvigorate Rathlin cultural life and the generous sharing of his knowledge by means of transatlantic telephone calls, I am deeply grateful. For more intensive linguistic analysis on Rathlin Irish see Nils M. Hulmer, *The Irish Language in Rathlin Island, Co. Antrim* (Dublin: Hodges, Figgis, 1942); T. F. O'Rahilly, *Irish Dialects Past and Present* (Dublin: Browne and Nolan, Ltd., 1932). Also see Clark, *Rathlin: Its Island Story*. I am also grateful to Dr. Kenneth Nilsen for these three references.

46. McCurdy, *Rathlin's Rugged Story*, 36, 77; and *Gaeilge Reachlann*, 7. McCurdy emphasizes that this intermixture of Scots-Gaidhlig and Irish was not exclusive to Rathlin. The coastal areas, from the Antrim glens to west Donegal, had a similar ethnic and language mix.

47. This difference in dialect was recorded by Swedish linguist Nils Hulmer. When he came to Rathlin in 1937, as Augustine McCurdy relates, he found "a remarkable difference between the dialect of the Upper End and the Lower End, chiefly in pronunciation, but also in grammar." Indeed, in the center part of the island

he noticed what he called "a more central form," which embodied features from both ends of the island. See *Gaeilge Reachlann*, 21. Notwithstanding these differences in dialect, the islanders were still able to converse with and to understand each other with ease, and differences seemed to dissolve whenever they found themselves under attack by outsiders.

48. McCurdy, *Gaeilge Reachlann*, 7.

49. Naming patterns for Rathlin families in Lubec, Trescott, and Pembroke, Maine, can be gleaned from the 1860 Federal Census, cited above.

50. Personal communication from Augustine McCurdy of Rathlin Island (son of the late Augustine McCurdy, recipient of the Sheriff's letters), 11 April 2003. While John McCurdy is remembered in oral tradition on Rathlin Island as being the "sheriff of Lubec," in Maine a Sheriff is a County officer.

51. Sidney A. Wilder, *Centennial Celebration of the town of Pembroke, 1832–1932*, unpublished mounted newspaper clippings (1932), Maine State Library, 21.

52. A puddler was a skilled artisan whose job it was to stir molten iron to the correct consistency in order to produce wrought iron.

53. Kevin Whelan, *The Killing Snows* (Cork, Ireland: Cork University Press, forthcoming).

54. Arnold Schrier, *Ireland and the American Emigration, 1850–1900* (Chester, PA: Dufour Editions, 1997), 28.

55. On this migration from northern New England, see Hal S. Barron, *Those Who Stayed Behind: Rural Society in Nineteenth Century New England* (Cambridge: Cambridge University Press, 1984). Concerning the movement of Irish from Maine and the Maritimes to the Midwest, see Joseph A. King, *The Irish Lumberman Farmer* (Lafayette, California: By the author, 1982).

56. 1860 Federal Census, Washington County, Maine, Series 653, Roll #455 (microfilm), Maine Historical Society, Portland, Maine.

57. Chris Crossman, "Drawing with Light," in Peter Ralston, *Sightings: A Maine Coast Odyssey* (Camden, ME: Downeast Books, 1997), x.

58. For an overview of the Franco-American traditions, see the work of Yves Frenette in Richard W. Judd, Edwin A. Churchill, and Joel W. Eastman, eds., *Maine: The Pine Tree State from Pre-History to the Present* (Orono: University of Maine Press, 1995), 457–59, 465–70; and on migration routes and settlement patterns his "Understanding the French Canadians of Lewiston, 1860–1900: An Alternate Framework," *Maine Historical Society Quarterly* 25, no. 4 (spring 1986): 198-229. On the workers of Hurricane Island, see Lawrence C. Allin, "Maine's Granite Industry," in Judd, Churchill, and Eastman, *Maine: The Pine Tree State*, 275–80; and Eleanor Richardson, *Hurricane Island: The Town that Disappeared* (Rockland, ME: The Island Institute, 1989), 28–30. For New Sweden, see Charlotte Lenentine Melvin, "The First Hundred Years in New Sweden," *The Swedish Pioneer Historical Quarterly* (Oct. 1970): 233–57.

59. A list of Washington County men drafted in August 1863 to serve in the Civil War included John McCurdy, Archibald Wilkinson, and L. McCurdy from Lubec, and John Bradley and John McFlail [McFall] from Pembroke. See *Vital Records from the Eastport Sentinel of Eastport, Maine 1818–1900* (Camden, ME: Picton Press, 1996) 198. At least two Irish soldiers from Lubec died during the Civil War. John Keive (born in New Brunswick of Donegal parents) was killed at the Battle of Fredericksburg in May 1863, and Daniel Keive, his twin brother, died at St. James Hospital in New Orleans in November 1863.

A BRAVE NEW WORLD:
THE IRISH AGRARIAN COLONY
OF BENEDICTA, MAINE

by Edward T. McCarron

In my travels over the New England states I have not seen such a place as
so likely to become flourishing and happy; would to God that all the Irish
in this Country had such a home and such favorable prospects before their
children
> –Thomas O'Sullivan to Bishop Benedict Fenwick, 28 January 1841

AMONG THE STONES in the old burying ground in Benedicta, Maine
is a monument to Patrick Brady, who died in 1860.[1] Carved in rough
marble common to country churchyards of the period, it stands overlooking Mt. Katahdin, in a fertile range of farms and pine wood. Like
most of his neighbors buried around him, Brady was a farmer, working
one hundred acres on the Molunkus River at the time he died. And, like
most of these neighbors, Brady was Irish-Catholic, an ethnic identity
proudly engraved on his tombstone. Crowned with "In Excelsis Deo,"
his epitaph tells us that "He was a native of County Cavan, the parish
of Kildorough."

The Irish origins of this early Maine farmer and the setting of a
Catholic churchyard in rural New England do not fit neatly into our
conception of ethnic America or the Irish. While volumes have been
written on the urban experience of Irish immigrants and their adaptive
responses to American cities, little historical research has touched upon
Irish settlements in rural farming communities.[2] This essay, which
investigates the family farms, community life, and religious identity of
Benedicta, Maine, will add to the growing evidence of Irish rural experience in America. To begin, we must travel to Boston. The year is 1833.

BISHOP BENEDICT FENWICK
AND HIERARCHICAL SUPPORT

Benedicta was the brainchild of Benedict Fenwick, the second bishop of Boston from 1825 to 1846.[3] Like other social observers of the time, Fenwick was concerned over the plight of the recent Irish immigrants in his city, many of whom lived in poor housing, earned low wages, and were frequently out of work. One solution, the bishop reasoned, would be the establishment of a rural colony where the Irish could take up farming and be free from the pitfalls of metropolitan life. An independent Catholic community, complete with its own church and resident clergy, would also ensure the survival of the faith amidst a growing threat from Protestant nativists. As a former parishioner wrote Fenwick from Albany: "It is not like Boston here. This is a home in comparison to your Down East Yankees. I would not fancy to live among such bigots. I saw enough of them at the time they burned the nunnery."[4] Indeed, the burning of the Ursuline convent in Charlestown, Massachusetts in 1834 coincided closely with Fenwick's increasing efforts to establish a Catholic colony in rural Maine.

For the site of his colony Fenwick settled upon a township far to the north, in the southern part of Aroostook County. Here his Irish colonists would be able to carve out a rural sanctuary free from the prejudice of their Yankee neighbors. What is more, Fenwick envisioned the Maine frontier as the ideal environment for the training of new clergy and the education of the laity. As early as 1825 he declared that "the thing I want most . . . is a seminary and a college. And for my part I have not a cent to build them with."[5] His Irish township offered him a solution. Profits from lumbering, milling, and church farms in Benedicta could be funneled into the construction and endowment of these institutions. The upcountry isolation of this Irish outpost would bring spiritual dividends as well. In a letter describing Benedicta, Bishop Fenwick remarked:

> It is there I shall erect a College into which no Protestant shall ever set foot; I cannot persuade myself that it is much to the advantage of Catholicity to have that mixture of boys of different creeds which prevails in all our Catholic establishments throughout the country. What is gained by removing the prejudices of Protestants is lost by impairing the devotion, and in some instances, the religion of the Catholics.[6]

Here, then, one begins to understand the motives that prompted the bishop to build his "New Jerusalem" in the wilds of Maine.

Fenwick's colony, in addition, was inspired by earlier Irish communities in northern New England. In particular, his model for Irish agrarian settlement can be found in North Whitefield, Maine, a community in the Kennebec region that boasted over 300 Irish Catholics in 1830. Whitefield was peopled in the early nineteenth century by Irish immigrants coming by way of the Maine timber trade. By 1818 they had established their own Catholic Church (only the third in the diocese outside of Boston) and a resident priest, Dennis Ryan. Ryan, a native of Kilkenny, operated a large farm and sawmill in Whitefield in addition to his ministerial duties. His energy and Irish identity acted as a magnet for new immigrants who sought to try their hand at farming.[7]

Ryan also attracted the favorable attention of Benedict Fenwick. Upon visiting Whitefield in 1832, Fenwick's enthusiasm was evident throughout his journal. He described a church that was filled to overflowing. Irish farms were flourishing as well. The bishop described going "into the field to see the people mowing and gathering in their hay. The crops of wheat, oats and hay were very abundant . . . [I] was greatly gratified to see the face of the country everywhere improved in cultivation."[8] Here then was an alternative to the precarious existence of Catholic newcomers in Boston. Whitefield's example inspired in Fenwick the wondrous possibilities that lay ahead in Benedicta.

The bishop advertised his scheme in *The Jesuit*, predecessor of the *Boston Pilot*. On April 27, 1833, he appealed to "industrious" families who would want to relocate to his Irish colony in Maine:

> [Bishop Fenwick] is aware that there are, at the present time, a great number of industrious individuals, who would be glad to purchase, and settle on farms with their families, and who would prefer...to remove to them, even under some disadvantage in the beginning, to living at great expense, and in a precarious manner in large cities, where they remain the half of their time out of employment, and with their children constantly exposed to the vices and seduction of the streets. He is aware, moreover, that nothing has hitherto deterred many decent Catholic families from thus establishing themselves, but the apprehension, were they to remove to any considerable distance, of being perpetually deprived of the benefits of their religion. . . . To obviate these strong objections . . . the Bishop intends, as soon as the land shall be secured by purchase, to proceed forthwith to the erection of a Catholic church in some central point, and to the establishment of a Catholic priest there.[9]

In November, 1833, Fenwick purchased 11,000 acres on the Aroostook frontier, which he noted "possesses every advantage that can recommend it for settlement, that of health, of fertility, and of convenience to market."[10] Much of the farmland was spoken for within the year—sold in lots of fifty or 100 acres, at attractive terms. Initially, 134 families engaged to move to the new settlement. As the Bishop was keen to point out, most "have been principally bred farmers. . . . Thus everything announces a successful settlement."[11]

Benedicta was one of the first examples of Catholic colonization in America, and remains today one of its most long lasting. Yet until recently little has been written concerning its history except for the occasional reference to a "unique community" or an "Irish-Catholic dream."[12] Indeed, the pioneering efforts of Benedict Fenwick have largely been forgotten beside those of later figures such as Archbishop John Ireland of St. Paul, who sponsored an ambitious program of Irish agrarian colonies in Minnesota during the 1870s.[13] The fact remains, however, that Fenwick is an important link in understanding the development of Catholic colonization in America. His experiment at Benedicta serves as an instructive lesson in the creation of a rural Catholic settlement and the promotional role of the Catholic hierarchy.

Bishop Fenwick, for example, was one of the first Catholic churchmen to promote actively the blessings of land ownership and rural life for Irish immigrants. Rural life, according to Fenwick, "gives to the inhabitants a robustness of constitution, and a vigor and vitality" which cannot be found in the cities.[14] What is more, land ownership engendered a feeling of independence and self-esteem. Fenwick, a product of the Jeffersonian era, envisioned for northern Maine a class of sturdy Catholic yeomen who would work their own farms and thus gain a measure of prosperity and respectability unattainable by the rank and file of urban workers. Indeed, Fenwick saw a link between rural agrarian pursuits and social betterment. By promoting Catholic colonization and land ownership, one uplifted those immigrants victimized by urban squalor, low wages, and strong drink. It was a lesson not to be lost on John Ireland fifty years later.[15]

Certainly the concept of a farming community as a solution to the Irish immigration problem was not entirely new to Fenwick. In 1817 representatives of the Irish emigrant-aid societies, including ex-patriot Thomas Addis Emmet, petitioned Congress for public lands in Illinois that could be settled by the new Irish immigrants.[16] Likewise, in 1822 Bishop John England of Charleston, South Carolina, a correspondent and friend of Benedict Fenwick, proposed an agrarian colony to aid the impoverished and unemployed Irish of his diocese.[17] Significantly, both of these schemes, although never fully realized, were built on the assumption that Irish Catholic farmers could prosper in rural environs. Certainly, this opinion helped shape Benedict Fenwick's Maine venture and his recruitment of "industrious" immigrants. In many regards, then, Benedicta can be seen as a test case for Irish agrarian settlement in the New World. Its progress, while slow and halting at times, speaks of the potential for Catholic communities on the frontier—a vision that lived on for the better part of the nineteenth century.

IRISH RECRUITMENT AND MIGRATION

It is tempting to remain with Bishop Fenwick, to explore his motivations and activities concerning this Catholic colony. Perhaps the more interesting story, however, concerns the settlers themselves who journeyed to Maine (which in the 1830s and 1840s comprised part of Fenwick's Diocese of Boston).[18] In the case of Benedicta we are fortunate to have a rich cache of documentary evidence—parish records, naturalization petitions, and, most significantly, a collection of letters written by Irish settlers to Fenwick which describe their farms, their family life, and their adjustment to life on the frontier during the 1830s and 1840s.[19] These letters range from clumsy to eloquent and as such provide a unique window on the Irish in rural America and their adaptive responses to life on the frontier.

Who were these voyagers to the North country? Sources suggest a number of revealing characteristics. Few of them, for example, were recent immigrants. Naturalization petitions, which specify date of arrival in America, confirm that most had resided in America for nine years or more before journeying to Maine.[20] This allowed them time to adjust to their new environment and, most importantly, to accumulate needed capital to support their agrarian ambitions. Thomas Casey, for example, left his native County Westmeath in 1821 to venture to Boston. For sixteen years he worked as a cooper along the waterfront before moving his family to northern Maine.

In fact, few of the Irish could be described as impoverished before taking up land in Maine. A survey of city records in Boston suggests that while some were identified as laborers, others appear as artisans and traders. Peter Boyle, who hailed from the Curragh of Kildare, worked as a carpenter. John McNamara tried his hand at shopkeeping. Perhaps most revealing was John Byrne who, although residing in Boston's North End, identified himself as a "farmer."[21] While it is doubtful he managed much of a harvest along the wharves and cobbled streets of Boston, his appellation does suggest a certain mindset that encouraged him (and others) to move beyond their urban surroundings.[22]

Other factors may have influenced some Irish, as opposed to others, to migrate to the farming frontier. The homeland origins of those settling in Benedicta, for example, are quite suggestive in this regard. Naturalization petitions and gravestone inscriptions reveal that the majority of Fenwick's Irish township came from settled and anglicized areas in the east and north of Ireland. The southeast, in particular, contributed over fifty percent, with the majority of these coming from Kilkenny, Laois, and the golden vale of Tipperary. Significantly, these regions were among the most fertile in Ireland. During the early nineteenth century they were characterized by large-scale mixed farming, a growing market economy, and upward mobility among Catholic farmers. Nonetheless, population growth and economic depression following the Napoleonic Wars forced many aspiring sons to seek their fortune in America, some of whom sought to adapt their agrarian experience to new settings.[23]

Boston and vicinity was the major recruitment ground for Benedicta settlers. Here Bishop Fenwick and parish priests were able to personally advertise the township and persuade families to take up the challenge.[24] News of the Irish colony was also carried further afield through family letters and newspaper advertisements in *The Jesuit*. Deeds held by Fenwick reveal subscribers sending money from as far as Canada and Alabama, although most of these distant recruits eventually backed out of the arduous undertaking.

Fenwick's colony likewise attracted support in Ireland during this period. The Reverend Thomas O'Flaherty, from Tralee, County Kerry, was just one example of those who inquired of land in Benedicta:

> Ere this letter can have reached you I shall God willing be on the ocean surge, bending my course for the Western World—Nine sturdy and staunch Catholics . . . will accompany me to your shores, determined

there to live and die—they may be said to form one family—I am anxious
to purchase one hundred acres of good arable land; one half of which to be
immediately ready for the plough. . . . I would be delighted to effect the
purchase in your little Catholic colony or township, would so much land
still there remain unoccupied.[25]

Although O'Flaherty eventually purchased one hundred acres in Benedicta, neither he nor his "sturdy and staunch Catholics" settled there.

Fenwick's colony, however, did attract several emigrants from
Britain. One well-documented example concerned George Green who
moved his family and possessions from Castle Douglas in the Scottish
lowlands. Green was certainly atypical of those who pioneered
Benedicta. A prosperous clothier in Scotland, his expressed desire was
to "retire from [my] public life...to an agricultural one in America."[26]
This gentleman farmer nonetheless shared many of the same motivations as his Irish neighbors. Writing to Fenwick in 1835, he expressed a
desire "to avail myself of the undoubted prospects of bringing up my
children Catholics and educating them for practical professions which
a Catholic and quiet settlement like yours [can provide]."[27] This sentiment echoed those of Irish settlers such as James McCoart who
acquired fifty acres of backland "for the benefit of his children."[28]

Providing for one's family and its future prosperity was an important
motive for those who traveled to the Aroostook. This is suggested in the
demographic profile of those moving north. Unlike the predominant
pattern of young, unattached Irish who traveled across the Atlantic during this period, those who migrated to Benedicta were middle-aged with
families. The average age for farmers upon arrival in Benedicta was thirty-
seven and, with one exception, they were all accompanied by family or
kin.[29] Networks of family and friends also played an important role in
promoting Irish settlement in Benedicta. James Kearns, for example,
acquired several plots of land for his brothers John and Thomas who
subsequently left their tenant farm in Kilkenny for a new life in Maine.
Similarly, Matthew Moran, a laborer in Salem, Massachusetts, asked
Fenwick in 1835 to reserve the lot of land next to Joseph Campbell and
Thomas Courtney. "We are all friends," he explained, "and [I] would
like to be near to them as possible."[30]

The most compelling example of chain migration into the North
country can be found out of Dover, New Hampshire, where at least five
families acquired property in Benedicta in the 1830s. Their surviving

letters to Fenwick reveal the intricate and often hidden networks of mutual assistance, information diffusion, and solidarity that enabled early immigrants to survive on the frontier. Hugh Gorman, for example, traveled to Boston to secure deeds on behalf of himself, James Magee, and John Holland. John Holland, in turn, journeyed to Benedicta, where he cleared land for both Magee and William McDavitt, who worked in the Dover textile mills. For his part, McDavitt acted as scribe—petitioning the Bishop on behalf of his Dover neighbors. He also recommended new recruits such as "Michael McGuiness of this town, a sober, industrious young man . . . He is . . . of an ingenious turn and can do anything that may be wanted in the cooper or carpenter line."[31]

This web of support and mutual assistance among the Dover Irish only makes sense if we dig a bit deeper into their backgrounds. Not only were they neighbors in Dover, but their family connections began much earlier in Ireland. With one exception, all of them were natives of the handloom region of Keady, County Armagh—an area whose small farms and weaving traditions were undermined by the mechanization of linen manufacturing in Ulster.[32] During the 1820s they were recruited to work in the mills of Dover, where they joined scores of other emigrants from parishes in Armagh and neighboring Monaghan.[33]

One traveler who made the voyage from Armagh to Dover was Martin Quealey, who went on to settle 100 acres in Benedicta. He first emigrated to Dover in 1826, finding work at the Cocheco mills. A decade later, Quealey and his eldest son made the first of several trips to Benedicta, cutting and clearing several acres of forest before returning to work in the mills. Progress was slow. It was not until 1840 that Quealey found the means to move his large family of ten to the Aroostook. Even then, as he explained to Bishop Fenwick, "I mean to leave one boy and two girls in Dover behind me, they are all to work in the factories and will try to save as much of their earnings as will pay you [for my land], before I move them down to the settlement."[34]

THE SETTLEMENT OF BENEDICTA

Martin Quealey and his family traveled by steamboat from coastal New Hampshire to Bangor, a day's journey in 1840. From there they forged north along the Aroostook Road, a pitted, muddy track that passed through vast stands of pine and hardwood forest "where ax never entered." In time, several outlying farms and clearings came into view, heralding their arrival in Benedicta. One of these plots belonged to Peter Plunkett, whose experience was typical of most new settlers. In 1838 Plunkett had begun transforming the landscape—cutting and clearing the forest, making fences around the perimeter of his holding, and building the beginning of a farmhouse. A Catholic priest passing through the township remarked, "Plunkett is hard at work clearing off his piece. I dined with him and eat [sic] a hearty meal of pork and bread. He has only a very poor camp in which he sleeps and eats—his wife and children stay at Mr. Bradys until he can have time to build a log house."[35]

Benedicta at this time was still a hardscrabble community. In 1840 the settlement numbered forty families, over two hundred people in all. Most, like Plunkett, lived on outlying farms but a small nucleus had clustered in the center of the township where the Bishop had laid out the church and ten acre lots in an effort to foster community cohesion. Here one would have found a contingent of artisans and traders: John McNamara, a tavern keeper who acted as postmaster and justice of the peace; his lodger John Rush, a carpenter by trade; Edward Sweeney, the blacksmith; and Henry Farrel, a stonemason and jack-of-all-trades who worked intermittently on the Catholic church.

The Catholic church was a rustic wood-framed building that remained without clapboards for several years. Its dilapidated state and its often empty pulpit were a frequent bone of contention among the Irish. James Magee, writing to the Bishop from Dover in 1837, relayed the message of one Benedicta settler who "complains bitterly of the neglect to which they have been doomed without either priest, church, or school. He says several families have left the settlement partly on that account."[36] A decade later the message was still the same. John Byrne observed:

> My Lord told me that you would put up a church . . . it is partly up but it is rotting . . . My Lord you have not left a priest here continually in consequence of which, there did a child die, without baptism . . . My Lord you have not put up a gristmill, in consequence of which we have often hungered for want of bread and at the same time had wheat a nough [sic] if we could get it ground.

Byrne added that the Kingdom of God "consists not in talk but in virtue."[37]

Perhaps the most important ingredient in the settler's complaints was the lack of a resident priest. This is somewhat ironic since Bishop Fenwick had earlier attributed the success of the Irish farming community in North Whitefield to its church and dynamic pastor Dennis Ryan. Besides ministering to his congregation, Ryan served as town selectman, chaired the school committee, and operated a sawmill that provided a source of cash and credit for the Irish lumberman-farmer.[38]

Benedicta, on the other hand, received only the best intentions of an absentee bishop and the complaints of part-time priests who considered farming duties and secular responsibilities beyond their ability. Father William Tyler complained in 1840 of having to supervise millwrights, farm labor, and road crews in the township. "I am not qualified for the situation . . . It is impossible for me to attend to these things and perform properly the duties of the ministry."[39] Fenwick responded by calling the priest home with no promise of replacement. Indeed, it was not until 1871 that Benedicta received its first resident pastor, Father Dennis McFaul.[40] In the interim it was served by Jesuit missionaries and later by visiting priests from Boston, Houlton, and even Woodstock, New Brunswick.

Perhaps we should not be too hard on the Bishop. At a time when the fledgling community was struggling toward self-sufficiency, his journals reveal a frequent concern for its welfare. In the 1840s Fenwick regularly sent barrels of pork, codfish, and flour to needy settlers and provided seed and farm tools to the community.[41] And despite complaints, Fenwick did pour time and money into the construction of a sawmill, only to see his energies foiled by incompetent millwrights and raging floods.

This patriarchal goodwill, however, was not enough for the neediest of settlers. The bishop's papers reveal frequent letters asking for money or loans. Typical was that of Charles Reilly, who requested $20 to purchase a cow, explaining that "it will be a great support for my family."[42] A few turned to more desperate measures in order to make ends meet. Blacksmith Edward Sweeney was rumored to be part of a counterfeiting ring operating between Bangor and Benedicta. Henry Farrell, who struggled to support a family of eight, attempted to rob the county bank in Bangor and landed in jail. The last we hear of him, the county sheriff had auctioned off his belongings in Benedicta and moved his family to relations in Fall River, Massachusetts.[43]

Conditions were far from stable during the early years—leading to a slow but steady exodus out of Benedicta. Some settlers, perhaps, began with too high expectations. George Green, for example, journeyed to Maine with dreams of a landed estate and life as a gentleman farmer. Within a year he and his family had returned to Scotland and his property was left to squatters. As neighbor John McNamara remarked, "Friend Green has got tired of this country . . . farming is poor speculation if a person has to hire all his help."[44] That same year William Croke, the bishop's hired farmer, left as well. Fenwick simply remarked that "he intends going to Ireland."[45]

Some Irish in Benedicta, particularly younger sons, joined the ranks of New England migrants who sought land and opportunities to the west. The family of Christopher Keegan, one of the original settlers, provides a notable example. In a letter to Bishop Fenwick in 1850, he lamented that "I am making ready to leave this place—alas not with joy. I came here with hart [sic] and hand fully determined to spend *all* my days." He explained that his two sons sought better land in the West and as "the prime and vigour of my life is gone I could not work my farm [without them]." Keegan, then close to seventy, moved with his family to St. Anthony Falls in "Mensota territory" where they joined other Irish immigrants who worked as lumbermen-farmers.[46]

Despite early struggles and out-migration one should pause before considering Benedicta a failure. Certainly for Bishop Fenwick his experiment on the Aroostook was a disappointment. Despite a steady outlay of funds, his dreams of a Catholic center in the wilderness went unfulfilled. In time, he turned his energies closer to home—building a Catholic College and Seminary in Worcester (now the College of the Holy Cross). By the time of his death in 1846, his Irish township in the north country was largely forgotten back in Boston.

Yet was life a failure for those who remained in Benedicta? The record suggests otherwise. Sixty-two percent of the families who resided in the township in 1840 were still listed on the 1850 census.[47] Their persistence and their sense of community can be ascribed to expanding kinship networks and the growing prosperity in agricultural production. While some Irish certainly fell short of success on the Aroostook frontier, others slowly adapted to their New World. They embraced a style of agriculture based on wheat and Indian corn and became acquainted with new methods of farming, such as the use of oxen as draught animals, unknown in their homeland.[48] Indeed, the agricultural census of 1850 reveals that Irish farm holdings and improved acreage were rough-ly comparable to their Yankee neighbors in the Aroostook region.[49]

The picture of agricultural adaptation and self-sufficiency in Benedicta runs against the grain of conventional wisdom concerning the Irish in America. Scholarship has traditionally stressed the urban nature of the Irish and their inability to adapt to rural conditions. Several writers, in fact, argue that the Irish settled in American cities precisely because they lacked the skills and knowledge that would allow them to cope with market-oriented farming in the New World.[50] While this may possibly apply to the famine emigrants who left small holdings in Connaught and Munster, it was not the case in Benedicta or earlier in North Whitefield, Maine. The Irish in these communities had emigrated from regions that were centers of commercial agriculture—notably the tillage and dairying areas of the southeast—a wide swath that cut from Wexford and south Kilkenny through Tipperary. Here they had been accustomed to mixed farming and a market economy, an experience that enabled them to modify and adapt successfully to new settings.[51]

It is important to note that Benedicta farmers also continued in cer-tain farming traditions from Ireland that distinguished them somewhat from their Yankee neighbors. Notably, they produced potatoes and oats in greater abundance than the non-Irish of nearby Golden Plantation.[52] This surplus was possibly based upon Irish cultural tradition and ethnic foodways. While both groups raised oats as feed for their animals, and consumed potatoes at their table, the Irish had traditionally relied heav-ily upon these crops for sustenance. Among the small farmer class in the homeland, oats, or "stirabout," was a mainstay of the diet. Potatoes, as well, were a dietary staple. Given only a small space of land they brought a prolific yield and could feed an entire family throughout the year (a feature that recommended them to the Aroostook frontier, where cool and temperamental summers could hinder corn production). Of course, potatoes became a major cash crop for northern Maine after the arrival of the railroad in 1870. For those Irish who remained in Benedicta, it spelled a boom that encouraged them to stay.[53]

LEGACY

Today, Benedicta retains much of its traditional character. Walking its rolling hills one can still see country lanes winding through abandoned orchards and several rustic farmhouses dating to the mid-nineteenth century. This rural community is still largely of Irish descent and locals take pride in pointing out their ancestors in the old graveyard over-looking Mt. Katahdin. Indeed, a 1984 celebration commemorating the 150th anniversary of the village brought out some of the original families who had settled the bishop's township. In the procession that wound its way into St. Benedict's Church, one could see the Rushes representing dairy farmers, the McAvoys for lumbering concerns, and the Quealeys representing potato growers. I suspect that Benedict Fenwick would have smiled.

1. An earlier version of this article appeared in *Records of the American Catholic Historical Society of Philadelphia* [now *American Catholic Studies*] 105, nos. 1–2 (Spring–Summer 1994): 1–15. It is reprinted with permission.
2. Most of the works that touch on Irish rural settlement pertain to Canada. They include John Mannion, *Irish Settlements in Eastern Canada: A Study of Cultural Transfer and Adaptation* (Toronto: University of Toronto Press, 1974); Donald Akenson, *The Irish of Ontario: A Study in Rural History* (Montreal: McGill-Queens University Press, 1984); see also Bruce Elliott, *Irish Migrants in the Canadas: A New Approach* (Montreal: McGill-Queen's University Press, 1988). On the rural Irish of Maine, see Edward T. McCarron, "Irish Migration and Settlement on the Eastern Frontier: The Case of Lincoln County, Maine, 1760–1820," *Retrospection: The New England Graduate Review in American History* 2 (1989): 21–31; and "In Pursuit of the 'Maine' Chance: The North Family of Offaly and New England, 1700–1776," in William Nolan and Timothy P. O'Neill, eds., *Offaly History and Society: Interdisciplinary Essays on the History of an Irish County* (Dublin: Geography Publications, 1998), 339–70.
3. Benedicta has been touched upon in several works. Most important is Sister Marie of the Visitation Nicknair, O.P., *Bishop Benedict Fenwick and the Origins of the Benedicta, Maine Community* (Augusta, ME: O'Ceallaigh Publications, 1992); see also Robert H. Lord, John E. Sexton, and Edward T. Harrington, *History of the Archdiocese of Boston in the Various Stages of its Development, 1604–1943* (New York: Sheed and Ward, 1944), Vol. 2, 152–55; and Sister Mary Gilbert Kelly, O.P., *Catholic Immigration Projects in the United States, 1815–1860* (U.S. Catholic Historical Society, Monograph Series, no. 17, 1939).
4. John Franklin to Bishop Fenwick, 1 September 1839; Benedicta Papers, Archives of the Archdiocese of Boston (hereafter AAB). On the burning of the Ursuline Convent see Nancy Lusignan Schultz, *Fire and Roses: The Burning of the Charlestown Convent, 1834* (Boston: Northeastern University Press, 2000).

5. Nicknair, *Bishop Benedict Fenwick*, 32.

6. Bishop Fenwick to Reverend George Fenwick, 29 November 1838; typescript copy in Benedicta Papters, AAB.

7. On the Irish community of Whitefield, Maine, see Edward T. McCarron, "The World of Kavanagh and Cottrill: A Portrait of Irish Migration, Entrepreneurship, and Ethnic Diversity in Mid-Maine, 1760–1820" (Ph.D. diss., University of New Hampshire, 1992), Chapter 6. See also McCarron's essay "Facing the Atlantic" in this book.

8. Bishop Benedict J. Fenwick, Memorandum, Mss, Vol. 2, 123, AAB.

9. *The Jesuit*, 27 April 1833.

10. Ibid., 5 October 1833.

11. Ibid., 27 April 1833; October 1833; and 9 August 1834. The purchase price of the land was $1.25 an acre, payable over a period of six years.

12. References and articles on Benedicta can be found in the *Boston Pilot*, 26 March 1987; the *Bangor Daily News*, 25 April 1987; and *Yankee Magazine* (March 1988): 54–63.

13. On Catholic colonization in Minnesota and the Midwest, see James P. Shannon, *Catholic Colonization on the Western Frontier* (New Haven: Yale University Press, 1957); Marvin R. O'Connell, *John Ireland and the American Catholic Church* (St. Paul, MN: Minnesota Historical Society Press, 1988); and Kelly, *Catholic Immigration Projects*.

14. Nicknair, *Bishop Benedict Fenwick*, 34.

15. On the philosophy and activities of John Ireland toward Catholic colonization see O'Connell, *John Ireland and the American Catholic Church*, Chapter 7.

16. Kerby Miller, *Emigrants and Exiles: Ireland and the Irish Exodus to North America* (New York: Oxford University Press, 1985), 188.

17. Reference to Bishop John England's interest in Catholic colonization may be located in Nicknair, *Bishop Benedict Fenwick*, 28.

18. Maine remained part of the Diocese of Boston until 1853, when the Diocese of Portland was founded under the direction of Bishop David Bacon.

19. These letters form a major portion of the Benedicta Papers, 1833–1875; the collection also includes bonds for deeds and administrative papers. AAB.

20. Primary declarations and naturalization petitions for the early decades of the nineteenth century regularly contain a variety of helpful data in the study of Irish immigrants. Court clerks, particularly in the original declaration of intention, often recorded the immigrant's place of birth (sometimes to the townland level), their age, occupation, date of departure, port and date of arrival, and years resident in the United States. For the Irish of Benedicta two major sources were consulted: Naturalization Petitions and Documents, Box 483 (Aroostook County), RG 85, National Archives, New England Branch, Waltham, MA; and primary Declarations of Intention, Boston Municipal Court (1822–1860), Massachusetts State Archives, Boston (hereafter MSA).

21. *Record Books*, 1837, Boston Municipal Court, MSA.

22. Ibid. Interestingly John Byrne in his naturalization petition identified his birthday as St. Patrick's Day. This would not be unusual except that four of his eventual neighbors in Benedicta also did the same. While this could be coincidence it possibly suggests that the Irish were refashioning a traditional identity in the New World.

23. Several works suggest that pre-famine Irish emigration was geographically selective. See William F. Adams, *Ireland and Irish Migration to the New World: From 1815 to 1840* (New York: Russell and Russell, 1967); and Miller, *Emigrants and Exiles*, 173–74. Ruth Ann Harris, in her work on the *Boston Pilot*, sees a sizeable Leinster migration up to the 1830s. See her "Characteristics of Irish Immigrants in North America Derived from the *Boston Pilot's* 'Missing Friends' Data, 1831–1850," *Working Papers in Irish Studies* (Northeastern University, 1988), 11.

24. See bonds for deeds, and manuscript letters in the Benedicta Papers, AAB.

25. Reverend Thomas O'Flaherty [Tralee, County Kerry] to Bishop Fenwick, August 1840; Fenwick Papers, Box 1, Folder 2.55, AAB. O'Flaherty later ministered at St. Mary's Church on Endicott Street in Boston.

26. George Green to Bishop Fenwick, 20 January 1840, Benedicta Papers, AAB.

27. George Green to Bishop Fenwick, 20 January 1840; also 9 March and 9 July 1839, Benedicta Papers, AAB.

28. Bond for deed to lot #42 east, 23 March 1836; Benedicta Papers, AAB.

29. Age data was derived by comparing naturalization declarations (which give age and date of arrival) with census schedules for Benedicta. These schedules include a census taken for Bishop Fenwick in 1837, and the 1840 federal population census.

30. Michael Moran to Bishop Fenwick, 20 August 1835; Benedicta Papers, AAB.

31. William McDavitt to Bishop Fenwick, 1 April 1839. Concerning the Dover Irish, also see William McDavitt to Bishop Fenwick, 28 February 1838, and James McGee to Bishop Fenwick, 7 July 1836; Benedicta Papers, AAB.

32. On linen weaving and the mechanization of linen manufacturing in Ulster, see the work of William H. Crawford, especially "The Evolution of the Linen Trade in Ulster before Industrialization," *Irish Economic and Social History* 15 (1988): 32–53; and *Handloom Weavers and the Ulster Linen Industry* (Belfast: Ulster Historical Foundation, 1994). Also see Marilyn C. Cohen, ed., *The Warp of Ulster's Past: Interdisciplinary Perspectives on the Irish Linen Industry* (London: Macmillan, 1996).

33. Interestingly, this chain migration from Armagh continues into recent years. The folk singer, Tommy Makem, from Keady, first arrived at Dover, New Hampshire and continues to live there. On the Dover Irish see Paul Bergen, "Occupation, Household and Family among the Irish of Nineteenth Century Dover, New Hampshire" (Master's thesis, University of New Hampshire, 1989). My data on places of origin for Irish families in Dover comes primarily from headstones in St. Mary's Cemetery, Dover, NH.

34. Martin Quealey to Bishop Fenwick, 1 April 1839; James Magee to Bishop Fenwick, 7 July 1836; Benedicta Papers, AAB.

35. Reverend William Tyler to Bishop Fenwick, 18 May 1838; Benedicta Papers, AAB.

36. James Magee to Bishop Fenwick, 7 July 1836; Benedicta Papers, AAB.

37. John Byrne to Bishop Fenwick, 1 June 1846; Benedicta Papers, AAB.

38. McCarron, "The World of Kavanagh and Cottrill," 312–15.

39. Reverend William Tyler to Bishop Fenwick, July 9, 1840; Benedicta Papers, AAB.

40. Reverend McFaul, from eastern Washington County, had Rathlin Island antecedents. Personal communication from Mr. Robert Black. On the connection

between Maine and Rathlin Island, see Fidelma M. McCarron's essay in this volume.

41. Fenwick, for example, imported four sacks of "good quality oats from Ireland," which he distributed in Benedicta. See Memoranda, April 6, 7, 21, 1838; AAB.

42. Charles Reilly to Bishop Fenwick, 6 March 1840; Benedicta Papers, AAB.

43. Reverend William Tyler to Bishop Fenwick, 18 May 1838; Michael Dunn to Bishop Fenwick, 10 April 1843; Benedicta Papers, AAB.

44. John McNamara to Bishop Fenwick, 18 August 1841; Benedicta Papers, AAB.

45. Bishop Benedict Fenwick, Memoranda, Vol. 2, 190.

46. Christopher Keegan to Bishop Fitzpatrick, 19 January 1850; Edward Sweeney to Bishop Fitzpatrick, 29 August 1852; Benedicta Papers, AAB. On the movement of Irish from Maine and the Maritimes into Wisconsin and Minnesota, see Joseph A. King, *The Irish Lumberman-Farmer: Fitzgeralds, Harrigans and Others* (Lafayette, CA: by the author, 1982).

47. Persistence rates remained relatively steady throughout the period, as revealed in census schedules for Benedicta:

PERSISTENCE RATES: BENEDICTA MAINE, 1837–1860

Date Range	Total No. of Families	No. Remaining	Persistence Rate (percent)
1837–1840	16	12	75%
1840–1850	40	25	62%
1850–1860	55	36	60%

Sources: 1837 Census of Benedicta and Federal Population Census for Benedicta, 1840, 1850, and 1860, Microfilm, Maine State Archives, Augusta, Maine.

48. Thirty-one out of forty-two Irish farmers in 1850 owned a pair of oxen. See 1850 Agricultural Census, Benedicta, Maine, Microfilm, Maine State Archives.

49. For total and improved acreage data in the 1850 Agricultural Census for Benedicta, neighboring Golden Plantation (largely Maine Yankee), Irish farmers in Whitefield, Maine and Yankee farmers in Whitefield were compared. The elevated average for total acres in Golden Plantation stems largely from three farmers who owned in excess of 350 acres each.

LAND AND CROP PRODUCTION, 1850

Town	Average Acres Improved	Average Total Acres
Benedicta	41.28	93.69
Golden Plantation	42.21	156.40
Whitefield Irish	41.80	78.10
Whitefield Yankee	36.50	79.17

Source: 1850 Agricultural Census, Microfilm, Maine State Archives, Augusta.

50. See Lawrence McCaffrey, *The Irish Diaspora in America* (Bloomington, IN: University of Indiana Press, 1976), 63–64. This point is continued in subsequent overviews of immigration, such as Roger Daniels, *Coming to America: A History of Immigration and Ethnicity in American Life* (New York: Harper Collins, 1989), 132. Daniels asserts that most Irish were "ill prepared for American agriculture."

51. On the regional character of Irish agriculture during the early nineteenth century, see T. Jones Hughes, "The Large Farm in Nineteenth Century Ireland," in Alan Gailey and D. Ó Hógáin, eds., *Gold Under the Furze* (Dublin: Glendale Press, 1982), 93–100; and Kevin Whelan, "Catholic Mobilization, 1750–1850," in P. Bergeron and Louis Cullen, eds., *Culture and Practiques Politiques en France et en Irlande* (Paris: Centre de Recherches Historiques, 1991), 246.

52. The 1850 Agricultural Census reveals that for the neighboring communities of Benedicta and Golden Plantation, Irish farmers produced a higher yield of potatoes and oats (but not the same abundance of Indian corn).

Mean Crop Production Among Irish and Non-Irish Farms (in bushels)
Town, Potatoes, Oats, Corn
Benedicta, 130.1, 157.6, 5.6
Golden Plantation, 83.7, 107.7, 23.9

Source: 1850 Agricultural Census (Microfilm, Maine State Archives, Augusta.

53. While nineteenth-century Irish immigrants may have consumed potatoes in greater volume than their Yankee neighbors in places like southern Aroostook County, one should not leap to the conclusion that the Irish were responsible for potato farming in Maine. There was a long tradition of potato farming in early America, and by the late eighteenth century, New England settlers, regardless of ethnicity, consumed potatoes at their table along with other staples such as corn and grain.

THE IRISH COMMUNITY AND IRISH ORGANIZATIONS OF NINETEENTH-CENTURY PORTLAND, MAINE

by Matthew Jude Barker

IRISH IMMIGRANTS settled in Portland in varying numbers from the 1790s until the 1930s. From the 1830s on, they formed numerous organizations and societies to aid and comfort the sons and daughters of Erin. These societies were created to serve a wide variety of purposes, including Irish nationalism, temperance, sports, literature, politics, entertainment, and culture. Many were also formed to accentuate the Irish-Americans' dedication and duty to the Catholic Church and their adopted country, and their desire to move up the ladder of success. Several of the societies were enormously successful, others transitory and abortive. Today, in Portland, there exist only two societies, although at the zenith of the popularity of Irish societies in Portland, at least half a dozen existed successfully at the same time.

EARLY IRISH SETTLERS

The first known Irishman in what is now Portland was Lt. Thaddeus Clark, who was here as early as 1662, when he married Elizabeth Mitton, granddaughter of George Cleeve, called by some the "Founder of Portland." Clark was killed in May 1690 by a band of Native Americans (Wabanakis) while in defense of Fort Loyall on Munjoy Hill.[1] For more than a century after Clark's death, Irish people were few and far between in Portland. There were notable exceptions. A Scotch-Irish family named McLellan was quite prosperous in Portland throughout much of the eighteenth and nineteenth centuries. The progenitor of the family was Bryce McLellan, who came here from County Antrim (now part of Northern Ireland) in 1727.[2] In 1767 an Irishman named William

McMahon (also spelled McMahan or Mahan) opened a school in Falmouth (Portland's name until 1786), which was later moved to Woodford's Corner. After the Revolution, his pupils included many boys who would later become leading citizens, including John Deering.[3] During the Revolution, James Sullivan (1744-1808), a lawyer and son of a Maine teacher from County Limerick, was in January 1777 appointed commissary to the several hundred men stationed at Falmouth under Colonel Joseph Frye. Along with Frye, he was engaged in constructing entrenchments for the town's protection. Sullivan later resigned his office, much to the chagrin of the town who wished him to become commander-in-chief of the forces in the area.[4] He went on to become a judge of the Superior Court and finished his days as the first Irish governor of Massachusetts, albeit not the first Catholic governor. James was the grandson of Major Philip O'Sullivan of Ardea, County Kerry, Ireland, a Catholic rebel who fled to France after the victory of William of Orange in 1691.[5] Philip was one of the "Wild Geese," Catholic expatriates who found refuge in the Catholic countries of Europe and offered their services to the monarchs of these countries, which included Spain, France, Austria, Italy, and Russia.[6] But James Sullivan's father John lost his Catholic religion in Maine, which often was the case when the Irish came to America prior to the nineteenth century, when, due in part to the absence of Catholic churches and priests, many Catholics converted to Protestantism. In 1795, James Sullivan was the first to write a history of Maine.

From the 1760s until the 1790s, many individuals with distinctly Irish surnames, including Flaherty, Ryan, O'Neal, McCormick, Murphy, O'Brien, Welch, Gallagher, O'Donnell, Mulligan, and Finnessy, appear in the church, town, vital, and court records of Portland. Most of these early Irish appear to have remained in Portland but a short time. It would not be until the first two decades of the nineteenth century that several Irish Catholic families would put down permanent roots in Portland.

By the early 1800s, several Irish Catholics were residing in Portland, mostly relatively new arrivals. Other Catholic families arrived by 1810, including Nicholas and Barbara Connolly Shea, Michael and Mary Gannon, Timothy and Nancy Mahoney, William and Margaret Mahoney Davis, and the families of John Buggy and John Driscoll.[7] These families represent the first positively identified Catholic families in Portland who thus created and developed the first, though quite small, Irish community in this city. By the 1820s, with the exception of the Shea family, it is difficult to find any record of their continuing influence locally.

CHEVERUS AND EARLY CATHOLICISM IN MAINE

In October 1796, a young émigré priest from England became associate pastor of the growing Catholic community in Boston. He was Father Jean Louis Anne Magdeleine Lefebvre de Cheverus, born in 1768 at Mayenne, in the French province of Maine. He had been ordained on December 18, 1790, in the last public ordination in Paris during the French Revolution.[8] Cheverus had charm, intelligence, and ambition, and was instrumental in the erection of the Church of the Holy Cross, dedicated in 1803 as Boston's first Catholic church.[9] In July 1798, Cheverus visited Portland, but apparently found few Catholics. He did baptize an Alexander Hayes, son of Alexander and Elizabeth, on that visit.[10] At any rate, he continued to stop in Portland on his annual visits to the Kavanaghs and Cottrills, prominent Irish Catholic families in Newcastle, Maine.[11]

Other early New England priests stopped in Portland to administer to the needs of what few Catholics were in the area. In 1802, Father Francois Matignon, another French émigré and called "the founding father of the Catholic Church in Boston,"[12] baptized eight children and one adult in Portland. A year later Father John S. Tisserant baptized Eleanor, daughter of Hugh and Anne Cusack, in Portland.[13] In a few months, Father Tisserant would officiate at the dedication of the Church of the Holy Cross in Boston, with Bishop John Carroll of Baltimore, the first American Catholic bishop, and others. The priest, from Connecticut, remarked that the communicants of the Holy Cross Church were mainly Irish, "who were drawn here by the miserable conditions that existed in their native country."[14]

Father James Rene Romagne, stationed with Passamaquoddy Native Americans at Pleasant Point, Maine, from 1799 to 1818, paid the small Catholic community of Portland several visits between 1811 and 1815, and baptized many children, including members of the Shea, Davis, Buggy, and Giffors families.[15] Romagne was from the same town in France as Father Cheverus.

According to historian Kerby Miller, between 800,000 and 1,000,000

Irish immigrated to North America between the end of the Napoleonic Wars (1815) and the eve of the Great Potato Famine (1844). Ireland's extended postwar economic crisis affected nearly all economic groups, over all parts of Ireland.[16] Due to an 1816 British legislative act that imposed heavy restrictions on U.S.-bound vessels, fares to the United States were more than double those to Canada. Thus most Irish emigrants in this era came to North America in the holds of Canadian timber ships. They landed in Quebec or the Maritime Provinces and untold numbers worked their way south to the United States. Many were known as "two-boater" Irish, as they had to first come to Canada, as it was less expensive, and then arrived in America later, in another boat.[17] We know from many sources that a great majority of the Portland Irish who came to Portland at this time indeed landed in Canada first and many spent several years at such places as St. John, New Brunswick, and Halifax, Nova Scotia.[18]

The precarious existence of the Irish tenant farmer grew steadily worse between 1815 and 1845. By the 1820s widespread poverty existed in Ireland along the Atlantic seaboard, from western Cork to Donegal, and in an area of poor soil that stretched eastward from Sligo Bay across northern Leinster and southern Ulster to the Mourne Mountains of the County Down.[19] When a famine struck the southern province of Munster and the western province of Connaught in 1822, many fled Ireland. As William Forbes Adams writes:

> Steadily and inexorably the pressure of population extended unemployment, reduced wages, and raised rentals to a ruined figure. Famine and disease swept over the country periodically, further endangering the lives already precariously insecure. Civil war, coupled with political and religious dissensions and agrarian friction, completed the forces of expulsion.[20]

The people of Portland were able to read firsthand accounts of the famine ravaging Ireland in 1822. The local newspaper *The Eastern Argus* on August 6, 1822 extracted a report from the *Dublin Evening Post* of June 8, 1822. It told of the sick and dying throughout Connaught and Munster.

> In one parish in Clare, 50 persons . . . were ill of fever, and 5 had died. The greater part of this parish [Clondegad] were totally destitute of provisions . . . We have quoted a paragraph from a Galway paper, which describes human beings reduced to the very verge of the grave for want of food . . .

In the county of Cork a typhus fever of a most malignant kind has already appeared. In Mayo the deaths from starvation continue to increase. In short, a great part of the west and south of Ireland present the shocking and appalling spectacle of a dense population in a state of famine, and upon the brink of a pestilence.[21]

The newspaper went on to describe the extent of this little known famine. "In the western part of Galway men, women, and children are dying of starvation, and so dreadful is the mortality, that every one who can quit are flying as from a plague."[22] The Dublin paper estimated that a million people were starving at the time.

We do not know how many Irish might have directly or indirectly come to Portland due to this famine.[23] It is known that same spring (1822) there were enough Roman Catholics residing in Portland to petition Jean Cheverus, now Bishop John Cheverus, first bishop of Boston, to visit them. The bishop came to visit the Portland Catholics soon after, spending several days with them. They were said to number either forty-three individuals or forty-three families. Before he left, two converts had been added to the growing community. Later, the bishop spent the weekend of July 13–14, 1822, with the Portland Catholics. A hall was secured for the purpose of saying Mass.[24]

Cheverus appointed Father Dennis Ryan to attend to their needs. The Irish-born priest had arrived in Boston in 1814 as a passenger on a Canada-bound British ship seized by an American privateer during the War of 1812. Bishop Cheverus ordained him in Boston in 1817, the first Catholic priest ordained in all of New England. Soon thereafter, Father Ryan was made pastor of St. Patrick's Church in Newcastle (near Damariscotta Mills), Maine (the oldest Roman Catholic Church still standing in New England). He became pastor of the newly created St. Dennis Catholic Parish (name later changed to St. Denis) in nearby Whitefield in 1819. Father Ryan visited the Portland Catholics between 1822 and 1827.[25]

The first Irish organization in Portland was the "Roman Catholic Society," a group that in actuality would become the first communicants of Saint Dominic Parish, the first Catholic parish and church in southern Maine, and the third oldest in the state. In 1823 the society held services on "Maine Street" (part of present day Congress Street) in Portland, according to the Portland City Directory for that year. At some point Masses, when possible, were held at Beethoven Hall, home of the Beethoven Musical Society, on Congress Street, in the vicinity of present-day Monument Square.[26]

On August 8, 1827, the second bishop of Boston, Benedict Joseph Fenwick, arrived in Portland, and spent some time with the Catholics of Portland. He celebrated Mass, heard confessions, confirmed people, and taught them vespers, "for there were none who understood how to chant them."[27]According to local prominent Irishman John O'Connor (usually rendered Connor), the Catholic population at the time was about 120 and Fenwick estimated 160 people attended a Mass held on August 12, 1827. Before he left, the bishop spent time with them looking for a place to build a house of worship and promised the communicants that he would soon send them their own permanent pastor.[28]

Fenwick kept his promise and sent Father Charles Daniel Ffrench, a native of County Galway, Ireland, and a convert to Catholicism. The son of an Anglican minister, Charles and his brother Edmund were banished from their father's home after secretly attending a midnight Mass on Christmas Eve and soon after converted. Father Ffrench studied in Portugal and was ordained as a Dominican in 1799. He was stationed in Ireland, New Brunswick, and New York before coming to Maine. His brother became the Catholic bishop of Kilmacduagh and Kilfenora in County Galway and County Clare.[29] The appointment of Ffrench to Portland is the first known example of a connection between County Galway and Portland that continues to this day.[30]

In May 1828, John Conner (Connor), Denis McCarthy (McCarty), and John Crease, of the newly created Catholic Committee, appealed to the citizens of Portland for help in erecting a "small chapel on their lot on State Street." They declared that they were too poor to complete the project themselves and asked for donations from the Portland people. They also opened a subscription list in Boston. The committee eloquently proclaimed:

> Religious instruction, if properly communicated, will not fail to inflame the youthful minds with high notions of religion, rather, with a love of temperance, of honesty and purity, to animate them with benevolent affections, with liberal views, with universal philanthropy, to impart genius to the rising population, and to be a popular star to conduct them through life as good men, useful members of society, and valuable citizens of this great republic of the world.[31]

The noted liberal writer John Neal of Portland wrote an editorial the next day in his newspaper, in which he stated, "Let the Catholics have a neat, comfortable, brick building for their purpose—instead of a wooden shed, and the town, *as a town,* will profit by the charity of those who contribute to the work."[32] He also stated that no "priesthood on earth exercise a more amiable and salutary guardianship over their flocks, than do the Catholics of this, and some other countries. They who are to be restrained in no other way, from idleness, drunkenness, debauchery, and violence, are as patient and submissive as little children, before the *father* of the church." Neal reminded the public that Roman Catholics are not permitted to attend services in Protestant churches, and "that therefore, unless he can find a catholic association, he is not very likely to worship at all."[33] Neal correctly realized that a Catholic Church would dictate moral authority to Portland's Catholics and help maintain order.

Between 1828 and 1833, Father Ffrench conducted four money drives and collected nearly $3,000 for his three new parishes (Portland and Eastport, Maine, and Dover, New Hampshire). It is said $1,300 of it was allotted to St. Dominic's. Ffrench was the Catholics' best benefactor, having sold his New Brunswick farm, and loaning $3,000 to them in order that they could pay their debts. The church eventually cost $7,000 to build.[34]

On June 13, 1828, the foundation stone of what would become Saint Dominic Catholic Church was laid on State Street. Enough work had been finished on the structure by November 1, 1830, that Mass could be celebrated. Work was not completed for some time, however, and it wasn't until 1833 that Bishop Fenwick dedicated the church, naming it in honor of the founder of Father Ffrench's order. By now the Catholic population of Portland, mostly Irish, numbered three hundred people.[35]

Considering the number of Irish in Portland by the time of the dedication of St. Dominic's, it is little surprise that a Hibernian Benevolent Society was formed in Portland early in 1832. It was perhaps the first such organization in Maine. James Mundy in his groundbreaking book, *Hard Times, Hard Men: Maine and the Irish, 1830-1860,* argued that the Bangor Irish, because of the great lumber trade in the region and the proximity to Canada, from which large numbers of Irish were leaving in the early 1830s, were "better organized socially than the Portland Irish."[36] But the Portland Irish had formed a temperance society in

1842, and by that same year they also had a very successful social organization in the form of the Hibernian Benevolent Society, which by then had already been in existence for ten years. The Portland Irish were as organized as their fellow Celts to the north and celebrated St. Patrick's Day with just as much fanfare, and apparently somewhat earlier. Incidentally, the Portland Hibernian Benevolent Society also predates the Ancient Order of Hibernians founded in New York in 1836.[37]

On St. Patrick's Day 1832, the Hibernian Benevolent Society met at the home of Thomas Owen, a County Meath emigrant who became one of the leading communicants of St. Dominic's Church, and enjoyed an "excellent repast" that had been prepared by a Mr. Daly and a Mr. Moore. John Connor, president of the society, was flanked by Father Charles Ffrench, St. Dominic's pastor, and by a Mr. Shea, who could not have been Nicholas Shea, the Irish merchant in whose house Mass was first said in Portland in 1822. Nicholas Shea had died in 1824, aged forty-eight.[38] He left two sons, including William, born in 1810, who was old enough to have been the "Mr. Shea" referred to. A County Wexford native, John Connor, who started a block making business with Dudley Cammett in Portland in 1817, gave the first toasts that evening:

> *The day we celebrate*—Sacred to christianity—to our native country long oppressed, may she with freedom soon be blessed.
> *America*—The birth place of freedom, the home, the asylum of the oppressed—May her stars, the emblem of strength, union, and light, visit every part of the world, and establish her dominion throughout the globe.
> *The memory of our glorious Patron Saint*—May the remembrance of his example and virtues always influence our conduct—may it perpetuate in our hearts an affection of the land we left, as well as for the country we have adopted.

The vice president of the society made another toast to *Insula Sacra*, an ancient name for Ireland, meaning the "holy isle."

> Ireland as she ought to be,
> Great, glorious and free—
> A sweet flower of the earth,
> And bright gem of the sea. [39]

The Hibernian Benevolent Society also made toasts to Daniel O'Connell, Irish mastiffs ("May they soon prove too strong for English

Bulls"), the society itself, and to the health of Father Ffrench. The priest thanked the group for their hospitality, and "wished prosperity to the society, and expressed a hope that it would erelong, not only emulate, but stand foremost among, the many benevolent associations, which form the ornaments of our Union."[40]

IRISH HISTORY AND HERITAGE

Although the Irish people of Portland and everywhere in 1832 had directly or indirectly experienced the pains of defeat and further subjugation at the hands of the British after abortive uprisings in 1798 and 1803, they were still hopeful. The 1798 Rising was led by United Irishmen, mostly Protestant, and the Defenders, the dominant secret Catholic society. They formed an uneasy alliance in hopes of freeing Ireland from British tyranny and misrule, aided, it was hoped, by a French invasion. The entire country was engulfed in turmoil during the 1790s. The French, as Catholics, had taken this opportunity to help out their Catholic brethren, but also to inflict as much damage as possible on their enemy, the English. They arrived off the coast of Ireland, ready to supply the Irish with much-needed fire power, but they were driven out to sea by powerful gales (ever after called the "Protestant Wind") and they never landed in Ireland.

Another French force came to Ireland in August 1798, under the command of General Humbert. The general and his army of about 1,400, half of whom were native Irish, captured the town of Castlebar, County Mayo, and appointed a local leading Catholic President of the Provisional Government of Connaught. But Humbert and his men were soon after routed by the combined British troops of Lord Cornwallis and General Lake, who had 10,000 men.[41] With their main support gone, the Irish rebels were not much good against Lord Cornwallis and his troops, who "hacked to pieces" the insurrectionists on Vinegar Hill in County Wexford.[42] Father John Murphy, who had witnessed the burning of his chapel, home, and many houses in his parish, often with the inhabitants still inside, had led that particular rising. Murphy began with an attack on three fronts, but when Father Michael Murphy, as the head of a fighting column, was killed, the battle turned from one of apparent success to utter defeat. In the words of a song about the 1798 Rising popular in the nineteenth century, "It's the most distressful country that ever I have seen . . . They're hanging men and women for the wearing of the green."[43] In Ulster, the Irish patriot Henry Joy McCracken, a Protestant, rose from his sick bed to lead an attack on Antrim town, but it ended in defeat and McCracken was promptly executed. Theobald Wolfe Tone, the celebrated Irish Protestant rebel and one of the leaders of the Rising and of the United Irishmen, was betrayed by an informer, and sentenced to death. Rather than suffer the great indignity of being strung from the gallows, he took his own life.[44]

Within a few weeks in 1798, it is estimated that 30,000 people, on both sides, were killed.[45] In the aftermath, Protestant reprisals forced many to emigrate.[46] The 1798 Uprising led the British Government to push for a Union, in which the Irish Parliament would be dissolved and the Irish then governed directly from the London Parliament, who would have little consideration for Ireland's affairs. The Act of Union was finally passed, signed by the king in August 1800, and officially put into effect January 1, 1801. Ireland was now annexed to Great Britain.[47] Another insurrection followed in 1803, but again proved fruitless, only providing more Irish martyrs to the litany of dead rebels, their names to be invoked for generations to come by Irish nationalists. The 1803 Rising ended with the public beheading of that great Irish patriot Robert Emmet.[48] But hope lingered for another generation. Much of this hope was manifested in the form of a man named Daniel O'Connell. The Portland Irish of the Hibernian Benevolent Society toasted O'Connell that St. Patrick's Day night in 1832 as one who might "obtain a full and ample concession of those civil and religious rights, upon which, for centuries past, her oppressors have trampled."[49]

DANIEL O'CONNELL: CATHOLIC EMANCIPATION AND REPEAL OF THE ACT OF UNION

A few years earlier, in 1829, Daniel O'Connell, a member of the Catholic gentry from County Kerry, had been responsible for the creation of the Catholic Relief Act, which opened up the Westminster Parliament and all but the highest offices to Roman Catholics throughout Great Britain and Ireland. But this was not enough. O'Connell, erstwhile mayor of Dublin and leader of the Catholic Association, continued to fight for the Catholics. By 1840 he had found a new cause, always hoping that in the end he could help his people through lawful means. The Portland Irish welcomed this next great cause, the Repeal Movement, with true enthusiasm. O'Connell, known as the Liberator, founded the Loyal National Repeal Association in 1840, with a sole purpose in mind: "the legislative independence of Ireland." He and his followers wanted to repeal the Act of Union of 1801. Repeal meetings were held throughout Ireland and the United States, from which vast amounts of money arrived in Dublin, the Repeal Association's headquarters.[50]

In 1843 prominent Portland Irishmen celebrated yet another St. Patrick's Day with a parade that started at Portland City Hall, where they had gathered inside, and which ended at St. Dominic's Church. The parade was led by a "Chief Marshall of the Day," Thomas Owen, who was followed by the Portland Brass Band, soldiers from Fort Preble (many of whom were Irish), the Catholic Temperance Society of Portland, and the Hibernian Benevolent Society. After church services, many went to the home of James McKinn (also Mackin), in the rear of Jones's Row in Portland, where a "sumptuous entertainment was prepared, conducted on Father Mathew's principal of strict Temperance."[51]

The assemblage at McKinn's place toasted many American and Irish heroes, including George Washington; General Andrew Jackson, "the patriotic Ex-President of the United States"; Father Theobald Mathew, the Irish temperance czar; and Edward Kavanagh, then governor of Maine and the first Catholic governor of a New England state. This was followed by the "Governor's March." The toasts continued by honoring the Irish patriot-poet Thomas Moore, which was followed by a rendition of "The Harp that once through Tara's Halls." Next to receive praise was Charles Carrol, of Carrolton, who was from an old American Irish Catholic family and was the last surviving signer of the Declaration of Independence. They also toasted the "Repeal of the Union," a union that fostered "British tyranny" and that destroyed the best interests of Ireland. Andrew McGlinchy, a native of Derry, toasted America, "the land of our adoption," and Ireland, "the land of our nativity," as well as Daniel O'Connell, "the restorer of Ireland of much of her ancient distinction." These were common toasts throughout the mid-nineteenth century. Many others also toasted O'Connell. William Arnold, a native of Cork and the Hibernian Benevolent Society's postmaster, toasted the Repeal of the Union as being "the only salve for the

wounds of the sons of Ireland."[52] Before the soirée ended, a soldier from
Fort Preble in Cape Elizabeth (now South Portland) who was of Irish origin read an ode he had composed for that night:

> Oh, Erin, mavourneen, loved land of my fathers,
> That floats like a gem on the foam of the sea,
> Far, far from the west, o'er the wide waste of waters,
> In sadness my thoughts often wander to thee.
> I think of the brave who once ranged on your mountains,
> I dream of the fair in your valleys that smiled,
> In fancy I stroll by the flowers and fountains,
> That cheered my light footsteps when I was a child.
> Oh, why should I leave those dear scenes of my childhood,
> Why leave the loved land that where the time-hallowed grave,
> Rankly turfed with green grass amid the dark wildwood,
> Affords its last rest to the noble and brave.[53]

Such emotions and Irish pride were aroused that St. Patrick's Day in
1843, combined with the excitement of the national and international
Repeal movement, that the Portland Irish gathered on July 12, 1843 to
officially form a Portland Repeal society. Father Patrick H. O'Beirne of
St. Dominic's Church was elected the chairman and John Crease, printer,
confectioner, writer, convert, and "lay-missionary" at St. Dominic's,
was chosen secretary. At the first meeting, a Mr. J. S. Murphy of Boston
addressed the group, as did a Mr. Abbot and General James Appleton of
Portland.[54]

In October 1843, *The Boston Pilot* printed the names of over eighty
Irish men and women who had donated money to the Portland Repeal
Society. The list gave the county of origin in Ireland for most of the
members, an invaluable piece of information in ascertaining the places
of origin for the Portland Irish at this time. According to various
sources, most of the Irish who had emigrated to America during this era
were from the northern Irish province of Ulster or the eastern coast of
Ireland. This holds true for the Irish in Portland, at least according to
the Repeal list. Derry, Meath, Tyrone, and Cork were the counties most
represented.[55]

Most of the Portland Irish gave a dollar towards Repeal, although
Father O'Beirne of County Leitrim, John Harney of County Waterford,
Philip Quinn of County Donegal, Owen Dirnam of the U. S. Army, and
John Connor of County Wexford, each gave five dollars. A substantial

number of local Irish ladies are mentioned in the list, including Judith McKinn, Ellen Launders (Landers), Mary Shea of Galway, Mary Ann Quinn, Joanna Cassels, Joanna Costello, Julia Connolly, and Catherine Carten—the last three from County Cork. Most of the Irishwomen donated a dollar, while Ann and Ellen Turner each gave two dollars.[56]

As was often the case with many Irish-American efforts to aid the "ould" country, Irish domestics and laborers contributed an enormous sum. Many of the Portland Irish listed in *The Boston Pilot* were indeed laborers and maids, but the list also provided the names of many of the early prominent Irish Catholics of Portland. These included Philip Cassidy (for whom Cassidy's Hill—near Portland's Western Cemetery—is named); Philip Quinn, a grocer and owner of the O'Connell House on Fore Street; Barney Daley (Daly), a labor contractor from Galway; John Haggerty, a Derry tailor; John Landers; Alice Landers; Lawrence Mullen; Thomas Owen; Michael Kelly; Thomas Haaffe; John Carten; Bernard Brannigan; Anthony Devine; Dennis McCarty; Francis and Andrew Larkin; William Arnold; Thomas Rice; Patrick Geehan; Manus Ward; James McKinn (Mackin); and John Connor.[57]

Throughout 1843 huge political rallies, or "monster meetings," were being held in Ireland in support of the Repeal movement, in which thousands of Repealers met to listen to Daniel O'Connell and other orators. One meeting in Castlebar, County Mayo had an attendance estimated at anywhere from 150,000 to 400,000, at least according to Repeal newspapers. One could find food and non-alcoholic drinks sold at these meetings. The Irish temperance priest, Father Mathew, while not directly involved in or endorsing Repeal, had enormous support. It is said that six million Irish people (out of an estimated population of eight million) had taken the temperance pledge by 1843.[58] Repeal wardens, led by Tom Steele, O'Connell's chief aide, controlled the throngs of Irish peasants who came to these meetings carrying branches and small trees ("the green bough of liberty"), and wearing green ribbons in their hats, coats, or around their necks.[59]

By September 1843, the Portland Repeal Society had sent $105 to Dublin.[60] But a month later the movement suffered a major blow when Daniel O'Connell was arrested for seditious oratory and then sentenced on May 30, 1844, to a year in prison. Later O'Connell became embroiled in internal difficulties among the Repealers. Thomas Francis Meagher, who had recently become a leader in the movement, and others, wanted total Repeal, and they would do anything to achieve their goal, even stage an armed uprising. O'Connell was strictly against violence. Meagher and his associates, including John Blake Dillon, William Smith O'Brien, and John Mitchel, became known as "Young Irelanders." O'Connell declared he was for "Old Ireland" and thought Old Ireland would stand behind him. But the Liberator's time had passed him by before he even noticed. He died a broken man in Genoa, Italy, on his way to Rome, in May 1847, during the year known as "Black '47," one of the worst years of the Great Potato Famine. It is not known what effect this internecine strife had on the Maine Repealers. It is known that by 1848 the movement had lost much of its steam in Portland and elsewhere in Maine.[61]

EARLY TEMPERANCE ORGANIZATIONS

St. Dominic's Catholic Church was the focal point of all the early Irish organizations in Portland. As already noted, the prominent communicants of this church were quite active in the Hibernian Benevolent Society of Portland. Sometime in 1842, St. Dominic's pastor Father Patrick H. O'Beirne formed a Catholic temperance society in Portland, known as the Catholic Total Abstinence Society. In January 1843, Patrick Donahue, senior editor of *The Boston Pilot*, "paid a visit to his friends" in Portland and was warmly greeted by Father O'Beirne. Donahue said that O'Beirne, whom he called "the respected and zealous Catholic Pastor," was "beloved and esteemed by all denominations in the city of Portland, and the wondrous success that has followed his exertions in behalf of temperance in that city, had endeared him to the whole community."[62] Donahue attended services at St. Dominic's and later attended a temperance sermon given by O'Beirne. At the end of the sermon, the Boston editor witnessed 250 people take the temperance pledge from Father O'Beirne, who "admonished them to adhere to it through life as the surest talisman of happiness and prosperity."[63]

George H. Shirley, a Maine temperance leader, reviewed the progress of the temperance movement in Portland for the year 1842 and up to and including February 28, 1843. On March 4, 1843, six weeks after Donahue's visit, a local newspaper published a report on the progress of Portland's temperance societies, which had been supplied to it by Shirley. The report on the Catholic Total Abstinence Society was very positive, reaffirming Donahue's earlier comments on Father O'Beirne. The paper noted that the society had about 260 members and that O'Beirne, president of the society, offered the pledge the first Sunday of each month.[64]

> He [Father O'Beirne] knew of not more than *twelve* in his little community that had not signed the pledge. Many notorious drunkards had been reclaimed; he knew of but *three* such at the present time among them. They had but *two* Rumsellers, and one of them seems inclined to give up the business! 'Sobriety,' he considered 'the first step to perfection.'[65]

One wonders if the rumseller that Father O'Beirne was referring to was Philip Quinn (1798-1853), a native of Donegal, who operated the "O'Connell House," a boardinghouse and grocery on Fore Street, from the 1830s until the 1850s. When Patrick Donahue stayed in Portland in January 1843, he stayed at Quinn's establishment. Donahue called Quinn a "warm-hearted host" and declared that the "sunshine of his countenance is always upon his guests, and his best efforts given to secure their comfort."[66] Philip Quinn came to Portland in his twenties and soon operated a retail shop on Exchange Street. He was an active member of the Hibernian Benevolent Society of Portland (he was vice president in 1839), the Portland agent for *The Boston Pilot* for some time, owned considerable property, and was regarded as an influential communicant of St. Dominic's Church.[67] But Quinn also had a bumpy ride in Portland.

Philip Quinn became one of the many Irishmen in Portland who sold liquor on the sly, as a semi-prohibition law had been passed in Maine in 1846, making it illegal to sell liquor locally. Quinn was brought before the local courts innumerable times for "rumselling"; and in 1848 a local temperance newspaper called him "one of the most incorrigible Rumsellers in this city."[68] The paper also stated that Quinn "persists in selling rum; and the reason is probably to be found in his own habits of drinking. He is an Irishman of considerable property, and will probably keep on selling and drinking until he is ruined."[69] Quinn, using his native Irish wit, accused Neal Dow, the Czar of Temperance in Maine who fought a fanatical battle against rumsellers, especially Irish rumsellers, of trying to "get all his money away for fines, and make a beggar of him."[70] Ironically, Philip Quinn had an insurance policy on his "O'Connell House" property to Neal Dow for at least $1,500 as collateral security. Dow received "full satisfaction" of the mortgage deed on the Fore Street property in 1843.[71] Quinn continued to have many battles in court in the next several years. On July 4, 1853, he disappeared from his home, and after a two-week search, he was found floating in Portland harbor, near Fort Preble.[72] Philip Quinn had led a paradoxical existence in his twenty-odd years in Portland, hovering between respectability and disrepute, and died tragically. His story is echoed many times over in the history of the nineteenth-century Portland Irish.

Patrick Donahue, friend of Father O'Beirne and Philip Quinn, was one of those remarkable Irishmen that grew up in the United States in the first half of the nineteenth century and became quite affluent. His father brought him to America when he was ten and he was apprenticed to the printing business at an early age. Many Boston newspapers employed Donahue before he became a co-editor and publisher of *The Boston Pilot.*[73] He was a staunch supporter of Father Mathew and his temperance cause, as well as most American and Irish movements of the 1800s. A merchant banker, Donahue "made and lost several fortunes" and was at one time regarded as "the richest and most influential Catholic in New England."[74] He and Henry L. Devereux began publication of the *Pilot* in 1834, a Catholic newspaper originally known as *The Jesuit* or *The Sentinel*, started by Bishop Fenwick.[75] This early newspaper was held in high esteem by the Portland Irish, and most Catholic households in Portland subscribed to it in the mid-1800s or at least read the latest edition. In 1843, Patrick Donahue, during one of his visits to the Portland Irish, remarked on their hospitality and literate status:

> The Irishmen of Portland are noble representatives of their generous country, and meet the stranger with that welcome,—the heart in the head—which an Irishman only knows how to extend. But we suspect they will not permit us to call ourselves strangers, for we were assured by those who never saw us before, that they were perfectly well acquainted with us, and that for years they had a weekly glimpse of the better part of us,—and that was the *Pilot.* They would not admit of our considering ourselves in that light, and every where received us as an old friend, with the warmth and fervor that distinguish the Irish heart.[76]

It is not known how long the Catholic Total Abstinence Society of Portland lasted. Accounts of its activities after the mid-1840s can not be located. The Portland Irish had more pressing concerns during this period when friends and relatives were dying on almost a daily basis in Ireland, as pestilence and famine ravished an already highly impoverished country. When Father James Maguire became pastor of St. Dominic's Catholic Church in 1846, the parish contained a thousand individuals. In 1847, "Black '47," some 500 Irish became communicants of the church.[77] Escaping famine, disease, callous landlords, an extremely ineffective land system, and an oppressive government, they found solace and security in Portland.

THE GREAT HUNGER (IRISH POTATO FAMINE)

The Great Irish Potato Famine, often called the Great Hunger (*An Gorta Mor*, in Gaelic Irish), was not, in the true sense of the word, a famine at all. Although some have called it nothing short of genocide, perpetrated by heartless men within the British government, it is a fact that Ireland had plenty of food in the mid- to late 1840s. The vast majority of the Irish depended on the potato for their very existence. The potato, a member of the nightshade family that also includes the tomato, reached Ireland in the late sixteenth century. It was used as a supplementary vegetable by all classes throughout Ireland, but by 1800, it had become a staple food of the poorer groups, such as the cottier (agricultural laborer) class.[78] About six million people out of a country of over eight million came to subsist on the potato, while their other crops, such as wheat, barley, and oats, and their cattle, sheep, and pigs, were all raised to pay the rent. These were subsequently sent to England and all parts of the British Empire to feed either the British people or British soldiers and diplomats stationed in India, Africa, Australia, South America, and elsewhere around the world.[79] For such a large population dependent on one crop, a crop that failed countless times in the past, it was inevitable that complete disaster would eventually occur.

Potato blight was an old story with the Irish. The potato crop had failed in part or in its entirety, in various locales in Ireland, in 1728, 1739, 1740, 1770, 1800, 1807, 1821, 1822, 1830, 1831, 1832, 1833, 1834, 1835, 1836, and 1837. The potato crop was also lost or failed in parts of Ireland in 1839, 1841, and 1844.[80] "Curl" and "dry rot" were the two commonest potato diseases. But starting in 1845–1846, an unknown blight caused by a fungus, which is now known as *Phytophthora infestans*, would shortly bring death to more than a million Irish people.[81]

Although the poorer Irish came to subsist largely on the potato, it was a great source of protein and nutrients. It contained important mineral elements such as iron, nitrogen, calcium, magnesium, sulfur, chlorine, and potassium. The potato was easily prepared, and with salt and buttermilk added to it, the vegetable prevented scurvy, helped build and maintain strong teeth, and supplied the daily dosages of energy needed to work the fields and care for the farm animals.[82] Visitors to Ireland often remarked in their journals of the Irishman's fine, strong, muscular build, and of the Irishwoman's beauty, which they invariably attributed to the potato diet. Arthur Young, a nineteenth-century traveler to Ireland, estimated that a barrel of potatoes containing roughly 280 pounds would feed a family of five for a week. This was the equivalent of eight pounds of potatoes a day for the average person and twelve to fourteen pounds a day for the father of an Irish family.[83] When Irish newspapers informed their readers that the potato crop at the start of the summer of 1845 appeared to be healthy, there must have been a collective sigh of relief perhaps even heard in England, where the Prime Minister, Sir Robert Peel, clenched his teeth in anticipation of anything that might occur to disrupt his empire. A Portland newspaper had carried an item a year earlier in which it was predicted that potatoes were "likely to be scarce in Ireland" the ensuing year and reported a drought that had "much impaired the yield of various crops and produced much anxiety among the farmers."[84] However, the reports in Ireland at the beginning of the season did appear optimistic. Unfortunately, that changed by the end of the summer. In August, blight appeared on the Isle of Wight that began to cause some concern. Subsequently, things only grew worse.[85]

It is not within the scope of this essay to expand on the Great Hunger, but some more highlights will be given to help the reader better understand this tragic epoch in Irish history that changed not only Ireland, but England, Canada, Australia, and America forever. Ironically, the Irish potato blight inadvertently came from America that summer of 1845, via European-bound vessels.[86] It spread throughout Ireland and Europe, but it devastated only Ireland. Sir Robert Peel privately acknowledged that Ireland seemed to be on the edge of a major disaster by October 1845.[87] The potato fungus would attack the leaves of the plant first, then spread to the actual potato. Almost immediately, the entire plant would decompose, "the potatoes withering, turning black and finally rotting, during which process a putrid smell emitted from them."[88] Farmers tried every conceivable measure to prevent the blight from spreading and to store as many healthy potatoes as they could find, but to no avail. The pestilence marched on, inadvertently bringing with it human diseases such as cholera, relapsing fever, famine dropsy (like scurvy), typhus, and dysentery.[89]

Tens of thousands died on the roadside, in their homes, along beaches, in the fields with green grass juice running down their faces. They ate anything to survive, from wild mushrooms and roots, seaweed, periwinkles, and sand eels, rotten vegetables and diseased potatoes. Even family pigs and eventually dogs would be consumed. They killed and ate the rats that fed off the dead animals or their dead relatives; the carcasses of diseased cattle were readily devoured.[90] Many took to bloodletting their cattle, whereby a small amount of blood was extracted from the animal and drained into jars to be added to what food was left as a fortifier. Some fried, salted and drank it as is.[91] In much of the country riots broke out as the sick and dying watched their food being shipped out of Ireland under armed guard.[92]

The British Government initially set up soup kitchens around Ireland, but these left much to be desired. Sir Robert Peel ordered that Indian corn (maize) from America be purchased and sent to the Irish. Many of the Irish did receive the maize, but few knew how to cook it, and many died a painful death by acute indigestion. One high point was the successful aid the Quakers, or Society of Friends, gave the sufferers. They set up the Central Relief Committee in Dublin in 1846 and from there many beneficial plans were formed.[93] But the British Government, after a few more half-hearted attempts to help the Irish, fell back on a policy they held dear to their hearts, whether they be Whig or Tory, i.e., *laissez-faire*, or free enterprise capitalism. This theory was the belief that the government should interfere as little as possible in private enterprise and in anything not directly related to the government. This system "gave the employer and the landlord freedom to exploit his fellow men."[94] Cecil Woodham-Smith best analyzed *laissez-faire* as it related to Ireland in her classic study of the Famine, *The Great Hunger*:

> The influence of *laissez faire* on the treatment of Ireland during the famine is impossible to exaggerate. Almost without exception the high officials and politicians responsible for Ireland were fervent believers in non-interference by Government, and the behavior of the British author-

ities only becomes explicable when their fanatical belief in private enterprise and their suspicions of any action which might be considered
Government intervention are borne in mind . . . The loss of the potato
crop was therefore to be made good . . . by the operations of private enterprise and private firms, using the normal channels of commerce . . . there
was to be "no disturbance of the ordinary course of trade." [95]

Perhaps the most malignant carrying-out of *laissez-faire* imaginable
was perpetrated by Charles Edward Trevelyan. As permanent head of
the British Treasury, Trevelyan did absolutely everything in his power
to not only not interfere during the course of the Great Hunger, but to
deny almost every scheme or act that might help Ireland. In 1846
Trevelyan blamed the Famine on the people themselves, whom he
called "selfish, perverse and turbulent." He cried that God Himself had
carried out retribution on the Irish. God was conveniently solving the
problem of Irish over-population and of Irish nationalism. Trevelyan
said of the Famine, "being altogether beyond the power of man, the cure
had been applied by the direct stroke of an all-wise Providence in a matter as unexpected and as unthought of as it is likely to be effectual."
Trevelyan decided to wait it out; he pitied the poor Irish who were ignorant of the fact that they "are suffering from an affliction of God's providence." [96] Sir Charles Trevelyan apparently did not figure the American
Irish into the equation, who, along with their non-Irish friends in the
United States, sent thousands of dollars in aid to their long-suffering kin.

Famine relief societies were formed all over the United States during
the Great Hunger. Mayor Josiah Quincy of Boston collected $50,000 in
that city for famine relief. The New York Relief Committee raised over
$100,000 in one month alone in 1847. Everywhere, the Irish and their
friends did what they could to help the sufferers in the Old Country. In
Washington, D.C., the vice president and members of Congress held a
public meeting for famine relief. Two American men-of-war set sail for
Ireland laden with supplies. Railroad and canal companies, not overlooking the fact that their enterprises had become so successful due to
the brawn of Irish men, carried relief packages free of charge.[97] Portland,
Maine, was no exception. Although they did not do nearly as much as
they would during the 1880 Irish Famine, Portlanders did come together
to help the sufferers to some degree.

In February 1847, a gentleman simply signing his name as "A
Subscriber" sent an eloquent plea to a local newspaper to beg everyone

so inclined to aid the sick and dying in Ireland. He wanted space enough in the papers to "ask our good fellow citizens, in the midst of our prosperity, to listen for a moment to the piercing cry of distress that reaches us from our fellow men across the water."[98] The subscriber went on:

> Surely it is not the spirit of Portland to slumber with the death cry of a starving people ringing in their ears, however remote that people may be, so long as they are not beyond the reach of philanthropic aid. I need not particularize. Enough is known of the *great distress for food* in Ireland, to arouse to action the liberal benevolence and diffusive charity which is so essential a characteristic of our people, and I believe all that is needed to set the good work going on, is for some one to start it—and who shall do it but the press? Will you not, then, come out, in company with all your brethren of the Press in the city, and call for an organized effort?[99]

The gentleman recommended that the local press call to order a public meeting in which citizens from all over southern Maine would meet and contribute to famine relief. He also assumed churches and philanthropic societies would "swell the amount" of the collections. He thus believed that "thousands will be saved from a lingering death by starvation, and live to pray for a blessing on us and our future prosperity, and the blessing of God shall indeed and in truth attend us and our interests."[100]

His call was apparently heeded. On February 26, 1847, several concerned individuals met at Portland City Hall, in the Mayor's Room, to discuss the famine in Ireland and Scotland. A relief committee was formed with William Swan, Esq., as president, and Benjamin Kingsbury, Jr., as secretary. Then a committee was appointed to receive the relief collections, which they would begin to gather on the first Sunday of March. The Collections committee included several prominent Portland Protestants such as John Mussey, Ether Shepley, William Swan, Joshua Osgood, Jedediah Jewett, and Byron Greenough, and influential Irish-Catholic citizen John Connor.[101] A motion was then made and passed, *viz.*, "That the Committee be authorized to receive and take charge of such contributions for the relief of the people of Ireland and Scotland, as may be forwarded to their care from other towns in this State."[102] The Committee hoped that after a substantial amount of contributions had been received, a ship could sail directly "from some port in Maine" and make its way to Ireland. It is interesting to note that those suffering from a famine in Scotland were included in the collections. Scotland did endure some troubles at the time, but they paled in comparison to the carnage being carried out in Ireland.

Thousands of Irish died on their way to America from Ireland, aboard so-called "coffin" ships. Conditions aboard these British ships were so terrible that a definition of their moniker is superfluous. Unsanitary, filth-ridden conditions, little or no edible food, long periods contained in the bowels of the ship (where one could hardly breathe), relentless storms, and a trip that took anywhere from three weeks to three months greatly speeded up the journey to the Afterlife for untold numbers of Irish emigrants. In 1847, 98,105 emigrants left Great Britain and Ireland and booked passage for Canada. Of that total, 5,293 died at sea, 8,072 perished shortly after arriving at Grosse Isle, the main disembarkation point in Canada and a quarantine station, and Quebec, and 7,000 died in and around Montreal. The numbers are astonishing. One Irish emigrant in every four succumbed on the way from Ireland or within six months after his or her arrival in Canada.[103] Joseph E. F. Connolly, a Portland lawyer and judge in the early twentieth century, wrote of these hardships for a history of St. Dominic's Church published in 1909:

> Hundreds of thousands of Irishmen with death from starvation staring them in the face took ship for America. Thousands of them were only exchanging a death from famine for that from ship fever and suffocation. They crowded aboard those ill-fitted emigrant ships that became sailing sepulchres before they reached their destined ports. Goose Island (sic), formed by the parting waters of the St. Lawrence, contains the graves of forty thousand of those poor Irish Emigrants of "47." A half acre of land in Montreal whose only mark of identification till lately was a huge rough boulder, contains the mouldering remains of six thousand more of those poor exiles of that Black "47".[104]

With so many dying on the way to America, a social problem soon became greatly apparent. Countless families were broken up and many children were left as orphans. Hundreds of young Irish boys and girls were left homeless in the area of Grosse Isle and adopted by local Catholic families, in mostly French communities.[105] The founder and editor of the *Portland Pleasure Boat*, Jeremiah Hacker, informed his readers of a Catholic priest named Father Harper who, after learning of a number of orphans in and around Grosse Isle, went there and inquired about the children. He was afterwards given permission to take fifty children and place them in homes in his parish. The priest was able to continue this work for some time. The editor wrote an editorial at the time that must have ruffled a few feathers. He said that he was not in favor of one religious sect over any other and repudiated the Protestants who "fear, or pretend to fear, that if more of them [Catholics] are permitted to land on our shores the country will be ruined." Hacker said that Protestants better first read of the story of Father Harper, before they "say more against Catholicism—To me, one *ism* appears quite as good as another." The editor said that man is still "the carnal man," no matter of what religion, possessed of "the spirit of Cain, and in the midst of religious offerings is ready to slay him who walks after a purer spirit." He said that he "had repeatedly advertised for orphan children who needed homes, and only one single family in all this protestant city has offered to befriend any of them." Hacker was in anguish over the fact that "not a single priest" in Portland had spoken to him about the orphans. The editor begged the citizens to help the orphans of the city by imploring, "Two orphan girls are now in want of a home: who will take them?"[106] Jeremiah Hacker did not make a lot of friends in Portland. A native of Brunswick and a member of the Society of Friends, Hacker operated his newspaper, which had a wide circulation, until the early 1860s.

Twenty-five years after he printed his unkind remarks about Protestants and others, a history of newspapers in Maine had choice words to print about him. Hacker's paper, it said, "dealt with great severity with what it claimed to be abuses in the religious, political, and moral customs of society." Hacker "had no civil words to spare for any man or cause that did not put their oars through the rowlocks of his Boat. It sailed on a turbulent sea."[107] When he began to make bold statements in opposition to "all military movements" at the beginning of the Civil War, he was practically forced to discontinue his newspaper, and he then moved to New Jersey.[108] But Hacker did have a point. Although most Irish orphans were taken in by family members or family friends, many were not. There would not be a Catholic orphanage in Portland for another generation.

FATHER MATHEW, TEMPERANCE,
AND PROHIBITION

As the Repeal movement died an inglorious death and the Irish of the Great Hunger continued to pour into Maine, another movement had been gaining momentum for years. Father Theobald Mathew, of County Tipperary gentry stock, had spent the 1840s traveling throughout the British Isles preaching total abstinence, declaring it would reduce crime and vice, and even be good for the political conflict in Ireland:

> The pledge I ask you to take does not enslave, it makes free. The fewer passions that rule us the freer we are, and no man is so free as the man who places himself beyond and out of reach of temptation, for 'those who court danger shall perish therein.' The freedom I advocate is one you can obtain without any sacrifice of health, of pleasure, of money, or of comfort. On the contrary, it will add to your health, your wealth, your pleasure and your comfort. Temperance brings blessing for eternity.[109]

In early July 1849 Father Mathew was in New York and soon after in Boston. A local newspaper reported his reception in Boston, where the governor and other dignitaries met him. In a few days, the "old hero in the war with King Alcohol" would stay with Most Rev. John B. Fitzpatrick, the third bishop of Boston. The paper declared that "we must have him in Portland," and unless it had already been taken care of, "our temperance Associations should see to it at once."[110] In early August it was announced that Father Mathew would visit Gardiner, Maine.[111] In September the good priest was in Providence, where he gave the temperance pledge to eight hundred.[112] In October the *Eastern Argus* was overjoyed when they stated:

> Fr. Mathew Coming—We are happy to announce that Fr. Mathew will be in Portland on the 25th inst. He cannot remain with us long, as he is to be at Bangor on the 28th. He proposes also to spend several days with the Indians in that section. We trust our city authorities will make preparations for a fitting reception.[113]

The various temperance organizations, as well as the Irish groups, prepared for Mathew's visit, but he never came. He would not be the last Irish celebrity who announced they would visit Portland, and not show, due to pressing matters elsewhere. Father Mathew was suffering from partial paralysis of his left side the last week of October, and was in Connecticut by the first week of November. The press said the Catholic crusader planned to spend the winter in the southern United States.[114]

Fr. Mathew admonished that drinking caused revelries, rows, idleness, and unthriftiness, and added to the Irish peoples' already impoverished state due to English misrule.[115] Another Mainer who felt as Mathew did, but who was not perceived by the Irish as being so kind, was Neal Dow, the "Father of the Maine Law." When the renowned author Anthony Trollope visited America, he stopped in Portland, roughly equating Portland harbor with Cork harbor in Ireland. He also called Neal Dow "the Father Mathew of the State of Maine."[116] James Mundy calls Dow "the Grand Poohbah of temperance" and states that Dow's name "became a curse on Irishmen's lips."[117] He was the author of the highly acclaimed "Maine Law" (as it was called) passed in 1851 as the first true prohibition law in the United States. It forbade the manufacture and sale of spirituous liquors not intended for mechanical or medicinal purposes. An earlier experimental prohibition act had been passed in Maine in 1846. As we saw with the sad case of Philip Quinn, the business of selling liquors on the sly was quite a profitable endeavor, but also a hazardous one. Many Portland Irish families rose up out of poverty due to the benefits of selling rum and other liquors in small, private rooms or in large grocery stores that posed as fronts for grog shops. Their children and grandchildren became prosperous and proper folk, with a law degree, a doctorate, a nursing degree, or a professional license of one kind or another. The initial finances it took to send their sons and daughters to private schools and colleges almost always came from bootlegging.

Unfortunately, many an Irish liquor dealer succumbed to his or her own products. Naturally, Neal Dow and his minions singled out the Irish for their selling and consuming of spirits. Irishmen and Irishwomen were almost always arrested, indicted, and convicted for selling rum and for drunkenness. If you had money for sureties, you could quickly remove yourself from jail. But most Irish invariably ended up doing thirty days or more in the county jail for being a habitual drunkard or on a "search and seizure" charge (liquors found on their property "proven" to be intended for sale). For instance, John Fleming and John Thornton both had to pay $6.17 "for getting drunk and making a disturbance" one Saturday night in 1866.[118] Another Irishman "indulged in a glorious drunk," but could not pay the four dollars and costs, so was immediately sent to jail.[119] In 1874, Michael Hogan and Sarah Brackett were each indicted for being "common sellers of intoxicating liquors," and both fined $100 and costs, which they paid.[120] Also in 1874, Patrick Plunkett was brought before the Superior Court after appealing a decision made against him on a charge of "search and seizure" in the Municipal Court. The Portland Police had seized two gallons of whiskey on his property, but Plunkett testified that he had purchased *four* gallons of whiskey, which had been prescribed by a doctor for his sick wife, and didn't sell any of it. The Superior Court upheld the lower court's guilty verdict.[121] Plunkett's defense attorney was the locally well-known Irish-born trial lawyer James O'Donnell. As one might imagine, many did not have the money to pay their fines.

It is true that Portland, like all major urban centers of the nineteenth century, had its fair share of crime, which was often induced by strong drink, especially when committed by Irish individuals. But the Portland Yankees clearly singled out the Irish for prosecution and commented negatively on them *ad nauseam* in their newspapers and journals. The Portland Irish and their susceptibility to alcoholism, their alleged low emotional intelligence (their tendency to act on emotion rather than reason), and their peculiar ways in both religious and social customs, was endless grist for local journalists well into the twentieth century.

NATIVISM AND THE KNOW-NOTHINGS

Neal Dow and his fanatical battle against Demon Rum only precipitated the onslaught of a nasty time in Maine and American history if you were foreign, especially if you were Irish Catholic. The Portland Irish soon became caught in the middle of the battle against "King Alchy" and the extremes of the Know-Nothing troubles of the mid-1850s. Animosity, to say the least, had existed between the Celt and the Anglo-Saxon for seven hundred years. Periodically, in America, the Saxons, now in the form of Yankees, renewed hostilities. The "native" Americans could digest small groups of Irish people, as they had before the 1820s. However, when hordes of Irish people, bringing with them disease, vice, filth, hostility, and crime, as the Yankees claimed, began pouring into the United States in unprecedented numbers, especially after 1845, "real" Americans had had enough.

As early as 1844 in Portland, one could sense the animosity, even the hatred, that some Yankee Portlanders felt towards the Irish. When *The Boston Pilot* wrote an editorial questioning the bravery of "native" Americans, saying, "every native ought to belong to a Peace Society,"[122] a Portland newspaper went on the defensive with a scathing editorial:

It is high time that a check were put to the impudence of foreigners. The work-houses and pest-holes of Europe boil over, and the scum is driven to the shores of America. Must we receive such materials into our arms to be stung and destroyed by them? Many American citizens have become so much incensed at the course pursued by foreigners, that they have resolved never to give them employment. It is true, they have the balance of power in their hands, and it belongs to them to decide who will be our rulers. Something must be done and rapidly, or we shall soon be completely under foreign influence, and obliged to acknowledge the Pope of Rome as the head of our nation. The God of Heaven preserve us from such a curse.[123]

And this was before the Great Potato Famine, which began a year later. The "God of Heaven preserve us from such a curse" indeed!, the Irish must have thought after reading a piece like that. Many Irish must have known that things were getting worse each year and they started to brace themselves for the inevitable boiling point.

In May 1848 a "native riot" broke out in Portland in which *The Boston Pilot* announced that all the principal "actors from the mother downwards were of the native school in politics and religion."[124] In March 1849, a week before St. Patrick's Day, another riot occurred in which an Irishman was left nearly dead. In fact a local paper was a little too quick to announce that "HE IS DEAD! The Irishman who was struck with a club, one night last week, in Fore Street, died at the Alms House on Tuesday from the effects of the blow. Has his murderer been arrested?"[125] The next day they had to retract their statement. "NOT DEAD—The man struck on the head in the riot on Fore Street last week, is fast resting from the injury received."[126] *The Boston Pilot* declared that this particular riot had been brought on by local prejudice against the Irish.[127]

The Boston Pilot also commented on the murder of Irishman Matthew Kincannon (probably Concannon) a few weeks later in Hallowell, Maine.[128] It appeared that "Mathew Kin'Kennan," as a local paper called him, was "stabbed on the front of the thigh by some one of a party of five or six Americans which caused his death in about ten minutes."[129] A jury of inquest found that Kincannon had succumbed to a wound that nearly severed his femoral artery in his right leg, inflicted with a dirk knife "willfully and felonously" by Samuel L. Blanchard. Blanchard, along with Elijah Barter, George Runnells, and John and Henry Leeman, had led "an aggravated and unprovoked assault upon several Irishmen" in the town of Hallowell.[130] It is not known what happened to these gentlemen, but obviously almost everyone, including the authorities, believed that the murder had been brought on by bigoted "native" Americans who were bent on smashing a few immigrants' heads, namely Irishmen. There were many more similar incidents across Maine in the late 1840s and early 1850s, but things still had not come to a head.

The inevitable boiling point came five years later, in 1854, when the Order of the Star-Spangled Banner (the American Party) was formed, a secretive political society against foreigners, Catholics, and especially the Irish. They became known as the "Know-Nothings," because when any member was asked questions about their organization, they would always reply "I know nothing."[131] Many prominent Americans were members, and they almost took over the political structure of the nation for a brief time. Many of the lower-class members wreaked particular havoc across the country. Portland did not escape the turmoil. According to local historian Allan R. Whitmore, some Protestants in Portland in 1854 believed that "secret Irish military companies" were forming and that some liberal-minded Protestants were joining them. Father John O'Donnell, pastor of St. Dominic's Church, began to grow uneasy, especially after he found it unsafe to walk the streets after dark. Even well-respected Portlanders "were seriously deliberating imagined dark designs of Irish-Catholics; nativist councils regularly assembled to develop defensive plans." In what today sounds ludicrous, Portland Protestants even spread a wild rumor that Father John O'Donnell had made a trip to Boston and returned with heavy boxes "overflowing with poison, which he intended to distribute to servant girls who would thus murder entire Protestant families on an already selected night to which wily Catholics referred only by a Latin password."[132] And with such a large number of Irish girls being employed as domestic maids, not a few Protestants refused to drink tea for some time. On June 17, 1854, Father O'Donnell cried out, in a formal letter, against the bigotry in the "City of Elms, the Forest City." He protested the number of societies that were formed "for the avowed purpose of persecuting Irishmen." O'Donnell, whose letter was printed in several newspapers, stated that "telegraph reports, grave newspaper articles and fanatical lectures are posted in public places, read in stores and counting rooms," and also placed in the work-shops where many Irish had gainful employment.[133]

Bigotry and prejudice against Irish Catholics in Portland reached a high that summer of 1854 when several young men threw rocks at Father O'Donnell, children hissed and cursed him, and the doors of St. Dominic's were stove in and smeared with horse manure. When in October someone launched a rock through O'Donnell's study, barely missing him, the priest went to the Mayor to seek some protection. After that a watchman, on the payroll of the city, was positioned near the church each night.[134]

The Know-Nothing movement came to a head in Maine with the tarring and feathering of Father John Bapst of Ellsworth and the burning of two Catholic churches in Ellsworth and Bath. (See gallery, plates 29–30.) The movement eventually subsided, but not until many Catholics were visibly and emotionally scarred. Portland did not see as much violence as some other Maine communities, and nothing compared to what erupted in some American cities. In any case, the Portland Catholics did decide to lay low in the 1850s, as there were very few Irish societies in Portland during that decade.

IRISH CATHOLIC SOCIAL AND POLITICAL ORGANIZATIONS

The most popular and perhaps only Catholic society in Portland in the 1850s was the Young Catholic Friends Society. The group tended to the needs of incoming immigrants, raised money for St. Dominic's through fairs and picnics, and held annual excursions to the islands of Casco Bay. Even many Protestants, before, during, and after the Know-Nothing troubles, attended many of these events. The great entrepreneur John Bundy Brown, owner of the Portland Sugar House, attended one such event in 1851. It is a shame he didn't comment more about it in his journal to allow us to learn what an important business magnate in Portland may have felt about the sectarian division then raging within Maine. On Wednesday, June 18, 1851, Brown wrote, "Weather very pleasant. Catholic picnic to the islands to-day . . ."[135] John Bundy Brown employed innumerable Irishmen at his sugar factory and also employed Irish maids, coachmen, and gardeners, such as Patrick Duffy, who later became the superintendent of Evergreen Cemetery in Portland.[136] In later years Brown kept an exact account of what his Irish employees did for him on his property and how much they received for such employment. For instance, Pat Noon received pay in the amount of $31.88 for twenty-one days of labor on Brown's farm in the 1860s.[137]

One of the most popular social events with the Portland Irish throughout the 1850s was the Erina Ball, usually sponsored by the Young Catholic Friends Society. It was almost always held each year on St. Patrick's Day Eve or the actual day. In 1859, the ball was held under the auspices of the Union Glee Club, at Lancaster Hall. Tickets were $1 and could be had by contacting the Committee of Arrangements, which included such local Irishmen as James McMaine (McMain), William Melaugh, John H. Mullen, David W. Kennedy, James Rooney, and William Dyer. Morse's Quadrille Band provided the music. This 1859 ball was "the largest and most brilliant of the season," according to a reporter for the *Portland Advertiser.* "The dancing was kept up with great spirit—in fact the company did not break up until 'St. Patrick's day in the morning' was well merged into the *next* morning."[138]

From the 1860s until the close of the century, myriad Irish organizations were formed in Portland. The dramatic increase in the number of societies was due to several factors. First, the Portland Irish, especially the families that had been here for at least a generation, were moving up the ladder of success, and many families were quite well off by the 1870s. It was only natural for them to imitate the "well-bred Yankees" by forming their own societies, which served a wide variety of purposes. Second, the population of the Portland Irish had swelled to more than 4,000 by the 1860s, and many different Irish groups, some in direct opposition to each other, were created to attend to the ever-growing population. There is no evidence of groups being formed solely on the basis of county of origin, as was the case in larger cities like New York and Boston. Third, from the 1860s onward, Ireland itself saw unprecedented nationalism that resulted in many Irish causes, movements, and societies. These societies were duly formed all over Ireland and America in the latter half of the nineteenth century.

Nationally, middle-class and upwardly mobile Irish formed the core membership of most Irish-American organizations. This holds true for Portland, and as we will see, members of Portland Irish societies were economically successful Irish who were simultaneously devout Catholics and ardent nationalists. There were, of course, poorer Irish who joined these groups, but the leadership of the societies was almost exclusively so-called "lace-curtain Irish." Many had arrived in this country poor, but had eventually built themselves a secure niche in Portland by entering various trades such as grocer, labor contractor, trader, mason, clothier, boilermaker, baker, blacksmith, undertaker, carpenter, harnessmaker, tailor, plasterer, or upholsterer. The Portland Irish men, many of whom were eventually successful, also became waiters, seamen, hackmen, bar owners, hostlers, stevedores and long-shoremen, railroad workers, iron founders, cordwainers, watchmen, gardeners, curriers, cooks, peddlers, painters, and hatters. By the end of the nineteenth century many Irish men had also gained employment as lawyers, doctors, booksellers, electricians, policemen, plumbers, postal clerks, barbers, telegraph operators, and firemen. Irish women were, in turn, usually domestic maids, cooks, washerwomen, and press feeders. Many also became boardinghouse keepers, seamstresses, grocers, and fancy goods dealers. By the end of the century we find Irish women who were clerks, teachers, and nurses.[139]

Irish societies in and of themselves promoted and developed Irish consciousness. An ethnic identity was created, separate from, yet a part of the American scene. One historian studied Irish-American organizations in detail and determined that although part of the Irish community was "Americanized," "paradoxically, an examination of these organizations shows that they also embodied many values commonly associated with the dominant Protestant culture. Members of ethnic associations were exhorted to be diligent, temperate, patriotic, and thrifty, to submit to civil authority, to educate themselves and their children, to adopt clean and orderly personal habits, and to be devout Christians." In other words they were urged to become good Americans, following the society's dominant ethics. [140]

From at least 1850 on, many Irish men were directors (managers) of the Protestant Widows' Wood Society in Portland for the Catholic churches. The society was established in 1830 "to furnish fuel during the winter season to destitute widows." It was graciously supported annually by contributions from the religious groups of Portland.

Between 1843 and 1871 the group raised $50,000.[141] Among the many Irish who became directors for the Catholics were Philip Cassidy and Michael Foley for St. Dominic's Church (early 1850s), William Doherty (St. Dominic's) and Hugh Dolan (the Cathedral of the Immaculate Conception) throughout the 1860s, Daniel Leo Bogan (St. Dominic's) and Patrick McGowan (Cathedral) in the 1870s, and Daniel O'Connell O'Donoughue in the 1880s. All of these men were highly successful and well-respected in Portland.[142]

In 1860, a St. Patrick's Society was formed in Portland, for "benevolent objects." They met on January 9, in Wardroom Number 2, to choose officers. P. E. McKeon ("physician and surgeon, R. C. C. E.") was elected president and physician, while Charles McCarthy, Jr. and James McGlinchy were picked for first and second Vice Presidents, respectively.[143] The other "Sundry influential Irishmen of Portland" who comprised the board of officers included Thomas Parker, John Kelly, and Terence McGowan.[144] Again, these men were all successful citizens of Portland. Charles McCarthy, Jr. was a Portland clothier and McGlinchy, brewer, trader, clothier, and grocer, would die at the age of fifty-eight in 1880 as the richest Irishman in the area, with an estate valued at $200,000.[145] Thomas Parker was a prosperous trader and Terence McGowan was the first Catholic bookseller in Portland. They were also ticket agents for all British steamers coming and going from the port of Portland.[146]

It is interesting to note that the St. Patrick's Society held their first meeting in a wardroom. By 1857, many Portland Irish, long ensconced in the Democratic Party, had made forays into local politics. The Portland Democratic Club in 1860 consisted of several local Irish, including Patrick Ward and Philip Cassidy, the only two Irish "Ward Vice-Presidents."[147] It also included influential Irishmen such as Patrick Rafferty, James McGlinchy, Thomas Parker, Terence McGowan, and John Carten. McGowan, McGlinchy, and Carten were members of the Democratic Nominations Committee, organized to select a candidate for mayor. They soon nominated Joseph Howard, who later won the election.[148] James O'Donnell (1817-1886), a Protestant native of Ireland, often spoke at the Democratic Headquarters. He was a trial attorney who frequently defended the Portland Irish and ran unsuccessfully on the Democratic ticket for county attorney in 1852. In March 1860, after forty-year old Thomas Parker spoke eloquently at a Democratic meeting, the Republican evening paper of the city called Parker "the keeper of an Irish grocery, and the candidate for Young Ireland for the Council."[149] The Democrats responded in their paper, *The Impending Crisis*, that they would compare Mr. Parker "with any Republican member of the present city council in point of ability and intelligence." The Democrats were tickled pink that Parker was "unfortunate enough" to have accounts of several years standing with many Republicans at his "Irish grocery," and noted that the Republicans had conveniently overlooked this.[150] Parker and his son Richard did eventually go on to become local politicians.

In April 1863, the Irish American Relief Association was organized in Portland. It was incorporated February 4, 1865 and became one of the most prominent Irish groups in the city throughout the 1860s–1880s. The association sponsored annual balls and St. Patrick's Day celebrations, endorsed noted speakers, and held annual summer trips to Sebago Lake, where the Irish participated in scull races, baseball games, dances, and foot and sack races. For instance, in April 1870, the Irish American Relief Association (hereafter the IARA) held their seventh annual Easter Ball. It was held in City Hall on April 18, 1870, with the floor director being J. E. Marshall, along with assistants E. H. Colman, J. W. Walsh, P. S. Doyle, R. Parker, Peter O'Connor, Maxine Taguet, and E. J. Sisk.[151] Chandler's Full Quadrille Band, under D. H. Chandler, provided the music and the Portland Brass Band performed a concert. Tickets were $1.25 for both performances. Refreshments were served in the Senate Chamber of City Hall. All members of the IARA could obtain tickets from William McAleney's harnessmaking shop.[152] In July 1876, the club held their annual excursion to Lake Sebago, where Chandler's Band again performed music. Attendees could dance a jig to the music of bagpipers and fiddlers, as well as participate in sack, foot, tub, and potato races, do the high jump (the first place jumper won a walking cane), and watch the West End and Atlantic Ball Clubs play each other. The best lady in the archery contest won an album.[153]

One of the first noted speakers to lecture at an Irish American Relief Association meeting was a figure well known to many of the Irish in Portland. The dark-haired, mustached, handsome young man who spoke to the group one night in January 1864 was Colonel Patrick Robert Guiney (1835-1877), who spent his formative years in Gorham's Corner. The Corner was a colorful section of Portland where the Irish had been settling since at least 1823. (See gallery, plate 42.) It was known for its clandestine activities and for its Irish "groggeries." The local papers never tired of reporting the nefarious goings on of the locality and often insisted nothing good ever came out of Gorham's Corner. So the Portland Irish must have been quite proud indeed when Guiney returned to Portland, an Irish boy who had made good. He was an attorney and a colonel in the United States Army who had helped organize the Ninth Massachusetts Volunteers, better known by their nickname, "Boston's Irish Ninth." Born in Parkstown, County Tipperary, Pat had come to Portland with his parents and brothers, where they settled at Cobb's Court. After a brief stint in a factory in Massachusetts, he returned to Portland and was employed in the machine shop of the Portland Company.[154] Inherently intellectual, Guiney left Portland for Worcester where, on October 20, 1854, he entered the College of the Holy Cross. Perhaps the deaths of his brother and father earlier that year finally convinced him his future lay elsewhere. His brother Thomas died on February 21, aged seventeen, due to injuries he received in an Irish row near their home a week earlier. His skull had been so badly injured that the boy had lapsed into a coma.[155] Tom and Pat's father James died on September 1, perhaps of a broken heart. Young Pat was off to college six weeks later. He did return, however, to study law in Portland, was admitted to the bar in 1856, and was an assistant editor of a paper in Lewiston. Then Guiney went back to Massachusetts, where he practiced law, entered local politics, married, and joined the Army in 1861, becoming a colonel in 1863. This had been the current of Patrick Guiney's life when he arrived in Portland in January 1864 to lecture on "The War, its origins, present appearance, and results."[156]

A large crowd gathered at Mechanics Hall on January 11, 1864 to listen to Guiney, who described the movements of the Army of the Potomac from the First Battle of Bull Run until that day. A Democrat-turned Lincoln Republican, he adamantly defended the Emancipation Proclamation and declared "that slavery was at an end, and the rebellion very nearly crushed out."[157] Most of the audience gave thunderous applause, but a few "Copperheads" (Southern sympathizers) huffed out of the room. An increasing number of Irish during the Civil War became virtual Copperheads, such as John Mullaly, a national newspaper editor, who argued that Lincoln was a dictator and the Bill of Rights had been trampled to the ground.[158] But many Irish fought valiantly in the war, in defense of the Union, such as Portlander John E. Downey, of Company D, 16th Maine Volunteers, who was killed at the Battle of Gettysburg July 1, 1863, at the age of twenty-one.[159]

Patrick Guiney's speech was well received, but Guiney himself suffered a great personal tragedy less than four months after his Portland lecture. On May 5, 1864, during the Battle of the Wilderness, he was struck through the eye with a bullet, which lodged in his head. The doctors feared for his life, but since Pat was a strong, clean-living young man, he survived. But he survived only after a fifty-nine-caliber rifle ball was removed from his head. (See gallery, plate 26.) After the war he went on to become Assistant District Attorney for Suffolk County, Register of Probate and Insolvency, an advocate for animals, and Major-General Commander of the Veteran Military League. Due to his wounds in the war, Patrick's life was shortened. He died suddenly in March 1877, aged forty-two. Guiney was the father of noted poet and writer Louise I. Guiney.[160]

Less than a week before St. Patrick's Day 1864, Father John O'Donnell, now Vicar-General of the Portland Diocese, and pastor of the Catholic Church in Nashua, New Hampshire, delivered a lecture before the IARA in Portland's newly finished City Hall. For the price of twenty-five cents, one could hear O'Donnell speak about St. Patrick's life, from his capture by Irish pirates somewhere in Britain, to his conversion to Christianity, and his eventual mission to take the Faith to Ireland. And one could hum along to Irish and American National Airs at the same meeting, performed by the Portland Brass Band.[161] Catholic priests were regular lecturers at IARA meetings, usually in connection with a religious holiday or national event. In the 1870s, Father Patrick Lunney, an assistant at St. Dominic's, broached a heated topic in the nineteenth century: evolution. In a lecture the priest titled "The Speculations of the Present Age," Lunney argued that even if the theory of evolution is true, "it does not disprove a Creator." He gave various points of evidence to make his case.[162] There was plenty of room for controversy that night at the IARA meeting!

Within a year after incorporation, the IARA had built up a sizable library, but it was lost in the Great Fire of July 4, 1866, in which a large part of Portland was reduced to ashes. In the next year the group was busy replenishing their library, with contributions coming in of books and funds. Prominent Portland Yankee, the Honorable Asa W. H. Clapp, donated $50 and the organization duly thanked him in a local newspaper.[163]

Members of the IARA had to pay an initiation fee of $5, followed by monthly dues of twenty-five cents. When a member took sick, they received $3 a week. Upon death, the member's wife, or next of kin, received $50 for funeral expenses. These were the conditions throughout the 1860s-70s. In 1871 the organization had 150 members, with "an invested fund of $2,500."[164] When teamster John Deehan "fell from his seat in a fit to the pavement," while carrying four hogsheads of molasses in his jigger, and was crushed to death, the IARA called for an emergency meeting. William Melaugh, president of the group, announced a special assembly to make arrangements to attend the funeral of their fallen member.[165] No doubt that meeting would also entail appropriating $50 for Deehan's funeral expenses. In this case the money would go to his elderly mother, her son being her sole support. Groups like the IARA were called to act in this way all too often in Portland in the nineteenth century.

There was no ladies' auxiliary of the IARA, but naturally Irish girls and women would have husbands, fathers, brothers, sons, and beaus in the group, so they often did what they could to contribute. In March 1867, a "large party of ladies" presented the organization with two large flags; one was the "Green flag of Erin" and the other the Star-Spangled Banner. After the presentation, the ladies began to play music and soon a fine dance was underway. The next day the flags were displayed above the association's new hall in McCarty's Block for all to see, just in time for St. Patrick's Day.[166]

The Irish American Relief Association was at the forefront of the many movements and causes the Portland Irish were engaged in from the 1860s until about 1890. But then popularity began to wane. William McAleney and Charles McCarthy, Jr. were the last surviving charter members, and the latter's obituary noted that membership had gradually dwindled until, by 1921, it had "ceased to be active other than [as] a business corporation."[167] The organization was largely superseded by the Ancient Order of Hibernians.

PORTLAND'S FENIANS

By 1865 many Portland Irish men had formed at least one local chapter of the Fenians, a group of revolutionary Irishmen who organized to attempt to rid Ireland of English rule once and for all. Officially formed on St. Patrick's Day, 1858, in Dublin, chapters or "circles" were established throughout Ireland, Great Britain, and America. The initial leaders in Ireland were James Stephens, Joseph Denieffe, Thomas Clarke Luby, Michael Doheny, and John O'Mahony.[168] In 1865 the Fenians in America splintered over several issues, including control of its treasury and whether it was feasible to invade Canada, which would cause a major blow to England.[169] In Portland, the Fenians split into two factions, one following the leadership of John O'Mahony, known as the O'Donoughue Circle for its local leader Daniel O'Connell O'Donoughue, and one loyal to national Fenian leader Col. William R. Roberts, known as the Roberts-Sweeny Circle. Harnessmaker William McAleney was the center of the latter group and led many Portland Fenians to St. Albans, Vermont, to participate in an abortive invasion of British North America there.[170] Daniel O'Connell O'Donoughue, a descendant of *the* Daniel O'Connell, was born in Caherciveen, County Kerry, and emigrated to New York about 1860. He served two years with the Army of the Potomac as an engineer. In 1865 he was appointed chief clerk of engineers in the U. S. Engineer's Office on Exchange Street in Portland, a post he held until his death in 1905. After being elected center of the O'Mahony Circle (known locally as the O'Donoughue Circle) of the local Fenians, he was appointed an agent to sell bonds for the hoped-for Irish Republic. On March 5, 1866, he placed the following advertisement in a local paper,

IRISH REPUBLIC,

Bonds in $10, $20, $50, $100, and $500, are now ready for delivery to the general public, redeemable six months after the acknowledgment of Irish Independence with 6 per cent interest, per annum. All orders should be addressed, D. O'C. O'Donoghue, Agent, 26 Free Street, Portland, Me.[171]

Several months later a notice appeared in the newspaper stating that William McAleney had been "appointed agent for the sale of Bonds of the Irish Republic for this city, and they will be for sale at the Grand Fenian Rally to-night."[172]

On March 26, 1866, a Fenian "rally" was held at the Mechanics Hall on Congress Street, with Daniel O'Donoughue (O'Donoghue is the spelling he seemed to use himself) presiding. He made a "stirring speech" and "believed that an Irish Republic virtually existed today, and James Stephens was its President."[173] Several other speakers followed him, including P. O'N. Larkin, fresh from Ireland, and Boston orator John E. Fitzgerald, who had only two years earlier survived the wreck of the *Bohemian*, a British steamer that sank off Cape Elizabeth with the loss of forty-two Irish immigrants. Following the speakers, "resolutions were passed endorsing Stephens and O'Mahoney, and asking for help to procure 50,000 stand of arms for the enrolled army of 200,000 men."[174]

In April 1866, the IARA and the Fenians made plans to welcome Colonel John O'Mahony himself to Portland. The former group planned their annual ball for the night of April 2, and expected O'Mahony to join the festivities. *The Eastern Argus* wrote, "Let there be a grand turn-out of the fairest and bravest of the descendants of those native to the 'gem of the seas'."[175] The next night, the Fenians were to meet at City Hall to hear O'Mahony speak on "Irish Independence." An impressive meeting was held by the Fenians, with several speakers, but O'Mahony did not show. [176] He was detained in New York City, busy with the news that Fenian leader James Stephens was coming to America to help broker peace between the factions of the American Fenians.

The Portland Fenians were active for some time after the failed Canadian invasions at St. Albans, Vermont, Buffalo, New York, and Eastport, Maine. They continued their summer picnics, entertained Irish speakers, and watched closely the goings-on of the national and international Fenians. Further Canadian invasions were planned; hope was not lost yet. In 1867, the Fenian Brotherhood in Ireland staged many local revolts and Fenians were active in a number of plots throughout Great Britain.[177] In June 1868, the Fenians of Portland had another large, impressive meeting at City Hall. Hugh Dolan, a successful local contractor, chaired the meeting. Dolan had replaced McAleney as Center of the Portland wing of the Roberts-Sweeny Circle in April 1867. When he was elected, that circle was said to be in a "flourishing condition."[178] The first speaker of the night was John Rafferty, Esq., of New York, followed by "General" John O'Neil, an American Fenian hero.[179]

The enthusiasm of the audience at the June 18, 1868 City Hall gathering forced O'Neil to stop many times during his speech, and he was barely able to take his seat afterward. When the meeting ended, many in the audience signed up to join the Circle. Then the crowd, with a band, serenaded O'Neil at the Preble House before he retired for the evening.[180] The Portland Fenians, along with other Maine members, issued a proclamation the day O'Neil spoke and inserted it in the newspapers:

> To the Irishmen of Maine. Portland, Me., June 16, 1868.
> Brothers and fellow-countrymen! To-day the Delegates of the Fenian Circles of the State of Maine, met in Convention to hear from our worthy and honored President, Gen. O'Neil, the prospects of the organization. After careful investigation of the affairs and condition of the present movement against British power, we are fully convinced of its feasibility,—and exhort our fellow-countrymen everywhere, to lay aside all issues that divide or distract them in the face of our common enemy; and make one bold, determined and systematic effort to break the shackles that bind our native land. Signed in behalf of the Convention,
> DANIEL A. MEEHAN, Portland.
> WM. McCARTHY, Bangor.
> DANIEL McGILLICUDY, Lewiston.
> JOHN BOLAIRD, Biddeford.
> EDWARD STAFFORD, Hallowell.
> Committee on Address.[181]

Of course the Irish republic would not come for at least another eighty years (1949), but the Portland Irish, along with Irishmen everywhere, were hopeful and confident for many years. The Portland Fenians were still active in 1870, but soon after became defunct.

LATE NINETEENTH-CENTURY ORGANIZATIONS

The 1870s and 1880s was an unprecedented time for Irish organizations in Portland. In the 1870s alone, Portland was home to the St. Patrick's Benevolent Society (founded in December 1869), the Greeley Guards (Montgomery Guards, formed in 1872), the Sheridan Cadets, the Portland Catholic Union (1874), the Ancient Order of Hibernians (organized February 1876), the Grattan Literary Association (organized October 30, 1877), the Celtic Club, the Wolfe Tone Association, the Young Men's Social Club, and the Independent Irish American political party (formed April 30, 1878).[182] In 1878, even a Gaelic prayer meeting group was formed and all were invited "who can understand the Gaelic language."[183] Other groups, while comprised mostly of Irish people, were directly connected to the Catholic Church, particularly either St. Dominic's Church or the Cathedral of the Immaculate Conception, dedicated in 1869 by Bishop David W. Bacon (installed as Portland's first bishop in 1855). These included the Portland Catholic Sunday School Union, the Assumption Sodality, Catholic Temperance Society, the Scapular Sodality of the Cathedral, the Altar Society of St. Dominic's, and the St. Theresa Literary Society. The last mentioned society was popular among the Catholic ladies of Portland. When Portland's second bishop, James A. Healy, returned from Rome in 1878, the society gave a "public literary entertainment" in his honor at Kavanagh Hall. Miss Lucy Leprohon welcomed him home in an address in English, while Miss Addie McAchorn welcomed him in French.[184]

A different kind of Irish organization was the boating-rowing associations created in Portland. They were extremely popular during the last three decades of the nineteenth century. One of the first was the Emerald Boat Club. Many of its members, like most Portland Irish groups, were members of other Irish organizations. They tended to the needs of their brethren much like the other groups. When Michael Noonan died in 1870, the Emerald Boat Club met and passed a number of resolutions on his death and inserted them in the local papers.[185] Other prominent boat or sculling groups at the time included the Cumberland Rowing Association (organized in March 1879), the Union Rowing Company, the Dirigo Boat Club, and the Argonaut Association (organized in October 1883).

By the 1880s and 1890s several Democratic organizations developed that included many Irish Catholics. In the late 1870s many Irish joined the Hancock Democratic Club. By the 1890s they had helped form, command, or joined such groups as the Cleveland Guards, Cleveland Longshoremen's Workingmen's Club, Cleveland Zouaves, Maintopmen, Ingraham Guards, and the Ward 4 Company.[186]

In January 1880, the Hibernians, the IARA, the Celtic Club, the Grattan Literary Society, and the Montgomery Guards invited Charles Stewart Parnell to Portland. Parnell was known as the "Uncrowned King of Ireland," because of his unprecedented efforts in the Land League agitation of the 1880s, but which did not prove as successful as hoped. Parnell accepted the invitation, on condition that troubles in Ireland would not force him to cut short his American trip.[187] When Michael Davitt, another land war agitator and founder of the Land League, was arrested in Ireland, Parnell went home and was unable to come to Portland.

In the 1880s Portland was home to an Irish Relief Committee of 1880 (for yet another famine then ravaging Ireland), an Irish National Land League (formed November 1880), a Ladies Land League, and many Democratic political groups comprised of a great many local Irish people.[188] A National Irish Athletic Association of Portland was active in the mid-1880s, when they held tournaments at Point of Pines.[189]

The 1890s saw the establishment of even more Irish groups, including the Irish American Union, a naturalization society, the Emerald Association, and the Columbian Club, called "one of Portland's leading social organizations" in 1897. Portland even had its own Tammany Hall, with a membership of over one hundred in 1892. They met at their hall at 95 Center Street.[190] The Ancient Order of Foresters of America (formed in Portland in June 1889 by mostly Irish Catholics), the Portland Longshoremen's Benevolent Society (formed in 1880), the St. Vincent de Paul Society, the Knights of Columbus, the Hibernian Cadets and Ladies Auxiliary of the Ancient Order of Hibernians, and several rowing associations and political entities continued to be successful in Portland well into the twentieth century.

THE TWENTIETH CENTURY

By the 1920s the Ancient Order of Hibernians (AOH) were among the only Irish groups still active in Portland, although there was a plethora of church and labor societies. The AOH left the area in the 1940s and did not return until the 1970s. St. Brendan's Associates was formed in Portland in 1961 by Martin J. Norton and was very popular until 1973, the year Norton became sick with age and could find no one to take it over.[191] The Irish-American Club took its place in Portland the same year. Thirty years later, in 2003, it is still quite viable and has a membership of over 600. The latter group and the AOH (Daniel O'Connell O'Donoughue Division) are the only Irish groups now remaining in Portland. These groups continue to sponsor Irish heritage and culture, St. Patrick's Day events, and Irish language and dance (*ceili*) classes. A new phase in the history of Irish associations occurred in the summer of 2002, when the Irish-American Club and other organizations purchased St. Dominic's Church, closed by the Portland Diocese in 1998, and announced their plans for a new Irish Heritage Center (IHC). Their plans to convert this building into an Irish social and community center make the future again look bright for the fostering and preservation of Irish culture and heritage in Portland and in Maine.

1. William Willis, *The History of Portland* (Somersworth, NH: New Hampshire Publishing Co., 1972), 283–85, 292. First published in 1833 in two volumes, a revised edition was printed in Portland in 1865. This is a facsimile of the 1865 edition.
2. See William David Barry, *Bryce McLellan and His Children, 1720–1776* (Portland: University of Southern Maine, 1973); William David Barry and John Holverson, "The Revolutionary McLellans," (unpublished manuscript, 1977), 1–4 (available at the Maine Historical Society, Portland, ME, hereafter MHS). Also see the essay on the Scotch-Irish by R. Stuart Wallace in this book.
3. Willis, *The History of Portland*, 374.
4. Thomas C. Amory, *Life of James Sullivan, With Selections from his Writings* (Boston: Phillips, Sampson and Company, 1859), 70–74.
5. See Amory, *Life of James Sullivan*, 412–13, for the origins of the Sullivans in Ireland.
6. See Seamus MacManus, *The Story of the Irish Race, A Popular History of Ireland* (Old Greenwich, CT: The Irish Publishing Company, 1921), 470–82.
7. This information is garnered from United States Census Records, 1800–1810 and also from "Baptisms, Funerals, and Confirmations of the Catholic Church at North Whitefield (St. Denis)" (1808), original volume in custody of the Portland Diocesan Archives, Portland, ME (hereafter PDA).
8. Walter Muir Whitehill, *A Memorial To Bishop Cheverus, With A Catalogue Of The Books Given By Him To The Boston Athenaeum* (Boston, MA: Boston Athenaeum, 1951), v–vi.
9. Thomas H. O'Connor, *The Boston Irish: A Political History* (Boston: Back Bay Books, 1995), 24–25.
10. "Records of Baptisms & Marriages, 1797–1816," extracted from records preserved at Cathedral of the Holy Cross, Boston, 1891 (manuscript copy at PDA).
11. William Leo Lucey, *The Catholic Church in Maine* (Francestown, NH: Marshall Jones, 1957), 66. For an excellent look at the Kavanaghs and Cottrills, see Edward Thomas McCarron, "The World of Kavanagh and Cottrill: A Portrait of Irish Emigration, Entrepreneurship, and Ethnic Diversity in Mid-Maine, 1760–1820" (Ph.D. diss., University of New Hampshire, 1992), as well as McCarron's essay "Facing the Atlantic" in this book.
12. Lucey, *The Catholic Church in Maine*, 24.
13. "Records of Baptisms & Marriages, 1797–1816," from Cathedral of the Holy Cross, Boston (manuscript copy at the PDA).
14. O'Connor, *The Boston Irish*, 25.

15. "Baptisms, Funerals, and Confirmations of the Catholic Church at North Whitefield (St. Denis)," manuscript copy, PDA.

16. Kerby A. Miller, *Emigrants and Exiles: Ireland and the Irish Exodus to North America* (NY: Oxford University Press, 1985), 193.

17. Lawrence F. Kohl, ed., *Irish Green and Union Blue: The Civil War Letters of Peter Welch* (Bronx, NY: Fordham University Press, 1986). For this reference I am indebted to William B. Jordan, Jr. by way of Michael C. Connolly.

18. Information from United States Census (Portland, Maine), 1850, 1860. Also St. Dominic's and Cathedral of the Immaculate Conception baptismal and marriage records, 1842–1880s.

19. Miller, *Emigrants and Exiles*, 38.

20. William Forbes Adams, *Ireland and Irish Emigration to the New World, from 1815 to the Famine* (New York: Russell and Russell, 1932), 336.

21. *Eastern Argus*, 6 August 1822, 2.

22. Ibid.

23. An Irish emigrant named Alice Carrigg Gillan came to Portland in 1910 by way of New London, CT. Ironically, she was the granddaughter of William Carrig, a survivor of the 1822 famine, who was a thirty-six-year-old farmer residing in Clondegad Parish, County Clare, the parish mentioned in the news article above. He never emigrated and died in Gortnamuck, Clondegad Parish, in 1866 at the age of eighty.

24. Lucey, *The Catholic Church in Maine*, 66.

25. Lucey, *The Catholic Church in Maine*, 46–49, 66. Edward McCarron's essay "Facing the Atlantic" in this volume covers many of these areas of early Catholic growth in Maine.

26. Matthew Jude Barker, "History of St. Dominic's Parish," in Michael and Marilyn Meoldy, eds., *Saint Dominic's: 175 Years of Memories, 1822–1997* (Portland, ME: Smart Marketing, Inc., 1997), 11 (available at the Maine Historical Society); Vincent A. Lapomarda, *Charles Nolcini: The Life And Music Of An Italian-American In The Age Of Jackson* (Worcester, MA: By the author, 1997), 12–13.

27. Benedict J. Fenwick (Joseph M. McCarthy, ed.), *Memoirs to Serve For the Future, Ecclesiastical History of the Diocese of Boston* (Yonkers, NY: U. S. Catholic Historical Society, 1978), 217.

28. Ibid.

29. Matthew Jude Barker, "History of St. Dominic's Parish," 11–14. See also Fr. Hugh Fenning, "The Conversion of Charles Ffrench," *The Watchman* 28, no. 53 (Summer 1961). Thanks to Michael C. Connolly for this reference.

30. For the connection between Portland and Galway in the late nineteenth through early twentieth centuries, see Seamus Grimes and Michael C. Connolly, "The Migration Link between Cois Fharraige and Portland, Maine, 1880s to 1920s," *Irish Geography* 22 (1989), 22–30. (Photocopy of this article at MHS).

31. Barker, "History of St. Dominic's Parish," 12; *Portland Sunday Telegram*, 4 July 1909, 11.

32. *The Yankee* (Portland), 14 May 1828.

33. Ibid.

34. Barker, "History of St. Dominic's Parish," 12–13.

35. *Souvenir History of St. Dominic's Parish* (Portland: 1909), 41. In possession of the author.

36. James Mundy, *Hard Times, Hard Men, Maine and the Irish, 1830–1860* (Scarborough, ME: Harp Publications, 1990), 38. Mundy states that Bangor's Irish "appear to have been more faithful in the celebration of St. Patrick's Day, at least in the formal sense of having parades and dinners that were public events in and of themselves." He further states that the Bangor Irish had created a Bangor Catholic Temperance Society and a Father Mathew Temperance Society by 1842.

37. Matthew Jude Barker, et al. "Ancient Order of Hibernians—Origins," *The Western Cemetery Project, 1997–2001, Irish-American History* (South Portland, ME: Ancient Order of Hibernians, 2001), 38.

38. William B. Jordan, Jr., *Burial Records of Eastern Cemetery, 1811–1890* (Bowie, MD: Heritage Books, 1987), 134.

39. *Daily Advertiser* (Portland), 31 March 1832, 2.

40. Ibid.

41. Gearóid ÓTuathaigh, *Ireland Before the Famine, 1798–1848* (Dublin: The Gill History of Ireland, 1972), Volume 9, 21–22.

42. O'Connor, *The Boston Irish*, 23.

43. Traditional street ballad of the United Irishmen Rebellion of 1798. See Ruth Bauerle, *James Joyce Songbook* (New York: Garland Publishing Co., 1982), 220. I am indebted to Thomas A. Wilsbach of the Portland Public Library and Michael C. Connolly for this reference.

44. MacManus, *The Story of the Irish Race*, 525.

45. ÓTuathaigh, *Ireland Before the Famine*, 23.

46. Miller, *Emigrants and Exiles*, 187.

47. ÓTuathaigh, *Ireland Before the Famine*, 30–41.

48. MacManus, *The Story of the Irish Race*, 532–37.

49. *Daily Advertiser* (Portland), 31 March 1832, 2.

50. ÓTuathaigh, *Ireland Before the Famine*, 185–89.

51. *The Boston Pilot*, 15 April 1843, 119–20. Collections of the Boston Public Library (hereafter BPL).

52. Ibid.

53. Ibid.

54. *The Boston Pilot*, 22 July 1843. For information on John Crease, see Lucey, *The Catholic Church in Maine*, 72, 81, 252–53, 256–57.

55. *The Boston Pilot*, 14 October 1843, 323, BPL.

56. Ibid.

57. The names of early prominent Portland Irish have been garnered from census and land records of Portland, articles on the Hibernian Benevolent Society found in *The Boston Pilot*, and from a list contained in *Souvenir History of St. Dominic's Parish*, 41.

58. Richard Stivers, *Hair of the Dog: Irish Drinking and Its American Stereotype* (University Park, PA: Pennsylvania State University Press, 2000), 39.

59. Thomas Keneally, *The Great Shame, and the Triumph of the Irish in the English-Speaking World* (New York: Anchor Books, 1998), 88–96.

60. *The Boston Pilot*, 23 September 1843.

61. See *The Boston Pilot* for 25 March, 24 June, and 11 November 1848 for information on the Bangor, Maine Repeal Society, which still seemed quite healthy at the time. Collections of BPL.

62. *The Boston Pilot*, 21 January 1843, 23, BPL.

63. Ibid.
64. *Portland Advertiser,* 4 March 1843, 2.
65. Ibid.
66. Ibid.
67. Matthew Jude Barker, "A Collection of Brief Biographies of Early Portland Irish," in Paul O'Neil, et al., eds., *The Western Cemetery Project, 1997–2001, Irish-American History,* 52.
68. *Washingtonian Journal,* 5 April 1848.
69. Ibid.
70. Ibid.
71. Cumberland County Registry of Deeds, Volume 128, 490 and Volume 141, 558, Registry of Deeds, Portland, Maine.
72. *Eastern Argus,* 21 July 1853. His gravestone located in Calvary Cemetery, South Portland, is still legible.
73. Carl Wittke, *The Irish in America* (Baton Rouge: Louisiana State University Press, 1956), 213.
74. Ibid.
75. Lucey, *The Catholic Church in Maine,* 79–80.
76. *The Boston Pilot,* 21 January 1843, 23.
77. *Souvenir History of St. Dominic's Parish,* 49–50.
78. Cathal Póirtéir, ed., *The Great Irish Famine* (Dublin: The Thomas Davis Lecture Series, published in association with Rádio Telefís Éireann (RTÉ) and Mercier Press, 1995), 5, 19.
79. Thomas Gallagher, *Paddy's Lament, Ireland, 1846–1847, Prelude To Hatred* (San Diego: Harcourt Brace, 1987), 20.
80. Cecil Woodham-Smith, *The Great Hunger, Ireland, 1845–9* (New York: Harper and Row, 1962), 32–33.
81. Christine Kinealy, *This Great Calamity: The Irish Famine 1845–52* (Dublin: Gill and Macmillan, 1994), 32–33.
82. Gallagher, *Paddy's Lament,* 22.
83. Ibid., 22–23.
84. *Portland Tribune,* 3 August 1844, 3.
85. See Woodham-Smith, *The Great Hunger,* 33–35.
86. Gallagher, *Paddy's Lament,* 7.
87. Kinealy, *This Great Calamity,* 34.
88. Ibid., 33.
89. For a graphic description of some of the Famine diseases, see Gallagher, *Paddy's Lament,* 57–66.
90. See Gallagher, *Paddy's Lament,* 35 and 108, for a description of how rats and dogs ate each other, and even attacked and ate people still clinging to life.
91. Gallagher, *Paddy's Lament,* 12.
92. Woodham-Smith, *The Great Hunger,* 120.
93. See Woodham-Smith, *The Great Hunger,* 151–54.
94. Woodham-Smith, *The Great Hunger,* 49.
95. Ibid.
96. Giovanni Costigan, *A History of Modern Ireland* (New York: 1969), 184. There are many fine books on the history of the Great Hunger beyond those cited, as well as several that were published during the 150th Anniversary of the Famine (c. 1994–2001). See also Overview to this book.

97. Wittke, *The Irish in America*, 8–9.

98. *Eastern Argus*, 22 February 1847.

99. Ibid.

100. Ibid.

101. *Portland Tribune and Bulletin*, 2 March 1847, 396.

102. Ibid.

103. Gallagher, *Paddy's Lament*, 207–11.

104. *Souvenir History of St. Dominic's Parish*, 49–50.

105. See Marianna O'Gallagher, *Gateway to Canada, 1832–1937* (Ste. Foy, Quebec: Livres Carraig Books, 1995), which lists the names of over 600 Irish children who were adopted and whose information was recorded by The Charitable Society of the Catholic Ladies of Quebec.

106. *Portland Pleasure Boat*, 7 November 1847. Collections of MHS.

107. Joseph Griffin, ed., *History of the Press of Maine* (Brunswick, ME: By the author, 1872), 59–60.

108. Ibid.

109. Frank J. Mathew, *Father Mathew: His Life and Times* (London: 1890), 38.

110. *Eastern Argus*, 26 July 1849, 2.

111. *Eastern Argus*, 6 August 1849, 2.

112. *Eastern Argus*, 25 September 1849. 2.

113. *Eastern Argus*, 16 October 1849, 2.

114. See *Eastern Argus*, 26 October, 3 and 27 November 1849.

115. Stivers, *Hair of the Dog*, 36–37.

116. Anthony Trollope, *North America* (NY: Harpers & Brothers, Publishers, 1862), 33–34.

117. Mundy, *Hard Times, Hard Men*, 99.

118. *Portland Daily Press*, 26 September 1866, 1.

119. Ibid.

120. *Portland Daily Press*, 21 January 1874, 3.

121. *Portland Daily Press*, 14 January 1874, 3.

122. *Portland Tribune*, 23 November 1844.

123. Ibid.

124. *The Boston Pilot*, 13 May 1848.

125. *Portland Advertiser*, 30 March 1849, 2.

126. *Portland Advertiser*, 31 March 1849, 2.

127. *The Boston Pilot*, 10 March 1849.

128. *The Boston Pilot*, 14 April 1849.

129. *Portland Advertiser*, 4 April 1849, 2.

130. Ibid.

131. William V. Shannon, *The American Irish* (New York: Macmillan and Co., 1963), 45–46.

132. Allan R. Whitmore, "'A Guard of Faithful Sentinels': The Know-Nothing Appeal in Maine, 1854–1855," *Maine Historical Society Quarterly* 20, no. 3 (Winter 1981): 153.

133. *State of Maine*, 17 June 1854; *The Boston Pilot*, 1 July 1854.

134. Whitmore, "A Guard of Faithful Sentinels," 154. For an account of Ellsworth and Father John Bapst see Mundy, *Hard Times, Hard Men*, Chapter 7 (especially 156–66). For an account of the burning of the Old South Church in Bath, see

William David Barry, "Fires of Bigotry," *Down East Magazine* 36, no. 3 (October 1989): 44–47, 77–78.

135. Journal and Accounts, 1851–1854, J. B. Brown Collection, Collection 1677, Box 2, MHS.

136. 1882 *Portland City Directory*, 121.

137. J. B. Brown Collection, Collection 1677, Box 2, in account with John Smith, MHS.

138. See *Portland Advertiser*, 12, 17, and 19 March 1859.

139. This information was garnered from Federal Census Records (Portland, 1850–1900), and Portland City Directories, 1823–1900.

140. Dale B. Light, Jr., "The Role of Irish-American Organisations in Assimilation and Community Formation," in P. J. Drudy, ed., *The Irish in America: Emigration, Assimilation and Impact* (London: Cambridge University Press, 1985), 114.

141. 1871 *Portland City Directory*, 307.

142. Information contained in the Portland City Directories, 1850–1885.

143. *Eastern Argus*, 18 January 1860, 2.

144. Ibid.

145. Diary of Charles McCarthy, Jr. (PDA, Book 1, 3) estimates that James McGlinchy's estimated worth in 1880 was $130,144.

146. See *Eastern Argus*, 21 April 1866, 4.

147. *The Impending Crisis And Irrepressible Conflict*, Portland, March 22, 1860, 1. Photocopy of original in Portland Irish Box 2, collections of MHS.

148. *Eastern Argus*, 23 and 26 March 1860.

149. *The Impending Crisis And Irrepressible Conflict*, 4.

150. Ibid.

151. *Eastern Argus*, 6 April 1870, 3.

152. Ibid.

153. *Eastern Argus*, 22 July 1876, 3.

154. For a fascinating look at Guiney and his life and times see Christian G. Samito, *Commanding Boston's Irish Ninth, The Civil War Letters of Colonel Patrick R. Guiney, Ninth Massachusetts Volunteer Infantry* (New York: Fordham University Press, 1998). See pages xi–xiii for Guiney's Portland origins.

155. See *Eastern Argus*, 13 February 1854; *Portland Advertiser*, 13 February 1854; and *Portland Transcript*, 25 February 1854. Also see Barker, "A Collection of Brief Biographies of Early Portland Irish," 48.

156. *Portland Daily Press*, 11 January 1864, 2.

157. Ibid.

158. Wittke, *The Irish in America*, 132–33.

159. This information was inscribed on the Downey headstone, Calvary Cemetery, South Portland, ME.

160. James B. Cullen, *The Story of the Irish in Boston* (Boston: J. B. Cullen and Co., 1890), 245–49, 263–71.

161. *Portland Daily Press*, 11 March 1864, 2.

162. *Portland Daily Press*, 20 January 1876, 2.

163. *Eastern Argus*, 18 February 1868, 3.

164. *Portland City Directory*, 1871, 308.

165. *Eastern Argus*, 2 January 1875, 3.

166. *Portland Daily Press,* 12 March 1867, 2.

167. *Portland Evening Express & Advertiser,* 2 April 1921.

168. See E. R. R. Green, "The Beginnings of Fenianism," in T. W. Moody, ed., *The Fenian Movement* (Cork: Mercier Press, 1968), 15–17.

169. For a detailed look at the American Fenians in Maine see Gary W. Libby's essay in this book, "Maine and The Fenian Invasion of Canada of 1866."

170. See *Eastern Argus,* 7 June 1866 and 20 June 1866, as well as Libby's essay in this book.

171. *Eastern Argus,* 5 March 1866, 3.

172. *Eastern Argus,* 7 June 1866, 3.

173. *Eastern Argus,* 28 March 1866, 3.

174. Ibid. The John E. Fitzgerald mentioned here is sometimes confused with John F. "Honey Fitz" Fitzgerald, the grandfather of future President John Fitzgerald Kennedy.

175. *Eastern Argus,* 2 April 1866, 3.

176. *Eastern Argus,* 4 April 1866, 3.

177. Keneally, *The Great Shame,* 459–63.

178. *Eastern Argus,* 27 April 1867, 3.

179. Keneally, *The Great Shame,* 440–43. On the night of May 31, 1866, O'Neil led an attack on Canadian forces near Fort Erie on the Niagara, outside Buffalo, New York. Fighting broke out, leaving between fifteen and twenty Canadian volunteers dead, as well as several Fenians. On June 3, O'Neil and his army retreated to the American side. Now, a year later, O'Neil was addressing the Portland Fenians. He was a red-headed young Irish American who had been commissioned a captain during the Civil War while a member of the 15th U.S. Colored Infantry.

180. *Eastern Argus,* 17 June 1868, 3.

181. Ibid.

182. From local newspapers and city directories of this period.

183. *Eastern Argus,* 7 November 1878, 4.

184. *Eastern Argus,* 13 July 1878, 4.

185. *Eastern Argus,* 10 January 1870, 3.

186. *Daily Eastern Argus,* 29 August 1892.

187. *Portland Daily Press,* 8 January 1880, 3.

188. For information on the efforts of Portlanders to help the Irish suffering in 1880 see Matthew Jude Barker, "The Time We Shared Stone Soup," *Portland City Magazine* (October 2000): 51–55.

189. See *Eastern Argus,* 7 July 1885, 4.

190. *Eastern Argus,* 7 April 1892.

191. *Portland Press Herald,* 15 March 1973, 17.

GALLERY

1. The *Jeanie Johnston*, replica of a ship built in Quebec in 1847 to transport Irish emigrants to America during famine years. The replica was constructed by the government of Ireland in the 1990s in Blennerville, Tralee, County Kerry. The *Jeanie Johnston* is shown here in Portsmouth, NH (August 9, 2003) during its maiden voyage. *(photograph courtesy of Michael Connolly)*

2. RMS *Bohemian* monument, Calvary Cemetery, South Portland. The Royal Mail Steamer *Bohemian* sank off Cape Elizabeth on February 22, 1864. This granite monument was erected by the Ancient Order of Hibernians to commemorate the loss of life of forty-two mostly Irish emigrants. Twelve unclaimed bodies were interred at this site. *(photograph courtesy of Michael Connolly)*

3. Arrival of the steamship *Oregon* in Portland, Maine, January 21, 1884. Pencil sketch by nineteenth-century Portland artist Frederic Goth. This wash-drawing depicts Irish immigrants debarking from this ship. *(photograph courtesy of Peabody Essex Museum, Salem, Massachusetts)*

4. John Ford (Feeney) played football at Portland High School from 1910 to 1914. *(photograph courtesy of Maine Historical Society, Maine Memory Network 5585)*

5. James Sullivan (1744–1808), born in Berwick, Maine; author of *History of the District of Maine* (1795); Governor of Massachusetts (1807–08). Engraving by H. Wright Smith, after a portait by Gilbert Stuart. *(photograph courtesy of Maine Historical Society)*

6. Coleman Patrick "Coley" Welch, Maine-born middleweight boxer in the 1930s and 1940s. Welch had a record of 108 wins, 26 losses, and 6 draws. *(photograph courtesy of Helen [Mrs. J. Donald] MacWilliams)*

7. Irish American cultural leaders. *Left to right:* Patrick H. Feeney, John Ford's elder brother; James Brendan Connolly (1868–1957), author of *Mother Machree* and other collections of short stories about Gloucester fishermen, and 1896 winner of the first Gold Medal in the modern Olympics; and James A. Healy (1890–1975), Portland-born philanthropist and bibliophile. Taken on Connolly's way to Colby College to receive an academic award. *(photograph courtesy of William and Deborah Barry)*

St. Joseph's Academy and Convent, Portland, Me.

8. Saint Joseph's Convent, c. 1930, main residence of the Sisters of Mercy, Portland. Designed by Timothy G. O'Connell (1868–1955). *(photograph courtesy of Collection of Maine Historic Preservation Commission)*

9. Rebecca McCobb. Oil on glass (reverse painting) ca. 1818, by Benjamin Greenleaf (1769–1821). *(photograph courtesy of the Maine Historical Society)*

10. Captain Parker McCobb. Oil on glass (reverse painting) ca. 1818 by Benjamin Greenleaf (1769–1821). *(photograph courtesy of the Maine Historical Society)*

11. Portrait of Mary McLellan (Mrs. Joseph McLellan), ca. 1795–1804. Mary (1740–1804) was the daughter of the third settler of Gorham, Maine. Oil on canvas, 30 5/8" x 25 1/16" (1972.70) by John Brewster, Jr. (attributed) (USA, 1766-1854). Museum Purchase, Portland Museum of Art, Portland, Maine. *(used with permission of the Portland Museum of Art)*

12. Captain Joseph McLellan, Sr., 1798. McLellan was the owner of the largest merchant fleet in Portland in the Federal Period, prior to the Embargo of 1807. Oil on canvas, 30 1/8" x 24 15/16" (1972.71) by Henry Sargent (USA, 1770–1845). Museum Purchase, Portland Museum of Art, Portland, Maine. *(used with permission of the Portland Museum of Art)*

13. Cottrill Headstone, St. Colmkille's Churchyard, village of Inistioge, County Kilkenny. *(photograph by Edward McCarron, used with permission)*

14. Kavanagh Farmhouse, Cluen, parish of Inistioge, County Kilkenny. *(photograph by Edward McCarron, used with permission)*

15. Matthew Cottrill House, Damariscotta, Maine. Built in 1801 by Nicholas Codd. *(photograph by Edward McCarron, used with permission)*

16. James Kavanagh House, Damariscotta Mills, Maine. Built in 1803 by Nicholas Codd, a Dublin-born housewright. *(photograph by Edward McCarron, used with permission)*

17. Portrait of Irish-born timber merchant Matthew Cottrill (ca. 1805). *(private collection)*

18. St. Patrick's Church, built by Nicholas Codd in 1808 in Damariscotta Mills, Maine. It is the oldest surviving Catholic Church in New England. *(photograph by Edward McCarron, used with permission)*

19. Rathlin Island, in the North Channel between Ireland and Scotland. Map drawn by Tracy Menard, after Augustine McCurdy, *Rathlin's Rugged Story. (used courtesy of Fidelma McCarron)*

20. West Lubec and Trescott, Maine, after Samuel Colby, *Atlas of Washington County, Maine*, 1881. *(map drawn by Fidelma McCarron, used with permission)*

21. Rathlin Harbor and Manor House. *(photograph by Kevin McCurdy, made available by his father Augustine McCurdy, and used courtesy of Fidelma McCarron)*

IRON WORKS AT PEMBROKE, MAINE.

22. Iron Works at Pembroke, Maine. *(photograph courtesy of Maine Historical Society, Maine Memory Network 1484)*

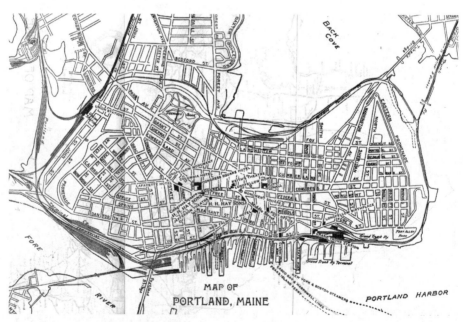

23. Map of Portland (1928) Hay's Guide to Portland (MP837100). *(photograph courtesy of Maine Historical Society)*

24. Saint Dominic's Church, corner of State and Gray Streets, Portland's oldest Catholic Church, built in 1833. The original building was dedicated on August 11, 1833, and the present building (depicted) was dedicated sixty years later on August 6, 1893. *(photograph courtesy of Michael Connolly)*

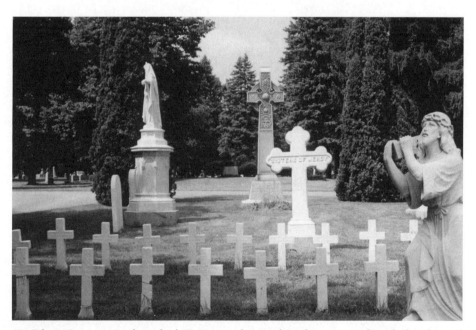

25. Calvary Cemetery, South Portland. Main entry showing the Celtic Cross marking the burial site of Bishop James Augustine Healy (Second Bishop of the Portland Diocese, 1875–1900), and the smaller white crosses of the Sisters of Mercy. *(photograph courtesy of Michael Connolly)*

26. Col. Patrick Robert Guiney (1835–77) from Portland's Gorham's Corner. Guiney was a student at Holy Cross College, Worcester, and a Civil War hero serving in the Ninth Massachusetts Regiment until badly wounded at the Battle of the Wilderness (1864). *(photograph courtesy of College of the Holy Cross Rare Books, Special Collections and Archives)*

27. McGlinchy's Brewery, located on Portland's Munjoy Hill at the corner of Fore and Waterville Streets, just below Adams Street. *(photograph courtesy of Maine Historical Society, Maine Memory Network 6677)*

28. Father John O'Donnell (1821–82). This popular priest served at St. Dominic's between 1850 and 1855. He is often credited with skillfully steering Portland's small, vulnerable Irish Catholic community through the dangerous Know-Nothing nativism of the 1850s. *(photograph courtesy of Maine Historical Society)*

29. Old South Church, Bath, burned by the Know-Nothings on July 6, 1854. Oil painting by John Hillings (1826–94). *(photograph courtesy of Maine Historical Society [A86-820])*

30. Old South Church, Bath, burned by the Know-Nothings on July 6, 1854. Oil painting by John Hillings (1826–94). *(photograph used courtesy of Maine Historical Society [A86-821])*

31. Irish immigrant workers clearing ice from Lewiston canals near Hill Mill 5, c. 1896. *(photograph courtesy of the Franco-American Center, USM/Lewiston-Auburn College)*

32. Lewiston, c. 1870, showing mills and canals. *(photograph courtesy of Collection of Maine Historic Preservation Commission)*

33. Lubec (in background) as seen from the north with Campobello Island (Canada) on left, and Pope's Folly (island) in center. *(photograph courtesy of Maine Historical Society)*

NAVAL RACE BETWEEN THE "WINOOSKI" AND "ALGONQUIN"—THE START, 3 P.M., FEBRUARY 13, 1866.—SKETCHED BY B. S. OSBON.—[SEE PAGE 142.]

34. Winooski and Algonquin in a naval race, February 13, 1866. The Winooski figured prominently in the American government's attempts to quell the Fenian skirmishes around Eastport in the spring of 1866. Image from *Harper's Magazine* (March 3, 1866, p. 348). *(private collection)*

35. James Stephens, Fenian Chief, at a grand reception at Jones's Wood, April 15, 1866. Image from *Harper's Magazine* (June 2, 1866, p. 348). *(private collection)*

36. Girls at recess at North School, c. 1911, near Munjoy Hill, Portland. *(photograph courtesy of Maine Historical Society, Collection 808, folder 5)*

37. Boys at recess at North School, c. 1911, near Munjoy Hill, Portland. *(photograph courtesy of Maine Historical Society, Collection 808, folder 5)*

38. Classroom at North School, c. 1911, near Munjoy Hill, Portland. *(photograph courtesy of Maine Historical Society, Collection 808, folder 6)*

39. Katharine O'Brien (d. 1998), head of the mathematics department at Deering High School in Portland, was also a published poet. *(photograph courtesy of the Maine Women Writers' Collection, Westbrook College, University of New England)*

40. The Ford/Feeney family at the filming of "Chicken Hearted Jim," directed by Francis Ford (1915). Back row (from left): Jack Ford, Unknown, Francis Ford, Phil Ford, John Feeney, Sr., Unknown, Eddie O'Fearna, Unknown. Front row (from left): Patrick Feeney, Cecil Mclean, Unknown, Josephine Feeney, Unknown. *(photograph courtesy of the family of Josephine Feeney and John Ford)*

41. Josephine Feeney at the wedding of the parents of Kathy MacDonald, February 11, 1946. *Left to right*: Emma Curran, Father McCoy, S. J., Julia Perkins, Josephine Feeney. *(photograph courtesy of the family of Josephine Feeney and John Ford)*

42. Gorham's Corner. This marks the intersection of York, Fore, Center, Cotton, Pleasant and Danforth Streets in the transition between Portland's Old Port and West End. *(photograph courtesy of Maine Historical Society, Maine Memory Network 6674)*

43. Bylaws of the Portland Longshoremen's Benevolent Society. This organization of mainly Irish laborers was founded in 1880. Its records are housed in the Maine Historical Society. *(photograph courtesy of Maine Historical Society, Maine Memory Network 6750)*

44. Mary Kilmartin (1913–2001) *(seated, front center)* and three other Irish-speaking women in Portland *(standing, from left)*: Kate Kilmartin, Claire Foley, and Margaret McMahon née Kilmartin. *(photograph courtesy of Claire Foley)*

45. Patrick (Pat) Malone, arguably the last of the great Irish story-tellers *(seanachi)*. A Portland longshore-man, Malone lived his later life with his family, the Busbys, in Stetson Court, a stone's throw from Saint Dominic's Church. *(photograph courtesy of Michael Connolly)*

46. Lawrence (Larry) Welch. As a Portland longshoreman Larry had two nicknames from his Irish-speaking parents: Dinish, from the birthplace of his mother, nee Loftus, from this island off Letermor; and Breathnach (Irish for Welch) from his father who was from Mace, near Carna in Connmara, County Galway. (*Photo courtesy of Michael Connolly*)

47. Irish Heritage Center board members and supporters, 2003. Back row (left to right): Joe Moran, Mary McAleney, Mike McAleney, Maureen Coyne Norris, Tony Owen, Patrick Nixon, Patricia Owen, Linda Hogan, Bob Kearney, and David Soule. Front row (left to right): Claire Foley, Ian O'Malley, Deehan McAleney, Sen. George Mitchell, and Bart Folan. (photograph courtesy of the photographer, Jim Daniels, P. Vincent "Vinny" O'Malley, and the Board of the Irish Heritage Center)

THE IRISH EXPERIENCE
IN LEWISTON, 1850–1880:
OPPORTUNITY AND SOCIAL MOBILITY
ON THE URBAN FRONTIER

by Margaret Buker Jay

"ON THE SEVENTEENTH OF EACH MARCH, it was a source of great pleasure and pride," reported the *Lewiston Evening Journal*, "for the late Patrick McGillicuddy to receive a little box of shamrock delivered to his home in Lewiston from his old home in Sneem, Ireland. The box was always packed with care and was fragrant with the fresh sweet scent of earth and springing leaves. The clinging roots, unbroken, told of the painstaking efforts of his friends who had gathered the shamrock in the fields and lanes in the vicinity of his old home in Sneem."[1] When Patrick McGillicuddy died on February 10, 1908, the local paper paid tribute to this prominent Lewiston citizen who had found in a new home a land of economic opportunity and success, but who never forgot the roots that connected him to the green fields of Ireland. His life in America mirrored the mythical rags-to-riches story where character, hard work, and luck—being in the right place at the right time—could bring financial and social fortune. At the end of his life, he had extensive real estate holdings, a place of respect in his adopted home, and an extended family that included lawyers, business leaders, contractors, and a former mayor and prominent political leader in Lewiston.[2]

Patrick McGillicuddy was born in County Kerry, Ireland, the oldest of a family of seven children left orphaned. Times were hard and prospects were poor, so Patrick decided in 1845, at the age of twenty, to set out for America. He left his brother, John, in charge of the family in Ireland, promising to send back the money to bring the rest of the children to America provided he made good in this country. Reluctant at first, his brother finally accepted the decision. The family horse was sold and the money used to purchase Patrick's ticket for the New World. His passage on the sailing ship *Susan E. Howell* was five pounds sterling, or about twenty-five dollars, not including his expenses for food en route. He left Liverpool, England, with fifty cents sewed into the waistband of his trousers. On the way over, his roommate was taken ill. When Patrick asked why he did not take some medicine, the young man responded that he had no money. As the story was told, Patrick took out his knife, cut the fifty cents from his waistband and gave it to his roommate to purchase the needed medicine from the ship's surgeon. He arrived in New York City in the spring of 1845 without material resources, but with a friend. His friend had a sister in New York who took them in, and having heard her brother's story, gave Patrick McGillicuddy a dollar bill. It was the first that he had ever seen and the biggest sum of money that he had ever had all for himself up to that time.[3]

The next morning, with the dollar in his pocket, he set out on his own. He followed a group of Irish immigrants into a local store, where a man was booking jobs for men to work in the mines. He signed up and received a ticket for the coalmines. One day in the deep coal pits convinced him that mining was not the kind of work that he had come to America to get. As luck would have it, his search for a job took him to a blacksmith's shop owned, as it turned out, by an Irishman from his hometown of Sneem, and a friend of McGillicuddy's father. Patrick worked in the blacksmith shop for more than a year. The first month he earned twenty-two dollars. As he had promised, he sent money to his brother and sisters in Ireland to be used to bring the family together in America.[4]

After a time he left his friend, the blacksmith, to go to Newport, Rhode Island, to work at his trade as a stone mason and to take contracts for building heavy stone walls. He continued to be successful, working in Newport and in Charlestown, South Carolina, where he was contracted to work on the masonry walls of Fort Sumter. While living in Newport, he was finally reunited with his family.[5] In the early 1850s, Patrick McGillicuddy made one last move. Now in his mid-twenties, with savings accumulated from his years as a stonemason and contractor, he relocated himself, his brother John, his sisters, and their families to a small town with big dreams on the Androscoggin River in Maine.

WATER POWER
AND THE GROWTH OF MANUFACTURING

At the beginning of the nineteenth century, Lewiston was still a pre-dominantly frontier community. Sparsely settled, isolated from any urban centers, the town was slow in developing. By mid-century, how-ever, it had begun a physical, social, and economic transformation, which in less than thirty years would make the city one of the leading manufacturing centers in Maine. Lewiston was a town of 3,500 in 1850; by 1854 it had more than doubled to 8,000 and was still growing.

Even in its early years, the town was not without attractions for man-ufacturing. Lewiston's greatest assets were the Androscoggin River and Lewiston Falls, which produced waterpower potential described by one observer in the 1850s as "unsurpassed in New England for safety and permanence, and cheapness of application to mechanical and manufac-turing purposes."[6] Early attempts were made to use this waterpower for local industry, but not until the 1830s were any efforts directed toward full-scale development. The Great Androscoggin Falls, Dam, Locks, and Canal Company was granted a charter in 1836 allowing it to construct dams, locks, canals, mills, works, machinery, and buildings on its prop-erty and to manufacture cotton, wool, iron, steel, and paper in the towns of Lewiston, Minot, and Danville. It was the vision of the direc-tors of this company to develop on a large scale the waterpower at Lewiston Falls, similar to the type of development that was being done in Massachusetts on the Merrimack River. In 1837, the company secured the services of a Boston civil engineer, B. F. Perham, who made a survey of the town and developed a plan for the construction of a series of dams and canals. The financial dislocations of the panic of 1837 and the inability of the company to attract viable interest from any large manufacturing enterprises hindered additional efforts to pro-mote development at that time.[7]

Eight years later, the corporation petitioned the Maine legislature to change its name to the Lewiston Water Power Company. The request was granted and the new company was formally established on November 19, 1845. Certificates of stock in the new company were issued to the shareholders, many of whom soon disposed of them to interested entrepreneurs in Boston. Control of Lewiston's future conse-quently passed into the hands of a new group of industrialists who were anxious to establish a series of large cotton textile firms. The Lewiston

Water Power Company made extensive real estate purchases from 1846 to 1850. By the spring of 1850, the company owned all waterpower rights in the area and over 1,000 acres of land, most of it on the Lewiston side of the river.[8]

The extension of the Androscoggin and Kennebec Railroad to Lewiston in 1849 removed the last major obstacle in the way of industrial expansion. Lewiston was no longer isolated from markets and sources of raw material. The railroad tied Lewiston into a broad network of transportation and communication with the major urban and market centers of America. The keys to the future of Lewiston as a cotton textile-manufacturing center were almost fully in place. The raw materials for industrial and infrastructure development were financial investment and labor. The nucleus of the financial investment was provided by a group of Boston and Providence entrepreneurs, including Benjamin E. Bates, Thomas J. Hill, Lyman Nichols, Alexander DeWitt, and Thomas Ward. The labor for the operation of the cotton textile mills would, at first, come from rural areas in Maine and northern New England; the same sources that provided the labor in Lawrence, Lowell, and Manchester. The unskilled labor for the construction of the canal system, mill sites and the laying out of streets in what was described by one observer as "a regular jungle, a mass of rocks and bushes that were almost impenetrable" would be largely provided by immigrants from Ireland.[9]

Albert H. Kelsey, who became known as the "god-father of Lewiston," recalled in an interview conducted in May of 1900 some of his first impressions when he came to Lewiston on the second day of May 1850. The small Lincoln Mill at the foot of the falls was the only mill in Lewiston at that time. But, Kelsey recalled, "a company called the Lewiston Water Power Company had got hold of the property and proposed to develop what they considered the great natural advantages of Lewiston. This company was composed mostly of Boston men. Lowell, Lawrence and other Massachusetts cities had been built up and developed by this time and capital was looking for other fields in which to do the same thing. I had quite important business interests of my own at that time in Boston and in other places in Massachusetts; but one of my friends was interested in the new company and in its project to develop this water power and land scheme down in Maine."[10] Kelsey was asked to look over the town and report on its possibilities. He spent a week in Lewiston and made a favorable report. Albert Kelsey was then asked to become the agent for the Lewiston Water Power Company and oversee the development of Lewiston. While Kelsey was at first reluctant to take on such a large challenge because of his other business interests, he eventually agreed to accept the position of agent.

The first step in the physical transformation of the town was the construction of a dam and a system of canals. Work was begun on the canal system in the spring of 1850. The task of building the canal and mill sites was a formidable challenge. Kelsey later recalled in detail some of the difficulties of those first months in the summer of 1850:

> That was a long and tedious job—that canal. Along that section where the Canal or Main Street Bridge is, we encountered solid ledge. In front of the Bates Mill there was a ledgy elevation some twenty feet above the present level. That had to be cleared away. I had the men put 19 casks of powder into the ledge and we sent her off with one crack. Where the DeWitt Hotel now stands was a hillock forty-five feet high. When I got ready to build the hotel all that had to be leveled.[11]

UNSKILLED IRISH LABOR

The bulk of the labor force engaged in the unskilled construction work was recruited from the Irish population of Boston. Patrick O'Donnell, one of the early leaders of Lewiston's Irish community, was hired as a labor contractor to furnish men to build the canal system. In the spring of 1850 he hired over 400 Irishmen to begin the unskilled work involved in blasting and digging the canal system and laying out mill sites.[12] When the 1850 census was conducted, barely a month after work had begun on the canal system, nearly seventy-five percent of all unskilled laborers living in Lewiston had been born in Ireland, and out of a population of approximately 3,500, the Irish numbered more than 700, or about 20 percent of the total population. In 1850, Lewiston had the highest ratio of Irish to its total population of any Maine city.[13]

The presence of such a large group of foreign-born laborers in Lewiston was primarily a result of the timing of Lewiston's economic development. Lewiston's industrial take-off coincided with the influx into New England of large numbers of Irish. The general economic dislocation of the Irish agricultural economy was aggravated in the mid-1840s by the appearance of the potato blight. Unable to pay their rents, and faced with the specter of starvation and misery, the evicted tenant had but one desire, to escape Ireland and English rule as quickly as possible. They came to America out of desperation and often, unlike Patrick McGillicuddy, with little hope that the future would offer a better life.[14]

The cost of transportation, even with the relatively low transoceanic rates, involved for the majority the expenditure of their last resources. The penniless newcomer arrived in Boston or New York with no alternative but to seek whatever work could be found. Desperation drove them to accept any type of employment that was offered. Consequently, they were a ready source of cheap labor for railroad or canal construction projects.[15]

The less fortunate, who lacked sufficient funds for passage to Boston or New York, were forced to go to Quebec, Nova Scotia, or New Brunswick in the empty holds of returning timber ships. From the Maritime Provinces, Irish families wandered down the coast toward Boston, until they reached a city where work could be found or a community whose charitable institutions would shelter them.[16]

Census information suggests that the Irish families who settled in Lewiston had been drawn from a variety of immigration routes. The manuscript census schedules for Lewiston reveal many instances of Irish children born in Nova Scotia or New Brunswick indicating that these Canadian provinces had been the point of debarkation for a large number of Irish families. An equally large number had lived in Massachusetts for several years before securing employment in Lewiston. From whatever geographical source, the majority arrived in the community with little, if any, accumulated savings and often without the types of skills and experience that would have assured them economic security.[17]

The very fact of urban growth generated a proliferation of employment opportunities. Albert Kelsey described Lewiston in the 1850s as "almost like a magic city. The expenditure of so much money, the building of the mills one after another as fast as we could hustle them along attracted the attention of the country and new inhabitants poured in from everywhere."[18] The cotton textile mills, Bates Mill 1 and 2, the Hill Mill, and the Androscoggin Mill provided large numbers of both skilled and semi-skilled positions; the Lewiston Bleachery and Dye Works, the Gas Works, and many machine shops and supportive manufacturing enterprises provided additional employment opportunities. A growing city also generated a constant demand for home and business construction and furnished unskilled work, skilled employment in the construction trades, and clerical jobs. The expanding population of the city created a direct demand for social services and, one would assume, a corresponding increased, albeit indirect, demand for the work of professionals and the products of both large and small businesses.

This was the community in which Patrick McGillicuddy chose to settle with his family and invest his skills, his influence, and his financial savings. It was a town—soon to become a city—in which Boston stockholders would make significant profits, local entrepreneurs would find opportunity for creating new businesses, thousands of individuals would find work in the cotton textile industry, skilled tradesmen would have steady work, and a class of professional and business leaders would emerge to provide social and political leadership in the 1860s.

Lewiston was also the community in which nearly three hundred of the unskilled laborers recorded in the 1850 census also chose to stake their lives and the security and future of their families. They were joined over the next decades by a continuing immigration of Irish-born laborers and families. Some of those additional immigrants, who became part of the Irish community of Lewiston in the 1850s and 1860s, came with labor skills, work experience, and modest financial savings. Their experiences and the opportunities for economic and social security over the next three decades were shaped by a variety of factors. The pattern of economic expansion in this urban frontier community was only one factor in determining the success of Irish-born residents in securing occupational advancement, property acquisition, residential security, and social and political acceptance over the next decades.

SOCIAL MOBILITY

What was the experience of Irish laborers in mid-nineteenth century Lewiston? How much opportunity was presented for Irish-born laborers and their families to rise from entry-level day labor to better-paying jobs in an expanding cotton textile manufacturing center? At the outset, the Irish controlled the lowest rungs of Lewiston's occupational ladder. In 1850, nearly seventy-five percent of all the unskilled laborers in the town were Irish-born. Yet more significantly, unskilled labor represented nearly ninety-five percent of all employment available to Irish males in the community. Only a small number held skilled jobs. In May 1850, when the federal census was conducted, Lewiston's Irish community included one contractor, one teacher, and one grocer.[19]

The manuscript census schedules for the succeeding decades, 1860 to 1880, reveal the occupational distribution of the Irish population at ten-year intervals, and gradual but modest improvement is reflected in the statistical information. The percentage of Irishmen still listed as day labor or laborer gradually declined over the years, although it never fell much below forty percent and averaged over sixty percent for the thirty-year period from 1850 to 1880.[20]

The majority of those who held skilled jobs or who established themselves as businessmen in the community did not emerge from the unskilled labor class, but rather moved into the community with savings and experience which enabled them to take advantage of the dynamic economic climate in Lewiston. While the experience of men like Patrick and John McGillicuddy indicates that the doors of opportunity for Irish immigrants were not locked, the research suggests that they were more the exception than the rule. How did their experience compare to the larger number of Irish immigrants who arrived in Lewiston to accept employment as common laborers? They represented the major portion of the Irish population of Lewiston. What, if any, were the opportunities available to them? In order to understand the tenuous position of the day laborer, it is important to outline some of the characteristics of unskilled or day labor:

1) Day labor was generally the lowest-paying work available. The rates for unskilled labor varied between a dollar a day and a dollar twenty-five cents a day over the 1850-1880 period. Those who worked for the city on road or sewer construction and maintenance were generally paid one dollar per day. The rates which the textile corporations paid for common labor varied from year to year but averaged only a little over one dollar per day.[21]

2) Day labor was irregular employment. The digging of ditches, grading of streets, and unloading of coal, cotton, or other cargo did not provide continuous employment. Individuals might be employed one day and unemployed the next. At most, the day laborer could expect to be employed for 240 days out of the year. The work was generally outdoor work that could be, and usually was, halted by bad weather. The work

was seasonal and there was a frequent shortage of employment during the winter months. Seasonal unemployment frequently necessitated some resort to charitable or welfare support to furnish food and fuel during the coldest winter months for many Irish families.[22]

3) The type of work done by the laborer was generally physically taxing, occasionally exposing the individual to crippling or fatal accidents. The local paper reported several incidents involving serious work-related accidents. Timothy Sullivan, employed by the Street Commissioner, was leveling gravel on upper Pine Street when he suffered a fatal concussion caused by a piece of granite trim which fell from a nearby building. He left a widow and seven children. John Sullivan was killed when a construction derrick collapsed; and Henry Murphy, while not killed in that same accident, sustained serious injuries. For men whose livelihood depended upon their ability to do physical labor, serious injuries were often cause for the family to become dependent upon charitable support.[23]

4) As the laborer advanced in age, his economic position could be expected to deteriorate. The older man simply could not compete physically with the younger job seeker. Consequently, the Irish laborer was faced with the specter of misery in his retirement, not infrequently becoming a public charge when there was no family to support him.

These factors combined to make such work the least desirable employment available. The Irish dominance of the unskilled labor pool was not challenged until the French-Canadian immigration of the 1870s.[24] If at all possible, the Irish laborer desired to move into a more secure and better-paying economic position. Those who had experience or skills in the various construction trades were often able to find work as brick- or stonemasons or carpenters. The booming construction industry offered many opportunities. Yet the majority of Irishmen lacked experience in this activity, and they were not in a position to learn a new trade. The major textile manufacturing corporations in Lewiston, the Bates Manufacturing Company and the Hill Manufacturing Company, provided some day labor for Irish laborers and employed some Irish women and children in the cotton mills. For first generation Irish immigrants in the 1850s and 1860s, however, there were few adult males reporting employment as cotton mill operatives or filling other semi-skilled or skilled positions in the cotton or woolen mills.

Employment and social discrimination were clear factors in the constriction of economic opportunities. The policy of the Lewiston Water Power Company, and its successor the Franklin Company, was to hire "American girls" to work in the mills and "American" men to fill most of the skilled, clerical, and management positions in the cotton mills and company businesses.[25]

NATIVISM

At least two experiences in the 1850s reflected the anti-Irish sentiment of some members of the community and some of the Boston directors. Both of these events were connected to the establishment of an Irish Roman Catholic church in Lewiston. The first Roman Catholic worship service in Lewiston was held in the home of Patrick McGillicuddy in 1850. By the mid-1850s, regular services were being held in a building on Lincoln Street that had been previously used by another congregation. Albert Kelsey, the agent of the Franklin Company, gave permission for the property to be used by Father McLaughlin and the local Irish Catholics. In 1855, during the height of Know Nothing and anti-Catholic and anti-Irish sentiment, the building was set on fire by a local mob. Albert Kelsey later recalled and reflected on the experience of that night:

> The alarm of fire was given and I hurried down to the scene. I found five or six hundred Lewiston people standing opposite the burning building. They were hooting and yelling and jeering. The fire engine had come to the scene but someone had cut the hose. At that juncture I ordered out the hose from the Bates, as the building was almost directly in the rear of the mill. I posted men along the hose and told them that if anyone attempted to cut it, to hold those men on the premises at all hazards. Then I went to the end of the hose and took the nozzle. First of all I turned it across the street and swept that crowd of persons who stood there shouting in such an insulting fashion. They scattered like flies before a shower. Then I put the water on the fire. The building was ruined.[26]

Albert Kelsey, a Yankee Protestant with no more interest in the Catholics than any other denomination, was willing to exert his personal influence to stop a mob. A short time later he showed an equal willingness to confront the very people who had selected him to be their agent in Lewiston. Soon after the loss of their place of worship, the priest came to see Mr. Kelsey and indicated his understanding that the company had voted to give a lot of land to each of the religious denominations and asked if the same arrangements could be made for the Catholic church. Kelsey recommended a place on Lincoln Street and the priest indicated he would be satisfied with that. When Kelsey laid the matter before the directors of the Franklin Company on his next visit to Boston, President Lyman Nichols and Director Benjamin Bates "immediately flew up and declared that they would not vote for such a gift and for their part would do all they could to keep the Catholics from having a lot." [27] The matter was dropped from consideration at that meeting, but Kelsey encouraged Fr. McLaughlin to make a personal appeal and even paid for his expenses to travel to Boston to meet with the Franklin Company directors. When he returned, the priest told Kelsey that he had been treated very rudely and would never consent to talk with either Mr. Nichols or Mr. Bates again even to get a lot for his church.

Albert Kelsey was provoked by the report of the meeting and, showing Fr. McLaughlin a map on his office wall of available properties, he pointed out a prime lot on Main Street. "There is the finest lot in the city of Lewiston," Kelsey said. "It is large enough for your church and for your parsonage, what will you give for it?" The priest indicated that he would be able to pay $1500 with ten percent down and the remainder in yearly installments of ten percent. The paperwork was drawn up and the documents sent to the directors in Boston, where the sale agreement was signed as part of the regular business transactions. On a subsequent visit, when Lyman Nichols discovered that the lot had been sold for significantly less than its value and to the Catholic society, he was furious. Albert Kelsey indicated that he had acted within his authority as agent and was exercising his legitimate power consistent with his values. "The right and the wrong of the matter," he challenged President Nichols, "the question as to whether you are justified in trying to keep the Catholic church out of Lewiston, we will not discuss. The land has been sold and the sale will stand. If you want me to resign, I will do so right here and now." Kelsey's resignation was not demanded. While it took more than a decade to complete, St. Joseph's Roman Catholic Church and rectory were built on the Main Street lot.[28]

Discrimination, both overt and subtle, was a fact of life for Irish Catholic immigrants in the mid-nineteenth century. Yet, as Irish families settled into Lewiston, the attitude of men like Albert Kelsey provided a balance to the bigoted perceptions on Lewiston streets and in

Boston boardrooms. The Irish laborers were hard-working men committed to providing a better life for themselves and their families. Their labor was transforming the physical topography of the city.

The policy of hiring only American-born employees for the cotton mills also began to give way to economic necessity. Over the three decades from 1850 to 1880, the employment situation of foreign-born workers improved somewhat as a larger number of laborers were able to move into semi-skilled factory employment. A job in the textile mills paid somewhat better than day labor; but even more important than the slight improvement in daily wages was the fact that mill employment was a year-round occupation and was not beset with the uncertainties that plagued unskilled labor. The Lewiston Bleachery and Dye Works employed a large number of Irish men. This may have been because the work was considered undesirable by native-born job seekers. The Irish also had a firm hold on jobs at the Lewiston Gas Works, probably because potential competitors considered the work there undesirable.[29]

If social mobility and economic success were tied only to more secure and lucrative employment, the vast majority of Lewiston's Irish laborers were unable to achieve by that measure. Most still reported their occupation as laborer on the 1860, 1870, and 1880 census enumerations. The number of occupational successes among the group of Irish immigrants identified as day laborers was small, but enough to encourage some optimism about the possibilities open even to the unskilled Irish immigrant. Several Irish laborers were able to secure sufficient monies to purchase their own farms. Timothy O. Callahan, a young single man of twenty-four in 1850, was listed on the census enumeration as a laborer. In 1860, now married and with a young family, he reported his occupation as grocer. By 1880, he had been able to build his grocery business into an investment worth nearly $20,000. Thomas Ward, a day laborer in his late teens in 1860, had a very successful clothing business in the 1870s and served several terms as a city councilman.[30]

Among the Irish laborers in the city, however, one of the most striking financial successes was Patrick Many. Sometime in the 1850s, he moved from being identified as an unskilled day laborer to become a truckman. By 1860, he reported to the census enumerator real and personal property assets valued at $3,000. Over the course of the next fifteen years, Patrick Many was one of the city's leading contractors. He supervised railroad work, did private contracting for home and business construction, built several tenements that he owned and rented, and on occasion worked for the city. He was the owner and proprietor of the Androscoggin Trotting Park, the city's only racetrack. By the mid-1870s, his property was valued by the local tax assessors at over $25,000.[31]

The great majority of Irish laborers, however, were occupationally immobile. Even after thirty years in the city, over sixty percent of foreign-born day laborers still were reported on census enumerations or city directories as laborers. Some were able to accumulate sizeable property holdings, but most had only a tenuous security in either occupation or residence. Yet, the geographic mobility of this group after the initial decade was surprisingly low. Stephan Thernstrom in a study of unskilled labor in Newburyport, Massachusetts found that economic and social forces were at work winnowing out the less successful. No such mechanism appears to have been operative in Lewiston. Certainly, the opportunity for employment and the distance of Lewiston from other major cities that might have siphoned off population were factors. An additional factor was the availability of public charity support in times of economic distress.[32]

The laborer who could turn to the community for periodic relief during periods of seasonal unemployment or hardship was much more likely to remain where he was than to venture elsewhere in search of uncertain employment. The connection between residential permanency and welfare availability seems unquestionable. Where public support was available, an individual was unlikely to uproot his family without fairly good assurances that moving would enhance their security. For many laborers in Newburyport, there had been little choice. Newburyport's charitable assistance was, Thernstrom tells us, "penurious in the extreme." The prospects for foreign-born laborers were made even less attractive in the mid-1850s by the passage of a state law in Massachusetts forbidding relief to alien paupers except in a few grim State almshouses. The harshness of relief prospects, coupled with the declining employment opportunities, were undoubtedly factors encouraging many laborers to leave.[33]

The situation in Lewiston was significantly different. There was no state law relieving the community of the responsibility for the relief of immigrants. Nor were there other communities on whom Lewiston could shift the burden of support. While laborers coming into the city from rural communities in Maine could be returned to their place of origin in cases of indigence, Irish laborers who were Lewiston residents or who had no other settlement within the state automatically became Lewiston's responsibility.

From the early 1850s through 1880, the general attitude as evidenced by the reports of the overseers of the poor and other public officials was one of support and concern. A tightening up of public relief in the early 1860s—a reaction against the lax and over-generous attitude of the late 1850s—tended to be fairly short-lived. By 1868, Mayor Isaac Parker was saying of the overseers of the poor:

> They should be men who combine business qualifications with Christian virtues—men of discrimination and large humanity—men, who, while they would consult economy, if they erred at all would err on the side of humanity, and bestow too much rather than too little,—men who would always remember that they have a humane and Christian, as well as a legal duty to perform toward the unfortunate poor.[34]

In that year there were thirty-seven Irish families receiving aid, by far the largest number of any nationality. The overseers were not particularly upset by this fact, and attributed it to the "more liberal *private* charities of other nationalities."[35]

THE ARRIVAL OF FRENCH-CANADIANS

The employment situation became even bleaker in the 1870s with the onset of an extended economic depression. The large influx of French-Canadian families recruited for work in the cotton mills and those who joined them, coupled with the fact that Irish laborers who had entered the city in the early 1850s were by now advanced in age and often unable to work regularly, increased the city's welfare responsibilities. Yet there was little evidence that public officials felt that the individuals out of work were completely responsible for their condition. In 1871, Mayor Garcelon admonished that:

> the large influx of non-residents seeking employment in our manufactories, will always be a source of expense to the city. The poor we have always with us, and not only justice but also humanity requires prompt and efficient protection. Let us remember that there are none

so wealthy or exalted but they may become the objects of public support, and that the measure we mete unto others may in like measure be meted unto us.[36]

In addition to direct charitable relief, the city assisted many by providing work on the city streets, sewers, and other public works. Mayor Farwell in his 1873 address suggested that the city provide "those destitute and temporarily out of employment with some occupation upon the city works or otherwise." The benefits of such a policy, he argued, would be twofold. Those helped would have an opportunity to earn their own support and thus feel less like dependents on the city's bounty. At the same time the expenses of the city would be reduced.[37] By 1880 all street work was being done by the day, under a city regulation which required that this work be given only to Lewiston residents. This regulation gave an advantage to Irish laborers over newly arrived immigrants who had no established legal residence in the community, and the passage of such a restriction reflected the growing political influence of the Irish.

If nineteenth-century Americans were optimistic about the immigrant laborer's chances for upward mobility, they were even more optimistic about his children's prospects for success. Was this optimism warranted? The frame of this study allows only a partial view of the experience of the second generation of Irish residents, some born in Ireland or on route, and many more born in Lewiston. The tenuous economic position of many of Lewiston's Irish families during the 1850-1880 period necessitated the employment of all available family members. Irish wives frequently took in washing or ironing, older daughters took positions as maids in the households of Lewiston's more affluent families; but the most frequent resort was the employment of Irish children in the city's cotton textile mills. From a young age—often nine or ten—many Irish children went to work in the cotton mills. The report of the overseers of the poor in 1872 was critical of the preparation that these children were receiving for self-supporting adult life:

There are, in our city, at least five hundred male and female minor children, that are growing up with very little education, and a great many without any at all; with no knowledge of labor, except that furnished by our mills, the result of which will be to increase the number of paupers to an alarming extent, just so fast as they go out into the world on their own account.[38]

The reports and pronouncements of public officials throughout the 1860s and 1870s were full of concern about the lack of preparation that the children of the poor were receiving. One major problem was the failure of the city to build sufficient school facilities to meet the ever-rising demand. As early as 1868 the School Committee had expressed serious alarm at the inadequacy of the facilities to meet the needs. The overcrowding of classrooms was most acute in the working class districts, where population growth was most intense, and where Irish and later French-Canadian families were most highly concentrated. Five primary schools on Lincoln Street were crowded to overflowing the School Committee reported, for all of these scholars had been rejected for want of room. From the school near the Gas Works, a strongly Irish residential area, twenty-five scholars were taken out at one time and sent into the streets to give room for the remainder to turn around. The conclusions of the Board were unequivocal:

> It is now a question as to whether we shall provide our children, particularly those of the lower grades, with the means to prepare themselves for the duties of life, or drive them into the streets where they may fit themselves for lives of idleness and, perhaps, crime. We may postpone other improvements and not materially suffer; but to postpone the construction of needed schoolrooms may forever put beyond our control hundreds of children, soon to become strong men and women and take upon themselves responsibilities as citizens.[39]

It became increasingly obvious, however, that the lack of sufficient classroom facilities was not the only factor involved in the alarmingly low rates of school attendance by lower-class children. One of the most penetrating criticisms of the educational system's inability to meet the needs of laboring children was offered by Dr. Alonzo Garcelon in his address as mayor in 1871:

> We have a law upon our statute books requiring the attendance of every scholar under the age of fifteen years employed in our mills, for at least three months in every year. This law, though of vital importance, is a dead letter practically. Enforced though it might and ought to be, to its full extent, I presume there would be hundreds of instances which demand especial consideration. We must bear in mind that by far the larger proportion of these scholars are children of the poor, and that their labor in the mills, or elsewhere, is absolutely essential to keep the wolf from

the door—that without that labor starvation or the poor-house would be the fate of many a family.[40]

The educational system, as it existed, was aimed at the preparation of middle-class children for adult life. One of Mayor Garcelon's major criticisms was that the system of graded schools discriminated against the poor, since they could attend only a small part of each year. Consequently, they became lost in the educational system, seldom meeting the requirements for advancement to higher grades, and often totally neglected. In a statement which is, perhaps, the clearest critique both of the inapplicability of the school system to this class of students and of the whole mobility thesis, Mayor Garcelon admonished: "It is idle to throw open gilded parlors and to expose to gaze tables covered with the choicest delicacies, and invite to the banquet those who are bound by the inexorable thongs of fate to a position from which they cannot extricate themselves."[41]

Dr. Garcelon further argued that "unless we would have growing up in our midst a class almost entirely devoid of the rudiments of education, vicious as well as ignorant, we must have especial provision for their accommodation."[42] He suggested that schools be set up where these children could learn the basic educational tools and that, in addition, the city promote some type of vocational education where working-class children could learn useful and marketable skills. These suggestions were not acted upon. The city did not have the money or interest in making special provisions for the education of the poor. For the most part, Irish children were exposed to formal education for only a few years, if at all, and then picked up what further training they required in the city's textile mills or elsewhere.

In spite of the pessimism expressed by some of the city's leading political figures, the situation was not as dismal as it might at first seem. While those occupations that required educational training—professions and a variety of white-collar positions—were effectively closed to all but a very small minority of Irish children, their economic position tended to be more secure than their father's. Unskilled day labor, which had furnished employment for the majority of Irish immigrants, accounted for only about twenty percent of the occupational distribution of the second generation. The majority, quite understandably, moved into semi-skilled factory employment. The cotton textile mills had furnished for most Irish children their earliest working experience.

Some individuals were able to move upward within the factory hierarchy to lower management positions. A larger number held skilled jobs as spinners, dyers, or section hands. The majority, however, were listed in the census schedules and city directories as simply factory operatives. The sons of Irish laborers also had greater access to skilled construction jobs. A fairly large number became brick masons or carpenters. Many of them undoubtedly served the construction demands within the Irish community. A number of sons of Irish immigrants became prominent businessmen. Timothy J. Murphy, founder of the T. J. Murphy Fur Co., was among those who emerged in the late nineteenth century as significant business leaders.[43]

While the economic position of the second generation hardly warrants excessive optimism, their occupational improvement was significant. Increased security and higher pay meant that a greater proportion of second-generation families were able to survive economically without the necessity of relying upon the employment of their children. The third generation was, therefore, in a position to avail itself of the types of educational training that would prepare them for more desirable and lucrative employment.[44]

HOME OWNERSHIP

In addition to the security of regular and remunerative employment, the Irish immigrant also sought residential security in the city. For some this involved the purchase or construction of their own home. For those forced to rent, residential security meant being able to afford healthy and sanitary accommodations for their families. The degree of success in meeting this objective varied considerably.

Home ownership represented both an avenue of upward social mobility into the property-holding class and an insurance against the vicissitudes of urban life. The Irish experience with eviction from their homes caused them to place an extremely high priority on property accumulation and home ownership. Many Irish families were willing to make great sacrifices—including the education of their children—in order to accumulate sufficient savings to purchase a city lot and construct a home. The earliest Irish immigrants who came to Lewiston to work on the canal system found themselves in a community that had little available housing facilities for them. The cotton mills planned for large brick boarding houses to be constructed to accommodate the girls who were recruited to work in the mills. The Lewiston Water Power Company also undertook the construction in the early 1850s of a hotel in Lewiston and made arrangements with the hotelkeeper to subsidize his expenses during the slow winter season. Personal homes, tenements, and private boarding houses were being constructed as quickly as possible, but in the early 1850s population growth outdistanced the supply of housing. A sizeable number of the Irish day laborers and their families were housed in "shanties" built on land owned by the Lewiston Water Power Company. The records of the Franklin Company, the successor to the Lewiston Water Power Company, include a Rent Roll of Lewiston Water Power Company Shanties. The typical monthly rent for a company owned shanty was a dollar a month, although Jerre Murphy paid an additional five dollars in 1856 to rent land for a garden for the season. The Rent Book list names and locations of the housing in places like Mill Dam, Tan Yard, Lower Level, Foundry, Gas Works, and Pine Tree Lot.[45] These company-owned properties and several other areas where Irish families built their own temporary housing were known as "patches"—Shingle Patch, Burnt Woods, Strawberry Patch, and Gas House Patch. In these locations, the Irish population crowded into small wooden cottages, some of them only one-room houses and others banked up with earth on the sides.[46]

These housing facilities, meagerly furnished, provided cheap and affordable housing. However, the excessive crowding of dwellings and unsanitary and unclean surroundings made them a potentially very serious health hazard. In the summer of 1854, the worst fears were realized when an epidemic of Asiatic cholera made its appearance in Lewiston. The disease outbreak, although it did not originate in the Irish community, got into Shingle Patch—one of the largest of the Irish settlements. As a health precaution and to prevent the spread of the disease, the selectmen ordered the dwellers on Shingle Patch to pull down their houses and move them into the country below the village. The other "patches" were less hard hit. Extensive efforts were made in those areas to clean up the buildings and surroundings. Although it lasted but a few weeks, the epidemic killed over 200 persons, the majority of them Irish.[47]

The undesirable nature of these rude accommodations, added to the strong desire for property ownership, encouraged those Irish laborers who could afford it to purchase or construct their own homes. The relatively low pay and irregular employment of many Irish immigrants prevented them from accumulating the necessary financial reserve to purchase land and construct a home. Even with the employment of several children, many families were barely able to supply their basic needs. Another factor that worked against the Irish was the relatively high cost of city lots. The dynamic nature of Lewiston's economy and the dramatic increase in population created a booming real estate market. The demand for city lots drove up the price. The most fortunate Irishmen were those who were able to make real estate purchases in the 1850s when 50 x 100 foot lots on some streets could be purchased for $200. By the mid-1860s, comparable lots could not be secured for less than $500 to $800.[48]

The manuscript census schedules for the 1850 through 1870 period indicate the value of real and personal property owned by the respondent. The process of property accumulation was extremely slow and the majority of Irish immigrants were never able to become homeowners. Those who did, however, often reported sizeable property holdings— generally in excess of $1,000. However, the census does not reveal the extent to which this property was mortgaged. The records of the Androscoggin Registry of Deeds reveal not only the amount of money involved in the various real estate transfers, but also whether the property was mortgaged and the terms for mortgage repayment. A review of selected real estate transfers suggests that it was unusual for Irish property owners to purchase their property without resort to a mortgage whether provided by a local bank or an individual. The process of meeting the financial obligations on the first mortgage often required the taking out of a second mortgage.[49]

The size of the property holdings of many Irishmen and information gathered from newspapers and other sources indicates that many of the Irish who owned property built tenement houses or multi-family homes that not only served the owner's family but also furnished, through rents, a second source of income. Income from rents often provided sufficient funds to meet the mortgage and other financial obligations on the property. There was a great demand for housing and rents tended to be rather high. This encouraged those who could to participate in this lucrative real estate market. In addition, Irish families who were forced to rent preferred, when possible, to rent from individuals who were extended family or who they knew and trusted.

Many tenement buildings, hastily and inexpensively constructed, were sub-standard; and the working-class and Irish residential areas suffered from inadequate sewage and sanitary facilities. In the early decades of urban growth, the city was without an adequate sewer system. Efforts were made in the late 1860s to overcome the inadequacies. However, the City Physician reported in 1871 that:

> notwithstanding [what] the city has done during the year by the construction of sewers, cleaning of streets, etc., for the sanitary improvements of the place, there yet remains much to be done. I cannot avoid the conclusion that very much of the sickness of the city, especially among the Irish and French population, is caused by the overcrowding of tenements, with the consequent impure atmosphere within doors, and by poisonous gases from decaying vegetable and animal matter about the dwellings.[50]

The situation tended to deteriorate, rather than improve, over the succeeding years as the growing population and the influx of large numbers of French-Canadians put increased pressure on already inadequate tenement facilities. In 1877 the City Physician reported in his annual review that:

> In some parts of the city, tenement houses are greatly overcrowded, so much so in our opinion as to constitute a prolific source of disease. In such localities especially, not only are the dwellings crowded and filthy, but the cellars and yards are, in many places, strewn with decaying organic matter, which not only offends the senses, but poisons the system and results in disease. In several instances families are living in apartments almost entirely below the level of the ground, the walls of whose rooms are seldom dry and the atmosphere always polluted with odors of mould and mildew. Such abodes may possibly afford health to some of the lower forms of animal life, but cannot aid the physical and moral advancement of a community.[51]

The historian surveying the residential position of the Irish immigrant might well be drawn to that small but impressive number who were able to make large gains. Individuals like Patrick Marshall, a common laborer, experienced no occupational mobility during the thirty-year period of this study. In 1856 he was listed on the Rent Roll as living in a company-owned shanty near the railroad depot and paying a dollar a month.[52] By 1880, however, he was able to report property holdings valued in excess of $7,000. His experience was repeated by others, yet the vast majority of Lewiston's Irish population failed to share in this success. The high cost of real estate and the inability of most families to accumulate sufficient savings for the purchase or construction of their own home meant that the majority was forced to rent. Throughout the period of this study, the Irish were residentially segregated in certain areas of the city—Irish Patch, Gas House Patch, Burnt Woods.[53]

Occupational and residential security represented two significant threads in the fabric of Irish immigrant experience in Lewiston. The creation of a secure, stable and vital religious, social and political life in the community was equally important. While historical and statistical tools enable a researcher to map out changes in occupation or property holdings over a particular period, the matrix of experiences and factors that contribute to social, religious, and political security and vitality are more subjective and difficult to quantify.

LATE NINETEENTH-CENTURY IRISH STABILITY

The development of a community of interest between the Irish and the city at large was a gradual and mutual process. Lewiston was a community in transition during this critical period. Physically, the city of Lewiston in 1880 was significantly transformed from the town of 1850. Socially and politically the transformation was more extensive. By 1880, the city had several Roman Catholic Churches and a significant and growing French-Canadian population. The employment opportunities available in 1880 were well beyond what was available for the first Irish residents who had come in 1850. The city had a system of public education that, while at times stressed and less than fully adequate, provided elementary and secondary educational opportunities. Lewiston could boast of its college, named for entrepreneur Benjamin Bates and open to both men and women. Time and shared experience reshaped some of the more virulent anti-Irish sentiment. While the local newspaper might report on the less than socially acceptable activities of some individuals in the Irish community with accounts of drunkenness, illegal sale of liquor, or other criminal behaviors, they were equally committed to reporting similar activities if conducted by native born.

The active participation of many Irishmen during the Civil War indicated their commitment to their new country and enhanced their acceptance into the social and political life of the community. Political power and influence were critical to Irish security and success. Ordinances, like that requiring that city workers be legal residents, secured jobs on the city streets, post office, police and fire departments. Political patronage and the opportunity to participate in lucrative contracts for public buildings further enhanced the position of Irish born residents and their children and grandchildren.

When the municipal elections were held in 1878, Patrick McGillicuddy was elected as an alderman and the City Council included Michael Eagan, Timothy J. Murphy, John Garner and Dennis J. Callahan. The Irish had political control of several wards in the city and a prominent voice in the political life of the local Democratic Party. Within another decade, the Irish community of Lewiston would have the political influence and power to place Daniel (D. J.) McGillicuddy on the ballot for Mayor and see him successfully elected. Daniel J. McGillicuddy was the son of John McGillicuddy and the nephew of Patrick McGillicuddy. John was the brother who had stayed in Ireland to watch over the family, while his older brother Patrick sought his fortune in America. In Lewiston, John bought a farm and raised his family. Daniel, was educated in the Lewiston schools and graduated from Bowdoin College in 1881, studied law and was admitted to the Maine bar in 1883. He was a prominent lawyer and politician, serving in the Maine legislature; then after three terms as Mayor, he served in the United States Congress, where he drafted the first Workmen's Compensation Act to pass Congress. [54]

When the city celebrated its 100th anniversary in 1895, the Irish were hailed in the local paper as including among them some of the prominent men of business and civic life. While it could not be said that by 1880 the Irish community of Lewiston had achieved full integration, occupational and residential security, and social acceptance and respectability, giant strides had been made. Although there were dramatic experiences of personal success, such as Patrick McGillicuddy, Timothy J. Murphy, and Patrick Many, the overall Irish experience in Lewiston represented no "rags to riches" phenomenon. Progress was slow and often slowest for those who had farthest to go. The majority of Irishmen who came to Lewiston in the 1850s and 1860s were poor, illiterate, and burdened by heavy family responsibilities. They adjusted to their condition as best they could, accepting the types of employment that were available, making advances when the opportunities arose. With the first three decades, most were able to secure for themselves and their families a life filled with greater possibilities and opportunities than they had experienced in mid-nineteenth century Ireland or dared to hope they might secure in a new country. They brought with them and retained a commitment to their religion, culture, music, and traditions that they continued to cherish in the city they helped to build.

1. *Lewiston Evening Journal*, 17 March 1908.
2. *Lewiston Evening Journal*, 10 February 1908.
3. Ibid.
4. Ibid.
5. Ibid.
6. John Hayward, *Hayward's New England Gazetteer* (Boston: Israel S. Boyd and William White, 1856), 295.
7. J. G. Elder, *History of Lewiston* (Lewiston, ME: A. G. Daniels, Printer, 1882), 10–25.
8. Ibid., 26.
9. Eunice Stevens, "Recollections of Lewiston" in *Newsletter of the Androscoggin Historical Society* 13 (September 1994).
10. *Lewiston Evening Journal*, 23 May 1900.
11. Ibid.
12. James Mundy, *Hard Times, Hard Men: Maine and The Irish 1830–1860* (Scarborough, ME: Harp Publications, 1990), 59.
13. Ibid.
14. Oscar Handlin, *Boston's Immigrants: A Study in Acculturation* (Cambridge, MA: Harvard University Press, 1959), 45.
15. Ibid., 49–50.
16. Ibid.
17. This essay is based on a longitudinal study of Irish residents in Lewiston with data from the manuscript census schedules for 1850, 1860, 1870 and 1880. This original census data provides information on names, ages, place of birth, occupations, and other information at ten-year intervals.
18. *Lewiston Evening Journal*, 23 May 1900.
19. This is a summary based on a more detailed study of occupational changes among Irish laborers in the 1850–1880 period.
20. Ibid.
21. *Tenth Census of the United States* (Washington, DC: Government Printing Office, 1886), 344–46.
22. Stephan Thernstrom, *Poverty and Progress: Social Mobility in a Nineteenth Century City* (New York: Atheneum Press, 1969), 20.
23. *Lewiston Evening Journal* articles, cross-referenced with reports of Lewiston Overseers of the Poor.

24. In 1870, Canadian immigrants accounted for only thirteen percent of the common labor force; by 1880 they were the largest single group with about forty-four per cent.

25. The Lewiston Water Power Company went through a financial crisis in the mid-1850s as the result of a forty-percent dividend paid to the shareholders and a heavy debt incurred for municipal improvements. The result was that the company was allowed to go under and the Franklin Company was created with the acquisition of the real estate and property rights. The management structure of the new company, including the major stockholders and directors, remained essentially unchanged.

26. *Lewiston Evening Journal*, 23 May 1900.

27. Ibid.

28. Ibid.

29. The Lewiston City Directories for 1860, 1864, 1872, and 1878–79 were used as a source for places of employment in addition to the Census data.

30. A combination of sources—manuscript Census reports, Lewiston City Directories, city reports, local property deeds, and *Lewiston Evening Journal* newspaper information—were used to fill in the careers of individuals. The success of Timothy O. Callahan may also have been assisted by his marriage to Mary McGillicuddy, a sister of Patrick McGillicuddy. Refer to *Lewiston Evening Journal*, 10 February 1908.

31. The information on Patrick Many is from manuscript Census reports, Lewiston City Directories, and *Lewiston Evening Journal* articles.

32. Thernstrom, *Poverty and Progress*, 25–26.

33. Ibid., 25.

34. "Mayor's Address," *Annual Report of the City of Lewiston for 1868*, 7–8.

35. "Report of the Overseers of the Poor," *Annual Report of the City of Lewiston for 1868*, 52–53.

36. "Mayor's Address," *Annual Report of the City of Lewiston for 1871*, 12.

37. "Mayor's Address," *Annual Report of the City of Lewiston for 1873*, 6.

38. "Report of the Overseers of the Poor," *Annual Report of the City of Lewiston for 1872*, 9.

39. "School Committee Report," *Annual Report of the City of Lewiston for 1868*, 84–86.

40. "Mayor's Address," *Annual Report of the City of Lewiston for 1871*, 8–9.

41. Ibid., 10.

42. Ibid.

43. Statistical analysis within the scope of this research (1850–1880) reveals that only about twenty percent of laborer's sons held unskilled jobs; about sixty percent were in semi-skilled (mostly factory operative) positions; and the remainder were in skilled or non-manual employment. These are only averages; the analysis indicates a wide percentage range depending on the age of the individuals. Clearly, employment positions filled by young men in their late teens and twenties are not an accurate indicator of mature adult occupational success.

44. A full study of second-generation families has not been conducted, but the Census information that is available indicates a reduction in child labor in those families.

45. Rent Roll of Lewiston Water Power Company Shanties 1856, Volume 7, Franklin Company Records, Lewiston Public Library.

46. *Lewiston Evening Journal*, 4 July 1895, 20.

47. Ibid.

48. *Lewiston Evening Journal*, 19 July 1876, 3.

49. The census schedules have provided some of this information; the remainder was secured from recorded deeds at the Androscoggin Registry of Deeds.

50. "Report of the City Physician," *Annual Report of the City of Lewiston*, 1871, 68.

51. "Report of the City Physician," *Annual Report of the City of Lewiston*, 1877, 70–71.

52. Rent Roll of Lewiston Water Power Company Shanties 1856 in Franklin Company Records, Lewiston Public Library.

53. Information on individuals, such as Patrick Marshall, has been gathered from Census records, City Directories, records of property transfers and deeds, Franklin Company papers, and random newspaper articles.

54. Obituary of Daniel J. McGillicuddy, *Lewiston Evening Journal*, 30 July 1936.

MAINE AND THE FENIAN INVASION OF CANADA, 1866

by Gary W. Libby

THIS ESSAY provides a chronology of the events that preceded and encompassed several attempts by the Fenian Brotherhood to invade Canada immediately after the American Civil War. These Fenian invasion attempts forced British North America to deal with the issue of defense in a coordinated fashion at a time when the formation of the Canadian Confederation was being hotly debated. This essay's primary focus is on the Fenians' attempt to invade New Brunswick from a base in Washington County, Maine, in the spring of 1866.

The Fenian Brotherhood was a secret revolutionary society organized in New York City in 1855 with the aim of achieving Ireland's independence from Britain by force. The organizational meeting, attended by a group of veterans of the 1848 Irish rising, took place at Michael Doheny's law office.[1] The name "Fenian" was derived from the Fianna (meaning warriors or soldiers) who were the legendary companions of Finn macCumaill and Oisin. (An alternate explanation of this name is the the Féne were a pre-Celtic people who lived in present-day Ireland.) The Fenians' guiding principle was "the conviction that the Irish people wanted separation and that the Fenians had the incontestable and inviolable right to get it for them by force of arms."[2]

After the organizational meeting, Joseph Denieffe, an American Fenian disgusted by the activities of the American Know-Nothing movement, returned to Ireland in 1856 and soon thereafter swore in Ireland's first Fenians.[3] By St. Patrick's Day 1858, Fenian leader James Stephens, who had joined the Irish Fenian Brotherhood soon after its beginning, had refined the organization's form and character, had written down its oath, and had begun recruitment in earnest.[4]

In Ireland and Britain, the Fenians were an oath-bound secret society. The oath had both external and internal application: "to make Ireland an independent democratic republic" and "to preserve inviolable secrecy regarding all the transactions of this secret society."[5] The American Fenians, however, were not bound by oath. American members merely had to sign a pledge, and even that was not required of military officers or persons of "position."[6] In Ireland, the requirement of an oath led to the condemnation of the Fenians by the Catholic Church, which excommunicated anyone who took the oath. The Fenians were officially denounced in two Papal Encyclicals. The Catholic Church apparently was troubled by the fact that the Fenians were a secular organization, influenced by the Protestant revolutionary Theobald Wolfe Tone. John O'Mahony, the Fenian leader in the United States, wrote, "Every individual born on Irish soil constitutes according to Fenian doctrine a unit of that nation, without reference to race or religious belief, and as such he is entitled to a heritage in the Irish soil, subject to such economic, political and equitable relations as shall seem fit to future legislators of a liberated Ireland."[7]

The Fenian Brotherhood in the United States grew explosively from forty members in 1858 to approximately 50,000 at the beginning of the American Civil War.[8] Membership recruitment continued with much success after the beginning of the war in both the Union and Confederate Armies.

During their exile in Paris following their participation in the abortive 1848 Irish rising, James Stephens, the Irish leader, and John O'Mahony, the principal organizer of the American branch, had studied continental secret societies, particularly the Italian. The Fenians were organized in "circles"; the head of each circle was called the "center." A circle theoretically consisted of 820 men, organized in multiples of nine. Each Center had nine "B"s (captains) under him. Each B had nine "C"s (sergeants) under him. Each C had nine "D"s under him. This structure, however, was largely ignored in practice.[9]

The American Fenians held their first convention in Chicago in November 1863, adopting a Constitution under which the government of the Brotherhood was led by a Head Center (O'Mahony) and a Central Council of five members, with secretaries and treasurers. This Convention proclaimed the virtual establishment of the Republic of Ireland and recognized James Stephens as the Brotherhood's representative in Europe.

In January 1865, shortly before the end of the American Civil War, at the second Fenian Convention held in Cincinnati, the Brotherhood began to split over two crucial issues. First was the control of its treasury. Second was the advisability of a Fenian invasion of British North America (as Canada was then called) in place of a Fenian invasion of Ireland itself. A faction lead by Colonel William Randall Roberts concluded that an attack on Ireland was unlikely to occur and, instead, urged an attack upon Canada. The Fenian Head Center, John O'Mahony, argued against an attack on Canada and suggested that the Brotherhood's efforts should continue to be directed toward Ireland itself. O'Mahony believed that if the Fenians could capture a beachhead in Ireland and hold out long enough, they could declare the Republic "virtually established" and then ask the Americans to recognize their government as a belligerent, as the British had recognized the Confederacy. Although at the end of the convention O'Mahony remained Head Center, the convention took steps to reduce his authority by increasing the size of the Central Council and electing O'Mahony's chief rival, Col. Roberts, as a Council member.

Following the Civil War, relations between Britain and the United States were at a low point. Britain had accorded belligerent status, one step from full diplomatic recognition, to the Confederacy and had allowed its ports to be used by Confederate raiders such as the *CSS Alabama*. At the end of the War, the Americans sought substantial compensation from the British for shipping lost to Confederate raiders built and operated out of British ports.

One manifestation of the low point was the American decision to abrogate the 1854 reciprocal treaty between the U.S. and Britain which allowed American fishermen to fish in British North American (Canadian) coastal waters and Canadian fishermen to fish in U.S. waters north of 36 degrees North latitude. That treaty also provided for free trade in a substantial list of natural products. A significant body of American opinion believed that the treaty favored British North America. On March 17, 1865, the U.S. gave the required one year's notice of its intent to abrogate the treaty. The abrogation took effect on March 17, 1866.

During 1865, the Andrew Johnson Administration sold weapons, including the *Ocean Spray*, a former Confederate raider, to the Fenians, knowing their intended use. At the time, Johnson was embroiled in a struggle with the Radical Republicans over Reconstruction. He needed the support of Irish America in the upcoming 1866 congressional elections; this bloc had generally supported the Democrats and opposed the Radical Republicans. The importance of the Irish vote had swelled as hundreds of thousands of Irish immigrated to the United States during the Great Irish Potato Famine of 1845–1850. In 1850 approximately a quarter of New York City's population, some 133,000 people, was Irish-born. By 1851 there were approximately one million people of Irish birth in the United States.[10]

Events in Ireland began to propel the Fenians toward military action. The British raided the offices of the Fenian newspaper, the *Irish People*, on September 14, 1865 and arrested some of the Fenian leaders. The British arrested James Stephens on November 11, 1865, but he escaped from jail two weeks later. He then fled the country. Meanwhile, those British regiments which had been heavily infiltrated by Fenian recruiters were posted overseas.

In October of 1865, Bernard Doran Killian, a prominent American Fenian, met with President Johnson[11] and Secretary of State William H. Seward[12] to sound out the administration's position on possible Fenian military activities. Killian asked how they would react if the Fenians seized some portion of Canada north of Maine. The two leaders led Killian to believe that the Johnson Administration would acknowledge the *fait accompli*.[13]

By the time of the third Fenian Convention, held in Philadelphia also in October 1865, the Brotherhood's internal fracture was almost complete. More than 600 delegates attended that convention and vigorously debated a proposal for an invasion of Canada. Delegates loyal to Col. Roberts supported the idea of a Canadian invasion that was just as vigorously opposed by delegates loyal to O'Mahony. The Roberts' wing of the Fenian Brotherhood made gains among the delegates that resulted in O'Mahony's being stripped of some of his powers. The Philadelphia convention abolished the position of Head Center as well as the Central Council and replaced them with a new structure based on the American Constitution, with a President and a General Congress consisting of a Senate and House of Delegates.[14] O'Mahony, however, retained the top spot, being elected President. He then appointed his own cabinet with a Secretary of War, an Agent of the Irish Republic, and an agent for the issue of bonds.[15]

By late autumn of 1865, the schism became irrevocable. The issue was control of the Fenian treasury, which consisted largely of the proceeds from the sale of bonds that were to be redeemed upon the success of the Fenian movement and the establishment of an Irish Republic.[16] The Senate wing's acting Treasurer, O'Rourke, was opposed to sending any more money to Ireland. Because O'Rourke was unable to post the $500,000 bond required by the Philadelphia Constitution, O'Mahony refused to recognize him as Treasurer and turned the Fenian money over to Killian instead. The Fenian Senate then declared that O'Mahony had acted unconstitutionally. Thereafter, there were two Fenian Treasurers. O'Rourke kept control over approximately $10,000. The O'Mahony wing controlled the rest of the Fenian treasury.[17]

After Stephens' arrest in Ireland, O'Mahony, without authority to do so, signed $68,000 of Fenian bonds and circulated them over the Senate's objections. [18] The Senate then passed a resolution forbidding O'Mahony to circulate those bonds. O'Mahony responded by claiming that the Senate had met illegally and refused to obey its resolution. The Senate retaliated by sending auditors to examine O'Mahony's Treasurer's books. Killian threw the Senate's auditors out of his office. By December 13, 1865, the Fenian Senate had published a Bill of Impeachment against O'Mahony.[19]

In the interim, Sir Frederick Bruce, the British Minister in Washington, had learned of the Fenian plans for a Canadian invasion. Bruce met with Secretary Seward, informing him orally of the substance of a British dispatch that instructed Bruce to maneuver the U.S. Government into a position to prevent an attack from U.S. soil. Seward responded by saying that he thought the Fenian affair was greatly exaggerated.[20] Bruce, however, was well supplied with intelligence gathered by British agents, including copies of O'Mahony's letters.[21] Seward assured Bruce that the U.S. Government had taken more precautions with respect to the Fenians than was supposed.[22] President Johnson told Bruce that the Fenian movement met with no sympathy on part of the U. S. Government.[23] Bruce reported back to his superiors in London describing Johnson as "our best friend in the administration."

About this time, the U.S. Army dismissed Gen. Thomas W. Sweeney, the Secretary of War in Roberts' wing of Fenians and an active duty army officer, from U.S. Army service. [24] Sweeney had asked for leave from the Army to visit Fenian Headquarters in New York City following his appointment as Fenian Secretary of War. U.S. Major General Thomas refused Sweeney's request for leave. Sweeney went to New York anyway.[25] Secretary of War Edwin Stanton then dismissed Sweeney from U.S. Army for having been "AWOL."[26] In reality, Stanton dismissed Sweeney for being an officer in the Fenian army.

The O'Mahony wing called for a congress to meet at Clifton Hall in New York City on January 3, 1866. About 600 delegates attended that Congress.[27] General Sweeney appeared before the Congress and admitted that the arms which O'Mahony had prevented him from buying were intended for an invasion of Canada and not of Ireland. The Congress ordered all Senators to appear before it. Only three (Meany, Mullin and Sennott) appeared; the rest were expelled from the Fenian Brotherhood. The Congress then rescinded the Philadelphia Constitution and re-adopted the Constitution drafted at the 1863 Chicago Constitution.[28] The new Constitution abolished the Senate and eliminated the title of President, replacing it with the old title of Head Center. O'Mahony was elected Head Center and given power to appoint a five-man Cabinet. As a check on the Head Center's power, the Congress elected a five-member Council to serve as an advisory and controlling body. The Head Center was named the chief financial agent. The five-member Council consisted of J. J. Rogers, Capt. J. Tobin, R. A. Sennott, James MaGrath and Jeremiah Cavanaugh.[29] The O'Mahony Congress endorsed an invasion of Ireland, not Canada.

After escaping from the British and before leaving Ireland, Stephens had issued a document denouncing the Roberts faction for "madly and treacherously" raising the cry of "to Canada instead of to Ireland" in defiance of the "wise and loyal O'Mahony." Stephens also wrote that the Roberts faction was guilty of cowardice and treason, and called on all right-thinking Fenians to cut and hack away the rotten branches.[30] Stephens had written letters to New York City newspapers calling the proposed Canadian Invasion "UnIrish."[31]

The Senate of the Roberts wing responded to the O'Mahony Congress and to Stephens' letters by holding a meeting on January 18, 1866. Speakers at that meeting claimed to have the support of two-thirds of the Fenian Circles and repudiated Stephens' attacks. The Roberts wing followed with an open membership meeting in February 1866 at a Pittsburgh Masonic Hall. That meeting decided on a three-pronged Canadian invasion involving 10,000 men to take place in winter so as to allow crossing of the ice-covered lakes and rivers. The three prongs were to be invasions launched from Detroit/Chicago; Buffalo, New York; and St. Albans, Vermont. General Sweeney, formerly of the U.S. Army and then serving as the Secretary of War in the Roberts Cabinet, gave an interview in which he said that a revolution in Ireland was impossible at present and that only those with no conception of warfare dreamed of such a possibility. According to Sweeney, sending detached parties of Americans to Ireland would be murder. Sweeney advocated the more practical plan of striking the British enemy in British North America, three thousand miles from Britain and within a few miles of the Fenians' base.[32]

Apparently, at least some Irish Fenians agreed with Sweeney. The *New York Tribune* reported that: "The people of Ireland who sympathize with Fenianism say they have only one hope—the only bright side of the picture that they can find to contemplate is that Canada must be captured."[33]

Events in Ireland continued to add impetus to events in America. The British suspended the Writ of Habeas Corpus in Ireland on February 17, 1866, perhaps as a result of reports of the *Cuba*, a Fenian privateer, putting to sea. News of the suspension reached New York City by March 1, causing O'Mahony to issue an Order calling on all Fenian Circles to gather together ready to take action. On Friday, March 2, 1866, the Portland *Daily Eastern Argus* reported the suspension of Habeas Corpus in Ireland. That day, Fenian Circles throughout New England met in response to an appeal from Messrs. Tobin and A. P. Sennott. Also, on March 2, Col. Roberts issued his own appeal for action: "Let men who will fight report to General Sweeney."

On March 3, Capt. John McCafferty, a former Irish prisoner and special envoy of James Stephens, "had a long and interesting interview with the President of the U.S." and "intended to call on him again at an early day."[34]

The media, especially the New York City press, greatly overstated the strength of the Fenian movement. That may have been done by design rather than by poor reporting. During the subsequent Fenian expedition to Campobello, the New Brunswick press alleged that the two correspondents covering the Fenians for the *New York Herald*, a Mr. Williams and a Mr. Fitzpatrick, were either Fenians themselves or Fenian sympathizers. They were accused of filing dispatches designed to arouse the sympathies of the American people in favor of the Fenians.[35] The *New York World's* Eastport correspondent meanwhile was none other than John Warren, a leader of the rival Roberts/Sweeney Fenians.[36] The *World* published wildly sensational accounts of the O'Mahony Fenians' Eastport adventure.

The March 5, 1866 issues of the *Portland Eastern Argus* carried a report from the *New York Express* that claimed that there were "nearly a million men ready to move." Some less gullible observers attempted to refute the New York newspapers' inflated claims. For example, a writer from Chicago, which had been described as a hotbed of Fenianism, described the demonstration there on St. Patrick's day as "in every respect a failure" since all the Fenians were able to muster after strenuous efforts were eight hundred men with muskets.[37]

Like the national Fenian Brotherhood, the Portland Fenians had split into two circles, one loyal to O'Mahony and the other loyal to Roberts/Sweeny. On March 6, Portland's O'Mahony Circle held a "large and enthusiastic meeting" at which "a large sum was subscribed, and considerable was contributed in small sums."[38] Daniel O'Connell O'Donoghue, who had been born in County Kerry, Ireland, on October 21, 1843, was the Center of Portland's O'Mahony Circle. O'Donoghue emigrated to New York City prior to the Civil War. He served two years as an engineer in the Army of the Potomac. After the War he moved to Portland, where he served as chief clerk of the U.S. Engineer's office. After the Fenian invasion, Governor Joshua Chamberlain appointed him Division Adjutant General of Maine. O'Donoghue went on to become the first Catholic elected to the Portland School Board in 1869. He died on April 9, 1905, a well-respected Portland citizen.

On March 7, at a Fenian meeting in New Haven, Connecticut, Brig. Gen. B. F. Mullen of Indiana, Secretary of Military and Naval Affairs for the O'Mahony wing of the Fenian Brotherhood, expressed himself "satisfied that the U.S. would follow the neutrality example set by England and would not block the progress of Fenianism." Gen. Mullen read a letter from James Stephens announcing that "he was ready to move the armies of Ireland when the signal should be given—Ireland had 325,000 men ready for the conflict and a signal corps as efficient as any in the world."[39] That same day, the *Eastport Sentinel* reported that a quantity of breech loading rifles, assumed to be intended for the Fenians, had been landed in Eastport by the steamer *New Brunswick*.

News of a coming Fenian invasion received a mixed reaction in New Brunswick. *The Standard*, the newspaper of St. Andrews, New Brunswick, vacillated between skepticism and fear. It confidently opined that, although General Sweeney said that his men planned "to make a demonstration against Canada about the middle of March with a small force and strike via the Maine frontier with his main column," it could not look on that as a threat because of the U.S. government's assurance to the British government that they would not permit any violation of neutrality.

Having confidently denied that any invasion would be forthcoming, however, *The Standard* went on to complain that St. Andrews had been left totally unprotected, having only a small Home Guard which had not been supplied with arms and two Volunteer Companies, one being described as "less efficient though zealous." Fort Tipperary's old guns had been sold in 1865 and not replaced. Moreover, the Artillery Company's field pieces had also been taken away during the Crimean War and never replaced, in spite of frequent requests for new guns. St. Stephen, New Brunswick, had a Volunteer Company and Home Guards that totaled about 200, and about another 160 organized in two newly formed Volunteer Companies. There were other units at Woodstock totaling almost 500, and the St. John's Volunteer Battalion had 578, plus a 300-man Volunteer artillery unit, of which Lt. Governor Arthur Hamilton Gordon had a rather low opinion.[40]

The Fenians hoped that their invasion of New Brunswick would trigger an insurrection among the locals. This aspiration was not quite as chimerical as it might seem, since the New Brunswickers were vigorously debating the issue of whether to join a proposed national confederation of the separate provinces. Early in March of 1866, the Fenians tried to encourage the anti-Confederation side by publishing and posting a circular at several locations in St. John, New Brunswick, which read:

CITIZENS OF NEW BRUNSWICK

Republican institutions have become a necessity to the peace and prosperity of your Province. English policy, represented by the obnoxious project of Confederation, is making its last efforts to bind you in effete forms of Monarchism. Annexation to the United States is not, necessarily, the only means of escape. Independence for the present is the best one, and will assure you of the supreme and sole management of your affairs. Mercenary bayonets cannot—shall not prevent you asserting this independence if you desire it. Signify your wishes and you become the founders of a Free State, untrammeled by Royalty, unchecked by Misrule and certain to secure all the lost benefits of Reciprocity.

By Order of Republican Committee of St. John

This appeal fell on deaf ears. Also, in early March, fear of the Fenians caused many of the common laborers of St. John, New Brunswick, to make a run on the banks, immediately drawing out thousands of dollars in gold and notifying the savings banks that they intended to withdraw more than $10,000 in gold over the next week.[41]

The British North American government took the Fenian invasion seriously and on March 7, 1866, called out 10,000 volunteers. At the time, British North America required universal militia service of all men between the ages of eighteen and sixty. This unpaid militia mustered only one day a year and was not provided with uniforms or arms. Accordingly, the militia had no real ability to defend the Province against an invasion. However, those citizens more inclined to patriotism and military service organized Volunteer units which were armed, equipped and trained by the government. In New Brunswick, the Volunteers called out to defend the Province from the Fenians were to be paid seventy-five cents per day, which included an amount in lieu of rations, and each good conduct man would receive an additional $6.00 at the end of each month's service.[42] In addition to the Volunteers, two regiments of British regulars who were about to leave Halifax, Nova Scotia, for deployment elsewhere, were detained.[43]

On the evening of March 7, the engineer of the British warship *HMS Pylades* was in the bar room of the Waverley House hotel in St. John, New Brunswick, when an animated discussion of Ireland and Fenianism erupted. Francis Kearney, who had been in a store on King Street earlier that evening attempting to recruit a man named Johnston to enlist as a Fenian, and three or four others were in the bar about 10:45 p.m. A disagreement resulted in Kearney's producing a pistol from his pocket. Someone convinced Kearney to return his pistol to his pocket. Kearney decided to leave, but refused to pay his bar tab. Upon being confronted by James Guthrie, the son of the proprietor of the Waverley House, Kearney began to argue. Mr. Guthrie and another patron forced Kearney down the stairs and out onto the street. As they tried to close the door, Kearney fired his pistol. The ball struck the door about three feet from the bottom and glanced off. Kearney was arrested. [44] This episode demonstrates that the atmosphere was charged; one such incident could set off the fuse.

The U.S. Cabinet discussed the Fenian situation on March 9, 1866 in response to the Canadian actions.[45] Secretary of War Edwin Stanton wanted to "crush" the Fenians, probably in an attempt to embarrass President Johnson. The badly divided Cabinet was unable to reach a decision.

Not all of the speculation focused on the Maine frontier. A March 12 dispatch from Albany to the *New York World* said that it had received information that uniforms for 5,000 men and 2,000 rifles were stored in Burlington, Vermont, waiting for the Fenians. On March 13, 1866, the U.S. Cabinet decided to send circulars to all U.S. Attorneys and Marshals urging increased vigilance.[46]

Because of the pressure resulting from the Roberts wing's proposed invasion, the O'Mahony wing held a military convention in New York City. Speaking before the delegates, Bernard Doran Killian, who had been serving as the Fenian Treasurer, proposed the capture of Campobello Island in New Brunswick to be used as a basis for the setting up of a provisional government of the Irish Republic. Once the Fenians had a beachhead in Canada, he envisioned that they would then be able to issue letters of marque for privateers.[47]

Patrick A. Sennott of Massachusetts, a native of New Brunswick who had earlier lived in St. John where he had taught school and kept a saloon, argued in support of the expedition.[48] In debate, a majority of the Fenian Council opposed the Campobello expedition. Most wanted to wait at least until Stephens arrived in New York. However, taking things into their own hands, impatient New York members erroneously informed O'Mahony that Campobello, located at the western entrance to Passamaquoddy Bay near the Maine coast, was neutral ground and not clearly property of the U.S. or Britain.[49]

The day after the convention convened, the March 14 issue of the St. Andrews *Standard* predicted that the scene of the Fenians' attack would be Campobello. That same day, Lt. Gov. Gordon wrote to General Doyle: "I know every move of the small Fenian circle at Calais and the names of all the members and have very good information at Eastport and Bangor also."[50] As a precaution the St. John, New Brunswick, garrison removed all of the powder and cartridges from the Fort House and the Carleton Tower to the bomb-proof magazine at Lower Cove.[51]

On St. Patrick's Day 1866 O'Mahony again summoned the Fenian Council that probably included a British spy. Soon thereafter, Sir Frederick Bruce wrote to Lord Clarendon that he had informed the Lt. Governors of Nova Scotia and New Brunswick of the Fenian invasion plans.[52] Bruce was aware that the Fenians had chartered an arms vessel and he knew of their arrival date at Eastport. The most likely source of Bruce's information was "Red Jim" McDermott, a confidant of O'Mahony.[53] Also, Sub-Inspector Doyle of the Royal Irish Constabulary was in the U.S. spying on the Fenians. He informed the British authorities in New Brunswick of a letter announcing an early attack on St. Stephen, New Brunswick. Henry J. Murray, British Consul at Portland, Maine, was instructed to notify the British vice-consuls at Eastport, Bath and Bangor to report on any signs of Fenian activity there. Murray reported that there was little interest in Fenianism in Portland. The Vice-consul at Eastport reported excitement in New Brunswick over rumored raids.[54] Fear of a Fenian invasion resulted in the cancellation of Montreal's St. Patrick's Day parade that was thought to be a signal for the Fenian invasion.

O'Mahony reluctantly backed the invasion of Canada when it became apparent that the faction led by Col. Roberts and Gen. Sweeney was going to forward with their invasion plans. On March 18, 1866, O'Mahony signed an authorization for Killian to proceed with the Campobello expedition.[55] The choice of Campobello, "neutral" or not, came as no surprise. New Brunswick Lt. Governor Gordon had written to Colonial Secretary Edward Cardwell that "Campobello I own I think a very likely place for a Fenian descent. It has capital harbours—it is close to the United States and its population is small—and it has no means of defense."[56]

The O'Donoghue-led O'Mahony Circle of the Portland Fenians met at their hall on Free Street on March 26 and held a torchlight procession at 7:00 p.m. to their rally at the Mechanics Hall. Once at the Mechanics Hall, the O'Mahony Fenians enjoyed American and Irish national airs provided by Chandlers Band and listened to a program of stirring speeches. Mr. O'Donoghue presided and made a short speech in which he called upon the assemblage to be generous in their contributions to the cause. O'Donoghue was followed by P. O. Larkin, who had just arrived from Ireland, J. E. Fitzgerald, and J. J. Crowley, of Boston. J. J. Mayberry, of Portland, filling in for George Francis Train, closed out the rally at about 11:00 p.m.[57] Following the adjournment of the rally, the O'Mahony Circle held a meeting. Portland's other Fenian Circle, loyal to the Roberts/Sweeny camp, of which William McAleney was the Center, did not participate in the agitation at the Mechanics Hall.[58]

McAleney, a native of Draine, County Derry, had emigrated from Ireland at age sixteen, arriving in Portland in 1849. Immediately upon his arrival he secured a job as helper to Father McGuire at St. Dominic's Church. He later became an apprentice harness-maker and went into the business on his own, continuing until 1910. Bishop David Bacon performed his marriage to Mary Mullen, also an emigrant from County Derry, on June 9, 1859. Within a month of the Roberts/Sweeney invasion from Vermont, he lost his home in the Great Portland Fire of July 4–5, 1866, but his harness-making shop did not burn.

After the Fenian invasion attempts, McAleney, during his more than sixty years in Portland, was active in Democratic Party politics, religious and Irish-American affairs, and charitable work. He was elected to the Portland City Council from Ward Two in the 1870s and from Ward Four in the 1880s. He helped Bishop Bacon organize Portland's Cathedral Parish and was a close friend and advisor to Bishop James Augustine Healy, Portland's second Roman Catholic bishop (1875–1900) and the first African American bishop in the United States. He was an organizer of Portland's Irish American Association, serving at times as its president and treasurer. He also was active in the Society for the Prevention of Cruelty to Animals and the Humane Society.[59]

By March 26 the whole volunteer force of New Brunswick had been ordered to report to Lt. Col. Inches at St. Stephen by 8:00 p.m, "Armed and equipped for active service."[60] The volunteers were ordered to march to St. Andrews. The British also began to mobilize the regulars for the defense of New Brunswick calling out the First Battalion of the Royal New Brunswick Regiment (Carleton and York). On April 3 Portland anticipated a speech by O'Mahony himself on the subject of Irish independence at City Hall. O'Mahony, however, never made it to Portland.[61] Nonetheless, the buzz created by O'Mahony's anticipated appearance resulted in a large meeting entertained by earnest speakers.

Apparently, O'Mahony had better things to do at the Fenian headquarters in New York City. He issued a Proclamation, dated April 5, 1866, in which he announced that James Stephens had just left Ireland for Paris on Fenian business and that Stephens shortly intended to come to the United States to try to restore harmonious counsel to the Fenian movement.[62]

The British Navy began to mobilize the fleet. The Troop transport *HMS Simoon* sailed for St. Andrews with a man-of-war escort. The British North American naval squadron was reinforced by the arrival of *HMS Tamar* that also brought troop reinforcements. The *HMS Pylades*, the *HMS Rosario* with sixteen guns and 250 men, and the *HMS Fawn* with seventeen guns and 250 men soon arrived.[63] Eventually, six British warships patrolled the Eastport area.[64]

While the British correctly anticipated Killian's arrival at Eastport, the New York newspapers breathlessly reported the sailing of a Fenian expedition to Bermuda. On April 5, 1866, the *New York Herald* reported:

> On Monday night, at about 12 o'clock, B. Doran Killian sailed an expedition for the capture of the Island of Bermuda, and on the following Tuesday night, at about the same hour, Colonel P. J. Downing sailed at the head of another expedition destined for the same place. Mr. Killian's expedition was composed of three magnificent iron steamers, with altogether three thousand desperadoes, all of whom had been soldiers in the United States Army. Colonel Downing had two steamers and two thousand five hundred men.

About the same time that they were reported to be sailing for Bermuda, Killian, Patrick J. Downing and others proceed by rail to Eastport.[65] Upon arrival, they checked into the Mabee Hotel where it was said that they attracted such unfavorable attention that they erased their names from the hotel's registration book.[66] Killian and company made free use of the telegraph, constantly sending and receiving dispatches. Killian applied for funds at the Frontier Bank, where he presented a telegram from New York certifying that his bankers held sixty thousand dollars at his credit. The prudent Yankee bankers, however, declined to advance him the requested money until the funds were placed in the Boston bank with which the Frontier Bank did business.[67] Foiled in his efforts to obtain ready cash, Killian then turned his efforts to the task of chartering vessels. He chartered the schooner *Sinbad* to leave for Machias on the afternoon of April 10. Again, Killian was foiled. The British Consul and prominent citizens of Eastport succeeded in getting the vessel's charter revoked.[68] Killian did, however, succeed in getting a small boat of about 15 tons out of the harbor.[69] Killian and his staff soon realized that the popular feeling of the better classes was against them. They began to observe great secrecy in their movements.[70]

As cover story for the large number of Fenians converging on the area, Killian hired the Eastport Town Hall for three nights and issued a manifesto stating that the Fenians were holding a convention in Eastport.

> The President of the Convention hereby thanks the Delegates for their promptness and discipline and trusts that, whilst waiting instructions from the Central Office, the Delegates will make due allowance for the civic inconveniences. All has been done that could be done to consult their comfort, and the President need only, in further sustainment of his zeal, allude to the very many downright hardships and sufferings necessarily undergone by our soldiers in the late war,—sufferings and privations lengthened and intensified owing to English Neutrality. He has no doubt, however, that the same spirit which animated our soldiers will inspire our civilians; and that the deliberations of their Convention will be marked by wisdom and decorum. On receipt of necessary intelligence, the President will proceed to develope the subject matters to be discussed by the Convention. For the time being the Delegates will fraternize with the good people of Eastport, and have opportunities of appreciating its many natural advantages, as the Frontier City of the representative Republic.[71]

Killian set up the two printing presses he had brought and printed a proclamation calling on the people of New Brunswick to resist Sir Fenwick Williams' efforts to impose a confederation on New Brunswick.[72] Speaking at Eastport, Killian boldly stated that the Fenian Brotherhood would side with the people of New Brunswick against the British government in its effort to force Confederation on the provinces. Killian added for effect that the Fenians would continue to hold conventions on the frontier until the question of Confederation was settled.[73]

Feelings were rising on the other side of the border as well. In a display of patriotic ardor at St. Andrews, New Brunswick, more than forty Canadian lads between the ages of fourteen and sixteen years had formed themselves into a company called the "Victoria Guards" and began to drill. On Saturday, April 7, 1866, they marched through town and went through the manual exercise and company movements with great credit to themselves and satisfaction to the spectators. When they arrived at the quarters of the Colonel Anderson, the Commander of the Frontier, they presented arms and marched past in both slow and quick time.[74] The company hoped that the general public would assist them in buying uniforms. That same day, New Brunswick called out 1,000 members of its militia.

The Fenians destroyed communications between St. John, New Brunswick, and western towns on the night of April 9, 1866. Also on that day, U.S. customs officers prevented the Fenian vessel *Ocean Spray* with its cargo of howitzers and their arms from leaving at midnight.

The April 10, 1866 edition of the *Eastern Argus* reported:

> The battalion of supposed Fenians, numbering some 80 men, which arrived in this city by the steamer from Boston Sunday morning, left for the eastward last evening in the steamer New Brunswick. Boxes said to contain arms and equipments, which arrived from New York a day or so since, consigned to a prominent Fenian this city were not taken on board. The reason given being that there was no room for them. There was quite an excitement on the wharf at the time of departure. The British Consul was present and a squad of police officers kept the crowd back from the steamer. The Fenians said nothing, but as soon as the gang plank touched the wharf, headed by their leader, they charged gallantly aboard. They were a fine, soldierly looking set of fellows, and so far as we learn behaved themselves like gentlemen while in town. It was stated on the street last evening, that a schooner had been chartered to take the arms and equipments eastward. We may hear some startling news from the border before many days.

The description of the Fenians depended on the point of view of the beholder as can be seen from the contrary item in the April 12, 1866 St. John, New Brunswick, *Morning Freeman*, which reported that "they were described by those who came as passengers with them from Portland as a most ruffianly looking set." The *St. Croix* (New Brunswick) *Courier* called the Fenians "in appearance the most villainous cut throat individuals we ever laid eyes on,—men who would be in their native element in the midst of rapine and murder, emphatically 'lewd fellows of the baser sort.'"[75]

By April 10, the British Consul and U.S. Marshals joined Killian and his staff as all lodged together at the Mabee Hotel.[76] The editor of the *St. Croix Courier* decided to do some investigative reporting to attempt to reconcile the conflicting rumors. He checked himself into the Mabee Hotel and, sitting with the British Consul, used breakfast as an opportunity to observe Killian, who was described as "a fine portly looking fellow, broad open countenance, but with a rather sinister expression of the eye."[77] The editor observed that Killian was attended by two secretaries, one described as "a rough Irish lad, evidently lacking in brains, judgment and experience."[78] The April 10 special dispatch to the *New York Herald* reported that there were bad feelings on both sides of Passamaquoddy Bay, with small arms and rockets continually being fired, causing great panic. Two companies of volunteers left Fredericton for St. Andrews.

Contention about confederation, meanwhile, was quite hot in New Brunswick, even though it did not reach the internecine pitch the Fenians had hoped for. On April 10, in the Lower House of the New Brunswick Parliament, the Government announced its resignation and the appointment of the opposition's Mr. Wilmont to form a new government.[79] However, although the anti-confederation administration's resignations were unconditionally accepted by Lt. Gov. Gordon, no new administration was formed.[80]

The Irish in Canada never became as enamored with the Fenian Brotherhood as had their fellow countrymen in the United States. In part, that was the result of a different settlement pattern. In British North America, which lacked heavily industrialized metropolitan centers,[81] Irish immigrants from rural agricultural backgrounds sought employment as farm laborers, maintaining rural social patterns similar to those they had experienced in Ireland.[82] In the U.S., Irish immigrants tended to congregate in the cities of the eastern seaboard where they were forced by economics and prejudice to work at unskilled labor and live in urban slums. In addition, British North America was home to a significant number of Protestant Irish who were well organized into Orange Order Lodges. Any attempt to organize a Fenian revolt would have faced not only government opposition, but also that of the Orange Order, to which many of the police belonged, and also of mob loyalism generally.[83] There were, however, active Fenians in Canada West, particularly centered in Toronto. More than five hundred Canadian Fenians marched as a unit in Toronto's 1866 St. Patrick's Day parade.[84]

On March 31, 1866 a Toronto telegraph clerk received a coded message addressed to a Mr. Cullen.[85] The clerk deciphered the simple code and brought the message to the attention of the authorities.[86] On April 9, Sir John MacDonald, the Attorney General of Canada West, received a telegraph informing him that Cullen, Michael Murphy, a Toronto tavern-keeper, who was President of the Hibernian Society and Head Center of the Canadian Fenians, and others had boarded a train bound for Montreal, presumably with the intention of going on to Portland, Maine, and joining the Fenian expedition there. MacDonald decided to have a detective board the train in Montreal and shadow the group to

Portland in hopes of obtaining evidence of an overt act which could serve as the basis for prosecution upon their return to Toronto.[87]

News of the Canadian Fenians' plans reached a group of cabinet ministers who were meeting in Montreal. They decided to countermand MacDonald's plans and ordered Murphy's arrest before he arrived at Montreal. They telegraphed Dr. Allen, the mayor of Cornwall, Ontario, seeking his assistance. Mayor Allen called out the town's entire force of approximately two hundred volunteers. When the train arrived at Cornwall on April 10, the Mayor, strongly escorted by the volunteers, called upon Murphy and his party to surrender to the Queen's authority. The Fenians did not resist; they were handcuffed and marched off to jail. The authorities confiscated their revolvers and ammunition.[88]

Their trial began on April 12 with the press and public excluded. The newspapers described the Government of Canada West as "straining every nerve to convict the alleged conspirators, and declare that the time has come to crush out every vestige of Fenianism in Canada."[89] The Canadians were afraid that a rescue raid would be attempted from the U.S. As a result, Mayor Allen, a member of the Orange Order, asked for reinforcements and obtained sixty stands of arms from Boston.[90] The mayor excluded the Catholic magistrates from his court.[91] On April 21, Col. Wheeler appeared for his examination in a most defiant manner, stating that he was an American citizen who would claim protection from Andy Johnson if the Canadians continued to keep him under arrest without producing the evidence against him. Col. Wheeler's threats apparently frightened the magistrates, who unanimously decided to let him go.[92]

The Canadians had a thin case and they delayed in bringing it to trial. Murphy and most of his remaining companions escaped from custody the following September, probably with at least the tacit cooperation of their jailers who were thereby saved the immense embarrassment of a possible not guilty verdict. The three Fenians who did not escape with Murphy were returned to Toronto and admitted to bail. They were never tried. Murphy, unable to return to Toronto, opened a tavern in Buffalo, New York, where he died April 11, 1868.[93]

Killian learned of these arrests and postponed his attack awaiting more men, money and arms from New York.[94] Meanwhile, residents of Campobello began moving to Eastport to avoid the anticipated invasion.[95] On April 11, fifty Fenians left Eastport in a schooner for an unknown destination. Two British war steamers patrolled Eastport Harbor and the St. Croix River with their gun ports open and everything ready. Within a week there would be "five British ships and five thousand British and New Brunswick troops in the vicinity." That British challenge must have driven the Fenians wild.[96]

The Fenians continued to maneuver Down East. Three hundred were reported to be using Castine as a rendezvous. Thirty more arrived at Calais in the afternoon by steamer from Eastport. The Fenians tried unsuccessfully to hire St. Croix Hall for a meeting. Three hundred to four hundred Fenians, without arms, arrived at Eastport by steamer with B. Doran Killian. Fifteen Fenians arrived at Calais by land from Bangor and left for Eastport with hired teams. The Calais authorities exercised extreme vigilance with respect to the Fenians.

Across the border, the New Brunswick volunteers at St. Stephen drilled industriously. However, rumors began to fly that the New Brunswick Volunteers were deserting and that many Irishmen had mysteriously disappeared from the frontier towns and were joining the Fenians.[97] During the afternoon of April 12, the British man of war *Pylades*, under the command of Capt. Hood, suddenly put to sea because of a rumored mutiny by fifty of its crew, who were clapped in irons.[98] The British Navy expressed concern that men of other crews also had been "tampered" with and expected similar difficulties with them.

Some British soldiers acted on their martial spirit by crossing from St. Stephen to Calais where they got into a dispute with Fenians. In the ensuing fight the British were driven over the bridge back to Canada. Thereafter, the town government of Calais cooperated with their New Brunswick neighbors, exhibiting a determination to prevent violence and to see that the laws were properly obeyed.[99] The April 14 issues of the St. John, New Brunswick, *Morning Telegraph* ridiculed the Fenians saying that "the only damage the Finnegans at Eastport and Calais are capable of doing at present will probably fall upon the boarding houses in case the American Militiamen cause them to decamp in hot haste."

Robert Kerr, the British Vice-Consul in Eastport, asked the American authorities to intervene. In response, the U.S. Government sent Commissioner L. G. Downes and Deputy U.S. Marshal B. F. Farrar to Eastport to enforce the neutrality laws.[100] The Gunboat USS *Winooski*, under Commander George H. Cooper, arrived the morning of April 16 and anchored off Eastport. The *Winooski* was a double-ended steamer of

974 tons, mounting 10 guns with a crew of about 150 sailors.[101] The Secretary of the Navy, Gideon Welles, instructed the captain of the *USS Winooski* to enforce the neutrality laws.[102] In addition to the *Winooski*, the U.S. War Department sent the ironclad *Mianbonomah* to the Eastport area to join the revenue cutter *Ashuelot* already stationed there.

Around 9:00 p.m. on April 4, 1866, an unknown steamer passed by Eastport via the eastern passage, steaming slowly until it was opposite town, then it ran up a green and a red light in place of the white light which it had carried and sailed on toward Lubec, anchoring opposite Friar's Head, Campobello. The steamer stopped there for about an hour and a half, and then proceeded seaward past Lubec at an estimated speed of fifteen or twenty knots.[103]

Proclaiming that "The spirit of liberty is abroad," a small number of Fenians crossed to Indian Island, New Brunswick, off Campobello, between midnight and 1:00 a.m., Sunday, April 15, and engaged in what amounted to a game of "capture the flag." The Fenians pointed their revolvers at the head of Mr. J. E. Dixon, the unarmed British deputy collector of customs, threatened to burn down his house, and compelled him to give up the British flag and the customs papers.[104] The *New York Herald* dispatch said there were nine Fenians in the raiding party, part of the crew of a Fenian privateer, from which they had lowered a boat and with muffled oars rowed under the guns of *HMS Pylades*. No shots were fired. Even though the Fenians had been in the area for days, there were no British soldiers on the island. Not until April 21 did an armed party from the *HMS Rosario* land to protect Indian Island.[105] After this incursion, Canadians at St. Stephen become nervous and, following the example of the citizens at Campobello, they crossed to U.S. side of the border at Calais to stay with American friends and relatives.[106]

On April 16, 1866 the Fenians circulated a broadside to British "Sailors & Marines:—U.S. citizens invite you ashore, where, if you leave behind the property and habiliments of slavery, you will find liberty, comrades and countrymen." The Fenians subsequently claimed that mutinies had indeed taken place and forty-six British servicemen had been placed in irons. Meanwhile, the revenue cutter *Ashuelot* arrived at Eastport with the brig *Sarah Bernice*, which was taken while attempting to land goods at Machias.

The Fenians held a mass gathering attended by about a thousand people, including many from across the border, at St. Croix Hall in Calais, addressed by Killian and A. P. Sennott.[107] Killian began by stating that the Fenians would respect U.S. laws. Killian then argued that the Americans owed a debt of gratitude to the Irish for their assistance in the Civil War. He asserted that now was the time to assist Ireland in the hour of her need. Americans could do that with sympathy and by furnishing arms or means to buy arms to the Fenian Brotherhood that now embraced one million men. Killian claimed it was the true policy of the U.S. to prevent establishment of a monarchy to its north as foreshadowed in the British scheme of confederation. Killian continued that if those opposed to that scheme in the provinces were to revolt on account of it, then the Fenians stood ready to step in and assist them. In so doing, they would be carrying out the true American policy. Killian declared the Fenians' intention to continue to hold "conventions" on the border until the confederation question was settled. According to Killian, every difficulty that arose under the British flag gave hope to the Irish rebels. Killian dwelt on the issue of British failure to observe strict neutrality during the Civil War and made a strong appeal to the people of Calais on that point. Killian also promised that the Fenians would see to it that the fisheries question resulting from the abrogation of the Reciprocity Treaty would be decided in their favor. The crowd at the meeting was attentive, but not enthusiastic. Applause came chiefly from a knot of Fenians in one corner of the hall who responded to signals from the podium. Both speakers emphatically stated that they did not intend to invade the provinces, although Killian refused after the meeting ended to answer why they were seeking to arm a force on the frontier.[108]

On April 17, the schooner *Ocean Spray*, loaded with 500 stands of arms for Killian, was sighted off Eastport. The revenue cutter *Ashuelot*, acting on orders of the local customs collector, Washington Long, immediately seized the *Ocean Spray*.[109] Collector Long, who had acted on his own authority, telegraphed the U.S. Attorney at Portland requesting advice. The U.S. Attorney ordered Collector Long to release the arms unless he could prove that they were destined for a foreign land.[110]

Soon thereafter, the *USS Winooski* arrived with Commander Cooper in charge. (See gallery, plate 34.) On learning of the arms, Cooper telegraphed Secretary of the Navy Gideon Welles to ask if he should allow the arms still on board the *Ocean Spray* to be landed. Secretary Welles, who was aware of the reluctance of Secretary of State Seward and

Secretary of War Stanton to take decisive action against the Fenians, sent word to Commander Cooper that he was content to leave the subject with Cooper until April 18, when Gen. Meade was expected to arrive.[111] As a contingency, Secretary Welles told Commander Cooper to cooperate with the civil authorities if Gen. Meade didn't arrive on the anticipated date.[112]

On April 18, 1866, U.S. Secretary of the Treasury Hugh McCullough, acting individually, ordered Collector Long to detain the *Ocean Spray* and its cargo until further orders.[113] When confronted, the Fenians aboard the vessel claimed that they had the arms because they intended to fish in "debatable waters."[114] Also, on April 18, New Brunswick's Lt. Gov. Gordon arrived in St. Andrews, the same day the Adjutant General of Maine arrived at Eastport.

The *HMS Duncan*, the eighty-one-gun flagship of Admiral Sir James Hope, arrived at St. Andrews on April 18, with Major General Hastings Doyle, his staff, and 570 men of the 2nd Battalion of the 17th Regiment of Foot, a company of Royal Engineers, and Capt. Newman's battery.[115] On April 19, the troops landed at Joe's Point and entered the city preceded by the band of the 17th Foot. The townspeople greeted the regulars with loud cheers as they reached the Public Square, where Major Simonds' Volunteer Battalion presented arms in their honor. After the entry parade, the engineers and artillery were quartered at Fort Tipperary, where the artillery placed its guns in position.

Gen. Doyle suggested that the British temporarily abandon the border area in hopes of enticing Fenians into following them into interior of New Brunswick where he would attack them. Lt. Gov. Gordon opposed Doyle's plan for fear that it would adversely affect local inhabitants' morale. Gen. Doyle also unsuccessfully urged that martial law be proclaimed.[116] Having been rebuffed in his plan, Gen. Doyle then established a strong defensive position at St. Andrews.[117]

The arrival of the *Duncan* set off a veritable social whirl for the inhabitants of St. Andrews. On Friday, April 20, Gen. Doyle reviewed the Volunteer Battalion and complimented them on their soldierly appearance and proficiency in drill. In addressing the volunteers, Gen. Doyle pointed to the barracks and said that he "had brought a few boys . . . who would give the Fenians two pence worth of powder" and that all those "Fenian bastards" wanted was "to take our gold and outrage our families."[118] The assembled volunteers and civilians vigorously cheered the General's remarks. Saturday, April 21, the 17th's band treat-ed the populace of St. Andrews to a concert in the Market Square. All Saints Church held a special service on Sunday, April 22, for the bene-fit of the troops who also filled the town's other churches.[119] The towns-folk's appreciation was not limited to the regulars. On Monday, April 23, the inhabitants of St. Andrews gave a public dinner in the Town Hall in honor of the York Volunteers. The hall was hung round with flags and the attendees gave more than a dozen toasts.[120]

All was not completely amicable and patriotic, however. The British troops complained that the civilians asked exorbitant prices for the common necessities of life, charging one soldier twenty cents for a half dozen eggs.[121] Back in Portland, the April 19, 1866 *Eastern Argus* edito-rial said that, although the Fenians attracted considerable attention, their chief object was to create a sensation and not a raid or battle.

Killian's military agent, an ex-Captain of the 6th Maine Regiment, made the rounds of the Eastport area buying up old cart wheels, worn-out swivels, and rusty cannon balls to be sent to the foundry. The Fenians also bought several kegs of gunpowder. A number of Fenians were seen daily in a conspicuous place making cartridges, but they didn't drill or make any movements as a military organization. The Fenians appeared in public as unarmed private citizens. Killian and others strolled across the international bridge to St. Stephen from Calais just as some people from New Brunswick crossed the bridge to Calais and chatted with the Fenians there.[122]

The Fenian Circle at Calais, Maine, consisted of about twenty men with Col. Dennis Doyle as the Center. He and other members of the Calais Circle hit upon a scheme to cause excitement on the other side of the St. Croix River. Eight Calais Fenians proceeded along the shore between the lower wharf in Calais up the river about four miles to the vicinity of Milltown, Maine. As they proceeded, they prepared bonfires, in some places only a few yards apart. They then went home to wait for nightfall. About 7:00 p.m. they returned to the riverside with torches and ignited the wood piles, giving the impression of the bivouac of a mighty army.[123] Having created that illusion, the Calais Fenians then began to fire shots in the air, causing panic at St. Stephens.[124]

A few days before, two small boats had crossed the St. Croix River just below St. Stephen, where they were noticed. "Old Joe" Young, who lived in St. Stephen, rode through the countryside yelling "Arm yourselves! The Fenians are upon you."[125] Center Doyle's activities brought him to the attention of the New Brunswick authorities, who kept him under close surveillance. Doyle's house on a Calais wharf was a gathering place for Fenians. Across the river in a St. Stephen hotel, Lt. Col. Anderson of the New Brunswick Volunteers had an excellent view of Doyle's home and kept a close watch on it.[126] During most of the time the Fenians were in the Eastport area they mysteriously left and returned, appearing at various places at various times in various numbers, sometimes along the river bank with weapons, often in the surrounding towns without weapons. The effect of these maneuvers was to create an exaggerated opinion of their numbers.

Gen. George G. Meade and staff arrived in Portland by train on April 19, 1866 and immediately boarded the chartered steamer *Regulator*. Meade's orders from Secretary of War Stanton were to "cool out" the Fenians with as little publicity as possible.[127] Also on board the *Regulator* were sixty-five men of Co. G, 1st Regiment U.S. Heavy Artillery. The *Regulator* then steamed off to Eastport. Its mission was described as both enforcement of neutrality laws and "to prevent John Bull from treading on that long tailed Fenian coat, being so invitingly flaunted under his nose at the border." Meade arrived at Calais at 1:00 p.m and was introduced to the citizens of Calais at 2:00 p.m. at St. Croix Hall. After that, aboard the *Regulator*, he met with Gen. Doyle, the British Commander at St. Andrews, who was an old friend.[128] Meade then left for Eastport at 3:00 p.m. Gen. Meade got in touch with the Fenian leaders and "gave them clearly to understand that any breach of the neutrality laws would be instantly followed by the arrest of every one of them."[129]

The New Brunswick press determined that the fact that Gen. Meade, the hero of Gettysburg, the son of an Irishman "and a Catholic to boot" was sent to the frontier was conclusive proof that the U.S. Government was in earnest in its efforts to preserve neutrality.[130]

On April 19, the Americans again seized the Fenian schooner *Ocean Spray*. However, before daybreak that morning, the Fenians rowed with muffled oars under guns of the *USS Winooski* and removed some of the arms aboard the *Ocean Spray*.[131] The U.S. authorities took the rest of the arms (which included rifles, revolvers, cannon and ammunition) to Ft. Sullivan by order of Gen. Meade.[132] The Fenians considered making an attack on the fort but were frustrated by a doubling of the guard there.[133] There was talk that the seizure of the weapons aboard the

Ocean Spray happened in the nick of time, since the Fenians had planned a simultaneous attack that very evening on St. Stephen and St. Andrews, New Brunswick, with the objective of taking control of the railway line to Woodstock and beyond.[134]

The Roberts/Sweeney wing made noise on April 19, when Col. Roberts, speaking to an assembly in New York City, stated that it would be his last public meeting before "the final blow for liberty would be struck."[135] April 20, four companies of troops from New York and one company from Ft. Independence in Boston Harbor were ordered to the eastern frontier. Gen. Meade said that he would line the coast with 50,000 men if necessary to prevent Fenian mischief.

On April 22, the Fenians raided Indian Island a second time and burned four stores, including the British customs warehouse and a warehouse stocked with liquor, fish and groceries that was owned by John Shields, an American citizen.[136] Mr. Shields subsequently filed a schedule of loss valued at $2,315.25.[137] A British man-of-war fired on the raiders as they returned to the United States.[138]

The American inhabitants of the Eastport/Calais area, who felt their summer's trade with their New Brunswick neighbors was being ruined, informed the U.S. authorities of vessels thought to be transporting Fenian arms. As a result, the Americans seized the Fenian-owned schooner *Perseverance* as well as the *J. N. M. Brewer* on suspicion of having arms and ammunition on board.[139] The St. John, New Brunswick, *Morning Freeman's* April 21, 1866 editorial opined that the Fenian invasion was not intended to be for real:

> The movements of the Fenians on our frontier are quite inexplicable. The O'Mahony Fenians repudiated the idea of invading the Provinces, and ridiculed the proposition made by General Sweeney; yet we find that the small bands now collected at Eastport and the neighborhood belong to that faction and that they are under the immediate control of the redoubtable B. D. Killian himself, once an intimate friend of the Hon. T. D. McGee and his associate in the management of the 'American Colt,' a rabid anti-British journal, now the right-hand man of O'Mahony and some time ago accused of furnishing information to the Canadian Government for a consideration.
>
> The way in which these men act shows conclusively—unless we can believe them all madmen—that they never meant to attempt an invasion. Instead of the rapidity and secrecy which would characterize a real movement, we see all the display and fuss and noise that usually characterize

feints or sham movements. They first take care that their intentions are made known to the world; then after a long delay they begin to come down in small squads. Their officers carry side arms and swagger and boast much. Their leader comes down and holds public meetings in Eastport and Calais. They give ample time to the British ambassador to send to the West Indies for the fleet, and to the fleet to return to this station; for the general in command at Halifax to send vessels and troops to the frontier; for our volunteers to turn out and organize thoroughly—and we may add, for a regiment to come all the way from Malta; and during this time they do not collect enough men to form a single regiment, and their only achievement is the cowardly attack on a Custom House officer living on a rocky island in Passamaquoddy Bay—a piece of mere wanton bravado, which could only be meant to insult and annoy.

Maj. Henry Chester Parry wrote a letter, dated April 21, 1866, to his father, Judge Edward Owen Parry, of Pottsville, Pennsylvania, referencing Fort Preble in Cape Elizabeth (now South Portland, Maine):

The Garrison of Fort Preble sailed for this place last Thursday night and went into Camp here on Friday night. Treat's Island is a picturesque little spot with a high rocky coast with a red slate stone beach—skirted here and there with dense clusters of fir trees. The island is owned by Mr. Treat who has a large herring fishery in the bay among the islands . . . Campobello is 2 miles across the water, and its borders are strictly watched by two powerful big black British men of war.

Gen. Meade and staff are at Eastport and Calais—and the Fenians thick and lively all over the neighborhood. They seemed chagrined because Col. Edwards seized quite a number of cases of their arms last night. This was done shortly after we went into bivouac. We crossed the water—long pull with muffled oars—boarded a small schooner, and took their muskets and ammunition. It was raining terribly, and we all got extremely wet. An enraged Fenian seized little Pettigrew, who was on board first, and threw him about 10' into the water. When the youngster came up from his sudden immersion, he sputtered out: 'You damned s— of a b——! You can't drown me!,' and quickly swam to one of the boats.

I used to lament my fate, shivering over the campfires in Virginia during the cold nights of winter, but camping out on the coast of Maine with a steady bitter cold wind from the sea blowing at you during this April month, exceeds any sleeping on the ground in a shelter tent that I have yet experienced. No officer or man is allowed to leave the island and we are worse off than Selkirk was at Yuan Fernandez.[140]

The British flag, stolen from the British customs post on Indian Island on April 15, was found within the week under the porch of the same Mr. J. E. Dixon from whom it was taken at gunpoint.[141]

On Monday evening, April 23, two Fenians attempted to cross the bridge into St. Stephen, New Brunswick, when the guards asked one of them, who was wearing a blue uniform, if he belonged to the American Army. The Fenian replied, "No, but we'll belong to another army soon, which will meet you at the point of the bayonet."[142] When the border guards prevented them from entering New Brunswick, the Fenians fired a revolver and ran back toward Calais where the U.S. authorities placed them in custody.[143] The Americans offered to surrender the Fenians to New Brunswick for trial but no demand was made for them.[144]

The *USS DeSoto* arrived at Eastport on April 23. Gen. Meade telegraphed Army Headquarters that he had captured a vessel loaded with arms, ammunition and uniforms intended for the Fenians.[145] (By April 21, all the American newspaper correspondents had gone home confident that nothing more would be done.[146]) The regulars raised the Union Jack at Fort Tipperary on April 24, presented arms and spiritedly sang "Rule Britannia" to the delight of the populace. On April 24, Gen. Meade told the Fenian leaders that "any breach of the neutrality laws would be instantly followed by the arrest of every one of them."[147]

The *Duncan* left for Halifax on the morning of April 25. Lt. Governor Gordon left for Fredericton the same morning. Although the U.S. troops were to remain, Gen. Meade also planned to leave in a few days. The whole number of Fenians along the border was recorded as three hundred.

Several weeks after the Fenians first arrived and promised to build up their business, the citizens of Calais were disenchanted with the Fenians' economic impact. The presence of hostile armed men in Calais and Eastport had brought trade on the river to a standstill. The *Calais Advertiser* called for enforcement of the state laws against carrying concealed weapons and for the federal government to "put a stop to these men congregating in any place to its injury."[148]

Some Fenians left town using free railroad tickets provided by the U.S. government. Others left on their own. Some were harassed by landlords for unpaid rent. On April 27, 1866, two hundred Fenians returned to Portland on the steamer *New Brunswick*. The Fenians had purchased cabin tickets but the vessel was so crowded that they could only get steerage. Although the vessel refunded the difference, the Fenians, who were armed with revolvers, appropriated the best accommodations for themselves. After docking in Portland, the vessel was ready to resume its voyage to Boston. Since several of the Fenians had gone ashore and had not returned, the Captain ordered the boat whistle to warn of the impending sailing. When the absent Fenians failed to return, the Captain said he could wait no longer and left for Boston. By the time the steamer had reached the entrance to Portland Harbor, the remaining Fenians on board drew their pistols and ordered the *New Brunswick* to put about or they would shoot somebody. The Captain put about and returned to Portland Harbor, where he requested assistance from the U.S. Marshal and the police. The law enforcement authorities, however, had insufficient numbers to arrest two hundred armed men in a bad mood. The Fenians came ashore and left for Boston on the next morning's train. The *New Brunswick* finally sailed for Boston at 9:00 p.m.[149]

On April 27, 1866, William H. Grace, a Fenian organizer and a Captain of the Eastport expedition, denounced O'Mahony as he arrived at Portsmouth, New Hampshire, on his way home. Grace said the expedition would have been a success if Killian had been sustained. Grace considered O'Mahony "an imbecile and a fraud on the public." According to Grace, the only hope of success was now Roberts and Sweeney. Grace told his Circle to send no more money to O'Mahony's headquarters at Union Square in New York City. By May 3, Capt. Grace had arrived in Boston where he said that Killian asserted that an iron vessel of war loaded with arms was supposed to have met the Fenians at Eastport with a landing on British territory scheduled for the night of their arrival. He claimed that O'Mahony had countermanded the sailing of the vessel and threw obstacles in the way that led to failure. Capt. Grace denounced O'Mahony and urged all good Fenians to rally to Sweeney.

About forty diehard Fenians continued to drill at Bog Brook near Calais. They tried to give the impression that they had British deserters in their ranks by having three or four men in red coats among them.[150] Col. A. P. Sinnott's First Massachusetts Fenian Regiment returned from Eastport to Boston on April 27 and 28. Most of them denounced O'Mahony but attached no blame to Killian or their own Col. Sinnott. They claimed that their efforts would have been successful if they had been properly supported. They stated that they had not abandoned the movement but had only "changed their base," and that they were still under orders and liable to be called upon at any time.[151] The First

Massachusetts pointedly expressed its willingness to join Gen. Sweeney and march across the border.[152]

By May 1 the comic opera invasion had run its course. Gen. Doyle conducted a grand review of his troops at 4:30 p.m. at the St. Andrews' Parade Ground. After watching the Royal Artillery and the 17th Foot march past the reviewing stand in both slow and quick time, Gen. Doyle told the assembled throng of civilians and regulars that he intended to send a portion of the troops to St. Stephen the next morning. He wished to say a few words to them before they parted:

> We must all bear in mind that our relations with the American Government and the people of the United States generally are, as I sincerely trust they ever will be, of the most friendly description, but there is, in the very centre of that great republic a very large Force organized and armed and calling themselves 'Fenians.' Most of you I suppose have heard of the play called 'Raising the Wind.' The hero of the piece is Jeremy Didler, whose life was spent borrowing money which never was repaid. Now the more appropriate name that these lunatics should have adopted would have been 'Jeremy Didlers' instead of Fenians.
>
> Well! The avowed object of these Jeremies is to dismember the British Empire, and subvert the authority of our beloved Queen by establishing that which they tell their dupes they intend to do, a Republic of Ireland, the idea of which is simply ludicrous. Like other madmen they have a good deal of 'method in their madness' and consider that discretion is the better part of valour and the means they therefore propose to adopt for the liberation of Ireland is to attack these peaceful Colonies which have never injured them in any way, simply because they fancy they are weak, instead of having the courage to proceed to that country which they profess to wish to liberate.
>
> Their hallucination also leads them to believe that these Provinces are desirous to throw off their allegiance to our Queen, let them if they dare attempt to put their feet upon our loyal shores, and they will find to their cost that these gallant and loyal Volunteers and militia and home guards, who have with so much alacrity and spirit to defend their homes, would be more than a match for them. It is not for us who are sent from the Mother Country to defend these her loyal children to boast of what we would do—but of this I feel as certain as I am sitting on my horse, that you wish no better amusement than to have the opportunity of being placed in a position to teach them, unworthy enemy as they would be, a lesson they would not easily forget—and if there should be any nervous Ladies amongst the inhabitants of this land, I would wish to calm their nervous fears, letting them know that the American Government have given the greatest proof of their friendly feeling towards us, and their

determination to preserve neutrality, by sending Men of War with a distinguished admiral to conduct them, and also regular troops to the Frontier, with General Meade at their head, than whom no more gallant or distinguished soldier ever drew a sword. I had the privilege of making his acquaintance during the War with the South while he was the head of the army of the Potomac, and altho' I cannot profess to say what orders he may have received from his Government, but of this I feel certain, that the Hero of Gettysburg will not allow a lawless and marauding band to invade our peaceful Territory—with the preparations made on both sides of the Frontier to give them a warm reception they will scarcely venture across, but, at any rate, the nervous ladies may put on their night caps if they wear such things, but I understand that they are now out of fashion, for being a bachelor I cannot speak with certainty upon the subject, but I am certain the ladies may go quietly to sleep in peace.[153]

Prior to Gen. Doyle's review and speech, he was to have received a visit from General Meade. Although the *Regulator* arrived at St. Andrews in the morning, Gen. Meade, who had suffered from a cold since his arrival, was too ill to land. He sent his Adjutant General to invite Gen. Doyle aboard. Gen. Doyle and several of his staff boarded the *Regulator* and held a lengthy audience with Gen. Meade. Gen. Doyle brought a guard of honor of about a hundred men of the 17th Foot with him to the wharf, as well as the regimental band that played airs while Gen. Doyle was on still the wharf. On his departure, Gen. Doyle had the band play *Auld Lang Sine*.[154] The 17th Regiment's band became such a hit with the inhabitants of St. Andrews that it performed in the Court House Square each Tuesday and Friday afternoon thereafter during its deployment.

On May 2, 1866, U.S. Customs Officers boarded a schooner at Eastport said to be a Fenian privateer. They discovered a large number of armed men on board. At 6:30 p.m., the Customs Officer at Lubec reported that there were Fenians aboard a small fishing schooner who transferred to a large schooner in back of Grand Manan, New Brunswick. On hearing the news, the *Winooski* left Eastport Harbor in pursuit of the suspected Fenian privateer.[155] The *Winooski* never located the vessel.

Also on May 2, some of the men who had gone to Eastport appeared at O'Mahony's New York Headquarters and demanded to be paid for their loss of time and employment. When O'Mahony refused, Col. Walsh and Capt. Gaynor held pistols to his head until he handed over $30 for each man in the party.[156] Three days later, seventy Circles of the Manhattan District sent delegates to O'Mahony's headquarters with instructions to "shift every wrong and outrage to the bottom."[157] After barring all salaried officers from the room, they called upon O'Mahony to explain the Eastport affair. At first he demurred, but then began. His inquisitors called him an "imbecile," a "spiritualist," and "Killian's dupe." The examination lasted two hours. O'Mahony admitted the expedition was a mistake but asked that he not be destroyed for making it. Several Fenians wanted to depose O'Mahony immediately but when he produced a letter from James Stephens stating that Stephens would be leaving soon for the U.S., they decided to permit O'Mahony to stay in office until Stephens arrived. In the meantime, the Fenians decided that a committee would "hold" the "books."[158]

Gen. B. F. Mullen, the former O'Mahony Secretary of Military and Naval Affairs, resigned his position and left for the west, where he began to deliver lectures calling the whole Fenian expedition a "humbug."[159] On May 3, the *Regulator* with Gen. Meade, his staff and Companies I and M of the 1st Regiment U.S. Heavy Artillery arrived at Portland. Company G remained at Calais. On May 4, the U.S. government released the *Regulator* from its charter. It was expected to be back in regular service between Portland and Bangor by May 14. Killian and the other Fenian leaders left town without paying their hotel bills and other debts in Eastport, which amounted to more than $1,000.[160] By the morning of May 7, the last of the Fenians left Calais. There were still a few at Eastport who, being frustrated in their attempt at an invasion, were planing to provoke trouble by another tactic. They were preparing in large numbers to go fishing intent on causing collisions with Canadian fishing vessels and causing a diplomatic crisis that might escalate to war.[161]

These diehards continued to harass British vessels in the schooner *Friend*. On the evening of May 8, the *Friend* cleared Eastport, pursued by the *Winooski*. The *Friend* eluded the *Winooski* and captured the British schooner *Wentworth*. The Fenians transferred their arms and cargo to the *Wentworth* and scuttled their own vessel. The *Winooski* came up on the *Wentworth* but was deceived by its name and appearance and allowed her to pass. The Fenians made a descent on Grand Manan Island, but decided against armed landing. Instead, they put ashore and returned the *Wentworth* to its crew.[162]

The final Fenian assault along the Maine border occurred on May 14 when nine armed Fenians landed on Marble Island, which is separated from Indian Island at high tide, and took possession of the Norwood house and defied the St. John Volunteers to dislodge them. The New Brunswickers wisely ignored the Fenians, who left the next morning.[163]

Killian refused to acknowledge defeat, stating: "My late enterprise is merely balked in one of several aims sought to be effected, and I see signs enough to convince me that the balking in this particular is merely temporary, and may be overcome."[164] He attributed his difficulties at Eastport to having been without funds until after the British warships had arrived and having less than seventy-five men until the real opportunity had passed.[165] The Roberts wing lost no time in ridiculing the O'Mahony invasion, calling it the "Eastport fizzle."[166] The *Toronto Globe* printed this doggerel: "Gen. Killian and all his men, marched up to Maine, and then—marched down again."[167]

On May 10, 1866, James Stephens arrived at New York City aboard the French steamship *Napoleon* expecting to embark on a mission to heal the wounds and to secure united action against the common enemy. That plan changed upon his arrival. Although he was met by thousands of Irishmen who escorted him to the Metropolitan Hotel, he arrived at a time of unprecedented turmoil in the Fenian movement. As one of his first official acts, Stephens accepted O'Mahony's resignation as Head Center and concurred in Killian's dismissal. Stephens appointed a committee to audit the accounts of O'Mahony's administration.[168] The committee found only $500 in the treasury and more than $30,000 in outstanding bills.[169] The cost to the Fenians of the Eastport fiasco was estimated at between $35,000 and $40,000.[170] The *Cleveland Leader* speculated that the whole Eastport expedition was intended as a screen for some deep swindle.[171]

During his interrogation, John O'Mahony said Killian was a traitor who sold out to the enemy. He claimed that Killian had engaged in a conspiracy with Thomas D'Arcy McGee, an exile from the 1848 Young Irelander Rebellion, who was then the Canadian Minister of Agriculture. Killian had worked for McGee while he lived in New York City between 1852 and 1856. Certain Canadian newspapers claimed that McGee had arranged the Eastport expedition in order to frighten New Brunswick into adopting Confederation. The newspaper reports claimed that Killian was to have been awarded with lifetime employment in the Canadian civil service. In early May the Fenian Council tried Killian on those charges and found him guilty, even though no conclusive evidence was produced. One of O'Mahony's last official acts was to remove Killian as Treasurer.[172]

As late as May 23, the St. Andrews, New Brunswick *Standard* predicted that the Fenians would be back to cause trouble in conjunction with the upcoming election at which the Confederation issue would be settled. *The Standard* referred to a letter from Killian in which he allegedly detailed his exploits at Eastport. Killian said he had not been defeated and that his men would remain on the border until the Confederation issue was settled.[173] *The Standard* advised that the citizens of New Brunswick keep a sharp lookout and to watch the movements of the "suspicious" persons said to be arriving at various points in the Province. Those predictions were inaccurate as to location, but prescient regarding the impending invasions by the Roberts/Sweeney Fenians. In Portland, the Roberts and Sweeney Circle held a meeting on May 25. The newspaper notice of that meeting also welcomed "all who are desirous of joining the company now forming."[174]

After accepting O'Mahony's resignation in disgrace, James Stephens toured the country on behalf of the former O'Mahony (official) wing trying to discourage assistance to the Roberts/Sweeney wing in its plan for another Canadian invasion. On May 26, 1866, Stephens spoke at Cooper Union in New York City, saying an invasion of Canada would be no more sensible than an assault on Japan.[175] Stephens said O'Mahony had shown patriotism by resigning and suggested that Roberts do likewise.[176] Stephens asked Roberts to give up his plans for a Canadian invasion. Roberts refused. Many wavering Fenian circles decided to support Roberts over Stephens.[177]

The Roberts/Sweeney Fenians held a mass meeting in Troy, New York, at which a speaker said that for once they were going to act like sensible men and attack England at its weakest point. He continued by saying that although there were British troops in Canada, many of them were members of the Fenian Brotherhood who had been stationed in Ireland until the suspension of Habeas Corpus there.[178] On June 1, the Portland Roberts and Sweeney Circle again advertized its upcoming regular meeting and repeated its call for persons desirous of joining the company now forming.[179]

Shortly after the dust settled following the failure of the O'Mahony wing's New Brunswick expedition, the Roberts/Sweeney wing began its long-awaited three-pronged invasion in late May and early June of 1866.

Their arms included approximately 4,000 muskets which they had obtained from the U.S. government's Bridesburg, Pennsylvania arsenal on May 3, 1866, during the O'Mahony faction's unsuccessful invasion of New Brunswick.[180] On June 2, about a thousand Fenians, under the command of Colonel John O'Neil, who had arrived from Nashville, Tennessee, at the head of the 13th Fenian Regiment, crossed the border, landing in the vicinity of Fort Erie on the Niagara Peninsula. The Fenians marched toward the Welland Canal and the railway line that ran parallel to it. They encountered a force of Canadian volunteers that had marched about three miles from the railroad station at Ridgeway, Ontario. The Fenians formed a line of battle in a field and the Canadian volunteers attacked, with the Queen's Own Rifles firing the first shot. Both sides exchanged several volleys, then the Fenians advanced at the double quick with fixed bayonets through thick brush toward the Volunteers who were ranged in an orchard on the other side of a swamp. Col. O'Neil concluded that the charge was useless and ordered a retreat. The Volunteers, believing that the Fenians had been routed, charged after the Fenians who turned and countercharged. The Volunteers broke and left the field of battle. The Fenians followed the retreating Volunteers for about two miles before stopping.[181]

Early in the battle, the Volunteers had captured a number of Fenians whom they took with them on their retreat. The Volunteers put their prisoners aboard the tug *Danville*. A party of about 200 Fenians came upon the *Danville* tied up at the Fort Erie dock. The Fenians fired into the tug that backed into the river and returned fire. The Fenians then turned their attention to a Volunteer artillery company that put up a brief resistance, then retreated down the river, and eventually surrendered to the Fenians.[182]

By June 3, 1866, the Volunteers were back in possession of Fort Erie without a fight. The main body of the Fenians had obtained intelligence to the effect that British troops armed with Armstrong guns were about to encircle their position. Since their reinforcements had been prevented by U.S. troops and picket boats from crossing the border, the Fenians evacuated Fort Erie and returned across the Niagara River to the United States. The U.S. gunboat *Michigan* was waiting and captured several hundred returning Fenians. The Canadians captured thirty-two Fenians.[183]

At St. Albans, Vermont, another force of Fenians gathered under the command of General Samuel P. Spear with the intention of invading

Quebec. As they had in Maine and Ontario, U.S. troops began to arrive in the St. Albans area with orders to prevent any violation of the U.S. neutrality laws. The U.S. regulars fanned out as far as Ogdensburg, New York. A "veteran" wrote to the *Eastern Argus*:

> Will you allow me to say to your Fenian friends that there is no doubt but that a very large majority of Americans favor their project, and wish to see English neutrality carried out to the letter, but it would be much better if they would keep their business more to themselves, and not allow it to be made public, and then our government would not be 'obliged' to run after them as they are at the present time.[184]

The "veteran" gave good advice and the entire Fenian campaign would have been potentially more successful if the Fenians hadn't allowed the newspapers to report their every move. For example, the New York newspapers reported that Gen. Spear, with 3,000 men, was to proceed from St. Albans via Phillipsburg, Quebec, and to cut off Montreal's railroad connections at St. John's Junction, St. Hilaire and St. Hyacinthe.[185]

Companies I and M of the 1st U.S. Artillery stationed at Fort Preble in Cape Elizabeth, Maine, which had been posted to Eastport to deal with the O'Mahony Fenian expedition there, were again drawn into the Fenian "war." On the morning of June 5, they left Portland by train for Ogdensburg where they expected to receive further orders. [186] Company G of the 1st U. S. Artillery left for the border on June 6 leaving no federal troops at Fort Preble.[187]

Portland's Roberts/Sweeney Fenian Circle held a rally on June 7,[188] with music provided by the Portland Band, and sent Company C, 2nd Infantry, Irish Republican Army, off to take part in the invasion of Quebec from St. Albans, Vermont.[189] Unbeknownst to the Portland Fenians, the U.S. authorities had already arrested Gen. Sweeney in his bed at the Tremont House Hotel in St. Albans about midnight on June 6.[190] Col. Roberts was arrested in New York City on June 7. He refused to post bail and was remanded to the custody of the U.S. Marshal and quartered at the Astor House Hotel.[191]

The Fenians continued to amass at Franklin, Vermont, for a reported reconnaissance at Stanbridge, Quebec. On June 7, about 500 to 1,000 Fenians crossed the border and occupied several positions. By June 9, the Canadians advanced and the Fenians decided to return to the United

States. About 200 Fenians encountered a force of Canadians at Pigeon Hill, Quebec. There was a brief skirmish in which the Fenians fought the Royal Guides, leaving several Fenians dead or wounded and sixteen captured.

General Meade, fresh from his duty on the Maine border, was assigned command of the U.S. forces along the Quebec and Ontario frontier. He immediately issued orders forbidding the railroads and express companies from transporting Fenians and their arms to the border. The U.S. Commissioner at St. Albans arraigned Gen. Sweeney on June 8. Sweeney waived examination. His bail was set at $25,000. The federal authorities also arrested several other Fenian officers.[192]

In an interview with Gen. Meade, Fenian Generals Murphy and Hefferman complained:

> We have been lured on by the Cabinet, and used for the purposes of Mr. Seward—They encouraged us on to this thing. We bought our rifles from your arsenals, and were given to understand that you would not interfere.[193]

Gen. Meade issued a proclamation on June 9 ordering all persons assembled "in connection with and in aid of the Fenian organization for the purpose of invading Canada" to desist from their enterprise and to disband. Any Fenians who could not afford to provide for their own transportation to return home were to be provided with such transportation on giving their names and addresses to the officer in command of the U.S. forces. Despite this offer, the Fenians issued a counter-proclamation:

> Stand comrades, stand! Ireland expects every man to do his duty. Blood has already flowed, and your countrymen are in the hands of your relentless foe. Will you desert them in the hour of need? Revenge and death, now or never.

Approximately 250 demoralized Fenians accepted the free transportation on June 9.[194]

For their part, the Portland Fenians returned home without having fired a shot in anger. They published a card of thanks in the June 20, 1866 issue of the *Eastern Argus*:

> The Roberts and Sweeney Circle of this city embrace this method of returning sincere thanks to John Shelleny, Centre of the Roberts and Sweeney Circle of Lawrence, Mass., also to Michael Casey, Thomas

Kallery and Michael O'Bryan, for their kind hospitality shown to Co. C, 2d Infantry, I.[rish] R.[epublican] Army, of this city, while en route home from St. Albans, Vt. Gentlemen, rest assured that your kindness on this occasion will not be soon forgotten by the members of this Circle.

CONCLUSION

While the 1866 Fenian invasion of Campobello was essentially a comic opera, it and the subsequent invasions led by the Roberts wing of the Fenian Brotherhood, had a profound effect on Canada, contributing to the adoption of the Canadian Confederation in 1867. Prior to the adoption of Confederation, British North America consisted of Canada West (Ontario), Canada East (Quebec)—both of which were under the Act of Union of 1841—and four separate provinces: Nova Scotia, New Brunswick, Prince Edward Island, and Newfoundland.[195]

The idea of a Confederation of the separate provinces of British North America into what became the Dominion of Canada had been discussed for decades. In 1864, Sir Samuel Leonard Tilley, a pharmacist from Gagetown, New Brunswick, who was New Brunswick's Premier, collaborated with Nova Scotia's Premier Charles Tupper to hold a meeting in Charlottetown, Prince Edward Island, which was attended by large delegations from Upper and Lower Canada. That meeting resulted in a decision to expand the proposed union and after another meeting in Quebec City, the seventy-two terms of union were announced.

Tilley's support for Confederation was not popular in New Brunswick, and the March 1865 election resulted in an overwhelming victory by the anti-confederation party lead by A. J. Smith. On March 6, 1865, Tilley resigned as Premier.[196] Although Lt. Governor Gordon had been anti-Confederation in the 1865 election, the British Government informed him that it supported Confederation. Moreover, the British had replaced the "uncooperative" Lt. Governor of Nova Scotia, Sir Richard MacDonnell, with the "more responsive" Sir William Fenwick.[197] Gordon then became a strong supporter of Confederation. An editorial in the *St. Croix Courier* opined:

> If there is one argument in favor of Union stronger than another it is the necessity that exists for a good and efficient system of mutual defense. We have sometimes regarded this as one of the weaker points in favor of Union, invasion or trouble seemed to be at so great a distance, but now when we see how soon sudden danger can threaten us, and how our ene-

mies may concentrate w/in a gunshot of our very doors, the man must be blind, infatuated, or prejudiced who can fail to recognize its force.[198]

The 1866 New Brunswick election campaign was fought between Tilley's pro-Confederation adherents and the anti-Confederation party of Albert Smith. The August 30, 1866 elections resulted in victory for Tilley's pro-Confederation party that won thirty-three seats to eight for A. J. Smith. Smith's eight seats were from areas remote from the Fenian invasion. The border areas voted heavily pro-Confederation. Tilley said that the effect of the Fenian raid had been "a most decided one, for when they came and said they were prepared to assist the Antis in preventing Confederation, the feeling in favor of Union at once became more general, for the people saw that in that alone was safety."[199]

On February 7, 1867, Lord Carnarvon introduced a draft bill in the House of Lords to unite the provinces of Upper Canada (Ontario), Lower Canada (Quebec), New Brunswick, and Nova Scotia, into the Dominion of Canada House of Lords. On March 8, 1867, that bill (the British North America Act–Confederation) was passed by Parliament. It received the royal assent on March 29, 1867, and on May 27, 1867, a Royal proclamation decreed that the Dominion would come into effect on July 1, 1867. Sir John A. MacDonald became Canada's first Prime Minister. Sir Samuel Tilley became the Confederation's Finance Minister.

Maine had played a role in these actions, but one that, in the fullness of time, had a more profound impact on our neighbor to the north than on our own state. This state had been a staging ground for the "Eastport fizzle." Maine's relationship with Canada, imprecisely defined as it was until the recently-passed Webster-Ashburton Treaty of 1842, had again, within one generation, become the subject of international intrigue. With the passage of time, Fenians in Maine and beyond, and Irish nationalists in America in general, would have to find other methods of demonstrating their loyalty to their ancestral homeland.

1. John Devoy, *Recollections of An Irish Rebel* (Shannon, Ireland: Irish University Press, 1969), 17.
2. D. George Boyce, *Nationalism in Ireland* (Baltimore, MD: The Johns Hopkins University Press, 1982), 176.
3. Devoy, *Recollections of An Irish Rebel*, 18.
4. Devoy, *Recollections of An Irish Rebel*, 19–20.
5. T. W. Moody, ed., *The Fenian Movement* (Cork: The Mercer Press, 1978), 17.

6. Leon O'Brion, *Fenian Fever* (New York: New York University Press, 1971), 2.

7. Moody, *The Fenian Movement*, 64.

8. O'Brion, *Fenian Fever*, 3.

9. O'Brion, *Fenian Fever*, 2.

10. Moody, *The Fenian Movement*, 13–14.

11. President Johnson had already expressed publicly his sympathy for the Fenians. See Joe Patterson Smith, *The Republican Expansionists of the Early Reconstruction Era* (Chicago: 1933), 80, 88–89.

12. Seward was a strong advocate of the U. S. annexation of Canada. After the purchase of Alaska from Russia in 1867, Seward argued that the Maritime Provinces of the newly created Dominion of Canada, tired of heavy taxation without much to show in return, would be willing to revolt and voluntarily join the United States. See also Francis Wayland Glen, *Annexation: The Ideas of the Late William H. Seward* (Brooklyn, New York: 1893).

13. O'Brion, *Fenian Fever*, 52.

14. O'Brion, *Fenian Fever*, 5.

15. O'Brion, *Fenian Fever*, 5–6.

16. Even though the Fenians never succeeded in their goal of establishing an Irish Republic, the Irish government under Eamon de Valera redeemed the Fenian bonds in 1940.

17. Mabel Gregory Walker, *The Fenian Movement* (Colorado Springs, CO: Ralph Myles Publisher, Inc., 1969), 60.

18. Walker, *The Fenian Movement*, 62.

19. Ibid.

20. O'Brion, *Fenian Fever*, 52–53.

21. Ibid.

22. O'Brion, *Fenian Fever*, 56.

23. O'Brion, *Fenian Fever*, 57.

24. Ibid.

25. Walker, *The Fenian Movement*, 72–73.

26. O'Brion, *Fenian Fever*, 57.

27. William D'Arcy, *The Fenian Movement in the U.S.: 1858–1886* (New York: Russell & Russell, 1947), 107.

28. Ibid.

29. Walker, *The Fenian Movement*, 65.

30. O'Brion, *Fenian Fever*, 65.

31. O'Brion, *Fenian Fever*, 42.

32. *St. John, NB, Morning Telegraph*, 1 March 1866.

33. Ibid.

34. Portland, Maine, *Eastern Argus*, 5 March 1866.

35. *St. John, NB, Morning Telegraph*, 26 April 1866 and 28 April 1866.

36. Harold A. Davis, "The Fenian Raid on New Brunswick," *Canadian Historical Review* 36 (December 1955): 321.

37. *St. John, NB, Morning Freeman*, 7 April 1866.

38. Portland, ME, *Eastern Argus*, 8 March 1866.

39. Ibid.

40. Davis, "The Fenian Raid on New Brunswick," 321.

41. *St. John, NB, Morning Telegraph*, 8 March 1866.

42. St. Andrews, NB, *The Standard*, 28 March 1866.

43. Brian Jenkins, *Fenians and Anglo-American Relations During Reconstruction* (Ithaca, New York: Cornell University Press, 1969), 117.

44. *St. John, NB, Morning Telegraph*, 10 March 1866.

45. Jenkins, *Fenians and Anglo-American Relations During Reconstruction*, 126.

46. Jenkins, *Fenians and Anglo-American Relations During Reconstruction*, 127.

47. Walker, *The Fenian Movement*, 81.

48. *St. John, NB, Morning Freeman*, April 5, 1866.

49. Walker, *The Fenian Movement*, 82. Actually, in 1814, the joint British/American Commission appointed under Article III of the Treaty of Ghent had awarded Campobello to Britain. See American State Papers, Foreign Relations, IV, 171.

50. Davis, "The Fenian Raid on New Brunswick," 322.

51. *St. John, NB, Morning Telegraph*, 17 March 1866.

52. D'Arcy, *The Fenian Movement in the U.S.*, 136.

53. O'Brion, *Fenian Fever*, 62.

54. D'Arcy, *The Fenian Movement in the U.S.*, 136.

55. Walker, *The Fenian Movement*, 82.

56. Gordon to Cardwell, 12 March 1866, Edward Cardwell Papers, Public Record Office.

57. Portland, ME, *Eastern Argus*, 28 March 1866.

58. Portland, ME, *Eastern Argus*, 7 June 1866.

59. Portland, ME, *Eastern Argus*, 26 September 1913; City of Portland, ME, Vital Records, Volume 11, 172; Portland, ME, *Evening Express*, 25 September 1913.

60. St. Andrews, NB, *The Standard*, 28 March 1866.

61. Portland, ME, *Eastern Argus*, 4 April 1866.

62. Portland, ME, *Eastern Argus*, 7 April 1866.

63. *St. John, NB, Morning Freeman*, 24 April 1866.

64. O'Brion, *Fenian Fever*, 62.

65. Walker, *The Fenian Movement*, 82.

66. *St. John, NB, Morning Freeman*, 12 April 1866.

67. Ibid. and *St. Croix, NB, Courier*, 14 April 1866.

68. *St. John, NB, Morning Freeman*, 12 April 1866.

69. Ibid.

70. Ibid.

71. St. Andrews, NB, *The Standard*, 18 April 1866.

72. Walker, *The Fenian Movement*, 83–84.

73. *St. John, NB, Morning Freeman*, 21 April 1866.

74. St. Andrews, NB, *The Standard*, 11 April 1866.

75. *St. Croix, NB, Courier*, 14 April 1866.

76. Terry Golway, *John Devoy, Irish Rebel* (New York: St. Martin's Press, 1998), 65.

77. *St. Croix, NB, Courier*, 14 April 1866.

78. Ibid.

79. Portland, ME, *Eastern Argus*, 11 April 1866.

80. *New York Herald*, 13 April 1866.

81. According to the 1851 Census, Montreal had a population of fewer than 60,000, Quebec about 42,000, and Toronto barely 30,000.

82. C. P. Stacey, "A Fenian Interlude: The Story of Michael Murphy," *Canadian Historical Review* 15 (1934): 134.

83. C. P. Stacey, "Fenianism and the Rise of National Feeling in Canada at the Time of Confederation," *Canadian Historical Review* 17 (1931): 240.

84. Stacey, "A Fenian Interlude," 144.

85. Stacey, "A Fenian Interlude," 146. The message as deciphered read: "Get twenty single men ready for orders by Tuesday choose drilled and temperance men if you can pack equipments and ammunition ready for expressing where men directed to follow. K"

86. Stacey, "A Fenian Interlude," 146.

87. Stacey, "A Fenian Interlude," 146–47.

88. Stacey, "A Fenian Interlude," 148–49.

89. *St. John, NB, Morning Freeman*, 14 April 1866.

90. Ibid.

91. *St. John, NB, Morning Freeman*, 24 April 1866.

92. Ibid.

93. Stacey, "A Fenian Interlude," 151–54.

94. Walker, *The Fenian Movement*, 84.

95. Ibid.

96. Jenkins, *Fenians and Anglo-American Relations During Reconstruction*, 136.

97. *St. John, NB, Morning Freeman*, 14 April 1866.

98. *New York Herald*, 13 April 1866.

99. *St. Croix, NB, Courier*, 14 April 1866.

100. W. S. Neidhardt, *Fenianism in North America* (University Park: Pennsylvania State University Press, 1975), 47.

101. Portland, ME, *Eastern Argus*, 18 May 1866.

102. Welles to Cooper, 14 April 1866, Gideon Welles Papers, Library of Congress.

103. St. John, NB, Morning Freeman, 17 April 1866.

104. Walker, *The Fenian Movement*, 84; *St. John, NB, Morning Telegraph*, 17 April 1866.

105. *St. John, NB, Morning Freeman*, 24 April 1866.

106. Neidhardt, *Fenianism in North America*, 47.

107. Davis, "The Fenian Raid on New Brunswick," 328.

108. Portland, ME, *Eastern Argus*, April 18, 1866.

109. Neidhardt, *Fenianism in North America*, 47.

110. Ibid.

111. H. K. Beale, ed., *Diary of Gideon Welles, 1861–1869*, 3 vols. (New York: 1960) 2:486, 17 April 1866.

112. Beale, *Diary of Gideon Welles*.

113. Neidhardt, *Fenianism in North America*, 48.

114. Walker, *The Fenian Movement*, 84.

115. St. Andrews, NB, *The Standard*, 25 April 1866.

116. Davis, "The Fenian Raid on New Brunswick," 329.

117. Neidhardt, *Fenianism in North America*, 47.

118. St. Andrews, NB, *The Standard*, 25 April 1866.

119. Ibid.

120. Ibid.

121. Ibid.

122. Neidhardt, *Fenianism in North America*, 49.

123. Calais, ME, *Weekly Times*, 4 January 1900.

124. Neidhardt, *Fenianism in North America*, 49.

125. Ibid.

126. Davis, "The Fenian Raid on New Brunswick," 330.

127. Neidhardt, *Fenianism in North America*, 48.

128. Neidhardt, *Fenianism in North America*, 50,48.

129. George G. Meade, *The Life and Letters of George Gordon Meade* (New York: 1913), 285.

130. *St. John, NB, Morning Freeman*, 24 April 1866. The report was incorrect. General Meade was an Episcopalian.

131. Portland, ME, *Eastern Argus*, 21 April 1866. The 21 April 1866 issue of the *St. John, NB, Morning Telegraph* reported that about twenty of the original 129 boxes of arms were removed by the Fenians before the alarm was sounded by the guards.

132. *St. John, NB, Morning Telegraph*, 21 April 1866.

133. Ibid.

134. *St. John, NB, Morning Telegraph*, 8 May 1866.

135. *St. John, NB, Morning Telegraph*, 21 April 1866.

136. Ibid. See also Walker, *The Fenian Movement*, 84, and Davis, "The Fenian Raid on New Brunswick," 330.

137. Walker, *The Fenian Movement*, 84.

138. *St. John, NB, Morning Telegraph*, 21 April 1866.

139. Ibid.

140. Maine Historical Society Collections S-572.

141. *St. John, NB, Morning Telegraph*, 21 April 1866.

142. *St. John, NB, Morning Telegraph*, 24 April 1866.

143. St. Andrews, NB, *The Standard*, 25 April 1866.

144. *St. John, NB, Morning Telegraph*, 24 April 1866.

145. *St. John, NB, Morning Freeman*, 24 April 1866.

146. Ibid.

147. *Eastport, ME, Sentinel*, 25 April 1866.

148. *St. John, NB, Morning Telegraph*, 1 May 1866.

149. Portland, ME, *Eastern Argus*, 28 April 1866.

150. *St. John, NB, Morning Telegraph*, 1 May 1866.

151. *St. John, NB, Morning Telegraph*, 3 May 1866.

152. Ibid.

153. St. Andrews, NB, *The Standard*, 2 May 1866.

154. Ibid.

155. *St. John, NB, Morning Freeman*, 5 May 1866.

156. Walker, *The Fenian Movement*, 84; *Cincinnati Enquirer*, 2 May 1866.

157. Walker, *The Fenian Movement*, 85.

158. Ibid.; *Cleveland Leader*, 5 May 1866.

159. *St. John, NB, Morning Telegraph*, 3 May 1866.

160. *St. John, NB, Morning Telegraph*, 8 May 1866.

161. *St. John, NB, Morning Telegraph*, 24 April 1866 & May 8, 1886.

162. *St. John, NB, Morning Telegraph*, 12 May 1866.

163. *St. John, NB, Morning Telegraph*, 19 May 1866.

164. Ibid.

165. *St. John, NB, Morning Telegraph*, 17 May 1866.

166. D'Arcy, *The Fenian Movement in the U.S.*, 141.

167. *Toronto Globe*, 28 April 1866.

168. Walker, *The Fenian Movement*, 87.

169. Ibid.

170. O'Brion, *Fenian Fever*, 62.

171. Walker, *The Fenian Movement*, 86.

172. Ibid.

173. St. Andrews, NB, *The Standard*, 23 May 1866.

174. Portland, ME, *Eastern Argus*, 25 May 1866.

175. Golway, *John Devoy, Irish Rebel*, 63.

176. Walker, *The Fenian Movement*, 88.

177. Walker, *The Fenian Movement*, 89.

178. *St. John, NB, Morning Telegraph*, 5 May 1866.

179. Portland, ME, *Eastern Argus*, 1 June 1866.

180. Golway, *John Devoy, Irish Rebel*, 62.

181. Portland, ME, *Eastern Argus*, 4 June 1866.

182. Ibid.

183. Ibid.

184. Portland, ME, *Eastern Argus*, 6 June 1866.

185. Ibid.

186. Portland, ME, *Eastern Argus*, 5 June 1866.

187. Portland, ME, *Eastern Argus*, 6 June 1866.

188. Portland, ME, *Eastern Argus*, 7 June 1866.

189. Portland, ME, *Eastern Argus*, 20 June 1866.

190. Portland, ME, *Eastern Argus*, 8 June 1866.

191. Ibid.

192. Portland, ME, *Eastern Argus*, 9 June 1866.

193. Portland, ME, *Eastern Argus*, 11 June 1866.

194. Ibid.

195. Walker, *The Fenian Movement*, 76.

196. Neidhardt, *Fenianism in North America*, 50.

197. Ibid.

198. *St. Croix Courier*, 19 May 1866.

199. Neidhardt, *Fenianism in North America*, 51.

MUTUALLY SINGLE: IRISH WOMEN IN PORTLAND, MAINE, 1875–1945

by Eileen Eagan and Patricia Finn

AT THE TURN OF THE TWENTIETH CENTURY, two images of Irish and Irish-American women were prominent in American popular culture: "Mother Machree" and "Bridget the domestic," the latter sometimes transformed into "Typhoid Mary." Bridget the domestic was frequently a negative stereotype of Irish working women, while "Mother Machree," a song popular at the beginning of the twentieth century, emphasized a sentimental but positive view of motherhood:

> There's a spot in me heart which no colleen may own
> There's a depth in me soul never sounded or known.
> There's a place in my memory, my life, that you fill.
> No other can take it, no one ever will.
>
> Sure I love the dear silver that shines in your hair
> And the brow that's all furrowed and wrinkled with care
> I kiss the dear fingers so toil-worn for me
> Oh, God bless you and keep you, Mother machree. [1]

Whether sentimentalized, as in the case of "Mother Machree," or demonized, as in the case of "Typhoid Mary," these two figures did represent two poles of women's experience in America. While the image of Irish motherhood and the Irish women's role in marriage has dominated the public consciousness in America in the form of memoirs and novels, as well as in songs and stories, there is another parallel reality. The experience of life as a single worker has, in fact, been a distinctive and determining part of the experience of many Irish women in the United States. In turn, this experience of singlehood has been influenced by American ideas and the actual roles of women. Irish and Irish-American women have adapted cultural values that were brought with them to the realities of their new environments.

A study of Irish immigrants to Portland, Maine shows how women were able to use permanent singlehood as a means of survival and social mobility. In doing so, they drew on family structures and ideas of mutuality that focused on collective as well as individual well-being. In this case, "singlehood" refers to being unmarried or unpartnered, not to being alone. This essay will analyze the history of Portland's Irish-American single women during the period from 1875 to 1945. We will look at the ways in which women in a variety of occupations were able to build successful lives and challenge the boundaries and spheres to which conservative ideology assigned them. Most of the discussion will involve the predominantly Catholic immigration in the period from the mid-nineteenth century through the early twentieth century, and will focus on the immigrants (first generation) and the second generation (the generation first born in the United States). In many respects—their cultural traditions, time of migration and urban environment—their experiences were similar to those in other cities as described by historians such as Hasia Diner, Janet Nolan, and Timothy J. Meagher.[2] In other ways, including occupations, mobility, and education, Portland's particular economic, geographic, and political settings shaped their lives.

Single womanhood in the United States is an experience that has been shaped by ethnicity and religion as well as by class.[3] This interaction begins with the immigration process itself. While most immigrant groups to the United States were predominantly single men or families, as historians Janet Nolan and Hasia Diner have noted, the late nineteenth century Irish were distinctive in the high percentage of single women migrating to North America, especially after 1870.[4] The occupations Irish women chose after arrival in the United States, their views on marriage and children, educational aspirations, and political beliefs and behavior continued to reflect the cultural values they brought with them. However, sometimes the values were themselves conflicting, and the conditions in which the immigrants found themselves led to new, if still sometimes contradictory solutions.[5] In particular, the experience of single life lived within the Irish and the Irish-American family set boundaries on women, but also allowed them choices they might not otherwise have had.

This pattern applies to the lives of Irish women immigrants in Portland, Maine. By the time of the Civil War, the Irish were the largest non-English group in the city, and they continued to come in substantial, if smaller, numbers well into the 1920s.[6] Many Irish came to this port city from Galway, an area that sent a particularly high percentage of female migrants.[7] In turn, these migrants sent money back to Ireland to bring over relatives in the process of chain migration. Women who obtained jobs as domestics often first brought over a sister for whom they could find work in the same or a nearby household. An oral history project in Portland records the story of Barbara McDermott Cloutier, who came to Maine from western Ireland after her older sister had come over and had obtained work as a domestic. Cloutier recalled, "I came to my aunt's. She was my mother's brother's wife. She had two children, my uncle was dead, and she welcomed me." Another sister followed.[8]

In nineteenth-century Portland, most Irish single women worked as domestics in private homes or in hotels. Others worked in factories, including a match factory and a screen factory near the port area where most Irish settled. The least well off, including many who spoke no English, worked as rag sorters.[9] Married women also found paid work necessary. They found that being married and being single were not necessarily opposite conditions. Irish men worked in dangerous jobs in construction and on the docks with high mortality and accident rates. Men's death or desertion left many Irish women as heads of households. In 1900, for example, in Portland's fourth ward, which included the heavily Irish Gorham's Corner neighborhood near the waterfront, 12.2% of heads of household were women—about 80% of those listed as widows.[10] In a time before the creation of even minimal social security nets, for many women, especially those with children, life became desperate. Despite ideology, for Irish and American women the route of marriage and children was not necessarily a way to survive or better themselves. Sometimes it was a road to poverty.

On the other hand, for young single women in Portland there were more opportunities, and these increased for the second generation of Irish-American women in the early twentieth century. Education and training for a variety of occupations became more available. However, by themselves, most Irish women could not have taken advantage of opportunities. Cultural inhibitions about women living alone limited their possibilities. Perhaps more to the point, even white-collar jobs did

not pay enough for women to support themselves alone.[11] Living with
other family members, a parent or parents or adult siblings, lessened
living expenses and allowed the family to pool resources for a variety of
purposes. The combination of being single with family ties and cooperation allowed some women to make a living and to expand their boundaries. Single Irish women found such opportunities in trades, small
businesses, and in professions such as nursing and teaching. They found
jobs in government and social services. Other women made their living
in the arts, including vaudeville.[12]

Teaching offered a particular opportunity to Irish women. In cities
with large Irish populations, teaching attracted many Irish-American
women. As Hasia Diner notes, "School teaching was for the second generation what domestic service had been for the first."[13] In Boston, New
York, and smaller cities like Worcester, Irish women had moved into
public school teaching in large numbers by 1900. They were often aided
in getting jobs in the public schools by the increasing role of the Irish
in municipal politics.[14]

In Portland, however, with a smaller percentage of Irish in its population, poverty and illiteracy, coupled with resistance by the basically
Protestant school board, limited the number of Irish Catholic teachers
in the public schools before 1880. Their numbers began to increase by
1900.[15] The problems Irish Catholic teachers faced in Portland were
similar to those experienced elsewhere. Describing the creation of
parochial schools in New York City, historian Jay Dolan notes that in
the nineteenth century Catholics confronted "common schools" that
"transmitted a clearly Protestant culture."[16] While in some cities like
New York, the public schools changed as a result of the influx of
Catholic immigrants, in Portland the schools maintained their
Protestant cast. An 1877 report of the school committee noted that one
of the duties of teachers was to open the school day with a reading of
"select portions of the Scriptures and the repeating of the Lord's prayer
in consort by the pupils."[17] Catholics responded in part by creating their
own school system.[18]

In the nineteenth century, first- and second-generation Irish women
found that their main opportunity for teaching was within religious
orders—the Sisters of Mercy in particular in Portland, whose members
taught in Catholic schools. In turn, the Sisters of Mercy established St.
Elizabeth's Academy for Girls in a central location near Portland's Irish

and other Catholic ethnic neighborhoods, which provided girls with more advanced education.[19] Appropriately enough, the first Catholic school for girls was the result of the philanthropy of Winifred Kavanagh, the single daughter of pre-famine immigrants who became rich and successful in Damariscotta Mills, Maine.[20]

By 1880, only a handful of Irish teachers had been employed in the public schools—and they were in the primary schools in Irish neighborhoods; their numbers increased by the turn of the century and continued to grow substantially in the next two decades. Between 1900 and 1910 the number of Irish women teachers doubled to about thirteen percent of the total Portland teaching staff. However, in those years, none was a high school teacher and only two were principals, both of kindergarten.[21]

As in other cities, an increasing political role for the Irish opened up public employment, including positions in the schools. The increase in numbers of Irish teachers beginning in the 1890s was partly the result of the election of two Irish men, Daniel O'Connell O'Donoghue and Patrick McGowan, to the Portland school committee.[22] O'Donoghue was appointed in 1869. McGowan was elected in 1880 following the change of the board structure in 1875 to election by wards. In addition, the city created a teacher training school that made it possible for local high school graduates to gain a teaching certificate. Finally, some second-generation Irish girls began going to the normal school in Gorham, Maine. It was, however, a long trek, physically and culturally, for girls from the Irish neighborhoods in Portland. The creation in that city of St. Joseph's College by the Sisters of Mercy in 1915 provided teacher training closer to home.[23]

A Catholic women's college that provided teacher training alleviated the problem of dealing with the basically Protestant character of the state normal schools. However, Catholic education posed other dilemmas for women who wanted to go into teaching as a profession or have other careers. Despite the continuing pattern of work for Irish single women (and the family need for their incomes), the Church's promulgation of the ideology of marriage and motherhood became even stronger in the early twentieth century. A representation of this can be seen in a graduation ceremony at St. Joseph's Academy in 1914. The student who won the gold medal for Latin gave a talk on "A Woman's Sphere in Life" and declared that women should look first to their domestic roles, seeking to create a home that was happy and pleasant.[24]

At the same time, Irish and Irish-American women continued to marry later than women of other ethnic groups and to remain single at a rate higher than the national average. This was reflected in their work experience. While nationally about one-quarter of women were employed outside the home in 1920, in Portland, one-third of first and second-generation Irish women were so employed. Almost all of these were single.[25] These figures hide the real employment statistics of married women whose work was often not counted because it was seasonal or not in the wage economy. However, there clearly was a distinctive pattern among the Irish.

Some working-class women lived in boarding houses outside of the Irish community and some professional women lived in residential homes; however, the majority of single Irish women lived in the Irish areas of Portland and continued to live with relatives. This was true for teachers as well as women in other occupations. An example is Elizabeth Walsh, who became one of the first Irish Catholic principals of a public school. She was born in 1853, the daughter of Irish immigrants, Thomas, a laborer, and Mary, who kept house. In 1880 at age seventeen, Walsh (then known as Lizzie Walsh) was already a teacher and lived with her parents, her twenty-two-year-old brother, and three sisters (one, Katie, was also a teacher). Lizzie had graduated from Portland High School and began teaching in 1878. She received training at the Portland Teacher Training School and was assigned to Staples School in Gorham's Corner; she would work there as a teacher and then as principal for fifty-seven years. Walsh continued to live with her parents until their deaths. Thereafter she resided with her sister, Delia, in a house on a street not far from school, still within the Irish neighborhood but on a block toward the more affluent west end of Portland.[26]

Elizabeth Walsh's sister Delia, who was seventeen years older than Elizabeth, seems to have never had outside employment, perhaps serving first to keep house for her parents and then her sister, who became the family wage earner. In this case, as in others, the roles of single women supported the collective and made possible individual and group survival and success. While the family did serve as an economic unit, Walsh also relied on her initiative in working two jobs, at Staples School and at Portland Evening School. She was still working this double shift in her early seventies.[27]

These roles sometimes took these women away from Portland, in search of more opportunity and perhaps adventure. Chain migration within the United States followed the pattern of migration from Ireland. Here, too, siblings helped each other. A dramatic example of this is the story of Josephine Feeney.[28] She was born in 1891, the daughter of Irish immigrants from Galway—Barbara Curran Feeney and John A. Feeney. Her mother worked as a domestic in a Portland hotel before marriage and then bore ten children, of whom only five survived childhood. John Feeney ran a saloon in Gorham's Corner, a center of Irish immigrant life. They did well enough financially to send Josephine to St. Joseph's Academy and then to Gorham Normal School. Graduating in 1912, she then taught at the North School (see gallery, plates 36–38.) near Munjoy Hill, a working-class and heavily Irish neighborhood of Portland, not far from her family home. She lived there with her parents and a variety of relatives.[29]

Then around 1920, Josephine Feeney moved to California and became a teacher in Beverly Hills. In moving west, she was following two brothers, Frank and John M. Feeney, who, like Frank, changed his last name to Ford and eventually became a successful film director in Hollywood.[30] (See gallery, plates 4 and 40–41.) Like her brothers, Josephine Feeney maintained her connections with her family in Portland. She also kept life-long ties with the schools she had attended.[31] Her family connection certainly helped her move. However, economic conditions in Portland were also relevant. Portland school reports in 1920 noted that the city had been losing teachers to other cities and businesses because of low pay. This might well have motivated Josephine Feeney, who after six years as a second grade teacher in Portland was making an annual salary of only $750.[32] Teaching was an occupation open to women but which paid them less than men were paid and also less than the unionized telephone workers in Portland. Telephone workers, another favorite occupational niche for Irish American women here, earned a minimum weekly wage of $10, with the possibility of $19 after seven years.[33]

Increasing numbers of Irish Catholic teachers in the public schools did not necessarily end discrimination. One focus of the Ku Klux Klan in Maine in the 1920s was the role of Catholic teachers in public education. A successful 1923 referendum, sponsored by upper- and middle-class reformers and supported by the Klan, eliminated the ward system of election for the Portland city council and school board. The subsequent election eliminated all the Catholic and Jewish members of the school board. In a speech preceding that election, Eugene Farnsworth, the leader of the Klan in Maine, declared: "We will not permit Catholics on the school board any more and we will not permit teachers who are Catholics to further hold these positions until they become Americans."[34]

While the educational system in Portland opened up some opportunities for women, it also set limits. Pay for teachers was less than in other cities. To increase pay and the possibility for promotion, teachers needed to move to other areas, as Josephine Feeney did, or to obtain degrees from liberal arts colleges and advanced degrees from colleges of education. For that, Irish and Irish-American women, like others, needed to leave Portland, and often Maine. Katharine O'Brien, for example, graduated from Deering High School in Portland, then went to Bates College in Lewiston, then on to receive a master's degree from Cornell and, ultimately, a Ph.D. in mathematics from Brown University in the 1930s.[35] After teaching at the College of New Rochelle (a Catholic college for women just outside of New York City), Dr. O'Brien returned to Maine and her family, and taught mathematics at Deering High School in Portland for thirty years, chairing the math department there. She also taught at the campus which is now the University of Southern Maine, and was a distinguished poet and musician.

Lack of access to professional education, shaped by direct discrimination, and by widespread American as well as Irish views of women's roles, limited Irish women's entry into the legal profession. While some Irish men were able to study law in Portland legal offices, and others went out of state to law schools, few Irish women in Portland became lawyers before 1970. Indeed, few women from any group did so.[36] An exception was Gail Laughlin. Of Scots and Irish descent, Laughlin graduated from Cornell Law School in 1898. She later returned to Portland and served in the state legislature in the 1920s.[37]

Women did obtain government jobs through other routes, sometimes through family connections. Rose Alice Henry, for example, began as a stenographer at the Customs House in 1899, and became secretary to the Immigration Inspector until her death in 1927.[38] Helen Cunningham Donahue became head of the Portland post office in the 1930s after the death of her husband, Judge Charles L. Donahue. She was also the daughter of James Cunningham, an Irish immigrant who was a successful contractor and prominent figure in the Catholic and Portland community.[39]

Some successful single Irish and Irish-American women born and raised in Portland moved beyond the Irish neighborhoods, but continued to live with single siblings and widowed parents and bought their own homes. Their lives in many ways reflect the qualities of the Nova Scotia female immigrants in New England described by Elizabeth Beattie, and the Irish and Irish American women described by Hasia Diner.[40] In particular, they exhibited in their lives a sense of family responsibility and attachment to the community. Census data, obituaries, and oral histories of some of these women give us a picture of their lives.[41] Besides their sense of responsibility to their parents and siblings, there was often a sense of obligation to their grandparents, nieces and nephews, aunts and uncles. In many cases this included their loyalty to the Catholic Church and their use of its institutions, including schools and orphanages. They combined interdependence with a strong sense of independence. This quality drove them to take control of their own lives. One example of their drive for independence was their desire for home ownership. This goal and the role of the family economy in making it possible can be seen in the following accounts of some single Irish women in Portland.[42]

In 1924, Mary, Delia, and Agnes Clarity moved into 45 Exeter Street in Portland. The house was new. It was painted white with green shutters and it had large windows looking in every direction.[43] It was two stories high and sat on a hill; facing east, it had a panoramic view of the city, distancing them from the working-class roots of their parents and grandparents.[44] Thirteen years earlier Mary and her sister Agnes had opened their corsetiere shop, "Clarity Corset Shop," in the downtown department store district.[45] They were then living in the Munjoy Hill section of Portland with their father Patrick and their sister Delia, who stayed home to care for the family members who worked outside of the home. The corset business in the early twentieth century was booming, and during the next twenty-five years the Clarity sisters were actively and successfully engaged in promoting this business.[46] Despite the strong competition in the undergarment industry from the emerging and well-financed department stores, this type of shop as a small retail business appealed to many single women of the day. There was a community of women shop owners who ran successful specialty stores, along with the increasing service-industry businesses, such as beauty salons with women shop owners that were rapidly emerging .[47]

While the Claritys were establishing themselves at home in the Deering neighborhood of Portland, only a few blocks away, Lauretta, Alice, and Agnes Sheehan were settling into their "new" home. Although the two-family house was over twenty-five years old when they bought it, it was solidly built and would prove to be a good long-term investment for the Sheehan sisters. After years of Lauretta and Agnes working in the millinery business in downtown Portland, and Alice additionally running numerous boarding houses, their hard work paid off. The Sheehan's Millinery Shop on Congress Street, within downtown Portland's main shopping district, would become a worthwhile investment for Lauretta and Agnes Sheehan, although they never did quite as well financially as the Clarity sisters.[48]

Hats, of course, were all the rage in the early twentieth century.[49] Everyone was outfitted in hats, from the family matriarch to the family pet, in color coordinates and matching plaids, or in all-feather creations; no one stepped out their door without a proper hat. Lauretta became involved in the millinery business at the age of fourteen when she worked at a local hat factory. She went on to work in a small millinery shop, perhaps performing a informal apprenticeship. Within three years, Lauretta and Agnes would own their own specialty shop.

Their father, Timothy Sheehan, a harness maker, had come to live with his brother's family in 1889 in Portland.[50] Because Timothy's wife, the mother of his children, had just died in Boston and he had no one to care for the children, he placed his three daughters in St. Elizabeth's Orphanage, run by the Sisters of Mercy.[51] Former residents testify to the nurturing environment provided by the nuns.[52] However, this experience may have helped form the girls' determination to take care of themselves, both financially and emotionally. This type of relationship with an institution of the Catholic Church demonstrates the connectedness through religion that was common with Irish immigrants and their families. In the cases of these families of sisters, this connection can best be explained through the access to Church support and especially of the Sisters of Mercy that was attained in their early years.[53] As part of the culture that provided a strong network of benevolence through daily contact and daily prayer, the efforts of the Catholic Church proved itself as a safeguard for these single Irish American women, as well as for married women.[54]

Within local late nineteenth and early twentieth century Portland, tourism, shipping, industrialization, and immigration all fired an economy centered on the waterfront. Then, most Portlanders held in common a sense of the importance of place, whether they were Yankees, Irish immigrants, or Italian, Jewish or Polish. In particular, the Yankee elite thought of Portland as their own "city by the sea" (to quote Portland's native poet Henry Wadsworth Longfellow). The Irish who were the first wave of non-English speaking immigrants felt that they had the right to move wherever they wanted in that city.[55] With the exception of the affluent living in their neighborhoods near the Eastern and Western Promenades, it was a city of working-class people and low-income housing. By the second decade of the twentieth century, the outer-lying areas of the city were quickly filling up with the middle-income residences like those of the Claritys and the Sheehans. The new houses were enviable. They were constructed with plumbing, electricity, oil heat, and plenty of room. There were back yards and front porches. There was a distance that set the owners apart from their jobs and their neighbors. There were streetcar lines that picked up the middle-class residents near their homes and dropped them off near their places of work. The people most able to buy homes usually had multiple incomes, as in the case of the Clarity and Sheehan families.[56]

In the time when the social and economic structure reflected gender as well as ethnic stratification, some single women challenged the marginalization of single women as "dependent old maids." The rapid mobility of some women was tied to educational attainments. When education of women was either discouraged or reserved for the upper class, few Irish-American women were able to see the advantages of schooling. Despite the obstacles, those who did achieve some education far surpassed the popular notion of what "Bridget" could achieve. By the early twentieth century, professionalization in social reform careers such as public health was becoming the norm rather than the exception.[57] This posed a new structural limitation. At the turn of the century, Irish-American women did not have access to formal medical training in Portland or elsewhere in the state of Maine. While there was training for nurses, it was necessary to go out of state for advanced medical education. [58]

In October 1918, Katherine Quinn joined the City of Portland Public Health Division at Portland City Hall. Like Katharine O'Brien, she had left Portland to get an education, in this case in the medical field. After graduating from the Catholic girls' high school in 1893, Quinn left her parent's home near Portland's east end, in the Munjoy Hill area, to attend college at New York City's St. Vincent's Hospital. After receiving her nursing degree from St. Vincent's, she went to Simmons College in Boston, while working at the Boston Lying-in Hospital, to gain further accreditation in the field of public health. Katherine returned to Portland in 1918, apparently to care for her aging parents and her younger brother William. Although William was employed as a boat carpenter in various establishments, he continued to live at the family home.[59] After her father's death in 1922, she moved her mother and brother to a nearby apartment on Morning Street and by 1932 had purchased a two-family home at 166 Eastern Promenade with a view of Casco Bay. Katherine Quinn would live there until her death in 1967.[60]

Other women found opportunities beside formal education to find relatively well-paid work through family connections. This was especially true in certain trades. After Alice Welch graduated from Portland High School in 1898, she went to work at the Portland Evening Express Company as a compositor. This was a desirable job for young women at the turn of the last century. At that time Portland Evening Express Company employed thirteen young women as compositors. At her home on Pleasant Street in Gorham's Corner, Alice lived with her father William, a compositor, and her younger siblings, Clara, Edward, and Margaret. Anna, her mother, had died years before. After her father's death in 1907 the siblings sold their home and eventually moved into a home near the Western Promenade.[61] By that time, Clara had become a matron at the telephone company, and at the same time Margaret became a telephone operator. The telephone company employed many local women, including numerous second-generation Irish Americans.[62] Indeed, the telephone workers were able to go beyond the family economy and develop larger collective action through unionization. In April 1919, the International Brotherhood of Electrical Workers' telephone operators, as "Hello Girls" at the telephone company's Portland office at 45 Forest Avenue, went on strike for better wages and working conditions. The strike resulted in a considerable pay raise and much better working conditions for these women workers. The strike was led by Cora Smith, an Irish-American woman from Portland.[63]

Examining the experiences of single women broadens the meaning of family as a mutual relationship. This mutuality persists through women's historic connection to nurturing activities and institutions. This is exemplified by the case of Katherine Quinn, a public servant working for the good of the family and the working-class community and the Sheehan sisters' connection to the Catholic Church. The Welch women's story speaks to both family economy and the creation of broader economic units to improve the community as a whole. The Clarity women's small-business success drew upon the family unit and their ties and connections with the more affluent in their Irish American community. Many of them were lifelong members of their church parishes and remained single women. Teachers like Elizabeth Walsh, Josephine Feeney, and Katharine O'Brien drew on their individual initiative and skills and on their family connections to expand their lives and boundaries. Women in unions like the telephone workers created, as did their brothers in the predominantly Irish longshoremen's union, a broader collective force, and developed sisterhood.

Considering the lives of single Irish-American women in Portland, we see that the interconnectedness with their family, friends, and community deeply enriched those around them through their mutually single lives. Despite the images of Mother Machree, Bridget the domestic, and Bridget's ominous alter-ego, "Typhoid Mary," a major experience of Irish and Irish-American women was the way in which those who were single were able to draw on traditional values of kinship and family to adapt and thrive in the new world. They used traditional means to justify what was, in some ways, a life outside of the traditional women's sphere.

1. William H. A. Williams, *"Twas Only an Irishman's Dream': The Image of Ireland and the Irish in American Popular Song Lyrics, 1800–1920* (Chicago: University of Illinois Press, 1996) 216; and Judith Waltzer Leavitt, *Typhoid Mary: Captive to the Public's Health* (Boston: Beacon Press, 1996). For the relation of her image to negative sterotypes of Irish women, especially domestic workers, see pages 1 and 164–66.
2. Hasia Diner, *Erin's Daughters in America: Irish Immigrant Women in the Nineteenth Century* (Baltimore: The Johns Hopkins University Press, 1983); Janet A. Nolan, *Ourselves Alone: Women's Immigration from Ireland 1885–1921* (Lexington: The University Press of Kentucky, 1989), 2; Timothy J. Meagher, *Inventing Irish America: Generation, Class, and Ethnic Identity in a New England City, 1880–1928* (South Bend, Indiana: University of Notre Dame Press, 2001). Sources for this essay include newspapers, oral interviews, and United States manuscript census data, including a comparison of women in one

predominantly first- and second-generation Irish ward in Portland, the fourth ward, in 1900 and 1920. See notes below.

3. This was obviously also true elsewhere. For a discussion of single Canadian women and their migration to Boston, see Elizabeth Beattie, *Obligation and Opportunity: Single Maritime Women in Boston, 1870–1930* (Montreal: McGill-Queen's University Press, 2000).

4. Nolan, *Ourselves Alone*, 2; Diner, *Erin's Daughters*.

5. For an examination of apparently conflicting views of women's work and motherhood, see Timothy J. Meagher, "Sweet Good Mothers and Young Women Out in the World: The Roles of Irish American Women in Late Nineteenth and Early Twentieth Century Worcester, Massachusetts," *U.S. Catholic Historian* 5, nos. 3–4 (1986): 325–44.

6. Michael C. Connolly, "The Irish Longshoremen of Portland, Maine, 1880–1923" (Ph.D. diss., Boston College, 1988), 38–39. See also James Paul Allan, "Catholics in Maine: A Social Geography" (Ph.D. diss., Syracuse University, 1970), 178–84.

7. For the lives and culture of the women of Galway see Maureen Langan-Egan, *Galway Women in the Nineteenth Century* (Dublin: Open Air Books, 1999); Diner, *Erin's Daughter in America*; and Connolly, "The Irish Longshoremen of Portland," 106.

8. Barbara McDermott Cloutier, interview, Portland, Maine, 16 April 1984, "Victoria Society of Maine Oral History Project" transcript, Maine Historical Society, Portland, Maine.

9. Eileen Eagan and Patricia Finn, "From Galway to Gorham's Corner: Irish Women in Portland, Maine," in Marli Weiner, ed., *Of Place and Gender* (Orono: University of Maine Press, 2004). For an assessment of the degree to which Irish (Gaelic) was spoken in Portland, see "The Galway Gaeltacht of Portland, Maine" by Kenneth Nilsen in this book.

10. *Twelfth Census . . . 1900*, Portland, Maine, Manuscript Census Schedules, United States Census Bureau (hereafter PMCS).

11. See the reports on working women's wages in the annual Maine labor reports, for example, "Women Wage earners," *21st Annual Report of the Bureau of Industrial and Labor Statistics for the State of Maine* (Augusta, ME: 1907).

12. See *Twelfth Census . . . 1900* and *Fourteenth Census, 1920*, PMCS.

13. Diner, *Erin's Daughters*, 96.

14. Diner, *Erin's Daughters*, 96–97. See also Polly Welts Kaufman, *Boston Women and City School Politics, 1872–1905* (New York: Garland Publishers, 1994) 232–33, 242–43.

15. *Directory of the City of Portland, 1857–1900*. The city directory each year listed the teachers and members of the school board. *Tenth Census . . . 1880; Twelfth Census . . . 1900*, PMCS. The Census lists occupations, birthplaces, and places of birth of parents. In some cases the teacher or school board member's religion can be determined through obituaries. See notes below.

16. Jay Dolan, *The Immigrant Church: New York's Irish and German Catholics, 1815–1865* (Baltimore: The Johns Hopkins Press, 1975), 101, 108. Dolan notes the creation of a ward system for the public schools in the early 1840s, in which teachers were selected by a local committee, and which opened up teaching jobs for Irish Catholics and ended the reading of the Protestant Bible in the local public school.

17. *Rules and Regulations of the School Committee of the City of Portland*, adopted June 15, 1877 (Portland, ME: Daily Press Printing House, 1877), 11. The use in the public schools of the Protestant version of the Bible and the Lord's Prayer had long been a subject of heated opposition by Maine Catholics.

18. See John S. Munroe, "Chronological History of Parochial Education in Portland, Maine" (Mandeville, LA: LaSalle University, 1996), unpublished manuscript, available at Saint Joseph's College library.

19. Sister Mary Raymond Higgins, *For Love of Mercy: Missioned in Maine and Andros Island, Bahamas 1883–1983* (Portland: Sisters of Mercy, 1995). See also the other sources cited in the Overview section of this book regarding the Sisters of Mercy.

20. For more information on the Kavanagh Family, see "Facing the Atlantic" by Edward McCarron in this book.

21. *Directory of City of Portland 1900* (Portland: Thurston Publishing) 1901; *Thirteenth Census . . . 1910*, PMCS.

22. *Report of the City of Portland, Portland Maine, 1895*. Daniel O'Donoghue figures prominently in Gary Libby's essay "Maine and the Fenian Invasion of Canada of 1866" in this book. Libby cites O'Donoghue as a leader of one of the two factions of Fenians in Maine's largest city. See "Daniel O'C. O'Donoughue" (obituary), *Portland Advertiser*, 10 April 1905; "Had Never Missed Voting Since Casting First Ballot in 1858" (obituary of Patrick McGowan, nephew of the school board's Patrick McGowan), *Portland Evening Express*, 20 October 1904; and *Report of the City of Portland* (Portland, ME, 1895). O'Donoughue's obituary asserts that he was "instrumental in securing the appointment of the first Catholic woman in the public schools" in Portland. For the role of Irish political power in opening up teaching jobs in public schools elsewhere, see Dolan, *The Immigrant Church*, 107–108; Diner, *Erin's Daughters*, 96–97; and Meagher, *Inventing Irish America*, 149, 152.

23. SJL (initials of the author as listed), "St Joseph's Academy," *Maine Catholic Historical Magazine* 4 (April 1914): 5–6; William Leo Lucey, *The Catholic Church in Maine* (Manchester: New Hampshire Catholic Press, 1957), 336. See also Durwood Ferland Jr., *Fortitudo et Spes: The Courage and Hope to Move a College* (Greenville, ME: Moosehead Communications, 1999) and Higgins, *For Love of Mercy*.

24. *Maine Catholic Historical Magazine* 3 (1914).

25. *Fourteenth Census . . . 1920*, PMCS; Joseph A. Hill, *Women in Gainful Occupations, 1890–1920* (Washington, D.C.: Government Printing Office, 1929), 76, 159.

26. "Veteran Teacher Dies Here at 81" (Elizabeth Walsh obituary), *Portland Evening Express*, 18 April 1942; *Tenth Census . . . 1880*, PMCS; *Directory of the City of Portland 1927, 1943*.

27. Elizabeth Walsh's salary for both jobs combined in 1917 was $725.00. *Fifty-eighth Annual Report, City of Portland* (Portland, 1917), 14.

28. On the Feeney/Ford family see Joseph McBride, *Searching for John Ford: A Life* (New York: St. Martin's Press, 2001) 1–74; Matthew Jude Barker, "John Ford and the Feeney Family of Galway and Portland, Maine," *Galway Roots/Clanna ná Gaillimhe* 5 (1998); "Josephine Feeney" (obituary), *Maine Sunday Telegram*, 27 January 1985, 7.

29. "Roster of teachers," *Annual Report of the City of Portland—1917* (Portland, Maine, 1918), 152; St. Joseph's Academy, *The Academia* (Portland, 1931), 94.

30. See Barker, "John Ford and the Feeney Family." See also earlier reference and citations about Ford in the Overview of this book.

31. Josephine Feeney bought a half-page ad in *St. Joseph's Fiftieth Jubilee Yearbook* in 1931 and again in 1967 (she died in 1987). She was a life member of the Gorham Normal Alumni organization. "Compliments of Miss Josephine Feeney Class of 1910," *St. Joseph's, Academia* (Portland, ME: 1931), 108; *Gorham Normal Alumni Directory* (Portland, ME: 1967).

32. *Sixty-Second Annual Report, City of Portland* (Portland, ME: 1921) 16, 28. Salaries in Portland ranged from $1,500 for a male liberal arts graduate teaching at Portland high to $400 for a female graduate of Portland Training School who taught kindergarten.

33. *Portland Evening Express* April 15–16, 1919, 1. The latter figure would represent a sizeable advantage ($988 v. $750) over a teacher like Josephine Feeney, who had an even longer tenure and a college certificate as well.

34. *Boston Herald*, 8 September 1923, 1. Another Klan leader in Maine was DeForest H. Perkins, who had been the Superintendent of Schools in Portland for eight years. Edward Bonner Whitney, "The Ku Klux Klan in Maine: A Study with Particular Emphasis on the City of Portland" (Thesis, Harvard College, 1966), 35–37; Rita Mae Breton, "Red Scare: A Study in Maine Nativism, 1919–1925," (Thesis, University of Maine, 1972), 202–203. See also John Syrett, "Principle and Expediency: The Ku Klux Klan and Ralph Owen Brewster in 1924," *Maine History* 39, no. 4 (Winter 2000–01): 215–39.

35. "Katharine E. O'Brien: Math Teacher, Poet, Musician" (obituary), *Portland Press Herald*, 11 April 1998. Like some others, she indicated her appreciation for the benefits of higher education by leaving a substantial part of her savings to the University of Maine system to improve its libraries ("Former Deering Teacher Wills Money to U Maine," *Portland Press Herald*, 3 March 1999). Katharine O'Brien's parents were both Irish born and moved to Portland from Massachusetts. Her mother, Katherine H. O'Brien, taught in a primary school in Portland in 1920. *Fourteenth Census, 1920* lists Katharine O'Brien as living at 130 Hartley Street in Portland with her father, Martin, her mother, Katharine, and her sister, Mary, aged twenty-two.

36. According to Lee Agger, as late as 1972 there were only thirty-one female lawyers in Maine (*Women of Maine* [Portland, Maine: Guy Gannett Publishing Co., 1982], 138). A more recent account estimates that there were only about eighteen women practicing law in Maine in 1972. One woman, Marguerite Fay, graduated from the Peabody School, a proprietary law school in the 1940s, but the University of Maine Law School (in Portland) did not graduate a woman between 1950 until 1961, and not another until 1968. Margaret Johnson, "Maine Women Attorneys: A Millennial Jubilee," *Law Interview* (July 2001). www.Lawinterview.com/interviewmaster_archive_07_01~ns4.html. *University of Maine School of Law, 1998 Alumni Directory* (Portland, Maine, 1998), 89–91.

37. Margaret Johnson, "Maine Women Attorneys: A Millennial Jubilee," *Law Interview*, July 2001. www.Lawinterview.com/interviewmaster_archive_07_01~ns4.html. Gail Laughlin, who was admitted to the bar in 1898, was the daughter of an Irish-born father and Canadian-born mother of Scots descent. After her wid-

owed mother moved the family to Portland, Laughlin graduated from Portland High School, studied at Wellesley and then Cornell and became active in the suffrage movement and the National Women's Party. She returned to Portland and served in the state legislature in the 1920s. Laughlin seems to have had no connection to the Irish community, but her experience (and her mother's) is like that of other Scots-Irish women. Some of her interest in domestic labor may have come from her familiarity with Irish domestics in her older brothers' homes in Portland. Ruth Sargent, "Gail Laughlin" in Barbara Sicherman and Carl Hurd Green, eds., *Notable American Women: The Modern Period* (Cambridge: Harvard University Press, 1980), 410–11. See entry for her brother Alexander Laughlin and his family and servant Margaret McGrath in *Twelfth Census of the United States*, Schedule No. 1—Population, 1900, Portland, Maine, Enumeration district 68.

38. "Rose Alice Henry" (obituary), 17 August 1927, Index 31, Maine Historical Society Obituary.

39. "Mrs. Helen C. Donohue, 95, Former Postmistress Dies," *Portland Press Herald*, 11 October 1974, 2.

40. Beattie, *Obligation and Opportunity*, 60; Diner, *Erin's Daughters*, 153.

41. See "Working Class Women of Portland's West End," Oral History Project, Archives, University of Southern Maine.

42. This is a complex and nuanced area much studied by historians and sociologists. Timothy J. Meagher states, "It was not a simple process of assimilation from one timeless essence to another: from 'Irishness' to 'Americanness.' Second generation Irish men and women, as we have noted, had not abandoned loyalties to Ireland, and they were probably as devoutly Catholic as their Irish ancestors" (*Inventing Irish America*, 11).

43. Photo obtained from the City's Assessors Office, 1924. In 1924 the City's Assessors Office photographed and detailed the condition of Portland's existing housing structures.

44. Patrick Claherty, her father, first appeared in Portland in 1851 according to the 1850–51 *Portland City Directory*. He was listed as a fisherman. At some point after the Civil War, they changed the spelling of their name, possibly to make pronunciation easier.

45. "At the Clarity Corset Shop, "Innovation Sale" of Nemo corsets the new styles 319 and 321 at $3.00. Correct fitting gives stylish, hygienic finish to these goods. Miss Mary E. Clarity, Corsetiere, Durant block, 536a Congress Street, Durant block, elevator, Phone 670." This advertisement appeared for the first time for the Clarity sisters in the *Portland Sunday Telegram*, 9 January 1911. Mary Clarity had worked for the former owners of this shop, perhaps in an apprentice role, for nearly five years. Before that she was employed in local department stores as a counter clerk.

46. As emphasis on the "hour glass" figure in fashion was changing to an affinity for a more comfortable style of clothing. Undergarments were becoming more diverse in recognizing all types of figures. Don Kirschner, *The Paradox of Professionalism: Reform and Public Service in Urban America, 1900–1940*, Contributions in American History Series No. 119 (New York: Greenwood Press, 1986), 153.

47. In the *City of Portland Directory* for 1910, three specialty corset businesses (all

women-owned) were listed along with fifty-one milliners, thirty-five of which had women owners; seventeen women manicurists; and nine women hair stylists.

48. As an indicator of their financial holdings, see *Portland City Directory* 1926 in the section "City Valuation and Taxes for 1925." Mary Clarity is listed as paying $198.41 (page 1317) and Lauretta, Agnes, and Alice Sheehan as paying $188.60 (page 1342).

49. See Wendy Gamber, *The Female Economy and Dress making Trades, 1860–1930* (Urbana: University of Illinois Press, 1997). On female owners of small businesses in Portland, see Candace Kanes, "Revisiting Main Street: Uncovering Women Entrepreneurs," in Polly Welts Kaufman and Katharine T. Corbett, eds., *Her Past Around Us: Interpreting Sites for Women's History* (Malabar, FL: Krieger Publishing Co., 2003), 189–203.

50. Sheehan, a harness maker, opened his own shop on Commercial Street. *Portland City Directory* 1906.

51. The Sheehan sisters probably stayed at St. Elizabeth's for long periods of time. Although Timothy would pass the orphanage each morning and had the opportunity to see his daughters on his way to work, there are no records to indicate that he did so.

52. See "Portland's Two Long Established Orphan Asylums Where Homeless Children are Tenderly Cared For," *Portland Sunday Telegram*, 22 January 1905, section 2, page 1. Also see Barbara Joyce, tape recording, 1988, "Working Class Women of Portland's West End," Oral History Project, Archives, University of Southern Maine.

53. Mary and Nellie Clarity attended St. Elizabeth's Academy (Mary E. Clarity obituary, *Portland Press Herald*, 2 January 1943; Lauretta Sheehan obituary, 2 September 1965). According to her 1936 obituary, Bridget Quinn, the mother of Katherine Quinn, was honored for her distinction of being the oldest member of the parish of the Cathedral of the Immaculate Conception. St. Elizabeth's Academy was located on Free Street and served in various functions since 1868 when it was purchased by Bishop Bacon for the Portland Roman Catholic Archdiocese. From 1878 to 1909, according to Mary Raymond Higgins in *From Love of Mercy*, many of the graduates went on to become nuns in the Sisters of Mercy.

54. Joseph Lee, *The Modernisation of Irish Society, 1848–1918* (Dublin: Gill and Macmillan, 1973). Lee explains how Ireland in the grip of massive emigration reorganized its church and state issues by redefining the role of women in Irish society to one of subservience to men; Irish leaders also discouraged marriage, thereby discouraging sexual relationships which could produce children. The role of religious orders would take precedence over marriage. While this reorganization was taking place in Ireland, the people used as examples in this article were migrating from Ireland, thus possibly carrying some of these beliefs with them. This suggests that the relationship between single women and the church and community was not without conflict. Women, single or married, who stepped outside the religious or moral boundaries of Catholic teaching on sex and marriage, for example, faced possible censure.

55. Robert Babcock, "The Rise and Fall of Portland's Waterfront, 1850–1920," *Maine Historical Society Quarterly* 22, no. 2 (fall 1982): 82–83.

56. Eventually the Claritys' real estate investments with their brother, Edwin, who lived across the street from them at 30 Exeter Street, proved to be a good investment.

57. Burton J. Bledstein, *The Cult of Professionalism: The Middle Class and the Development of Higher Education in America* (New York: W. W. Norton & Company, 1978) 84–88.

58. For discussion of Irish women and nursing in Portland, see Eagan and Finn, "From Galway to Gorham's Corner," in Weiner, *Of Place and Gender*. Men, including Irish men, were able to go to The Medical School of Maine from 1909 to 1921. According to the *Portland City Guide* (Portland: Forest City Printing, 1940), The Medical School of Maine, founded in 1820, was under the control and supervision of Bowdoin College. In 1899 this institution decided the last two years of courses should be given in Portland. Between 1909 and 1921, when Bowdoin College discontinued its medical curriculum, the Maine School of Medicine continued at 132 Chadwick Street in Portland. Thanks go to Nicholas Noyes of the Maine Historical Society library staff for this reference.

59. An older brother, David, left home many years before and was successfully employed at The Portland Company. David was married by this time and starting a family, as well as participating in city government as a councilor from his district.

60. "Miss Quinn, 91, Public Health Pioneer Dies," *Portland Evening Express*, 17 May 1967, 2.

61. Records from the Cumberland County Register of Deeds indicate only one record of co-ownership for property at 37 Thomas Street in 1931 and make no further mention of Alice Welch's investment. There was no will filed in the Cumberland County Probate office for Welch.

62. See *1920 Manuscript Census*. By 1910, almost all of the Boston Telephone Company's operators were Irish-American women. Their union conducted a successful strike in 1919. See Sarah Deutsch, *Women and the City: Gender, Space, and Power in Boston, 1870–1940* (New York: Oxford University Press, 2000), 192, 206, 211.

63. *Portland Evening Express*, 15–16 April 1919, 1.

NATIONALISM AMONG EARLY TWENTIETH-CENTURY IRISH LONGSHOREMEN IN PORTLAND, MAINE

by Michael C. Connolly

PORTLAND, MAINE was a significant and prosperous shipping port between the mid-nineteenth and early twentieth centuries. During this period, Portland's waterfront workers formed an ethnically cohesive and predominantly Irish longshoremen's union, the Portland Longshoremen's Benevolent Society (PLSBS) to negotiate their wages and work conditions. This essay will focus on the ethnicity of these dock laborers, specifically gauging the nature and degree of their Irish nationalism. It will also attempt to place this local group into the larger context of Ireland's history and the history of Irish longshoremen in other American ports, primarily New York. What emerges is a balancing act—between old and new, first and second generation, Irish and Irish-American. In short, an overview of these years, especially the transition into the postwar 1920s, provides a lens through which we can analyze larger issues such as American immigration, ethnic identity, and assimilation.

The emergence of Portland as a major Atlantic port can be dated from its mid-nineteenth century linkage by rail to Montreal and, by extension, to the fertile grain-producing regions of Canada's western provinces. In July 1853, the Atlantic and St. Lawrence Railway completed the rail link between Montreal and Portland, especially useful during the winter months, November through April, when the Saint Lawrence River would often be inaccessible due to ice. For over seventy years, this link provided the means of transporting Canadian grain to Portland, where it was loaded onto steamships bound for Europe. Due to cost overruns, the Atlantic and St. Lawrence Railway was leased to the Grand Trunk Railway just three weeks after opening service.[1]

John Alfred Poor, a Portland lawyer and entrepreneur, had envisioned a transportation hub centered in Portland that would link North America with the major cities of Europe by steamship and rail. Poor could never be accused of being timid in his "vision" of Portland and its future role:

> a vision, in which I saw the whole line pass before me like a grand panorama, and in continuation a vast system of railroads permeating the whole country . . . with new cities with a dense population, with every facility for ocean steamships from every country; and the coast of Maine lined with cities rivaling the cities on the coast of the Baltic.[2]

Poor's vision was ultimately more fully realized by Saint John, New Brunswick than by Portland, Maine. In the nearly seventy years between the Grand Trunk Railway link to Portland from Montreal in 1853 and the development of Saint John as Canada's new "winter port" in the early 1920s, Portland enjoyed seven decades of export-driven trade with Europe, largely because of the single commodity of Canadian grain. Neither city could effectively compete with Boston, "the Hub," but, for a variety of reasons, compared to Saint John, "Portlanders were perhaps a bit more fortunate overall." Furthermore, according to Maine and Canadian historian Robert Babcock, "Portlanders had turned landward and concentrated upon providing goods and services for their more populous environs . . . Despite the boundary that separated them, both communities had industrialized under remarkably similar circumstances on the rim of the North Atlantic economy."[3]

Before this Grand Trunk rail connection to Montreal, work along Portland's waterfront had been unpredictable. The West Indies trade in molasses and rum had provided irregular (casual) and poorly-paid work for a small group of African American dock workers, but they had largely been displaced by the more numerous Irish, who arrived in mid-nineteenth century Portland, hungry for work at almost any wage or condition.[4] By 1880, this group of predominantly Irish longshoremen, seeking a level of occupational security in their newly chosen home, formed the Portland Longshoremen's Benevolent Society (PLSBS), whose records today form a major labor collection at the Maine Historical Society in Portland. [5]

There are many references to Irish nationalist causes in the recorded minutes of the PLSBS. The first occurred within the opening pages of one of the earliest record books of the union. This entry referred to a scheduled meeting in support of the Land League in Ireland.[6] A concern for Ireland within the union would continue throughout the latter years of the nineteenth century and into the first two decades of the twentieth century as shown in the recorded minutes of the PLSBS. This concern was always balanced by a focus on the more parochial, economic pressures facing the union, such as wages, work rules, and conditions. Although difficult to prove, it would seem plausible that the younger, American-born members were more concerned with these domestic issues than were the older, Irish-born founders of the union. This is not to say that the Irish-born members were not strong union advocates or any less diligent about maintaining work rules. If anything, they were equally diligent; but they managed to mix this strong unionism with an abiding concern for Irish nationalist causes. This duality of interest is a central thesis of this essay.

Membership in the union varied widely in its first two decades, but by 1899, it had reached a high of 868 members. During the first decade of the twentieth century, however, PLSBS membership witnessed a sharp steady decline, as a weakening economy required fewer laborers to handle goods into or out of the port of Portland. Locally this was reflected primarily in a sharp decrease in the volume of Canadian grain being exported via Portland to Europe. Membership in the PLSBS was cut in half to 425 between the years 1899 and 1910.[7]

The union would survive the economic recession of the early 1890s and the slack time leading up to a World War I all-time high in 1919 when war-related exports would eventually boost union membership to 1,366. Although the years immediately preceding and following the war marked an era of growth and confidence for the Irish dock workers in Portland, events across the Atlantic in the land of their birth or ancestry increasingly preoccupied Portland's Irish community as a whole and the predominantly Irish PLSBS specifically. This essay will examine how the Portland longshoremen balanced their economic and political realities in America with their nationalist dreams and hopes concerning Ireland.

Before considering twentieth century examples of Irish nationalism among this group of laborers, we will briefly focus on a few of the nineteenth-century antecedents in order to demonstrate that the Portland Irish never lost sight of their country of origin, or its travails.[8] As the Irish Catholic flock in Portland grew dramatically in the years after the

Irish Potato Famine (1845–50) and the American Civil War (1861–65), there were many expressions of their continued interest in the affairs of their native country. At times this nationalist enthusiasm ran counter to the expressed wishes of the Catholic hierarchy in America. Historian Kerby Miller states, "although most Irish immigrants were loyal to [the Democratic Party, the Catholic Church, and Irish-American nationalism, particularly the Fenian movement], relations between these institutions were largely utilitarian and competitive, sometimes hostile."[9]

The Irish in Portland, as in other American cities in the late nineteenth century, kept the faith politically as well as religiously.[10] Although politically active within the Democratic Party, the Irish in Portland were neither numerous nor powerful enough to unseat the Yankee, Protestant, Republican majority in the city, and certainly even less powerful or numerous in the state of Maine as a whole. Political events in Ireland in the early 1880s directly affected Portland. Although the source of Irish immigration into Maine in the eigtheenth and early nineteenth centuries varied widely within Ireland, in the decades following the Famine, County Galway appears to have been the major source of Portland's Irish immigrants through the process known as chain migration. Many of these "greenhorns" came from Galway and other parts of Ireland's western province of Connaught where land agitation, and the Land League organization itself, was most advanced.[11]

In the late nineteenth century, the two most important nationalistic movements in Ireland were the Irish Parliamentary Party, a constitutional political movement led by Charles Stewart Parnell, and the Land League, a more radical agrarian movement led by Michael Davitt. By 1880, these two groups had joined with the Irish Republican Brotherhood (IRB), known in America as the Clan na Gael, or Fenians, in a "New Departure" to bring Home Rule to Ireland.[12]

Evidence of the interest of local Irish Americans in the political events in Ireland could be seen in the extensive coverage given by a major Portland newspaper to the trial of the leaders of the Irish Land League. Two major Irish nationalist leaders were the subjects of an 1880 article found in Portland's *Eastern Argus* newspaper:

TRAVERSERS TRIALS

The Land Leaguers at Last Before the Court.
So superior did the defense seem within doors, and so popular was Mr.
Parnell without, that the government seemed to be on trial rather than
the traversers . . . Mr. Michael Davitt [attempted to show] that notwithstanding the sufferings and distress through which Ireland has passed, the
percentage of attacks upon individuals has been unusually small.[13]

The coverage of news from Ireland was supplemented by political
activity locally. Early in the 1880s, an Irish Land and Industrial League
(ILIL) in Portland claimed to have 170 members "with a good sum in
the treasury. The interest in the cause seems to be daily increasing as is
shown by the manifest enthusiasm at each meeting." [14] This group met
on the third Monday of each month at the Irish American Relief
Association hall. Late in 1880, James Cunningham was elected president, and a mass meeting was proposed for the Portland City Hall. A
poem appeared in a Portland newspaper in 1882, allegedly from one
Phelim McGee to his son, Patrick, in Portland. The colloquial poem
spoke favorably of the American Land League (ALL) and made specific
reference to this city:

> An' the next [letter] dated at Portland,
> Givin' the job ye's had won
> We tould all around to the naybors—
> So proud av our tilinted son.[15]

Another group active in Portland even before the Land League was
the Irish American Relief Association (IARA) which had incorporated in
1863. The IARA served essentially as a local benevolent society, and as
such did not represent the same degree of connection to Ireland as the
Land League. A Ladies Land League was also active locally.[16]

These and other similar cultural and political groups provided the networks through which Portland's Irish community functioned in the late
nineteenth and into the early twentieth century. The struggle by the Irish
and Irish-Americans in Portland for recognition and full acceptance,
however, was primarily a domestic economic battle. The first requirement of the immigrant was to survive; the second was the more difficult
task of finding a method of prospering in this new land so that the second
and subsequent generations might not have to fight the same battles:

Immigrant nationalism thus had as one of its sources the all too human melancholia and sense of loss suffered by those who have irrevocably broken with the past that nurtured them. For most, it would probably pass, but for some the ache would be permanent; they would always be aliens in their new land . . . But the immigrant nationalist was something more than a dreamer, and he was driven by more than nostalgia for the Old Country. Indeed, it was the ruling passion for many second- and third-generation Irishmen who knew only America.[17]

One method of economic survival was to concentrate on the natural, geographical advantages that Portland offered to its citizens. Chief among these advantages was Portland's location on a deep, natural, ice-free harbor, geographically closer to Europe than any other major American port. Having largely achieved their goal of providing a secure place of employment along Portland's waterfront through their union, the PLSBS, these mainly Irish laborers experienced the World War I economic boom. Membership swelled to an all-time high of 1,366 in the year after the end of the war (1919). Would economic prosperity and occupational security in America prompt a decline in the degree of Irish nationalism for these workers? The evidence seems to support the contention that it did not decline; instead, Irish nationalism survived into the twentieth century in Portland.

The years 1919 through 1921 were of crucial importance to Ireland as they delineate the period of its War of Independence, often called the Anglo-Irish War. The PLSBS, as a predominantly Irish labor union, demonstrated its continued interest in the affairs of Ireland throughout these "Troubles." Portland was clearly of enough significance to be among the larger American cities visited by Irish and Irish-American dignitaries who spoke of Ireland's travails and attempted to raise money for its relief. Portland's foreign-born population had remained high in the years between 1870 and 1920, averaging around 20%, but the ethnic mix was changing. The Irish, as a percentage of all foreign-born Portlanders, had declined over these years from a high of 57% in 1870 to 24% in 1910, and only 18.2% by 1920.[18] This should not be taken to imply that concern for the "mother country" had waned. Portland in 1920 was a city nearly evenly divided between native and foreign stock, and, with the exception of English-speaking Canada, Ireland was still the source of most of its foreign population.[19]

The Irish longshoremen of Portland had apparently given unqualified support to the American effort in World War I. Although many of its members were by now second or later generation Irish Americans, the historical evidence, including union records, clearly demonstrates a continued concern for Ireland and its fate in the early 1920s.[20] The union had by now been in existence for forty years, and by this time many of its active members were the sons or even grandsons of first-generation charter members. In many ways the Irish were being assimilated into the Portland community by the 1920s, but there were still nagging reminders of their second-class status. The Ku Klux Klan re-emerged in this period, with a healthy contingent of anti-foreign, anti-Catholic supporters in Portland and Maine as a whole.[21] Thus while the process of Americanization or assimilation was underway within Portland's Irish community, there were also valid reasons for keeping an eye out for the defense of one's own ethnic identity, religion, and love of one's country of origin. The first commitment given to the "Irish Republic" by the Portland longshoremen in this period was in the form of financial aid. On April 6, 1920 the local union voted unanimously to purchase $2,000 worth of bonds of the Irish Republic, symbolically exchanging a Liberty Bond in order to facilitate the purchase.[22] An announcement was also made at this meeting that reported a lecture to be given at the Portland City Hall on April 11, 1920 on the topic of the Irish Republic.

All of this occurred at a particularly trying time for Ireland. Local newspapers were reporting that several Sinn Fein (republican) hunger strikers were facing death. The action of the PLSBS, in a small and symbolic way, paralleled that of the Irish Trades Union Congress and Labor Party (ITUC&LP) which had only recently called for a general strike in Ireland over the treatment of the political prisoners.[23] The PLSBS voted to inform the stevedores, the group responsible for employing dock workers, that no work would be done after 6 p.m. on April 11 so that longshoremen might attend the Portland City Hall lecture.[24]

The anticipated lecturer, referred to earlier in the union records, was the Honorable Daniel F. Cohalan, Justice of the New York Supreme Court, and one of the country's most notable Irish-American nationalists. In America, the major organization sponsoring the Irish republican ideal (Ireland as a separate, independent republic rather than simply a vestige of Great Britain with a degree of autonomy, or home rule) was the Clan na Gael. The Clan was known widely as the Fenians, and it

would be the "main American contact with the militant IRB." The Irish
Republican Brotherhood would be the main group sponsoring and facil-
itating the Easter Rebellion in Dublin on April 24, 1916. After 1916,
these pro-republican forces would coalesce in support of Sinn Fein,
which would win a monumental electoral victory in the December
1918 general election. On January 21, 1919, Sinn Fein proclaimed a de
facto Irish Republic in the form of Dáil Éireann (the Irish Assembly).
Britain's rejection of this legitimate political choice by the vast majority of Irish people precipitated the Anglo-Irish War (1919–20) and resulted,
ultimately, in the partition of Ireland.[25]

Local newspapers in April 1920 wrote of a "big mass meeting" which
so filled the City Hall that "hundreds [were] turned away." Archbishop
Louis S. Walsh introduced Judge Cohalan. "Today Ireland is before the
world and simply asks for life, liberty and the pursuit of happiness . . .
No true Christian will raise a hand against Ireland's protest and in
England herself, she is opposed solely by the English government, the
vast majority of the English people nobly championing her cause." [26]
Judge Cohalan was accompanied to Portland by a seemingly unlikely
supporter, the Honorable Robert Lindsay Crawford, past President of
the Independent Order of Orangemen.[27] Crawford revealed what he
termed "the secret": "Ireland wants Ireland for herself. Ireland was a
cultured people when England had scarcely emerged from the primal
state of barbarism."[28]

R. Lindsay Crawford was an "exceptional" case. "Most Protestant
Irishmen in North America were strongly opposed to any measure of
Irish self-government," but Crawford was a radical ex-Orangeman who
had emigrated to Canada where he became a journalist and founder of a
society named the Protestant Friends of Irish Freedom (1919–1921). In
Ireland Crawford's "attempt to transform his Independent Orange
movement into a nonsectarian, working-class alliance foundered on the
rocks of religious tribalism, and Crawford himself felt obliged to emigrate to Canada."[29] In North America, Crawford fought this quixotic
fight at a time when the "Anglophile native middle-class" had as its
spokesperson none other than President Woodrow Wilson who could
trace his ancestry to Ulster Presbyterian stock.[30] The enthusiasm of
Catholic Irish-Americans, however, was not something that could
always be taken for granted:

> To the amazement and consternation of British ambassadors and pro-English Americans, in the late nineteenth and early twentieth centuries Irish nationalism still stirred Irish-America's soul. To be sure, large numbers of Irish-Americans cared little or nothing about either home rule or the Irish republican dream . . . Catholic Irish-Americans were rarely hostile to Irish nationalism, but many were indifferent.[31]

This swing into Maine by Judge Cohalan and Lindsay was for the purpose of addressing this potential indifference and, by the way, for collecting money for the Irish Republic. The degree of organization revealed was impressive. A headquarters was established at 100 Free Street and staffed by a five-person committee with the assistance of a fifty-person advisory committee. At this City Hall meeting, team captains were named for each of Portland's nine wards. Pledges and contributions from that one night alone reportedly totaled nearly $20,000.

In a remark calculated to appeal to the anti-English sentiment of the audience, Judge Cohalan praised Maine's Senator Fernald for his vote against what Cohalan called the "English made League of Nations."[32] It seems peculiar that at least on that issue some Anglophobic Irish Americans had found common ground with Henry Cabot Lodge and other mainstream and largely isolationist Republican Party leaders in America. A later Irish-American historian, Doris Kearns Goodwin, framed this issue quite differently:

> And if [Mayor John F. "Honey Fitz"] Fitzgerald had become the Senator from Massachusetts in 1916 instead of Lodge, the history of the country and indeed of the entire world might have been different, for it was from that very Senate seat that Lodge played his decisive role in the crushing defeat of the Covenant of the League of Nations, the defeat that, in President Woodrow Wilson's words, "broke the heart of the world."[33]

This essay will now attempt to step back and view these reported episodes within a larger context—considering what was happening in the rest of Irish America, and how these local events, especially concerning the Irish longshoremen, fit into this broader picture. Portland's significant Irish community was not unique in its support for Irish freedom. Up and down the Atlantic coast and in small towns and large cities within the Irish diaspora in America, from Chicago to Butte, Montana and on to Pacific coast cities such as San Francisco, support for Ireland in its time of peril took many forms. One of the most significant and revealing of these was the "Irish Patriotic Strike" of New York City longshoremen between August and September, 1920. Its importance to this essay is its demonstration of the nationalism of a very similar group of Irish and Irish-American longshoremen in a neighboring, albeit much larger, East-coast port.

This strike was apparently a spontaneous response to British atrocities in the Anglo-Irish War (1919–1921) and other, more local affronts to Irish sensibilities. Two disparate figures played central roles in initiating this drama. The first was the Lord Mayor of Cork, Terence MacSwiney, who in August 1920, after his arrest for support of the Irish republican movement, began a hunger strike. This fast would last for seventy-four days and lead to his death as an Irish republican martyr. The second figure in this historic event was Daniel Mannix, the Roman Catholic Archbishop of Melbourne, Australia. Mannix was, by 1920, perhaps the foremost episcopal supporter of Sinn Fein and the cause of an Irish Republic. In the midst of Ireland's war of independence, Mannix commenced a trip that would take him halfway around the globe via America for the alleged purpose of visiting his "venerable mother" back in the old country. A crowd of 200,000 saw him off in Australia and additional thousands gathered to see him on his trip across America from San Francisco to New York. The Irish community of New York sent 15,000 enthusiastic supporters to hear Mannix's address at Madison Square Garden.

On July 31, 1920 Archbishop Mannix, having traversed the American continent, boarded the White Star liner *Baltic* bound from New York for Liverpool. By his side on the New York docks was the President of the Irish Republic, Eamon de Valera, himself *persona non grata* with the British government. Along with thousands of Irish supporters on the pier that day was the band of the famous "Fighting 69th"—the predominantly Irish regiment that was highly decorated for its heroic action during the Civil War. The *New York Times* hailed the occasion as "marked by disorders rarely if ever equaled at an American transatlantic passenger pier."[34]

The disorder, it seems, was largely caused by a rift between the predominantly English cooks and stewards on the *Baltic* and the largely Irish coal heavers over whether Archbishop Mannix should be allowed on board. This episode would become a classic clash of rival ethnicities that involved competing national loyalties and more than a little socio-economic class rivalry thrown in for spice. Although Mannix was allowed to board the *Baltic*, the drama was only beginning. After the *Baltic* set sail, British Prime Minister David Lloyd George affirmed that Mannix would not be allowed to disembark in Ireland. Liverpool was also deemed an inappropriate point of visitation for this potentially catalytic clergyman because of its huge Irish neighborhoods "ablaze with Sinn Fein flags and banners, and . . . tense with excitement." Eventually a British destroyer intercepted the *Baltic* before its arrival and escorted Mannix, against his will, to the English naval port of Penzance in Cornwall. Predictably, Irish protesters in Britain, Ireland and America decried this as an aggressive act of "the Pirates of Penzance."[35]

Across the Atlantic, in New York as well as in Boston and other American ports, the protest reached a crescendo upon the return trip of the *Baltic* to New York. The "Irish Patriotic Strike" that resulted was unique. It was not fought over economic issues; rather, it commenced with a picket by thirty Irish and Irish-American nationalist women. It eventually resulted in a major port-wide work stoppage involving other ethnic dock workers, including a significant number of African American longshoremen. African American nationalist leader Marcus Garvey was a prominent supporter, having been inspired by the example of the Irish nationalist struggle, despite the fact that his constituents often bitterly clashed with Irish longshoremen and other common laborers along New York's piers and work sites.[36] Claude McKay, a black Marxist who would join the American Communist Party in 1921, recalled attending a monster Sinn Fein rally in London in 1920 when, "for that day, at least, I was filled with the spirit of Irish nationalism." This Irish affinity, for McKay at least, had deep roots:

> I react more to the emotions of the Irish people than to those of any other whites; they are so passionately primitive in their loves and hates. They are quite free of the disease which is known in bourgeois phraseology as Anglo-Saxon hypocrisy. I suffer with the Irish. I think I understand the Irish. My belonging to a subject race entitles me to some understanding of them.[37]

Back in Portland, Lord Mayor Donal O'Callaghan of Cork addressed another large public meeting the following year, on March 30, 1921. [38] O'Callaghan's address followed by only five months the death by hunger strike of his predecessor, the former Lord Mayor of Cork,

Terence MacSwiney, on October 25, 1920. MacSwiney, a veteran of the Irish Republican Army (IRA), had been arrested in August 1920 and charged with the possession of "revolutionary documents." His protest to incarceration in London's Brixton Prison took the form of a hunger strike, which resulted in his death. International attention was directed toward Ireland by MacSwiney's heroic struggle and by the British execution of eighteen-year-old Kevin Barry just one week later, on November 1, 1920. The tragic events in Ireland and England created a swelling commotion within Irish-American communities in this country, especially as they occurred in the last few days leading up to the presidential election of November 2, 1920. The MacSwiney case "was bigger news in the American press than the presidential election." According to the former editor of the *London Daily News*, the Irish were a "formidable political mass" in America who "have come across the Atlantic with bitterness in their hearts." He went on to make a political connection with the recent deaths of MacSwiney and Barry:

> The Irish vote is the crucial element of every election. No candidate, whether for a mayoralty, a state governorship, the Senate, or the Presidency, can ignore it . . . The Atlantic bridge that Anglo-American good will must erect must have Ireland as the keystone of its central arch. Without a reconciled Ireland there can be no enduring reconciliation with America. That is why the tragedy at Brixton Jail has such momentous reverberations across the Atlantic.[39]

Lord Mayor Donal O'Callaghan of Cork had arrived at Newport News, Virginia in January 1921 without a British passport, which Irish citizens at that time were legally bound to use. He had come to testify about the British burning of Cork City as a reprisal for IRA actions in that area.[40] A local newspaper reported an IRA attack at Ross Carbery, County Cork. This would have been one of the raids made by the "flying squadrons" of IRA Commandant Tom Barry, and others, and made famous in Barry's autobiographical memoir of this period, *Guerilla Days in Ireland*.[41]

The previous month the British government had refused to allow a group of distinguished Americans to visit Ireland for the purpose of investigating conditions there related to the Anglo-Irish war. This affront did not prevent this distinguished group, The Committee of 100, from releasing its report that predictably blamed the British government for the disorder in Ireland. They reported that "the Imperial British army in Ireland has been guilty of proved excesses, not incomparable in degree and kind with those alleged, by the Bryce report on Belgium Atrocities, to have been committed by the imperial German army."[42] While he was in America, Mayor O'Callaghan publicly testified before this group, the American Commission on Conditions in Ireland.[43]

O'Callaghan's welcome to America was not universal, however, and some of his detractors only barely hid their anti-Irish nativism. While O'Callaghan was in America, nativist and Anglophile groups, such as the Loyal Coalition, attempted to silence him. The Loyal Coalition asked President Warren G. Harding to deport the Lord Mayor, stating that "We have the greatest confidence in the wisdom and patriotism of your administration in this issue, because of your well known attitude towards hyphenated agitation."[44] Despite these protests, Mayor O'Callaghan continued his visit. He addressed the National Press Club and toured American cities, including Portland, where he spoke to enthusiastic crowds.

In Portland on March 30, 1921, Lord Mayor Donal O'Callaghan was treated to an afternoon luncheon at the Lafayette Hotel arranged by Archbishop Louis S. Walsh and presided over by Father T. J. Houlihan. A large parade down Congress Street preceded an evening lecture at the Portland City Hall, which was filled for the occasion. In his address the Lord Mayor spoke of how eighty-four percent of the Irish people in 1918 had voted for a republic (Sinn Fein), a figure which increased to ninety percent one year later, but to no avail.[45]

The impact of speakers such as Judge Cohalan and Mayor O'Callaghan on the longshoremen's union could be witnessed one and one-half months later. The PLSBS at its meeting of May 17, 1921 provoked dissention on the issue of a contribution to the Irish Relief Fund (IRF). This fund had originated shortly after the Easter Rebellion of 1916 in order to gather money for those suffering from the effects of the devastating British suppression of that uprising. This was especially needed in Dublin's city center, where 179 buildings had been destroyed, leaving 100,000 people, roughly one-third of Dublin's population, dependent upon public relief.[46] When a motion was made at a May 1921 meeting of the PLSBS to contribute $1,000 to the IRF, some members complained that they had already given individual donations, and when the treasurer was threatened with an injunction, the president withdrew this motion.[47]

This controversy was caused, in all likelihood, by a feeling that there was a financial limit to which the Society and its members could go to aid Ireland. The controversy apparently originated with those who had already contributed as individuals to this cause, and so while there was clearly still much support for the Irish nationalist cause, the support was not without limits. It may be conjectured that this controversy could have been a reflection of the ambivalence of a union that by 1920 was neither purely American nor purely Irish, but a combination of both. In this sense their ethnic sensibilities were torn by both influences, and thus, symbolically at least, somewhat "mid-Atlantic."

There was no direct evidence of opposition from the few non-Irish longshoremen or from second or later-generation Irish union members who may have felt a less direct attachment to Ireland. Between the bonds for the Irish Republic and Judge Cohalan's visit in 1920, and the earlier visit by Lord Mayor O'Callaghan in 1921, individual financial resources must have been stretched quite thinly. Portland's Irish were probably similar to those in other American cities where, according to historian Kerby Miller, "Many emigrants simply grew cynical after repeated pleas for money by Irish-American and visiting Irish nationalists failed to produce promised results. '[If the Irish] People are getting all the money that is sent to them from this Country they Ought to be rich.'" [48] At the next meeting, on May 24, 1921, a similar motion that members be assessed to pay for the IRF was not entertained by union president Michael McDonough. This local rejection by the PLSBS occurred even though the IRF had widespread endorsement, including the support of America's three Catholic cardinals as well as forty bishops and archbishops, although it was nominally an organization in support of a revolutionary cause.[49]

On November 8, 1921, a Mr. Curley addressed a PLSBS meeting for fifty-two minutes "regarding the situation in Ireland." Curley requested all members to join the American Association for Recognition of the Irish Republic (AARIR). The AARIR had been founded one year earlier, in November 1920, by Eamon de Valera, the titular leader of the still-ephemeral Irish Republic. This occurred during de Valera's crucial American tour in the very midst of the Anglo-Irish War (1919–1921). The AARIR was designed to replace the Friends of Irish Freedom (FOIF), over which the Irish, and de Valera in particular, had lost control. The AARIR's growth was phenomenol.

At the center of this battle for the "hearts and minds" of Irish America was a struggle between de Valera and his Irish entourage, on the one hand, and "the eastern establishment of the national FOIF, in particular Judge Cohalan, on the other hand. The dispute resulted in de Valera severing all ties with the FOIF and creating this new organization, the American Association for the Recognition of the Irish Republic (AARIR)."[50] The AARIR had raised upwards of $5 million by August 1921, although it seems that much of that money failed to reach republican hands in Ireland.[51] Finally, on April 25, 1922, the PLSBS voted unanimously to draw up a resolution, and to send a copy to Ireland and another copy to British Prime Minister [David] Lloyd George, "to try and halt the atrocities in Ireland."[52]

The "Irishness" of Portland's longshoremen was demonstrated in these many ways during the first two decades of the twentieth century. For these workers, though, the day-to-day struggles along Portland's waterfront proved to be a more intense and immediate interest, both to themselves and to their families. As Mr. Curley was addressing the Portland longshoremen concerning the Irish Republic in November 1921, these same Irish longshoremen were about to enter into their most important confrontation with the combined might of the transatlantic shipping agents doing business out of Portland. Nothing more clearly depicts the duality of interest among these dockers. They were, as has been demonstrated, keenly interested in the fate of Ireland, but they were also, as would soon be seen, primarily concerned with their own economic survival and well-being in a bitter strike which threatened not only their union but also the prosperity of Portland as a whole.[53]

The early twentieth century, especially the years 1919 to 1923, marked a period of transition along the waterfront of Portland, Maine. The wartime economic boom was over, and never again would the PLSBS reach the record-high membership achieved in 1919. The steady decline in membership was caused by a multitude of factors, not the least of which was the Canadian decision to develop major port facilities at both Halifax, Nova Scotia and Saint John, New Brunswick, while Portland's business elite focused on the allure of the tourist dollar.[54]

Another transition seemed to be generational in nature. Although the PLSBS remained overwhelmingly Irish, even after World War I, the percentage of Irish-born workers declined in relationship to American-born Irish workers of second and subsequent generations. Those who had come to America in the post-Famine wave of emigration of the early 1880s were by now being replaced on Portland's docks by their sons and grandsons. Could the link with Ireland be maintained through this significant generational transition? Timothy Sarbaugh writes, "Perhaps one could conclude, therefore, that the more Americanized the Irish community, the stronger the appeal of Irish nationalism, which was predicated upon ease and success and not conflict and crisis in the assimilation process." [55] In the early 1920s, at least, the evidence seems to demonstrate that the Irish longshoremen of Portland, Maine could, to borrow a current slogan, "Think globally and act locally." They were patriotic American workers who supported their families, their church, their political party, and their union, but who simultaneously also found the time, money and energy to demonstrate their continued love for "the Isle of Inishfree."

1. Michael C. Connolly, "To 'Make This Port Union All Over': Longshore Militancy in Portland, 1911–1913," *Maine History* 41, no. 1 (spring 2002): 41–43. See Michael C. Connolly, "The Irish Longshoremen of Portland, Maine, 1880–1923" (Ph.D. diss., Boston College, 1988): 19. This dissertation is available at the University of Southern Maine Library (Portland) and Portland Public Library, and may be ordered from University Microfilms International (order #8904006) by calling U.M.I. at 1-800-521-0600. See also David B. Pillsbury, "The History of the Atlantic and St. Lawrence Railroad Company," Fogler Library (Special Collections) of the University of Maine, Orono; Michael J. Sheehy, "John Alfred Poor and International Railroads: The Early Years to 1860" (Master's thesis, University of Maine at Orono, 1974); and Archibald W. Currie, *The Grand Trunk Railway of Canada* (Toronto: University of Toronto Press, 1957).
2. Connolly, "To 'Make This Port Union All Over,'" 43. Laura E. Poor, ed., *The First International Railway and the Colonization of New England: Life and Writings of John Alfred Poor*, 26, as cited in Charles E. Clark, *Maine: A Bicentennial History* (New York: Norton Publishing Co., 1977), 96. See also two articles by Robert H. Babcock, "Economic Development in Portland (Me.) and Saint John (N.B.) During the Age of Iron and Steam, 1850–1914," *American Review of Canadian Studies* 9 (spring 1979): 3–37; and "The Rise and Fall of Portland's Waterfront, 1850–1920," *Maine Historical Society Quarterly* 22, no. 2 (fall 1982): 63–98.
3. Babcock, "Economic Development," 29–30.
4. Michael C. Connolly, "Black Fades to Green: Irish Labor Replaces African-American Labor Along a Major New England Waterfront, Portland, Maine, in the Mid-Nineteenth Century," *Colby Quarterly* 37, no. 4 (December 2001): 357–73.
5. The records of the PLSBS (ILA local 861) together with some volumes of the pre-

dominantly Italian Freight Handlers' Union (ILA local 912) total over ninety volumes and are housed at the Maine Historical Society in Portland, Maine. See
MHS Manuscript Collections 359 (MS 85-15) and 360. Recently the four oldest
volumes of this collection were graciously returned to the collection from
which, over time, they had become estranged. This reuniting was due in large
part to Dr. Charles E. Burden of Dresden, Maine and Nathan R. Lipfert, Library
Director of the Maine Maritime Museum in Bath, Maine. The union, the Maine
Historical Society, and future generations of historians are very grateful for this
gesture. Nicholas Noyes, Head of Library Services at the MHS, recently referred
to this as an act of "archival integrity."

6. This occurred at a rare Sunday Special Meeting of the PLSBS where it was
"Moved and Seconded that the letter from the Land League be accepted." PLSBS
Records, 18 December 1881, 96. A committee of five was "appointed to consult
with the Land League committee." Its members were Robert Ward, L. B. Howard
(President), Daniel Leonard, Daniel Tobie, and P. J. Higgins (Financial Secretary).
Follow-up mentions of contact with the Land League occurred on 12/20/81 (97);
12/27/81 (99); and 1/10/82 (103).

7. Connolly, "To 'Make This Port Union All Over,'" 43; and "The Irish Longshoremen of Portland, Maine 1880–1923," Appendices C and M.

8. See Matthew Barker's essay in this book for a more complete depiction of nineteenth-century Irish-American nationalism and the major social and cultural
organizations within Portland's Irish community.

9. Kerby A. Miller, *Emigrants and Exiles: Ireland and the Irish Exodus to North
America* (New York: Oxford University Press, 1985), 328.

10. "Irish-American politics was the politics of realism, free of the American liberal's moralizing and distrust of the uses of power." Thomas N. Brown, *Irish-
American Nationalism* (Philadelphia: Lippincott Co., 1966), 134.

11. Seamus Grimes and Michael C. Connolly, "The Migration Link between Cois
Fharraige and Portland, Maine 1880s–1920s," *Irish Geography* 22 (1989): 22–30.
This is the journal of the Geographical Society of Ireland, headquartered in
Dublin. Another version of this appeared as "Emigration from Connemara to
America" in *Galway Roots/Clanna na Gaillimhe: Journal of the Galway Family
History Society* 2 (1994): 40–43. Also see Michael C. Connolly, "The Next Parish
West of Galway: The Irish Diaspora of Portland, Maine," *House Island Project*
(1996), 6–9. This is a publication of Portland Performing Arts (now the Center for
Cultural Exchange).

12. See Gary Libby's essay in this book for a discussion of the activities of the
Fenians in Maine in the mid-nineteenth century.

13. *Eastern Argus*, 30 December 1880, 2.

14. *Eastern Argus*, 1 December 1880, 3.

15. See *Eastern Argus*, 14 January 1882, 3 for a full reference to this poem.

16. *Eastern Argus*, 5 August 1881, 3. Matthew Barker's essay in this book deals
extensively with the IARA and other similar Irish nationalist organizations in
nineteenth-century Portland.

17. Brown, *Irish-American Nationalism*, 21.

18. *Fourteenth Census of the United States (1920)*, Volume II, Population,
762–63. See also Babcock, "Economic Development," 29.

19. *Abstract of the Fourteenth Census (1920)*, 115. In Portland those with native

parentage totaled 51.9% while "foreign white stock" (foreign-born and children of foreign-born or "mixed" parentage) totaled 47.6%. The Irish trailed only English-speaking Canada in this area, and many of the latter were undoubtedly the children of Irish-born parents who had emigrated to Canada.

20. In this year the number of foreign-born Portlanders (19.1%) still outnumbered those born to foreign parents (18.2%), but when added to those born of "mixed" parentage (10.3%) it is clear that second and subsequent generation ethnic citizens in Portland (28.5%) were of greater importance. This would be even more true among the Irish who, having been in Portland longer than other groups such as the Italians, Russians and Poles, would have an even greater percentage of later-generation representatives. See *Abstract of the Fourteenth Census* (1920), 115.

21. For a study of mid-nineteenth century nativism in Maine see Allan R. Whitmore, "'A Guard of Faithful Sentinels': Know Nothing Appeal in Maine, 1854–1855," *Maine Historical Society Quarterly* 20, no. 3 (winter 1981): 151–97. See also John Syrett, "Principle and Expediency: The Ku Klux Klan and Ralph Owen Brewster in 1924," *Maine History* 39, no. 4 (winter 2000–01): 215–39. For a reference to race relations on the docks of Portland in the mid-nineteenth century see Connolly, "Black Fades to Green."

22. Ironically, in San Francisco, the Friends of Irish Freedom (FOIF) tempered their pronouncements immediately before the U.S. entry into the war in April 1917. To demonstrate their "100% Americanism" they strongly supported the four Liberty Loan campaigns. By 1920, however, the FOIF in San Francisco had redoubled their efforts in support of the Irish bond campaign, raising over $500,000 in one drive alone. See Timothy Sarbaugh, "Exiles of Confidence: The Irish-American Community of San Francisco, 1880 to 1920," in Timothy J. Meagher, ed., *From Paddy to Studs: Irish-American Communities in the Turn of the Century Era, 1880 to 1920* (Westport, CT: Greenwood Press, 1986), 168–69.

23. *Portland Evening Express*, 12 April 1920, 6.

24. PLSBS Records, Volume 7, 6 April 1920, 280.

25. Timothy Sarbaugh, "Exiles of Confidence," 168. See also William M. Leary, "Woodrow Wilson, Irish Americans, and the Election of 1916," *Journal of American History* 54, no. 1 (1967): 58–59. Leary states that the Revolutionary Directory of the Clan was composed of John Devoy (New York), Joseph McGarrity (Philadelphia), and John T. Ryan (Buffalo). Leary further states that "they usually followed the advice of New York Supreme Court Justice Daniel F. Cohalan." One of the best works on Cohalan is Charles Callan Tansill, *America and the Fight for Irish Freedom, 1866–1922* (New York: Devin-Adair Co., 1957). Again, see Gary Libby's essay in this book regarding the Fenians in Maine during the earlier period (mid-nineteenth century).

26. *Portland Evening Express*, 12 April 1920, 15.

27. The Orange Order was a militantly pro-British, sectarian (pro-Protestant) organization founded in Ireland (1795) in the years just prior to the United Irishmen's Rebellion of 1798. Its name derived from William of Orange (King Billy) who defeated the Catholic King James II at the Battle of the Boyne (July 12, 1690), a victory celebrated every year on that date by Orangemen in Northern Ireland and other Orange strongholds.

28. *Portland Evening Express*, 12 April 1920, 15.

29. Miller, *Emigrants and Exiles*, 453, 535–36.

30. "The Irish-American press had been urging repudiation of Wilson, whom it characterized—at least in its milder moments—as an 'Ulster Orangeman.'" See Leary, "Woodrow Wilson, Irish Americans, and the Election of 1916," 57. See also Miller, *Emigrants and Exiles*, 535.

31. Miller, *Emigrants and Exiles*, 536.

32. *Portland Evening Express*, 12 April 1920, 15.

33. See Doris Kearns Goodwin, *The Fitzgeralds and the Kennedys* (New York: Simon and Schuster, 1987), 252 as cited in Michael C. Connolly, "The First Hurrah: James Michael Curley versus the 'Goo-Goos' in the Boston Mayoralty Election of 1914," *Historical Journal of Massachusetts* 30, no. 1 (winter 2002): 74.

34. Bruce Nelson, *Divided We Stand: American Workers and the Struggle for Black Equality* (Princeton, NJ: Princeton University Press, 2001), 27.

35. Nelson, *Divided We Stand*, 28.

36. Nelson, *Divided We Stand*, 31. Nelson, who teaches history at Dartmouth College, also focused on this issue in "The 'Irish' Waterfront and Insurgent Nationalisms: New York, 1920," a paper presented at the American Conference for Irish Studies (ACIS) 39th Annual Meeting, Fordham University, New York, June 7, 2001. I am indebted to the author for a copy of this paper. Again, see Connolly, "Black Fades to Green," for a discussion of race on Portland's waterfront.

37. Wayne Cooper, ed., *The Passion of Claude McKay: Selected Poetry and Prose, 1912–1948* (New York: Shocken Books, 1973), 58–62 as cited in Nelson, *Divided We Stand*, 34.

38. PLSBS Records, Volume 7, March 22, 1921, 343.

39. Alan J. Ward, *Ireland and Anglo-American Relations, 1899–1921* (Toronto: University of Toronto Press, 1969), 229–30.

40. Ward, *Ireland and Anglo-American Relations*, 239–41.

41. *Portland Evening Express*, 31 March 1921, 1. This book by IRA commandant Tom Barry has recently become something of a cult work, especially favored by liberation movements and their supporters in developing countries and those fighting anti-imperial struggles against overwhelming odds. It was, at one point, out of print and difficult to obtain, even in Ireland, but lately it has again become widely available.

42. Ibid.

43. *The American Commission on Conditions in Ireland: Interim Report*, in possession of the author. The Committee of One Hundred on Ireland was the parent body of this group, and its members represented people from thirty-six different states.

44. *Portland Evening Express*, 30 March 1921, 17.

45. *Portland Evening Express*, 31 March 1921, 1.

46. Samuel Levenson, *James Connolly: A Biography* (London: Martin, Brian and O'Keeffe, 1973), 325. The devastation in city center Dublin would later become the focus of some of the most revered theatrical works of the Irish labor activist and dramatist Sean O'Casey, such as *Juno and the Paycock* and *The Plough and the Stars*.

47. PLSBS Records, Volume 7, 17 May 1921, 355.

48. Miller, *Emigrants and Exiles*, 536.
49. Ward, *Ireland and Anglo-American Relations*, 112, 128–29.
50. Sarbaugh, "Exiles of Confidence," 169.
51. Ward, *Ireland and Anglo-American Relations*, 234.

52. PLSBS Records, Volume 7, 25 April 1922, 434. These atrocities occurred during the Anglo-Irish War, just before the start of the Irish Civil War:

1919–1921, The Anglo-Irish War
Jan. 21, 1919, Anglo-Irish War begins
Oct. 25, 1920, Death of Terence MacSwiney
Nov. 21, 1920, "Bloody Sunday"
Dec. 11–12, 1920, Cork sacked by Black and Tans
Dec. 23, 1920, Government of Ireland Act—creation of No. Ireland (partition)
July 9, 1921, Truce between IRA and British Army
Jan. 7, 1922, Treaty ending Anglo-Irish War narrowly approved by Dáil Éireann
June 28, 1922, Civil War begins
Aug. 12, 1922, Assassination of Michael Collins (Béal na mBláth, Co. Cork)
May, 1923, End of Civil War

53. See Connolly, "The Irish Longshoremen of Portland, Maine," 199–212, for a narrative about the strike of December, 1921 and the critical mediation role played by Portland's Catholic Bishop, Louis S. Walsh. This conclusion regarding domestic concerns is remarkably similar to that of Leary, "Woodrow Wilson, Irish Americans, and the Election of 1916," 72. "Certainly [Irish Americans] sympathized with their cousins across the sea, but they were now citizens of a different country, and their fortunes were linked to their new homeland. Their leaders, who gained and retained power by emphasizing Irish issues, did not understand this distinction."
54. Babcock, "Economic Development" and "The Rise and Fall of Portland's Waterfront, 1850–1920."
55. Sarbaugh, "Exiles of Confidence," 173.

"THE LANGUAGE THAT THE STRANGERS DO NOT KNOW": THE GALWAY GAELTACHT OF PORTLAND, MAINE IN THE TWENTIETH CENTURY

by Kenneth E. Nilsen

IT IS ONLY IN RECENT YEARS that some researchers of the Irish in America have begun to turn their attention to the question of the language of Irish immigrants. It is no longer acceptable to assume that the Irish arrived on the shores of North America with a solid knowledge of English, as was done by historians of the American Irish in past decades. There is now a growing, if gradual, realization on the part of some researchers that many of the Irish who immigrated here were actually native speakers of Irish Gaelic who had widely varying levels of competency in English.[1]

Even today native speakers of Irish from Ireland's various Gaeltacht (Gaelic-speaking) regions can be found in different concentrations across the Continent, with the greatest number in the Northeastern United States. The Greater Boston area, for instance, is home to Irish speakers from Aran, Cois Fharraige, Connemara and, to a lesser extent, West Kerry. Springfield, Massachusetts and Hartford, Connecticut also have relatively large numbers of West Kerry Gaeltacht people. A number of Mayo Irish speakers reside in Holyoke, Massachusetts, and southern Connecticut. New York has a large sprinkling of native speakers from every Gaeltacht region. Brooklyn, Staten Island, New Jersey, and Philadelphia seem to have been preferred by Donegal Irish speakers. From the 1880s to the 1920s, Portland, Maine was a favored destination for Irish speakers from three neighboring regions of West Galway: Cois Fharraige,[2] Connemara and Corr na Móna. In fact, due to the large number of immigrants from that particular geographical locale, it is quite possible that Portland had the highest percentage of Irish speakers among its Irish-born residents of any American city in the twentieth century.

Irish speakers were undoubtedly arriving in Maine decades before the 1880s. In 1838 Nathaniel Hawthorne noted on a visit to Augusta that other than French, the foreign language he heard was that of the "wild Irish" and "he concludes that some of the workers on the Mill Dam can speak nothing else."[3] In the 1840s and 1850s, large numbers of famine immigrants arrived in Maine, many of whom came from Irish counties with a large percentage of Irish speakers. However, although we may assume many of them spoke Irish, there is very little hard evidence. Most Irish speakers came from the poorer districts and had no training in reading or writing Irish or English. The Irish language had no official status in Ireland and was being rapidly replaced by English. Although the reading of Irish was taught by a number of proselytizing Bible societies and also in some of the schools in Connacht under the control of Archbishop MacHale, it was not until 1879 that the British government allowed "Celtic" to be taught in the National Schools and even then only under severely limited restrictions. The situation for the language was far worse in North America. Other than a column or two in a few Irish-American weeklies, the Irish language had no voice in the North American press.[4] As for the Catholic Church in America, the evidence for the use of Irish, especially during the decades of heaviest Gaeltacht emigration, is sparse indeed. In recent times, Irish Studies Programs in North America have increasingly begun to include the Irish language as part of their curricula, but in spite of this, they rarely include any research into or contact with the local community of native Irish speakers.

There is evidence to suggest that immigration from West Galway to Portland was well underway in the 1850s, just after the Great Famine. Unskilled Irish workers were attracted to various construction enterprises that were commencing at that time.[5] Also at this time, Irish laborers were starting to replace African Americans as longshoremen.[6] One of the major projects in Maine was the railway that was being built from Portland to Island Pond, Vermont, where it was to join with its counterpart originating in Montreal. Island Pond is credited as being the first International Railroad Junction in the United States.[7] In his history of St. James Catholic Church, Island Pond, John Carbonneau writes:

Six hundred immigrant Irish laborers were brought to Portland, Maine from New York to build the first international railway in North America. The Catholic faith came to Island Pond in the hearts and minds of these hardworking laborers who came tie by tie, rail by rail, and arrived on a cold winter Saturday, January 29, 1853. [Many] of these remained locally to run the railway, to work in lumbering, to go into business and to become good farmers.[8]

The names of some of those who remained in Island Pond were Thomas Foley, Patrick Foley, Thomas Gill, Patrick Flaherty, John Holleran, Patrick Curran, and Martin Donohue—all names that were and still are common in Cois Fharraige, Connemara, and Portland. [9] Carbonneau tells us that the Island Pond parish records "began on October 16, 1856 with the baptism of Marguerite Flaherty, daughter of Patrick and Sobina Connor Flaherty by Reverend J. Daly" and "the first recorded marriage was that of Miss Sarah Foley to Martin Donohue on October 28, 1858."[10] That the Island Pond-Portland connection continued for these West Galway immigrants is indicated by the fact that several of them who died in Island Pond were sent back to Portland for burial. Thus a Sabina O'Connor Flaherty (clearly identical to the woman mentioned above) who died in Island Pond in 1861 is buried in the Catholic cemetery in Portland.[11] A Michael Foley, quite possibly a native of Cois Fharraige or Connemara, who died on July 23, 1857 at the age of twenty-five in Island Pond, was later buried in Portland's Western Cemetery.[12]

By the 1880s, the Irish-born population of Portland was approaching ten percent of the city's population. Many of these were Irish speakers from West Galway.[13] Portland was one of several favorite destinations for West Galway immigrants. One ship manifest, that of the SS *Hibernian*, which steamed from Glasgow, Derry, and Galway and arrived at the port of Boston on June 3, 1896, has some very interesting details about its passengers and may serve as a window into immigration from West Galway at that time. In addition to the usual categories of name, sex, nationality, and occupation, this manifest lists "last residence" and "destination." Approximately forty-eight of the 221 steerage passengers were from locations in West Galway identifiable as Irish-speaking districts. These are, from east to west, Barna, Spiddal, Costello, Lettermullan, Rosmuc, Kilkerrin, Carna, Mynish, Callowfeenish, Cashel, and the Aran Islands. Twenty-nine of the forty-eight West Galway passengers were destined for Boston. Seven of them were going to Pittsburgh and another five were headed for Portland. The Portland destinees were sixteen-year-old domestic Delia Curran and eighteen-year-old domestic Hannah Quincannon from Spiddal, twenty-year-old laborer James Mulkerin from Kilkerrin, and twenty-year-old domestic Abbie Green, and eighteen-year-old domestic Margaret McDonough from Carna.[14]

Facts and figures such as these help to give us some picture of the immigrants, and researchers may yet be able to obtain additional statistics about America's nineteenth-century Irish speakers. For instance, close scrutiny may yet reveal whether sixteen-year-old Delia Curran from Spiddal arrived safely in Portland after the SS *Hibernian* landed in Boston. We might even be able to discover whether she was Delia A. Curran who married Michael R. Feel in Portland on January 22, 1901 or Delia B. Curran who married Martin A. Sullivan on November 26, 1901.[15] Or perhaps she was the Delia Curran who married Coleman Concannon on November 10, 1914. But even though we may be able to compile a good deal of statistical data about this individual, we will never be able to know exactly what it felt like for Delia and thousands like her to leave home at such a young age. We can never be sure what thoughts, what words and phrases, what songs were in her mind as she started a new life in America. Nineteenth-century Irish speakers in Portland, like their counterparts in many other U.S. cities, left little trace of their linguistic heritage.[16]

In the twentieth century, what distinguished Portland from many other U.S. cities was the percentage of Gaeltacht people to be found among its Irish-born population. In terms of numbers, more Irish-speaking immigrants may have gone to Boston and New York, but, as has been noted, it appears that the percentage of Irish speakers coming to Portland was the highest of any American city.[17] This gave Portland's Irish community a unique flavor. Due largely to Portland's thriving longshore industry, Gaeltacht immigration to Portland continued for the first three decades of the twentieth century. The flow of this immigration to Portland waned in the 1930s[18] and came to a virtual halt in the 1940s when emigration to England became more popular.[19] In the 1950s and 1960s, only a few individuals from Cois Fharraige emigrated to Portland.[20] In spite of this drop, Portland's strong Gaelic-speaking community continued throughout the first half of the twentieth century, and if Nathaniel Hawthorne could have visited the Portland docks or strolled the streets of certain of Portland's neighborhoods during these years, he might have been surprised to hear "the wild Irish" being spoken in Maine's major city in the twentieth century.

By the 1980s, the Irish language in Portland had ceased to be a vibrant force in the city. Yet many remained who still spoke Irish on a regular basis with their spouses and with a certain network of relatives and friends. In 1984 I was introduced to this Portland Irish community by Michael Connolly, who had come to know many of the Irish speakers through his research into the longshore industry. Michael had the vision to realize that the stories of the remaining Irish speakers' "Portland experience" should be recorded in their own language. From 1984 to the present, Michael and I have recorded on videotape and audiotape interviews with sixteen of Portland's Irish speakers.[21] We have also done interviews in English with six individuals who were familiar with the Portland Gaeltacht, and who were in regular contact with Irish speakers.[22]

Of the sixteen Irish speakers, fourteen were from Cois Fharraige and two were from Joyce Country (one from Seana-Farachain and one from Corr na Móna).[23] Many of those we interviewed were ninety years of age or older. Catherine ("Ceata") Concannon, whom we interviewed twice in 1988, we visited again and recorded in 1997 when she was 103!

The interviews provide actual first-hand accounts of what it was like for these Irish speakers to leave Ireland and start life in a new country. They give us information in their own words and in their own language that cannot be supplied by bare statistical data. The interviews were typically conducted in Irish. That those interviewed had no difficulty in understanding the questions is apparent from the instant responses they made. However, some of the interviewees responded readily in Irish, while others, from lack of practice speaking Irish gave some answers in English and some answers in Irish, or moved back and forth from one language to the other. Their Irish was typical Galway dialect Irish. Most had been totally unaffected by any modern artificial school Irish. Only a few of them gave any indication of having had Irish in school. Several of them showed a remarkably high level of Irish fluency. Two of the interviewees, Mary Kilmartin and Pat Malone (see gallery, plates 44–45), had very impressive stores of Irish folklore and tradition.[24]

Over the course of the next few pages excerpts from the interviews will be presented. These reveal the thoughts of the interviewees on a variety of subjects: family history, life in Ireland, leaving Ireland, work and daily life in the U.S., and much more. The excerpts are presented in an English translation. Italics are used to indicate words, phrases and sentences spoken in English. Punctuation, or lack thereof, and grammar is used to reflect the speech rhythms of the interviewees, and, therefore, intentionally does not reflect standard English usage.

FAMILY HISTORY

While most of those we interviewed gave some interesting details about their family background, **Mary Kilmartin** (*Máire Ní Mhárta* in Irish[25]), born in 1913, was a veritable genealogist. Born and raised in Minna, Cois Fharraige, Mary was one of the few interviewees who had kept up an active interest in Irish. In her youth she had learned from books long pieces of poetry in Irish such as "Aithrí Raiftearaí" ("Raftery's Repentance") and Michael Burke's "Oíche na Gaoithe Móire" ("The Night of the Great Wind"). She also recited for us a poem which she learned in school about a husband and wife who emigrated to New York, which begins, "Céad Slán leat, a Éire, is tú Cuisle mo Chroí" ("Farewell to you, Ireland, you are the love of my heart"). Perhaps even more interesting were the snatches of Cois Fharraige poetry she had, such as the one composed by a Mogan of Cor na Rón which is given below. We interviewed Mary on two occasions (audiotape, December 17, 1989 and videotape, March 1, 1997). It was her information about her great-grandfather James Kilmartin that led me to investigate the Portland-Island Pond connection. Note also that her grandfather Patrick Kilmartin had been in the States, but returned to Ireland with enough money to buy property.[26]

Mary Kilmartin: Ulick Costello was my [maternal] *great-great-grandfather*. He owned all of Baile na mBroghach. They [i.e., the Costellos] started the fair in Spiddal. They had so many cattle. They owned all of Baile na mBroghach. Then the children got married. None of those daughters came out here. It was considered a great disgrace to let daughters come out here. They would give them a dowry and they would stay at home and they would marry.

K. Nilsen: Who did you hear this from?

MK: You know, there is nothing that I heard that I do not remember. When I was going to school, everything the schoolmistress would say, I would remember it, like Patrick Malone. You remember Patrick, Pat

Malone. When I was young I always liked to listen to the old people because there was insight in their speech. My father was Philip Kilmartin [Feilipe Ó Márta], his was father was Patrick [Pádhraic] and his father was James [Séamas]. That James Kilmartin is buried here, I believe in Shrove[27], New Hampshire or some place like that.

KN: Is he?

MK: Yes, my *great-grandfather*, James. He was working on the first *railroad* that was built between America and Canada and they met at Island Pond. And I think there is a sign up there, but I do not know if their names are on it or not. That is the place where they met.

KN: Was he killed?

MK: No, he lived after that. They were *very tough*, you know. The Irish were.

KN: But did they go home to Ireland?

MK: No, the *great-grandparents* stayed out here. But my grandfather was out here also but he went back and he bought the place that we have now in Minna.

KN: Was Patrick, your grandfather, raised in this country?

MK: *No,* he was raised in Ireland, his mother died young. She was a Conroy [Conaire]. She died and left two children after her. [Now concerning the Kilmartins] my father was the youngest of seven sons and one daughter. That daughter was the oldest and she was Pat Malone's mother.

KN: What was her name?

MK: Catherine Kilmartin [Cáit Ní Mhárta].

KN: What was your own mother's name?

MK: Barbara O'Toole was her name. Her mother was a Flaherty [Fátharta].

KN: Where were they from?

MK: From our place, from Minna, *yeah*, they were and then her grandmother was Mary Ulick [Máire Uilioc], part of these Ulicks from Baile na mBroghach.

KN: What other relations were there?

MK: My father's mother was a Malone and her mother was a Mogan and from those Mogans came the people who could compose songs and who had the traditional material and it is from them that Patrick Malone got it. One of the Mogans from Cor na Rón, you know this is a couple of hundred years ago, one of the Mogans was coming over and he was thirsty, he was on the boat named the *Chieftain*. Now these Mogans had some land near the Crumlin River [in Cois Fharraige] and they could get a drink of water there any time they wanted it. So this Mogan composed a song satirizing the ship the *Chieftain*. And some of these Mogans probably never went to school and yet they were superb at composing songs. He made a piece of a song and he said:

> "Nach iomú lá aoibhinn a bhí mise ag abhainn Chroimlinn,
> Agus an t-uisce ag dul síos thart dhom fairsing go leor
> Shíl mé nach dtiocfadh sé sa saol seo
> Go mbeinn sínte sa *Chieftain* is tart ar mo scóig."

> (It is many the pleasant day I was at Crumlin River,
> with the water streaming past me as plentiful as could be
> I never thought it would come to pass
> that I would be lying aboard the *Chieftain* and thirst in my throat.)

But when the captain heard it, he did not like it and Mogan had to make another song praising the boat.[28]

KN: Did you hear the other song?

MK: No.

KN: Who did you hear this one from?

MK: From some old person in Ireland, and, *of course*, Patrick Malone had it too from his mother. You know, his mother was excellent, she could go back two hundred years and she was *eighty-six* when I saw her and she was so *bright*. And Patrick Malone's father was Michael [Micil] Malone. My aunt, you know, Catherine Kilmartin, was married to a Malone and her mother was a Malone too. Michael Malone's father was Peter Malone [Peadar Ó Maoileoin] and a brother of Michael's is buried in Arlington Cemetery.

Another interviewee who had a considerable amount of information about his family background was **Jim Brown,** whom we recorded on videotape on May 4, 1988. Jim was a native of Corr na Móna and said that his parents did not speak Irish to the children in his house. In spite of this, most of the interview was conducted in Irish, and Jim proved to have an excellent command of Corr na Móna Irish, with no hint of school Irish, with the possible exception of the phrase "cóiste tineadh"[29] for "train." In this piece Jim also refers to the aversion certain families had to letting their children emigrate.

Jim Brown: My grandfather was out here in Scranton. He worked in the coal *mines* in Scranton. His name was Patsy Brown.

KN: How long was he here?

JB: He went *back* to Ireland again.

KN: Who were your mother's people?

JB: She was a Philbin, Nora Philbin [Nóra Filibín], from Dubhachta.

KN: And her mother?

JB: Her mother was a Kane [Caodháin], her people were out by Recess, Corr west of Maam. My grandfather was William Philbin. None of the Philbins came to this country, there were five brothers and none of them came to this country. They were very much against coming to this country. They didn't like that you would be coming over to this country.

KN: Why was that?

JB: Well, they prefered that you would stay at home. That is the reason they had. They didn't go there, they never left home, that is why. That is the biggest reason, I believe. They never went anywhere. They went to school for a while, then they married, that is all. The old people they were fantastic at arranging weddings. *They used to marry, try and marry them off over there, you know. They didn't like to see them emigrate either. They were against that in a way, yeah.*

Of the fourteen Irish speakers we interviewed, one, **Mrs. Nan Foley** (née Connolly) surprised us by saying that she was born in Portland in 1897 but raised in Na Creagáin near Minna, Cois Fharraige. She surprised us even further when she told us that her father, Martin Connolly, had been born in West Virginia! [30]

KN: Where were you born?

Nan Foley: *Right down 67 York Street.*

KN: What age were you when you went to Ireland?

NF: I was *almost three years old.*

KN: When did your father and mother come out?

NF: My mother came out, I think, in *eighteen eighty-eight*. And my father was from West Virginia but he went after that to Ireland when he was young, but I do not know what age he was. And he stayed in Ireland until he was about nineteen or twenty and he came out here. *And then,* he married. They were here until *nineteen hundred.*

KN: What was your father's name?

NF: Máirtín Connolly.

KN: Where was he born?

NF: In Walker's Station, West Virginia.

KN: Where were his people from.

NF: Well, from Minna, *really*.

KN: Did your father have Irish?

NF: Yes, ach, *I think* he was *more at ease* speaking English.

KN: How did he pick up the Irish he had?

NF: I don't know, the way I did, *I guess*.

KN: And when did he come to Portland?

NF: He came to Portland, *I think*, in *eighteen eighty-nine*, a year after my mother.

KN: Where was he before that?

NF: In Minna. *Also* his father bought land and they built a house there and, *you know*, he stayed there until he came out here. And he was here until *nineteen hundred* and they went back *and bought the land and built a house.*

KN: Do you remember going over on the boat?

NF: I don't remember anything about that but I remember when we went to Na Creagáin.

KN: What was it like?

NF: *I thought* that it was cold *and, you know, of course,* our house was new. Everyone thought it was fine, *you know, because* it was new and had big windows.

THE FAMINE

Naturally a few of our interviewees had heard accounts of the Great Famine from older relatives and friends. Below are two brief accounts, one from Steve Concannon and the other from Mary Kilmartin. Steve Concannon was born in Doire Locháin, several miles east of Spiddal in 1900. We interviewed him in December 1984, December 1987, and September 1997.

Steve Concannon: Well, *you know*, at the time of the famine they were very poor. We were poor when I was growing up but we were no way as poor as those people. There was a man up on the Tamhna in our village whom they called "Maitiú na Tamhnaí." He had worked in England for a while. But he said (he was *probably* close to eighty) that when he was a young man about fifteen, he would take a basket of turf to Galway during the time of the famine and he would buy turnips and bring them home. *You know*, he didn't have any money to buy flour or anything he said. But that is how they were *living*, I believe. They were very poor.

Mary Kilmartin: The famine, I heard Patrick Malone talking about it. He said he was seventeen when his grandfather was telling him about it. His grandfather told him they used to take the eyes out of the potatoes and plant them and then they would eat the rest of the potatoes. And that is the time a lot of the names down by the shore were changed. People came from the towns and from other counties and moved down to the shore. "They could always get food at the shore," he said.

LEAVING IRELAND;

THE TRIP TO AMERICA;

ARRIVAL IN THE U.S.

Some of the most touching accounts we heard were the ones which dealt with leaving home. Most of the emigrants never saw their parents again.

Catherine ("Ceata") Concannon (née Foley[31]**)** was born in Teach Mór, Cois Fharraige in 1894 and was a younger sister of Philip Foley. She came to the U.S. in 1913 and worked as a domestic for about ten years before she married Peter F. Concannon.[32] We recorded Catherine in February and May 1988 and again in September 1997 when she was 103 years old. The following account begins with a description of a custom that was often referred to as an "American wake." The send-off party for emigrants had an atmosphere that was filled with a mixture of the strongest emotions.[33]

KN: Did they have a *party* the night before you left?
Catherine Concannon: Oh, gosh, *yes*, they were all drunk. There was a *party, all right*. That's when they would get their fill of drink, the poor things. And I *hated* my father and I remember, I can see the road now outside the house, where we stood and said *goodbye* and he said to me,

"I'll never see you again." That is so *clear* to me today as it was that day. *And* I *feel very guilty* that I did not go home to see him *because* I could have gone, *but that's youth for you.* It is *sad*, the poor creatures over there. You don't know it until you have children yourself.

KN: Do you remember coming out to America?

CC: Do I remember when I first came out? Indeed I do. [When I arrived in Portland] I came out at Union Station and my brother was there. They were over at Union Station. "Oh, gosh," said my brother, "There's Ceata over there." And I said to the person who was with me, "Look, there's our Philip." So we got together and he took me to where I was going to live, to my aunt's house. And he said, "Go up now and *surprise* them." And up I went and it was as dark as the devil, they didn't keep the light *on.* It was so dark and I put my head inside and my sister said, "Oh, my, *look, hi, Catherine." That's all. So anyway*, it was nice.

But *the next day, you know,* some of these people were hard on the creatures who had just arrived (and I could never be hard to anyone) and she took me to work and I said to myself, "It is a pity that I do not have five hundred dollars and I would go home to my Dad. *And so* I worked until I had five hundred dollars and by that time I preferred to stay in America to going home to Ireland.

Steve Concannon gave us one of the fullest accounts of what it was like for him in the years leading up to his departure. In the year 1918 at the time of the influenza epidemic, he found himself being called upon by three different neighbors to help with planting potatoes and various other chores. For every eight days he worked, the neighbors would give his mother a pound sterling.

Steve Concannon: There was one man, the poor man, who had six children, and he was over fifty years old and after dinner his wife would come out to the gate and say, "Oh, he wants to take a rest." But he wanted me to keep going all the time. "Hey, Steve," he would say, "I ate two potatoes too many, but you keep working." Then he would lie down and take a rest for a half-hour.

So I was working for three of them. That is why when *1919* came I was kind of tired. Everyone wanted me to work, you know, and everyone wanted to get as much out of me as they could. So I said to my mother in the potato-digging season in *October 1919,* "I would like to go to East

Galway and earn enough to buy a suit of *tweed*." Because at that time it was all homespun west of Galway and I didn't like it because it was so *thick*. But I liked *tweed*. So my mother said, *"All right*, if you want to go." *So* I went to East Galway. I took my shovel, *of course*, and a couple of pairs of socks and a couple of shirts and we went east to the Square.[34] Well that is where you would have to stand at that time and that is where they would come to hire you, because they knew that that was where all the spalpeens [itinerant farm laborers] would be, everyone of them with his shovel and his *bundle*. I waited there until Mrs. Flanagan and John Flanagan came. They hired me and another lad named Stephen Welby from Minna. *So* I went to East Galway and I liked the area and I stayed for a year and a half and I learned how to plow and how to handle horses.

So I came to Galway one day, I believe it was the next autumn, the potato digging season again in *1920* and I gave my mother ten pounds and a bag of wool. And my mother said to me, "Steve, your are wasting your life here. You would be better off to go to America than to stay here." *So*, she gave me the idea of going to America. *So*, that's when I wrote to my uncle out here and he sent me my passage in March *1921* and I came out in April *1921*.

Patrick Malone (1897–1985) was from Rosaveal-Casla, at the western end of Cois Fharraige. He had retained a large amount of traditional Irish language material: songs, stories, rhymes, riddles and anecdotes. In Ireland he had spent several years sailing and fishing along the coast of Galway Bay. He had also been active in the old Irish Republican Army (IRA) before coming to America in 1923. After arriving in New York at Ellis Island, he took the train to Pittsburgh, and after several years moved to Portland.[35] He begins his account of coming to the States by referring to the prophecy of Colm Cille (St. Columba).

Pat Malone: At that time, you would laugh about it. I heard that Colm Cille said that you would eat your breakfast in Ireland and that you would eat your dinner in America. Well that came to be. At that time it could take half a year to come to America, it could take some of the boats half a year. They ran out of water and everything long ago, the little sailing ships.

KN: Do you remember coming over on the boat?

PM: *Yeah, oh sure.*

KN: How long did it take?

PM: Eight days.

KN: Was it nice?

PM: *Oh, yeah.*

KN: What boat did you come on?

PM: The *Baltic* of the Cunard Line.

KN: From what place?

PM: From Queenstown.

KN: How did you go to Queenstown?

PM: I went on a *jaunt* to Galway and on a train to Queenstown.

KN: Was anyone with you?

PM: Oh, there were a lot of passengers coming out.

KN: From Galway? Connemara?

PM: *Yeah,* from every place. I didn't know them except for one man who was coming out along with me. He was a fine fellow, it was his second trip out here. I was all right, I wasn't seasick at all, but some of the poor creatures were quite bad with seasickness.

KN: Why? Was it rough?

PM: *Yeah,* and these people were not used to the sea, *the smell, you know.*

KN: Was the food good?

PM: *Yeah.*

KN: So you were satisfied.

PM: *Oh, yeah.* We had a bottle of stout every day.

KN: Was there dancing and music?

PM: *Yeah,* accordions and violins. There were a lot of *foreigners* on board also. I knew they were *foreigners* because I heard them talking to each other, up on *deck* in groups, walking around.

KN: And you came in where?

PM: To New York.

KN: Did you go to Ellis Island?

PM: We went through Ellis Island. We were kind of afraid of it, but it didn't bother me. But they were sending some of them *back* from Ellis Island, *you know.* It was kind of *hard* in *1923.* They were very strict at that time. Then I went to Pittsburgh.

KN: Was there anyone to meet you in New York?

PM: No.

KN: Did you stay in New York a night or two?

PM: On the boat. We were kept on the boat for a week. The *quota* was full.[36] And only *so much* were being let out. Well, I was walking on the boat. It was being loaded and unloaded, you know, *discharging*. I talked to a *longshoreman*. "Well," he said, "*what the hell are you doing there?*" "I don't know," says I, "the quota's full." "*I'll come down tonight and you'll come down on the net and to hell with them. I'll take care of you.*" But I thought about it. "No," I said, "*I'll never be able to become an American citizen if I do that. No, I'll wait. I'll go through everything.*"

KN: You stayed there.

PM: I stayed there. *I should thank him, you know.*

KN: Just the same, if you had been caught it would have been bad.

PM: *Yeah, yeah* and that's the way half of the people came into America. Half of those who are in America, *senators'* and *presidents'* people, that is how they got in, half of them. It was all English that were on the *Mayflower*. There was no Irishman on her.

Mrs. Nan Foley (née Connolly), as mentioned above, was born in Portland in 1897 and was taken to Ireland in 1900 when her parents returned there. Fifteen years later Nan herself returned to Portland at the age of eighteen! **PF** refers to Philip Foley, Nan's husband, whom we actually interviewed first.

KN: What year did you come out?

NF: *1915.*

KN: What place did you come to?

NF: To Portland.

KN: Directly in to Portland?

NF: Well, we *landed* in Boston. My two aunts were at Union Station.

KN: Do you remember the boat?

NF: Do I remember? Oh, I remember, *twelve days.*

KN: Quite long.

PF: What was the name of the boat, he is asking.

NF: *I think The American, I think* that that was the name of the boat.

KN: But you didn't like the boat?

NF: No, *no.*

KN: Why?

NF: *Well, I don't know,* I was *seasick and* I was *lonesome. I was sick, I was really sad.*

KN: What did you think?

NF: I thought it was *horrid.* I thought it was *horrid.* And we got *the trolley pass* at Union Station to Oak Street *and I thought Oak Street was the worst place in the whole wide world.*

KN: Why?

NF: *I don't know* why.

KN: Did you go to work then?

NF: Well, I didn't go to work *for a while.* I stayed with my aunt. *And then* I went to work along with *friends,* with my aunt *for a while.*

KN: How was the work?

NF: *Hated it.*

PF: Women worked *hard* at that time, brother.

Patrick O'Malley [Pádhraic Ó Máille] was born in Baile Logáin, Inveran, Cois Fharraige in 1901. He came to this country in 1924. Previous to his departure he had been active in the East Connemara branch of Óglaigh na hÉireann (the old IRA). He spent over six months in prison in Galway and his brother spent two years in prison in Kildare during the Irish Civil War. In Portland he was a longshoreman for over fifty years. We interviewed Patrick on May 23, 1986.

KN: Have you been here a long time?

Pat O'Malley: Sixty, more than sixty years.

KN: Do you think about the old country?

PO'M: Oh, all the time.

KN: Did you ever go home?

PO'M: No.

KN: Do you remember coming out.

PO'M: Oh, *yes,* I remember.

KN: How did you come?

PO'M: By boat.

KN: How long did it take?

PO'M: Seven days.

KN: Did you enjoy it?

PO'M: No, it seemed to me that it was very cold.

KN: Where did the boat leave from in Ireland?

PO'M: Queenstown.

KN: What year was that?

PO'M: *'24,* 1924.

KN: Did the boat come in here?

PO'M: Oh, *no,* Boston.

KN: Was there anyone to meet you?

PO'M: A cousin and my sister.

KN: Did you come to Portland that night?

PO'M: I came to Portland *right away.*

KN: What did you think?

PO'M: *If,* if there had been a road going to Ireland, I would have walked it. I was six months without work.

KN: Where were you staying?

PO'M: I was staying with a cousin of my mother's.

KN: Where was that?

PO'M: *Right* in Portland here, in Portland, Gray Street. I was staying with a Connolly from Connemara who was married to a cousin of my mother's.

KN: You were without work for six months.

PO'M: I was waiting for six months.

KN: What work did you finally get?

PO'M: I went to work for a *contractor, you know.* But if there had been a road going to Ireland, I would have walked it.

Jim Brown came to the U.S. at the age of eighteen in the early 1930s, at the height of the Great Depression. In spite of this he was able to get a job as a helper in construction and later on became a longshoreman.

KN: Where did you start your journey from?

JB: I got the "cóiste tineadh" in Ballinrobe and I went *all the ways* on the "cóiste tineadh," that's a train, in to Cork and I went from Cork to Queenstown.

KN: What was the name of the boat you sailed on?

JB: *Santa Cecilia.* I can't say *White Star* in Irish, I can't say *Santa Cecilia* in Irish.

KN: What kind of a boat was it?

JB: It was a luxury boat, one of the big ones, *yes.*

KN: Did you like it?

JB: Sure, I had never seen a boat until then. I was in that *country* [Ireland] and they wouldn't let me out. You had to be in at *nine o'clock* at night or "God help you" *after that*. God forbid, it was *strict*. They were right, *of course*. We lads were crazy about playing *football*.

KN: Were you sick on the boat?

JB: Yes, indeed. I was seasick *all the ways*. I was *homesick*. I wasn't yet *twenty* when I came out, I was eighteen years, I believe. But you are *lonesome*, you are lonely. You are with strangers and no one talks to you. No one will talk. No one knows who you are and you don't know who the other man is either. It took me a long time before I knew who anybody was. Well, it takes a while, in a *strange* lonely land you are a stranger.

KN: Why did you leave?

JB: You couldn't get any work in Ireland, you had to go to England or to America. Half of the people of Ireland are over in England working and they are fighting with England. They are out of line with England. Sure, England has never been beaten and she never will be beaten.

KN: Where did the boat come in?

JB: South Boston, *army base*.

KN: Were you let in right away? Was there immigration to go through?

JB: Oh, one had to go past the doctors. There was a doctor looking at your teeth *even*, another one taking your shoes off to see whether you had any *corns*. [laughs] They had a great *time* with me.

KN: Was anyone with you?

JB: Yes, a sister of my father's was with me. She went over from this country. I came out with her. I couldn't have made my own way. I was *very bashful*. I had no *gall*. I couldn't talk to anyone, to strangers. I had never seen anything but the lads I went to school with and played *football* with. That's all.

KN: What did you think when you arrived?

JB: A brother was waiting for me here. Yes, John. He died there a couple of years ago, he died in Boston.

KN: Did you stay in Boston a couple of nights?

JB: I didn't stay at all in Boston. I came to this town the same day I arrived in Boston. I can't translate Boston to Irish either. I can say "Boston," that's all.

KN: How long were you here before you got work?

JB: Oh, maybe a week.

KN: Where did you go to work?

JB: I went to work out on Forest Avenue building a garage there, for the Cunninghams. Joe Moloney was the *super*. They gave me work, *plenty*.

KN: What kind of pay was there?

JB: Oh, *eighty cents an hour*. There were no dollars at that time. If it weren't for the *Union*, they still wouldn't have any pay. It's the *Union* that made the pay *really*. A policeman said to me, "*Jim Brown*, if it weren't for the *Union*," he says, "you wouldn't have any pay yet and we wouldn't have anything either," he says. *Twenty-seven dollars a week* they were getting at that time, the Portland police.

LONGSHORE

The domination of the longshore industry in Portland by the Irish has been thoroughly documented by Michael Connolly and indeed was the genesis of the project to interview and record the Portland's Irish speakers. Nearly all the men we interviewed had been longshoremen, some for a few years and some, like Patrick O'Malley, for half a century. It was hard, backbreaking work, and yet many of those we spoke to said they enjoyed it. From 1853 to the early 1920s, Portland was assured of an extensive winter trade with Canada due to the fact that the ports of Montreal and Quebec were frozen in the winter. Canadian grain was transported by rail to Portland where it was loaded on ships bound for Europe. Portland boasted in those days that it was "Canada's winter port." But, Connolly states, "between 1923 and 1934 Canadian exports through Portland virtually dried up."[37] The industry had a brief revival during the Second World War but continued to decline after that.

Philip Foley (1891-1989) was born in Teach Mór, Cois Fharraige, and was the older brother of Catherine ("Ceata") Concannon. He came to the U.S. in 1913 and returned to Ireland after a few years here. He came back to the U.S. around 1916 and was in the U.S. Army in World War I and served in France. He started on longshore in 1923. We interviewed Philip and his wife Nan on May 23, 1986; Philip was nearly ninety-six years old.

KN: Were there many Irish here at that time?

PF: There was nothing but Irish. Women and men, going back and forth on Congress Street, *after Mass* on Sunday. *All* west *from Galway to Connemara and Mayo all over,* Corr na Móna *they used to call them.*

KN: And when you got the job working on longshore were there many Irish there?

PF: They were all Irish. All Irish, most of them. And the *bosses* also, the *bosses* were Irish.

KN: Did you ever hear any Irish when you were working?

PF: *Sure.* Irish was all there was. They were all Irishman working at that time who had immigrated.

KN: What kind of work was it?

PF: *Running the grain over to England,* bread for England, and *freight,* every kind, pigs' feet and everything was *going to England* at that time. They couldn't go into Canada. It was *frozen,* Canada. *And then* they got a boat that could cut the *ice* and everything. No boat is coming here now.

KN: And you said that they would be speaking Irish when they were working?

PF: That's what they spoke. They were all Irishmen.

KN: And did the Corr na Móna people have Irish?

PF: *Oh, yes.* Irish as good as the Cois Fharraige people had.

KN: How many people do you think were here who had Irish? A couple of hundred, a couple of thousand?

PF: There were a couple of thousand, *anyway.*

KN: And where did they live?

PF: *All over Portland, South Portland, Munjoy Hill, St. Patrick's.*

KN: Do you remember any of the bosses you had? Were they good, were they bad?

PF: Some of them were quite hard. They would try to get the *gang* to work at its utmost.

KN: Why was that?

PF: Oh, to brag that they had the best *gang.* And they would be the first to get the next job.

Jim Brown worked longshore both before and after World War II. His uncle John Brown was an important figure in the longshore union (officially named the Portland Longshoremen's Benevolent Society, or PLSBS, founded in 1880), having held the office of President in 1900, from 1917 to 1919, and in 1935.[38]

KN: When did you start on longshore?

JB: Oh, it was after *'33*, *'34* I think. Then I got *off*, they put me in the army in *1941* or *two*.

KN: What was the work like?

JB: Oh, we worked hard, *really*. Every hatch in the boat had a *boss*. There were seventeen men, they called it a *gang* and three or four *bosses*. And they would have to know you well before they would allow you to work either. But you would have to be in the *Union* to go to work with them. It was the *longshore* [union] that sent the *longshoremen* to work. The *Union* was *hiring* and sending the men to work. You would have to join the *Union* before you started to work. It was *fifty* dollars to join also.

KN: What time did you start in the morning?

JB: Eight, *eight o'clock*. Eight o'clock till *five*, five, *straight time*.

KN: Was there lunch time?

JB: Oh, there was. Twelve to one o'clock. An hour for lunch. And at night you would go in at *six o'clock*. There used to be a lot of *overtime*. That's where there was big pay.

KN: How were the bosses? Were they hard?

JB: It's for that reason they were put there, to *drive* you. They were terrible for *driving*. There was a John Feeney from *around Clifden* and he was good to me and *my brother John*. He was very good to me. He was from Roundstone or Clifden, Feeney, Seán Ó Fíne. *John Feeney and he used to go to Montrehall* [Montreal]; he would go to Montrehall in the summer. The boats used to go into Montrehall in the summer to load up, and they came down here in the winter to load. Montrehall would be *frozen*, you couldn't go there because of the snow and frost. They could not go in to load the boats.

KN: You were saying that some of the bosses were hard.

JB: Some of them were, *yeah*. They were *ignorant*, that is why. That's all. But Feeney wasn't like that. Feeney could talk to his men. When you talk to a man, that is better than *driving* him. When you see a man *driving*, he doesn't know anything about the work.

Steve Concannon worked for the railroad when he first arrived in Portland but soon moved on to longshore. In both occupations he spoke Irish on a daily basis with his fellow workers. For his first five years he lived in South Portland with his uncle Mark Concannon, who had come to Portland in the 1890s and was also a longshoreman.

SC: Oh, brother, when I first came out here, the first job I had was working on the railroad, *you know*, down here they called it *Yard Eight* at that time. And there was a *roundhouse* there and the *steam engines* used to be there. And they were all Irish there. The crowd I was with was always speaking Irish together. There were a couple of people working with us, one from Nova Scotia, *you know*, I am *sure* he was *Scotch*, but a very nice man who was always telling me a lot of jokes about the Irish. But there were four or five of us who were called *greenhorns*, we had only recently come from Ireland, and we spoke Irish all the time. Well, then we were laid off, we were laid off in *November* and my uncle took me and I *joined longshore* and sure when I went to work *longshore*, we were all speaking Irish. Everyone was speaking Irish in *longshore*. Everyone. Some of the Irish worked *longshore* all their lives and didn't pick up much English ever. Some of them had poor English *because* they never spoke it, but Irish always.

KN: If I had been there fifty years ago, would I have heard much Irish?

SC: Oh, you would have heard Irish, brother. You would have heard Irish unless there was a *country-born* there. [39] They would be speaking English to each other always and if an Irishman like me were working with them, we would, I would speak English along with them. But if I were down in the hatch along with men from Cois Fharraige, we would all be speaking Irish.

KN: What would you be talking about?

SC: Oh, well, *you know*, some of them used to tease each other, *of course*. There was one thing about *longshore*, as *long* as you were doing your work the *boss* didn't mind, you know. *You know*, it is not the same as working in a factory. *So*, they'd be *kidding* each other and have a lot of *jokes* about each other and teasing. My uncle once told me about a man who had money. And they said he was married three times. And another fellow said when he heard that, "Well, it's no wonder for him to have money," he says, "he got three dowries," he says, "and we only got one dowry." *That's, 'He got three dowries.'*

KN: When you would be working, would they say to each other things like, "Ó, beir air sin" (Oh, take hold of that) or "Tabhair dhom é sin" (Give me that)?

SC: Oh, *yes, sure,* brother. "Breathnaigh amach" (watch out), *you know,* and "coinnigh isteach ón *digger*" (keep in from the *digger*). Or if you were working on coal. You know, I used to hear them talking about that Irishman who didn't pick up much Irish [English], *you know,* some old Irishman who was shoveling coal over where *Prince of Fundy is now.* There were four big *diggers* there and coal was coming in all the time there and there used to be *gangs* working *steady* there almost all the time. But when a *greenhorn* would come around, *you know* they used to call a new lad from Ireland a *greenhorn,* they would put him in the *wing,* what they called the *wing, you know.* So, the *digger* would come down this way and if you could stay *close* to the *digger,* you were *all right.* But if you were in the *wing,* you would have to *swing* out. It was more difficult to get the coal that they would throw. *So,* someone asked this [old] man, *"How is the greenhorn making out?" You know, he'd ask in English, "How was the greenhorn making out?" "Ah, yes, he's all right,"* he says, *"he's all right but he has no 'come west' in him." You know, he was trying to say the meaning. He was unable to translate it, you know, 'come west,' he had no energy. But the way they say that in Irish* "níl aon tíocht aniar ann." *But he was trying to answer the fellow who asked him in English and he said, "He is all right but he has no 'come west' in him." Well, of course, that was a great joke, we used to have great fun on that, you know, and kidding each other like that, you know.*

KN: Who was the man who said that?

SC: I don't know but I heard stories about him. I heard one once about Frank O'Toole. He was always speaking Irish, *poor* Frank. During the *war,* that is the *last war,* there were boxes of *lard* coming in and they were very slippery. And Frank would be *piling* them up and sometimes he wouldn't be *careful* and the *whole breech* would fall down on him. And the *boss* was watching him, his name was Peadairín Breathnach, and it was getting on his *nerves* watching Frank. Finally he called out to Frank to be *careful, you know, they'd fall* down. But *anyway,* a big *breech* came down on him. *"Hey, Frank,"* he says, *"you are fired. Get out of the hole." "No, sir,"* says Frank, *"because I won't fire for you." So,* we used to have a great *joke* about that, you know, Frank said, *"I won't fire for you,"* says Frank, you know, *and he didn't either. But that was a great joke over there, you know, they used to kid, you know.* And with Peadairín after that and if someone was down in the hole, and the hole was, you know, *forty feet deep, you know,* you'd be down there *and they'd holler up to* Peadairín, *they'd say, "I won't fire for you,* Peadairín*." You know, you wouldn't feel the day.*[40]

We used to work fourteen hours a day, from seven o'clock in the morning to eleven at night during the *war* and you wouldn't feel the day going by if you were with a good *gang.* You wouldn't feel the day going by, *you know.* One time there was a boat from Cuba with sugar. You know, when they loaded the sugar on board in Cuba, the first *process,* it was kind of *wet,* wet. Every bag was two hundred weight. We worked with hooks. But if you were working on that from seven in the morning till eleven at night, seven days a week, it took us three weeks to *empty* it. You could only put in the *sling* ten bags, I don't want to tell a lie, *either* ten bags or twenty, maybe twenty, but I think it was ten bags that we would put in the *sling,* but it took us very long to empty the boat. And we were working seven days a week, Sunday and *all.* And I saw some of them giving up on that *job.* That was *tough,* you know. It was *hard, you know. Yeah, but, yeah, so,* I worked, *you know, that way.* I liked it but I know that there is no assurance in the *longshore,* you know, because it is only for a while when there is a *boom* or something like that. They do a lot of *loafing.* And you know, working *longshore* long ago it is like a person who smokes *cigarettes* who couldn't give them up and in the end you are down there and you are *loafing* for so long so often that in the end you don't want to go to work on a *steady job because* you don't want to be *confined* like that.

DOMESTIC SERVICE

Most of the Irish immigrant women in Portland got work as domestic servants. Many of them arrived at an early age such as Delia Curran, who was destined for Portland at age sixteen. Even in the twentieth century, some of the women immigrants were quite young, such as Mary Kilmartin, who came to Portland in 1930 at the age of sixteen. It must have been difficult for these young women to adapt to life in the houses of wealthy people, and there are many stories that illustrate the unfamiliarity of the domestics with the customs and even the language of their employers. Their duties could include cleaning, washing, cooking, waiting on tables, and looking after children.[41] Some of the domestics formed close life-long bonds with their employers. Others had stormy, difficult relations with mean, stingy "Poncáin" (Yankees), the word used by all of Portland's Irish speakers to refer to the well-to-do families. The Irish domestics worked every day except Sunday and Thursday afternoon. On Thursdays they would visit their relatives or go for a stroll on the Eastern or Western Promenade, where they would frequently be joined by young Irishmen when they finished their work. Many of the Irish domestics were allowed to invite friends into the kitchen of their employers' house for tea. As a result, the men knew a great deal about the work situation of the women.

Jim Brown was one of the men who spent a fair amount of time with the Irish domestic workers. I asked Jim if he had any stanza of the "Óró mhíle grá" type. This is a ditty with no set text which was very popular in Cois Fharraige and Connemara and to which extemporaneous stanzas could be added at will. In fact, the only Portland-composed piece of Irish we heard was the following: "Óró mhíle grá, siar is aniar Congress Street and back the Promenade" ("Oh, my love, back and forth Congress Street and back the Promenade"). I asked Jim Brown if he had any of these little stanzas.

Jim Brown: I had to come to this *country* before I heard that song "Óró mhíle grá." I heard a girl from near Spiddal singing that song. There were a lot of girls in my time who could sing that song. I had to come to this *country* before I heard the song, *though*. I never heard that song over in Ireland.

KN: Where did you hear it?

JB: They used to be singing it over on the Promenade when they would have *an evening off*. The Western Promenade at that time used to be full of girls from Ireland.

KN: What were you doing there?

JB: I was going with the girls. I had a woman there every night. What do you think? They were good. They were working for the people who had the big money. They gave them *jobs*, these people, the *millionaires*. They wanted girls from Ireland to be working for them. They were *honest*.

KN: Did they talk to you about their work?

JB: When it would get to be *midnight*, one o'clock in the morning, they would give an *invitation* into the house and they would prepare a cup of tea or coffee. And they had permission from their employers to bring their *friends* in any time for a cup of tea. The girls used to tell me that. There's no one like that now. No one is coming out now.

KN: Did they work every day of the week.

JB: I think they used to have one day a week, the fourth day or the fifth day to go out, it was Thursday.

KN: What would they do on that day?

JB: Well, they would visit their relatives. If they had relatives they would pay them a *call* in the evening. But they preferred to be over at the Promenade waiting for the boys. We'd all be over there every night.

KN: Did the girls have a difficult time?

JB: Maybe you'd hear one of these girls and maybe she didn't know what a *radiator* was and stuff like that, *you know what I mean*. But you would have to hear both sides of the story. I wouldn't pay attention to one side of the story. But some of them were able to pick things up more readily than some others.

KN: Were there *jokes* about it?

JB: The woman of the house told Margaret that she would put the stuff on the *dumbwaiter*. And sure the *dumbwaiter* was there and Margaret didn't know it. So, "Heavens, where is the *dumbwaiter*," says Margaret, "I've been here for a half hour waiting for the *dumbwaiter*." She thought it was a man. "Why don't you open the door," says the woman, "the *dumbwaiter* is in there." "I didn't know," says Margaret, "what a *dumbwaiter* was."

But they [i.e., the employers] would show them everything and give them the names of everything in the house. They knew well that the girls did not know. Most of them were the children of farmers. They had never seen a city until they were put on the boat in Dublin. As for me, they kept me in until I was eighteen. Then they put me on the boat in Queenstown. They said, "Go out to America." "Go out to America now," they used to say.

Steve Concannon was quite aware of the work the Irish immigrant women did and had a number of humorous stories about their predicaments. As mentioned above, Steve lived for five years with his uncle,

Marcas Concannon and Marcas's wife. Married women like Mrs. Marcas Concannon, in addition to their own children, frequently had several boarders to look after, usually recently-arrived relatives.

Steve Concannon: The women who came from Ireland from my place, almost all of them worked up there for the *Yankees, as, I'll say it* in English, *domestics. They were all domestics I would say, you know.* But the ones who are coming out now, the girls, they have much better education. They don't do *domestic* work any more.

KN: But at that time . . .

SC: That is the work they did *because* they had no education. Ireland was so poor and there was no farmer *hardly* who could send a son or a daughter to college at that time. There was no money, brother.

KN: Were there stories about the women?

SC: [Yes. There was a house with a statue of Oliver Cromwell]. Ceata didn't know what *statue* it was. Catherine [the woman of the house] says to Ceata, *"when you're down there, dust off that statue." "By the way,"* says Ceata to her, *"who's this one here?" "Oh,"* she said, *"that's Oliver Cromwell." "Oh, to Hell with him,"* says Ceata, *"I won't dust him off." And you know, of course, the Yankee laughed at her, you know. But we used to get fun, you know.* We used to have a laugh, you know, we did.

Of course, the girl from Cois Fharraige at that time when there were potatoes, fish, and milk, you could eat four or five potatoes, there was no substance to them as in meat. The first thing I noticed when I came to this *country* was that you could only eat two potatoes when you had meat. *So,* there was this girl, *anyways,* I heard them talking about it, she was working for Yankees (we call the Yankees Poncáin) and there were three of the Yankees, a man, his wife, and the daughter. "Well," she says, *"Mary, we'll have one baked potato for each of us and what-ever you need for yourself. But we'll have one apiece." And, of course, the Yankee lady, about eleven o'clock or before the dinner was cooked, she came out to supervise, you know, how Mary was making out. She looked in the oven. She saw nine potatoes in there. "Oh," she said, "I told you," she said, "all we wanted is one apiece." "Well, that's what I did," she said, "one apiece for you and six for myself." You know, because she was so used to it in the old country, eating so much pota-toes. She didn't realize that she couldn't eat six because . . . They used to have a lot of fun on the Irish girls, you know.*

I heard a joke, you know, of course it was really tough on the girls. They were raised in Cois Fharraige or Connemara, *they never heard a word of English and you know "adhastar," do you know "adhastar an asail?" They used to call it the ass's head-stole, you know "adhastar an asail."*[42] *So*, long ago the *icebox* used to be down in the cellar. *And this Yankee lady* said to this girl, she was teaching to *cook, "Go down,"* she says, *"and get me the oysters." The oysters was in the icebox. But she didn't know and she came up with a piece of a clothesline. She said, "This is the only adhastar I could find." So* we had a great time with the girls like that, *you know.*

PROHIBITION AND POITÍN IN PORTLAND

The people of West Galway who settled in Portland maintained for several decades their language and various aspects of their Gaelic culture. When Prohibition came, it could have put a halt to the tradition of having alcoholic beverages at parties and weddings. However, there were some Irish speakers in Portland who had learned the traditional craft of making "poitín" (moonshine) in Ireland, and when the need arose during Prohibition, they did not abstain from putting their expertise to use.

Pat Malone, as mentioned earlier, had a fine repertoire of Irish traditional folklore including a number of songs. One of the songs he sang had several references to poitín. The song ended with this reference to poitín: "leigheasfadh sé casacht na hoíche is dhíreodh sé daoine bheadh cam" ("it could cure the night cough and it could straighten people who were crooked"). Pat then commented, "Agus dhéanfadh sé cam daoine a bheadh díreach freisin" ("it could make straight people crooked too"). These references to poitín[43] led me to ask the following naïve question:

KN: Did you ever taste poitín?
PM: I made it myself. *Oh, yeah.*
KN: You made it.
PM: *Yeah.* I made it here too. Well, I bought barley here. Well, I had a *friend* here, Eddie Coffey, who had traveled most of Ireland. We were going east one day on Commercial. We were working *longshore.* He said that he had never seen a drop of poitín being made. Well, on our way home, I went into the *Grain* and I bought a fifty weight of barley. It will

take you a month, from the time you steep the barley in water until you will have a glass of poitín. You have to put it in water for *forty-eight hours*. Then you take it out, then you put it on a level surface and it will begin to *sprout*. You have to keep turning it every morning so that it won't stick together and form lumps. You have to keep it *separated*. Then you have to harden it, you know, put it in a kiln. *I was doing it on top of a boiler*. Then you have to grind it. And when it is ground you put boiling water over it. You extract its juice from it. Then you make *beer* from that water, you add *yeast*. Then you put the "back" on it, like a cover. Then when the "back" falls in the barrel, you make a singling of it, just like whiskey. Well you put the singling through again to double it and then you have your whiskey. Ah, there's a lot of bother to it.

KN: Was it as good here as it was in Ireland?

PM: *Oh, all right*. It wasn't as good, the *still* wasn't half as big. We had a *fifty-gallon still* in Ireland, the *still* was big, you know, more air.

KN: How did you learn how to do it in the first place?

PM: By watching another man making it, *just like everything else*.

Patrick O'Malley was another Portlander who was acquainted with the art of making poitín.

KN: Did the Irish here have parties and weddings?

PO'M: Weddings, yes. It would be in a house. They would have bread, butter, eggs, and poitín.

KN: Did they have poitín here?

PO'M: Here? They were making poitín here also, some of the Irish. There were a couple of fellows out in South Portland who were making poitín. One was working on the *railroad. He used to sell it.* He was making money on it.

KN: Did you taste it?

PO'M: He gave me a gallon. I paid for it.

KN: Was it any good?

PO'M: Oh, it was good. I was working for a man who made poitín in Ireland for over a year. He was making poitín almost every week.

KN: Did you ever see poitín being made?

PO'M: I sold it.

THE IRISH LANGUAGE IN PORTLAND, 1880–1960

All the testimony we received from our interviewees indicates how omnipresent Irish was in Portland's Irish communities. Similar evidence was given to us by the children of Irish speakers and by individuals who visited these communities in years gone by. The following accounts refer principally to the use of Irish in a number of settings.

One of the leading Irish speakers in Portland was Mrs. Catherine Flaherty, usually referred to as Ceata Bhreathnach. It is most unfortunate that we did not get an opportunity to interview her. She passed away in 1985 at the age of 87. [44] In this excerpt, Steve Concannon reminisces about Ceata's singing ability.

Steve Concannon: There was a woman here, Ceata Bhreathnach. Well, she was superb at singing the old songs. When we were *greenhorns*, we would go out there. She was working for Yankees out by the Western Promenade. And the two women she was working for were kind of deaf. And we would be in the kitchen, four or five of us, and we would be *happy*. And I'd ask poor Ceata to sing a song for us, she was superb at singing the old songs, "Nach aoibhinn do na héiníní éiríonns go hard is a bhíonns a' cruinniú le chéile ar aon chraoibhín amháin" ("Isn't it splendid for the little birds that fly on high and gather together on one small little branch"). That's a nice song and a real old song, but I can't remember it now. And "Anach Cuain (Annaghdown)" and "Sé fáth mo bhuartha nach bhfaighim cead cuarta i ngleanntaí uaigneach sa bhíonn mo ghrá" ("It is the cause of my sorrow that I cannot get leave to visit the lonely glens where my love is"). That is another old song. There were a lot of fine old songs and I used to enjoy listening to them. And sometimes I think a woman is able to sing a song better than a man if she has a nice voice. And this woman was excellent at singing for us. Her name was Ceata Bhreathnach.

Patrick O'Toole (1892-1989) was a native of Cois Fharraige who emigrated to Norwood, Massachusetts around 1914. After a year there, he moved to Portland. He was in the U.S. Army and served in France during the First World War. He spent a number of years working on the Grand Trunk Railway and also was a longshoreman for five or six years. We interviewed him in December 1986.

KN: Did you speak any Irish since coming out?

Patrick O'Toole: Oh, *all* Irish.

KN: Was there much Irish here in Portland?

PO'T: You wouldn't hear anything around here but Irish at that time *because* they were all *Irish* in this *section. All Gaelic.*

KN: Would you hear Irish on the street?

PO'T: You would hear Irish on the street. You would hear Irish on Congress Street. It didn't make any difference where you went, you'd hear Irish. Irish, Irish *here,* Irish *there. Even the ones that was born here, they had the* Gaeilge *too. They learned it from them, because that's all they heard is* Gaeilge.

As the older generation of Irish speakers passes on, the memory of an Irish-speaking Portland becomes fainter and fainter. But as mentioned above, the children of those Irish speakers still have vital memories of their parents' Irish-speaking neighborhoods. While it is true that Irish was only rarely passed on to the next generation, nevertheless the children of Irish speakers sometimes recalled interesting details that the Irish speakers themselves never thought to mention.

Larry Welch (see gallery, plate 46) was born in Portland, the son of two Connemara Irish speakers. He worked for several years in the 1920s on longshore and later worked for the telephone company. He recalled a number of stories about Finn MacCool (Fionn MacCumhaill) and Cúlán and was full of anecdotes about Portland's Irish communities in the period 1915–1950. The following excerpt touches on a number of points: the distinction between Connemara and Cois Fharraige, the use of Irish, the Western Promenade, and the greenhorn versus native-born distinction. Michael Connolly (MC) and I recorded Larry Welch on January 6, 1990. The interview was conducted in English.

Larry Welch: Yeah, all those Irish around here were right from Connemara section where we come from. There was no Cois Fharraiges here. The Cois Fharraiges were always up at the other end of the city.

MC: Near St. Dominic's?

LW: In that parish, yeah. Whereas Gorham's Corner and all that were a mixture.

KN: And you mentioned a man named Green.

LW: Pat Green, yeah. They called him Robert Emmett because he used, he could spout the Gaelic to beat Hell. He was real good and he was educated too. His brother was Mike Green that your father [Michael Francis Connolly, father of MC] worked for. There was a number of Greens. They were cousins of my father's, I think, or my mother. We were pretty close cousins all around here, Christ.

KN: You mentioned, was it your uncle's funeral?

LW: At my Uncle Larry's funeral up in Montgomery Street, just about World War I, about 1917, I guess.

MC: What happened there, Larry?

LW: Well, he told this Gaelic, spouted Gaelic for about fifteen or twenty minutes, in a declamatory way, you know, just like he was on stage. And everybody was there listening to him. The only one that understood him, I guess, was my father, I think, he still understood the Gaelic. Oh, my other uncle Tom, but it must have been some kind of a poem or story, you know, that's all I knew. I just sat there and watched him. Of course, he had, you might say, a drop taken, you know, he was beechers, they say. He had his speech. That's what they used to say, you know, when you get a little garrulous with the booze. "He had a drop taken."

KN: You also mentioned that there used to be a lot of Irish spoken when you were young.

LW: When I was a little kid, just when my mother died there and a little while afterward, my father did what they used to call bringing out a greenhorn, advancing the fare, helping them out and they'd pay him back, see? Now they did that and they used to come down to our house Sunday afternoon, on their afternoon off and have tea and cake and all that and talk and every one of them, of course, spoke the Gaelic. They were all from Connemara, back in the west part of Galway.

KN: Did you ever hear of anyone coming out who didn't know English?

LW: No, but most of them when I was a kid there they had quite a brogue, what we called a brogue. But they all could speak English. A lot of them couldn't, my father couldn't read or write, no, neither could my mother. In those days when they were, the English schools were considered changing the religion, you know. . . . God damned sure they would not go there. That's a sad thing too. That's the time when the English had those laws against the Irish.

MC: What about, you know hundreds of nicknames. Do you know any nicknames that were in Irish? Any of the longshore Irish?

LW: Paudeen na gCruc. I don't know what the "gCruc" means.

KN: Of the hills.

LW: Padeen of, he was a Joyce.

KN: He must have been from the hill country.

LW: Corr na Móna. Padeen na gCruc. There was Cois Fharraige Mike. I don't know if he was Cois Fharraige or not but they called him that.

MC: That was Mike Connolly, wasn't it?

LW: Yeah.

MC: What about, did you know Cac an Éinín?

LW: Oh, Cac an Éiní, I worked with him for years. That's "bird shit," isn't it? Boy, . . . I wouldn't call it to his face. He was a little, little teeny guy, but he was feisty, a tough little bastard. He worked, he never missed a day or an hour. Pulling all those boxes of meat in those days with seven or eight hundred pounds on your truck, pull that fourteen hours a day. Chris' sake, we did, and on the last night, that's when all those ships come in from, when Montreal would freeze up in the winter and they'd work all night Friday night right up to Saturday afternoon after working all week fourteen hours a day. Hey, I carried a hundred and forty. . . . This shoulder of mine is wider than this side. A hundred and forty pound bags of flour all day long.

MC: When you started longshore did you hear any Irish spoken at all?

LW: Sure they spoke Irish, sure. But it was fading out. You know, when I first went down there they talked a lot of it.

KN: When would that be then?

LW: What was it, 1923 when I joined the union? 1923, yeah.

MC: That was the heyday.

LW: They were all Irish in the gangs, in the steady gangs.

KN: Did you hear stories about the men on longshore or the women, the women of course worked for the Yanks?

LW: Well, it could be. They congregated up on the Western Promenade. That was a "happy hunting ground" there for the servant girls and the young Irish from Ireland. They didn't mix much with what we called us "natives," born here, we were natives. As I say there was a little feeling there, something, it seems between, in those days, you thought, the first generation kind of looked down on them, you know. And it took some time before when they died out there and these young ones, so-called natives, got in the union, for Chris' sake, the union went downhill from a militant standpoint. The old-country Irish were pretty god damned good union men. They made a good union there.

KN: When did you notice that Irish people stopped coming to Portland in general?

LW: Well I think the immigration laws changed, didn't they?

Sister Mary de la Salle O'Donnell grew up as the youngest of nine children on Salem Street, Portland in the 1930s. Her parents, Anne Scahill and Michael O'Donnell, were natives of Carraroe, at the western edge of Cois Fharraige, who emigrated to Portland and married there in 1912. She heard a good deal of Irish growing up from her parents and the neighbors. As the youngest she picked up only a few phrases of Irish, but she shared with us some valuable reminiscences of Portland's Irish community.

Sr. O'Donnell: In our family, my mother and father talked Gaelic together most of the time even in our presence so that my older brothers and sisters could speak a little bit of the Gaelic. I could just understand a little bit of what they were saying if an English word were inserted, then I put 2 and 2 together and was able to decipher this for myself. I picked up "muise" [indeed] and "dún do bhéal" [close your mouth] and "suigh síos ansin" [sit down there]. Oh, of course, cé chaoi bhfuil tú? [how are you?], maith go leor [well enough], cé chaoi bhfuil tú fhéin? [how are you, yourself?].

KN: Did you ever hear singing in Gaelic?

Sr. O'D: I can tell you two stories where singing in Gaelic was involved. The first is on rainy days, my mother would kind of remove herself from the rest of us and she'd go to a room, usually it was a front bedroom and she'd sit by the window and she would sing Gaelic songs and we never interrupted her. She never said anything about, you know, "Be quiet." We just tiptoed or if we noticed her in the bedroom we would withdraw. So she had a reputation of knowing so many of the traditional Irish songs and she had a marvelous memory for them. The second, again, concerns my mother and it was an Irish wedding. As I understand it there would be very few men at the party itself until they came back from work and so in this instance my mother was there at the wedding with my sister, who must have been about five or six years old at the time, and anyway my mother was singing all of the songs and they were all in a circle and my father came home, washed up and raced to the party. And when he saw my sister Mary, she was the oldest girl, she looked very sad, and so he went over to her and took her aside, and he says, "What's the matter, Maura?" And she said, "Papa, Mama is singing holding hands with Mr. So-and-So." And that was what they were doing, all in a circle, you know, and holding hands. Well he says, "Ah," he says, "it's all right. It's all right. Don't you worry. They're just having a nice time." So that's how he took care of it. So it was all happening within the Gaelic. And of course when she came over on the boat she did a lot of the entertaining but I didn't find out much of that until I was older.

KN: Do you think Gaelic was ever used officially, maybe at the Hibernians?

Sr. O'D: I'm just guessing that the meetings would be held in English but when they got together they must have talked because they were all Gaelic-speaking. I don't know of anyone in the neighborhood of the adults who did not speak Gaelic.

KN: How many Irish speakers were there in Portland, Mike?

MC: Because of where they came from they were predominantly Irish speaking, as Sister says. I think that's what makes Portland unique.

KN: Several hundred or a thousand?

MC: I think more.

Sr. O'D: Well there's something about Portland that reminds the Irish of their village, and I'm just guessing, you know, they must have communicated this to the people in Ireland and they just gravitated toward us. So even to the fish and the dulse, in August my father would go dulsing and in, I guess it's May and June he would fish for cunners and you'd see a whole group of Irishmen out there, on the rocks, Cape Elizabeth. And the cunners would be salted and in my family every Christmas my mother would send a box of salted fish to our relatives in Norwood and they in return would send us cranberries.

MC: That's a name I hadn't heard for a while, cunners, because when I was raised on Munjoy Hill, the Rock, which is officially called Pomeroy Rock, I never knew it as that, I only knew it as Cunners Rock and it's a little island right off the East End beach. [45]

KN: Could you say more about dulse?

Sr. O'D: The dulse is a kind of seaweed, only it's a beautiful deep purple, red type of seaweed and it clings to the rocks and you pick it at the turn of the tide. It has to be low tide but you pick it at the turn and it's plentiful out in Cape Elizabeth, I don't know whether it's still plentiful, but it would take them about an hour to get maybe a couple of pillow cases of the dulse. They'd spread it on the rocks until it dried and then they'd put it back into a clean pillowcase and take it home. Now the Irish love dulse but I just learned recently that dulse is one of the best foods going. It has all of the minerals and the Irish at home, my mother didn't do this, but the Irish in, back in Galway, they would make puddings out of it.

Dr. Bart O'Connor ("Beachla Tom Bheachla") was born in the Bronx, New York, in the late 1920s. His father was Thomas O'Connor, a native of New Village, Barna in Cois Fharraige. His mother was a Coyne, from An Cnocán Glas, near Spiddal. Growing up in the Bronx, he heard a fair amount of Irish from his parents and had some command of the language until he started school. His mother's older sister, Delia Coyne, married Thomas Coyne in Portland in 1915. Bart and his mother frequently visited his Aunt Delia in the 1930s and 1940s. Here is what Bart remembers about Portland in that period.

Dr. Bart O'Connor: Delia had four children. Tom, a priest; a nun; and James and John.

Mr. Coyne worked down on the railroad; that's where the two sons worked.

As a kid I loved to go to Portland, my aunt loved to go to the movies.

Congress Street was where the main movie, the main area was and they'd walk on Congress Street and they'd meet and talk to people. I remember, see Congress Street ends toward South Portland around Eighth Street and all that area going down toward the water to the docks and to the railroad and they would be talking on the street in Gaelic, absolutely. The whole area was all really Gaelic-speaking and I was fortunate because I remembered some of the Gaelic when I was a kid. So I remember what they were talking about. That always annoyed my aunt that I'd know what they were saying, that I could remember. She didn't know that I could remember any Gaelic.

KN: Where did your mother first come out from?

BO'C: My mother came to Portland, I think up around that area, I don't know, Boston or New York. All I know is that from Ireland she went to Scotland, she was in Glasgow, she went there and lived there and was in service maybe a year, a year and a half then she came to the U.S. and she, I think, came to Portland. I'm positive she came to Portland. She stayed with Aunt Delia and Tom until she got herself a job in service again. Then she came right down to New York where she met my father.

KN: What village was your father from?

BO'C: My father was from Barna, New Village; that's what it's called. What was most striking about Portland, it did have a very strong culture and that was Irish, very Irish, very Catholic. They would cook on Fridays breams[46] that were mailed from Ireland. I don't know if you know that dried fish, brown and they would get it in brown paper bags. I remember they always had that. My mother used to get it at Christmas time from her sister but Aunt Delia got it all the time. I think it was from Uncle Tom's family. And they would cook bream. I hated it. That white gunky stuff. But, they ate it; they loved it. And she made all her own bread. She did a lot of her own cooking.

Her house was small but they had a lot of little rooms and we used to stay up in those rooms and we were put to bed early and then, like about 8:30, we'd be in bed and then we'd start hearing the Gaelic and the drone, you know. I don't know, my impression of the Irish speech coming upstairs in the bedroom very monotonous, it would almost put you to sleep. They spoke all night long, well into the night. I think they used to break up maybe one or two o'clock. They were hungry for the language and that kind of exchange.

EPILOGUE

The vigorous Gaeltacht of Portland survived for decades due principally to a constant stream of Irish-speaking immigrants. Once immigration started to decrease due to the immigration laws of the 1920s and the decline of the longshore industry, the number of Irish speakers also decreased. And though "they may have been hungry for the language," in the twentieth century, Irish speakers only rarely passed Irish on to the second generation. For Portland's Irish speakers, Irish was an oral language spoken only within a certain network of acquaintances, namely relatives and friends who had been raised in Ireland. In Portland, as in many American cities, the Irish language received no institutional support of any kind, and in such a setting it must have seemed point-less to hand the language down to the next generation. There is no evi-dence to suggest that the Catholic Church and clergy gave any recogni-tion to the language in Portland. Catholic schools and colleges offered no instruction in Irish. Irish was not officially the language of the Portland Longshoremen's Benevolent Society (PLSBS) even though many of its members regularly spoke Irish to each other both on and off the docks. Nor was Irish used in an official capacity by the Ancient Order of Hibernians, another organization to which many Irish immi-grants belonged. As mentioned earlier, there was very little Irish lan-guage material in the Irish American press; and to date no example of Irish printed in Portland has come to light. In spite of the large numbers of Irish speakers in Portland, the Irish government never made any attempt to support the Irish language in the city.

Thus, what was once an energetic Irish-speaking community might have passed into oblivion if it were not for the current on-going project. This study has preserved a permanent record of an active Irish-speaking community in detail that we only wish we had for the nineteenth cen-tury. The tape recordings of our interviews will be available for future generations to hear what the Irish language sounded like in Portland and see what the Irish speakers looked like. In recent years more and more Irish Americans have been interested in learning the ancestral language.[47] Irish language classes have now been taught in Portland for nearly twenty years by Máire Concannon, whose parents emigrated from Cois Fharraige. These classes are held at the Irish Heritage Center, formerly St. Dominic's Church, which has historically played such an important part in Portland's Irish community.

Part of the evidence has been collected in this project but there is more work to be done. As stated above, the children of Irish speakers have a valuable contribution to make as well. Their reminiscences about the Irish-speaking communities of Portland will help to dispel the long-held belief that all Irish immigrants arrived in this country as monolingual English speakers. Work of this kind must be done if we are to have an accurate picture of Irish immigration to this country.

1. Gaeltacht filmmakers, journalists and broadcasters have done some excellent work on Gaeltacht communities in the U.S. Breandán Feiritéar has produced several documentaries on the Kerry Irish speakers in Springfield, Massachusetts in addition to one on Patrick Ferriter, a collector of Irish language material who emigrated to Massachusetts in 1895. Bob Quinn's five-part series "Pobal i mBoston" documented the Connemara-Cois Fharraige-Boston connection and was shown on Radio Telefís Éireann in the early 1990s. A more recent Quinn production chronicled the Connemara settlement in Minnesota in the 1880s. Radio na Gaeltachta has a large archive of interviews that they recorded with Gaeltacht emigrants to North America.

2. Tomas De Bhaldraithe, *The Irish of Cois Fhairrge, Co. Galway, a Phonetic Study* (Dublin: The Dublin Institute for Advanced Studies, 1945), ix, explains that there are two definitions of Cois Fharraige. "Cois Fhairrge," as far as one can ascertain from the people of the Gaedhealtacht of West Galway, is applied to that area that stretches along the coast from about Bearna, itself a few miles west of Galway City, to somewhere about Casla. Some people limit its extension to the districts immediately surrounding the villages in question in the present work, An Teach Mór and An Lochán Beag, which are situated about fifteen miles west of Galway. These villages are on the coast road, and are in the center of Cois Fhairrge, if the name is given its broader interpretation. [Editorial note: De Bhaldraithe (1945) uses the Classical Irish spelling "Cois Fhairrge." Modern standard Irish uses the spelling "Cois Fharraige." Both are pronounced "kush ARR-ig-uh."]

3. Nathaniel Hawthorne, *The American Notebooks* (New Haven, CT: Yale University Press, 1932), 10, as quoted in James H. Mundy, *Hard Times, Hard Men: Maine and the Irish, 1830–1860* (Scarborough, ME: Harp Publications, 1990), 15.

4. For information regarding Irish language publishing in the U.S., see several works by Kenneth E. Nilsen, "Irish Gaelic Literature in the U.S. in the Nineteenth Century," in Marc Shell, ed., *American Babel: Literatures of the United States from Abnaki to Zuni* (Cambridge: Harvard University Press, 2002), 188–218; "The Irish Language in the U.S.," in Michael Glazier, ed., *The Encyclopedia of the Irish in America* (Notre Dame, IN: Notre Dame Press, 1999), 470–74; "The Irish Language in Nineteenth Century New York City," in Ofelia García and Joshua A. Fishman, eds., *The Multilingual Apple: Languages in New York City* (New York: Mouton de Gruyter Publishing, 1997), 52–69; "The Irish Language in New York City 1850–1900," in T. Meagher and R. Bayor, eds., *The New York Irish* (Baltimore: Johns Hopkins University Press, 1995), 252–74; "Thinking of Monday: The Irish Speakers of Portland, Maine," *Éire/Ireland* 25 (1991): 6–19; and "Collecting Celtic Folklore in the United States," in Gordon W. MacLennan, ed., *Proceedings of the First North American Congress of Celtic Studies, 1986* (Ottawa: University of Ottawa, 1988), 55–74.

5. See Mundy, *Hard Times, Hard Men*, Chapter 3, especially 52–54.

6. Michael C. Connolly, "Black Fades to Green: Irish Labor Replaces African-American Labor Along a Major New England Waterfront, Portland, Maine, in the Mid-Nineteenth Century," *Colby Quarterly* 37, no. 4 (December 2001).

7. See Michael C. Connolly, "The Irish Longshoremen of Portland, Maine" (Ph.D. diss., Boston College, 1988), 16–20 for the background on the Portland-Montreal rail link and for Irish immigration at that time: "Chronologically this peak in Irish immigration occurred simultaneously with the rail linkage to Montreal" (37).

8. J. Carbonneau. *Centennial Anniversary St James Catholic Church, Island Pond, Vermont 1871–1971* (Littleton, NH: Courier Printing Co., Inc., 1971), 13.

9. Ibid.

10. Ibid., 14. Until 1858, Portland Catholics would have been buried in "the Catholic ground" at the Western Cemetery, near Cassidy's Hill, or in the Eastern Cemetery, at the foot of Munjoy Hill. By 1858–1861, however, Calvary Cemetery in South Portland was considered "consecrated ground" and would continue to be the main Catholic burial ground for Portland to this day. William B. Jordan, Jr., the local historical expert on Portland's cemeteries, believes that records at Calvary suggest that some Catholics were, in fact, re-interred there from the Western Cemetery.

11. E-mail communication dated January 14, 2003 from Mrs. Mary Coyne who states that, according to family tradition, this Mrs. Sabina Flaherty had first been married to a man named Coyne who died in Ireland, and that Sabina Coyne and her children then emigrated from Spiddal, County Galway. Sabina had a sister in New York, and she and her family stayed with her when they arrived in 1856. The family is not sure when and where Sabina Coyne married Patrick Flaherty. It is believed that Patrick had relatives in Portland, and this would explain why his wife's remains were sent there for burial in 1861. Mrs. Mary Coyne also mentions that some of the Coyne children eventually settled in Lancaster, New Hampshire and Guildhall, Vermont, both of which are on or near the railway line to Island Pond, Vermont.

12. See Matthew Jude Barker, et al., *The Western Cemetery Project 1997–2001: A Celebration of 125 years of service to the Portland Irish-American Community* (Portland: 2001) Appendix A: Catholic Burials in the Western Cemetery, 92. The continuation of the Portland-Island Pond, Vermont connection is suggested in the obituary of Violet C. Coolbrith in the *Portland Press Herald*, 3 April 2003, 10B. Coolbrith was born to Nicholas and Rose O'Gorman in St. Gilles, Province of Quebec, but after a fire destroyed the family home they moved to Island Pond, Vermont, where she was raised. During World War II, Violet served as a welder on the Liberty Ships at the South Portland shipyards and subsequently moved to Long Island, in Casco Bay, where she raised her family. At the time of her death, Rose left two sisters still in residence in Island Pond.

13. Connolly, "The Irish Longshoremen of Portland, Maine," 43.

14. See http://istg.rootsweb.com/1800/hibernian960603.html from the National Archives and Records Administration LDS Microfilm #1404145. Transcribed by Sheila Tate for The Immigrant Ships Transcribers Guild, November 7, 1998.

15. The Maine State Archives website has a searchable index for marriages and deaths in the state of Maine. See http://thor.dafs.state.me.us/pls/archives.

16. For an excellent fictitious portrayal of a "typical" Irish immigrant in Portland at the turn of the twentieth century, see Connolly, "The Irish Longshoremen of Portland, Maine," 107–48. Matthew Barker, in his essay in this book, uncovered an intriguing morsel from 1878 when a "Gaelic prayer group" was formed for those "who can understand the Gaelic language." See *Eastern Argus*, 7 November 1878, 4.

17. Connolly, "The Irish Longshoremen of Portland, Maine," 95.

18. Máire Uí Churraoin, *Máire Phatch Mhóir Uí Churraoin: A Scéal Féin*, Eagarthóir: Diarmaid Ó Gráinne (Baile Átha Cliath: Coiscéim, 1995), 28. Uí

Churraoin, who was born in Cois Fharraige in 1912, says (my translation) "Nobody was going to America when I was eighteen years old" (i.e., in 1930).

19. De Bhaldraithe, *The Irish of Cois Fhairrge*, ix, describes the linguistic and emigration situation he found in Cois Fharraige during World War II: "Cois Fhairrge, apart from the street in the villages of Bearna and An Spidéal, is practically one hundred per cent Irish-speaking . . . The majority of the people understand a certain amount of English, and can manage to carry on their business with outsiders in 'English,' although there are at least two intelligent middle-aged men in Teach Mór, who understand no English. The younger people during the 1930s usually make a much poorer attempt to speak English to the stranger than do their parents, who for the most part have been abroad. The recent mass emigration to England will undoubtedly change the position." See also S. Ó Conghaile, *Cois Fharraige le mo Linnse* (Baile Átha Cliath: Clódhanna, 1974), 16, written in 1960 (my translation): "Until about twenty years ago, Cois Fharraige people did not talk much at all about going to England. It was America they all had in mind when they would think of emigrating. Then during the last war there was plenty of work in England and good money to be earned by men and women. Married men as well as single men went. That is happening ever since then and every autumn and winter a large amount of Cois Fharraige people go to England during the beet season. It is mostly married men who go over to work on the beets and they spend four or five months there. They are happy to have this work and it is good it exists."

20. An interesting anecdote relating to the end of emigration to Portland from Connemara was narrated to me by a couple, natives of Connemara, who emigrated separately to Boston and later married there in the early 1950s. The day before he was to leave for America, the young man visited his fiancée and her family. Upon hearing that the young man was intending to go to Maine, his fiancée's father said: "Ná téirigh go Maine mar níl tada ansin ach seandaoine." ("Don't go to Maine because there is nothing there but old people.")

21. List of Irish Speakers Recorded:

NAME	BORN	PLACE	DEATH	WORK	ARRIVAL
Brown, Jim	c. 1908	CM	1997	Longshore	1930
Cloutier, Barbara	1900	CF	1996	Domestic	c. 1918
Concannon, Catherine	1894	CF	2000	Domestic	1913
Concannon, Steve	1900	CF	2001	Longshore	1920
Costello, Mary	1902	CF	1993	Domestic	c. 1919
Feeney, Joe	1909	CF	1991	Restaurant Work	1955
Folan, Bart	1927	CF	——	Gas Company	1950
Foley, Nan	1897	Portland	1994	Domestic	1915
Foley, Philip	1891	CF	1989	Longshore	1911
Joyce, Sr. Malachy	1909	SF	1994	Domestic, Nun	1930
Keane, Patrick	1932	CF	——	Construction	1960
Kilmartin, Mary	1913	CF	2001	Domestic	1930
Malone, Patrick	1897	CF	1985	Longshore	1923
O'Malley, Patrick	1901	CF	1988	Longshore	1924
O'Toole, Patrick	1892	CF	1989	Railroad, Longshore	1914
Walsh, Nora	1904	CF	1996	Domestic	c. 1920

CF = Cois Fharraige; CM = Corr na Móna; SF = Seana-Faracháin

22. I would like to thank Michael C. Connolly for arranging these interviews. I am also greatly indebted to Mrs. Claire Foley for her support of the project and for arranging, hosting, and participating in several of the interviews. I would also like to thank all those we interviewed and their families for their kind hospitality and support of the project. The five interviewed in English were Claire Foley, Sister Mary de la Salle O'Donnell, Larry Welch, and Mary Joyce, all of Portland, and Bart O'Connor of New York.

23. We were unable to locate any Irish speakers from Connemara, i.e. the area west of Cois Fharraige. Also, inquiries about Aran Islanders in Portland yielded the memory of only one man, known as "Stiofán Árann," and his wife. We have since discovered that the grandmother of Maureen Coyne Norris, Mary Helen Coyne née McDonagh, was from Inishmór on the Aran Islands. She emigrated first to Chicago where she married John J. "Chicago" Coyne from Illauneeragh, an island in Kilkerrin Bay which lies east of Callowfeenish and Carna. They then both moved to Portland, where John became a longshoreman and a member of the PLSBS.

24. See Nilsen, "Thinking of Monday" and "Collecting Celtic Folklore" for descriptions of Pat Malone's folklore repertoire.

25. Irish forms of names are given only if they occur at some point in the recordings.

26. On return emigration to Cois Fharraige, see Seamus Grimes and Michael Connolly, "The Migration Link between Cois Fharraige and Portland, Maine, 1880s to 1920s, *Irish Geography* 22 (1989).

27. Apparently, this is Groveton, New Hampshire. "The village of Groveton owes its existence primarily to the Atlantic and St. Lawrence railway, now known as the Canadian National, which located a station there in 1852." Information from http://www.greatnorthwoods.org/northumberland/history/1969008.htm.

28. This anecdote clearly suggests that the captain of the ship understood Irish. For references to entire shiploads of Irish-speaking emigrants, see Kerby Miller, *Emigrants and Exiles: Ireland and the Irish Exodus to North America* (New York: Oxford University Press, 1985), 298.

29. See Patrick S. Dinneen, *An Irish-English Dictionary* (Dublin: Educational Company of Ireland, 1927), 231, where "cóiste teineadh" is given as the Irish for "locomotive engine."

30. The records of the State of Maine list the marriage of Annie J. [Nan] Conley of Portland to Philip Foley of Portland on November 3, 1920.

31. Most of the Galway Foleys are actually Folans. The current Irish form is Ó Cualáin that apparently derives from MacFhualáin or MacThuathaláin .

32. According to Maine State Archives, Catherine Foley of Portland married Peter F. Conconnon [sic] of Portland on June 14, 1923.

33. For some interesting material on the "American Wake," see Miller, *Emigrants and Exiles*, 556–68.

34. Eyre Square in Galway is where the "spailpíní" from Cois Fharraige and Connemara would assemble to be hired by farmers from East Galway. This was referred to as a "hiring fair." Spailpín is the Irish name for an itinerant farm laborer.

35. Patrick J. Malone of Portland married Margaret Ridge of Portland on April 17, 1929 (Maine State Archives).

36. The Dillingham Act (1921) and the Reed-Johnson Act (1924) drastically curtailed immigration to the U.S. See Connolly, "The Irish Longshoremen of Portland, Maine," 222–26.

37. Ibid., 221.

38. Ibid., Appendix R—PLSBS Presidents (1880–1980).

39. "Country-born" is what the Irish immigrants of Portland called those who were born and raised in the U.S.

40. Anecdotes of this kind are common among bilingual immigrant groups and reflect, of course, the difficulty the older generation had in dealing with a new linguistic atmosphere. I have heard anecdotes of this kind in every Gaeltacht area about members of the older generation who had a poor command of English.

41. See Nilsen, "Thinking of Monday," 10–11. See also the essay in this book by Eileen Eagan and Pat Finn regarding domestic service and other typical occupational niche jobs for Irish women in Portland.

42. The Irish word "adhastar" means a horse's or donkey's halter, or as Steve Concannon translates it, "an ass's head-stole." The word is pronounced "eyester" which is exactly how the English word "oyster" is pronounced in West Galway English. The Irish word for "oyster" is "oistre."

43. See Ó Conghaile, *Cois Fharraige le mo Linnse*, 50–67, for a description of the process of distilling poitín.

44. We met Ceata Bhreathnach at a party held in honor of the Irish speakers of Portland on April 1, 1984 at the home of Dr. Jack Hayden and his wife Margaret (Peggy) née Keane (Peig Ní Chatháin), herself an Irish speaker from Furbo in Cois Fharraige, near Spiddal. Ceata was clearly the matriarch of those remaining Irish speakers in Portland, then numbering around fifty.

45. A cunner is a bottom feeder. Its buckteeth enable it to eat shellfish (crustaceans). It is described by a local fisherman as "bony, but good eating." He called it a "hook polisher"—a fish known to be able to skillfully nibble the bait off the hook without being caught. Thanks to the Tackle Shop on India Street, Portland, for this reference.

46. Breams were very popular in Cois Fharraige and Connemara. Aran fishermen would exchange a load of breams for a load of turf with Connemara boatmen. See Finnín Ní Chonceanainn, *Tomás Bán* (Baile Átha Cliath: Conradh na Gaeilge, 1996).

47. Nancy Stenson cites Portland's Irish-speaking community in "Beagáinín: The Use of Irish Among Immigrants to the United States," *New Hibernia Review/Iris Éireannach Nua* 2, no. 2 (samhradh/summer 1998): 117–18 .

EPILOGUE

They Change Their Sky: The Irish in Maine has presented a multifaceted glimpse at the fortunes of the Irish in this state from their earliest arrival to the present time. It is an inspiring story in which the courage and hope of this group was both tested and rewarded. In this book several themes have been explored. Maine is on the eastern frontier of North America, just as Ireland is on the western frontier of Europe. Frontier areas always present challenges, but the rewards are potentially great for those who succeed. Frontier boundaries change, of course, and as the settlements continued to push further northward and eastward through Maine, different towns and regions experienced this change in their own unique ways.

The Irish in Maine rose to the challenge, whether in Portland, or Lewiston, or Bangor, or Benedicta, or along the coast; they often served as facilitators for other groups that would subsequently arrive. The Irish seemed well-prepared for this task, as they had often been both geographically and politically marginalized in Ireland itself. Coping skills, which were learned in dealing with a socially and politically dominant ruling class in Ireland, were relevant in the New World. Other than African Americans, many of the first of whom came as slaves, the Irish in Maine, as in America as a whole, were often the first non-WASP (white, Anglo-Saxon, Protestant) group to arrive in large numbers. Their marginality was a hurdle, but also a potential advantage. Historians have referred to the choice that the Irish were forced to make—to lead the "outs" or to join the "ins." In the case of Maine, the Irish did both, and did well.

In acting as facilitators for other groups, the Irish were able to use their similarities with the "outs," i.e., a minority religion (Roman Catholicism, or in the case of the earliest arrivals, Presbyterianism), and prejudicial treatment (especially during the nativist outbreaks of the 1850s and 1920s). But there were important distinctions, as well. In religion, the Irish were often able to dominate the hierarchy of the Roman Catholic Church in Maine, New England, and, indeed, America as a whole. In terms of language, even with the findings of Kenneth Nilsen's essay, most Irish were at least somewhat proficient in the use of the English language; certainly they had an advantage over the later-arriving French speakers of the mid-nineteenth century and beyond.

Historian Kerby A. Miller in his two major works on Irish immigration to America, as well as other American historians, has concluded that where no "entrenched elite" existed in the New World, the Irish thrived. Certainly Maine represented just such a place of opportunity. Maine's elites were less dominant than those in more developed areas such as Boston or Philadelphia. It is interesting to speculate whether Maine's Irish had more in common, in this regard, with the Irish in the mid-west and west than with their sisters and brothers just south of Maine along the Atlantic seaboard.

The ultimate success of the Irish in Maine should not be misinterpreted as a "glossed-over" version of history. The struggles were real and they were intense. When this book presents a positive view of these struggles, it is done in the spirit of highlighting a group that faced and dealt with a new and challenging environment ("They change their sky") while not losing their essence or culture ("but not their soul") when they came to America ("who cross the ocean"). When the book presents a negative view, it does so in hopes of highlighting the intensity of this struggle, especially difficult in the mid-nineteenth and early twentieth centuries. If there is any bias toward presenting successes, perhaps this represents the tendency of the authors and the editor to analyze the resiliency of the Irish in Maine over these years, especially considering the humble origins of the vast majority of them. This positive analysis has, perhaps, been the major accomplishment of this book.

Failures, struggles, and conflicts and also part of the story of the Irish in Maine. Although many of these have been addressed in these essays, there are many avenues open for future research in this area of history, both positive and negative. Suggestions for future research and publication would include:

– the Irish experience in Maine as unique or similar to that of the Irish in other states or regions;

– the relationship of the Irish in Maine with other ethnic or racial groups, including areas of conflict, e.g., Franco-American, Italian,

African American, Yankee (WASP) elites, or Yankee non-elites;

– the issue of socio-economic status and class, along with social mobility;

– the Irish role in institutions or occupations, e.g., the Church, politics, business, sports, etc.;

– Irish women in Maine and their uniqueness or similarity with other Irish-American women;

– the Irish experience in other Maine cities, towns, or regions beyond those included in this book;

– the Irish in Maine labor, both organized and unorganized;

– the Irish who ran afoul of the law or legal system, especially concerning alcohol and its abuse;

– the Irish in the arts, broadly defined.

It is hoped that the essays in *They Change Their Sky: The Irish in Maine* will engender important unexplored historical and cultural questions, as well as provide data or alternative explanations for long-held assumptions. To the extent that the authors of *They Change Their Sky* have opened up new areas for future research, their book will find its measure of success.

CONTRIBUTORS

MATTHEW JUDE BARKER is a Portland native and for over twenty years has been a genealogical and historical researcher. He is a part-time employee of the Portland Public Library and the Maine Historical Society (MHS), where you may find him assisting researchers at the Society library on any given Saturday. From 1995 to 1998 he compiled and edited "The Shamrock Connection," a newsletter devoted to Irish heritage in New England. Copies of the newsletter are available at the MHS. He has had numerous articles published on local and Irish history, including pieces in the *Journal of the Galway West Family History Society* and *Portland Magazine*. His history of Saint Dominic's Church was abridged and published in 1997 in *Saint Dominic's: 175 Years of Memories, 1822–1997*. Barker was a major contributor to *The Western Cemetery Project*, published in 2002 by the Ancient Order of Hibernians (Division 1, Portland, Maine). He is currently working on a major social history of the Portland Irish.

MARGARET BUKER JAY grew up in the Lewiston-Auburn area, graduating from Edward Little High School in Auburn and Bates College in Lewiston. At Bates, her undergraduate thesis was "The Greenback Labor Party in Maine." While a graduate student in history at the University of Virginia, she began a research study on the social mobility of day laborers in Lewiston, Maine during the early decades of the city's industrialization and urban transformation, 1850–1880. This research led to the publication of "The Irish in Lewiston: Social Mobility on the Urban Frontier," *Maine Historical Society Quarterly* 13, no. 1A (Special Edition, 1973): 3-25. Following her graduate studies, Buker Jay moved to Connecticut and participated in several research projects with the Connecticut Humanities Council. In 1989 she completed a Master of Divinity degree at Yale, was ordained in the United Church of Christ in 1990, and has served since in both local church and conference ministries in Connecticut. She is currently serving the First Congregational Church of Wallingford, Connecticut as Minister of Outreach and Program Development. In addition to the update of her research paper on the Irish in Lewiston, Buker Jay is currently pursuing a research and writing project on the role of laywomen in the Congregational Church in the eighteenth and nineteenth centuries.

MICHAEL C. CONNOLLY is a lifelong resident of Portland's Munjoy Hill and the grandson of a charter member of the Portland Longshoremen's Benevolent Society, a predominantly Irish labor union founded in 1880. He is Associate Professor of History and former Director of the Honors Program at Saint Joseph's College in Standish, Maine. His Ph.D. from Boston College (1988) was largely based on research and a dissertation on these Irish longshoremen. Two of his most recent publications deal with that subject: "Black Fades to Green: Irish Labor Replaces Afro-American Labor Along a Major New England Waterfront, Portland, Maine in the Mid-Nineteenth Century," *Colby Quarterly* 37, no. 4 (December 2001): 357–73; and "To 'Make this Port Union All Over': Longshore Militancy in Portland, 1911–1913," *Maine History* 41, no. 1 (spring 2001): 41–60. In the spring of 2004 he taught for the Semester at Sea program on its around-the-world floating university/ship, the *Universe Explorer*. *They Change Their Sky* is his first book.

EILEEN EAGAN is an Associate Professor of History at the University of Southern Maine. She received her B.A. from D'Youville College in Buffalo, New York, her M.A. in History from the University of Wisconsin-Milwaukee, and her Ph.D. in History from Temple University. At USM she teaches in the History Department and is a member of the Women's Studies Council. In addition to teaching twentieth-century U.S. history and the history of women in the U.S., she has taught "Crossing Borders: Irish Women's Migration to America." The author of *Class, Culture and the Classroom: The Student Peace Movement in the 1930s* (Temple University Press), her recent research has focused on the experiences of Irish and Irish-American women in Maine, focusing on the intersection of gender, class, and ethnicity. She is the co-author, with Patricia Finn, of "From Galway to Gorham's Corner: Irish Women in Portland, Maine" in *Of Place and Gender: Women in Maine History*

(Orono: University of Maine Press, forthcoming 2004), and of "The Irish in Maine" in Michael Glazier, ed., *The Encyclopedia of the Irish in America* (South Bend, Indiana: University of Notre Dame Press, 1999). Her other current research is in the area of public memory and historic commemoration. Her article "Immortalizing Women: Finding Meaning in Public Sculpture" is included in Polly Kaufman and Katharine Corbett, eds., *Her Past Around Us* (Krieger, 2003). She is part of a group that has developed the Portland Women's History Trail.

PATRICIA FINN is the co-author, with Eileen Eagan, of "Galway to Gorham" in *Of Place and Gender: Women in Maine History* (Orono: University of Maine Press, forthcoming 2004). Finn is also one of the co-founders of the Portland Women's History Trail and over the last six years has unfailingly piloted large and small groups of people up and down the brick-lined sidewalks of the city of Portland conveying recent research. Finn is currently enrolled in the Master of Science program in adult education in USM's College of Education, where she also serves as a teaching assistant. She is employed as a staff person in the University of Southern Maine History Department.

GARY W. LIBBY was born in Portland and educated in the Portland public schools. In 1969 he received a B.A. in political science from the University of Southern Maine, and in 1973 a J.D. from Duke University School of Law. He also received degrees from the Episcopal Theological School and Georgetown University School of Law's LL.M. program. Since 1976 he has been engaged in private law practice in Portland. Libby is a Trustee of the Portland Water District and the Maine Historical Society, which he has served as Secretary of the Board of Trustees. In 2003 he helped to coordinate a successful conference at the MHS on the Chinese in Maine, resulting in the compilation of "Biographical Sketches of Maine's Chinese" (2003, MHS Collections).

EDWARD T. McCARRON is Associate Professor and Chair of the History Department at Stonehill College, North Easton, Massachusetts. He holds a Ph.D. in Early American History from the University of New Hampshire. He has published several works on Irish immigration and early New England, including "In Pursuit of the 'Maine' Chance: The North Family of County Offaly and New England, 1700–1776," in

Offaly History and Society (1998). He is also co-author, with Richard B. Finnegan, of *Ireland: Historical Echoes, Contemporary Politics* (Westview Press, 2000). He has recently moved with his wife Fidelma and their family into a home in the Munjoy Hill area of Portland.

FIDELMA MCCARRON is an independent scholar living in Portland, Maine. She holds a B.A. in Archaeology and Old Irish from University College, Dublin. She is author of two essays: "The Cot Fisherman of the River Nore," and, with John Mannion, "Old World Antecedents, New World Adaptations: Inistioge Immigrants in Newfoundland." Both essays appear in William Nolan and Kevin Whelan, eds., *Kilkenny History and Society: Interdisciplinary Essays in the History of an Irish County* (Dublin: Geography Publications, 1990). She is a native of Drogheda, County Louth, and grew up in a family that owned and operated a traditional Irish pub within a stone's throw of the River Boyne.

KENNETH E. NILSEN is a professor of Celtic Studies and chairman of the Department of Celtic Studies at Saint Francis Xavier University in Antigonish, Nova Scotia. He received his doctorate in Celtic Studies from Harvard Unversity. His major field of research involves the Celtic languages in North America. He has made extensive audio- and video-recordings of Irish and Scottish Gaelic speakers throughout the northeastern United States and eastern Canada. He has published articles in journals such as *Éigse, Éire-Ireland, Béaloideas, Harvard Celtic Colloquium* and *Celtica* and in collections such as *The New York Irish* (Baltimore: The Johns Hopkins University Press, 1995), *The Multilingual Apple: Languages in New York City* (New York: Mouton de Gruyter Publ., 1997), 52–69; *The Encyclopedia of the Irish in America* (Notre Dame, IN: Notre Dame University Press, 1999), 470–74; *and American Babel: Literatures of the United States from Abnaki to Zuni* (Cambridge, MA: Harvard University Press, 2002), 188–218. A previously published essay on Portland appeared as "Thinking of Monday: The Irish-Speakers of Portland, Maine," *Éire-Ireland* 25, no. 1 (spring 1990): 6–19.

R. STUART WALLACE of Plymouth, New Hampshire holds a Ph.D. in American History from the University of New Hampshire, where his dissertation topic was "The Scotch-Irish of Provincial New Hampshire."

Dr. Wallace has served as Editor of the magazine *Historical New Hampshire*, Director of the New Hampshire Historical Society, and Director of the New Hampshire Division of Historical Resources, where he also served as the State Historic Preservation Officer. He also served as the Director of the London Town House and Gardens in Maryland, and as Director of the Christa McAuliffe Planetarium in Concord, NH. He has published several articles in scholarly journals, and most recently, contributed to the *Encyclopedia of the Irish in America*, published by the University of Notre Dame Press. He currently is Assistant Professor of History at the New Hampshire Technical Institute.

BIBLIOGRAPHY

Note: [MHS] at the end of an entry indicates that the item can be found at the Maine Historical Society, Portland.

Aalen, F. H. A., Kevin Whelan, and Mathew Stout. *Atlas of the Rural Irish Landscape*. Cork: Cork University Press, 1997.

Abbott, Cheryl, and J. Fraser Cocks, III, eds. *James Augustine Healy Collection of Nineteenth and Twentieth Century Literature*. Waterville, ME: Colby College, 1978.

Adams, William Forbes. *Ireland and Irish Emigration to the New World, From 1815 to the Famine*. New York: Russell and Russell, 1932.

Agger, Lee. *Women of Maine*. Portland, Maine: Guy Gannett Publishing Co., 1982.

Akagi, Roy Hidemichi. *The Town Proprietors of the New England Colonies*. Philadelphia: University of Pennsylvania Press, 1924.

Akenson, Donald. *The Irish Education Experience: The National System of Education in Ireland in the Nineteenth Century*. Toronto: University of Toronto Press, 1970.

————. *The Irish of Ontario: A Study in Rural History*. Montreal: McGill-Queens University Press, 1984.

Albion, Robert G. *Forests and Sea Power: The Timber Problems of the Royal Navy, 1652–1862*. Cambridge: Harvard University Press, 1926.

————. "The Port of Portland, Maine." *Ships and the Sea* 4, no. 22 (August 1954).

Albion, Robert G., William A. Baker, and Benjamin W. Labaree. *New England and the Sea*. Middletown, CT: Wesleyan University Press, 1972.

Allan, James Paul. "Catholics in Maine: A Social Geography." Ph.D. diss., Syracuse University, 1970.

Allen, Frederick L. *Only Yesterday: An Informal History of the Nineteen-Twenties*. New York: Harper and Row, 1964.

Allen, Neal W., Jr., ed. *Province and Court Records of Maine* 6. Portland, ME: Maine Historical Society, 1975.

Allin, Lawrence C. "Maine's Granite Industry." In *Maine: The Pine Tree State from Prehistory to the Present*, edited by Richard W. Judd, Edwin Churchill, and Joel Eastman, 275–80. Orono: University of Maine Press, 1995.

————. "Shipping and Shipbuilding in the Period of Ascendancy." In *Maine: The Pine Tree State from Prehistory to the Present*, edited by Richard W. Judd, Edwin Churchill, and Joel Eastman, 297–305. Orono: University of Maine Press, 1995.

Allswang, John. *A House for All Peoples*. Lexington: University of Kentucky Press, 1971.

American Commission on Conditions in Ireland. *American Commission on Conditions in Ireland: Interim Report*. By Commission, 1921.

Amory, Thomas C. *Life of James Sullivan with Selections of His Writings.* Boston, MA: Phillips, Sampson, and Co., 1855.

———. *The Military Services and Public Life of Major John Sullivan of the American Revolutionary Army.* Boston, MA: Wiggen and Lunt, 1868.

Anbinder, Tyler. *Five Points.* New York: The Free Press, 2001.

———. "From Famine to Five Points: Lord Lansdowne's Irish Tenants Encounter North America's Most Notorious Slum." *American Historical Review* 107, no. 2 (April 2002).

———. *Nativism and Slavery: The Northern Know Nothings and the Politics of the 1850s.* New York: Oxford University Press, 1992.

Anderson, Hayden L. V. *Canals and Waterways of Maine.* Portland, ME: Maine Historical Society, 1982.

Anderson, Will. *Was Baseball Really Invented in Maine?* Portland, ME: By author, 1988. [MHS]

Angus, Murray E. "The Politics of the 'Short Line.'" Master's thesis, University of New Brunswick, 1958.

Anti Negro Riots in the North, 1863. 1863. Reprint, Salem, NH: Ayer Company Publishers, 1969.

Appel, J. J. "From Shanties to Lace Curtain: Irish Image in Puck." *Comparative Studies in Society and History,* vol. 13 (October 1971).

Appleby, R. Scot. *Church and Age Unite: The Modernist Impulse in American Catholicism.* Notre Dame, IN: University of Notre Dame Press, 1992.

Asher, Robert. "Union Nativism and the Immigrant Response." *Labor History* 23, no. 3 (1982).

Ashlet, Robert P. "The St. Alban's Raid." *Civil War Times Illustrated* 6 (November 1967): 18–27.

Augustine, H. R. *In the Footprints of Father Matthew.* Dublin: Gill and Son, 1947.

Babcock, Robert. "Economic Development in Portland (Me.) and Saint John (N.B.) During the Age of Iron and Steam, 1850–1914." *American Review of Canadian Studies* 9 (spring 1979): 3–37.

———. *Gompers in Canada: A Study in American Continentalism Before the First World War.* Toronto: University of Toronto Press, 1974.

———. "The Rise and Fall of Portland's Waterfront 1850–1920." *Maine Historical Society Quarterly* 22, no. 2 (fall 1982): 63–98.

Bailyn, Bernard. *The People of British North America.* New York: Vintage Books, 1988.

Baker, Donald G. *Race, Ethnicity and Power: A Comparative Study.* Boston: Routledge and Kegan Paul, 1983.

Baker, Richard L. *Historical Synopsis of Economic Development in Portland, Maine.* Portland: 1959.

Baker, William. *A Maritime History of Bath, Maine and the Kennebec River Region.* Bath, ME: Marine Research Society of Bath, 1973.

Ball, Joseph H. *Government-Subsidized Union Monopoly: A Study of Labor Practices in the Shipping Industry.* Washington, DC: Labor Policy Association, 1966.

Banks, Ronald F. *A History of Maine: A Collection Readings on the History of Maine, 1600–1970.* Dubuque, IA: Kendall/Hunt Publishing Company, 1973.

———. *Maine Becomes a State: The Movement to Separate Maine from*

Massachusetts, 1785–1820. Somersworth, NH: New Hampshire Publishing Company, 1973.

———. *Maine During the Federal and Jeffersonian Period: A Bibliographical Guide*. Portland: Maine Historical Society, 1974.

Banton, Michael. *Racial and Ethnic Competition*. Cambridge: Cambridge University Press, 1983.

Barbrook, Alec. *God Save the Commonwealth: An Electoral History of Massachusetts*. Amherst: University of Massachusetts Press, 1973.

Barker, Matthew J. "A Collection of Brief Biographies of Early Portland Irish." In *The Western Cemetery Project: A Celebration of 125 Years of Service to the Portland Irish-American Community*, edited by Paul O'Neil, et al. (The Daniel O'Connell O'Donoughue Division – Division 1 of the AOH.) South Portland: Waterfront Graphics and Printing, 2001. [MHS]

———. *The Descendants of Patrick Greaney of Cummer Parish*: Galway, Ireland, 1800–1989. South Portland, ME: 1989. [Manuscript at MHS]

———. "From Galway to Maine: The Story of an Immigrant Family." *Galway Roots/Clanna na Gaillimhe: Journal of the Galway Family History Society* 4 (1996): 21–22.

———. "John Ford and The Feeney Family of Galway and Portland, Maine." *Galway Roots/Clanna na Gaillimhe*, vol. 5 (1998).

———. "The Last Time We Shared Stone Soup." *Portland Monthly Magazine* (October 2000).

———. "The Maine Summer of Eugene O'Neill." *Portland Monthly Magazine* 18, no. 3 (May 2003): 25–31.

———. "Munjoy Hill's Unsinkable Kitty Kentuck." *Portland Monthly Magazine* (December 1996).

———, ed. "The Shamrock Connection." Newsletter/magazine. 1995–1998. [MHS]

Barnes, Albert S. *Greater Portland Celebration 350*. Portland: Gannett Books, 1984.

Barnes, Charles B. *The Longshoremen*. 1915. Reprint, New York: Arno Press, 1977.

Barrett, Andrea. *Ship Fever and Other Stories*. New York: Norton, 1996.

Barron, Hal S. *Those Who Stayed Behind: Rural Society in Nineteenth-Century New England*. New York: Cambridge University Press, 1984.

Barry, Coleman. *The Catholic Church and German Americans*. Milwaukee: Bruce, 1953.

Barry, Tom. *Guerilla Days in Ireland*. Dublin: Anvil Books, 1981.

Barry, William David. "The Brush'uns: A Portland, Maine Art Group." *Maine Antique Digest* (April 1979): 18c–19c. [MHS]

———. "Bryce McLellan and his Children, 1720–1776." Portland: University of Southern Maine, 1973. [MHS]

———. "Fires of Bigotry." *Down East Magazine* 36, no. 3 (October 1989): 44–47, 77–78.

———. *The History of Sweetser Children's Home*: A Century and a Half of Service to Maine Children. Portland, ME: The Anthoensen Press, 1988.

———. "James Healy, We Hardly Knew You." *Portland Monthly Magazine* 9, no. 3 (May 1994): 9–17.

———. *A Passionate Intensity: The Life and Work of Dorothy Healy*. Portland: The Baxter Society, 1992. [Multiple authors, co-edited with Gael May McKibben.]

———. *Rum, Riot and Reform: Maine and the History of American Drinking*. Portland: Maine Historical Society, 1998.

———. "A Vignetted History of Portland Business, 1632–1982." Portland: The Newcomen Society in North America, no. 1176, 1982.

Barry, William David, and Arthur J. Gerrier. *Munjoy Hill Historic Guide*. Portland: Greater Portland Landmarks, 1992.

Barry, William David, and John Holverson. *The Revolutionary McLellans: A Bicentennial Project of the Portland Museum of Art*. Portland, ME: Portland Museum of Art, 1977. [MHS]

Barry, William David, and Stephanie Philbrick. "From the Collections: The Persis Sibley Andrews Black Diaries, Manuscript Collection 206." *Maine History* 40 (winter 2001–02): 333–36. [MHS]

Barth, Frederick. *Ethnic Groups and Boundaries: The Social Organization of Cultural Difference*. Boston: Little, Brown, 1969.

Bauerle, Ruth. *James Joyce Songbook*. New York: Garland Publishing Co., 1982.

Bayor, Ronald, and Timothy J. Meagher, eds. *New York Irish*. Baltimore: Johns Hopkins University Press, 1996.

Beale, Howard K., ed. *Diary of Gideon Welles, 1861–1869*. New York: W. W. Norton & Co., 1960.

Beals, Carleton. *Brass-Knuckle Crusade: The Great Know-Nothing Conspiracy, 1820–1860*. New York: Hastings House, 1960.

Beattie, Elizabeth. *Obligation and Opportunity: Single Maritime Women in Boston, 1870–1930*. Montreal: McGill-Queen's University Press, 2000.

Beatty, Jack. *The Rascal King: The Life and Times of James Curley, 1874–1958*. Reading, MA: Addison-Wesley, 1992.

Bedford, Henry. *Socialism and the Workers in Massachusetts, 1886–1912*. Amherst: University of Massachusetts, 1966.

Beem, Edgar Allen, "Carry on Francis: When You Talk to F. M. O'Brien You're Talking to History." *Maine Times*, 17 April 1987. [MHS]

Belcher to Richard Waldron, 5 June 1732. *Collections of the Massachusetts Historical Society* 56. Boston: By the Society, 1893. [MHS Collections]

Belknap, Jeremy. *The History of New-Hampshire*. 3 vols. Dover, NH: J. Mann and J. K. Remick, 1812.

Bell, Daniel. "The Racket-ridden Longshoremen." *Dissent* 6 (autumn 1959).

Bennett, David H. *The Party of Fear*. Chapel Hill: University of North Carolina Press, 1988.

Bennett, Sari J., and Carville V. Earle. "Labor Power and Locality in the Gilded Age: The Northeastern United States, 1881–1894." *Social History* (Canada) 15, no. 30 (1982).

Bergen, Paul. "Occupation, Household and Family Among the Irish of Nineteenth Century Dover, New Hampshire." Master's thesis, University of New Hampshire, 1989.

Berlanstein, Lenard, ed. *Rethinking Labor history: Essays on Discourse and Class Analysis*. Urbana: University of Illinois Press, 1993.

Berlin, Ira. *Slaves Without Masters: The Free Negro in the Antebellum South*. New York: Pantheon Books, 1974.

Berlin, Ira, and Ronald Hoffman, eds. *Slavery and Freedom in the Age of the American Revolution*. Charlottesville: University of Virginia Press, 1983.

Bernstein, Irving. *The Lean Years: A History of the American Worker, 1920–1933*. Baltimore: Penguin Books, 1966.

Bernstein, Iver. *The New York Draft Riots: Their Significance for American Society and Politics in the Age of the Civil War*. New York: Oxford University Press, 1990.

Betit, Kyle J., and Dwight A. Radford. *Ireland, a Genealogical Guide for North Americans*. Salt Lake City, UT: The Irish at Home and Abroad, 1995.

Betts, John R. "The Negro and the New England Conscience in the Days of John Boyle O'Reilly." *Journal of Negro History* 51 (October 1966): 246–61.

Bew, Paul. *Land and the National Question in Ireland*. Atlantic Highlands: Humanities Press, 1979.

Bibeault, Real. "Le Syndicat ces Debardeurs de Montreal" [A study of ILA local 375]. Master's thesis, University of Montreal, 1954.

Billington, Ray Allen. *The Origins of Nativism in the United States, 1800–1844*. New York: Arno Press, 1974.

———. *The Protestant Crusade, 1800–1860: A Study of the Origins of American Nativism*. New York: Macmillan, 1938.

Birmingham, Stephen. *Real Lace: America's Rich Irish*. New York: Harper and Row, 1973.

Biscoe, Mark Wyman. "Damariscotta-Newcastle Ships and Shipbuilding." Master's thesis, University of Maine at Orono, 1967.

Blanchet, Joseph P. *The View from Shanty Pond: An Irish Immigrant's Look at Life in a New England Mill Town*. Charlotte, VT: Shanty Pond Press, 1999.

Bland, Sister Joan. *Hibernian Crusade, The Story of the Catholic Abstinence Union of America*. Washington, DC: Catholic University Press, 1951.

Blanshard, Paul. *The Irish and Catholic Power: An American Interpretation*. Boston: Beacon Press, 1953.

Bledstein, Burton J. *The Cult of Professionalism: The Middle Class and the Development of Higher Education in America*. New York: W. W. Norton & Company, 1978.

Blessing, Patrick J. *The Irish in America: A Guide to the Literature and Manuscript Collections*. Washington, DC: The Catholic University Press, 1992.

———. "'West Among Strangers': Irish Migration to California, 1850 to 1880." Ph.D. diss., University of California at Los Angeles, 1981.

Blodgett, Geoffrey. *The Gentle Reformers: Massachusetts Democrats in the Cleveland Era*. Cambridge: Harvard University Press, 1966.

———. "Yankee Leadership in a Divided City." In *Boston 1700–1980: The Evolution of Urban Politics*, edited by Ronald Formisano and Constance Burns. Westport, CT: Greenwood Press, 1984.

Bodnar, John. *Immigration and Industrialization: Ethnicity in an American Mill Town, 1870–1940*. Pittsburgh: University of Pittsburgh Press, 1977.

———. *Remaking America: Public Memory, Commemoration and Patriotism in the Twentieth Century*. Princeton, NJ: Princeton University Press, 1966.

———. *The Transplanted: A History of Immigrants in Urban America*. Bloomington: Indiana University Press, 1985.

Bodnar, John, Roger Simon, and Michael Weber. *Lives of Their Own: Blacks, Italians, and Poles in Pittsburgh, 1900–1960*. Urbana: University of Illinois Press, 1982.

Bogdanovich, Peter. *John Ford*. Berkeley: University of California Press, 1968.

Boller, Paul F. *Presidential Campaigns*. New York: Oxford University Press, 1996.

Bolster, W. Jeffrey. *Black Jacks: African American Seamen in the Age of Sail.* Cambridge: Harvard University Press, 1997.

———. "An Inner Diaspora: Black Sailors Making Selves." In *Through a Glass Darkly: Reflections on Personal Identity in Early America,* edited by Ronald Hoffman, Mechal Sobel, and Fredrika J. Teute, 419–48. Chapel Hill: University of North Carolina Press, 1997.

———. "'To Feel like a Man': Black Seamen in the Northern States, 1800–1860." *Journal of American History* 76 (March 1990): 1173–99.

Bolton, Charles Knowles. *Scotch Irish Pioneers in Ulster and America.* Boston: Bacon and Brown, 1910.

Bolton, Ethel Stanwood. *Immigrants to New England, 1700–1775.* Salem: The Essex Institute, 1931.

Booth, Glenn Gordon. "The Maine Door to Canada: Immigration to Canada via Portland, Maine, 1907–1930." Master's thesis, University of Maine (Orono), 1995.

Boulger, John. *Handbook of Irish Genealogy.* Dublin: Heraldic Artists, Ltd., 1984.

Bourke, Joanna. *Husbandry to Housewifery: Women, Economic Change, and Homework in Ireland, 1890–1914.* New York: Clarendon Press, 1993.

Boyce, D. George. *Nationalism in Ireland.* Baltimore: The Johns Hopkins University Press, 1982.

———, and Alan O'Day, eds. *The Making of Modern Irish History: Revisionism and Recent Controversy.* London: Routledge, 1996.

Boyd, Andrew. *Holy War in Belfast.* Tralee, Ireland: Anvil Books, 1969.

———. *The Rise of Irish Trade Unions, 1729–1970.* Tralee, Ireland: Anvil Books, 1972.

Boyle, Harold. *The Best of Boyle.* Portland, ME: Guy Gannett Publishing Co., 1980.

———. "When the Klan Campaigned in Maine." *Maine Sunday Telegram,* 23 April 1978.

Brault, Gerard. *The French-Canadian Heritage in New England.* Hanover, NH: University Press of New England, 1986.

Breton, Raymond, and Pierre Savard, eds. *The Quebec and Acadian Diaspora in North America.* Toronto: Multicultural History Society of Ontario, 1982.

Breton, Rita Mae. "Red Scare: A Study of Maine Nativism, 1919–1925." Master's thesis, University of Maine (Orono), 1972.

Brody, David. *Workers in Industrial America: Essays on the Twentieth Century Struggle.* New York: Oxford University Press, 1980.

Brown, Irene Quenzler, and Richard D. Brown. *The Hanging of Ephraim Wheeler.* Cambridge, MA: Harvard University Press, 2003.

Brown, Raymond. *Waterfront Organization in Hull, 1870–1900.* Hull, England: University of Hull, 1972.

Brown, Richard H. *I am of Ireland.* New York: Harper and Row, 1974.

Brown, Stewart J., and David W. Miller. *Piety and Power in Ireland 1760–1960.* Belfast, Northern Ireland: The Institute of Irish Studies at The Queen's University, 2000.

Brown, Thomas N. *Irish American Nationalism, 1870–1890.* Philadelphia: J. B. Lippincott, 1966.

———. "The Origin and Character of Irish-American Nationalism." In *Irish Nationalism and the American Contribution,* edited by Lawrence McCaffrey. New York: Arno Press, 1976.

Browne, Henry J. *The Catholic Church and the Knights of Labor.* Washington, DC: Catholic University Press, 1949.

Brundage, David. *The Making of Western Labor Radicalism: Denver's Organized Workers, 1878–1908.* Urbana: University of Illinois Press, 1994.

Buchanan, Roger B. *History of the 1934 Waterfront Strike in Portland, Oregon.* Master's thesis, University of Oregon (Eugene), 1964.

Buchley, R. W., R. M. Drake, and Lester Breslow. "Height, Weight, and Mortality in a Population of Longshoremen." *Journal of Chronic Disease* 7, no. 5 (1958).

Buckley, Patrick J. *The New York Irish: Their View of American Foreign Policy, 1914–1921.* New York: Arno Press, 1976.

Buel, Charles Chauncey. "The Workers of Worcester: Social Mobility and Ethnicity in a New England City." Ph.D. diss., New York University, 1974.

Buenker, John. *Urban Liberalism and Progressive Reform.* New York: Charles Scribner's Sons, 1973.

Buhle, Paul. "The Knights of Labor in Rhode Island." *Radical History Review* 17 (1978).

Buker Jay, Margaret. "The Irish in Lewiston, Maine: A Search for Security on the Urban Frontier, 1850–1880." *Maine Historical Society Quarterly* 13, no. 1/A (Special edition, 1973): 3–25.

Bukowcyk, John. *"And My Children Did Not Know Me": A History of Polish Americans.* Bloomington: Indiana University Press, 1987.

Bunker, Benjamin. *Bunker's Text Book of Political Deviltry, With Jack-Knife Illustrations, Maine's Small Bore Politicians, and Facts About Temperance Hypocrites.* Waterville, ME: Kennebec Democrat Office, 1889.

Bunting, W. H. *A Day's Work: A Sampler of Historic Maine Photographs 1860–1920, Part I.* Gardiner, ME: Tilbury House Publishers and Maine Preservation, 1997. [MHS]

————. *A Day's Work: A Sampler of Historic Maine Photographs 1860–1920, Part II.* Gardiner, ME: Tilbury House Publishers and Maine Preservation, 2000. [MHS]

————. *Portrait of a Port: Boston, 1852–1914.* Cambridge: The Belknap Press of Harvard University Press, 1971.

Burchell, R. A. "The Historiography of the American Irish." *Immigrant and Minorities* (Great Britain) 1, no. 3 (1982).

————. *The San Francisco Irish: 1848–1880.* Berkeley: University of California Press, 1980.

Bush, Edward F. "The Canadian 'Fast Lane' on the North Atlantic, 1886–1915." Master's thesis, Carleton University, 1969.

Butler, Joyce. "Rising Like a Phoenix: Commerce in Southern Maine, 1775–1830." In *Agreeable Situations: Society, Commerce, and Art in Southern Maine, 1780–1830,* edited by Laura Fecych Sprague. Kennebunk, ME: The Brick Store Museum, 1987.

Butler, Richard J. *Dock Walloper.* New York: G. P. Putnam's Sons, 1933.

Byrne, Cyril, and Margaret Harry. *Talamh an Eisc: Canadian and Irish Essays.* Halifax, Nova Scotia: Nimbus Publishing, 1986.

Byrne, Frank L. *Prophet of Prohibition: Neal Dow and His Crusade.* Gloucester, MA: Peter Smith, 1969.

Cahill, Robert Ellis. *The Old Irish of New England.* Peabody, MA: Chandler-Smith, 1985. [MHS]

Cahill, Thomas. *How the Irish Saved Civilization*. New York: Anchor Books, 1995.

Cahill, Thomas P. *A Short Sketch of the Life and Achievements of Captain Jeremiah O'Brien of Machias, Maine*. Worcester, MA: Harrigan Press, Inc., 1936.

Callahan, Bob, ed. *The Big Book of American Irish Culture*. New York: 1987.

Cameron, Ardis. *Radicals of the Worst Sort: Laboring Women in Lawrence, Massachusetts, 1860–1912*. Urbana: University of Illinois Press, 1993.

Candee, Richard. "John Langdon's Unusual Census of 'Mechanical Labor': The 1820 Artisans of Wiscasset, Jefferson, Alna, Edgecomb, and Whitefield, Maine." *Maine Historical Society Quarterly* 27, no. 1 (summer 1987): 24–37.

———. "Maine Towns, Maine People." In *Maine in the Early Republic: From Revolution to Statehood*, edited by Charles E. Clark, James S. Leamon, and Karen Bowden. Hanover, NH: University Press of New England, 1988.

Canny, Nicholas P., ed. *Europeans on the Move: Studies on European Migration, 1500–1800*. New York: Oxford University Press, 1994.

———. "The Ideology of English Colonization: From Ireland to America." *The William and Mary Quarterly* 30, no. 4 (October 1973): 575–98.

———. *Kingdom and Colony: Ireland in the Atlantic World, 1560–1800*. Baltimore and London: The Johns Hopkins University Press, 1988.

Carbonneau, J. *Centennial Anniversary St. James Catholic Church, Island Pond, Vermont 1871–1971*. Littleton, NH: Courier Printing Co., Inc., 1971.

Carola, Leslie Conron, ed. *The Irish, a Treasury of Art and Literature*. New York: Hugh Lauter Revin Associates, Inc., 1993.

Carroll, Aileen M. *The Cathedral of the Immaculate Conception and Its Bishops* (Written for the Observance of Its 125th Anniversary Celebration, 8 and 11 December 1994). Portland, ME: Diocese of Portland, 1994. [MHS]

———. *Heavenly Light: The Stained Glass Windows of the Cathedral of the Immaculate Conception*. Portland, ME: Dale Rand Printing, 1996. [MHS]

Carroll, Francis M. *American Opinion and the Irish Question, 1910–1923: A Study in Opinion and Policy*. New York: St. Martin's Press, 1978.

———. *A Good and Wise Measure: The Search for the Canadian-American Boundary, 1783–1842*. Toronto: University of Toronto Press, 2001.

———. *Money for Ireland: Finance Diplomacy, Politics, and the First Dail Eireann Loans, 1919–1936*. Westport, CT: Praeger Publishers, 2002.

Carter, Richard. "Behind the Waterfront Rackett." *Compass* (December 1951).

Cartwright, Frederick F. *Disease and History*. New York: Crowell, 1972.

Catholic Diocese of Portland. "Memorable Events of the Catholic Church in Portland." *Maine Catholic Historical Magazine* 8 (1919–1928).

Chafe, Edward. "A New Life on 'Uncle Sam's Farm': Newfoundlanders in Massachusetts, 1846–1859." Master's thesis, Memorial University (St. John's), 1982.

Chambers, J. S. *The Conquest of Cholera*. New York: Macmillan Co., 1938.

Chaplin, Ralph. *Wobbly*. Chicago: University of Chicago Press, 1948.

Chase, Fanny S. *Wiscasset in Pownalborough*. Portland: The Anthoensen Press, 1967.

Child, Irwin. *Italian or American? The Second Generation in Conflict*. New Haven: Yale University Press, 1943.

Chinnici, Joseph. *Devotion to the Holy Spirit in American Catholicism*. New York: Paulist Press, 1985.

———. *Living Stones: The History and Structure of Catholic Spiritual Life in the United States*. New York: Macmillan, 1989.

Churchill, Edwin A. "Too Great the Challenge: The Birth and Death of Falmouth, Maine, 1624–1676." Ph.D. diss., University of Maine (Orono), 1979.

Clancy, Mary, John Cunningham, and Alf MacLochlain, eds. *The Emigrant Experience*. Galway: Galway Labour History.

Clark, Charles E. *The Eastern Frontier: The Settlement of Northern New England, 1610–1763*. New York: Alfred A. Knopf, 1970.

———. *Maine: A Bicentennial History*. New York: Norton Publishing Company (The States and the Nation Series), 1977.

———. *Maine During the Colonial Period: A Bibliographical Guide*. Portland: Maine Historical Society, 1974.

Clark, Charles E., James S. Leamon, and Karen Bowden, eds. *Maine in the Early Republic: From Revolution to Statehood*. Hanover, NH: University Press of New England, 1988.

Clark, Dennis. *Hibernia America: The Irish and Regional Cultures*. Westport, CT: Greenwood Press, 1976.

———. *The Irish in Philadelphia: Ten Generations of Urban Experience*. Philadelphia: Temple University Press, 1974.

———. *Irish Relations: Trials of and Immigrant Tradition*. East Brunswick: Associated Press, 1982.

Clark, Roy. *Longshoremen*. North Pomfret, VT: David and Charles, 1974.

Clark, Samuel. *Social Origins of the Irish Land Warrior*. Princeton, NJ: Princeton University Press, 1979.

Clark, Wallace. *Rathlin: Its Island Story*. Coleraine: Northwest Books, 1988.

Clarke, Brian. *Piety and Nationalism: Lay Voluntary Associations and the Creation of an Irish Catholic Community in Toronto, 1850–1895*. Toronto: McGill Queen's University Press, 1993.

Clarke, Kathleen. *Revolutionary Woman*. Dublin: O'Brien Press, Ltd., 1991.

Clayton, W. Woodford. *History of Cumberland County, Maine*. Philadelphia, PA: Everts and Peck 1880. [MHS]

———. *History of York County, Maine*. Philadelphia, PA: Everts and Peck 1880. [MHS]

Coben, Stanley. *Rebellion Against Victorianism: The Impetus for Cultural Change in 1920s America*. New York: Oxford University Press, 1991.

Coburn, Carol K., and Martha Smith. *Spirited Lives: How Nuns Shaped Catholic Culture and American Life, 1836–1920*. Chapel Hill: University of North Carolina Press, 1999.

Coffey, Lorraine. "The Rise and Decline of the Port of Newburyport." Ph.D. diss., Boston University, 1975.

Coffin, Robert P. T. *Captain Abby and Captain John*. New York: Macmillan, 1939.

———. *Kennebec: Cradle of Americans*. New York: Ferrar and Reinhart, Inc., 1937.

Coghlan, Ronan. *Pocket Guide to Irish First Names*. Belfast: 1985.

Cohen, Bruce. "The Worcester Machinist Strike of 1915." *Historical Journal of Massachusetts* 16, no. 2 (summer 1988).

Cohen, Marilyn, ed. *The Warp of Ulster's Past: Interdisciplinary Perspectives on the Irish Linen Industry, 1700–1920*. London: Macmillan, 1996.

Cohen, Michael. "Jerusalem of the North: An Analysis of Religious Modernization in Portland, Maine's Jewish Community 1860–1950." Honors thesis, Brown University, 2000. [MHS]

Cole, Donald. *Immigrant City: Lawrence, Massachusetts, 1845–1921*. Chapel Hill: University of North Carolina Press, 1963.

Cole, Ronald. "Music in Portland, Maine, from Colonial Times Through the Nineteenth Century." Ph.D. diss., Indiana University, 1975.

Coleman, Terry. *Going to America*. Garden City, NJ: Anchor Books, 1973.

Collections of the Maine Historical Society. Portland, ME: By the Society, 1865–1916.

Collins, Sarah. "Francis O'Brien: Portland's Philosopher-Bookman." *Salt* 28 (October 1986): 50–60. [MHS]

Comerford, R. Vincent. *The Fenians in Context: Irish Politics and Society, 1848–1882*. Dublin: Wolfhound Press, 1985.

Commission on the Restoration of the Irish Language. Dublin: Stationary Office, 1963.

Conforti, Joseph A. *Imagining New England: Explorations of Regional Identity from the Pilgrims to the Mid-twentieth Century*. Chapel Hill: University of North Carolina Press, 2001.

Conk, Margo A. "Immigrant Worker in the City, 1870–1930: Agents of Growth or Threats to Democracy?" *Social Science Quarterly* 62, no. 4.

Connell, K. H. *Irish Peasant: Four Historical Essays*. Oxford: Clarendon Press, 1961.

Connellan, Leo. *Death in Lobster Land*. Fort Kent, ME: Great Raven Press, 1978. [MHS]

———. *New and Collected Poems*. New York: Paragon House, 1989. [MHS]

Connolly, Michael C. "Black Fades to Green: Irish Labor Replaces African-American Labor Along a Major New England Waterfront, Portland, Maine, in the Mid-Nineteenth Century." *Colby Quarterly* 37, no. 4 (December 2001): 357–73.

———. "The First Hurrah: James Michael Curley versus the 'Goo-Goos' in the Boston Mayoralty Election of 1914." *Historical Journal of Massachusetts* 30, no. 1 (winter 2002): 50–74.

———. "The Irish Longshoremen of Portland, Maine, 1880–1923." Ph.D. diss., Boston College, 1988.

———. "The Next Parish West of Galway: The Irish Diaspora of Portland, Maine." *House Island Project*. Portland: Portland Performing Arts, 1996: 6–9.

———. "To 'Make this Port Union all over': Longshore Militancy in Portland, 1911–1913." *Maine History* 41, no. 1 (spring 2002): 41–60.

Connolly, Michael C., and Seamus Grimes. "Emigration from Connemara to America." *Galway Roots: The Journal of the Galway Historical Society* 2 (1994).

Connolly, Michael C., and Seamus Grimes. "The Migration Link between Cois Fharraige and Portland, Maine, 1880s to 1920s." *Irish Geography* 22 (1989): 22–30. [MHS]

Connolly, S. J. *Priests and People in Pre-famine Ireland, 1780–1845*. Dublin: Gill and Macmillan, 1982.

Connors-Carlson, Shirlee. "A Pocketful of Irish Settlements in the Woods." In *The County: Land of Promise, A Pictorial History of Aroostook County, Maine*, edited by Anna Fields McGrath. Norfolk, VA: The Donning Co., 1989. [MHS]

Considine, Robert B. *It's the Irish*. Garden City, NY: Doubleday, 1961.

Constitution and By-Laws of the Grattan Literary Association of Portland, ME Organized October 30, 1877. Portland: Tucker Printing House. 1882. [MHS]

Constitution and By-Laws of the Irish-American Relief Association of Portland Organized May 4, 1863. Portland: David Tucker, Printer, 1867. [MHS]

Constitution and By-Laws of the Portland Catholic Union Organized January, 1874. Portland: Eustis & Castell, Printers, 1874. [MHS]

Constitution and By-Laws of the St. Patrick's Benevolent Society, Portland, Maine. Portland: Stephen Berry, Printer, 1871. [MHS]

Conyngham, David Power. *The Irish Brigade and Its Campaigns*. Boston: Donahue, 1869.

Conzen, Kathleen Neils. "Ethnicity as Festive Culture: Nineteenth Century German America on Parade." In *The Invention of Ethnicity*, edited by Werner Sollors. New York: Oxford University Press, 1989.

———. "Immigrants, Immigrant Neighborhoods and Ethnic Identity: Historical Issues." *Journal of American History* 66 (December 1979).

Cook, Adrian. *The Armies of the Streets: The New York City Draft Riots of 1863*. Lexington: University Press of Kentucky, 1974.

Cooper, Brian E., ed. *The Irish American Almanac and Green Pages*. New York: Pembroke Press, 1986.

Cooper, S. Josephine, ed. *A Bicentennial History of Sullivan, Maine*. Camden, ME: The Sullivan-Sorrento Historical Society, 1989.

Cooper, Wayne, ed. *The Passion of Claude McKay: Selected Poetry and Prose, 1912–1948*. New York: Shocken Books, 1973.

Corby, William. *Memoirs of Chaplain Life*. New York: Fordham University Press, 1992.

Corish, Patrick. *Radicals, Rebels, and Establishments*. Belfast: Appletree Press, 1983.

Corkery, Daniel. *The Fortunes of the Irish Language*. Cork: Mercier Press, 1968.

———. *The Hidden Ireland*. Dublin: Gill and Macmillan, 1983.

Costigan, Giovanni. *A History of Modern Ireland*. New York: Pegasus, 1969.

Cousens, S. H. "Demographic Change in Ireland, 1851–1861." *Economic History Review* 14 (spring 1961).

———. "The Regional Variations in Population Changes in Ireland, 1860–1881." *Economic History Review*, no. 17 (1964).

Couvares, Frank M. *The Remaking of Pittsburgh: Class and Culture in an Industrializing City, 1877–1919*. Albany: State University of New York Press, 1984.

Crapol, Edward P. *James G. Blaine: Architect of Empire*. Wilmington, DE: Scholarly Resources Inc., 2000.

Crawford, William H. "The Evolution of the Linen Trade in Ulster Before Industrialization." *Irish Economic and Social History* 15 (1988): 32–53.

Croker, T. Crofton. *Researches in the South of Ireland*. New York: Barnes and Noble, 1969.

Cronin, Mike, and Daryl Adair. *The Wearing of the Green*. New York: Routledge Press, 2001.

Cronin, Sean. *Washington's Irish Policy 1916–1986*. Dublin: Anvil Books, 1987.

———, ed. *The McGarrity Papers*. Tralee, Ireland: Anvil Books, 1972.

Crosby, Donald F. *God, Church and Flag: Senator Joseph R. McCarthy and the Catholic Church, 1950–1957*. Chapel Hill: University of North Carolina Press, 1978.

Cross, Robert. *The Emergence of Liberal Catholicism in America*. Cambridge: Harvard University Press, 1967.

Crossman, Chris. "Drawing with Light." In *Sightings: A Maine Coast Odyssey*, by Peter Ralston. . Camden, ME: Downeast Books, 1997.

Cullen, James B. *The Story of the Irish in Boston*. Boston, MA: J. B. Cullen and Co., 1889.

Cullen, Louis. *The Emergence of Modern Ireland, 1600–1900*. Dublin: Gill and Macmillan, 1981.

———. "The Irish Diaspora of the Seventeenth and Eighteenth Centuries." In *Europeans on the Move: Studies on European Migration, 1500–1800*, edited by Nicholas P. Canny. New York: Oxford University Press, 1994.

———. *Six Generations of Life and Work in Ireland from 1790*. Cork: Mercier Press, 1970.

———. "The Social and Economic Evolution of South Kilkenny in the Seventeenth and Eighteenth Centuries." *Decies* 13 (January 1980).

Culligan, Matthew J., and Peter Cherici. *The Wandering Irish in Europe: Their Influence from the Dark Ages to Modern Times*. London: Constable and Co., Ltd., 2000.

Cumbler, John T. *Working-Class Community in Industrial America: Work, Leisure and Struggle in Two Industrial Cities, 1880–1930*. Westport, CT: Greenwood Press, 1957.

Curran, Joseph M. *Hibernian Green on the Silver Screen*. Westport, CT: Greenwood Press, 1989.

Curran, Philip E. *Genealogies of Philip Edward Curran and his wife Nancy Ann Joy*. Westbrook, ME: By author, 1997.

Curran, Robert. *Michael Augustine Corrigan and the Shaping of Conservative Catholicism in America, 1878–1902*. New York: Arno Press, 1978.

Currie, Archibald W. *The Grand Trunk Railway of Canada*. Toronto: University of Toronto Press, 1957.

Curtis, L. Perry, Jr. *Apes and Angels: The Irishman in Victorian Caricature*. Washington, DC: The Smithsonian Institution Press, 1971.

Cushman, David Quimby. *Ancient Sheepscot and Newcastle*. Bath, ME: Upton and Son, 1882.

Daly, Marie E. "Rathlin Islanders Downeast." *Nexus* 6, no. 6 (December 1989): 196–98.

Daniels, Roger. *Coming to America: A History of Immigration and Ethnicity in American Life*. New York: Harper Collins, 1989.

Dannenbaum, Jed. *Drink and Disorder: Temperance Reform in Cincinnati from the Washington Revival to the W.C.T.U.* Urbana: University of Illinois Press, 1984.

D'Arcy, William. *The Fenian Movement in the United States, 1858–1886*. Washington, DC: Catholic University of America Press, 1947.

Davis, Albert. *A History of Ellsworth*. Lewiston, ME: Journal Print Shop, 1927. [MHS]

Davis, Harold A. "The Fenian Raid on New Brunswick." *Canadian Historical Review* 36 (December 1955).

———. *An International Community on the St. Croix*. Orono: University of Maine Press,1950.

Davis, Ronald L. *John Ford: Hollywood's Old Master*. Norman: University of Oklahoma, 1995.

Davis, Susan. *Parades and Power: Street Theater in Nineteenth Century Philadelphia*. Philadelphia: Temple University Press, 1986.

Davitt, Michael. *The Fall of Feudalism in Ireland*. New York: Harper and Brothers, 1904.

Dawley, Alan. *Class and Community: The Industrial Revolution in Lynn*. Cambridge: Harvard University Press, 1976.

Dawson, A. A. P. "The Stabilization of Dockworkers' Earnings." *International Labour Review* 63 (March–April 1951).

Dawson, William L. "A Bibliographic Study of the Life of Neal Dow, 1804–1897." *Maine Historical Society Quarterly* 25, no. 3 (winter 1986).

Day, Clarence. *History of Maine Agriculture, 1604–1860. University of Maine Bulletin* 56, no. 11 (April 1954).

de Bhaldraithe, Tomás. *Gaeilge chois Fhairrge: an Deilbhíocht*. Baile Átha Cliath: Institiúid Árd-Léinn Bhaile Átha Cliath, 1953.

———. *The Irish of Cois Fhairrge, Co. Galway, A Phonetic Study*. Dublin: The Dublin Institute for Advanced Studies, 1945.

Debrow, Gail, ed. *Restoring Women's History through Historic Preservation*. Baltimore: Johns Hopkins Press, 2003.

de Fréine, Seán. *The Great Silence*. Cork: Mercier Press, 1978.

Delaney, Mary Murray. *Of Irish Ways*. New York: Barnes & Noble, 1973.

Demaris, Ovid. *America the Violent*. New York: Cowles Book Co., 1970.

Demeter, Richard. *Irish America: The Historical Travel Guide*. Pasadena, CA: Cranford Press, 1997.

Detmer, Josephine H., and Patricia N. Pancoast. *Portland*. Portland, ME: Greater Portland Landmarks, Inc., 1972.

Deutsch, Sarah. *Women and the City: Gender, Space, and Power in Boston, 1870–1940*. New York: Oxford University Press, 2000.

Devoy, John. *Recollections of an Irish Rebel*. Shannon, Ireland: Irish University Press, 1969.

Dezell, Maureen. *Irish America, Coming into Clover*. New York: Anchor Books/Random House, 2002.

Dickson, J. Margaret, ed. *A History of the Island of Rathlin, by Ms. Gage*. Coleraine: J. Margaret Dickson, 1995.

Dickson, R. J. *Ulster Emigration to Colonial America 1718–1775*. Belfast: Ulster Historical Foundation, 1976.

DiFazio, William. *Longshoremen: Community and Resistance on the Brooklyn Waterfront*. South Hadley, MA: Bergin and Garvey Publishers, 1985.

Dineen, Maurice. *The Catholic Total Abstinence Movement in the Archdiocese of Boston*. Boston: Grimes Publishers, 1908.

Diner, Hasia. *Erin's Daughters in America: Irish Women in the Nineteenth Century*. Baltimore: Johns Hopkins University Press, 1983.

Dinneen, Joseph. *The Purple Shamrock: The Honorable James Michael Curley of Boston*. New York: W. W. Norton, 1949.

Dinneen, Patrick S. *An Irish-English Dictionary*. Dublin: Educational Company of Ireland, 1927.

Divine, Robert A. *American Immigration Policy, 1924–1952*. New Haven: Yale University Press, 1957.

Dolan, Jay. *The American Catholic Experience: A History from Colonial Times to the Present*. Garden City, NJ: Doubleday, 1983.

———. *Catholic Revivalism: The American Experience, 1830–1900*. Notre Dame, IN: University of Notre Dame Press, 1978.

————. *The Immigrant Church: New York's Irish and German Catholics, 1815–1865.* Baltimore: Johns Hopkins University, 1975.

Dolan, Jay, Scott Appleby, Patricia Byrne, and Debra Campbell. *Transforming Parish Ministry: The Changing Roles of Catholic Clergy, Laity, and Women Religious.* New York: Crossroads, 1990.

Dominic, Randolph, and William David Barry. *Pyrrhus Venture.* Boston: Little, Brown Publishers, 1983.

Donnelly, James, and Samuel Clark, eds. *Irish Peasants: Violence and Political Unrest, 1780–1914.* Madison: University of Wisconsin Press, 1983.

Donohoe, J. M. *The Irish Catholic Benevolent Union: 1869–1893.* Washington, DC: Catholic University Press, 1951.

Donovan, George F. *The Pre-Revolutionary Irish in Massachusetts, 1620–1775.* Menasha, WI: George Banta Publ. Co., 1932.

Donovan, K. "Good Old Pat: Irish-American Stereotype in Decline." *Eire-Ireland* 15, no. 3 (fall 1980).

Dow, George, and Robert Dunbar. *Nobleboro, Maine: A History.* Nobleboro: Nobleboro Historical Socety, 1988.

Dow, Neal. *The Reminiscences of Neal Dow.* Portland, ME: Evening Express Publ. Co., 1898.

Dowling, P. J. *The Hedge Schools.* Cork: Mercier Press, 1968.

Dowling, William C. "John Ford's Festive Comedy: Ireland Imagined in *The Quiet Man.*" *Eire-Ireland* 36, nos. 3–4 (fall/winter 2001): 190–211.

Downs, Jacques. *The Cities on the Saco.* Norfolk, VA: Donning Co., 1985.

Doyle, David N. *Ireland, Irishmen and Revolutionary America, 1760–1820.* Cork: The Mercier Press, 1981.

————. *Irish America: Native Rights and National Empires, 1890–1901.* New York: Arno Press, 1976.

————. "The Regional Bibliography of Irish America 1880–1930: A Review and Addendum." *Irish Historical Studies* 13, no. 1 (May 1983).

Doyle, David N., and Owen Dudley Edwards, eds. *America and Ireland, 1776–1976: The American Identity and the Irish Connection.* Westport, CT: Greenwood Press, 1976.

Drudy, P. J., ed. *The Irish in America: Immigration, Assimilation, and Impact.* New York: Cambridge University Press, 1985.

Dunleavy, Janet. *Douglas Hyde: A Maker of Modern Ireland.* Berkeley: University of California Press, 1991.

Dwyer, T. Ryle. *Irish Neutrality and the USA, 1939–47.* Dublin: Gill & MacMillan, 1977.

Eagan, Eileen. *Class, Culture, and the Classroom: The Student Peace Movement of the 1930s.* Philadelphia: Temple University Press, 1981.

————. "Immortalizing Women: Finding Meaning in Public Sculpture." In *Her Past Around Us: Interpreting Sites for Women's History,* edited by Polly Welts Kaufman and Katharine T. Corbett. Malabar, FL: Krieger Publishing Co., 2003.

Eagan, Eileen, and Pat Finn. "From Galway to Gorham's Corner: Irish Women in Portland, Maine." In *Of Place and Gender,* edited by Marli Weiner. Orono: University of Maine Press, 2004.

Eastman, Joel W. "Entrepreneurship and Obsolescence: Owen W. Davis, Jr. and the Katahdin Charcoal Iron Company 1876–1890." *Maine Historical Society Quarterly* 17, no. 2 (fall 1977): 69–84.

Eaton, Cyrus. *Annals of the Town of Warren*. Hallowell, ME: Masters, Smith and Co., 1851.

Eckstorm, Fannie H. *Indian Place Names of the Penobscot Valley and Maine Coast*. Orono: University of Maine Press, 1941.

Eckstorm, Fannie H., and Mary W. Smyth. *Minstrelsy of Maine*. Boston, MA: Houghton Mifflin, 1927.

Edsall, Thomas Byrne. *Chain Rection: The Impact of Race, Rights, and Taxes on American Politics*. New York: Norton, 1991.

Edwards, George Thornton. *Music and Musicians of Maine*. Portland: The Southworth Press, 1978. [MHS]

Edwards, Ruth Dudley. *Patrick Pearse: The Triumph of Failure*. New York: Taplinger Publishing Co., 1978.

Ehrlich, Mark. *With Our Hands*. Philadelphia: Temple University Press, 1986.

Elder, J. G. *History of Lewiston*. Boston: A. G. Daniels, Printer, 1882; Bowie, MD: Heritage Books, 1989. [MHS]

Eliel, Paul. "Labor Peace in Pacific Coast Ports." *Harvard Business Review* 19 (summer 1941).

————. *The Waterfront and General Strikes, San Francisco, 1934*. San Francisco: Hooper Printing Company, 1934.

Elliot, Bruce. *Irish Migrants in the Canadas: A New Approach*. Montreal: McGill-Queens University Press, 1988.

Ellis, John Tracey. *American Catholicism*. Chicago: University of Chicago Press, 1969.

————. *The Catholic Priest in the United States: Historical Investigations*. Collegeville, MN: St. John's University Press, 1971.

————. *The Life of James Cardinal Gibbons: Archbishop of Baltimore, 1834–1921*. 2 vols. Milwaukee: Bruce, 1952.

Elwell, Edward H. *Portland and Vicinity*. Portland, ME: Greater Portland Landmarks, 1975. (A facsimile of the 1876 edition.)

Emmons, David M. *The Butte Irish: Class and Ethnicity in an American Mining Town, 1875–1926*. Urbana: University of Illinois Press, 1989.

Erie, Steven P. *Rainbow's End: Irish Americans and the Dilemmas of Urban Machine Politics, 1840–1985*. Berkeley: University of California Press, 1988.

Esman, Milton J. *Ethnic Politics*. Ithaca, NY: Cornell University Press, 1994.

Evans, A. A. *Technical and Social Changes in the World's Ports*. Geneva: International Labour Office (Studies and Reports, New Series, no. 74), 1969.

Evans, E. Estyn. *Ireland and the Atlantic Heritage*. Dublin: The Lilliput Press, 1996.

Eyman, Scott. *Print the Legend: The Life and Times of John Ford*. New York: Simon and Schuster, 1999.

Fairfield, Roy. *Sands, Spindles, and Steeples*. Portland, ME: House of Falmouth, 1956. [MHS]

Fairly, Lincoln. *Facing Mechanization: The West Coast Longshore Plan*. Los Angeles: U.C.L.A. Industrial Relations (Monograph #23), 1971.

————. "Longshore Contract." *Dissent* 9 (1962).

Fallows, Marjorie R. *Irish Americans: Identity and Assimilation*. Englewood Cliffs, NJ: Prentice Hall, Inc., 1979.

Fanning, Charles, ed. *The Exiles of Erin: Nineteenth Century Irish-American Fiction*. Chester Springs, PA: Dufour Editions, 1997.

———. *The Irish Voice in America: 250 Years of Irish-American Fiction.* Lexington: University Press of Kentucky, 2000.

———, ed. *New Perspectives on the Irish Diaspora.* Carbondale: Southern Illinois University Press, 2000.

———, ed. *Selected Writings of John V. Kelleher on Ireland and Irish America.* Carbondale: Southern Illinois University Press, 2002.

Fenning, Fr. Hugh. "The Conversion of Charles Ffrench." *The Watchman* 28, no. 53 (summer 1961).

Fenwick, Benedict J. *Memoirs to Serve for the Future, Ecclesiastical History of the Diocese of Boston.* Yonkers, New York: U.S. Catholic Historical Society, 1978.

Ferguson, Donald. *Munjoy Hill: Portland's Scenic Peninsula.* Portland: By author, 1981.

Ferland, Durwood, Jr. *Fortitudo et Spes: The Courage and Hope to Move a College.* Greenville, ME: Moosehead Communications, 1999.

Fink, Leon. *Workingmen's Democracy: The Knights of Labor and American Politics.* Urbana: University of Illinois Press, 1983.

Finke, Roger, and Rodney Starke. *The Churching of America, 1776–1990: Winners and Losers in Our Religious Economy.* New Brunswick, NJ: Rutgers University Press, 1992.

Finlay, William. "One Occupation, Two Labor Markets: The Case of Longshore Crane Operators." *American Social Review* 48, no. 3 (1963).

Finnegan, Richard B., and Edward T. McCarron. *Ireland: Historical Echoes, Contemporary Politics.* Boulder, CO: Westview Press, 2000.

Fitzgerald, Margaret E., and Joseph A. King. *The Uncounted Irish in Canada and the United States.* Toronto: P. D. Meany, Publishers, 1990.

Fitzpatrick, David. "Emigration, 1801–70." In *A New History of Ireland: Ireland under the Union,* Vol. 5, edited by W. E. Vaughn. Oxford: Clarendon Press, 1989.

———. *Irish Emigration, 1801–1921.* Dublin: The Economic and Social History Society of Ireland, 1984.

———. "'A peculiar tramping people': The Irish in Britain, 1801–70." In *A New History of Ireland: Ireland under the Union,* Vol. 5, edited by W. E. Vaughn. Oxford: Clarendon Press, 1989.

———, ed. *The Reynolds Letters: An Irish Emigrant Family in Late Victorian Manchester.* Cork: Cork University Press, 1999.

Fitzpatrick, David, and W. P. Vaughn. *Irish Historical Statistics: Population, 1821–1971.* Dublin: Irish Academy, 1978.

Flanagan, James M. *Builders of Maine.* Mt. Desert, ME: Windswept House, 1994.

Flynn, Elizabeth Gurley. *The Rebel Girl: An Autobiography of my First Life 1906–1926.* New York: International Publishers, 1973. (Originally *I Speak my Own Piece,* 1955.)

Foley, Albert S. "Bishop Healy and the Colored Catholic Congress." *Interracial Review* 28 (May 1954): 79–80.

———. *Bishop Healy, Beloved Outcaste: The Story of a Great Priest Whose Life Has Become a Legend.* New York: Ferrar, Straus and Young, 1954.

———. *Dream of an Outcaste: Patrick F. Healy.* Tuscaloosa, AL: Portals Press, 1989.

———. *God's Men of Color: The Colored Catholic Priests of the United States, 1854–1954.* New York: Farrar, Straus and Company, 1955.

Folsom, Burton W. *Urban Capitalists, Entrepreneurs, and City Growth in Pennsylvania's Lackawanna and Lehigh Regions, 1880 to 1970.* Baltimore: Johns Hopkins University Press, 1981.

Foner, Eric. "Class, Ethnicity, and Radicalism in the Gilded Age: The Land League and Irish America." *Marxist* Perspectives 1, no. 2 (summer 1978).

Foner, Philip. "The Industrial Workers of the World." In *History of the Labor Movement in the United States* (vol. 4), by Philip Foner. New York: International Publishers, 1965.

Fones-Wolf, Kenneth, and Martin Kauffman, eds. *Labor in Massachusetts: Selected Essays.* Westfield, MA: Institute for Massachusetts Studies, 1990.

Ford, Dan. *Pappy: The Life of John Ford.* Englewood Cliffs, NJ: Prentice-Hall Inc., 1979.

Formisano, Ronald. "The Invention of the Ethnocultural Interpretation." *American Historical Review* 99, no. 9 (April 1994).

Formisano, Ronald, and Constance Burns. *Boston 1700–1980: The Evolution of Urban Politics.* Westport, CT: Greenwood Press, 1984.

Foster, Roy F. *Modern Ireland 1600–1972.* London: Viking Penquin, 1988.

———. *Paddy and Mr. Punch: Connections in Irish and English History.* London: A. Lane, 1993.

Francis, Robert C. A. "History of Labor on the San Francisco Waterfront." Ph.D. diss., University of California, 1934.

Frank, Elizabeth. *Louise Bogan: A Portrait.* New York: Alfred A. Knopf, 1985.

Freeman, Frederic W. *Mother Goose Comes to Portland.* Portland: Southworth Printing Co., 1918. [MHS]

Frenette, Yves. "Understanding the French Canadians of Lewiston, 1860–1900." *Maine Historical Society Quarterly* 25, no. 4 (spring 1986): 198–229.

Frisch, Michael H. *Town into City: Springfield, Massachusetts and the Meaning of Community, 1840–1880s.* Cambridge: Harvard University Press, 1972.

Fuchs, Lawrence. *John F. Kennedy and American Catholicism.* New York: Meredith Press, 1967.

Funchion, Michael. *Chicago Irish Nationalists.* New York: Arno Press, 1976.

Gabaccia, Donna. *Militants and Migrants: Rural Sicilians Become American Workers.* New Brunswick, NJ: Rutgers University Press, 1988.

Gaffey, James P. *Citizen of No Mean City: Archbishop Patrick Riordan of San Francisco, 1841–1914.* Wilmington, NC: Consortium, 1976.

Gaffney, Thomas L. "Maine's Mr. Smith: A Study of the Career of Francis O. J. Smith, Politician and Entrepreneur." Ph.D. diss., University of Maine (Orono), 1979. [MHS]

Gallagher, Tag. *John Ford: The Man and His Films.* Berkeley: University of California Press, 1986.

Gallagher, Thomas. *Paddy's Lament: Ireland, 1846–1847, Prelude to Hatred.* San Diego, CA: Harcourt Brace, 1987.

Gamber, Wendy. *The Female Economy and Dressmaking Trades, 1860–1930.* Urbana: University of Illinois Press, 1997.

Gamm, Gerald H. *The Making of New Deal Democrats: Voting Behavior and Realignment in Boston, 1920–1949.* Chicago: University of Chicago Press, 1990.

Gans, Herbert. *The Urban Villagers: Group and Class in the Life of Italian-Americans.* New York: Orbus Press, 1962.

Garlock, Jonathan. *Guide to the Local Assemblies of the Knights of Labor.* Westport, CT: Greenwood Press, 1982.

Garvin, Tom. "The Anatomy of a Nationalist Revolution: Ireland, 1858–1928." *Society for Comparative Study of Society and History* 28, no. 3 (1986).

———. *The Evolution of Irish Nationalist Politics.* New York: Holmes and Meier, 1981.

Gaughan, J. Anthony, ed. *Memoirs of Senator Joseph Connolly (1885–1961): A Founder of Modern Ireland.* Blackrock, Co. Dublin: Irish Academic Press, 1996.

———. *Thomas Johnson, 1872–1963: First Leader of the Labour Party in Dail Eireann.* Mount Merrion, Co. Dublin: Kingdom Books, 1980.

Geary, James W. *We Need Men: The Union Draft in the Civil War.* Dekalb, IL: Northern Illinois University Press, 1991.

Gelderman, Carol. *Mary McCarthy: A Life.* New York: St. Martin's Press, 1988. [MHS]

Gerber, David. "Ambivalent Anti-Catholicism: Buffalo's American Protestant Elite Faces the Challenge of the Catholic Church, 1850–1860." *Civil War History* 30, no. 2 (1984).

———. *The Making of an American Pluralism: Buffalo, 1825–1860.* Urbana: University of Illinois Press, 1989.

Gerrier, Arthur J. "Nicholas Codd." *A Bibliographical Dictionary of Architects in Maine* (vol. 6). Augusta, ME: Maine Historic Preservation Commission, 1991.

Gerstle, Gary. "Race and the Myth of the Liberal Consensus." *Journal of American History* 82, no. 2 (September 1995).

———. *Working Class Americanism: The Politics of Labor in a textile City, 1914–1960.* New York: Cambridge University Press, 1989.

———. "The Working Class Goes to War." *Mid-Americans* 75, no. 3 (October 1993).

Gibb, George S. *The Saco-Lowell Shops.* Cambridge: Harvard University Press, 1950.

Gibson, Ralph. *A Social History of French Catholicism, 1789–1914.* New York: Routledge, 1989.

Gienapp, William E. "Nativism and the Creation of a Republican Majority in the North Before the Civil War." *Journal of American History* 72 (December 1985): 529–59.

Ginger, Ray. *The Bending Cross: A Biography of Eugene Victor Debs.* New Brunswick, NJ: Rutgers University Press, 1940.

Glasgow, Maude. *The Scotch-Irish in Northern Ireland and the American Colonies.* New York: G. P. Putnam's Sons, 1936.

Glazier, Michael, ed. *The Encyclopedia of the Irish in America.* Notre Dame, IN: University of Notre Dame Press, 1999.

Gleason, Angela B. "Adamnan in the Tenth and Eleventh Centuries: A Literary Revival." M. Phil. thesis, Trinity College Dublin, 1997.

———. "Entertainment in Early Ireland." Ph. D. diss., Trinity College Dublin, 2002 (a published version of this is forthcoming).

Gleason, Philip. "The New Americans in Catholic Historiography." *US Catholic Historian* 11, no. 3 (summer 1993).

Gleeson, David T. *The Irish in the South 1815–1877.* Chapel Hill: University of North Carolina Press, 2001.

Glen, Francis Wayland. *Annexation: The Ideas of the Late William H. Seward.* Brooklyn, New York: 1893.

Goldberg, Joseph P. "Longshoremen and the Mechanization of Cargo Handling in the United States." *International Labor Review* 28, no. 3 (1973).

Goldscheider, Calvin, and Sidney Goldstein. *Jewish Americans: Three Generations in a Jewish Community*. Englewood Cliffs, NJ: Prentice Hall, 1968.

Goldstein, Judith S. *Crossing Lines: Histories of Jews and Gentiles in Three Communities*. New York: William Morrow and Co., 1992. [MHS]

Golway, Terry. *John Devoy, Irish Rebel*. New York: St. Martin's Press, 1998.

Goodwin, Doris Kearns. *The Fitzgeralds and the Kennedys*. New York: Simon and Schuster, 1987.

Goold, William. *Portland in the Past with Historical Notes of Old Falmouth*. Portland: B. Thurston and Company, 1886.

Gordon, Michael. "Studies in Irish and Irish American Thought and Behavior in Gilded Age New York City." Ph.D. diss., University of Rochester, 1977.

Gordon, Milton. *Assimilation in American Life: The Role of Religion and National Origins*. New York: Oxford University Press, 1964.

Goulart, Ron, ed. *The Encyclopedia of American Comics*. New York: Facts on File (A Promised Land Production), 1990.

Gould, Alberta. *George Mitchell: In Search of Peace*. Farmington, ME: Heritage Publ., Inc., 1996. [MHS]

Gower, Karen E. Sherrard. *John Sherrard and Decendants*. [Camden, ME]: Penobscot Press, 1993.

Grady, Joseph L. *From Ireland, Land of Pain and Sorrow: Saga of Six Generations of Irish-Americans*. Phoenix, AZ: Erin Go Braugh Books, 1984.

Grady, William. "Footprints of Early Irishmen and Others on the Penobscot and Its Environs, Miscellaneous Papers." Manuscript, Bangor, ME: 1942–46. [MHS Collection 1960]

———. "Irish Immigration on the Penobscot and Its Environs: 1735–1865." Manuscript, Bangor, ME: 1940–45. [MHS Collection 1960]

Graff, Harvey L. *The Literacy Myth: Literacy and Social Structure in the Nineteenth Century City*. San Diego: Academic Press, 1979.

Grattan, William J. *The Spires of Fenwick: A History of the College of the Holy Cross, 1843–1963*. New York: Vantage Press, 1966.

Greeley, Andrew M. *The Irish Americans: The Rise to Money and Power*. New York: Harper and Row, 1981.

———. "The Success and Assimilation of Irish Protestants and Catholics in the United States." *Social Science Research* 72, no. 4 (1985).

———. *That Most Distressful Nation: The Taming of the American Irish*. Chicago: Quadrangle Books, 1972.

Greeley, Andrew M., William McCready, and Kathleen McCourt. *Catholic Schools in a Declining Church*. Kansas City: Sheed and Ward, 1976.

Green, E. R. R. "The Beginnings of Fenianism," in T. W. Moody, ed. *The Fenian Movement*. Cork: Mercier Press, 1968.

Greene, Francis B. *History of Boothbay, Southport and Boothbay Harbor, Maine, 1623–1905*. Portland, ME: Loring, Short and Harmon, 1906.

Greene, Lorenzo J. *The Negro in Colonial New England*. New York: Atheneum Publishers, 1968.

Greenhaus, John. *Clans and Families of Ireland*. Secaucus, NJ: The Wellfleet Press, 1993.

Grenham, John. *Tracing Your Irish Ancestors: The Complete Guide*. Dublin: Gill and Macmillan, 1992.

Griffin, Joseph, ed. *History of the Press of Maine*. Brunswick, ME: Press of J. Griffin, 1872. [MHS]

Griffin, Patrick. *The People with No Name: Ireland's Ulster Scots, America's Scots Irish, and the Creation of a British Atlantic World, 1689–1764*. Princeton, NJ: Princeton University Press, 2001.

Griffin, William D. *The Book of Irish Americans*. New York: Times Books, 1990.

———. *A Portrait of the Irish in America*. New York: Scribner, 1981.

Grimes, Robert R. *How shall we sing in a foreign land?* Notre Dame, IN: University of Notre Dame Press, 1996.

Grimes, Seamus, and Michael C. Connolly. "Emigration from Connemara to America." *Galway Roots: The Journal of the Galway Historical Society* 2 (1994).

Grimes, Seamus, and Michael C. Connolly. "The Migration Link between Cois Fharraige and Portland, Maine, 1880s to 1920s." *Irish Geography* 22 (1989): 22–30. [MHS]

Groneman, Carol. "Working Class Immigrant Women in Mid-Nineteenth Century New York: The Irish Woman's Experience." *Journal of Urban History* 4, no. 3 (May 1978).

Gubin, Sidney N. "Technical Changes and Trade Union Policy." Ph.D. diss., University of California, 1938.

Guignard, Michael J. *La Foi, La Langue, La Culture: The Franco-Americans of Biddeford, Maine*. Biddeford: Privately printed, 1982.

———. "Maine's Corporation Sole Controversy." *Maine Historical Society Quarterly* 12, no. 3 (winter 1973).

Guinnane, Timothy. "Rethinking the Western European Marriage Pattern: The Decision to Marry in Ireland at the Turn of the Century." *Journal of Family History* 16, no. 1 (1991).

———. *The Vanishing Irish: Households, Migration, and the Rural Economy in Ireland*. Princeton, NJ: Princeton University Press, 1997.

Gulliver, P. H., and Marilyn Silverman. *Merchants and Shopkeepers: A Historical Anthropology of an Irish Market Town, 1200–1991*. Toronto: University of Toronto Press, 1995.

Gutman, Herbert S. *Work, Culture and Society in Industrializing America: Essays in American Working-Class and Social History*. New York: Alfred A. Knopf, 1976.

Hachey, Thomas. *Britain and Irish Separatism: From the Fenians to the Free State, 1867–1922*. Washington, DC: Catholic University of America Press, 1984.

Hachey, Thomas, and Lawrence McCaffrey, eds. *Perspectives on Irish Nationalism*. Lexington: University Press of Kentucky, 1989.

Hackett, J. D., and Charles Montague. *Early Passengers lists from Ireland*. Baltimore: Genealogical Publishers, Co., 1965.

Hagel, Otto, and Louis Goldblatt. *Men and Machines*. San Francisco: International Longshoremen's and Wharehousemen's Union and the Pacific Maritime Association, 1963.

Halpine, Charles G. (AKA Miles O'Reilly). *Poetical Works of Charles G. Halpine (Miles O'Reilly)*. New York: Harper & Brothers, 1869.

———. *To Uncle Sam: Cry from the American Soldiers in Mountjoy Prison, near Dublin by Private Miles O'Reilly*. Ireland: c. 1866.

Hamilton, Gail [M. A. Dodge]. *Biography of James G. Blaine*. Norwich, CT: The Henry Bill Publishing Co., 1895.

Hammack, David C. *Power and Society: Greater New York at the Turn of the Century*. New York: Russell Sage Foundation, 1982.

Hammond, Otis G., ed. *Letters and Papers of Major General John Sullivan*. Concord, NH: New Hampshire Historical Society, 1930.

Handlin, Oscar. *Boston's Immigrants: A Study in Acculturation*. New York: Atheneum, 1997.

———, ed. *The Children of the Uprooted*. New York: G. Braziler, 1966.

Handloom Weavers and the Ulster Linen Industry. Belfast: Ulster Historical Foundation, 1994.

Hanna, Charles A. *The Scotch Irish*. New York: G. P. Putnam's Sons, 1902.

Hanna, William F. "The Boston Draft Riot." *Civil War History* 36 (September 1990): 262–73.

Hannerz, Ulf. *Exploring the City: Inquiries Toward an Urban Anthropology*. New York: Columbia University Press, 1980.

Hansen, Marcus L. *The Atlantic Migration, 1607–1860*. Cambridge, MA: Harvard University Press, 1940.

———. *The Immigrant in American History*. New York: Harper and Row, 1940.

———. "The Second Colonization of New England." *The New England Quarterly* 2 (1929): 539–60.

Hardt, John P. "Port Changes in Pacific Coast Ports." Master's thesis, University of Washington, 1948.

Hareven, Tamara. *Family Time and Industrial Time: Relationship between Family and Work in a New England Industrial Community*. New York: Cambridge University Press, 1982.

———, ed. *Family and Kin in Urban Communities: 1790–1930*. New York: Viewpoints, 1977.

Hareven, Tamara, and John Modell. "Urbanization and the Malleable Household: An Examination of Boarding and Lodging in American Families." *Journal of Marriage and the Family* 35 (1973).

Hareven, Tamara, and Maris Vinoskis. "Martial Fertility, Ethnicity, and Occupation in Urban Families: An Analysis of South Boston and the South End in 1880." *Journal of Social History* 8 (1975): 69–93.

Harrigan, Margaret Connors. "Their Own Kind: Family and Community Life in Albany, New York, 1850–1915." Ph.D. diss., Harvard University, 1975.

Harris, Ruth Ann. "'Characteristics of Irish Immigrants in North America,' Derived from the Boston Pilot's 'Missing Friends' Data, 1831–1850." *Working Papers in Irish Studies*. Boston: Northeastern University, 1988.

Harris, Ruth Ann, and Donald M. Jacobs, eds. *The Search for Missing Friends*. Vol. I, 1831–1850. Boston: New England Historic and Genealogical Society, 1989.

Hatch, Louis C. *Maine: A History*. New York: American Historical Society, 1919; Somersworth, NH: New Hampshire Publ. Co., 1974.

Hawthorne, Nathaniel. *The American Notebooks*. New Haven, CT: Yale University Press, 1932.

Hayes, Ernest R. "The Development of Courtney Bay, Saint John, New Brunswick, 1908–1913." Master's thesis, University of New Brunswick, 1969.

Haynes, George. "A Chapter from the Local History of Know-Nothingism." *New England Magazine* 13, no. 1 (September 1896).

Hayut, Yehuda. "Containerization and the Load Center Concept." *Economic Geography* 57, no. 2 (1981).

Hayward, John. *The New England Gazeteer.* Concord, NH: Israel S. Boyd and William White, 1839. [MHS]

Headley, Joel. *The Great Riots of New York: 1712–1873.* New York: Irvington Publishers, 1970.

Healy, John (writer) and John Ewing (photographer). "Irish Roots: From Galway to Casco Bay." *Maine Sunday Telegram,* 22 December 1991, 1A, 13–14A; *Portland Press Herald,* 23 December 1991, 6A; *Portland Press Herald,* 24 December 1991, 1A, 6A; *Portland Press Herald,* 25 December 1991, 1A.

Healy, Kathleen. *Frances Warde: American Founder of the Sisters of Mercy.* New York: Seabury, 1973.

Hechter, Michael. *Internal Colonialism: The Celtic Fringe in British National Development, 1536–1966.* Berkeley: University of California Press, 1975.

———. "Towards a Theory of Ethnic Change." *Politics and Society* (fall 1971).

Henderson, Thomas McLean. *Tammany Hall and the New Immigrants, 1910–1921.* Charlottesville: University of Virginia Press, 1973.

Henning, Calvin. *James Fitzgerald.* Rockland, ME: William A. Farnsworth Library and Art Museum, 1984. [MHS]

Henretta, James. "The Study of Social Mobility: Ideological Assumption and Conceptual Bias." *Labor History* 18 (spring 1977): 165–78.

Hensey, Brendan. *Health Services of Ireland.* Dublin: Institute of Public Administration, 1979.

Herberg, Will. *Protestant, Catholic, and Jew: An Essay in American Religious Sociology.* Garden City, NJ: Doubleday, 1955.

Herron, Sr. Mary Eulalia. "The Work of the Sisters of Mercy in the New England States: Diocese of Portland, 1858–1921; Diocese of Manchester, 1884–1921." *Records of the American Catholic Historical Society* 35 (Mar 1924): 57–100. [MHS]

Hickey, D. J., and J. E. Doherty. *A Dictionary of Irish History Since 1800.* Totowa, NJ: Gill and Macmillan, 1980. [MHS]

Higgins, Mary Raymond, R.S.M. *For Love of Mercy: Missioned in Maine and Andros Island, Bahamas 1883–1983.* Portland: Sisters of Mercy, 1995.

Higham, John. "Another Look at Nativism." *Catholic Historical Review* 44, no. 2 (1958).

———. *Strangers in the Land: Patterns of American Nativism, 1860–1925.* New Brunswick, NJ: Rutgers University Press, 1955.

Hill, Joseph A. *Women in Gainful Occupations, 1890–1920.* Washington, DC: Government Printing Office, 1929.

Hill, Stephen. *The Dockers: Class and Tradition in London.* London: Heinemann Printing Company, 1976.

History of Penobscot County, Maine. Cleveland, OH: Williams, Chase and Co., 1882.

Hobsbawn, Eric and Terence Ranger. *The Invention of Tradition.* Cambridge: Cambridge University Press, 1985.

Hoffman, Miles E. *International Longshoremen's Association: A Contemporary Analysis of a Labor Union.* Philadelphia: Temple University Press (Labor Monograph no. 7), 1966.

Hogan, Peter. *The Catholic University of America: The Rectorship of Thomas J. Conaty*. Washington, DC: Catholic University of America Press, 1949.

Hollingsworth, Jeffrey D. *Magnificent Mainers*. North Attleborough, MA: Covered Bridge Press, 1995.

Holt, Jeff. *The Grand Trunk in New England*. Toronto: Railfare Enterprises Ltd., 1986.

Horton, James O., and Lois E. Horton. *Black Bostonians: Family Life and Community Struggle in the Antebellum North*. New York: Holmes and Meier Publishers, Inc., 1979.

Hotten-Somers, Diane M. "Relinquishing and Reclaiming Independence: Irish Domestic Servants, American Middle-Class Mistresses, and Assimilation, 1850–1920." *Eire-Ireland* 36, nos. 1–2 (spring–summer 2001): 185–201.

Houston, Cecil J., and William J. Smyth. *Irish Emigration and Canadian Settlement: Patterns, Links, and Letters*. Toronto: University of Toronto Press, 1990.

Hudson, Susan. "Les Soeurs Grises [The Gray Nuns] of Lewiston, Maine, 1878–1908: An Ethnic Religious Feminist Expression." *Maine History* 40, no. 4 (winter 2001–2002): 309–32.

Hughes, T. Jones. "The Large Farm in Nineteenth Century Ireland," in Alan Gailey and D. O'Hogain, eds. *Gold Under the Furze*. Dublin: Glendale Press, 1982.

Hull, John T., ed. *Centennial Celebration 1786–1886, Portland, Maine*. Portland: Owen, Strout and Company, 1886.

Hulmer, Nils M. *The Irish Language in Rathlin Island, Co. Antrim*. Dublin: Hodges, Figgis, 1942.

Hutcheson, Michael. "Deforestation in Ireland, c. 1500–1800." Ph.D. diss., Boston College, forthcoming 2004.

Ignatiev, Noel. *How the Irish became White*. New York: Routledge, 1995.

Ihde, Dr. Thomas W., ed. *The Irish Language in the United States: A Historical, Sociolinguistic, and Applied Linguistic Survey*. Westport, CT: Bergin and Garvey, 1994.

———. "Language Report: Irish Language Courses at American Colleges." *Eire-Ireland: A Journal of Irish Studies* 30, no. 4 (1996): 181–86.

Institute for Practical Democracy. *Stories We Must Tell Ourselves*. Portland, ME: Directives, Ltd., 2002.

Isenberg, Michael T. *John L. Sullivan and His America*. Urbana: University of Illinois Press, 1988.

Issell, William. "Citizens Outside the Government: Business and Urban Policy in San Francisco and Los Angeles, 1890–1932." *Pacific Historical Review* 57, no. 2 (spring 1988).

Ives, Edward D. *Larry Gorman: The Man Who Made the Songs*. Bloomington: Indiana University Press, 1964. [MHS]

Jackson, J. B. *American Space: The Centennial Years, 1965–1876*. New York: Norton Press, 1972.

Jacobs, Donald M. "A Study of the Boston Negro from Revolution to Civil War." Ph.D. diss., Boston University, 1968.

Jacobson, Matthew Frye. *Barbarian Virtues: The United States Encounters Foreign Peoples at Home and Abroad, 1876–1917*. New York: Hill and Wang, 2000.

———. *Special Sorrows: The Diasporic Imagination of Irish, Polish, and Jewish Immigrants in the United States*. Cambridge: Harvard University Press, 1995.

————. *Whiteness of a Different Color: European Immigrants and the Alchemy of Race*. Cambridge: Harvard University Press, 1998.

Jaffee, David. "Peddlers of Progress and the Transformation of the Rural North." *Journal of American History* 78, no. 2 (September 1991).

Jenkins, Brian. *Fenians and Anglo-American Relations During Reconstruction*. Ithaca, NY: Cornell University Press, 1969.

Jenkins, William. "In the Shadow of a Grain Elevator: A Portrait of an Irish Neighborhood in Buffalo, New York, in the Nineteenth and Twentieth Centuries." *Eire-Ireland* 37, nos. 1–2 (spring–summer 2002): 14–37.

Jennings, Francis. *The Invasion of America: Indians, Colonialism, and the Cant of Conquest*. Chapel Hill: University of North Carolina Press, 1975.

Jensen, Vernon H. *Decasualization and Modernization of Dock Work in London*. New York: New York School of Industrial Relations (I.L.R. Paperback Series: no. 9), 1971.

————. *Hiring of Dock Workers and Employment Practices in the Ports of New York, Liverpool, London, Rotterdam and Marseilles*. Cambridge: Harvard University Press, 1964.

————. *Strife on the Waterfront: The Port of New York Since 1945*. Ithaca: Cornell University Press, 1974.

Johnson, Arthur L. "Boston and the Maritimes: A Century of Steam Navigation." Ph.D. diss., University of Maine (Orono), 1971.

Johnson, Daniel. *Vital Statistics from New Brunswick (Canada) Newspapers 1893–1894*. Saint John, NB: By author, 2002. [MHS]

Johnson, Margaret. "Maine Women Attorneys: A Millennial Jubilee." *Law Interview* (July, 2001).

Johnson, Paul E. *A Shopkeeper's Millennium: Society and Revivals in Rochester, New York, 1815–1837*. New York: Hill and Wang, 1978.

Johnston, John. *A History of Towns of Bristol and Bremen*. Albany, NY: Joel Munsell, 1873.

Jones, Herbert G. *Portland Ships are Good Ships*. Portland: Machigonne Press, 1945.

Jones, Howard Mumford. *O Strange New World, American Culture: The Formative Years*. New York: Viking Press, 1964.

Jones, Maldwyn A. "The Scotch-Irish in British America." In *Strangers Within the Realm: Cultural Margins of the First British Empire*, edited by Bernard Bailyn and Phillip D. Morgan. Chapel Hill: University of North Carolina Press, 1991: 284–313.

Jones, Paul John. *The Irish Brigade*. Washington, DC: Robert B. Lute, 1969.

Jordan, Donald. "Land and Politics in the West of Ireland: County Mayo, 1846–1882." Ph.D. diss., University of California at Davis, 1982.

Jordan, William B., Jr. *Burial Records, 1717–1962, of the Eastern Cemetery, Portland, Maine*. Bowie, MD: Heritage Books, 1987.

————. *Burial Records 1811–1890 of the Western Cemetery in Portland, Maine*. Bowie, MD: Heritage Books, 1987.

————. *A History of Cape Elizabeth, Maine*. Portland, ME: House of Falmouth, 1965; Bowie, MD: Heritage Books, 1987.

————. *Index to Portland Newspapers: 1785–1835*. Bowie, MD: Heritage Books, 1994.

————. *Maine in the Civil War: A Bibliographical Guide*. Portland: Maine Historical Society, 1976.

————. *Red Diamond Regiment: The 17th Maine Infantry, 1862–1865*. Shippensburg, PA: White Mane Publishing Co., 1996.

————, ed. *The Civil War Journals of John Mead Gould, 1861–1866*. Baltimore: Butternut and Blue, 1997.

Jordan, Winthrop D. *White Over Black: American Attitudes Toward the Negro, 1550–1812*. Chapel Hill: University of North Carolina Press, 1968.

Joyce, P. W. *English As We Speak It In Ireland*. London: Longmans, Green, and Co., 1910.

Judd, Richard W., Edwin Churchill, and Joel Eastman, eds. *Maine: The Pine Tree State from Prehistory to the Present*. Orono: University of Maine Press, 1995.

Kane, Paula. *Separatism and Subculture: Boston Catholicism, 1900–1920*. Chapel Hill: University of North Carolina Press, 1994.

Kanes, Candace. "Revisiting Main Street: Uncovering Women Entrepreneurs," in Polly Welts Kaufman and Katharine T. Corbett, eds. *Her Past Around Us: Interpreting Sites for Women's History*. Malabar, FL: Krieger Publishing Co., 2003.

Kantowicz, Edward. *Corporation Sole: Cardinal Mundelein and Chicago Catholicism*. Notre Dame, IN: University of Notre Dame Press, 1983.

Kaplan, Ron. "The Sporting Life: The Irish Influence in Baseball." *Irish America* 19, no. 1 (February–March 2003): 54–56.

Kauffman, Christopher. *Faith and Fraternalism: The History of the Knights of Columbus, 1882–1982*. New York: Harper & Row, 1982.

Kaufman, Polly Welts. *Boston Women and City School Politics, 1872–1905*. New York: Garland Publishers, 1994.

————. *Women Teachers on the Frontier*. New Haven, CT: Yale University Press, 1984.

Kaufman, Polly Welts, and Katharine T. Corbett, eds. *Her Past Around Us: Interpreting Sites for Women's History*. Malabar, FL: Krieger Publishing Co., 2003.

Kaufman, Polly Welts, Eileen Eagan, and Patricia Finn. *A Women's History Walking Trail in Portland, Maine*. Portland: Portland Women's History Trail, 1997. [MHS]

Kaufman, Polly Welts, Eileen Eagan, and Patricia Finn. *Working Women of the Old Port: A Portland Women's History Trail*. Portland: Portland Women's History Trail, 2003. [MHS]

Kavanagh, Edward. "Autographed Letter Signed (A.L.S.), 1795–1844, Washington, to William Allen, Norridgewock." Maine Historical Society Manuscripts, 1:88, 89, 90, 94, 95, MHS Collections 420–22.

————. "Autographed Letter Signed (A.L.S) Fr. John Cheverus to E. Kavanagh, 20 March 1821." Maine Historical Society Collection 420, vol. 1.

————. "Letter to (Hon. William King) 7th January 1832 4 pp. (William King, b. 1796, d. 1852. Governor of Maine) -With Cheverus' Letter Under C." [MHS]

Kearney, Richard, ed. *Migrations: The Irish at Home and Abroad*. Dublin: Wolfhound Press, 1990.

Keating, Anne. *Building Chicago: Suburban Developers and the Creation of a Divided Metropolis*. Columbus: Ohio State University Press, 1988.

Kee, Robert. *The Green Flag: The Turbulant History of the Irish National Movement*. New York: Delacorte Press, 1972.

Keegan, Gerald. *Famine Diary: Journey to a New World*. Dublin: Wolfhound Press, 1991.

Keller, Morton. *The Art and Politics of Thomas Nast*. New York: Oxford University Press, 1968.

Kelley, James. "Labor Problems of the Longshoremen in the United States." Ph.D. diss., Boston University, 1941.

Kellogg, Elijah. *A Strong Arm and a Mother's Blessing*. Boston: Lothrop, Lee and Shepherd, Publishers, 1880.

Kelly, James. "The Resumption of Emigration from Ireland After the American War of Independence: 1783–1787." *Studia Hibernica* 24 (1984–1988).

Kelly, Josephine. *Dark Shepherd*. Paterson, NJ: St. Anthony Guild Press, 1967.

Kelly, Sr. Mary Gilbert, O.P. *Catholic Immigration Projects in the Unites States, 1815–1860*. New York: The U.S. Catholic Historical Society (Monograph Series 17), 1939.

Kelly, Richard D., Jr. "The Descendants of Dennis T. Cullinan of Ennis, County Clare, Ireland." Augusta, ME: By author, 1976. [MHS]

Keneally, Thomas. *The Great Shame, And the Triumph of the Irish in the English-Speaking World*. New York: Anchor Books/Random House, 2000.

Kenneally, James. *The History of American Catholic Women*. New York: Crourvads, 1990.

Kennedy, Lawrence. "Power and Prejudice: Boston Politics, 1885–1895." Ph.D. diss., Boston College, 1989.

Kennedy, Robert E., Jr. *The Irish: Emigration, Marriage, and Fertility*. Berkeley: University of California Press, 1973.

Kenny, Kevin. "Diaspora and Comparison: The Global Irish as a Case Study." *The Journal of American History* (June 2003): 134–62.

———. *Making Sense of the Molly Maguires*. New York: Oxford University Press, 1998.

Kerr, Clark. "Collective Bargaining on the Pacific Coast." *Monthly Labor Review* 64 (April 1947).

Kerr, Clark, and Lloyd Fisher. "Conflicts on the Waterfront." *Atlantic Monthly* 184 (September 1949).

Keyes, Charles, ed. *Ethnic Change*. Seattle: University of Washington Press, 1986.

Keysar, Alexander. *Out of Work: The First Century of Unemployment in Massachusetts*. New York: Cambridge University Press, 1986.

Kinealy, Christine. *The Great Irish Famine: Impact, Ideology and Rebellion*. New York: Palgrave, 2002.

———. *This Great Calamity: The Irish Famine, 1845–1852*. Dublin: Gill and Macmillan, 1994.

King, Joseph A. *The Irish Lumberman-Farmer, Fitzgeralds, Harrigans and Others*. Lafayette, CA: By author, 1982.

Kingsley, Elbridge. *Picturesque Worcester*. Springfield: W. F. Adams, 1895.

Kirkland, Edward C. *Men, Cities, and Transportation: A Study in New England History*. 2 vols. Cambridge: Harvard University Press, 1948.

Kirkpatrick, Gabriel W. "Influenza 1918: A Maine Perspective." *Maine Historical Society Quarterly* 25, no. 3 (winter 1986).

Kirschner, Don. *The Paradox of Professionalism: Reform and Public Service in Urban America, 1900–1940* (Contributions in American History, no. 119). New York: Greenwood Press, 1986.

Kivisto, Peter, and Dag Blanck, eds. *American Immigrants and Their Generations: Studies and Commentaries on the Hansen Thesis After Fifty Years*. Urbana: University of Illinois Press, 1990.

Kleppner, Paul. *Continuity and Change in Electoral Politics, 1893–1928*. Westport, CT: Greenwood Press, 1987.

———. *The Cross of Culture: A Social Analysis of Midwestern Politics, 1850–1900*. New York: Free Press, 1970.

———. *The Third Electoral System, 1853 to 1982*. Chapel Hill: University of North Carolina Press, 1979.

Knights, Peter R. *Plain People of Boston, 1830–1860*. New York: Oxford University Press, 1971.

Knobel, Dale T. *Paddy and the Republic*. Middletown, CT: Wesleyan University Press, 1986.

Kohl, Lawrence F., ed. *Irish Green and Union Blue: The Civil War Letters of Peter Welch*. Bronx, NY: Fordham University Press, 1986.

Kolesar, Robert. "The Politics of Development: Worcester, Massachusetts in the Late Nineteenth Century." *Journal of Urban History* 16, no. 1 (November 1989).

Kornbluh, Joyce L., ed. *Rebel Voices: And I.W.W. Anthology*. Ann Arbor: University of Michigan Press, 1964.

Kosmuin, Barry A., and Seymore Lachma. *One Nation Under God: Religion in Contemporary American Society*. New York: Harmony Books, 1993.

Krichels, Deborah Tracey. "Reaction and Reform: The Political Career of James Phinney Baxter, Mayor of Portland, Maine, 1893–1897, 1904–05." Master's thesis, University of Maine (Orono), 1986. [MHS]

Lamoreaux, Naomi. "Bank Mergers in Late Nineteenth Century New England: The Contingent Nature of Structural Change." *Journal of Economic History* 53, no. 1 (September 1991).

———. *Banks, Personal Connections, and Economic Development in Industrial New England*. New York: Cambridge University Press, 1994.

Lampman, Robert J. "Collective Bargainings of West Coast Sailors, 1885–1947: A Study in Unionism." Ph.D. diss., University of Wisconsin, 1950.

Lamson, R. "1951 New York Wildcat Dock Strike." *Social Science Quarterly* 34 (1954).

Land Owners in Ireland, 1876. Baltimore: Genealogical Publishing Co., 1988.

Landale, Nancy S., and Stewart Tolnay. "Generation, Ethnicity, and Marriage: Historical Patterns in the Northern United States." *Demography* 30, no. 1 (February 1993).

Langan-Egan, Maureen. *Galway Women in the Nineteenth Century*. Dublin: Open Air Books, 1999.

Lapomarda, Vincent A. *The Catholic Church in the Land of the Holy Cross: A History of the Diocese of Portland, Maine*. Strasbourg, France: Les Editions du Signe, 2003.

———. *Charles Nolcini: The Life and Music of an Italian-American in the Age of Jackson*. Worcester, MA: By author, 1997.

Larkin, Emmett. "The Devotional Revolution in Ireland, 1850–1875." *American Historical Review* 77, no. 3 (June 1972): 625–52.

———. *The Roman Catholic Church in Ireland and Fall of Parnell, 1888–1891*. Chapel Hill: University of North Carolina Press, 1979.

Larkin, Sr. Mary Teresita. "The History of the Devolution of Catholic Education in the Province, District and State of Maine From 1604–1933." Master's thesis, University of Maine (Orono), 1934.

Larrowe, Charles P. "The Great Maritime Strike of '34." *Labor History* 11, no. 4 (fall 1970).

———. "The Great Maritime Strike of '34, Part II." *Labor History* 12, no. 1 (winter 1971).

———. *Harry Bridges: The Rise and Fall of Radical Labor in the United States.* New York: Lawrence Hill Publishers, 1972.

———. *Maritime Labor Relations on the Great Lakes.* East Lansing, MI: Michigan State University Labor and Industrial Relations Center, 1955.

———. *Shape-up and Hiring Hall: A Comparison of Firing Methods and Labor Relations on the New York and Seattle Waterfronts.* Berkeley: University of California Press, 1955; Westport, CT: Greenwood Press, 1976.

Lascelles, E. C., and S. S. Bullock. "Dock Labour and Decasualization." *Studies in Economics and Political Sciences*, no. 75, London School of Economics and Political Science, 1924.

Laslett, John H. M. "DeLeonite Socialism and the Irish Shoe Workers of New England." In *Labor and the Left: A Study of Socialist and Radical Influence in the American Labor Movement, 1881–1924.* New York: Basic Books, 1970.

Laxton, Edward. *The Famine Ships: The Irish Exodus to America.* New York: Henry Holt and Co., 1996.

Leach, Douglas Edward. *Arms for Empire: A Military History of the British Colonies in North America, 1607–1763.* New York: Macmillan, 1973.

———. *The Northern Colonial Frontier: 1607–1763.* New York: Holt, Rinehart and Winston, 1966.

Leamon, James S., Richard R. Wescott, and Edward O. Schriver. "Separation and Statehood, 1783–1820." In *Maine: The Pine Tree State from Prehistory to the Present*, edited by Richard W. Judd, Edwin Churchill, and Joel Eastman. Orono: University of Maine Press, 1995.

Lears, T. Jackson. *No Place of Grace: Antimodernism and the Transformation of American Culture, 1880s to 1920.* New York: Pantheon, 1981.

Leary, William M., Jr. "Woodrow Wilson, Irish Americans and the Election of 1916." *Journal of American History* 54, no. 1 (June 1967): 57–72.

Leavenworth, Peter S. "'The Best Title That Indians Can Claime': Native Agency and Consent in the Transferal of Penacook-Pawtucket Land in the Seventeenth Century." *The New England Quarterly* (June 1999): 275–300.

Leavitt, Judith Waltzer. *Typhoid Mary: Captive to the Public's Health.* Boston: Beacon Press, 1996.

Lee, Joseph. *Ireland, 1945–1970.* Dublin: Gill and Macmillan, 1979.

———. *The Modernisation of Irish Society, 1848–1918.* Dublin: Gill and Macmillan, 1973.

Leinenweber, Charles. "The Class and Ethnic Bases of New York City Socialism, 1904–1915." *Labor History* 22, no. 1 (1981).

Lemke, William. *A Pride of Lions: Joshua Chamberlain and Other Maine Civil War Heroes.* North Attleborough, MA: Covered Bridge Press, 1997.

———. *The Wild, Wild, East: Unusual Tales of Maine History.* Camden, ME: Yankee Books, 1990.

Leonard, Ira M., and Robert D. Parmet. *American Nativism, 1830–1860*. New York: Van Nostrand Reinhold, 1971.

Leonard, William C. "Vigor in Arduis: A History of Boston's African-American Catholic Community, 1788–1988." Ph.D. diss., Boston College, 1999.

Levenson, Samuel. *James Connolly: A Biography*. London: Martin, Brian and O'Keefe, 1973.

Levin, Murray B. *The Compleat Politician: Political Strategy in Massachusetts*. Indianapolis: Bobbs-Merrill, 1962.

Levine, Ben. *Waking Up French, Réveil: The Repression and Renaissance of the French in New England*. Rockland, ME: Watching Place Productions, 2003. Film.

Levy, Bill. *John Ford: A Bio-Bibliography*. Westport, CT: Greenwood Press, 1998.

Lewis, Samuel. *A Topographical Dictionary of Ireland*. 1837. Reprint, Baltimore: Genealogical Publ. Co., 1984.

Leyburn, James G. *The Scotch-Irish: A Social History*. Chapel Hill: University of North Carolina Press, 1962.

Libby, Gary W. "Biographical Sketches of Maine's Chinese." (2003). [MHS]

Licht, Walter. *Getting Work: Philadelphia, 1840–1950*. Cambridge: Harvard University Press, 1992.

Liebes, Richard A. "Longshore Labor Relations on the Pacific Coast, 1934–1942." Ph.D. diss., University of California, 1942.

Light, Dale B., Jr. "Class, Ethnicity, and the Urban Ecology in a Nineteenth Century City: Philadelphia's Irish, 1840–1910." Ph.D. diss., University of Pennsylvania, 1979.

———. "The Role of Irish-American Organisations in Assimilation and Community Formation." In *The Irish in America: Emigration, Assimilation and Impact*, edited by P. J. Drudy. New York: Cambridge University Press, 1985.

Lincoln, William. *History of Worcester, Massachusetts from Its Earliest Founding to September 1836*. Worcester, MA: Hersey, 1862.

Linderman, Gerald F. *Embattled Courage: The Experience of Combat in the American Civil War*. New York: The Free Press, 1987.

Lindholdt, Paul J., ed. *John Josselyn, Colonial Traveler: A Critical Edition of Two Voyages to New-England*. Hanover, NH: University Press of New England, 1988.

Linehan, John C. *The Irish Scots and the "Scotch-Irish."* Concord, NH: The American Irish Historical Society, 1902.

Litt, Edgar. *Ethnic Politics in America: Beyond Pluralism*. Glencoe, IL: Scott, Foresman, 1970.

Litwack, Leon F. *North of Slavery: The Negro in the Free States, 1790–1860*. Chicago: University of Chicago Press, 1965.

Longfellow, Henry Wadsworth. *Poetical Works*. Oxford: Oxford University Press, 1904.

Lord, Robert H, John E. Sexton, and Edward T. Harrington. *History of the Archdiocese of Boston: In the Various Stages of Its Development, 1604–1943*. 3 vols. Boston, MA: The Pilot Publishing Company, 1945.

Loveitt, Lillian F. "The Social History of Portland, Maine from 1820 to 1840." Master's thesis, University of Maine, 1939. Special Collections, Fogler Library, University of Maine, Orono.

Loveitt, Rosella A. "The Social History of Portland, Maine from 1840 to 1860." Master's thesis, University of Maine, 1940. Special Collections, Fogler Library, Univeristy of Maine, Orono.

Lovell, John C. *Stereotypes and Dockers: A Study of Trade Unionism in the Port of London, 1870–1914.* New York: A. M. Kelley, 1969.

Lowell, Robert. *The Mills of the Kavanaughs.* New York: Harcourt, Brace and World, Inc., 1951.

Lownes, Richard. *Technical Innovation: Capital and Labour: Two Case Histories of the Port Industry of California.* Romford, England: Anglican Regional Management Centre, 1976.

Lubell, Samuel. *The Future of American Politics.* New York: Harper, 1952.

Lubove, Roy. *Community Planning in the 1920s.* Pittsburgh: University of Pittsburgh Press, 1963.

Lucey, William Leo. *The Catholic Church in Maine.* Francestown, NH: Marshall Jones, 1957.

———. *Edward Kavanaugh: Catholic Statesmen Diplomat from Maine, 1795–1844.* Francestown, NH: Marshall Jones Company, 1946.

———. "A Late Report of the Ship 'Hibernia' Captured by a French Privateer in the year 1800." *The New England Quarterly* 17 (March–December 1944): 101–106.

———. "Longfellow's Kavanagh: A Forgotten Tale." *America* 62 (March 1940): 690–91.

———. "Two Irish Merchants of New England." *The New England Quarterly* 14, no. 4 (December 1941): 633–45.

Luria, Daniel D. "Wealth, Capital, and Power: The Social Meaning of Home Ownership." *Journal of Interdisciplinary History* 7, no. 2 (autumn 1976).

Lynch-Brennan, Margaret. "The Servant Slant: Irish Women Domestic Servants and Historic House Museums." In *Her Past Around Us: Interpreting Sites for Women's History,* edited by Polly Welts Kaufman and Katherine Corbett. Malabar, FL: Krieger Publ. Co., 2003.

Lyons, F. S. L. *Charles Stewart Parnell.* New York: Oxford University Press, 1977.

———. *Culture and Anarchy in Ireland, 1890 to 1939.* Oxford: Clarendon Press, 1979.

MacCurtain, Margaret, and Doncha O'Currain. *Women in Irish Society: The Historical Dimension.* Westport, CT: Greenwood Press, 1979.

MacDonagh, Oliver. *States of Mind: A Study of Anglo-Irish Conflict, 1800–1980.* London: George Allen Press, 1983.

MacDonagh, Oliver, W. F. Mandle, and Pauric Travers, eds. *Irish Culture and Nationalism, 1750–1950.* New York: St. Martin's Press, 1983.

MacDonagh, Thomas J. "The Origins of the Parochial Schools of This City." *The Catholic Directory and History of Worcester and Suburbs* (1887).

Macdonald, Fergus. *The Catholic Church and the Secret Societies in the United States.* New York: U.S. Catholic Historical Society, 1946.

MacLysaght, Edward. *The Surnames of Ireland.* Dublin: Irish Academic Press, 1980. [MHS]

MacManus, Seamus. *The Story of the Irish Race.* New York: The Irish Publishing Company, 1921; Old Greenwich, CT: The Devin-Adair Co., 1966.

MacWilliams, J. Donald. *A Time of Men.* Lewiston, ME: Twin City Printery, 1967.

———. *Yours in Sport: A History of Baseball, Basketball, Boxing and Bowling in Maine.* Lewiston, ME: Twin City Publishers for the Monmouth Press, 1967.

Maddock, Fidelma. "The Cot Fishermen of the River Nore." In *Kilkenny History and Society: Interdisciplinary Essays on the History of an Irish County,* edited by William Nolan and Kevin Whelan. Dublin: Geography Publications, 1990: 541–66.

Maguire, John F. *The Irish in America*. New York: Arno Press, 1969.

Maine Catholic Historical Magazine. Waterville, ME: The Catholic Bishop and the Maine Catholic Historical Society 8 vols., 1913–1928. [MHS]

Malcolm, Elizabeth. "Catholic Church and Irish Temperance." *Irish Historical Studies* 23 (1982).

———. *"Ireland Sober, Ireland Free": Drink and Temperance in Nineteenth-Century Ireland*. Syracuse: Syracuse University Press, 1986.

Malm, F. T. "Wage Differentials in Pacific Coast Longshoring." *Industrial and Labor Relations Review* 5 (October 1951).

Malone, Joseph J. *Pine Tree and Politics: The Naval Stores and Forest Policy in Colonial New England, 1691–1775*. Seattle: University of Washington Press, 1964.

Mandle, W. F. *The Gaelic Athletic Association and Irish Nationalist Politics, 1884–1924*. Dublin: Gill, 1987.

Mannion, John. "Irish Merchants Abroad: The Newfoundland Experience, 1750–1850." In *Negoce et Industrie en France et en Irlande aux XVIII et XIX siecles*, edited by L. M. Cullen and P. Butel. Paris: Centre de Recherches Historiques, 1980.

———. *Irish Settlements in Eastern Canada: A Study of Cultural Transfer and Adaptation*. Toronto: University of Toronto Press, 1974.

———. "Migration and Upward Mobility: The Meagher Family in Northern Ireland and Newfoundland, 1780–1830." *Irish Economic and Social History* 15 (1988).

———. "Patrick Morris and Newfoundland Irish Immigration." In *Talamh an Eisc: Canadian and Irish Essays*, edited by C. Byrne and M. Harry. Halifax, NS: 1986.

———. "The Waterford Merchants and the Irish-Newfoundland Provisions Trade." In *Negoce et Industrie en France et en Irlande aux XVIII et XIX siecles*, edited by L. M. Cullen and P. Butel. Paris: Centre de Recherches Historiques, 1980.

Mannion, John, and Fidelma Maddock. "Old World Antecedents, New World Adaptations: Inistioge Immigrants in Newfoundland." In *Kilkenny History and Society: Interdisciplinary Essays on the History of an Irish County*, edited by William Nolan and Kevin Whelan. Dublin: Geography Publications, 1990.

Marshall, William F. *Ulster Sails West: The Story of the Great Emigration from Ulster to North America in the Eighteenth Century*. Baltimore: Genealogical Publ. Co., 1977.

Martin, Kenneth R., and Ralph Linwood Snow. *The Pattens of Bath: A Seafaring Dynasty*. Bath, ME: Maine Maritime Museum and Patten Free Library, 1996. [MHS]

Marvin, A. P. *History of the Catholic Church in the United States*. Notre Dame, IN: University of Notre Dame Press, 1969.

Massbarger, Paul. *Fiction with a Parochial Purpose: Social Uses of American Catholic Literature, 1884–1900*. Boston: Boston University Press, 1971.

Mathew, Frank J. *Father Mathew: His Life and Times*. London: Cassell, 1890.

Mathews, Lois K. *The Expansion of New England*. Boston: Houghton Mifflin, 1909. [MHS]

Matsumoto, Valerie. *Farming the Home Place: A Japanese American Community in California*. Ithaca, NY: Cornell University Press, 1993.

Matthews, Samuel W. "Report of the special agent." Augusta, ME: Burleigh and Flynt, 1889.

McAuliffe, John J. *Timothy G. O'Connell, 1868–1955: A Biographical Dictionary of Architects in Maine.* Vol. 6. Augusta: Maine Historic Preservation Commission, 1991.

McAvoy, Thomas. *A History of the Catholic Church in the United States.* Notre Dame, IN: University of Notre Dame Press, 1969.

McBreairty, Darrell M. *Conversations with A'nt Ev': An Oral History of the Allagash.* Allagash, ME: Allagash Publishing Co., 1982.

McBride, Joseph. *Searching for John Ford: A Life.* New York: St. Martin's Press, 2001.

McBride, Theresa. "Social Mobility for the Lower Classes: Domestic Servants in France." *Journal of Social History* 4, no. 4 (fall 1974).

McCaffrey, Lawrence J. *The Irish Diaspora in America.* Bloomington, IN: Indiana University Press, 1976.

———. *Textures of Irish America.* Syracuse: Syracuse University Press, 1992.

———, ed. *The Irish in Chicago.* Urbana: University of Illinois Press, 1987.

———, ed. *Irish Nationalism and the American Contribution.* New York: Arno Press, 1976.

McCarron, Edward T. "Altered States: Tyrone Migration to Providence, Rhode Island, During the Nineteenth Century." *Clogher Record* 16, no. 1 (1997): 145–61.

———. "A Brave New World: The Irish Agrarian Colony of Benedicta, Maine in the 1830s and 1840s." *Records of the American Catholic Historical Society of Philadelphia* 105 (spring/summer 1994): 1–15.

———. "Famine Lifelines: The Transatlantic Letters of James Prendergast." In *Ireland's Great Hunger: Silence, Memory and Commemoration,* edited by David A. Valone and Christine Kinealy. Lanham, MD: University Press of America, 2002: 41–62.

———. "In Pursuit of the 'Maine' Chance: The North Family of Offaly and New England, 1700–1776." In *Offaly History and Society: Interdisciplinary Essays on the History of an Irish County,* edited by William Nolan and Timothy P. O'Neill. Dublin: Geography Publications, 1998: 339–70.

———. "Irish Migration and Settlement on the Eastern Frontier: The Case of Lincoln County, Maine, 1760–1820." *Retrospection: The New England Graduate Review in American History* 2 (1989): 21–31.

———. "The World of Kavanagh and Cottrill: A Portrait of Irish Emigration, Entrepreneurship, and Ethnic Diversity in Mid Maine, 1760–1820." Ph.D. diss., University of New Hampshire, 1992.

McCouaig, Sean. "McCouaig Family Ships." *The Glynns: Journal of the Glens of Antrim Historical Society.* Coleraine, Co. Derry: Impact Printing, 1998.

McCourt, D. "County Derry in New England." *County Londonderry Handbook.* Coleraine, Northern Ireland, 1964. 87–101.

McCracken, Eileen. *The Irish Woods Since Medieval Times.* Newton Abbot, England: David and Charles, 1971.

———. "Notes on Kilkenny Woods and Nurserymen." *Old Kilkenny Review* (1970).

McCrum, R. G. *Dear Mom: World War II Remembered in a Sailor's Letters.* Orono: University of Maine Press, 1994.

McCrum, Robert, William Cran, and Robert MacNeil. *The Story of English*. New York: Viking Press, 1986.

McCurdy, Augustine. *Gaeilge Reachlann: A History of Rathlin Irish*. Rathlin: An tEach Ceannann Dubh Publications (By author), 2002.

———. *Rathlin's Rugged Story: From an Islander's Perspective*. Coleraine, County Antrim: Impact Printing, 2000.

McDannell, Colleen. *Material Christianity*. New Haven: Yale University Press, 1995.

McDonald, Terrence J. *The Parameters of Urban Fiscal Policy: Socio-Economic Change and Political Culture in San Francisco, 1860–1906*. Berkeley: University of California Press, 1986.

McGee, Thomas D'Arcy. *A History of the Irish Settlers in North America*. Boston: P. Donahoe, 1852.

McGrath, Anna Fields, ed. *The County: Land of Promise, A Pictorial History of Aroostook County, Maine*. Norfolk, VA: The Donning Co., 1989. [MHS]

McGrath, Francis C. *Brian Friel's (Post) Colonial Drama: Language, Illusion, and Politics*. Syracuse: Syracuse University Press, 1999.

———. *Ireland's Field Day Theatre Company* (forthcoming).

———. *The Sensible Spirit: Water Pater and the Modernist Paradigm*. Tampa: University of South Florida Press, 1986.

McGreevy, John T. *Parish Boundaries: The Catholic Encounter with Race in the Twentieth-Century Urban North*. Chicago: University of Chicago Press, 1996.

McKelvey, Jean T. *Dock Labor Disputes in Great Britain: A Study in the Persistence of Industrial Unrest*. Ithaca, NY: Cornell University (State School of Industrial and Labor Relations), 1953.

McKenna, James E., Joseph R. McKenna, and Peter A. McKenna. *Sign of the Stag: A Chimera*. Rumford, ME: Northeast Folklore 32, 1997.

McLaughlin, Francis M. "The Development of Labor Peace in the Port of Boston." *Industrial and Labor Relations Review* 20 (1967).

———. "Industrial Relations in the Boston Longshore Industry." Ph.D. diss., Massachusetts Institute of Technology, 1964.

McLaughlin, Virginia Yans, ed. *Immigration Reconsidered*. New York: Oxford University Press, 1990.

McLellan, John. "Bryce McLellan (1690–1776), An Immigrant to Maine, His Children and Grandchildren." New Orleans: By author, 1987. [MHS]

McLeod, Hugh. "Catholicism and the New York Irish: 1880 to 1910." In *Disciplines of Faith: Studies in Religion, Politics, and Patriarchy*, edited by Jim Obelkevich, Lyndal Roper, and Raphael Samuel. New York: Routledge and Kegan Paul, 1987.

———. *Piety and Poverty: Working Class Religion in Berlin, London and New York, 1870–1914*. New York: Holmes and Meier, 1996.

———. *Religion and the People of Western Europe*. Oxford: Oxford University Press, 1981.

McMahon, Eileen. *What Parish Are You From? A Chicago Irish Community and Race Relations*. Lexington: University Press of Kentucky, 1995.

McNickle, Chris. *To Be Mayor of New York: Ethnic Politics in the City*. New York: Columbia University Press, 1994.

McSeveney, Samuel. *The Politics of Depression in the Northeast, 1893–1896*. New York: Oxford University Press, 1972.

Meade, George G. *The Life and Letters of George Gordon Meade*. New York: Charles Scribner's Sons, 1913.

Meagher, Timothy J. *From Paddy to Studs: Irish American Communities at the Turn of the Century, 1880 to 1920*. Westport: Greenwood Press, 1986.

———. *Inventing Irish America: Generation, Class, and Ethnic Identity in a New England City, 1880–1928*. Notre Dame, IN: University of Notre Dame Press, 2001.

———. "'Irish All the Time': Ethnic Consciousness among the Irish in Worcester, Massachusetts, 1880–1905." *Journal of Social History* 19, no. 2 (winter 1985).

———. "'The Lord is Not Dead': Cultural and Social Change Among the Irish in Worcester, Massachusetts." Ph.D. diss., Brown University, 1982.

———. "Sweet Good Mothers and Young Women Out in the World: The Roles of Irish American Women in Late Nineteenth and Early Twentieth Century Worcester, Massachusetts." *U.S. Catholic Historian* 5, no. 3–4 (1986): 325–44.

———. *Urban American Catholicism: Culture and Identity of the American Catholic People*. New York: Garland Press, 1988.

Mears, David Otis. *An Autobiography*. Boston: Pilgrim Press, 1920.

Mellish, Michael. *The Docks After Devlin: A Study of the Effects of the Recommendations of the Devlin Committee on Industrial Relations in the London Docks*. London: Heinemann Educational Press, 1972.

Melody, Michael, and Marilyn Melody, eds. "History of St. Dominic's Parish." *Saint Dominic's: 175 Years of Memories, 1822–1997*. Portland: Smart Marketing, Inc. 1997. [MHS]

Melvin, Charlotte Lenentine. "The First Hundred Years in New Sweden." *The Swedish Pioneer Historical Quarterly* (October 1970): 233–57.

Merk, Lois Bannister. "Massachusetts and the Women's Suffrage Movement." Ph.D. diss., Radcliffe College, 1956.

Merwick, Donna. *Boston Priests, 1848–1910: A Study of Social and Intellectual Change*. Cambridge, MA: Harvard University Press 1973.

Mettres, Seamus. *The Irish American Experience: A Guide to the Literature*. Washington, DC: University Press of America, 1981.

Mezy, Phiz. "West Coast Waterfront Showdown." *Nation* 16 (November 1948).

Miller, David W. *Church, State, and Nation in Ireland, 1898–1921*. Pittsburgh: University of Pittsburgh Press, 1973.

———. "Irish Catholicism and the Great Famine." *Journal of Social History* 9, no. 1 (1975).

———. *Queen's Rebels: Ulster Loyalism in Historical Perspective*. Dublin: Gill and Macmillan, 1978.

Miller, Kerby A. *Emigrants and Exiles: Ireland and the Irish Exodus to North America*. New York: Oxford University Press, 1985.

Miller, Kerby A., Arnold Schrier, Bruce D. Boling, and David N. Doyle. *Irish Immigrants in the Land of Canaan: Letters and Memoirs from Colonial and Revolutionary America, 1675–1815*. Oxford: Oxford University Press, 2003.

Miller, Kerby A., and Paul Wagner. *Out of Ireland: The Story of Irish Emigration to America*. Washington, DC: Elliott and Clark Publishing, 1994.

Miller, Randall, and Thomas D. Marzik, eds. *Immigrants and Religion in Urban America*. Philadelphia: Temple University Press, 1977.

Miller, Robert Ryal. *Shamrock and Sword: The Saint Patrick's Battalion in the U.S.–Mexican War*. Norman: University of Oklahoma Press, 1989.

Miner, A. A. "Neal Dow and His Life Work." *The New England Magazine* 10, no. 4 (June 1894).

Mitchell, Albert Gibbs. "Irish Family Patterns in Nineteenth Century Ireland and Lowell, Massachusetts." Ph.D. diss., Boston University, 1976.

Mitchell, Arthur, ed. *Ireland and Irishmen in the American War of Independence.* Dublin: The Academy Press, 1978.

———. *Labour in Irish Politics, 1890–1930: The Irish Labour Movement in an Age of Revolution.* Dublin: Irish University Press, 1974.

———. *Revolutionary Geovernment in Ireland: Dail Eireann, 1919–1922.* Dublin: Gill & Macmillan, 1995.

Mitchell, Brian C. *The Paddy Camps: The Irish of Lowell, 1821–1861.* Urbana: University of Illinois Press, 1988.

Mitchell, George J. *Making Peace.* Berkeley: University of California Press, 1999.

Mokyr, Joel. *Why Ireland Starved: A Quantitative and Analytical History of the Irish Economy, 1800–1850.* Winchester, MA: Allen and Unwin, Inc., 1983.

Mollenkopf, John. *The Contested City.* Princeton, NJ: Princeton University Press, 1989.

———. *Dual City: Restructuring New York.* New York: Russell Sage, 1991.

Moloney, Deirdre M. *American Catholic Lay Groups and Transatlantic Social Reform in the Progressive Era.* Chapel Hill: University of North Carolina Press, 2002.

Monaghan, Jay. *The Great Rascal: The Life and Adventures of Ned Buntline.* Boston: Little, Brown, 1952.

Montgomery, David. *Beyond Equality: Labor and the Radical Republicans, 1862–1872.* New York: Alfred A. Knopf, 1967.

———. *The Fall of the House of Labor.* New York: Cambridge University Press, 1987.

———. "The Irish and the American Labor Movement." In *America and Ireland, 1776–1976: The American Identity and the Irish Connection,* edited by David Doyle and Owen Dudley Edwards. Westport, CT: Greenwood Press, 1979.

Moody, T. W., ed. *The Fenian Movement.* Cork: Mercier Press, 1978.

———. *Michael Davitt and Irish Revolution, 1846–1882.* New York: Oxford University Press, 1981.

Moogk, Peter. "Reluctant Exiles: The Problems of Colonization in French North America." *William and Mary Quarterly* 46 (July 1989).

Mooney, Thomas. *Nine Years in America: A Series of Letters to his Cousin, Patrick Mooney, A Farmer in Ireland.* Dublin: James McGlashan Publishers, 1850.

Moore, Deborah Dash. *At Home in America: Second Generation New York Jews.* New York: Columbia University Press, 1989.

Moorhouse, B. "Researching the Irish-Born of New York City." *The New York Genealogical and Biographical Record* 112, no. 2 (April 1981): 65–71.

Morison, Samuel Elliot. *The Maritime History of Massachusetts, 1783–1869.* Boston: Northeastern University Press, 1979.

Morris, James M. *Our Maritime Heritage: Maritime Developments and their Impact on American Life.* Lanham, MD: University Press of America, 1979.

Moss, Kenneth. "St. Patrick's Day Celebration and the Formation of the Irish American Identity, 1845–1875." *Journal of Social History* 29, no. 9 (fall 1995).

Mulholland, Elaine M. "The Irish Stereotype and Its Significance During the 1863

New York City Draft Riots and the Orange Riot of 1871." Master's thesis, University of Maine (Orono), 1999.

Mulkern, John R. *The Know-Nothing Party in Massachusetts: The Rise and Fall of a People's Movement.* Boston: Northeastern University Press, 1990.

Mundy, James H. *Bygone Bangor.* Bangor, ME: Bangor Daily News, 1976.

———. *Hard Times, Hard Men: Maine and the Irish 1830–1860.* Scarborough, ME: Harp Publications, 1990.

———. "Hard Times, Hard Men: Maine and the Irish 1830–1860." Ph.D. diss., University of Maine (Orono), 1995.

———. "Heroes by Appointment." Master's thesis, University of Maine (Orono), 1970.

———. *No Rich Men's Sons: The Sixth Maine Volunteer Infantry.* Cape Elizabeth, ME: Harp Publications, 1994.

———. *Second to None: The Story of the 2nd Maine Volunteer Infantry: "The Bangor Regiment."* Scarborough, ME: Harp Publications, 1992.

Mundy, James H., and Earle G. Shettleworth, Jr. *The Flight of the Grand Eagle.* Augusta, ME: Maine Historic Preservation Commission, 1977.

Munroe, John S. "Chronological History of Parochial Education in Portland, Maine." Unpublished manuscript. Mandeville, LA: LaSalle University, 1996.

Murdoch, Eugene C. *One Million Men: The Civil War Draft in the North.* Madison: State Historical Society of Wisconsin, 1971.

Murphy, Francis. *Sketches of the Life and Work of Captain Cyrus Sturdivant.* New York: Willis McDonald and Co., Printers, 1882.

Murphy, Frank, ed. *The Bog Irish, Who They Were and How They Lived.* Ringwood, Victoria, Australia: Penquin, 1987.

———. "The Irish and Afro-Americans in the United States History." *Freedomways* 22, no. 1 (1982).

Murphy, Robert T. *Patrick C. Keely, 1816–1896: A Biographical Dictionary of Architects in Maine.* Augusta, ME: Maine Historic Preservation Commission 4, no. 7 (1987). [MHS]

Myers, John F. Audio tapes (5) regarding emigration from New Brunswick to Maine. Northeast Archives of Folklore and Oral History, University of Maine (Orono).

Myrdal, Gunnar. *An American Dilemma: The Negro Problem and Modern Democracy.* 2 vols. New York: Harper, 1944.

Nahirny, Vladimir, and Joshua Fishman. "American Immigrant Groups, Ethnic Identification, and the Problem of Generations." *Sociological Reviews* 13, no. 3 (December 1965).

Nash, Gary B. "Forging Freedom: The Emancipation Experience in the Northern Seaport Cities, 1775–1820." In *Slavery and Freedom in the Age of the American Revolution,* edited by Ira Berlin and Ronald Hoffman. Charlottesville: University of Virginia Press, 1983.

———. *The Urban Crucible: Social Change, Political Consciousness and the Origins of the American Revolution.* Cambridge: Harvard University Press, 1979.

National Maritime Union. "N.M.U.- 40 Years on a True Course." *N.M.U. Pilot* 42 (May 1977).

Neal, John. *Portland Illustrated.* Portland: W. S. Jones, Publisher, 1874.

Neidhardt, W. S. *Fenianism in North America.* University Park: Pennsylvania State University Press, 1975.

Nelson, Bruce. *Divided We Stand: American Workers and the Struggle for Black Equality*. Princeton, NJ: Princeton University Press, 2001.

———. *Workers on the Waterfront: Seamen, Longshoremen, and Unionism in the 1930s*. Urbana: University of Illinois Press, 1988.

Nevins, Allan. *Ordeal of the Union, 1890–1971*. NewYork: Scribner, 1947.

New York Committee of Merchants for the Relief of Colored People Suffering from the Late Riots, 1863 Report. Salem, NH: Ayer Company Publishers, 1969.

Ní Chonceanainn, Finnín. *Tomás Bán*. (Ciarán Ó Coigligh a chuir in eagar agus a scríobh an brollach.) Baile Átha Cliath: Conradh na Gaeilge, 1996.

Nicknair, Sr. Marie of the Visitation, O.P. *Bishop Benedict J. Fenwick and the Origins of the Benedicta, Maine Community*. Augusta, ME: O'Ceallaigh Publications, 1992.

Nilsen, Kenneth E. "Collecting Celtic Folklore in the United States." In *Proceedings of the First North American Congress of Celtic Studies, 1986*, edited by Gordon W. MacLennan. Ottawa: University of Ottawa, 1988: 55–74.

———. "Irish Gaelic Literature in the U.S. in the Nineteenth Century." In *American Babel: Literatures of the United States from Abnaki to Zuni*, edited by Marc Shell. Cambridge: Harvard University Press, 2002. 188–218.

———. "The Irish Language in the U.S." In *The Encyclopedia of the Irish in America*, edited by Michael Glazier. Notre Dame, IN: Notre Dame Press, 1999: 470–74.

———. "The Irish Language in New York City 1850–1900." In *The New York Irish*, edited by T. Meagher and R. Bayor. Baltimore: The Johns Hopkins University Press, 1995.

———. "The Irish Language in Nineteenth Century New York City." In *The Multilingual Apple: Languages in New York City*, edited by Ofelia García and Joshua A. Fishman. New York: Mouton de Gruyter Publ., 1997. 52–69.

———. "Thinking of Monday: The Irish Speakers of Portland, Maine." *Eire/Ireland* 25, no. 1 (spring 1990): 6–19.

Nolan, Janet A. *Ourselves Alone: Women's Immigration from Ireland, 1885–1921*. Lexington: The University Press of Kentucky, 1989.

Norris, Martin J. *Law of Maritime Personal Injuries*. Rochester, NY: Lawyers Cooperative Publishing Company, 1975.

North, James. *The History of Augusta*. 1870. Reprint, Somersworth, NH: New England History Press, 1981.

Northrup, H. "New Orleans Longshoremen." *Political Science Quarterly* 57 (1942).

Norton, Mary Beth. *In the Devil's Snare*. New York: Knopf, 2002.

Noyes, Sybil, Charles T. Libby, and Walter G. Davis. *Genealogical Dictionary of Maine and New Hampshire*. Baltimore: Genealogical Publishing Co., Inc., 1988. [MHS]

Oates, Mary J. "The Professional Preparation of Parochial School Teachers, 1870s to 1940s." *Historical Journal of Massachusetts* 12, no. 1 (January 1984).

O'Brien, Anthony Patrick. "Factory Size and Economies of Scale and the Great Merger Wave of 1898–1902." *Journal of Economic History* 48, no. 3 (December 1988).

O'Brien, Conor Cruise. *Parnell and His Party, 1880–1890*. Oxford: Oxford University Press, 1964.

O'Brien, David. *The Renewal of American Catholicism*. New York: Oxford University Press, 1972.

O'Brien, Francis M. "F. M. O'Brien Views the World of Books in Portland." *Maine Antiquarian Booksellers Association Book Fair.* 9 October 1994. [MHS]

———. *Francis M. O'Brien, A Backward Look: 50 Years of Maine Books and Bookmen.* Portland: Anthoensen Press, 1986. [MHS]

O'Brien, John. "Exertions of the O'Brien Family, at Machias in the American Revolution." *Collections of the Maine Historical Society* 2. Portland: By the Society, 1847: 242–49.

O'Brien, Michael J. "The Early Irish in Maine." *Journal of the American Irish Historical Society* 10 (1911): 162–70.

———. *A Hidden Phase of American History: Ireland's Part in America's Struggle for Liberty.* New York: Dodd, Mead and Co., 1921.

———. *In Old New York, the Irish Dead in Trinity and St. Paul's Churchyards.* New York: The American-Irish Historical Society, 1928.

———. *The Irish at Bunker Hill.* Greenwich, CT: Devin Adair, 1968.

———. *The Irish in America, Immigration, Land, Probate, Administrations, Birth, Marriage, and Burial Records of the Irish in America in and about the 18th Century.* Baltimore: Genealogical Publishing Co., 1965.

———. "The Lost Settlement of Cork, Maine." *Journal of the American Irish Historical Society* 7 (1913): 175–84.

———. *Pioneer Irish in New England.* New York: P. J. Kennedy & Sons, 1937.

O'Brien, Simon P. "Longshoremen Stabilize Their Jobs." *American Federationist* 34 (May 1927).

O'Broin, Leon. *Fenian Fever: An Anglo-American Dilemma.* New York: New York University Press, 1971.

O'Carroll, Ide. *Models for Movers: Irish Women's Emigration to America.* Dublin: Attic Press, 1990.

Ó Conghaile, S. *Cois Fharraige le mo Linnse.* Baile Átha Cliath: Clódhanna, 1974.

O'Connell, Marvin R. *John Ireland and the American Catholic Church.* St. Paul: Minnesota Historical Society Press, 1988.

O'Connor, Harvey. *Revolution in Seattle.* Seattle: Left Bank Books, 1981.

O'Connor, Joseph. *Star of the Sea: A Novel.* Orlando, FL: Harcourt, Inc., 2002.

O'Connor, Thomas H. *Boston Catholics: A History of the Church and Its People.* Boston, MA: Northeastern University Press, 1998.

———. *The Boston Irish: A Political History.* Boston: Back Bay Books, 1995.

———. *Civil War Boston: Home Front and Battlefield.* Boston, MA: Northeastern University Press, 1997.

———. *Fitzpatrick's Boston, 1846–1866: John Bernard Fitzpatrick, Third Bishop of Boston.* Boston: Northeastern University Press, 1984.

———. "The Irish in New England." *New England Historical and Genealogical Register* 139 (July 1985): 187–95.

ÓCuív, Brian. "The Gaeltacht - Past and Present." In *Irish Dialects and Irish-Speaking Districts.* Dublin: Institute for Advanced Studies, 1951.

———. *A View of the Irish Language.* Dublin: Stationery Office, 1969.

O'Dea, John. *History of the Ancient Order of Hibernians and Its Auxiliary.* New York: National Board of the AOH, 1923.

O'Dwyer, George F. "Captain James Howard, Col. William Lithgow, Col. Arthur Noble, and other Irish Pioneers in Maine." *Journal of the American Irish Historical Society* 19 (1920): 71–91.

O'Dwyer, Riobard. *Who Were My Ancestors?* Astoria, IL: Stevens Publishing Co., 1976.

O'Farrell, Patrick. *Letters from Irish Australia, 1825–1919.* Sydney: New South Wales University Press and Belfast: Ulster Historical Foundation, 1984.

O'Gadhra, Nollaig. "The Irish Language Revival in 1966." *Eire/Ireland* 4, no. 4 (1969).

O'Gallagher, Marianna. *Grosse Isle: Gateway to Canada, 1832–1937.* Ste. Foy, Quebec: Carraig Books, 1995.

———. *The Shamrock Trail: Tracing the Irish in Quebec City.* Ste. Foy, Quebec: Livres Carraig Books, 1998.

O'Grada, Cormac. "Across the Briny Ocean: Some Thoughts on Irish Emigration to America, 1800–1850." In *Ireland and Scotland, 1650–1850,* edited by T. M. Devine and David Dickson. Edinburgh: John Donald Publishers, Ltd., 1983.

———. *Ireland: A New Economic History, 1780–1939.* New York: Oxford University Press, 1994.

O'Grady, John. *How the Irish Became Americans.* New York: Twayne, 1973.

O'Leary, Charles J. "A History of Organized Labor in Maine During the New Deal." Special Collections, Fogler Library, University of Maine, Orono.

O'Leary, Wayne M. "The Maine Sea Fisheries, 1830–1890: The Rise and Fall of a Native Industry." Ph.D. diss., University of Maine (Orono), 1981.

Olson, James S. *Catholic Immigrants in America.* Chicago: Nelson-Hall Publishers, 1987.

Olzak, Susan, and Joanne Nagel, eds. *Comparative Ethnic Relations.* Orlando: Florida Academic Press, 1986.

O'Neil, Paul, et al., eds. *The Western Cemetery Project: A Celebration of 125 Years of Service to the Portland Irish-American Community.* (The Daniel O'Connell O'Donoughue Division – Division 1 of the AOH.) South Portland: Waterfront Graphics and Printing, 2001. [MHS]

O'Neill, Kevin. *Family and Farm in Pre-Famine Ireland: The Parish of Killashandra.* Madison: University of Wisconsin Press, 1984.

O'Rahilly, T. F. *Irish Dialects Past and Present.* Dublin: Browne and Nolan, Ltd., 1932.

Oram, R. B. *The Dockers Tragedy.* London: Hutchinson, 1970.

Oram, R. B., and C. C. Baker. *The Efficient Port.* Elmsford, NY: Pergamon, 1971.

Ordinance Survey Memoirs of Ireland: North Antrim Coast and Rathlin. Vol. 24. Belfast: The Institute of Irish Studies, 1994.

Orel, Harold, ed. *Irish History and Culture.* Lawrence: University of Kansas, 1976.

Ormond, Douglas S. *The Roman Catholic Church in Cobequid, Acadie, 1692–1755, and Colchester County, Nova Scotia, 1828–1978.* Truro, Nova Scotia: 1979. Includes data on the Kavanaghs, 1778–1830. [MHS]

O'Rourke, Kevin. *Currier and Ives, The Irish and America.* New York: Harry N. Abrams, Inc., Publisher, 1995.

Orsi, Robert. *The Madonna of 115th Street: Faith and Community in Italian Harlem, 1880–1950.* New Haven: Yale University Press, 1985.

———. *Thank You St. Jude: Women's Devotion to the Patron of Hopeless Causes.* New Haven: Yale University Press, 1996.

O'Toole, James M. *Militant and Triumphant: William Henry O'Connell and Catholicism in Boston, 1859–1944.* Notre Dame, IN: University of Notre Dame Press, 1992.

————. *Passing for White: Race, Religion, and the Healy Family, 1820–1920*. Amherst: University of Massachusetts Press, 2002.

O'Tuama, Sean, ed. *The Gaelic League Idea*. Cork: Mercier Press, 1972.

ÓTuathaigh, Géaróid. *Ireland Before the Famine, 1798–1848*. The Gill History of Ireland, vol. 9. Dublin: Gill and Macmillan, 1972.

————. "Language, Literature, and Culture in Ireland Since the War," in Joseph Lee, *Ireland, 1945–1970*. Dublin: Gill and Macmillan, 1979.

Owen, Henry W. *The Edward Clarence Plummer History of Bath, Maine*. Bath, ME: The Times, 1936. [MHS]

Padden, Michael, and Robert Sullivan. *May the Road Rise to Meet You: Everything You Need to Know about Irish American History*. New York: Penguin-Putnam, 1999.

Palmer, Dwight L. "Pacific Coast Maritime Labor." Ph.D. diss., Stanford University, 1935.

Pancoast, John. "The Irish Are Coming." *Portland Landmarks Observer* (September–October 1979). [MHS]

Paradis, Wilfred. *Upon This Granite: Catholicism in New Hampshire, 1647–1997*. Portsmouth, NH: Peter Randall, 1998.

Parker, Edward L. *The History of Londonderry, Comprising the Towns of Derry and Londonderry, N.H.* Boston: Perkins and Whipple, 1851.

Parsons, Carolyn. "'Bordering on Magnificence':Urban Domestic Planning in the Maine Woods." In *Maine in the Early Republic: From Revolution to Statehood*, edited by Charles E. Clark, James S. Leamon, and Karen Bowden. Hanover, NH: University Press of New England, 1988.

Peck, Henry A. *Seaports in Maine: An Economic Study*. Orono: University of Maine Studies (Second series, no. 2), 1955.

Penhallow, Samuel. *The History of the Wars of New England with the Eastern Indians*. Boston: R. Fleet and Cornhill, 1726.

Peterson, Gardner. *Docker*. New York: Atheneum, 1980.

Petrin, Ronald A. *French Canadians in Massachusetts Politics, 1885–1915: Ethnicity and Political Pragmatism*. Philadelphia: Temple University Press, 1983.

Pilcher, William W. *The Portland Longshoremen: A Dispersed Urban Community*. New York: Holt, Rinehardt and Winston, 1972. [About Portland, Oregon]

Pillsbury, David B. "The History of the Atlantic and St. Lawrence Railroad Company." Special Collections, Fogler Library, University of Maine, Orono.

Poirteir, Cathal, ed. *Famine Echoes*. Dublin: Gill and Macmillan, 1995.

Poor, Laura E. *First International Railroad and the Colonization of New England*. New York: G. P. Putnam's, 1892.

"Portland Custom House and Its Collectors." *Portland Board of Trade Journal* 12 (1899).

"Portland in a Nutshell." *Portland Board of Trade Journal* 5, no. 1 (May 1892).

Portland Longshoremen's Benevolent Society, Records and Minutes. Maine Historical Society Manuscript Collections 359 (MS 85-15) and 360.

Potter, George. *To the Golden Door*. Westport, CT: Greenwood Press, 1974.

Powderly, Terence V. *The Path I Trod*. New York: Columbia University Press, 1940.

————. *Thirty Years of Labor, 1859 to 1889*. 1890. New York: A. M. Kelley, 1967.

Powers, Vincent. "Invisible Immigrants: The Pioneer Irish of Worcester, Massachusetts, 1826–1860." Ph.D. diss., Clark University, 1976.

Prude, Jonathan. *The Coming of the Industrial Order: Town and Factory Life in Rural Massachusetts, 1810–1860.* Cambridge: Cambridge University Press, 1983.

Purcell, Richard J. "Maine: Early Schools and Irish Teachers." *The Catholic Educational Review* 33 (April 1935): 467–79.

Purvis, Thomas. "The European Ancestry of the United States Population, 1790." *The William and Mary Quarterly* 41 (January 1984): 85–101.

Quin, Mike [Paul W. Ryan]. *The Big Strike.* Olema, CA: Olema Publishing Company, 1949; New York: International Publishers, 1979.

Quinlan, Michael, ed. *Guide to the New England Irish.* Boston: Quinlan Campbell, Publishers, 1987.

Radford, Dwight A., and Kyle J. Betet. *Discovering your Irish Ancestors: How to Find and Record Your Unique History.* Cincinnati, OH: Betterway Books, 2001. [Portland Public Library]

Radin, M. "The Case of Harry Bridges: A Deportation Case." *Social Service Review* 14 (1940).

———. "Harry Bridges Case Again." *Social Service Review* 16 (1942).

———. "The Unfinished Case of Harry Bridges." *Social Service Review* 19 (1945).

"Record of Labor Work Done Here Since 1836." *Board of Trade Journal* 15 (1902–1903).

Redmond, Dick. *The Maine Boxing Records Book, 1922–2000.* Greenville, ME: Moosehead Communications, 2000.

Reed, Merl E. "Lumberjacks and Longshoremen: The I.W.W. in Louisiana." *Labor History* 13, no. 1 (winter 1972).

Reiche, Howard C., Jr. *Closeness: Memories of Mrs. Munjoy's Hill.* Falmouth, ME: Long Point Press, 2002.

Renshaw, Patrick. *The Wobblies.* Garden City, NJ: Doubleday Publishers, 1967.

Rice, James R. "A History of Organized Labor in Saint John, New Brunswick, 1813–1890." Master's thesis, University of New Brunswick, 1968.

Rich, Louise Dickinson. *Happy the Land.* Philadelphia: Lippencott Co. 1946.

———. *We Took to the Woods.* Philadelphia: Lippencott Co., 1942.

Richards, Eric. "Scotland and the Atlantic Empire." In *Strangers Within the Realm: Cultural Margins of the First British Empire,* edited by Bernard Bailyn and Philip D. Morgan. Chapel Hill: University of North Carolina Press, 1991.

Richardson, Eleanor. *Hurricane Island: The Town that Disappeared.* Rockland, ME: The Island Institute, 1989.

Rielly, Edward J. *Baseball: An Encyclopedia of Popular Culture.* Santa Barbara, CA: ABC-CLIO, 2000.

Riley, Arthur J. "Catholicism in New England to 1788." Ph.D. diss., The Catholic University of America (Washington, DC), 1936.

Ring, Elizabeth. *Maine in the Making of the Nation, 1783–1870.* Camden, ME: Picton Press, 1996. [MHS]

———. *The McArthurs of Limington, Maine.* Falmouth, ME: Kennebec River Press, 1992. [MHS]

Rischin, Moses. "Immigration, Migration and Minorities in California: A Reassessment." *Pacific Historical Review* 41, no. 1 (1972).

Roberge, Robert A. "Three-Decker: Structural Correlate of Worcester's Industrial Revolution." Master's thesis, Clark University, 1965.

Robertson, Diana Forbes. *My Aunt Maxine: The Story of Maxine Elliott.* New York: The Viking Press, 1964.

Robinson, Robert M. "Maritime Labor in San Francisco, 1933–1937." Ph.D. diss., University of California, 1937.

Robinson, Tim. *Connemara*. Roundstone, County Galway: Folding Landscapes, 1990.

———. *Mapping South Connemara*. Roundstone, County Galway: Folding Landscapes, 1985.

———. *Stones of Aran: Pilgrimage*. New York: Penquin, 1990.

———, ed. *Connemara After the Famine: Journal of a Survey of the Martin Estate by Thomas Colville Scott*. Dublin: Lilliput Press, 1995.

Rodechko, James. *Patrick Ford and His Search for America: A Case Study of Irish-American Journalism, 1870–1913*. New York: Arno Press, 1976.

Roe, Mícheál D. "Contemporary Catholic and Protestant Irish America: Social Identities, Forgiveness, and Attitudes Toward *The Troubles*." *Éire-Ireland* 37, nos. 1–2 (spring–summer 2002): 153–74.

Roediger, David. *The Wages of Witnesses: Race and the Making of the American Working Class*. New York: Routledge, 1995.

Rosen, Ruth. *The World Split Open: How the Modern Women's Movement Changed America*. New York: Viking Press, 2000.

Rosenbaum, Edward. "The Expulsion of the I.L.A. from A.F. of L." Ph.D. diss., University of Wisconsin at Madison, 1955.

Rosenberg, Daniel. *New Orleans Dockworkers: Race, Labor, and Unionism, 1892–1920*. Cambridge: Cambridge University Press, 1983.

Rosenburg, Charles E. *The Cholera Years*. Chicago: University of Chicago Press, 1987.

Rosenthal, M. L. *Selected Poems and Three Plays of William Butler Yeats*. New York: Collier Books, 1986.

Rosenzweig, Roy. *Eight Hours for What We Will: Workers and Leisure in an International City, 1870–1920*. New York: Cambridge University Press, 1983.

Ross, Steven G. *Workers on the Edge: Work, Leisure, and Politics in Industrializing Cincinnati, 1788–1890*. New York: Columbia University Press, 1985.

Rovere, Richard H. *Senator Joe McCarthy*. New York: Harcourt, Brace, 1959.

Rowe, William H. *The Maritime History of Maine: Three Centuries of Shipbuilding and Seafaring*. New York: W. W. Norton, 1948.

Royce, Anya Patterson. *Ethnic Identity: Strategies and Diversity*. Bloomington, IN: Indiana University Press, 1982.

Rubin, Lester. *The Negro in the Longshore Industry*. Philadelphia: University of Pennsylvania Press, 1974.

Ruddy, Michael. "An Irish Army in America." *Civil War Times* 42, no. 1 (April 2003): 32–40.

Ryan, Dennis P. *Beyond the Ballot Box: A Social History of the Boston Irish, 1845–1917*. Rutherford, NJ: Fairleigh Dickinson University Press, 1983.

Ryan, James G. *Irish Records, Sources for Family and Local History*. Salt Lake City, UT: Ancestry Publishing, 1988.

Sacred Heart Parish: Seventy-Fifth Anniversary. Portland: 1972. [MHS]

Sadik, Marvin, et al. *Seven Essays in Memory of Francis M. O'Brien*. Portland, ME: Private printing, 1995. [MHS]

Saint Dominic's Parish. *Souvenir History of St. Dominic's Parish, 1822–1909*. Portland, ME: 1909.

Salvatore, Nicholas. *Eugene V. Debs: Citizen and Socialist*. Urbana: University of Illinois Press, 1984.

———. *We All Got History: Memory Books of Amos Webber*. New York: Random House, 1996.

Samito, Christian G. *Commanding Boston's Irish Ninth: The Civil War Letters of Colonel Patrick R. Guiney, Ninth Massachusetts Volunteer Infantry*. New York: Fordham University Press, 1998.

Sanders, James W. *The Education of an Urban Minority: Catholics in Chicago, 1833–1965*. Chicago: University of Chicago Press, 1977.

Sarbaugh, Timothy J. "Exiles of Confidence: The Irish-American Community of San Francisco, 1880 to 1920." In *From Paddy to Studs: Irish American Communities at the Turn of the Century, 1880 to 1920*, edited by Timothy J. Meagher. Westport: Greenwood Press, 1986: 161–79.

———. "Father Yorke and the San Francisco Waterfront, 1901–1916." *Pacific History* 25, no. 3 (1981).

Sargent, Ruth. "Gail Laughlin." In *Notable American Women: The Modern Period*, edited by Barbara Sicherman and Carl Hurd Green. Cambridge: Harvard University Press, 1980.

Saunders, S. A. *The Economic History of the Maritime Provinces*. Ottawa: Royal Commission on Dominion-Provincial Relations, 1939.

Saxton, Alexander. *The Indispensable Enemy: Labor and the Anti-Chinese Movement in California*. Berkeley: University of California Press, 1971.

Scally, Robert J. *The End of Hidden Ireland: Rebellion, Famine, and Emigration*. New York: Oxford University Press, 1995.

Schlegel, Donald N. *Passengers from Ireland: Lists of Passengers Arriving in American Ports between 1811 and 1817*. Baltimore: Genealogical Publishing Co. Inc., 1980.

Schlereth, Thomas. "Columbia, Columbus, and Columbianism." *Journal of American History* 79, no. 3 (December 1992).

Schneiderman, William. *The Pacific Coast Maritime Strike*. San Francisco: Western Worker Publisher, 1937. Pamphlet.

Schrier, Arnold. *Ireland and the Irish Emigration, 1815–1900*. Minneapolis: University of Minnesota Press, 1958.

Schultz, Nancy Lusignan. *Fire and Roses: The Burning of the Charlestown Convent, 1834*. Boston: Northeastern University Press, 2000.

Scontras, Charles A. *Organized Labor and Labor Politics in Maine, 1880–1980*. Orono: University of Maine Press (University of Maine Studies, Series 2, no. 83), 1966.

———. *Organized Labor in Maine: Twentieth Century Origins*. Orono: University of Maine Press (Bureau of Labor Education), 1985.

———. *Organized Labor in Maine: War, Reaction, Depression, and the Rise of the CIO 1914–1943*. Orono: Bureau of Labor Education, University of Maine, 2003.

———. *The Socialist Alternative: Utopian Experiments and the Socialist Party of Maine, 1895–1914*. Orono: University of Maine Press (Bureau of Labor Education), 1985.

———. *Two Decades of Organized Labor and Labor Politics in Maine, 1880–1900*. Orono: University of Maine Press, 1962.

Scott, Geraldine Tidd. *Ties of Common Blood: A History of Maine's Northeast*

Boundary Dispute with Great Britain, 1783–1842. Bowie, MD: Heritage Books, Inc., 1992. [MHS]

Scott, Kenneth. *British Aliens in the United States During the War of 1812*. Baltimore: Genealogical Publishing Co. Inc., 1979.

Scott, Reva. *Samuel Brannan and the Golden Fleece*. New York: The MacMillian Company, 1944.

Scwartz, Harvey. *The March Inland: Origins of the International Longshoremen's and Warehouse Division, 1934–1938*. Los Angeles: U.C.L.A. Industrial Relations (Monograph Series no. 19), 1978.

Seidman, J., Jack London, and Bernard Karen. "Leadership in a London Union." *American Journal of Sociology* 56, no. 3 (1951).

Shannabruch, Charles. *Chicago's Catholics: The Evolution of an American Identity*. Notre Dame, IN: University of Notre Dame Press, 1981.

Shannon, James P. *Catholic Colonization on the Western Frontier*. New Haven: Yale University Press, 1957.

Shannon, William. *The American Irish: A Political and Social Portrait*. New York: Macmillan Co., 1963.

Shaw, Douglas. *The Making of an Immigrant City: Ethnic and Cultural Conflict in Jersey City, 1850–1877*. New York: Arno Press, 1976.

Shea, Christina. *Moira's Crossing: A Novel*. New York: St. Martin's Press, 2000. [MHS]

Shea, John Gilmary. *The Life and Times of the Most Reverend John Carroll*. New York: John G. Shea, 1888.

Sheehy, Michael J. "John Alfred Poor and International Railroads: The Early Years to 1860." Master's thesis, University of Maine (Orono), 1974.

Shefter, Martin. "The Electoral Foundations of the Political Machine: New York City, 1884–1897." In *The History of American Political Behavior*, edited by Joel Sibley, Alan G. Bogue, and William Flanigan. Princeton, NJ: Princeton University Press, 1978: 263–98.

Sherman, Andrew M. *Life of Captain Jeremiah O'Brien, Machias, Maine*. Morristown, NJ: The Jerseyman Office, 1902.

Sherman, Rexford B. "The Bangor and Aroostook Railroad and the Development of the Port of Searsport." Special Collections, Fogler Library, University of Maine, Orono.

Shettleworth, Earl G., Jr., and William David Barry. *Mr. Goodhue Remembers Portland: Scenes From the Mid-Nineteenth Century*. Augusta, ME: Maine Historic Preservation Commission Publications, 1981.

Shorey, Henry A. *The Story of the Maine Fifteenth*. Bridgton, ME: Press of the Bridgton News, 1890. [MHS]

Sicherman, Barbara, and Carl Hurd Green, eds. *Notable American Women: The Modern Period*. Cambridge: Harvard University Press, 1980.

SJL. "St. Joseph's Academy." *Maine Catholic Historical Magazine* 4 (April 1914).

Skelton, Brenda K. "The Buffalo Grain Shovellers' Strike of 1899." *Labor History* 9, no. 2 (spring 1968): 210–38.

Smith, David C. *A History of Lumbering in Maine, 1861–1960*. Orono: University of Maine Press (University of Maine Studies, no. 93), 1972.

———. "Maine's Changing Landscape to 1820." In *Maine in the Early Republic: From Revolution to Statehood*, edited by Charles E. Clark, James S. Leamon, and Karen Bowden. Hanover, NH: University Press of New England, 1988.

Smith, Joe Patterson. *The Republican Expansionists of the Early Reconstruction Era.* Chicago: University of Chicago Libraries, 1933.

Smith, Judith E. *Family Connections: A History of Italian and Jewish Immigrant Lives in Providence, Rhode Island, 1900–1940.* Albany: State University of New York Press, 1985.

Snyder, Don J. *Night Crossing: A Novel.* New York: Alfred A. Knopf, 2001. [MHS]

Snyder, Robert. *The Voice of the City.* New York: Oxford University Press, 1990.

Sollors, Werner. *The Invention of Ethnicity.* New York: Oxford University Press, 1989.

Solomon, Barbara. *Ancestors and Immigrants: A Changing New England Tradition.* Cambridge: Harvard University Press, 1956.

Sorrelle, Richard. "The Sentinelle Affair and Militant Survivance: The Franco-American Experience in Woonsocket, Rhode Island." Ph.D. diss., University of Buffalo, 1975.

Southgate, William S. "The History of Scarborough, from 1633 to 1783." *Collections of the Maine Historical Society* 3 (1853).

Spear, Marilyn. *Worcester's Three Deckers.* Worcester: Bicentennial Commission, 1977.

Spear, Verne Raymond. *The Descendants of Redmond Peter Fahey and Cecelia Haverty and John Sweeney and Mary Dineen, 1810–1984.* West Springfield, MA: The Trade Press, 1984.

Sprague, Laura Fecych, ed. *Agreeable Situations: Society, Commerce and Art in Southern Maine, 1780–1830.* Kennebunk, ME: The Brick Store Museum, 1987.

———. *The Mirror of Maine: One Hundred Distinguished Books that Reveal the History of the State and the Life of Its People.* Orono: The University of Maine Press and the Baxter Society, 2000.

Stacey, C. P. "A Fenian Interlude: The Story of Michael Murphy." *Canadian Historical Review* 15 (1934).

———. "Fenianism and the Rise of National Feeling in Canada at the Time of Confederation." *Canadian Historical Review* 17 (1931).

Stackpole, E. S. "Character of the Irish Emigrants Who Helped Colonize This State." [Manuscript in MHS Collection 862]

Stakeman, Randolph. "Slavery in Colonial Maine." *Maine Historical Society Quarterly* 27, no. 2 (fall 1987).

Stanley, R. H., and G. O. Hall. *Eastern Maine and the Rebellion.* Bangor, ME: R. H. Stanley and Co., 1887.

Stellman, Louis J. *Sam Brannan: Builder of San Francisco.* New York: Exposition Press, 1953.

Stenson, Nancy. "Beagánín: The Use of Irish Among Immigrants to the United States." *New Hibernia Review* 2, no. 2 (summer 1998): 116–31.

Stern, Boris. *Cargo Handling and Longshore Labor Conditions.* Washington, DC: United States Government Printing Office, 1932.

Stevens, Eunice. "Recollections of Lewiston." *Newsletter of the Androscoggin Historical Society* 13 (September 1994).

Stilgoe, John R. *Common Landscape of America, 1580 to 1845.* New Haven: Yale University Press, 1982.

Stivers, Richard. *Hair of the Day, Irish Drinking and Its American Stereotype.* University Park: Pennsylvania State University, 2000.

Stoddard, Harry Gilpin. *The Seventy-Year Saga of a New England Enterprise in Industrial Worcester*. New York: Newcomen Society of North America, 1952.

Stonequist, Everett. *The Marginal Man: A Study in Personality and Culture Conflict*. New York: Scribner's, 1937.

Stott, Richard. *Workers in the Metropolis: Class, Ethnicity, and Youth in Antebellum New York City*. Ithaca, NY: Cornell University Press, 1990.

Sturdivant, Cyrus. *Sketches of the Life and Work of Capt. Cyrus Sturdivant*. New York: Willis McDonald and Co., 1882.

Sugrue, Thomas J. "Crabgrass Politics: Race, Rights, and the Myth of the Liberal Consensus." *Journal of American History* 82, no. 2 (September 1995).

Sullivan, Catherine, et al., eds. *Sacred Heart Church, 1896–1996: Celebrating 100 Years of Parish Life Through Narrative, Remembrances, and Images*. South Portland, ME: Brownie Press, 1998. [MHS]

Sullivan, James. *History of the District of Maine*. 1795. Reprint, Augusta: Maine State Museum, 1970.

Sullivan, Mary C. *Catherine McAuley and the Tradition of Mercy*. Notre Dame, IN: University of Notre Dame Press, 2000.

Sullivan, Robert E., and James M. O'Toole, eds. *Catholic Boston: Studies in Religion and Community, 1870–1970*. Boston: Archdiocese of Boston, 1985.

Survey Memoirs of Ireland: North Antrim Coast and Rathlin 24. Belfast: The Institute of Irish Studies (1994).

Sutherland, Daniel E. *The Expansion of Everyday Life, 1860–1876*. New York: Harper & Row, 1989.

Swados, Harvey. "West-coast Waterfront—The End of an Era." *Dissent* (autumn 1961).

Swankey, Ben, comp. *Man Along the Shore: The Story of the Vancouver Waterfronts as Told by Longshoremen Themselves (1860–1975)*. Vancouver: International Longshoremen's and Warehousemen's Union, Local 500 Pensioners, 1975.

Swanstrom, Edward E. *The Waterfront Labor Problem*. New York: Fordham University Press, 1938.

Swift, Roger, and Sheridan Gilley. *The Irish in the Victorian City*. Dover, NH: Croom Helm, 1985.

Syrett, John. "Principle and Expediency: The Ku Klux Klan and Owen Brewster in 1924." *Maine History* 39, no. 4 (winter 2000–01): 214–39.

Tansill, Charles Callan. *America and the Fight for Irish Freedom, 1866–1922*. New York: Devin-Adair Co., 1957.

Taplin, Eric L. *The Dockers' Union: A Study of the National Union of Dockworkers, 1889–1992*. New York: St. Martin's Press, 1986.

———. *Liverpool Dockers and Seamen, 1870–1890*. Hull: University of Hull Publications, 1974.

Taves, Anne. *The Household of Faith: Roman Catholic Devotions in the Mid-Nineteenth-Century America*. Notre Dame, IN: University of Notre Dame Press, 1986.

Taylor, Alan. "Centers and Peripheries: Locating Maine's History." *Maine History* 39 (spring 2000).

———. "'A Kind of Warr': The Contest for Land on the Northeastern Frontier, 1750–1820." *The William and Mary Quarterly* (1989): 3–26.

———. *Liberty Men and Great Proprietors: Revolutionary Settlement on the Maine Frontier, 1760–1820*. Chapel Hill: University of North Carolina Press, 1989.

Taylor, Linda Maule, ed. *Limerick: Historical Notes*. Limerick, ME: Town of Limerick, 1975.

Taylor, Paul S., and Norman Leon Gold. "San Francisco and the General Strike." *Survey Graphic* 23 (September 1934).

Teaford, Jon. *The Unheralded Triumph: City Government in America*. Baltimore: Johns Hopkins University Press, 1986.

TeBrake, Janet Kahrer. "Peasants and Politics: Local Origins of the Irish Land League Movement." Ph.D. diss., University of Maine (Orono), 1984.

Tentler, Leslie Woodcock. "Present at the Creation: Working Class Catholics in the United States." In *American Exceptionalism: U.S. Working Class Formation in an International Context*, edited by Rick Halperin and Jonathan Morris. New York: St. Martin's Press, 1997.

————. *Seasons of Grace: A History of the Catholic Archdiocese of Detroit*. Detroit: Wayne State University Press, 1990.

The Irish in New England, Immigration of the Irish to New England, Sources of Irish-American Genealogy, The Kennedys of Massachusetts. Boston: New England Historic Genealogical Society, 1985. [MHS]

Theriault, Reg. *Longshoring on the San Francisco Waterfront*. San Pedro, CA: Singlejack Books, 1978.

Thernstrom, Stephan. *Poverty and Progress: Social Mobility in a Nineteenth Century City*. Cambridge: Harvard University Press, 1964.

————. *The Other Bostonians: Poverty and Progress in an American Metropolis 1860– 1970*. Cambridge: Harvard University Press, 1973.

Thibadeau, W. J. *The Irishman: A Factor in the Development of Houlton*. Augusta, ME: The Kennebec Journal, c. 1910.

Thoman, Richard. "Portland, Maine: An Economic-Urban Appraisal." *Economic Geography* 27 (1951).

Thomas, M. Hasley, ed. *The Dietary of Samuel Sewall, 1684–1729*. 2 vols. New York: Farrar, Straus and Giroux, 1973.

Thompson, Bryan. "Cultural Ties as Determinants of Immigrant Settlement in Urban Areas." Ph.D. diss., Clark University, 1971.

Thompson, Deborah. *Bangor, Maine, 1769–1914, An Architectural History*. Orono: University of Maine Press, 1988.

Thornley, David. *Isaac Butt and Home Rule*. London: MacGibbon & Kee, 1964.

Tibbetts, Margaret Joy. "The Irish Neighborhood in Greenwood, Maine." *The Bethel Courier* 5, no. 1 (March 1981). [Journal of the Bethel Historical Society]

Tincker, Mary Agnes. *The House of Yorke*. New York: The Catholic Publication Society, 1872. [A novel dealing with the Father Bapst affair; MHS]

Townshend, Charles. *Political Violence in Ireland: Government and Resistance Since 1848*. Oxford: Clarendon Press, 1983.

Trask, Willian Blake, ed. *Letters of Colonel Thomas Westbrook and Others Relative to Indian Affairs in Maine, 1722–1725*. Boston: George E. Littlefield, 1901.

Trollope, Anthony. *North America*. New York: Harpers & Brothers, Publishers, 1862.

Truxes, Thomas. *Irish-American Trade, 1660–1783*. New York: Cambridge University Press, 1987.

Tuchman, Barbara W. *The Proud Tower: A Portrait of the World Before the War, 1890–1914*. New York: Macmillan Company, 1966.

Tuckel, Peter, and Richard Maisel. "Voter Turnout among European Immigrants to the United States." *Journal of Interdisciplinary History* 24, no. 3 (winter 1994).

Tyrrell, Ian R. *Sobering Up: From Temperance to Prohibition in Antebellum America, 1800–1860.* Westport, CT: Greenwood Press, 1979.

Uí Churraoin, Máire. *Máire Phatch Mhóir Uí Churraoin: A Scéal Féin.* (Eagarthóir, Diarmaid Ó Gráinne.) Baile Átha Cliath: Coiscéim, 1995.

"Union Labor: Less Militant, More Affluent." *Time,* 17 September 1965.

Valone, David A., and Christine Kinealy, eds. *Ireland's Great Hunger: Silence, Memory and Commemoration.* Lanham, MD: University Press of America, 2002.

Vecoli, Rudolph J. "European Americans: From Immigrants to Ethnics." In *The Reinterpretation of American History and Culture,* edited by William H. Cartwright and Richard L. Watson, Jr. Washington, DC: National Council for the Social Studies, 1973.

———. "The Resurgence of American Immigration History." *American Studies International* 17 (winter 1979).

Velie, Lester. "Big Boss of the Big Port." *Colliers* 129 (February 9, 1952).

Vinyard, Jo Ellen. *The Irish on the Urban Frontier: Detroit, 1850–1880.* New York: Arno Press, 1976.

Vital Records from the Eastport Sentinel of Eastport, Maine 1818–1900. Camden, ME: Picton Press, 1996.

Vorse, Mary Heaton. *Labor's New Millions.* New York: Arno Press, 1969.

———. "The Pirate's Nest of New York." *Harper's* 204 (April 1952).

Wade, Mason. *The French Canadians: 1760–1917.* Toronto: Macmillan, 1968.

Wagner, H. *Linguistic Atlas and Survey of Irish Dialects.* Vol. 3, The Dialects of Connaught, 1958–1969. Dublin: Dublin Institute for Advanced Studies.

Walker, Mabel Gregory. *The Fenian Movement.* Colorado Springs, CO: Ralph Myles Publisher, Inc., 1969.

Walkowitz, Daniel. *Worker City, Company Town: Iron and Cotton Worker Protest in Troy and Cohoes, New York, 1855–1884.* Urbana: University of Illinois Press, 1981.

Wallace, R. Stuart. "The Scotch Irish of Provincial New Hampshire." Ph.D. diss., University of New Hampshire, 1984.

Walsh, Victor. "'Across the Big Wather': Irish Community Life in Pittsburgh and Allegheny City, 1850–1885." Ph.D. diss., University of Pittsburgh, 1983.

———. "A Fanatic Heart: The Cause of Irish American Nationalism in Pittsburgh During the Gilded Age." *Journal of Social History* 15, no. 2 (winter 1981).

Ward, Alan. *Ireland and Anglo American Relations 1899–1921.* Toronto: University of Toronto, 1969.

Ward, Estolv E. *Harry Bridges on Trial.* New York: Modern Age Books, 1940; New York: A.M.S. Press, 1976.

Warner, Sam Bass. "If All the World Were Philadelphia: A Scafolding in Urban History, 1774–1930." *American Historical Review* 74 (1968).

Washburn, Charles G. *Industrial Worcester.* Worcester: Davis Press, 1917.

Waters, Mary C. *Ethnic Options: Choosing Identities in America.* Berkeley: University of California Press, 1990.

Wayman, Dorothy G. *Cardinal O'Connell of Boston: A Biography of William Henry O'Connell 1859–1944.* New York: Farrar, Straus and Young, 1954.

Weiner, Marli, ed. *Of Place and Gender*. Orono: University of Maine Press, 2004.

Weinstein, James. *The Decline of Socialism in America, 1912–1925*. New York: Vintage, 1969.

Wells, Dave, and Jim Stodder. "A Short History of New Orleans Dockworkers." *Radical America* 10 (January–February 1976).

Westcott, Richard R. *New Men, New Issues, The Formation of the Republican Party in Maine*. Portland, ME: Maine Historical Society, 1986.

"The Wharves of Portland, Maine." *Portland Board of Trade Journal* 179 (1912–1913).

Wheeler, George Augustus, and Henry Warren Wheeler. *History of Brunswick, Topsham, and Harpswell, Maine*. Boston: Alfred Mudge and Son, 1878.

Whelan, Kevin. "Catholic Mobilization, 1750–1850." In *Culture and Practiques Politiques en France et en Irlande*, edited by P. Bergeron and Louis Cullen. Paris: Centre de Recherches Historiques, 1991.

———. *The Killing Snows*. Cork: Cork University Press (forthcoming).

Whitehill, Walter Muir. *A Memorial to Bishop Cheverus, With A Catalogue of the Books Given by Him to the Boston Anthenaeum*. Boston: Anthenaeum, 1941.

Whitmore, Allan R. " 'A Guard of Faithful Sentinels': The Know-Nothing Appeal in Maine, 1854–1855." *Maine Historical Society Quarterly* 20, no. 3 (winter 1981).

Whitney, Edward Bonner. "The Ku Klux Klan in Maine: A Study with Particular Emphasis on the City of Portland." Master's thesis, Harvard University, 1966.

Whittemore, Charles P. *A General of the Revolution, John Sullivan of New Hampshire*. New York: Columbia University Press, 1961.

Whyte, W. Hamilton. *Decasualization of Dock Labor*. Bristol, England: Arrowsmith, Ltd., 1934.

Wiggin, Edward. *History of Aroostook*. Presque Isle, ME: Star-Herald Press, 1922.

Wiggin, Frances Turgeon. *Maine Composers and Their Music: A Biographical Dictionary*. Rockland, ME: Maine Federation of Music Clubs, 1959. [MHS]

———. *Maine Composers and Their Music*, Book II. Portland: Maine Historical Society, 1976. [MHS]

Wilde, Lady. *Quaint Irish Customs and Superstitions*. Cork: Mercier, 1988.

Wilder, Sidney A. *Centennial Celebration of the Town of Pembroke, 1832–1932*. Unpublished mounted newspaper clippings, 1932. [Maine State Library]

Wilentz, Robert Sean. "Industrializing America and the Irish: Towards the New Departure." *Labor History* 20, no. 4 (fall 1979).

Williams, William H. A. *'Twas Only an Irishman's Dream: The Image of Ireland and the Irish in American Popular Song Lyrics, 1800–1920*. Urbana: University of Illinois Press, 1996.

Williamson, Joseph. *History of the City of Belfast in the State of Maine, From Its First Settlement in 1770 to 1875*. Portland, ME: Loring, Short, and Harmon, 1877.

Williamson, William D. *The History of the State of Maine: From Its First Discovery, A.D. 1602, to the Separation, A.D. 1820, Inclusive*. 1832. Freeport, ME: Cumberland Press, 1966.

Williard, Benjamin J. *Captain Ben's Book*. Portland: Lakeside Press, 1895.

Willis, William. *The History of Portland*. 1833, 1865. Portland, ME: Maine Historical Society, 1972. [Reprint of the 1865 edition]

———. "Scotch Irish Immigration to Maine, and a Summary History of Presbyterianism." *Collection of Maine Historical Society* 6. Portland, ME: By the Society, 1859. 1–37.

Wilson, Andrew J. *Irish America and the Ulster Conflict 1968–1995*. Washington, DC: Catholic University of America, 1995.

Wilson, Hazel. *Tall Ships*. Boston: Little, Brown and Co., 1958.

Winks, Robin. "Raid at St. Albans." *Vermont Life* 15 (spring 1961): 40–46.

Wittke, Carl. *The Irish in America*. Baton Rouge: Louisiana State University Press, 1956.

———. *The Irish in America: A Students' Guide to Localized History*. New York: Teachers College Press, Columbia University, 1968.

Wood, Richard G. *A History of Lumbering in Maine, 1820–1861*. Orono: University of Maine Press (University of Maine Studies, no. 33), 1961.

Woodbury, Gordon, "The Scotch-Irish Presbyterian Settlers of New Hampshire." *Proceedings of the New Hampshire Society* 4. Concord, NH: 1906.

Woodham-Smith, Cecil. *The Great Hunger, Ireland, 1845–1849*. New York: Harper and Row, 1962.

Wright, Allan J. "'The Methods of Friendly Approach': Portland, Maine as Canada's Winter Port." Master's thesis, University of New Brunswick, 1976.

Writers' Program of the W.P.A. *Maine: A Guide "Down East."* St. Clair Shores, MI: Scholarly Press, Inc., 1976.

Writers' Program of the W.P.A. *Portland City Guide*. The American Guide Series. Portland: Forest City Printing Company, 1940.

Wuthnow, Robert. *The Restructuring of American Religion: Society and Faith Since World War II*. Princeton, NJ: Princeton University Press, 1988.

Wynn, Graeme. *Timber Colony: A Historical Geography of Early Nineteenth Century New Brunswick*. Toronto: University of Toronto Press, 1981.

Yancey, William, Eugene Erickson, and Richard Juliani. "Emergent Ethnicity: A Review and Reformation." *American Sociological Review* 4, no. 3 (June 1976).

Yerxa, Donald A. "The Burning of Falmouth, 1775: A Case Study in Imperial Pacification." *Maine Historical Society Quarterly* 14, no. 3 (winter 1975): 119–60.

Yurdan, Marilyn. *Irish Family History*. Baltimore: Genealogical Publishing Co., Inc., 1990.

Zunz, Oliver. *The Changing Faces of Inequality: Urbanization, Industrial Development, and Immigrants in Detroit, 1880 to 1920*. Chicago: University of Chicago Press, 1982.

———. *Making America Corporate, 1870 to 1920*. Chicago: University of Chicago, 1990.

INDEX

H

Haaffe, Thomas, 151
Hacker, Jeremiah, 160–61
Haggerty, John, 151
Halifax, Nova Scotia, 101–2, 142, 222
Hallowell, 81, 83, 166
Hamilton, Alexander, 48
Hancock Democratic Club, 178
Hanley, Patrick, 65
Hanley, Roger, 74
the Hanleys, 65
Hannaford, Reg, xvi
Hannibal (privateer), 10
Harding, Warren G., 289
Harney, John, 150
Hawthorne, Nathaniel, 298, 301
Hayes, Alexander, Jr., 141
Hayes, Alexander, Sr., 141
Hayes, Elizabeth, 141
Healy, Dorothy, xviii
Healy, James Augustine, 8–9, 13–14, 178, 225
Hebrides, Scotland, 98
Heffernan, Hugh, 82
Henry, Hugh, 49
Henry, Rose Alice, 264
Heskett, Christine Qualey, xviii
Hester, 80
Hibernian Benevolent Society, 145–46, 148–49, 152
Hibernian Cadets and Ladies Auxiliary of the Ancient Order of Hibernians, 179
Hibernia (privateer), 10, 68
Hill, Thomas J., 190
Hill Mill, 192, 195
Hitchcock, Becky, xv
HMS Duncan, 234
HMS Fawn, 226
HMS Pylades, 222, 226, 231–32
HMS Rosario, 226, 232
HMS Simoon, 226
HMS Tamar, 226
Hogan, Linda, xvii
Hogan, Michael, 164
Holland, John, 128
Holleran, John, 299
Holmes Hole, 103
home ownership, 204–8
Hope, James, 234
Horan, Alexander, 108
Horan, John, 108–9
Horan, John, Jr., 108
the Horans, 109, 114
Houlihan, T.J., 289
Houlton, 8
House Island Project, 15
Howard, Joseph, 170
Hutchinson, Thomas, 45, 47

I

Indian Island, New Brunswick, 232, 237
Ingraham Guards, 178
Inistioge, Ireland, 62, 82
Ireland, John, 124
Irish-American Club, xvii, 14, 179–80
Irish American Relief Association, 171, 173–74, 281
Irish American Union, 179
Irish Heritage Center, xii, xvii, 15, 180
Irish Land and Industrial League, 281
Irish National Land League, 179
Irish Relief Committee of 1880, 179
Irish Relief Fund, 289–90
Irish Republican Army, 288
Irish Republican Brotherhood, 280
Irish Trades Union Congress and Labor Party, 283
Island Pond, VT, 298–99

J

Jackson, Andrew, 85
Jackson, Elizabeth, 72
Jamaica, 69
Jefferson, Thomas, 69
Jeffries, David, 45
Jerome, William, 12
Jewett, Jedediah, 159
J & J Cooke shipping firm, 101
J.N.M. Brewer, 237
John and Edward, 68
Johnson, Andrew, 215–17, 223, 230
Jordan, William B., Jr., xix
Joyce, Anastasia, 63
Joyce, Malachy, 337

K

Kallery, Thomas, 248
Kavanagh, Edward, 85, 149
Kavanagh, James, 6, 62–66, 69–76, 79–81, 84–85
Kavanagh, Winifred, 261
the Kavanaghs, 17, 86, 141
Keady, Ireland, 128
Keane, Margaret (Peggy), 339
Keane, Patrick, 337
Kearney, Bob, xvii, 15
Kearney, Francis, 222
Kearns, Anthony, 82
Kearns, James, 127
Kearns, John, 127
Kearns, Thomas, 127
Keegan, Christopher, 131
Keegan, Patrick, 74
Keive, Charles, 108

Kelly, John, 170
Kelly, Michael, 151
Kelly, Robert, 78
Kelsey, Albert H., 190–92, 196–97
Kennebec Railroad, 190
Kennebec River, 71, 81
 settlements, 45–46, 48
Kennedy, David W., 168
Kerr, Robert, 231
Kerry, Ireland, 148
Kildorough, Ireland, 121
Kilfenora, Ireland, 144
Kilkenny, Ireland, 62–63, 70, 102, 123,
 126–27, 132
Kilkerrin, Ireland, 299
Killian, Bernard Doran, 216–17, 223–24,
 226–28, 230–31, 233, 235, 237, 243–45
Kilmacduagh, Ireland, 144
Kilmartin, Catherine, 303–4
Kilmartin, James, 302–3
Kilmartin, Mary, 301–4, 306–7, 320
Kilmartin, Patrick, 303
Kilmartin, Philip, 303
Kilpatrick, Ireland, 106
Kimball, Kris, xvi
Kincannon, Matthew, 165–66
King George's War, 55
Kingsbury, Benjamin, Jr., 159
Kinsale, Ireland, 78
Knights of Columbus, 179
Knights of Labor, 9
Knox, Henry, 75
Knox, William, 75–76
Ku Klux Klan, 9, 283

L

Ladies Land League, 179
laissez-faire policy, 157–58
Landers, Alice, 151
Landers, John, 151
land proprietors, 45, 50–52, 54–55
language. See Gaelic language; Gaelic lan-
 guage speakers
Laois, Ireland, 126
Larkin, Andrew, 151
Larkin, Francis, 151
Larkin, P.O., 176, 224
Laughlin, Gail, 264
Launders, Ellen, 151
Law, James, 46
Leeman, Henry, 166
Leeman, John, 166
Leinster, Ireland, 100, 142
Leprohon, Lucy, 178
Lettermullan, Ireland, 299
Lewiston, 4, 187–210
Lewiston Bleachery and Dye Works, 192, 198

Lewiston Falls, 189
Lewiston Gas Works, 198
Lewiston Water Power Co., 189–91, 196, 205
lime, 55
Limerick, 76
Limerick, Ireland, 64
Limerick County, Ireland, 140
Lincoln County, 61–86
Lincolnshire Proprietors, 50–52, 54–55
Lisbon, Portugal, 69
Liverpool, England, 69–71, 78
Londonderry, Ireland, 46, 75, 79
Londonderry, NH, 44, 49, 52, 56
Long, Washington, 233–34
longshoremen, 277–92
Lowell, Robert, 85
Lower Cluen, Ireland, 63
the Loyal Coalition, 289
Loyal National Repeal Association, 149
Lubec, 97, 99, 101, 104, 106, 109–10,
 112–14, 232
Luby, Thomas Clarke, 175
Lunney, Patrick, 173
Lydia, 68
Lyng, Sylvanus, 12

M

Maccalum, 46
MacDonald, John, 229–30, 250
MacDonnell, Richard, 249
MacGregor, James, 43–44
Machias, 10, 232
Mackin. See McKinn, James
MacMahan's Island, 65
MacSwiney, Terence, 286, 288
Maddock, Fidelma, 100
Madigan, Catherine, 82
Madigan, Edmund, 74
Madigan, John, 74–75
Madigan, Walter, 74, 82–83
Magee, James, 128–29
Maggie and Jiggs, 10
MaGrath, James, 218
Maguire, James, 155
Mahoney, Nancy, 140
Mahoney, Timothy, 140
Maine Irish Children's Program, 15
Maintopmen, 178
"Major Jack Dowling," 6
Maliseet Indians, 114
Mallon, Michael, 82
Malmude, Jonathan, xvi
Malone, Michael, 304
Malone, Pat, xix
Malone, Patrick, 301, 303–4, 307, 309–11, 324
Malone, Peter, 304
Malone, Richard Joseph, 9

Mogan, Patrick, 304
Molloy, John, 74
Molunkus River, 121
Montezuma, 83
Montreal, Canada, 278
Mooney, William, 74–75
Moore, Julie, xvi
Moore, Thomas, 146, 149
Moran, Joe, xvii
Moran, Matthew, 127
Moran, Ralph, 81–82
the Morrisons, 114
Morton, Eileen, xvi
"Mother Machree," 257, 269
"Mr. Dooley," 6
Mulholland, Jackie, xvi
Mulkerin, James, 300
Mullaly, John, 172
Mullen, B.F., 220, 243
Mullen, John H., 168
Mullen, Lawrence, 151
Mullen, Mary, 225
Mull of Kintyre, Scotland, 99, 106
Mundy, James, 145
Mundy, James H., xiv
Munjoy Hill, 12
Munroe, John, xviii
Munster, Ireland, 46, 142
Murphy, Cindy, xiv
Murphy, Henry, 195
Murphy, Jerre, 205
Murphy, John, 147
Murphy, J.S., 150
Murphy, Michael, 147, 229–30
Murphy, Suzanne, xvi
Murphy, Timothy J., 204, 209
Murray, Henry J., 224
Murray, John Gregory, 8
Muscongus Proprietors, 50
Mussey, John, 159
Mynish, Ireland, 299

N

Nabby, 69
Na Creag·in, Ireland, 305–6
Napoleon, 244
Nast, Thomas, 10
National Irish Athletic Association of
   Portland, 179
Native Americans, 47–48, 51, 54–55
nativism, 164–67, 196–200
Neal, John, 145
New Bedford, MA, 103
New Brunswick, 240
Newburyport, MA, 199
Newcastle, 6, 17, 61–62, 65–66, 73, 76, 78,
   84, 141, 143

New Ross, Ireland, 63–64, 71
New Waterford, 65, 75, 77
New York, passenger trade, 79
New York City, 103
Nichols, Lyman, 190, 197
Nickels, Thomas, 73
Nilsen, Kenneth, xviii, xix, 11, 342
Nobleboro, 65–68
Nolan, Janet, 258
Noon, Pat, 168
Noonan, Michael, 178
Nore River, Ireland, 63
Norris, Maureen Coyne, 338
North Star, 79
North Whitefield, 7–8, 123, 130, 132
Norton, Martin J., 179
Norwood, MA, 14
Nowlan, Daniel, 82
Noyes, Nicholas, xiv
Noyes, Oliver, 45–46

O

O'Beirne, Patrick H., 150, 152–54
O'Brien, Francis M., xix, 13–14
O'Brien, Jeremiah, 10
O'Brien, John, 10, 65
O'Brien, Katherine, 264, 267, 269
O'Brien, Morris, 10
O'Brien, William, 82
O'Brien, William Smith, 152
O'Bryan, Michael, 248
O'Callaghan, Donal, 287–89
Ocean Spray, 228, 233–34, 236
O'Connell, Daniel, 146, 148–49, 151
O'Connell, William Henry, 7–8
O'Connor, Bart, 332–33
O'Connor, John, 144
O'Connor, Peter, 171
O'Connor, Thomas, 332
O'Dea, John, xvii
O'Dee, John, 71, 74
O'Donnell, Denis, 103
O'Donnell, James, 164, 170
O'Donnell, John, 166–67, 173
O'Donnell, Michael, 330
O'Donnell, Patrick, 191
O'Donoughue, Daniel O'Connell, 170,
   175–76
O'Dono(u)ghue, Daniel O'Connell, 220, 224,
   261
O'Flaherty, Thomas, 126–27
O'Gorman, Nicholas, 336
O'Gorman, Rose, 336
O'Hara, John, 82
Old Town, 8
O'Leary, Charles, 5
O'Leary, Edward Cornelius, 9

Y